HISTORICAL DICTIONARIES OF SPORTS
Jon Woronoff, Series Editor

Historical Dictionary of Basketball

John Grasso

Historical Dictionaries of Sports, No. 2

The Scarecrow Press, Inc.
Lanham • Toronto • Plymouth, UK
2011

R
796.323
G7694 h

Published by Scarecrow Press, Inc.
A wholly owned subsidiary of The Rowman & Littlefield Publishing Group, Inc.
4501 Forbes Boulevard, Suite 200, Lanham, Maryland 20706
http://www.scarecrowpress.com

Estover Road, Plymouth PL6 7PY, United Kingdom

British Library Cataloguing in Publication Information Available

Library of Congress Cataloging-in-Publication Data

Grasso, John.
  Historical dictionary of basketball / John Grasso.
    p. cm. — (Historical dictionaries of sports ; no. 2)
  Includes bibliographical references.
  ISBN 978-0-8108-6763-5 (cloth : alk. paper) — ISBN 978-0-8108-7506-7
(ebook)
  1. Basketball—History—Dictionaries. I. Title.
  GV883.G73 2011
  796.323—dc22

                                                              2010024468

Contents

Editor's Foreword

Basketball is certainly one of the most popular sports in the world. It is played in virtually all countries, at all levels, from primary, to high school, to college. It is played by young and old, men and women, and there are countless professional teams that vie for national and international trophies, to say nothing of being included in the Olympics. That is already not bad for a sport. But what makes basketball really stand out is that the professionals have not taken over while the rest of us become spectators, watching it in stadiums or on television, although we do that as well. Wherever there is a basketball, and they seem to be everywhere, and wherever there is a patch of pavement big enough and some place to hang the basket, people almost naturally join in. So it is obvious that basketball should be one of the sports highlighted in this series, although this volume will deal more with the professional and semiprofessional level and the international tournaments. In just more than a century since it was "invented" by James Naismith, it has indeed conquered the world very peacefully but convincingly in ways he could never have imagined.

Historical Dictionary of Basketball traces the history of basketball, reaching back to the earliest times and emphasizing its situation at present. This is done twice, actually, first in the chronology, and then in the introduction, which tells us more about its intriguing career. The dictionary section focuses more sharply on some of the prominent people involved, pioneers in the sport, outstanding players, and also coaches. Naturally, there is considerable attention to the major teams at various levels and some of the schools that have regularly fielded particularly good teams. Other entries present the main leagues and associations as well as some of the technical aspects. The appendixes provide records and rankings of various sorts, including national league championships and Olympic Games. The bibliography is more than just an afterthought. It includes numerous books readers may wish to consult to round out and supplement the information found here.

John Grasso bears out some of the comments above. He is not a former basketball player on a major team, but one of countless fans, only he was a fan who took an unusually serious interest in this sport. He has written extensively on basketball and is a member of the Association for Professional Basketball Research. Over the years, he has watched countless matches in the United States and other countries while attending seven Olympic Games. He is also an Olympic historian and treasurer of the International Society of Olympic Historians. As a writer, he produced two monographs of his own on basketball, *The Absurd "Official" Statistics of the 1954–1955 NBA Season* and *Olympic Games Basketball Records*, while also contributing to *Total Basketball*, *The Compendium of Professional Basketball*, and *Harvey Pollack's NBA Statistical Yearbook*. Of course, you can follow the sport without this book, but it is infinitely more interesting when you know more about its genesis and history and can look up players and teams and consult the main records. So this is a nice companion to have.

Jon Woronoff
Series Editor

Preface

It is impossible in a book of this size to cover all aspects of an activity that has been practiced worldwide for more than 100 years. The first draft originally contained more than 1,500 pages and still omitted many people and teams. For the dictionary entries I have selected players, coaches, contributors, teams, leagues, and phrases covering domestic and international, men's and women's, scholastic and professional basketball from the sport's beginnings to modern times. In doing so, I've limited entries to colleges that won National Collegiate Athletic Association (NCAA) Championships, countries that competed in more than one Olympic Games tournament, professional teams in the major United States' leagues, and selected individuals from all eras. Space limitations have restricted entries to brief sketches, but readers interested in more details are advised to make use of the extensive bibliography section. It is hoped that the information contained within this book will provide the neophyte reader with a general introduction to basketball and that some of the anecdotal details will be of interest to the reader with a broader background.

I'd like to thank Dorothy A. Grasso, interior decorator, for putting up with my reclusive hobbies for more than forty years. Thanks also to Steve Grasso, manufacturing engineer, my Beijing companion and the future Dr. L. A. McMonkey, aka Laurel Zeisler, speech therapist, for their encouragement and support. Many thanks to Dr. Tomasz Małolepszy, mathematics professor and European sports expert, and Stuart Demsker, New York Jets fan extraordinaire and college sports expert, for their help with the text. And thanks to Dr. Bill Mallon, orthopedic surgeon and Olympic Games expert for getting me involved with this project; and the staff at Scarecrow Press, including Jon Woronoff, series editor, Andrew Yoder, production editor, April Snider, acquisitions editor, and Nicole McCullough, copyeditor, for helping to bring it to fruition.

ix

Acronyms and Abbreviations

AAU	Amateur Athletic Union
ABA	American Basketball Association
ABAUSA	Amateur Basketball Association of the United States of America
ABL	American Basketball League (several)
AIAW	Association for Intercollegiate Athletics for Women
AKA	also known as
BAA	Basketball Association of America
BFUSA	Basketball Federation of the United States of America
BYU	Brigham Young University
C	center
CBA	Continental Basketball Association
CBL	Central Basketball League
CCNY	City College of New York
CIAW	Commission on Intercollegiate Athletics for Women
CIS	Commonwealth of Independent States
EBA	Eastern Basketball Association
EBL	Eastern Basketball League
F	forward
FIBA	Fédération Internationale de Basketball (originally Fédération Internationale de Basketball Amateur)
FIBB	Fédération Internationale de Basket-Ball
G	guard
HRL	Hudson River League
IAAUS	Intercollegiate Athletic Association of the United States
IBL	International Basketball League
IOC	International Olympic Committee
LIU	Long Island University
LSU	Louisiana State University

MBC	Midwest Basketball Conference
NAIA	National Association of Intercollegiate Athletics
NAIB	National Association of Intercollegiate Basketball
NBA	National Basketball Association
NBADL	National Basketball Association Development League
NBC	Nashville Business College
NBL	National Basketball League (several)
NCAA	National Collegiate Athletic Association
NFL	National Football League
NHL	National Hockey League
NIBL	National Industrial Basketball League
NIT	National Invitation Tournament
NPBL	National Professional Basketball League
NYSL	New York State League
PBL	Philadelphia Basketball League
PBLA	Professional Basketball League of America
PF	power forward
PG	point guard
PSAL	Public School Athletic League (New York City)
SF	small forward
SG	shooting guard
SPHA	South Philadelphia Hebrew Association
UCLA	University of California, Los Angeles
ULEB	Union of European Leagues of Basketball
UNLV	University of Nevada, Las Vegas
USA	United States of America
USBL	United States Basketball League
USC	University of Southern California
USMA	United States Military Academy (Army)
USSR	Union of Soviet Socialist Republics (Soviet Union)
UTEP	University of Texas at El Paso
WBL	Women's Professional Basketball League
WBL	World Basketball League
WNBA	Women's National Basketball Association
YMCA	Young Men's Christian Association
YMHA	Young Men's Hebrew Association

Chronology

1891 United States December: Dr. James Naismith invents basketball. **21 December:** Eighteen students at Springfield College in Springfield, Massachusetts, participate in the first game of basketball.

1893 United States 21 March: The first women's basketball game is played at Smith College in Northampton, Massachusetts, using rules adapted by Senda Berenson.

1895 United States: Clara Baer publishes the first women's basketball rules called "Basquette." **United States 9 February:** The first men's intercollegiate basketball game is played at Hamline College in St. Paul, Minnesota. The Minnesota School of Agriculture defeats Hamline, 9–3.

1896 China 11 January: A basketball game is played at the YMCA in Tianjin, China. **United States 16 January:** The first men's intercollegiate basketball game with five players to a side is played between the University of Chicago and the University of Iowa. Chicago wins, 15–12.

1897 United States: The 23rd Street YMCA wins the first Amateur Athletic Union tournament in New York City.

1898 United States 30 July: The National Basket Ball League (NBL), the first professional basketball league, is organized. **United States 1 December:** The first professional league basketball game is played. Trenton defeats the Hancock Athletic Association, 21–19, in Philadelphia before 900 fans in the opening game of the NBL.

1902 United States 2 November: Harry "Bucky" Lew is the first black player to play in a professional basketball game when he plays for Lowell against Marlborough in a New England League game.

1903   United States 5 January: The professional Philadelphia Basketball League (PBL) begins play in direct competition with the NBL. Eight teams in the Philadelphia area form the league that schedules doubleheaders with the clubs' junior teams playing in the first game.

1904   United States 2 January: Due to competition from other professional leagues the NBL plays its last game. **United States 15–16 July:** At the Olympic Games in St. Louis, Missouri, a basketball tournament is held. The tournament is won by the Buffalo Germans, who defeat five other teams from various cities within the United States. Olympic historians consider this basketball tournament a "demonstration" event.

1906   United States 3 February: The Intercollegiate Athletic Association of the United States (IAAUS) is founded as a result of President Theodore Roosevelt requesting the presidents of three major Ivy League schools to take steps to improve the safety of collegiate athletics. In 1910, the organization becomes known as the National Collegiate Athletic Association (NCAA). **United States November:** The professional Central Basketball League (CBL) is organized with six teams in the Pittsburgh and eastern Ohio areas. After a successful 30-game season is played, a second 20-game postseason is held.

1909   United States 2 January: The first recorded death in a professional basketball game occurs when Charles Ritter of the North Wales team dies in a game against Stratton in the PBL. **United States 9 January:** The PBL terminates play, as four of the league's six teams drop out for financial reasons. **United States 16 March:** In the CBL, Johnstown defeats Alliance by the score of 110–9 on 55 field goals. Bill Keenan scores 38 field goals for 76 points. The individual total points is not surpassed in a professional basketball game until 1961, and the individual total field goals has never been topped. **United States 18 September:** The Hudson River League (HRL) begins play. **United States November:** Sportswriter-promoter William J. Scheffer organizes the Eastern Basketball League with teams in Pennsylvania and New Jersey and including some of the former PBL teams. This league is one of the most successful of the early professional leagues and lasts until 1923.

1912   United States 20 January: The HRL terminates operations. **United States 12 November:** The CBL disbands.

1913   Philippines 4–12 February: The first Far Eastern Championship Games are contested in Manila. Six countries enter the multisport festival—the Philippines, Japan, China, Malaysia, Thailand, and Hong Kong. The Philippines wins the basketball tournament.

1923   Japan May: Luis Salvador of the Philippines scores 116 points in a game against China in the Far Eastern Championship Games in Osaka. **United States 3 November:** The New York Renaissance plays their first game. Over the next 26 years, the all-black team plays more than 3,000 games and wins more than 80 percent of the time.

1925   United States 27 April: The American Basketball League (ABL) is formed in Cleveland, Ohio. This is the first professional basketball league with teams in major cities. Professional football executive Joseph F. Carr organizes the league. Eleven clubs apply for membership, and nine began the season.

1926   United States 7–9 April: The ABL holds a best-of-five game championship series billed as the "World Series of Basketball." The first half champion Brooklyn Arcadians lose to the second half champion Cleveland Rosenblums in three straight games.

1932   Palestine 28 March–6 April: The first Maccabiah Games are held. Jewish athletes from around the world are invited to participate in a series of sports competitions. **Switzerland 18 June:** The Fédération Internationale de Basket-Ball (FIBB) is organized in Geneva by representatives from seven European nations and one from South America. Leon Bouffard is named president. The organization's name is later changed to the Fédération Internationale de Basketball Amateur (FIBA).

1934   United States 29 December: Promoter Edward "Ned" Irish stages the first college doubleheader at Madison Square Garden in New York City. More than 16,000 fans watch New York University defeat Notre Dame University, 25–18, and Westminster College defeat St. John's University, 37–33. The success of the event causes Madison Square Garden to frequently schedule college basketball programs over the next 50 years.

1935   Switzerland 2–7 May: The first FIBA men's European Championships are held in Geneva. Latvia defeats Spain, 24–18, in the championship game. Czechoslovakia defeats Switzerland for third place. **United States November:** The Midwest Basketball Conference is created by Akron Firestone Tire and Rubber Company athletic director Paul "Pepper" Sheeks and Indianapolis businessman Frank Kautsky. The league, composed of nine company-sponsored teams, proves to be successful and evolves, two years later, into the National Basketball League (NBL).

1936 Germany 7–14 July: The first Olympic basketball tournament is held at the Berlin Olympics. Twenty-three nations are scheduled to compete, but Spain withdraws at the last minute due to its civil war. The Hungarian team also withdraws prior to the tournament. Initial matches for both countries are considered as forfeits. The United States defeats Canada 19–8 in the final match played outdoors in the rain. Mexico defeats Poland for third place. Dr. James Naismith is invited and attends the Games.

1938 United States 9–16 March: The first National Invitation Tournament (NIT) is held at Madison Square Garden in New York City. Temple University defeats the University of Colorado, 60–36, in the final game to win the championship. **Italy 12–16 October:** The first FIBA women's European Championships are held outdoors in Rome, with Italy finishing first and Lithuania second.

1939 United States 17–27 March: The first NCAA National Championship tournament is held. Oregon State University defeats Ohio State University, 46–33, at Evanston, Illinois, in the final game to win the championship. **United States 28 March:** The New York Renaissance defeats the Oshkosh All-Stars 34–25 to win the first World Professional Basketball Tournament in Chicago.

1942 United States 26 November: The Sheboygan Redskins of the NBL defeat the Chicago Studebakers, 53–45, in Sheboygan, Wisconsin. The Studebakers team consists of four white players and six black players. This is the first integrated game in the NBL.

1945 United States 7 February: In a regular-season college game between Columbia and Fordham, experimental rules are used. One of these rules provides for three points for field goals taken from beyond 21 feet.

1946   United States 23 April: The Eastern Pennsylvania Basketball League is organized, with play to begin in the fall of 1946. The minor league, with several name changes, survives until 2001. **United States 6 June:** The Basketball Association of America (BAA) is formed at a meeting of the Arena Managers Association of America in the Hotel Commodore in New York City. The 11-team league will begin play in November. **Canada 1 November:** The newly formed BAA begins play in Toronto, Ontario, as the New York Knickerbockers defeat the Toronto Huskies, 68–66, in the league's first game. **United States 11 December:** The Chicago Stags defeat the Cleveland Rebels, 88–70, in a BAA experimental game played with 15-minute quarters instead of the usual 12-minute ones.

1947   United States 22 April: The Philadelphia Warriors defeat the Chicago Stags, 82–80, in Philadelphia, Pennsylvania, to win the BAA's first league championship. **United States 24 October:** The 16-team Professional Basketball League of America (PBLA) begins play with a game in Wichita, Kansas, between the Atlanta Crackers and Oklahoma City Drillers and is won by Atlanta, 44–43. The league features the Chicago American Gears and George Mikan. **United States 13 November:** The PBLA disbands citing losses of more than $600,000.

1948   United States 10 May: Four of the NBL's strongest teams re-sign from the league and join the BAA. **England 30 July–13 August:** The Olympic basketball tournament is held in London. Twenty-three nations compete, including several who are not proficient at the sport. The team from Iraq loses games by scores of 102–30, 100–18, 98–20, 120–20, 125–25, and 77–28. The Irish team loses games by scores of 71–9, 73–14, and 55–12. The United States, which was nearly defeated by Argentina in a preliminary round, defeats France in the final, 65–21. Brazil defeats Mexico for third place. **United States 17 December:** The Detroit Vagabond Kings of the NBL disband and are replaced by the New York Renaissance, who play as the Detroit Rens. The Rens are the first all-black team in an integrated professional basketball league.

1949   United States 10 February: Joe Fulks of the Philadelphia Warriors scores 63 points in a BAA game against the Indianapolis Jets to set a league record that stands for 10 years. **United States 3 August:** The

BAA and the NBL merge to form the National Basketball Association (NBA). A 17-team league plays the 1949–1950 season.

1950 United States 28 March: City College of New York defeats Bradley University, 71–68, to win the NCAA National Championship. They had defeated Bradley two weeks earlier to win the NIT and become the first (and only) school to win both events in the same year. **United States 25 April:** Walter A. Brown, owner of the Boston Celtics, selects Charles "Chuck" Cooper in the second round of the NBA draft. When told by an associate that Cooper was black, Brown replies, "I don't care if he's striped, plaid, or polka dot, Boston selects Cooper." Cooper was the first black player to be chosen in the NBA draft, but Earl Lloyd is also chosen in a later round, and other black players are invited to several teams' training camps as the NBA decides to integrate. **United States 31 October:** Earl Lloyd of the Washington Capitols becomes the first black player in an NBA game. He scores six points against the Rochester Royals in an otherwise uneventful game in Rochester, New York. Chuck Cooper on 1 November, Nat Clifton on 4 November, and Hank DeZonie on 3 December are the other three black players to play in the NBA this year. **Argentina 22 October–3 November:** The first FIBA men's World Championship is held in Buenos Aires and is won by Argentina. Ten nations enter, with the United States finishing second and Chile third. **United States 1 November:** The eight-team National Professional Basketball League (NPBL) begins play. Four of the former NBL teams that played the 1949–1950 season in the NBA but were expelled following that season are joined by four other Midwestern teams in the new league. **United States 22 November:** The Fort Wayne Pistons defeat the Minneapolis Lakers, 19–18, in Minneapolis, Minnesota, in the lowest-scoring game in NBA history. George Mikan scores 15 of the loser's 18 points.

1951 United States 6 January: The Rochester Royals and Indianapolis Olympians play six overtimes in the longest game in NBA history. Indianapolis defeats Rochester, 75–73. Three of the six overtimes are scoreless. Only 19 personal fouls are called on the two teams, still a league record. **United States 17 January:** New York City district attorney Frank Hogan has five people arrested on charges of bribery and conspiracy for fixing college basketball games. Over the next several months, the scandal spreads and seven colleges and 32 people are eventually involved. **United States 21 January:** Milt Schoon of Denver scores 64 points in a NPBL game, the most by a professional since the early years of basketball. **Argentina 25 February–8 March:** The first Pan American Games men's basketball tournament is held in Buenos Aires. The United States wins, Argentina is second, and Brazil is third. There is no women's basketball tournament. **United States 2 March:** The first NBA All-Star Game is played in Boston, Massachusetts. The East defeats the West, 111–94, before 10,094 fans. **United States 24 March:** The NPBL disbands. **United States 21 April:** The Rochester Royals defeat the New York Knickerbockers, 79–75, in the seventh and deciding game in the NBA Finals. The Knicks had fought back from a three games to none deficit to require a seventh game.

1952   United States 10 February: The Baltimore Bullets use only five players in an NBA game and defeat the Fort Wayne Pistons, 82–77. **United States 31 May:** The Harlem Globetrotters begin a four-month around-the-world tour, the first ever for a basketball team. **Finland 14–18 July:** An Olympic qualifying tournament is held at Helsinki immediately prior to the Olympic Games. Thirteen nations compete, and six qualify to continue in the regular Olympic tournament. **Finland 25 July–2 August:** Sixteen nations compete in the Olympic Games at Helsinki. Teams are divided into four groups for the preliminary round, with the best two teams from each group advancing to the quarter-final round. The United States defeats the Union of Soviet Socialist Republics (USSR, also known as the Soviet Union), 36–25, in the final match, after the Soviet Union plays a possession-type offense in an attempt to be competitive. The third-place match is won by Uruguay over Argentina.

1953   United States 10 January: Jack Molinas of the Fort Wayne Pistons of the NBA is suspended for life by Commissioner Maurice Podoloff for betting on his own team. It later is disclosed that Molinas was heavily involved in fixing college games, and a decade later he is sentenced to prison. **Chile 7–22 March:** The first FIBA women's World Championship tournament is held in Santiago. Ten nations enter, and the United States wins, followed by Chile and France. **United States 9 January:** Bevo Francis of Rio Grande College scores 116 points in a game against Ashland Junior College. The record is later not recognized by the NCAA, as it was not set against a four-year school. **United States 21 March:** The Boston Celtics defeat the Syracuse Nationals,

111–105, in four overtimes in a playoff game. Bob Cousy makes 30 of 32 successful free throws and totals 50 points.

1954 United States 2 February: Bevo Francis scores 113 points against Hillsdale College. This record is accepted by the NCAA. **United States 7 March:** The NBA experiments with 12-foot baskets in a game at Milwaukee, Wisconsin, between the Minneapolis Lakers and Milwaukee Hawks, won by the Lakers, 65–63. **United States 8 March:** A regular-season doubleheader between the same two teams is experimented with by the NBA in Baltimore, Maryland. The Milwaukee Hawks defeat the Baltimore Bullets, 64–54, and, 65–54, in both games of the doubleheader played before 3,000 fans at the Baltimore Coliseum. Games consist of four 10-minute periods instead of the regular 12-minute periods. **United States 21 March:** Milan High School, with an enrollment of only 161 students, wins the Indiana State High School Championship. **United States 23 April:** The NBA adopts the 24-second shot clock to be used in the 1954–1955 season. **Brazil 22 October–5 November:** The United States wins the FIBA men's World Championship at Rio de Janeiro. Brazil is second and the Philippines third of the 12 competing nations. **United States 27 November:** The Baltimore Bullets of the NBA disband. The league rules that the 14 games the Bullets played will not count in the standings and some (but not all) of the individual statistics achieved in those games will count.

1955 United States 27 February: In the lowest-scoring NBA game played with a 24-second shot clock, the Boston Celtics defeat the Milwaukee Hawks, 62–57, on a slippery floor before 6,068 fans at the Providence Auditorium in Providence, Rhode Island. **Mexico 12–26 March:** The second Pan American Games is contested, and the first women's Pan American Games basketball tournament is held. The United States women's team is undefeated in eight contests and wins the gold medal. Chile is second, and Brazil is third. The men's team is defeated by Argentina in one game but, although tied with Argentina and Brazil, each with records of four wins and one defeat, is declared the winner based on the difference between points scored and allowed. Argentina is placed second and Brazil third.

1956 Australia 22 November–1 December: The Olympic basketball tournament is held in Melbourne. Sixteen nations are invited, but Israel withdraws at the last minute due to the Suez Crisis and is not replaced. Bill Russell leads the United States to victory over the Soviet Union in the final match, 89–55. Uruguay again finishes in third place by defeating France.

1957   United States 23 March: The University of North Carolina defeats the Wilt Chamberlain–led University of Kansas, 54–53, in triple overtime to win the NCAA Championship tournament. **United States 13 April:** The Boston Celtics win the NBA Championship by defeating the St. Louis Hawks in double overtime, 125–123, in the seventh game of the championship series. **Brazil 13–26 October:** The second FIBA women's World Championship is held in Rio de Janeiro. The United States finishes first of the 12 entrants, followed by the USSR and Czechoslovakia.

1958   United States 9 March: George Yardley of the Detroit Pistons scores 26 points in a game against the Syracuse Nationals and becomes the first player to score 2,000 points in an NBA season, as he concludes the season with 2,001. **United States 12 April:** The St. Louis Hawks defeat the Boston Celtics in six games to win the NBA Championship. Boston does not lose the title again until 1967.

1959   Chile 16–31 January: Brazil wins the FIBA men's World Championship in Santiago. The United States is second and Chile third of the 13 competing nations. **United States 27 February:** The Boston Celtics, without Bill Russell, set an NBA record by scoring 173 points in one game and defeat the Minneapolis Lakers, 173–139, before 6,183 fans at Boston Garden. The Celtics score 52 points in the fourth quarter, also a league record. **Soviet Union 10–18 October:** The United States does not enter the third FIBA women's World Championship, and only eight nations, all Communist, participate. The Soviet Union wins, followed by Bulgaria and Czechoslovakia. **United States 24 October:** Wilt Chamberlain makes his NBA debut with 43 points and 28 rebounds. Neither figure has since been surpassed by an NBA player in his first league game. **United States 8 November:** Elgin Baylor scores 64 points in one game to set a new NBA single-game scoring record, as the Minneapolis Lakers defeat the Boston Celtics, 136–118, at the Minneapolis Auditorium.

1960   Philippines 15–28 January: The first FIBA men's Asian Basketball Confederation Championships are held in Manila, with the

Philippines defeating the Republic of China to claim the championship. **Italy 26 August–10 September:** The Olympic basketball tournament is held in Rome. Sixteen nations are invited. The U.S. team, one of the best in the history of the sport, is led by Oscar Robertson, Jerry West, Jerry Lucas, and Walt Bellamy and easily wins the tournament. The Soviet Union is again second and Brazil third. Tournament host Italy finishes in fourth place. **United States 15 November:** Elgin Baylor breaks his own single-game NBA scoring record by scoring 71 points as the Los Angeles Lakers defeat the New York Knickerbockers, 123–108, at Madison Square Garden in New York City. **United States 24 November:** Wilt Chamberlain sets the NBA record by getting 55 rebounds in a game against Bill Russell and the Boston Celtics in a losing effort, as the Celtics beat Chamberlain's Philadelphia Warriors, 132–129, at Convention Hall in Philadelphia.

1961   United States March: A second college basketball scandal unfolds, and 37 players from 22 colleges are eventually arrested. Former NBA player Jack Molinas is later arrested and sentenced to ten to fifteen years in prison. **United States 27 October:** The San Francisco Saints defeat the Los Angeles Jets, 99–96, in San Francisco, as the American Basketball League (ABL) begins play. Among the league innovations is a three-point field goal if taken from more than 25 feet from the basket. **United States 6 November:** A four-cent postage stamp is issued by the United States commemorating the 100th anniversary of the birth of Dr. James Naismith, the inventor of basketball. **United States 8 December:** Wilt Chamberlain scores 78 points for the Philadelphia Warriors for a new NBA single-game record, and Elgin Baylor scores 63 points for the Los Angeles Lakers, who defeat the Warriors, 151–147, in a triple overtime game at Convention Hall in Philadelphia. Chamberlain also has 43 rebounds in the losing effort.

1962   United States 3 January: Wilt Chamberlain is ejected from a game in Los Angeles with 8:38 remaining in the fourth quarter. This is the only action he misses in the entire season, as he plays the complete duration of every other game. **United States 2 March:** Wilt Chamberlain scores 100 points in a game against the New York Knickerbockers played before 4,124 fans in Hershey, Pennsylvania, won by Chamberlain's Philadelphia Warriors, 169–147. Chamberlain makes 36 of 63 field goals and 28 of 32 free throws. He also has 25 rebounds and two assists. **United Arab Republic 24–31 March:** The first FIBA Men's Africa Championships are held in Cairo, Egypt. Five countries compete, with the United Arab Republic finishing first and Sudan second. **United States 14 April:** Elgin Baylor scores 61 in an NBA Finals game against the Boston Celtics to set a Finals scoring record.

1963   United States 1 January: The ABL suspends operations, citing losses in excess of $1,000,000. **Brazil 11–23 May:** Host nation Brazil wins the FIBA World Championship. Yugoslavia finishes in second place, the Soviet Union third, and the United States fourth of the 13 entrants.

1964   Japan 11–23 October: The Olympic basketball tournament is held in Tokyo, the first time it is held in Asia. Sixteen nations are invited. The United States again has a powerful team and is undefeated in nine matches. They defeat the Soviet Union, 73–59, for the gold medal. Brazil wins its second consecutive bronze medal by defeating Puerto Rico.

1965   Korea 20 April–2 May: The first FIBA women's Asian Basketball Confederation Championships are held in Seoul. Korea defeats Japan for the title.

1966   United States 19 March: Texas Western University defeats the University of Kentucky to win the NCAA National Championship. Texas Western is the first team to start five black players in an NCAA Final game. Kentucky, as is typical of the era, has an all-white team. **Guinea 10–18 April:** The first FIBA Women's Africa Championships are held in Conakry, with the United Arab Republic finishing first and Guinea second. **United States 18 April:** Bill Russell is named coach of the Boston Celtics for the coming season. Russell is the first black coach in the NBA. **United States 28 April:** The Celtics, under retiring coach Red Auerbach, win their seventh consecutive NBA Championship.

1967   United States 2 February: The American Basketball Association (ABA) is organized at a meeting in Pittsburgh, Pennsylvania. **United States 28 March:** The NCAA bans the use of the dunk shot in college games. **Uruguay 27 May–11 June:** The Soviet Union wins the FIBA World Championships in Montevideo. Yugoslavia finishes in second place, Brazil in third, and the United States in fourth among the 13 entrants. **United States 13 October:** The Oakland Oaks defeat the Anaheim Amigos, 134–129, in Oakland, California, before 4,828 fans in the first game in the ABA.

1968   United States 17 February: The Naismith Memorial Basketball Hall of Fame building is opened on the campus of Springfield College in Springfield, Massachusetts. Although the Hall of Fame was established in 1959, with annual induction ceremonies this marked the erection of a building open to the public housing the Hall of Fame's displays. **Mexico 13–25 October:** The Olympic basketball tournament is held in Mexico City. Sixteen nations are invited. The United States does not have its strongest possible team, as several top players, including Lew Alcindor, honor a black Olympic boycott and do not try out for the team. Nonetheless, college sophomore Spencer Haywood leads the United States to another undefeated record and the gold medal. Yugoslavia defeats the Soviet Union in the semifinals but is defeated by the United States in the final game. The Soviet Union wins the bronze medal by defeating Brazil. **United States 27 November:** In a regular ABA game in Louisville, Kentucky, five-foot, three-inch female jockey Penny Ann Early plays for the Kentucky Colonels. She enters the game in the second quarter following a time out, inbounds the basketball, the Colonels immediately call another time out and she is removed from the game. Her name, nonetheless, appears in the game's box score.

1970   United States 7 March: Austin Carr of Notre Dame University scores a record 61 points against Ohio University in an NCAA tournament first-round game. **United States 12 April:** The Indiana Pacers defeat the Pittsburgh Pipers, 177–135, in Indianapolis, to set the all-time ABA single-game scoring record. **Yugoslavia 10–24 May:** Host country Yugoslavia wins the FIBA World Championship in Ljubljana. Brazil finishes in second place, the Soviet Union in third, Italy in fourth, and the United States in fifth. Thirteen nations enter the tournament.

1972   United States 1 July: The Association for Intercollegiate Athletics for Women (AIAW) is created to oversee women's collegiate sports and administer national championships. It is dissolved on 30 June 1983, after the NCAA assumes control. **Germany 27 August–10 September:** The Olympic basketball tournament is held in Munich.

Sixteen nations are invited. The United States' Olympic winning streak is halted in the final game, won by the Soviet Union in a controversial ending. Although the United States appears to have won the game in a last second rally, 50–49, the last three seconds of the game are required to be repeated by the intervention of R. William Jones, president of the FIBA, and the Soviet Union scores the winning basket to win the gold medal, 51–50. The U.S. team feels they were cheated and refuses to accept the second-place silver medals. Cuba defeats Italy by one point, 66–65, for the bronze medal.

1974   United States 19 January: Notre Dame University defeats UCLA, 71–70, in South Bend, Indiana, and ends UCLA's 88-game winning streak. **Puerto Rico 3–14 July:** The Soviet Union wins the FIBA World Championship in San Juan. Yugoslavia is second and the United States third. The tournament is expanded to 14 teams.

1975   United States 1 January: The Amateur Basketball Association of the United States of America (ABAUSA) is formed. This organization is recognized by FIBA as the one responsible for American international basketball competition and replaces the Amateur Athletic Union in that capacity. **United States 14 February:** The San Diego Conquistadors defeat the New York Nets, 176–166, in four overtimes before 2,916 fans at the San Diego International Sports Arena in the highest scoring game in ABA history. Julius Erving scores 63 points for the Nets.

1976   United States 31 March: The NCAA reinstates the dunk shot for the 1976–1977 college basketball season. **United States 4 June:** The Boston Celtics defeat the Phoenix Suns, 128–126, in three overtimes before 15,320 fans at Boston Garden in a game sometimes called the "greatest game in NBA history. **United States 17 June:** The NBA accepts four teams from the ABA, the New York Nets, Indiana Pacers, Denver Nuggets, and San Antonio Spurs, and the ABA ceases to exist. **Canada 18–27 July:** The Olympic basketball tournament is held in Montreal. Twelve nations are invited for this and all subsequent men's Olympic tournaments. Yugoslavia again defeats the Soviet Union in the semifinal. The United States easily wins the gold medal by defeating Yugoslavia, 95–74. The Soviets defeat the host Canadians for the bronze medal. After the Olympic Games have begun, most of the African nations withdraw in protest over a tour of South Africa by the New Zealand rugby team. Egypt withdraws from the basketball tournament after losing its opening game and forfeits the remaining six games. A women's Olympic basketball tournament is held for the first time with six nations competing. The Soviet Union easily outclasses the field and wins the gold medal. The United States wins the silver medal and Bulgaria the bronze.

1978   United States 9 April: In an effort to win the league scoring championship, David Thompson of the Denver Nuggets scores 73 points in a 139–137 loss to the Detroit Pistons in Cobo Arena in Detroit in an afternoon game. That evening, George Gervin of the San Antonio Spurs scores 63 points against the New Orleans Jazz in a 153–132 loss to the Jazz at the Louisiana Superdome in New Orleans to win the championship. **Philippines 1–14 October:** Yugoslavia defeats the Soviet Union, 82–81, in overtime in the final game of the FIBA World Championships in Quezon City, Metro Manila. Brazil wins the bronze medal, Italy finishes in fourth place, and the United States, represented by the Athletes in Action team, is fifth. Fourteen teams compete. **United States 9 December:** The Women's Professional Basketball League begins play in Milwaukee, Wisconsin.

1979   United States 23 March: The Philadelphia 76ers defeat the New Jersey Nets, 123–117, at The Spectrum in Philadelphia in the conclusion of a suspended game that was begun on 8 November 1978. In the time between the initial game and its conclusion, three players were traded, Ralph Simpson, Eric Money, and Harvey Catchings, and consequently play for both teams in the game.

1980   Soviet Union 20–30 July: The Olympic basketball tournament is held in Moscow. More than 60 nations boycott the Olympics in protest of the Soviet invasion of Afghanistan in December 1979. As a result of the boycott, the 12 nations qualifying for the men's basketball tournament include such countries as Sweden and India, not exceptionally strong teams. The host Soviet Union is defeated by both Italy and Yugoslavia in preliminary rounds. Yugoslavia defeats Italy and wins the gold medal for the first time. The Soviet Union defeats Spain for the bronze medal. In the women's basketball tournament, the powerful Soviet Union team, led by seven-foot, two-inch Uljana Semjonova, again dominates the tournament and wins the gold medal by defeating Bulgaria in the final match, 104–73. Yugoslavia defeats Hungary for the bronze medal. **United States 29 November:** In the first college basketball game since 1945 to use the three-point field goal rule, Ronnie Carr of Western Carolina University makes the first one in a victory over Middle Tennessee State University.

1982 United States 12–28 March: The first NCAA Division I women's national basketball championship is held. Louisiana Tech defeats Cheyney State, 76–62, in the final game held at Old Dominion University in Norfolk, Virginia. **Colombia 15–28 April:** The Soviet Union defeats the United States, 95–94, in the final game and wins the FIBA World Championship. Yugoslavia defeats Spain by two points, 119–117, and is third. Host nation Colombia receives a bye in the preliminary round and even though winless for the tournament finishes in seventh place of the thirteen entrants in the tournament held in Cali.

1983 United States 13 December: The Detroit Pistons defeat the Denver Nuggets, 186–184, in triple overtime at McNichols Sports Arena in Denver, Colorado, before 9,655 fans in the highest-scoring game in NBA history. Four players each score more than 40 points in the game.

1984 United States 29 July–10 August: The Olympic basketball tournament is held in Los Angeles, California. In retaliation for the 1980 boycott, the Soviet Union and 13 other Communist nations boycott these Olympics ostensibly because of "security concerns." Romania defies the boycott and competes (although not qualifying for basketball), as does Yugoslavia (which did qualify in both men's and women's events). China returns to the Olympic Games for the first time since 1952 and competes in both men's and women's basketball. The United States, with one of its strongest teams, including Michael Jordan, Patrick Ewing, and Chris Mullin, easily wins the gold medal by defeating Spain in the gold medal game, 96–65. Yugoslavia defeats Canada for the bronze medal. In the women's competition, without the challenge from the Soviet team, the United States easily wins the gold medal over Korea, and China, led by the 17-year-old, six-foot, eight-inch, 254-pound Zheng Haixia defeats Canada for the bronze. **United States 21 December:** Six-foot, seven-inch Georgeann Wells becomes the first female to dunk a basketball in an NCAA game, playing for the University of West Virginia against the University of Charleston and using a regulation-sized basketball.

1986 Spain 5–19 July: The United States defeats the Soviet Union, 87–85, to win the FIBA World Championship in Madrid. Yugoslavia defeats Brazil for the bronze medal. Twenty-four nations are entered in the two-week tournament.

1988 Georgia, SSR 25 July: The first NBA preseason game ever contested outside North America is played in Tbilisi in the Soviet Republic of Georgia. The Atlanta Hawks (from Georgia in the United States) defeat the Soviet National Team, 85–84. **Korea 17–30 September:** The Olympic basketball tournament is held in Seoul. This is the first Olympic Games in 12 years in which both the United States and Soviet Union compete. The Soviets upset the United States in the semifinal round, 82–76, and then defeat Yugoslavia in the final, 76–63. The United States defeats Australia, 78–49, to win the bronze medal. Oscar Schmidt of Brazil sets Olympic individual scoring records with 55 points in one game on 24 September and an average of 42.3 for the tournament. In the women's competition, the field is expanded to eight teams, and the United States defeats the Soviet Union in the semifinal round and in the final round defeats Yugoslavia, 77–70, to win the gold medal. The Soviet Union defeats Australia to win the bronze.

1989 United States 9 November: The Milwaukee Bucks defeat the Seattle Supersonics, 155–154, after five overtime periods in the longest NBA game after the institution of the 24-second shot clock.

1990 Argentina 8–20 August: Yugoslavia defeats the United States in the semifinals and the Soviet Union in the finals to win the FIBA World Championships held in Buenos Aires. The United States defeats Puerto Rico by two points to win the bronze medal. Sixteen teams are entered. **Japan November 2:** The Phoenix Suns and Utah Jazz open the NBA season with a game in Tokyo. A capacity crowd of 10,111 see the Suns defeat the Jazz, 119–96. A second game between the two teams is played the following night. This marked the first time that two North American professional sports teams played a regular-season game outside of North America. **United States 10 November:** The Phoenix Suns score an NBA record 107 points in the first half of a game with the Denver Nuggets. The Suns are limited to 30 points in the third period and win the game, 173–143, at the Arizona Veterans' Memorial Coliseum in Phoenix before 14,487 fans.

1992   Spain 26 July–8 August: The Olympic basketball tournament is held in Barcelona. For the first time, professional basketball players are allowed to compete. The United States entry, called the "Dream Team," consists of 12 players, 10 of whom would be included in the 1996 NBA list of the 50 Greatest Players in NBA History. The team easily wins the gold medal with an average score of 117–73. This tournament, the first since the breakup of the Soviet Union and Yugoslavia, has teams from Lithuania and Croatia enter for the first time. The former Soviet Union enters a team consisting of players from its former republics under the name "Commonwealth of Independent States," also referred to as the "Unified Team." The United States defeats Croatia in the gold medal match, and Lithuania defeats the Unified Team for the bronze medal. In the women's competition, the Unified Team defeats China for the gold medal, and the United States defeats Cuba for the bronze.

1994   Canada 4–14 August: The United States with "Dream Team II," a collection of NBA professional players not nearly as talented as their 1992 predecessors, easily wins the FIBA World Championship in Toronto. They defeat Greece in the semifinal round and Russia in the finals. Croatia defeats Greece for third place. Sixteen teams are entered.

1995   United States February: A new women's professional basketball league—the American Basketball League (ABL)—is announced with play to begin in 1996.

1996   United States 16 April: The Chicago Bulls defeat the Milwaukee Bucks, 86–80, for their 70th regular-season NBA victory and set a new league record for most wins in a season. They win two more games before the season ends and finish with an all-time NBA record of 72–10. They then win 15 of 18 playoff games to win the NBA Championship. **United States 24 April:** The NBA announces the formation of the Women's National Basketball Association (WNBA) to begin play in 1997. **United States 20 July–3 August:** The Olympic basketball tournament is held in Atlanta. The U.S. "Dream Team III," although not quite as formidable as the 1992 version, again dominates the competition and wins easily by defeating Yugoslavia in the final match.

Lithuania again wins the bronze medal with a win over Australia. In the women's competition, 12 teams are invited for the first time and will be in all subsequent Olympic basketball tournaments. The U.S. team practices together for more than one year in preparation for the Games and wins the gold medal by defeating Brazil in the final, 111–87. Australia defeats the Ukraine for the bronze. **United States 18 October:** The women's American Basketball League (ABL) begins play with three games. The New England Blizzard defeat the Richmond Rage, 100–73, in Hartford, Connecticut, the Colorado Xplosion defeat the Seattle Reign, 82–75, in Denver, Colorado, and the San Jose Lasers defeat the Atlanta Glory, 78–70, in San Jose, California.

1997 United States 21 June: The WNBA begins play. The New York Liberty defeat the Los Angeles Sparks, 67–57, before 14,284 fans at the Forum in Inglewood, California. Penny Toler, Los Angeles guard, scores the first WNBA basket.

1998 United States 1 July: The NBA fails to reach agreement for a new collective bargaining agreement with the NBA Players Association and calls a lockout. **Greece 29 July–9 August:** Yugoslavia defeats Russia in the final game, 64–62, to win the FIBA World Championship in Athens. The United States is unable to send NBA players due to an NBA labor dispute but still defeats Greece for the bronze medal with a team consisting of American professional players who had been playing in Europe. Eleven of the 12 players on the team have or will have NBA experience but none are of star quality. Sixteen nations are entered. **United States 22 December 1998:** The women's ABL disbands.

1999 United States 20 January: The NBA and NBA Players Association reach an agreement, and the lockout is ended. The NBA All-Star Game is canceled, and the 82-game regular season is shortenened to 50 games and begins on 5 February. **United States 3 August:** Isiah Thomas purchases the entire Continental Basketball Association (CBA).

2000 Australia 17 September–1 October: The Olympic basketball tournament is held in Sydney. The U.S. team is challenged by Lithuania in the semifinal match and is fortunate to win, as a potential winning three-point field goal attempt by Šarūnas Jasikevičius of Lithuania just misses at the buzzer. The United States defeats France in the gold-medal game, and Lithuania again wins the bronze medal by defeating host nation Australia. The U.S. women's team defeats Australia for the gold medal, and the team from Brazil wins the bronze by defeating Korea.

2001 United States 8 February: The CBA discontinues operations after 55 years and files for bankruptcy shortly afterward. **United States 27 June:** Kwame Brown of Glynn Academy (high school) in Brunswick, Georgia, is selected by the Washington Wizards as the first overall selection in the NBA draft. He is the first player without college experience to be taken as the number one overall choice. The first four players drafted this year have no college experience.

2002 United States 26 June: Yao Ming, a seven-foot, five-inch player from China, is chosen by the Houston Rockets and becomes the first international player to be selected as the first player overall in the NBA draft. **United States 30 July:** Six-foot, five-inch Lisa Leslie of the Los Angeles Sparks becomes the first player in the WNBA to dunk the ball in league play. **United States 29 August–8 September:** The United States has its worst showing in international basketball competition, as the American team, composed of NBA players, finishes in sixth position in the FIBA World Championship tournament held in Indianapolis, Indiana. They are defeated by Argentina in a preliminary round, by Yugoslavia in the knockout quarter-final round, and by Spain in the consolation match for fifth place. Yugoslavia defeats Argentina in overtime to win the gold medal, and Germany defeats New Zealand to win the bronze.

2003 United States 25 June: LeBron James is selected by the Cleveland Cavaliers directly from high school in the NBA draft. He is the second high school player to be chosen as the first overall NBA draft selection.

2004 Greece 15–28 July: The Olympic basketball tournament is held in Athens. The U.S. team has its poorest showing and loses three games in the competition. Argentina defeats the United States in the semifinal and wins the gold medal by defeating Italy in the final, 84–69. The United States makes a recovery and defeats Lithuania, who had defeated them in a preliminary round match, in the bronze medal game, 104–96. The U.S. women's team continues their winning streak and defeats Australia for the gold medal, 74–63. Russia defeats Brazil for the bronze medal. **United States 19 November:** An NBA game at the Palace of Auburn Hills in Michigan between the Detroit Pistons and the Indiana Pacers ends in a fight between players and spectators. With less than one minute to play in the game, a fight between several players escalates to a brawl between players and spectators after a fan throws a cup of beer at Pacer Ron Artest. Nine players are suspended, and five fans are also legally charged.

2006   Japan 19 August–3 September: Spain defeats Greece, 70–47, to win the men's FIBA World Championship held in Saitama. The United States defeats Argentina, 96–81, to win the bronze medal. Twenty-four nations take part for the first time since 1986.

2007   United States 11 March: In a minor league game in Rockville, Maryland, the Maryland Nighthawks feature the world's tallest lineup. They start the seven-foot, nine-inch Sun Ming-Ming at center, the seven-foot, seven-inch former NBA player Gheorghe Muresan at one forward, and seven-foot, one-inch Ayo Adigun at the other forward. Seven-foot tall Deng D'Awol and six-foot, eight-inch Barry Mitchell are the guards. The starting five are only on the court together for a few minutes at the beginning of the game. The Nighthawks defeat Cape Cod, 132–128, on a half-court shot at the buzzer worth four points under the league's special rules. **United States 1 April:** Jordan Farmar plays a game in the NBA Development League in the afternoon and plays another in the evening in the NBA. He is the first player ever to play for these two leagues in the same day. **United States 9 July:** NBA referee Tim Donaghy resigns amid reports that the Federal Bureau of Investigation has been studying allegations that he placed bets on games that he officiated. **United States 15 August:** Donaghy pleads guilty to two federal charges.

2008   United States 29 July: Former NBA official Tim Donaghy is sentenced to 15 months imprisonment for his previous year's conviction. **China 10–24 August:** The Olympic basketball tournament is held in Beijing. The U.S. team practices together for three years prior to the Olympic Games and is referred to by sportswriters as the "Redeem Team." They win all eight contests in the tournament, but Spain gives them a battle in the final game before losing, 118–107. Argentina defeats Lithuania for the bronze medal. In the women's tournament, the U.S. team raises its undefeated streak to 33 consecutive Olympic matches and defeats Australia in the final game. Russia defeats China and wins the bronze medal.

2009   United States 20 January: Barack Obama is sworn in as the 44th president of the United States. He is the first U.S. president to have a strong interest in basketball. **United States 11 September:** Michael Jordan, David Robinson, John Stockton, Jerry Sloan, and C. Vivian Stringer are inducted into the Naismith Memorial Basketball Hall of Fame. **United States 8 October:** President Obama and several cabinet members play a basketball game at the White House against a bipartisan team of members of the House of Representatives.

2010   United States 4 June: John Wooden dies of natural causes just four months shy of his 100th birthday. **United States 8 July:** Lebron James in a one-hour television special announces that he would sign with the Miami Heat for the coming season to join former Olympic teammates Dwyane Wade and Chris Bosh. James' contract with the Cleveland Cavaliers had expired on 30 June and he had become a free agent. **Turkey 28 August–12 September:** The men's FIBA World Championship is played in Ankara, Istanbul, Izmir, and Kayseri. Twenty-four teams compete with teams from Iran, Jordan, and Tunisia participating for the first time. The United States, although many of their best players are not on the team, defeats Turkey for the championship, 81–64. Lithuania defeats Serbia for third place, 99–88. **Czech Republic 23 September–3 October:** The FIBA World Championship for women is scheduled. Sixteen teams will participate with games to be played in Brno and Ostrava.

Introduction

In less than 120 years, an activity invented by one man to alleviate winter boredom for a college gym class has evolved into a worldwide multibillion-dollar enterprise. It is impossible for Dr. James Naismith, basketball's inventor, to have envisioned the extent to which his simple game would reach. Without major changes to his original 13 rules, basketball is now played in more than 200 countries by people of all ages.

BASKETBALL'S BEGINNINGS

James Naismith was born 6 November 1861, in Almonte, Ontario, Canada. In 1869, his father, John Naismith, moved his family to Grand Calumet Island in Quebec, to build a sawmill there. The following year was a disastrous year for the Naismith family, as first a fire destroyed the sawmill, then a typhoid epidemic struck and eight-year-old James lost both parents, his father in October and his mother on his ninth birthday, 6 November 1870. He, his brother, and sister, were taken to live with their grandmother in the village of Bennie's Corners, Ontario. Less than two years later, she too, passed away, and the three orphans were entrusted to their uncle, Peter J. Young.

After graduating from Almonte High School in 1883, James Naismith attended McGill University in Montreal, Quebec, Canada, graduating with honors in 1887, with a bachelor's degree in philosophy. At McGill, the five-foot, ten-inch Naismith participated in football, soccer, and gymnastics, but his original intention was to be a clergyman. He studied theology at the Presbyterian Theological College in Montreal and was licensed for the ministry in 1890. An advocate of "muscular Christianity," he decided to couple his religious calling with physical education and become an instructor for the Young Men's Christian Association (YMCA).

In 1890, he enrolled at the International YMCA Training School in Springfield, Massachusetts. The school's function was to train students to become YMCA secretaries and physical directors. There, he met fellow student Amos Alonzo Stagg, a Yale graduate, who also had originally studied for the ministry but changed careers and was studying to become a physical educator. Stagg organized and coached Springfield's football team that fall, and Naismith played center for him. The following year, Naismith again played on the team and invented the first football helmet, although it was strictly for his own personal protection. Stagg, who would live to 102 years of age, coached college football until age 98 and was one of the major figures in the development of football.

Dr. Luther Gulick headed the athletic department at the school. He was aware that his students were bored with the calisthenics that usually comprised their winter physical activity and needed a new, more interesting physical activity. In 1891, Naismith, as one of his pupils, was challenged to create one.

In a book entitled *Basketball: Its Origin and Development*, published posthumously in 1941, Naismith describes how he created the game. "Dr. Gulick made the statement: 'There is nothing new under the sun. All so-called new things are simply recombinations of the factors of things that are now in existence.' The doctor used as an illustration the recombining of elements to make new chemical substances, such as synthetic drugs and dyes. Mentally applying this principle to our need for a new game, I made the remark: 'Doctor, if that is so, we can invent a new game that will meet our needs. All that we have to do is to take the factors of our known games and recombine them, and we will have the game we are looking for.' . . . Dr. Gulick asked the class to try out my idea and to bring a plan for a new game to the next session. Little did I think at that time what effect my suggestion would have in the field of sports and on my own life. The fact that this was assigned to us as a problem has led to the statement sometimes made that basketball was invented in one night. It was many weeks later that basketball actually came into existence." Naismith goes on to say that there were two groups of students at the school, prospective YMCA physical directors and prospective YMCA secretaries. The secretaries were not particularly interested in the hourly physical education class, as they felt it was not needed for their future profession. After two other instructors failed to motivate the secretaries, Dr. Gulick assigned the task to Naismith adding, "Now would be a good time for you to work on that new game that you said could be invented." (Although a student, Naismith was assigned to teach several classes during his second year at Springfield.)

Naismith states that he first attempted to modify the sport of football, but the restrictions he placed on tackling did not appeal to the men who preferred the rough outdoor game. An attempt at indoor soccer was abandoned for fear of breaking windows with errant shots. He then tried lacrosse, one of his favorite sports, but it, too, did not lend itself to being played indoors. After two weeks of failure with his class, he approached the problem philosophically. "My first generalization was that all team games used a ball of some kind." He decided that a large ball would be preferable to a small one, since a small ball could easily be hidden and it would be difficult for a large group to play with one. He then looked at rugby and realized that the tackling that eliminated its choice as an indoor game was the result of allowing players to run with the ball. His first principle for the new game was that a player could not run with the ball. He then sought an objective, such as the goal used in lacrosse and hockey, but he envisioned attempts at goal as being too rough (although the modern game of team handball is essentially that and is not an exceptionally rough sport). He then recalled an old childhood game called "Duck on a Rock."

Each player got a large stone (called a "duck"). One player, named the "guard," placed his "duck" on a large rock, and the others took turns standing behind a base line throwing their "ducks" at it in an attempt to knock it off. When a player missed, he had to retrieve his "duck" before being tagged by the guard. Naismith remembered that players who threw their ducks as hard as they could had much farther to go to retrieve their duck and had a greater chance of being tagged. Those who threw their ducks in an arc could retrieve theirs more readily. Said Naismith, "With this game in mind, I thought that if the goal were horizontal instead of vertical, the players would be compelled to throw the ball in an arc, and force, which made for roughness, would be of no value." He then decided that a box at each end of the floor would be the goal. He realized that with nine men surrounding the box, it would be impossible to score a goal, but he thought if the box were elevated above the players' heads it would work. "I now had a team game with equipment and an objective. My problem now was how to start it." He thought of a rugby throw-in but realized it was too rough and decided that throwing the ball up between one player from each team would minimize the roughness. Naismith's choice of ball was between a football and soccer ball. He realized that a football was shaped for ease in carrying the ball, and since there would be no carrying the ball in his new game, he chose a soccer ball.

The next step in the game's development has earned a place in sports history for the school's janitor, a Mr. Stebbins. Naismith went in search of two boxes and upon meeting the janitor asked if he had two boxes about 18 inches square. He was told that he didn't have boxes but did have two old peach baskets. "I told him to bring them up, and a few minutes later he appeared with the two baskets tucked under his arm. They were round and somewhat larger at the top than at the bottom. I found a hammer and some nails and tacked the baskets to the lower rail of the balcony, one at either end of the gym." Naismith then realized he needed a set of rules. He returned to his office and in less than one hour wrote out his set of 13 rules, brought them to Miss Lyons, the stenographer, and had them typed (see appendix A).

Shortly afterward, Naismith's class arrived at the gymnasium. "When the class arrived, I called the roll and told them that I had another game, which I felt sure would be good. I promised them that if this was a failure, I would not try any more experiments. I then read the rules from the bulletin board and proceeded to organize the game. There were eighteen men in the class; I selected two captains and had them choose sides. When the teams were chosen, I placed the men on the floor. There were three forwards, three centers, and three backs on each team. I chose two of the center men to jump, then threw the ball between them. It was the start of the first basketball game and the finish of the trouble with that class."

The game was probably played on 21 December 1891, although Naismith did not record the date in his memoirs. The 18 student/players included Lyman W. Archibald, William R. Chase, William H. Davis, Eugene S. Libby, Frank Mahan, Finlay G. MacDonald, T. Duncan Patton, Edwin P. Ruggles, and John G. Thompson on one team, and Fred E. Barnes, W. E. Carey, George E. Day, Benjamin S. French, Henri Galen, E. G. Hildner, G. S. Ishikawa, Raymond P. Kaighn, and G. R.

Weller on the other team. The final score was 1–0, with Chase being the player who scored the only goal. The game was a success and became a popular endeavor for the class. Shortly after the historic game, Frank Mahan removed the original rules from the bulletin board. He gave them to Naismith, who retained them until his death. The rules remained in the Naismith family until 2007, when Naismith's memorabilia was sold at auction.

Mahan also asked Naismith what the game was to be called. "Frank insisted that it must have a name and suggested the name of Naismith ball. I laughed and told him that I thought that name would kill any game. Frank then said: 'Why not call it basketball?' 'We have a basket and a ball, and it seems to me that would be a good name for it,' I replied. It was in this way that basketball was named." (The name was originally spelled as two words but by the early 20th century had evolved to its present spelling.)

EARLY DEVELOPMENT

In January 1892, the Springfield school newspaper *The Triangle* printed the rules under the heading "A New Game." The paper was distributed to YMCAs across the country, and the game spread rapidly. On 11 March 1892, a public demonstration of the game was held at the International YMCA Training School, with Naismith, Gulick, Stagg, and four other instructors playing against a team of seven students. Stagg scored the only goal for the instructors who were defeated, 5–1. This game and one other when Naismith was at the University of Kansas in 1898 were the only two times that Naismith ever played his own game.

The new game quickly spread countrywide, although its structure by modern terms was quite loose. College students played games against students from other schools, YMCAs, high schools, or local town teams. Rules were also still being evolved and varied from game to game. The first college basketball game with five players a side took place in Iowa City on 16 January 1896, between the University of Chicago and the University of Iowa, with Chicago winning, 15–12. In 1901–1902, a formal college conference was organized with Yale, Trinity, and Wesleyan, comprising the Triangular League. Other conferences followed during the next decade. In 1906, the Intercollegiate

Athletic Association of the United States (IAAUS) was founded as a result of President Theodore Roosevelt requesting the presidents of three major Ivy League schools to take steps to improve the safety of collegiate athletics. In 1910, the IAAUS was renamed the National Collegiate Athletic Association (NCAA), but it wasn't until 1939 that it began sponsoring a national championship tournament.

The Amateur Athletic Union (AAU), founded in 1888, also became involved with sponsoring basketball and in 1897 held its first tournament in New York City. Organized nonprofessional basketball during these early years was primarily held under the jurisdiction of the YMCA and AAU. The international YMCA organization also helped spread the game throughout the world. On 11 January 1896, the Tianjin, China, YMCA held one of the first basketball games in China.

THE EARLY PROFESSIONALS

Professional basketball began in Trenton, New Jersey, in 1896. A Trenton YMCA team with Fred Cooper as captain held a game at the Masonic Temple in Trenton against the Brooklyn YMCA on 7 November 1896, in which admission was charged—25 cents for seats and 15 cents for standing room. Basketball rules at this time still awarded an out-of-bounds ball to the first player to touch it, and this game was played with a 12-foot wire fence surrounding the court so the ball would never go out of bounds and the players would not be mingling with the spectators in attempts to retrieve it. It was also noted that there would be fewer delays and the game would move more quickly. In later years, Cooper said the idea for a cage was the result of a sports editor claiming that the Trenton team played like monkeys and should be put in a cage. Regardless of its origin, the fact is that early Trenton games used a cage, although other teams did not.

On 20 July 1898, at a meeting in the Hotel Vendig in Philadelphia, Pennsylvania, several men organized the first professional basketball league. William E. Morgenweck of Camden, New Jersey, James McMurray of Millville, New Jersey, H. W. Junghurth, representing the Germantown Big Five of Philadelphia, and sports editor Peter E. Wurfflein, representing Frank Smith of Trenton, were among those present. Horace S. Fogel of Philadelphia was elected league president.

The league, called the National Basket Ball League (NBL), began play in Philadelphia on 1 December 1898. Six teams began the season, three from New Jersey, the Trenton Nationals, Camden Electrics, and Millville Glassblowers, and three from the Philadelphia area, the Clover Wheelmen, Germantown Nationals, and Hancock Athletic Association. Both Germantown and Hancock dropped out prior to the season's end. Trenton had been the only team that used a cage but insisted on its use for league play, and it became the league standard.

The NBL lasted until 3 January 1904. Other professional leagues were begun and ended in the interval. Another Philadelphia-based league, the American Basketball Association, existed briefly in 1900. An American Basketball League, Massachusetts Basketball League, and New England Basketball League were other short-lived attempts. The Philadelphia Basketball League, from 1902–1909, was the second professional league that had any longevity. It was followed by the Central Basketball League (1906–1912), Eastern Basketball League (1909–1923), Hudson River League (1909–1912), New York State League (1911–1923), Pennsylvania State League (1914–1921), and Interstate League (1915–1920). Nearly all these leagues suspended play for one or more seasons during World War I, as most teams played their games in armories that were then needed for the military. In addition, many of the leagues' players were in military service. Each of these leagues attracted the top players, with many players playing in several leagues during the same season. Leagues were relatively local, with teams within 100 to 200 miles of each other.

WOMEN'S BASKETBALL

Shortly after basketball was invented, two women contributed to promote and popularize the game for females. Senda Berenson was hired as a teacher at Smith College to teach physical education in 1892. After learning of Dr. James Naismith's new game of basket ball, she introduced it to her students. She modified the rules to adapt the sport to women. Her rules variation, with six players to a team, the court divided into three sections and only limited movement permitted, remained the women's rules for more than half a century. On 22 March 1893, the first organized women's basketball game was held at Smith College (with no male spectators allowed). In 1899, she became editor of the official rules and retained this position for the next 18 years.

Clara Baer established a physical education department at Newcomb College in New Orleans, Louisiana, in 1891. While there, she introduced the new sport of basketball in 1893. In 1895, she published the first women's basketball rules using the name "Basquette." Her rules were designed to adapt Dr. Naismith's rather physical sport of basket ball to women's physiques and capabilities and minimized player movement. She divided the court into sections, although it is thought that she might have done so because she misread Dr. Naismith's drawings of the basketball court. She also invented a game called "Newcomb Ball," a volleyball offshoot and is credited as being the originator of netball. The women's game was played in schools and colleges but had declined by the 1920s due to administrators' overzealous attempts at preserving "femininity." It survived in some areas, notably Iowa high schools, where girls' basketball was extremely popular. AAU teams and national tournaments also survived, especially in the southeastern states, but on the whole scholastic basketball was a male sport.

THE FIRST TRUE MAJOR LEAGUE

In 1925, the first attempt at a league with a wider scope occurred. The American Basketball League (ABL) was organized by George Preston Marshall, George Halas, and Joseph Carr, all executives with the National Football League. It was the first league based in the larger cities throughout the eastern half of the United States, with teams mostly in cities that had Major League Baseball teams. Teams in the league for the first season were the Boston Whirlwinds, Brooklyn Arcadians, Buffalo Bisons, Chicago Bruins, Cleveland Rosenblums, Detroit Pulaski Post Five, Fort Wayne Caseys, Rochester Centrals, and Washington Palace Five.

The league was split in two halves and played 16 games in the first half and 14 in the second. Since basketball rules were still in the process of development, variations existed in different parts of the country. The league agreed on a uniform set of rules, eliminated the two-handed dribble, and required backboards. Players were required to sign exclusive contracts and not jump teams, as had been the custom.

The ABL survived for six seasons. Its downfall in 1931 was primarily due to the national economic depression. Nearly all the best players participated, with one notable exception. As was the case in Major League Baseball at the time, there were no black players. The ABL was resurrected in 1933 and continued in operation on a smaller scale for the next 20 years, with teams primarily on the Eastern Seaboard.

SHOWTIME: THE HARLEM GLOBETROTTERS AND OTHERS

In addition to league teams, there were many other independent basketball teams in existence. Some of the better ones traveled extensively for games and became well-known and prospered. The Original Celtics were one such team. Although at times they joined various leagues, and usually dominated play, they fared better as an independent team from 1914 to 1940.

Another of the best independent teams was the all-black New York Renaissance or Rens. They began play on 3 November 1923, and were organized by Bob Douglas. Over the next 26 years they traveled extensively and played more than 3,000 games, winning more than 80 percent of the time.

The Harlem Globetrotters, another all-black independent team, was organized in the late 1920s. (Their legendary first game in Hinckley, Illinois, on 7 January 1927, has since been proven to be a myth.) Like the Rens, the Globetrotters traveled extensively and played all-comers, but unlike the Rens, the Trotters found that they widened their appeal by mixing comedy into their games. By the 1950s, the Trotters relied mostly on comedy for their appeal and in the 21st century are still a successful comedy attraction.

Other touring teams, also known as barnstorming teams, of the 1920s and 1930s include Olsen's Terrible Swedes, the House of David, and the all-female All-American Red Heads.

THE GROWTH OF THE INTERNATIONAL GAME

Basketball has been played outside the United States since the mid-1890s, when the international YMCAs introduced the sport. As early as January 1896, basketball was played in China. In Brazil, in 1896, U.S. professor Shaw of Mackenzie College of São Paulo introduced the game. G. Carlson of the United States introduced the game in Chile in 1919. The YMCA was responsible for introducing the game in Argentina in 1912, Australia and Canada around 1900, Cuba in 1906, Egypt in 1920, Greece in 1919, Hong Kong in 1920, India between 1905 and 1910, Korea in 1907, New Zealand in the 1920s, the Philippines shortly after 1900, Portugal in 1913, Puerto Rico in 1913, Romania in 1920, Uruguay in 1912, and Yugoslavia in 1920.

Bulgaria learned the game in 1916, from students who had studied abroad. Czechoslovakia saw its first exhibition game in 1897, introduced by Josef Klenka, who had studied in the United States. In 1924, a group of youths who had studied in the United States introduced the game to Ecuador. In England, surprisingly, the sport was introduced in 1895, at a women's physical training college by an American physical education teacher. The game, however, has never caught on there, although Great Britain did field a men's team in the 1948 Olympic Games. In 1893, Mel Rideout returned from a training session in Springfield, Massachusetts, and working with the YMCA in Paris, introduced the game. Germany took to the sport rather late, and even though they competed in the 1936 Olympic basketball tournament in Berlin the game did not catch on until the 1950s. Norway is another country that did not play the game until the 1960s.

In Italy, basketball was introduced by Miss Ida Nomi Venerosi Pesciolini, who taught the game to girls in Siena. Hyozo Omori, a graduate of the Springfield International YMCA Training school, introduced the Japanese to the sport in 1908. The Mexican Basketball Federation claims to be the second nation to play the sport (although this is most likely an exaggeration). In an article written for the 1972 Fédération Internationale de Basketball book *The Basketball World*, the authors state, "It is almost certain that Mexico was the second country in the world in which basketball was played after its invention in 1891 by Dr. Naismith. It was introduced by the YMCA . . . at the turn of the century." Since it has been documented that it was played in China in 1896, this statement may be the result of an overenthusiastic national federation.

Peru learned the game from two North American missionaries, Joseph Byrne Lockey and J. A. MacKnight, in 1911. Poland learned the game from a Miss M. Germanowna, who discovered the game while studying in England. Spain learned the game from a Roman Catholic priest, Father Eusebio Millan, who came to Spain from Cuba in 1921. In Turkey, it was introduced in 1904, by an American teacher at Robert College in Istanbul. The Union of Soviet Socialist Republics first played the game in 1906.

By the 1930s, the game was being played in more than 30 countries. In 1932, the Fédération Internationale de Basket-Ball (FIBB) was created in Geneva, Switzerland with eight founding members Argentina, Czechoslovakia, Greece, Italy, Latvia, Portugal, Romania and Switzerland. The organization's name was later changed to Fédération Internationale de Basketball Amateur (FIBA) and, in 1989, the word *amateur* was dropped from its name, although the acronym FIBA was retained. It attempted to standardize the rules and oversee international tournaments. It quickly grew and today has more than 200 members. R. William Jones was one of the cofounders of FIBA and worked toward basketball's inclusion in the 1936 Olympic Games in Berlin. He was the secretary-general of the FIBA from 1932 until 1976 and helped create the European Championships and World Championships.

In 1936, basketball was played at the Olympic Games for the first time. Twenty-three nations took part in the tournament, which was played outdoors. The championship final between the United States and Canada was played in a rainstorm with a court that quickly became muddy. The United States won, 19–8, and did not lose another Olympic Games basketball game until 1972.

COLLEGES AND THE ORIGINS OF THE NBA

High school and college basketball continued to be played extensively and, in December 1934, sports writer Edward "Ned" Irish began promoting college basketball doubleheaders at Madison Square Garden. They proved to be very successful and became a winter staple for large indoor arenas. In 1938, the Metropolitan Basketball Writers Association in New York City organized a postseason men's collegiate basketball tournament called the National Invitation Tournament, quickly shortened by headline writers to the NIT. The tournament was played at Madison Square Garden in New York City following the regular college basketball season. Six teams were invited for the first NIT: Temple University, the University of Colorado, Oklahoma A&M College, New York University (NYU), Long Island University (LIU), and Bradley Tech. The tournament began on 9 March 1938, with Temple University meeting Bradley Tech and NYU playing LIU. The two winners, NYU and Temple, advanced to the following week's games with Colorado and Oklahoma A&M, with Temple winning the initial tournament.

The NCAA followed suit in 1939 and held its first national championship tournament in Evanston, Illinois. Eight teams were invited, including the University of Oregon, the University of Texas, Oklahoma University, Utah State University, Villanova University, Brown University, Wake Forest University, and Ohio State University. Oregon defeated Ohio State to win the inaugural NCAA National Championship. The two tournaments grew in size and stature until the 1970s, when the NCAA's rules prohibited the best schools from participating in the NIT. The NCAA tournament now features 65 schools, and the NIT has 32 that were not selected for the more prestigious NCAA event.

The 1930s also saw many businesses sponsoring company basketball teams, especially in the Midwestern United States. This led to the formation of the Midwest Basketball Conference (MBC), created by Akron Firestone Tire & Rubber Company athletic director Paul "Pepper" Sheeks and Indianapolis businessman Frank Kautsky in November 1935. The nine-team league, consisting mostly of corporate-sponsored teams, did not have a fixed schedule, although teams were required to play a minimum of eight games against at least four league opponents. It comprised the Akron Firestones, Buffalo Bisons, Chicago Duffy Florists, Dayton Metropolitans, Detroit Hed-Aids, Indianapolis Kautskys, Indianapolis U.S. Tire, Pittsburgh YMHA, and Windsor Cooper Buses. The MBC can be considered to be the grandfather of the present-day National Basketball Association (NBA). After two successful years, the MBC was renamed the National Basketball League (NBL) for the 1937–1938 season and became the premier professional league for the next 12 years.

Internationally, the 1930s saw the birth of FIBA, the inclusion of basketball in the 1936 Olympic Games, and the inception of the FIBA European Championships.

WARTIME BASKETBALL AND POSTWAR PROSPERITY

World War II saw many changes in American life. Professional sports, for the most part, continued, although with modification. The ABL survived with just four or five teams from 1942–1944, and the NBL also had only five in 1942–1943 and four in 1943–1944.

One innovation in the 1942–1943 season in the NBL was its use of black players. Although baseball was not yet integrated, the Chicago Studebakers NBL team of 1942–1943 used 12 players who were members of the United Auto Workers union employed at the Studebaker plant in Chicago—eight black former Harlem Globetrotters and four white players. The Toledo Jim White Chevrolet team also began the season with several black players. Unlike Major League Baseball's integration in 1947, with Jackie Robinson, there was little publicity or celebration with the basketball integration, and it was carried out successfully. Ironically, during the war years due to their manpower shortage, the Harlem Globetrotters actually employed a white player, Bob Karstens.

With many athletes involved in military service, some of the best basketball of that time was played by Armed Forces teams. In addition to playing other military teams, they also played college teams and usually came out on top. From 1942–1945, the Great Lakes Naval Training Station won 100 games, while losing only 11. Other top squads were Norfolk Naval Training Station, Camp Grant Army Base, Valley Forge Military Hospital, and Mitchel Field.

After the war, one of the most important events in the history of basketball occurred. The Basketball Association of America (BAA) was organized on 6 June 1946, at a meeting of members of the Arena Managers Association of America. Representatives of the Boston Garden (Walter A. Brown), Cleveland Arena (Al Sutphin), Chicago Stadium (James D. Norris and Arthur Wirtz), New York's Madison Square Garden (Edward "Ned" Irish), Philadelphia Arena (Pete Tyrell), Pittsburgh Arena (John Harris), Providence Arena (Lou Pieri), St. Louis Arena (Emery Jones and Arthur Wirtz), Toronto's Maple Leaf Gardens (Lew Hayman), Washington's Uline Arena (Mike Uline), and a group representing Indianapolis attended the meeting. Each prospective owner contributed $10,000 as a franchise fee. Maurice Podoloff, president of the American Hockey League and operator of the New Haven Arena, was named league president. The season began on 1 November 1946, in Toronto, Ontario, Canada, with a game between the New York Knickerbockers and Toronto Huskies, won by New York, 66–64. The other teams in the league were the Boston Celtics, Chicago Stags, Cleveland Rebels, Detroit Falcons, Philadelphia Warriors, Pittsburgh Ironmen, Providence Steamrollers, St. Louis Bombers, and Washington Capitols.

That same year, the NBL expanded to 12 teams, and professional basketball, like most American sports, enjoyed the postwar prosperity. Several minor leagues, including the Eastern Pennsylvania Basketball League, Pacific Coast Basketball League, and New York State Basketball League also were in operation. In 1947, Maurice White, owner of the NBL's champion Chicago American Gears, attempted to organize yet another professional league, the Professional Basketball League of America (PBLA). The ambitious venture began operation on 24 October 1947, with 16 teams throughout the Midwestern and southeastern parts of the United States. George Mikan of the Gears was the league's star attraction, but other top professionals also played. In less than one month, the league's losses surpassed $600,000, and the Gears filed for bankruptcy. On 13 November 1947, the league was disbanded.

After the failure of the PBLA, the Minneapolis Lakers of the NBL signed Mikan. The bespectacled six-foot, ten-inch, 245-pounder was virtually unstoppable once he established himself in the pivot, and the Lakers began a string of six league championships in seven seasons, beginning with the 1947–1948 season and ending with Mikan's retirement after the 1953–1954 season. Mikan, referred to as Mr. Basketball, was voted by the Associated Press as the greatest basketball player in the first half of the 20th century and was often featured on the marquee at Madison Square Garden as "Tonite: Mikan vs. the Knicks." He led his league in scoring in nearly every season he played and set league records for total points scored and highest average in a season.

The BAA, meanwhile, lost four of its original 11 teams but added the ABL's Baltimore Bullets, contracted its schedule from 60 to 48 games, and continued in operation. It continued to provide an opportunity for the best graduating college players and began to attract players from the rival ABL and NBL as well. As the NBL continued to lose players to the BAA, Fort Wayne Zollner Pistons' owner Fred Zollner attempted to promote a merger between the two leagues. As a first step toward that goal, Fort Wayne and three of the NBL's strongest teams, the Lakers, Indianapolis Kautskys, and Rochester Royals, joined the BAA on 10 May 1948. The NBL managed to continue in operation and added several new teams, including one in Detroit. On 17 December 1948, the NBL's new Detroit franchise, the Vagabond Kings, disbanded. The league offered the franchise to the all-black New York Renaissance team, who played as the Detroit Rens, and assumed the Vagabond Kings' record of 2–17. Following the 1948–1949 season, the NBL and BAA formally merged, and on 3 August 1949, the 17-team NBA was created.

After a season with 17 teams, an unbalanced schedule, and extensive travel, the NBA established a minimum arena seating capacity requirement that effectively eliminated several of the former NBL teams, and the association began the 1950–1951 season with just 10 teams. Most of those teams eliminated from the NBA attempted to form a new league—the National Professional Basketball League—in 1950–1951. The new league completed its season but disbanded in the midst of its postseason playoffs.

INTEGRATION, SCANDALS, AND THE NEAR DEATH OF THE NBA

While the NBL had been integrated since 1942, and the minor league Eastern and American leagues and the United States 1948 Olympic team as well as many colleges were also integrated, the BAA did not contain any black players. The first year of the NBA did not have any either. Although there were no written prohibitions, an unwritten agreement among the team owners upheld the ban. But in 1950, NBA Celtics owner Walter A. Brown drafted Charles "Chuck" Cooper of Duquesne University, and Washington Capitols owner Mike Uline drafted Earl Lloyd of West Virginia State University. Brown's famous quote after being told that "Cooper was a colored boy" was, "I don't care if he's striped, plaid, or polka dot, Boston selects Cooper of Duquesne." NBA owners had been afraid of alienating Abe Saperstein, owner of the all-black Harlem Globetrotters, whose team often performed in NBA preliminary games and frequently drew the largest crowd of the season for them. Integration still proceeded relatively slowly during the next 10 years, and teams rarely had more than two black players in that time.

During the postwar era, the college game continued to rise in popularity. Madison Square Garden and other large arenas often scheduled college doubleheaders and held midseason tournaments. The Holiday Festival in New York was one such event and was often sold out. In 1950, City College of New York (CCNY) defeated Bradley University to win the NIT at the Garden and two weeks later repeated the performance there by again defeating Bradley to win the NCAA National Championship.

Less than one year later, on 17 January 1951, New York City district attorney Frank Hogan had five people arrested on charges of bribery and conspiracy for fixing college basketball games. Over the next several months the scandal spread, and seven colleges and 32 people were eventually involved. CCNY was one of the hardest hit by the scandal, and Long Island University and the University of Kentucky were also affected. As a result, the NBA permanently banned several players, and two then-current NBA stars, Ralph Beard and Alex Groza, were suspended for life. Kentucky star seven-foot-tall Bill Spivey, even though acquitted by a jury, was among those banned, as were LIU's Sherman White and Bradley player Gene Melchiorre. In separate incidents, NBA referee Sol Levy was arrested for fixing professional games, and NBA star Jack Molinas received a lifetime suspension in 1953 for betting on his own team. (It was subsequently disclosed that Molinas was also involved with fixing college games and, a decade later, his problems surfaced in a second college fixing scandal and he was imprisoned.) Levy, on the other hand, was acquitted on a technicality in 1954.

Although the NBA no longer had competition from the NBL, it still did not achieve status as a major sport in the United States. One factor was the constant stalling and strategic fouling. On 22 November 1950, the Fort Wayne Pistons defeated the Minneapolis Lakers, 19–18. The Fort Wayne coach realized that the best way to play the champion Lakers was to restrict their opportunities to score and consequently instructed his players to hold the ball. The strategy worked, but league commissioner Maurice Podoloff instructed all teams never again to use that approach.

During the 1953–1954 NBA season, the league tried a few experiments. In one, they played a regular-season game with 12-foot-high baskets, but this proved to be a failure since the taller players still had the advantage and neither team could shoot well. They also tried a game where the two officials sat in high chairs on the sidelines similar to those used by a tennis umpire. That, too, was unsuccessful. By 1954, the incessant fouling and consequent stoppages caused Dan Biasone, owner of the Syracuse Nationals, to promote the use of a shot clock that would require teams to shoot within a fixed period of time or relinquish the ball. A 24-second clock and limits on team fouls were used for the 1954–1955 season, and its use saved the league. The game was played at a faster pace, scoring improved, and players were required to be more athletic. The Boston Celtics, led by Bob Cousy and Bill Sharman, played at a fast pace and took every opportunity to fast break. During the 1954–1955 season, they became the first NBA team to average 100 points per game.

BILL RUSSELL, WILT CHAMBERLAIN, AND THE BOSTON CELTICS

When Bill Russell joined the Boston Celtics in December 1956, after leading the United States to the Olympic championship, he essentially revolutionized the sport. He emphasized shot-blocking and defense and, coupled with the Celtics fast-breaking style of play, the astute leadership of coach Arnold "Red" Auerbach, and an unselfish team, they won nine NBA Championships over the next 11 seasons.

In 1959, the NBA gained the services of Wilt Chamberlain, a seven-foot, one-inch, 275-pound player unlike any other that had ever played in the league. Had the NBA not had a rule prohibiting teams from signing players who were not four years past their high school graduation, he would have joined the NBA four years sooner. He was far and away the best high school player in the nation in 1956, when he played for Overbrook High School in Philadelphia and was recruited by more than 100 colleges. Eddie Gottlieb, owner of the NBA's Philadelphia Warriors had a special draft rule passed that enabled teams to have first choice of any high school player in their area and was rewarded four years later when he was able to sign Chamberlain to a Warriors' contract.

Wilt enrolled at the University of Kansas and according to NCAA rules of the era was not eligible to play varsity basketball until his sophomore year. That year he led Kansas to the final of the NCAA

Championship tournament, where they were defeated in triple overtime. He was injured in his junior year at school, and consequently Kansas did not qualify for the NCAA tournament. After the frustrations of playing college basketball, he left school after his junior year and signed with the Harlem Globetrotters for one year.

His first NBA game, on 24 October 1959, was against the New York Knickerbockers, and Chamberlain quickly showed that he was in a class by himself. He scored 43 points and had 28 rebounds. Neither figure has since been matched by any NBA player in his debut. Chamberlain continued his impressive scoring and rebounding and by the end of his first season had 2,707 points, a 37.6 points per game average, and 1,941 rebounds, a 27.0 rebound per game average. He shattered the previous NBA records, which were Bob Pettit's 2,105 points and 29.2 points per game average, and Bill Russell's 1,612 rebounds and 23.0 rebound average. Chamberlain continued to improve and two years later scored the unheard total of 4,029 points, averaging 50.4 points per game. That season he also scored an even 100 points in a game.

Although Chamberlain's scoring and rebounding were much greater than anyone had ever achieved, his inability to lead the Warriors to the league championship was constantly highlighted. While Bill Russell was leading the Celtics to one NBA Championship after another (nine in eleven years), Chamberlain's teams failed to win even one title. In 1967, after he had been traded to the Philadelphia 76ers and had several other outstanding players on his team, he modified his game, minimized his scoring, and concentrated on assists. Playing the role of center-playmaker, he averaged 7.8 assists per game while still scoring 24.1 points and capturing 24.2 rebounds and led the 76ers to a league-record 68 victories and the NBA Championship.

INTERNATIONAL BASKETBALL IN THE 1960s

As the sport's popularity grew in the United States, it also grew internationally. Basketball leagues in Europe were primarily organizations of competing sports clubs and consequently were considered "amateur" by the FIBA, thus their participants were also able to compete for their national teams in such international competitions as the Olympic Games and World Championships. Several Americans, including future New

York Knickerbocker and U.S. senator Bill Bradley, competed in Europe. European students began attending colleges in the United States and returning to their homelands to play in their national leagues. Hall of Famer Krešimir Ćosić was one such player. He attended Brigham Young University, was selected for All-American teams, and was drafted by the NBA, but he preferred to play in Yugoslavia and remain eligible for Olympic competition. The Italian and Spanish leagues were two of the strongest national leagues.

THE AMERICAN BASKETBALL ASSOCIATION: THE NBA'S GREATEST CHALLENGE

While Russell and Chamberlain continued their duels, 1967 saw the birth of a new professional league, the American Basketball Association (ABA). Although an attempt at a third major league occurred in 1961, with Abe Saperstein's American Basketball League, it succumbed after only one and one-half years and did not present a major threat to the NBA. The ABA, on the other hand, was a different story. It used several innovations to compete with the NBA. The main difference was a three-point field goal. Successful baskets taken from beyond an arc that was 25 feet from the basket were worth three points. A 30-second shot clock was employed instead of the NBA's 24-second clock, and a red, white, and blue basketball was used. Eleven teams began the league's first season in 1967, and former NBA great George Mikan was the ABA's first commissioner.

Although the league did not have the best players at first, they did have wealthy team owners who in just a few years were able to offer college stars lucrative contracts to join them. While some ABA teams struggled at the gate and franchises changed cities often, several of their teams, such as the Indiana Pacers, Kentucky Colonels, Denver Rockets, and New York Nets, did well. The ABA also began signing players whose college eligibility had not expired and caused more pressure on the NBA. While the ABA often resorted to gimmicks at first, such as bikini-clad ball girls, the quality of play after just a few years rivaled that of the NBA, especially after they successfully caused some NBA stars, for example, Rick Barry, Billy Cunningham, Zelmo Beaty, and Joe Caldwell, to switch leagues.

By the early 1970s, the NBA sought a merger. The NBA Players Association, seeing players' salaries rise astronomically due to the competition, successfully sued to stop the merger, and it was not until 1976 that the suit was settled and four ABA teams joined the NBA. The ABA changed the NBA's outlook and some of their innovations (three-point field goal, slam dunk competition, signing college players prior to their graduation) were adopted and play a major role in today's game.

THE 1972 OLYMPIC GAMES

The 1972 Olympic Games in Munich, Germany, saw the United States finally lose an Olympic game, although its finish was quite controversial. The Soviet Union led for most of the game, but the United States went ahead, 50–49, in the last seconds on two free throws by Doug Collins. With three seconds remaining, the Soviet Union inbounded the ball, time expired, and the United States thought they were the victors, once again. But there was confusion at the official scorer's table, and the Soviet Union claimed they had called time out.

R. William Jones, head of the FIBA, intervened and ordered the last three seconds to be replayed. A second attempt to inbound the ball occurred, and the Soviet Union attempted a length-of-the-court pass, but the timer's horn sounded as soon as the player passed the ball inbounds, prior to the three seconds expiring. A third attempt at playing the last three seconds was ordered. Ivan Edeshko passed the ball the length of the court to Aleksandr Belov, who made the winning shot as time expired. The furious U.S. team lodged a protest that was not upheld, and they refused to accept the second place silver medals, which still reside in a Swiss bank vault.

THE RETURN OF WOMEN'S BASKETBALL

As a result of the passage of the Education Amendment of 1972, with its section labeled "Title IX," basketball again became a popular sport for females in the 1970s. Title IX basically prohibited educational institutions from discrimination based on gender. This carried into sports, and consequently colleges and high schools began fielding women's basketball teams. The Association for Intercollegiate Athletics for Women (AIAW), created in 1972, began holding national championships but was dissolved in the 1980s as the NCAA took over women's collegiate sports administration.

Although there were a few independent women's professional teams as early as the 1930s (e.g., the All-American Red Heads, Hazel Walker's Arkansas Travelers), the first successful attempt at a women's professional league occurred in 1978, when the Women's Professional Basketball League began play. The league lasted for three seasons but then failed. Several other unsuccessful attempts at a women's league occurred during the next decade, but it was not until 1996 that another league succeeded. The American Basketball League (ABL) did well, but after the NBA created and sponsored their own Women's National Basketball Association (WNBA) in 1997, the ABL was not able to compete and terminated operations in December 1998. The WNBA continues to thrive, although the fact that is subsidized by the NBA is a major factor in its continuing operations.

BIRD AND MAGIC

The post–ABA NBA should have prospered since basketball was still a popular sport and there was no direct competition, but two factors contributed to additional headaches for league ownership. The first was the increased number of black players in the league. During the 1950s, when the league first integrated, an unofficial maximum of three black players per team was the norm. The next decade saw the elimination of the unofficial quotas, and teams with five black players in their starting lineup were not unusual, although most teams, such as the New York Knicks, had a racial balance and harmony. By the 1970s, the proportion of blacks had exceeded 50 percent, and some teams, for example, the Golden State Warriors and Detroit Pistons, fielded rosters with just one or two whites and 10 or 11 blacks. By the 1980s, society had accepted integration, and black players seldom faced discrimination. The paying audience was still more than 90 percent white, and while unspoken, still would have preferred to see more white players.

The second major problem in the 1980s was the increased use of drugs in society and in sports. Quite a few of basketball's stars succumbed to drug addiction, and consequently the sport's image was damaged. Fortunately for the NBA, the 1979 NCAA Championship matched two teams with charismatic players, the Indiana State Sycamores with the Caucasian Larry Bird and the Michigan State Spartans with African American Earvin "Magic" Johnson. Both joined the NBA in 1980, and the next decade saw either Bird's Boston Celtics or Johnson's Los Angeles Lakers reach the NBA Championship Finals every year from 1980–1989, with the teams meeting on three occasions. Their friendly rivalry and the battles between the Celtics and the Lakers helped keep fan interest alive during the 1980s. NBA commissioner Lawrence O'Brien also implemented an antidrug policy that helped alleviate the drug problem, although not completely.

With the rise of cable television and its need for programming, the NBA received much better television coverage and it, too, helped promote their product. When David Stern took over as NBA commissioner in 1984, his keen marketing sense helped the NBA to prosper. By the end of the decade, the league added four more teams and by 1990 had a 27-team league.

MICHAEL JORDAN AND THE DREAM TEAM

Michael Jordan was selected as the third pick in the 1984 draft behind Hakeem Olajuwon and Sam Bowie after leading the University of North Carolina to the 1982 NCAA Championship and the United States to the 1984 Olympic gold medal. Although one of the country's best players, he had yet to achieve the legendary status that would be his a decade or two later. With the Chicago Bulls during the 1980s, he led the NBA in scoring seven times in his first eight seasons, but it was not until Phil Jackson became the Bulls' coach in 1989 that the Bulls would become NBA champions. The Bulls won the title three consecutive years from 1991–1993. Jordan then decided he needed another challenge in his life and quit basketball to play professional baseball. After two years in the minor leagues, where he learned that he could not hit a curve ball, he returned to the NBA late in the 1994–1995 season. The following year he, along with Scottie Pippen, Dennis Rodman, and Toni Kukoc, led the Bulls to a league-record 72-victory season. The Bulls went on to win the league championship and had similar seasons the following two years. Following the 1997–1998 season, coach Jackson resigned, as did Jordan.

Another major event during the 1990s was the change in international regulations to allow the use of professional players in Olympic competition. The United States, after losing the 1988 Olympic Games tournament to the Soviet Union, jumped on this opportunity and fielded a team for the 1992 Olympic Games in Barcelona, Spain, that consisted of 11 of the best NBA players and the top college player of 1992. That team, dubbed the "Dream Team" by sportswriters, easily dominated the Olympic tournament and won their eight games by an average score of 117–73. "Dream Team II," put together for the 1994 FIBA World Championships, did not have nearly the same caliber of players but also still easily won that tournament. For the Atlanta Olympics in 1996, a third "Dream Team" was constructed. This one featured five players from the 1992 team and seven other quality NBA players. They also easily won the tournament.

INTERNATIONAL BASKETBALL IN THE 21ST CENTURY

As the sport's popularity has increased worldwide, professional basketball has also grown internationally. During the 1990s, the NBA often looked to other parts of the globe to recruit players. In the 1988–1989 season, 23 of the roughly 400 NBA players were born outside the United States. A decade later there were 40. The league increasingly signed non-U.S.-born players, and during the 2006–2007 season, 87 of the NBA players were nonnatives, more than 20 percent of the total players in the league.

Through the 2009–2010 season, there have been 285 NBA players from 74 different countries. Conversely, American collegians who were unable to play in the NBA often played overseas, and virtually every European professional basketball league employed Americans. As the FIBA has relaxed the restriction on "amateur" participation, overseas leagues have increased their players' salaries to be almost on par with the United States. Added to this is the fact that most professional leagues outside the United States have much shorter schedules than the roughly 100-game NBA schedule, and playing in Europe has a strong appeal for many Americans. Most non-American leagues had limitations on the number of "imported" players that each team could sign, and Americans often became naturalized citizens of their team's nation to help their team avoid this restriction. In women's basketball, since the American WNBA plays a summer schedule, its players often sign to play in winter leagues overseas.

KOBE, LEBRON, AND THE MULTIMILLIONAIRES

Following a labor disagreement that shortened the 1998–1999 season from 82 to 50 games, it would have seemed that public backlash against a group of multimillionaire owners disagreeing with a group of multimillionaire players would have occurred, but this simply was not the case. The NBA continued to prosper during the first 10 years of the new millennium; however, the league's source of players changed. The quality of international players had greatly increased, and the 2002 World Championships, 2004 Olympic Games, and 2006 World Championships saw foreign teams defeating the United States' best. More and more international players were hired, and natives of more than 40 countries played in the league during the decade, including several from China, such as the seven-foot, five-inch Yao Ming.

The NBA also no longer waited for players to graduate college, and many were selected in the draft directly from high school. The decade's top stars included Kobe Bryant, LeBron James, Kevin Garnett, and Dwight Howard, none of which attended college. The league, through its worldwide marketing, has become global and has scheduled a few games overseas. There will probably be a day in the not too distant future that an international league will be created that includes teams from six continents. Basketball is no longer just an American sport played overseas but a truly international one. There is no doubt that Dr. James Naismith would look at today's game and marvel at the changes that have occurred to his simple indoor winter pastime.

The Dictionary

– A –

ABDUL-JABBAR, KAREEM (née FERDINAND LEWIS "LEW" ALCINDOR, JR.). B. 16 April 1947, New York, New York. As a seven-foot, two-inch student at Power Memorial High School in New York, Lew Alcindor led his team to 71 consecutive victories and was highly recruited by colleges nationwide. He selected the **University of California, Los Angeles,** helped lead them to three consecutive **National Collegiate Athletic Association (NCAA)** Championships, garnered an 88–2 record in his three years on varsity, and was named Most Outstanding Player of the NCAA tournament each year. After the 1967 season, the NCAA banned the **dunk** shot to theoretically make it more difficult for exceptionally tall players like Alcindor to score, but it turned out to be advantageous for him, as he developed a **hook shot** (dubbed a "sky hook" by sportswriters because of its high arc) and thus had one more unstoppable shot.

Although Alcindor would have been selected for the 1968 **U.S. Olympic** team, he chose not to make himself available since there was some pressure by the black community that the United States was using its black athletes improperly. Selected by the **Milwaukee Bucks** as the first selection in the 1969 **National Basketball Association (NBA) draft**, he was also selected by the **New York Nets** of the **American Basketball Association** as their first choice. Alcindor signed with the Bucks, even though he would have preferred to play in his hometown. He helped them improve their won–lost record by 29 games and was named Rookie of the Year. The next season, after acquiring future Hall-of-Famer **Oscar Robertson**, the Bucks had a league-record (since broken) 20-game winning streak, won three playoff series, and became NBA champions. On 1 May 1971, the day after the Bucks' final game, Alcindor announced that he was adopting the Muslim faith and changing his name to Kareem Abdul-Jabbar.

By 1974, Abdul-Jabbar had had enough of the small-town environment of Milwaukee and expressed a desire to be traded to either Los Angeles or New York. In June 1975, his wish was granted, and he was traded to the **Los Angeles Lakers**. From 1975 until his retirement in 1989, Abdul-Jabbar helped lead the Lakers to eight NBA Finals and five NBA Championships. When he retired after 20 NBA seasons, he had set NBA career records for most points, **field goals** made, field goals attempted, and **minutes** played. He was the league's Most Valuable Player six times, was the Finals Most Valuable Player twice, and was selected to the All-NBA first team 10 times and All-NBA second team five times. He was chosen for the NBA **All-Star Game** in 19 of his 20 seasons. Being based in Los Angeles for much of his career, he was able to appear in several Hollywood films and has been on several television situation comedies. As a history major with diverse interests, he has also written more than a half-dozen books. While still an active player, he was one of 12 players selected to the NBA's 35th Anniversary Team in 1981. In 1995, Abdul-Jabbar was enshrined in the **Naismith Memorial Basketball Hall of Fame** and in 1996 was named one of the 50 Greatest Players in NBA History.

ABDUL-RAUF, MAHMOUD (née CHRIS WAYNE JACKSON). B. 9 March 1969, Gulfport, Mississippi. Chris Jackson attended Gulfport High School and **Louisiana State University**. He left school after his sophomore year and was selected by the **Denver Nuggets** in the 1990 **National Basketball Association (NBA) draft**. The six-foot-tall, 160-pound **guard** played in the NBA from 1990–1996 for Denver and from 1996–1998 with the **Sacramento Kings**. In 1991, he converted to Islam and changed his name to Mahmoud Abdul-Rauf. He played in Turkey with Fenerbahçe in 1998–1999 and then returned to the NBA for the 2000–2001 season with the Vancouver Grizzlies. In 1993, he was voted the NBA's Most Improved Player.

Although afflicted with Tourette's syndrome, Jackson is an excellent **free throw** shooter and led the NBA twice in that category. In

1993–1994, he had the second highest free throw percentage in NBA history, making 219 of 229 free throws for a .956 percentage. His NBA career totals for nine years are 586 games, a 14.6 points per game average, and a free throw percentage of .905, one of a very few NBA players with a career free throw percentage greater than 90 percent. He returned to Europe in 2003 and played in **Russia** in 2003–2004, **Italy** in 2004–2005, and **Greece** in 2006–2007.

AIR BALL. An air ball is the term used for a shot at the **basket** that does not hit either **backboard** or rim. It generally occurs because the player rushes the shot without positioning himself properly on a **field goal** attempt. Although it seldom occurs on a **free throw** attempt, when it does happen it is extremely embarrassing to the shooter. On 28 December 1974, in Atlanta, Georgia, Elmore Smith of the **Los Angeles Lakers** incurred three consecutive air balls on free throw attempts. He managed only one free throw in 11 attempts that night. The term is a relatively new one, and it is claimed that the **Duke University** student fans originated it in the mid-1970s. *See also* HEARN, FRANCIS DAYLE "CHICK."

ALCINDOR, LEW. *See* ABDUL-JABBAR, KAREEM.

ALL-AMERICAN. An All-American is a scholastic player selected as being among the best for a season in American sport. The term was originated in the 1890s by sportswriters Caspar Whitney and Walter Camp, who selected "All-American football teams" beginning in 1889. **Basketball**'s earliest All-American teams were named following the 1928–1929 season.

ALL-AMERICAN RED HEADS. The All-American Red Heads were a women's touring **basketball** team organized in 1936 by C. M. "Ole" Olson, a promoter who headed a men's touring team called "Olson's Terrible Swedes." The Red Heads played men's rules and defeated more than half of their opponents, usually men's teams. All team members appeared with red hair, either natural or dyed. As with the **Harlem Globetrotters** and many other touring teams, comedy was added once a large lead was established. Special halftime shows were also included for additional spectator entertainment.

In 1955, Orwell Moore purchased the team from Olson. His wife, Lorene "Butch" Moore, was one of the team's stars. Others included Jolene Ammons, Jessie Banks, Barb Hostert, Red Mason, Pat Overman, Hazel Walker, and Sue Whitten. At the height of the Red Heads' success, they maintained three teams and sponsored a girls' camp. The Title IX federal law requiring equal opportunity for men's and women's college sports brought about the demise of the Red Heads as women's college basketball became much more prevalent.

ALL-STAR GAME. Most sports leagues have an annual exhibition game in which the best players from the league participate. Major League Baseball began the tradition in 1933. The **National Basketball Association (NBA)** played its first annual All-Star Game in 1951 at **Boston Garden**. Selection for the game has varied between **coaches** and players voting and fans voting. In recent years, the NBA has had fans vote for the starting five for Eastern Conference and Western Conference teams, and the coaches select the remainder of the team. A Most Valuable Player in the All-Star Game is also selected, and at one time, *Sport* magazine awarded that player a new car. Since the mid-1980s, the NBA has held an All-Star Weekend with other activities, including skills contests, **three-point** shooting competitions, and **slam dunk** competitions.

ALLEN, FORREST CLARE "PHOG." B. 8 November 1885, Jamesport, Missouri. D. 16 September 1974, Lawrence, Kansas. Phog Allen began playing **basketball** shortly after it was invented. He attended Independence High School in Independence, Missouri, and played on their basketball team. In 1903, he met the game's inventor, **James Naismith,** who was then teaching at the **University of Kansas.** Allen attended the University of Kansas and began **coaching** there in 1908. He then coached at Warrensburg Normal College and returned to Kansas in 1920, remaining there until his retirement in 1956. His record at Kansas was 591–219, and his overall record was 771–233.

Allen was largely responsible for having basketball included in the **Olympic Games** beginning in 1936. His 1952 Kansas team won the **National Collegiate Athletic Association** Championship, and seven of its members were added to the 1952 U.S. Olympic team that Allen coached to the **gold medal**. A practicing osteopath, he was given the nickname "Phog" by sportswriters for his foghorn voice. The 16,300-seat basketball arena at the University of Kansas, built in 1955, was named Allen Fieldhouse in his honor. He was inducted into the **Naismith Memorial Basketball Hall of Fame** in 1959 with its inaugural class.

ALLEN, WALTER RAY "RAY." B. 20 July 1975, Castle Air Force Base, Merced, California. Ray Allen attended Hillcrest High School in Dalzell, South Carolina, and the **University of Connecticut**. He left college after his junior year and was taken in the 1996 **National Basketball Association (NBA) draft** by the **Minnesota Timberwolves**, who immediately traded his **draft rights** to the **Milwaukee Bucks**. The six-foot, five-inch **guard** played for the Bucks from 1996 until February 2003, when he was traded to the Seattle Supersonics. He remained with the Sonics through the 2006–2007 season and set a league record with 269 **three-point field goals** in 2006. This was the third time he had led the NBA in three-point field goals, the only player ever to lead the league three times in that category.

Although only an 80 percent **free throw** shooter in college, Allen improved dramatically in the NBA, and in eight different seasons shot 90 percent or better. In June 2007, he was traded to the **Boston Celtics** in a trade that paved the way for the Celtics to acquire **Kevin Garnett**. The Celtics, with Allen, Garnett and **Paul Pierce**, won the 2007–2008 NBA Championship. Through the 2009–2010 season, he was second all-time in the NBA in career three-point field goals and three-point field goal attempts. He was selected for nine NBA **All-Star Games** and won a **gold medal** with the **United States** in the 2000 **Olympic Games**. In the 1998 Spike Lee film *He Got Game*, he had a cofeatured role.

AMATEUR ATHLETIC UNION (AAU). In the words of its website, "The Amateur Athletic Union (AAU) is one of the largest, nonprofit, volunteer sports organizations in the **United States**. A multisport organization, the AAU is dedicated exclusively to the promotion and development of amateur sports and physical fitness programs. The AAU was founded in 1888 to establish standards and uniformity in amateur sport. During its early years, the AAU served as the leader in international sport representing the United States in the international sports federations. The AAU worked closely with the **Olympic** movement to prepare athletes for the Olympic games." In 1978, the U.S. Congress passed the Amateur Sports Act, which chartered the U.S. Olympic Committee and provided for national governing bodies for each Olympic sport. Prior to that act, the AAU exerted much more influence, at times controversial, over American athletes' international participation. Since 1897, the AAU has sponsored annual **basketball** tournaments in the United States (although in its early years they were not always held annually) and in 1926 added a women's tournament. *See also* USA BASKETBALL.

AMATEUR BASKETBALL ASSOCIATION OF THE UNITED STATES OF AMERICA (ABAUSA). *See* USA BASKETBALL.

AMERICAN BASKETBALL ASSOCIATION (ABA). The American Basketball Association (ABA) was a men's professional major **basketball** league that began operation in 1967 and ceased operations in 1976, when four of its then seven teams joined the **National Basketball Association (NBA)**. The ABA began play in 1967, with the New Jersey Americans, Pittsburgh Pipers, Minnesota Muskies, **Indiana Pacers**, **Kentucky Colonels**, New Orleans Buccaneers, Dallas Chaparrals, Denver Rockets, Houston Mavericks, Anaheim Amigos, and Oakland Oaks. The first game was played on Friday, 13 October 1967, in Oakland, California, and was won by the Oakland Oaks, 134–129, over the Anaheim Amigos.

The league employed the **three-point field goal**, originated by the **American Basketball League** in 1961; used a 30-second **shot clock**; and employed the league's most distinctive feature, a red, white, and blue basketball. The league's first commissioner was former NBA star **George Mikan**, who served from 1969–1971. Subsequent commissioners included James Gardner, Jack Dolph, Bob Carlson, Mike Storen, Tedd Munchak, and **Dave DeBusschere**. During the league's nine-year existence, only the Indiana, Kentucky, and Denver franchises did not relocate. One of the league's innovations was the concept of regional franchises. In 1969, the Houston Mavericks relocated to North Carolina, as the Carolina Cougars and played home games in Charlotte, Greensboro, Raleigh, and

Winston-Salem. The Oakland Oaks, after two seasons in Oakland and one in Washington, D.C., moved to Virginia in 1970, as the **Virginia Squires** scheduled home games in Roanoke, Richmond, Norfolk, and Hampton Roads. Other regional franchises were attempted in Florida and Texas.

In the league's first season, 1967–1968, the ABA employed several players who had been blacklisted by the NBA for alleged involvement with gamblers, including New York City high school stars **Connie Hawkins** and Roger Brown. Hawkins had an outstanding year and led his Pittsburgh Pipers to the ABA Championship Finals.

The ABA carried on a running battle with the NBA to acquire players. At that time, the NBA had a requirement that prospective players could not be signed until they had been out of high school for four years. In 1969, the ABA signed undergraduate collegian **Spencer Haywood** and established a precedent that the NBA reluctantly followed. The competition between the two leagues caused player salaries to increase dramatically, and after its initial two seasons the ABA was successful in signing many of the best collegiate players. As salaries began to escalate, the NBA and ABA began initial discussions toward a merger, but the NBA Players Association filed an antitrust suit in 1970 (known as the **Oscar Robertson** suit, since Robertson was head of the NBA Players Association) and effectively blocked the merger. The suit was settled in 1976, and a merger then took place.

Although the league at times featured some zany characters and outlandish promotions, such as having a female jockey (**Penny Ann Early**) play in one game, or employing bikini-clad cheerleaders for the **Miami Floridians** team, the league played some high-quality basketball, especially after its first two years. One innovation that the NBA uses today is the "slam-dunk" contest, which began as half-time entertainment at the 1976 ABA **All-Star Game** in Denver. When the leagues merged and the NBA accepted four ABA franchises, the New York Nets, Indiana Pacers, **Denver Nuggets**, and **San Antonio Spurs**, many of basketball's best players were in the ABA. A website, www.remembertheaba.com, created and maintained by Denver attorney Arthur Hundhausen, continues to keep the league's legacy alive. *See also* APPENDIX B (for a list of league champions).

AMERICAN BASKETBALL LEAGUE (ABL) (1925–1931). The American Basketball League (ABL) was a men's professional **basketball** major league that began operation in the fall of 1925 and terminated operations in 1931. It was organized by George Preston Marshall, George Halas, and Joseph Carr, all executives with the National Football League, and was the first professional basketball league with teams based in the larger cities in the eastern **United States**. Teams in the league for the first season were Brooklyn Arcadians, Washington Palace Five, Cleveland Rosenblums, Rochester Centrals, Fort Wayne Caseys, Boston Whirlwinds, Chicago Bruins, Detroit Pulaski Post Five, and Buffalo Bisons.

Since basketball rules were still in the process of development, variations existed in different parts of the country. The league agreed on a uniform set of rules and eliminated the two-handed **dribble**, required **backboards**, and signed players to exclusive contracts. The ABL lasted six full seasons with between 30 and 50 games per team each season. Most seasons were split into two halves, with the two winners competing in a postseason "World Series." During its six-year existence, both the New York **Original Celtics** and **Philadelphia SPHAs** were members at times. After three seasons, Carr resigned as league president, and **John J. O'Brien**, president of the Metropolitan League, took over. The league's final season, 1930–1931, was played in the midst of the Great Depression. O'Brien felt that fans were tired of seeing the same players and added a league rule that each team would have to employ two rookies. A three-second rule was also added, limiting players from holding the ball in the foul lane for more than three seconds. Following the season, O'Brien suspended operations.

In 1933, the ABL was reorganized and resumed play with teams in the New York City metropolitan area only. That league is generally treated by basketball historians as a separate entity. During its six-year existence, the ABL featured virtually all the best (Caucasian) professional basketball players of the era at one time or another. *See also* AMERICAN BASKETBALL LEAGUE (ABL) (1933–1953), APPENDIX B (for a list of league champions).

AMERICAN BASKETBALL LEAGUE (ABL) (1933–1953). The American Basketball League (ABL) was a men's professional basketball league that began operation in 1925, with teams in major cities throughout the eastern **United States**. It suspended operations following the 1930–1931 season and was reorganized by League President **John J. O'Brien** as a regional league, with teams mainly in the New York City metropolitan area. From 1933–1946, this version of the American Basketball League remained solvent and was the major professional league in the eastern United States, until the **Basketball Association of America (BAA)** was created in 1946.

From 1946–1953, the ABL was still a viable entity, but its quality was diminished, as the best players played in the BAA. One innovation of the ABL was dividing games into three 15-**minute** periods in an attempt to give fans more for their money. The **Philadelphia SPHAs** were one of the league's best teams. Others included the Trenton Moose, Brooklyn Jewels, Brooklyn Visitations, Jersey Reds, and Kingston Colonials. Most seasons were played in two halves, with the two winners meeting for the league championship in a postseason playoff.

During World War II, the league survived with just four or five teams. After the war, the league began to be integrated, and in the early 1950s a mostly black team, the New York Harlem Yankees (which later became the Saratoga Yankees) competed and other teams also employed black players. During the league's final season, 1952–1953, a conflict arose among some team owners who wanted to hire players implicated in the point-shaving scandals and other owners who wanted to uphold the ban. As a result, several teams dropped out, and the league finished with just five teams. In 1953, the league was disbanded. *See also* AMERICAN BASKETBALL LEAGUE (ABL) (1925–1931); APPENDIX B (for a list of league champions).

AMERICAN BASKETBALL LEAGUE (ABL) (1961–1962). In April 1960, **Harlem Globetrotter** owner **Abe Saperstein**, after being rebuffed in an attempt to obtain an **National Basketball Association (NBA)** franchise, announced plans to form a new men's professional basketball major league starting in October 1961. The American Basketball League (ABL) began play on 27 October 1961, in San Francisco's Civic Auditorium, where the San Francisco Saints defeated the Los Angeles Jets, 99–96.

The league employed several innovations: No **foul** shot was awarded if a player was fouled in the act of shooting and the basket was good, a 30-second **shot clock** was used, and, the most important one, three points were awarded for **field goals** made beyond an arc that was 25 feet from the backboard (23 feet, nine inches from the center of the basket). This was the first basketball league to do this, a rule that the NBA would not employ for another 18 years. Other teams in the league were the Chicago Majors, Cleveland Pipers, Hawaii Chiefs, Kansas City Steers, Pittsburgh Rens, and Washington Tapers. Saperstein owned the Chicago team and employed several former Globetrotters, including former NBA star **Nat "Sweetwater" Clifton**. The Pipers and Tapers had competed in the **National Industrial Basketball League** the previous year. Several players, including Sy Blye, **Connie Hawkins**, Tony Jackson, and **Bill Spivey** had been blacklisted by the NBA for alleged influence by gamblers. Hawkins became the league's leading scorer, with Spivey second. Cleveland was league champion but after the season dropped out of the ABL in a failed attempt to join the NBA. Six teams began the league's second season in November 1962, but on 31 December 1962, Saperstein decided to fold the league. Losses were said to have been about $1,000,000. Kansas City was declared the league's second season champion.

During its brief existence, the league employed 135 different players, including 47 who also had or would have NBA experience and 10 others who would later play in the **American Basketball Association** a few years later. Of the 81 players whose only major league pro basketball experience was the ABL, there were several noteworthy ones—the aforementioned Spivey and Blye; Kelly Coleman, a legendary high school star in Kentucky; **Clarence "Bevo" Francis**, a college star at Rio Grande College in Ohio who holds the **National Collegiate Athletic Association (NCAA)** individual game scoring record with 113 in a game; Rick Herrscher, who later played Major League Baseball with the New York Mets; R. C. Owens, who played professional football; and John Berberich, who later earned a doctorate in psychology and as a police psychologist profiled serial killer Ted Bundy. Among the players with NBA experience were Dick Barnett, Bill Bridges, Gene Conley, Archie Dees, Andy Johnson, **Neil Johnston**, Kenny Sears, **Bill Sharman**, Larry Siegfried,

Charlie Tyra, and **George Yardley**. *See also* APPENDIX B (for a list of league champions).

AMERICAN BASKETBALL LEAGUE (ABL) (1996–1998). The American Basketball League (ABL) was a women's professional **basketball** major league created by Steve Hams, Anne Cribbs, and Gary Cavalli in February 1995, and began league play on 18 October 1996. The league was created to capitalize on the success of the undefeated 1996 U.S. women's national team that were **Olympic** champions. Seven members of that team played in the ABL. Teams that began the initial season included the Atlanta Glory, Colorado Xplosion, Columbus Quest, New England Blizzard, Portland Power, Richmond Rage, San Jose Lasers, and Seattle Reign.

The league used several different rules from the **National Collegiate Athletic Association (NCAA)**. A standard 30-inch circumference basketball was used rather than the 29-inch one used by the NCAA. Four 10-**minute** periods were played rather than two 20-minute halves. Players were allowed six personal **fouls** before **disqualification** rather than the NCAA's limit of five. And a 25-second **shot clock** was used. The league played a 40-game schedule during the 1996–1997 season, with Columbus defeating Richmond in the finals of the postseason playoffs.

During the summer off-season, the **National Basketball Association (NBA)** began its own women's league, the **Women's National Basketball Association (WNBA)**, in competition with the ABL. For the ABL's second season in 1997–1998, a 44-game season was played; Columbus defeated Long Beach in the playoff finals. The league's third season began but was disbanded on 22 December 1998, after teams had played between 12 and 15 games.

While it lasted, the league featured some of America's best female basketball players. On 8 December 1996, diminutive (five-foot, three-inch) Debbie Black recorded a **quadruple-double**—10 points, 14 **rebounds**, 12 **assists**, and 10 **steals**—a feat only accomplished four times in the NBA and by players more than a foot taller. *See also* APPENDIX B (for a list of league champions).

ANAHEIM AMIGOS. *See* UTAH STARS.

ANDERSON PACKERS. The Anderson Duffey Packers were a **basketball** team that competed from 1946–1949 in the **National Basketball League (NBL)**. They were owned by Ike W. Duffey, a self-made millionaire, owner of a meatpacking company in Anderson, Indiana. In 1945–1946, the company sponsored an independent professional basketball team called the Anderson Chiefs. They received a franchise in the NBL for the 1946–1947 season and renamed the team the Duffey Packers.

Their best season was 1948–1949, when they were league champions. In 1949, they became part of the **National Basketball Association (NBA)**. As the NBA did not allow the use of sponsors' names, they were known simply as the Anderson Packers. In the unwieldy 17-team, three-division league that year they finished second in the Western Division with a record of 37–27 but lost in the league semifinals to the **Minneapolis Lakers**. After the season, in an effort to streamline the league, the NBA established minimum requirements that effectively caused six Midwestern franchises, including the Packers, to drop out of the league. A new league, the **National Professional Basketball League**, was formed by the Packers and several of the dropped franchises. Among the best players with the Chiefs and Packers were Bob Bolyard, Frankie Brian, Elmer Gainer, Milo Komenich, Howie Schultz, Charley Shipp, and Ed Stanczyk.

ANGOLA. Angola joined the **Fédération Internationale de Basketball (FIBA)** in 1979, and has since become the best African men's **basketball** team in international competition. In the 15 FIBA Africa Championships from 1980–2007, they finished first nine times, second twice, and third twice. They have competed in every **Olympic Games** since 1992, with their best results coming in 1992, when they finished 10th of 12 teams. In that tournament, they were overwhelmed in their opening game against the U.S. **Dream Team**, 116–48, but rebounded from that loss to defeat **Spain** and lose to **Germany** by only one point. They also competed in six **World Championships**, with a best finish of 10th in 2006. Among their best players have been Jean-Jacques Conceição; the Victoriano brothers, Angelo, Edmar, and Justino; Antonio Carvalho; and Joaquim Gomes. Through 2010 there has yet to be an Angolan in the **National Basketball Association (NBA)**.

ARCAIN, JANETH DOS SANTOS. B. 11 April 1969, Carapicuiba, Saõ Paulo, **Brazil.** Janeth Arcain was selected for four **Olympic basketball** teams for Brazil from 1992–2004 and won a **silver medal** in 1996 and a **bronze medal** in 2000. The five-foot, 11-inch **forward** appeared in 29 games in four Olympics and averaged 18.4 points per game. She is the all-time career Olympic record-holder in several categories, including most **minutes,** two-point **field goal** attempts, total field goal attempts, **free throws,** free throw attempts, **steals,** and total points. She is the runner-up to **Lisa Leslie** in two-point field goals, defensive **rebounds,** personal **fouls,** and total field goals and is the runner-up to **Teresa Edwards** in **assists.**

Arcain played for the Brazilian national team in the 1990 Goodwill Games, 1987 (silver medal) and 1991 **(gold medal)** Pan American Games, and five **World Championships** from 1990–2006, winning a gold medal in 1994. She was with the Brazilian national team in the South American Championships in 1989, 1991, 1993, 1995, and 1999, and won gold medals in each of those tournaments. She also played for the Houston Comets in the **Women's National Basketball Association** from 1997–2005 and won four championships with them. She has played for Ros Casares Valencia in **Spain** and in the Brazilian league has won championships with Leite Moça, Polti, Santo Andrée, Vasco da Gama, and São Paulo/Guaru. Arcain owns a computer store and runs a gymnasium in Brazil.

ARCHIBALD, NATHANIEL "NATE," "TINY." B. 2 September 1948, New York, New York. Nate Archibald attended DeWitt Clinton High School in the Bronx, New York; Arizona Western Junior College; and the **University of Texas at El Paso.** The six-foot, one-inch **point guard** was selected by the Cincinnati Royals in the 1970 **National Basketball Association (NBA) draft.** He started slowly, averaging 16 points and five **assists** per game in his first season but in his second year increased his scoring and assists by more than one and one-half times. Before his third NBA season, in 1972–1973, the Cincinnati Royals relocated and played as the Kansas City–Omaha Kings. That year, Archibald had one of the best individual years in NBA history, scoring 2,719 points and recording an NBA record 910 assists. His 34.0 points per game average led the league, as did his 11.4 assists per game, the only player ever to lead the NBA in both categories in the same season. He also led the league in **minutes played**, **field goals** made and attempted, and **free throws** made and attempted. Despite his efforts, the Kings only won 36 of 82 games, and Archibald was not named Most Valuable Player. Injuries in the 1973–1974 season limited him to just 35 games. For the rest of his career, although he had some flashes of brilliance, injuries prevented him from achieving his previous excellence.

From 1976–1984, Archibald was with the New York Nets, Buffalo Braves, **Boston Celtics**, and Milwaukee Hawks. He helped the Celtics win the NBA Championship in 1981. He was selected for the NBA **All-Star Game** six times in his career and was named its Most Valuable Player in 1981. In 1991, he was enshrined in the **Naismith Memorial Basketball Hall of Fame** and in 1996 was chosen as one of the 50 Greatest Players in NBA History.

ARGENTINA. Argentina joined the **Fédération Internationale de Basketball (FIBA)** in 1932 as one of the eight founding federations. **Basketball**, although second to football (soccer), has been extremely popular in this South American country. They are one of only three countries to win the men's **Olympic gold medal** in basketball, doing so in 2004. They were also Olympic **bronze medalists** in 2008. In their first Olympic basketball tournament, in 1948, they narrowly missed upsetting the **United States** in a preliminary round game. On 3 August 1948, they had a seven-point halftime lead but lost the game by two points, 59–57.

During the 1950s, the Juan Perón government was overthrown, and the political situation resulted in the rapid decline of the basketball program. Argentina did not compete in the Olympic Games again until 1996. The country won the inaugural **World Championships** held in Buenos Aires in 1950 and finished second in 2002. In the Pan American Games, Argentina finished second in 1951 and 1955 and first in 1995. In the 43 South American Championships that have been held, the country has medaled in 35 of them and finished first 12 times. In the newer FIBA Americas tournament, Argentina won the gold in 2001.

Among the best men's players for Argentina have been Leopoldo Contarbio, Oscar Furlong, Ricardo González, Rafael Lledo, Ruben Menini, and Juan Carlos Uder of the 1948–1952 teams. Eight of the players on the 2004 Olympic team have played in the **National Basketball Association**—Carlos Delfino, **Emanuel "Manu" Ginóbili**, Walter Herrmann, Andrés Nocioni, Fabricio Oberto, Juan "Pepe" Sánchez, Luis Scola, and Rubén Wolkowyski.

The Argentinean women's team has not fared as well as the men's. They have never qualified for the Olympic Games, their best finish in the World Championships has only been sixth in 1953, they won the gold medal in the 1948 South American Games and have finished in second place 12 times, have a best finish of fifth in the Pan American Games, and came in third in the 2001 FIBA Americas tournament.

ARIZIN, PAUL JOSEPH. B. 9 April 1928, Philadelphia, Pennsylvania. D. 13 December 2006, Springfield, Pennsylvania. Paul Arizin attended La Salle High School in Philadelphia. He did not play **basketball** in high school or in his freshman year at college. He began playing in his sophomore year for **Villanova University** and on 12 February 1949 scored 85 points against the Philadelphia Naval Air Material Command Center team in a 117–25 victory for Villanova. At the time this was the most points ever scored in one game by a college player.

Selected by the Philadelphia Warriors in the 1950 **National Basketball Association (NBA) draft**, although he suffered from asthma, Arizin led the NBA in scoring in his second season, with a 25.4 points per game average. He spent the next two years in the U.S. Marine Corps playing for the Quantico Marines team. Upon his discharge, he returned to the NBA, played for the Warriors until 1962, and helped lead them to the 1956 NBA Championship. When the team announced plans to move to San Francisco, Arizin decided to retire rather than relocate. He played on weekends in the Eastern Basketball Association (EBA) the next three seasons for Camden, continued to average more than 25 points per game, and was named the EBA's Most Valuable Player in 1963.

Arizin was selected for the NBA **All-Star Game** 10 times during his career and was named its Most Valuable Player in 1952. In the 16 years that he played organized basketball, three in college, 10 in the NBA, and three in the EBA, he failed to average 20 or more points per game in only two seasons—his sophomore year in college and his rookie year in the NBA. After retiring from basketball he worked for International Business Machines as a customer executive in Philadelphia. In 1970, he was selected to the NBA 25th Anniversary Team and in 1996 was named one of the 50 Greatest Players in NBA History. In 1978, he was enshrined in the **Naismith Memorial Basketball Hall of Fame.**

ARIZONA, UNIVERSITY OF. The University of Arizona in Tempe began its men's **basketball** program in 1904. Since 1973, home games have been played at the 14,545-seat McKale Memorial Center. The most accomplished **coaches** in school history were Fred Enke, who won 520 games and lost 316 from 1926–1961, and Robert "Lute" Olson, who won 589 games while only losing 188 from 1983–2008. The Wildcats won the **National Collegiate Athletic Association** Championship in 1997 and were runners-up in 2001. They also were semifinal losers in 1988 and 1994. Their best players include Gilbert Arenas, Mike Bibby, Sean Elliott, Richard Jefferson, Steve Kerr, Damon Stoudamire, and Jason Terry.

ARKANSAS, UNIVERSITY OF. The University of Arkansas is located in Fayetteville. Even though the school was established in 1871, the men's **basketball** program only began in 1923. From 1958–1993, they played at the John Barnhill Arena, but since 1993 home games have been played at the 19,368-seat Bud Walton Arena. The top basketball **coaches** in school history have been Nolan Richardson, Glen Rose, and Eddie Sutton. In 1994, the Razorbacks won the **National Collegiate Athletic Association** Championship, with Corey Beck, Clint McDaniel, Dwight Stewart, Scotty Thurman, and Corliss Williamson leading them. The following year they were the runners-up to the **University of California, Los Angeles.** Ron Brewer and his son, Ronnie Brewer; Todd Day; Marvin Delph; Joe Johnson; Joe Kleine; Lee Mayberry; Sidney Moncrief; Alvin Robertson; and Darrell Walker have been among the best players.

ASSIST. An assist is credited to a player for a pass to a teammate that results in an immediate **field goal.** The definition is vague enough that individual official scorers' interpretations vary, and consequently this statistic has not been uniformly credited during **basketball**'s history.

Modern-day interpretation tends to be more liberal than in earlier years. Only one assist (unlike in ice hockey and some other team sports) can be credited on a field goal. The **National Basketball Association (NBA)** record for most assists in one game is 30 and was set on 30 December 1990, by Scott Skiles of the **Orlando Magic**. **John Stockton** of the **Utah Jazz** holds the NBA career record with 15,806, nearly 5,000 more assists than the second-place **Jason Kidd**. Stockton also has the three highest single-season performances, with a high of 1,164 assists in a season.

ASSOCIATION FOR INTERCOLLEGIATE ATHLETICS FOR WOMEN (AIAW). The Association for Intercollegiate Athletics for Women (AIAW) was created on 1 July 1972, to oversee women's collegiate sports and administer national championships. It superseded its predecessor organization the Commission on Intercollegiate Athletics for Women (CIAW), which was founded in 1966. The AIAW had 280 member schools when it began in 1971 and grew to nearly 1,000 member schools. The **National Collegiate Athletic Association (NCAA)** at that time was not interested in administering women's sports, but as women's sports became more popular throughout the 1970s, the NCAA began to offer championships in them. From 1973–1982, the AIAW sponsored a national collegiate championship. In 1982, the NCAA also began holding a women's national collegiate championship and caused schools to choose between organizations. Being a much wealthier organization, the NCAA enticed schools with such benefits as payment of transportation costs to national tournaments and in essence put the AIAW out of business. On 30 June 1983, after an unsuccessful antitrust suit against the NCAA, the AIAW ceased to exist.

ATLANTA HAWKS. The Atlanta Hawks are a team in the **National Basketball Association (NBA)**. The team had its origin in the **National Basketball League (NBL)** in 1946 as the Buffalo Bisons and have since played as the Tri-Cities Blackhawks in the NBL (1946–1949), and in the NBA as the Tri-Cities Blackhawks (1949–1951), Milwaukee Hawks (1951–1955), St. Louis Hawks (1955–1968), and Atlanta Hawks since 1968.

Buffalo Bisons. In 1946, the Buffalo Bisons entered the NBL. They only lasted until Christmas, when the team was sold to a group from Moline, Illinois, and were renamed the Tri-Cities Blackhawks.

Tri-Cities Blackhawks. The three cities represented by the team's name are Moline, Illinois; Rock Island, Illinois; and Davenport, Iowa. Nearly all their home games were played at the 6,000-seat Wharton Field House in Moline, Illinois. Among their most notable players in the NBL were Joe Camic: **William "Pop" Gates**, one of the first black players in the NBL; Ward Gibson; Billy Hassett; Ed Lewinski; **Bobby McDermott**; Don Otten; Don Ray; Whitey Von Nieda; and Stan Waxman. After three relatively unsuccessful seasons in the NBL, they were part of the merger that formed the NBA on 3 August 1949. They played in the NBA at Moline for two seasons before moving to Milwaukee, Wisconsin, in September 1951. Among their most notable players were Frankie Brian, Dike Eddleman, Don Otten, Warren Perkins, Mike Todorovich, and Gene Vance. Hank DeZonie became the NBA's fourth black player when he played for them briefly in 1950.

Milwaukee Hawks. Home games were played at the 11,000-seat Milwaukee Arena. They finished in last place in the Western Division in each of their four seasons there, but in that time they participated in several historic games. On 7 March 1954, at the Milwaukee Arena, they were defeated by the Minneapolis Lakers, 65–63, in a regular-league game played with 12-foot-high baskets. The following day they and the **Baltimore Bullets** played the only doubleheader featuring the same two teams in NBA history. They defeated the Bullets in two games on the same night at the Baltimore Coliseum by nearly identical scores, 64–54 and 65–54. The games were shortened to 10-**minute** periods. After the 24-second **shot clock** was incorporated in the league rules for the 1954–1955 season, the Hawks played the lowest-scoring NBA game on 27 February 1955. They were defeated by the **Boston Celtics** in Providence Auditorium on a slippery floor, 62–57. Among their most notable players were Bill Calhoun, Bob Harrison, Lew Hitch, Mel Hutchins, Jack Nichols, **Bob Pettit**, George Ratkovicz, Chuck Share, Don Sunderlage, and **Bill Tosheff**. They were among the first NBA teams to play black players and gave **Chuck Cooper**, Ken McBride, Dave Minor, Jackie Moore, Isaac

"Rabbit" Walthour, and Bob Wilson an opportunity to play in the NBA. On 11 May 1955, they moved to St. Louis, Missouri.

St. Louis Hawks. Home games were played at the 15,000-seat St. Louis Arena and at the 10,000 seat Kiel Auditorium. Among their most notable players were Zelmo Beaty, Bill Bridges, Al Ferrari, Richie Guerin, **Cliff Hagan**, Lou Hudson, **Clyde Lovellette**, **Ed Macauley**, Bob Pettit, Chuck Share, Paul Silas, and **Lenny Wilkens**. Their best seasons were 1956–1957, when they reached the seventh game of the NBA Finals but lost to the Boston Celtics in double overtime, and 1957–1958, when they won the franchise's only league championship. In May 1968, team owner Ben Kerner sold the team to a group of Atlanta investors, and the team was moved again.

Atlanta Hawks. Home games were played at Alexander Memorial Coliseum, the Omni, the Georgia Dome, and Philips Arena. Their most notable players have been Mookie Blaylock, John Drew, Alan Henderson, Lou Hudson, Eddie Johnson, Joe Johnson, **Pete Maravich**, Wayne "Tree" Rollins, Dan Roundfield, **Dominique Wilkins**, and Kevin Willis. Their best seasons were 1986–1987 and 1993–1994, when they finished first in the Central Division with a record of 57–25 each year but lost in the second round of the playoffs both times. In Atlanta, the Hawks have never advanced past the second round of the playoffs. The franchise's NBA record from 1949–2010 is 2,376–2,454.

ATTLES, ALVIN A., JR. "AL." B. 7 November 1936, Newark, New Jersey. Al Attles attended Weequahic High School in Newark and North Carolina A&T College. Selected by the Philadelphia Warriors in the 1960 **National Basketball Association (NBA) draft**, he played from 1960–1971 for the Philadelphia Warriors and then the San Francisco Warriors. On 2 March 1962, he was the second high scorer on his team, with 17 points, when teammate **Wilt Chamberlain** scored 100. The 117-point total is still the NBA record for most points by two teammates in a game. In 1964 and 1967, the six-foot-tall **guard** was a member of the losing team in the NBA Championship Finals. His NBA career totals for 11 years are 712 regular-season games and an 8.9 points per game average. In 1969, he was named player-**coach** of the Warriors (only the third black coach in the NBA) and performed the dual role for two seasons before retiring from playing. He led them to the NBA Championship in 1975 in four straight games over the highly favored Washington Bullets and continued as coach through the 1982–1983 season. Attles has remained with the Warriors' organization in an executive capacity.

AUERBACH, ARNOLD JACOB "RED." B. 20 September 1917, Brooklyn, New York. D. 28 October 2006, Washington, D.C. Red Auerbach attended Eastern District High School in Brooklyn, Seth Low Junior College, and George Washington University. When the **Basketball Association of America** began in 1946, he was hired by the Washington Capitols as **coach** and led them to a record of 49–11, but they lost in the playoffs to the **Chicago Stags**. In 1949, they again finished at top of their division but were defeated by the Minneapolis Lakers in the playoff finals. At the conclusion of that season, after a dispute with Capitols' owner Mike Uline, Auerbach resigned. He was hired by Ben Kerner, owner of the Tri-Cities Blackhawks, but after one year Auerbach again resigned. He was then hired by **Walter A. Brown**, owner of the **Boston Celtics**, and remained a Celtic for the next 56 years. Although Auerbach was the Celtics' coach from 1950–1956, it was not until they acquired **Bill Russell** in December 1956 that the team became successful. They won the league championship in 1957 and from 1957–1966 won nine of 10 **National Basketball Association (NBA)** Championships.

Auerbach was known for his feuds with several NBA referees and his trademark cigar. When he felt the Celtics had an insurmountable lead in a game, he would light up a cigar while still coaching on the bench. After the 1965–1966 season, Auerbach retired from active coaching but remained a Celtics' executive. Auerbach, who had been the first NBA coach to regularly play five black players, named Bill Russell as coach, the first black coach in the NBA. Auerbach created a winning tradition for the Celtics, and from 1957–1986 the Celtics won 16 NBA titles. In 1969, he was enshrined in the **Naismith Memorial Basketball Hall of Fame**. In 1980, he was voted by the Professional Basketball Writers Association of America as the greatest coach in NBA history.

AUSTRALIA. Australia has been a **Fédération Internationale de Basketball (FIBA)** member since 1947. They are in the FIBA Oceania zone, but of the 21 federations in that zone nearly all of them, except for **New Zealand**, are small nations with limited populations. Consequently, Australia has been able to compete in every men's **Olympic basketball** tournament since 1956, with the exception of 1960 and 1968. Their best showing has been fourth place in 1988, 1996, and 2000, when they lost the **bronze medal** game in 1988 to the **United States** and in 1996 and 2000 to **Lithuania**. They have not done as well in the **World Championships**, with fifth place being their best effort in ten attempts. In the FIBA Oceania Championships, they have placed first in 17 of the 18 times they entered, losing only in 2001 to New Zealand.

They have produced some notable Olympians, including **Eddie Palubinskas**; **Andrew Gaze**; Lindsay Gaze, Andrew's father who played for the 1964 team and **coached** four others (1972–1984); and four-time Olympians Ray Borner Mark Bradtke, Shane Heal, Larry Sengstock, Phil Smyth, and Andrew Vlahov. The 10 Australians who have played in the **National Basketball Association** are David Andersen, Chris Anstey, Andrew Bogut, Mark Bradtke, Andrew Gaze, Shane Heal, Nathan Jawai, Luc Longley, Patrick Mills, and Luke Schenscher.

The Australian women's team has been even more successful than the men's team. They have competed in six Olympic Games and won the bronze medal in 1996 and the **silver medal** in the next three Olympics, 2000–2008. They won the World Championships in 2006 and placed third in 1998 and 2002. They have also won all 11 of the FIBA Oceania Championships in which they have entered. Sandy Brondello has competed in four Olympics, and three-time Olympians include Trish Fallon, Shelley Gorman Sandie, Robin Gull Maher, Kristy Harrower, **Lauren Jackson**, Rachel Sporn, and Michele Timms. Brondello, Fallon, Harrower, Jackson, Sporn, and Timms have all also competed in the **Women's National Basketball Association (WNBA)**. Other Australian Olympians who played in the WNBA include Suzy Batkovic, Tully Bevilaqua, Carla Boyd, Michelle Brogan Griffiths, Annie Burgess LaFleur, Belinda Snell, Laura Summerton, Penny Taylor, and Jenny Whittle.

– B –

BACKBOARD. The backboard is a rectangular board on which the **basketball hoop** is hung. It is usually six feet horizontally by three and one-half feet vertically, with a three-inch border around the edge. For indoor games, it is often made of glass and is transparent. Outdoor backboards are often made of metal or Plexiglas. A 24-inch by 18-inch rectangle two inches wide is usually marked behind the rim of the **basket**. The backboard is used most often when shooting from an angle to either side of the basket. Shots using the backboard are called "bank shots."

BACKCOURT. A **basketball** court is divided into two halves. The **frontcourt** is the half that contains the basket at which the offense shoots. The backcourt is the half that contains the opponent's basket. Teams change ends after the first half of the game. There are several specific rules pertaining to the backcourt. A team must move from backcourt to frontcourt within a certain time limit (eight seconds in the **National Basketball Association**, 10 seconds in most other jurisdictions) after inbounding the ball. Once the team has possession of the ball in their frontcourt they may not move into the backcourt. **Guards** are sometimes referred to as "backcourt" players, since they usually bring the ball from backcourt to frontcourt. In the rules for girls' six-player basketball, certain players were prohibited from crossing from backcourt to frontcourt.

BALTIMORE BULLETS (1947–1954). The Baltimore Bullets were a team in the **Basketball Association of America (BAA)** and **National Basketball Association (NBA)** from 1947–1954. They joined the BAA in 1947 after having played in the **American Basketball League**. Home games were played at the 4,500-seat Baltimore Coliseum. Among their most notable players were **Don Barksdale**, Walt Budko, Ray Felix, Rollen Hans, Paul Hoffman, **Buddy Jeannette**, Grady Lewis, Ed Miller, Chick Reiser, Red Rocha, and Fred Scolari. Their best season was 1947–1948, when they won the league title.

On 10 February 1952, the Bullets used only five players and defeated the Fort Wayne Pistons, 82–77. On 8 March 1954, the Bullets played the only doubleheader in league history featuring the same two teams. At the Baltimore Coliseum they lost twice to the Milwaukee Hawks by scores of 64–54 and 65–54. On 27 November 1954, the team disbanded after playing just 14 games in the 1954–1955 season. League statistics for that season were very inconsistent. Statistics from several of their games were not included but varied with each player and team. In their brief existence, the Bullets' record was 161–303 (although official NBA records omit their 3–11 mark of 1954).

BALTIMORE BULLETS (1963–1973). *See* WASHINGTON WIZARDS.

BALTIMORE CLAWS. *See* MEMPHIS SOUNDS.

BARKLEY, CHARLES WADE "SIR CHARLES." B. 20 February 1963, Leeds, Alabama. Charles Barkley attended Leeds High School and Auburn University. In college, although only six-feet, five-inches tall, he weighed nearly 300 pounds. Despite his size, he was light on his feet and could jump. An excellent **rebounder**, he was known as the "Round Mound of Rebound." He left school after his junior year and was drafted by the **Philadelphia 76ers** in the 1984 **National Basketball Association (NBA) draft**. He played for the 76ers, **Phoenix Suns**, and **Houston Rockets** from 1984–2000.

Although he played on some excellent teams, Barkley was only able to reach the NBA Finals once, in 1992–1993 with Phoenix, where they were defeated by the **Chicago Bulls**. He was selected as the NBA's Most Valuable Player in 1993 and named to the All-NBA First Team five times, All-NBA Second Team five times, and All-NBA Third Team once. Selected to play in the NBA **All-Star Game** 11 times, he was the Most Valuable Player in the 1991 game. When he retired he was one of only four players in NBA history to have recorded more than 20,000 points, 10,000 rebounds, and 4,000 **assists**. He played in 1,073 regular-season games and averaged 22.1 points and 11.7 rebounds per game.

Barkley was a member of the U.S. 1992 **Olympic Dream Team** and won a **gold medal** with them. In the 1996 Olympics, he won a second gold medal. He is known for his outspokenness and has been a regular on a weekly pregame **basketball** show. In 2006, he was enshrined in the **Naismith Memorial Basketball Hall of Fame.**

BARKSDALE, DONALD ARGEE "DON." B. 31 March 1923, Oakland, California. D. 8 March 1993, Oakland, California. Don Barksdale's middle name is often erroneously cited as "Angelo," but he was, in fact, named "Argee" after his father. He attended Berkeley High School in Berkeley, California, Marin Junior College, and the **University of California, Los Angeles.** He was selected for the 1948 **gold medal**-winning U.S. **Olympic basketball** team as a member of the Oakland Bittner **Amateur Athletic Union (AAU)** team and was the first black ever to play for the U.S. Olympic basketball team. After the Olympics he continued to play AAU basketball and was a member of the 1951 U.S. national team in the Pan American Games.

Barksdale established some precedents in the San Francisco area: He was its first black radio disc jockey, first black television host, and first black owner of a beer distributorship. In 1951, the six-foot, six-inch **forward-center** signed with the **Baltimore Bullets** of the **National Basketball Association (NBA)** and played for them for two years, and he also played for the **Boston Celtics** for two years before retiring in 1955. In four years in the league, he averaged 11.0 points per game. He became the first African American to play in an NBA **All-Star Game** in 1953. After retiring from basketball, Barksdale purchased an Oakland nightclub.

BARRY III, RICHARD FRANCIS DENNIS, "RICK." B. 28 March 1944, Elizabeth, New Jersey. Rick Barry attended Roselle Park High School in Roselle Park, New Jersey, and the University of Miami. In college, he led all **National Collegiate Athletic Association** players in scoring in his senior year, 1965, with a 37.4 points per game average in 26 games. Selected by the San Francisco Warriors in the 1965 **National Basketball Association (NBA) draft**, he played in the NBA from 1965–1967 and 1972–1978 for the Warriors and from 1978–1980 for the **Houston Rockets.** Barry also played in the **American Basketball Association (ABA)** from 1968–1972 for the Oakland Oaks, Washington Capitols, and New York Nets. He was NBA Rookie of the Year in 1966. The next year he led the league in scoring with a 35.6 points per game average and led the Warriors to the NBA Finals. After signing with the ABA in 1967, he was required to not play in the 1967–1968 season, as the Warriors still had a one-year option on his services. In 1969, with Oakland, he was a member of the ABA league championship team, although he injured his knee and only played in 35 regular-season games. In those 35 games, he averaged 34.0 points per game and was the ABA scoring leader. In 1975, he led the NBA in **steals** and led the Warriors to the league championship. His NBA career totals for 10 years are 794 regular-season games, a 23.2 points-per-game average, and a **free throw** percentage of .900. His ABA career totals for four years are 226 regular-season games, a 30.5 points-per-game average, and a free throw percentage of .880. He was selected for eight NBA and four ABA **All-Star Games** and was the Most Valuable Player in the 1967 NBA All-Star Game. He was selected to the All-NBA First Team five times and the All-NBA Second Team once. An excellent free throw shooter, he led the NBA six times and ABA three times in free throw percentage and was one of the last professional players to shoot free throws underhanded. Barry once made 60 consecutive free throws and held the record that has since been broken.

After retiring from active play, Barry **coached** Fort Wayne in the **Continental Basketball Association** from 1992–1994 and New Jersey and Florida in the **United States Basketball League** from 1998–2000. He has worked as a broadcaster and has had a radio show in the San Francisco area. He was enshrined in the **Naismith Memorial Basketball Hall of Fame** in 1987. In 1996, he was named one of the 50 Greatest Players in NBA History. His first wife, Pam Hale, was the daughter of former pro player and coach Bruce Hale. All four of their sons, Scooter, Jon, Brent, and Drew, have played professional **basketball**, with the latter three in the NBA.

BASKET. The basket is a metal ring 18 inches in diameter with a net of 15 inches to 18 inches in length. It is attached to the **backboard** at 10 feet from the ground and is the goal at which players shoot the **basketball**. The goal was originally a peach basket, hence the name. *See also* NAISMITH, JAMES A.

BASKETBALL. Basketball is a sport invented by Dr. **James A. Naismith** in 1891. The ball used in the game is also called a basketball. It is generally about 30 inches in circumference and is orange, although from 1967–1976 the **American Basketball Association** used a red, white, and blue ball. Women's basketball under both the **National Collegiate Athletic Association** and **Women's National Basketball Association** rules uses a 29-inch circumference basketball, but international rules mandate the same size ball for both men and women.

BASKETBALL ASSOCIATION OF AMERICA (BAA). The Basketball Association of America (BAA) was a men's professional **basketball** major league from 1946–1949, when it merged with the **National Basketball League (NBL)** on 3 August 1949, to form the **National Basketball Association (NBA)**. It was organized on 6 June 1946, at a meeting of members of the Arena Managers Association of America. Representatives of the **Boston Garden (Walter A. Brown)**, Cleveland Arena (Al Sutphin), Chicago Stadium (James D. Norris and Arthur Wirtz), New York's **Madison Square Garden (Edward "Ned" Irish)**, Philadelphia Arena (Pete Tyrell), Pittsburgh Arena (John Harris), Providence Arena (Lou Pieri), St. Louis Arena (Emery Jones and Arthur Wirtz), Toronto's Maple Leaf Gardens (Lew Hayman), Washington's Uline Arena (Mike Uline), and a group representing Indianapolis attended the meeting. On 20 August 1946, the Indianapolis franchise was replaced by one in Detroit at the Olympia Arena owned by Norris and Wirtz. Each prospective owner contributed $10,000 as a franchise fee. **Maurice Podoloff**, president of the American Hockey League and operator of the New Haven Arena, was named league president.

The season began on 1 November 1946, in Toronto, Ontario, **Canada**, with a game between the **New York Knickerbockers** and **Toronto Huskies**, won by New York, 66–64. The other teams in the league were the **Boston Celtics, Chicago Stags, Cleveland Rebels, Detroit Falcons**, Philadelphia Warriors, **Pittsburgh Ironmen, Providence Steamrollers, St. Louis Bombers**, and **Washington Capitols**. A 60-game schedule was played with the league split into the Eastern Division and Western Division. The top three teams in each division engaged in postseason playoff series to determine the league champion. The Warriors defeated the Stags in the final round of the playoffs and became league champions.

Before the league's second season, four teams dropped out, including Cleveland, Detroit, Pittsburgh, and Toronto dropped out, and the **Baltimore Bullets** of the **American Basketball League** were added. The 1947–1948 season was played with just eight teams. They played a 48-game schedule with unusual results. Philadelphia won the Eastern Division with a record of 27–21, one game ahead of the New York Knicks at 26–22. Providence won just six of 48 games. In the Western Division, St. Louis won with a record of 29–19, just one game better than the other three teams in the division, who finished in a three-way tie for second place at 28–18. When the playoffs were completed, Baltimore was the surprise winner.

For the 1948–1949 season, four of the best teams from the rival NBL, the Minneapolis Lakers, Rochester Royals, Fort Wayne Zollner Pistons, and Indianapolis Kautskys, were enticed to join the BAA and made it a 12-team league. The Kautskys and Zollner Pistons were required to drop their sponsors' names and became the **Indianapolis Jets** and Fort Wayne Pistons. Minneapolis defeated Washington and won the 1949 league championship. On 3 August 1949, the two leagues merged, forming the NBA with 17 teams playing the 1949–1950 season. *See also* APPENDIX B (for a list of league champions).

BAYLOR, ELGIN GAY. B. 16 September 1934, Washington, D.C. Elgin Baylor attended Phelps Vocational High School and Spingarn High School, both in Washington. He attended the College of Idaho for one year and then transferred to Seattle University. As a transfer student in 1955–1956, he was ineligible to play for Seattle, so he played for the Westside Ford **Amateur Athletic Union** team that season. In his senior year at Seattle, he led the team to the **National Collegiate Athletic Association** Championship game, where they lost to the **University of Kentucky**. He was chosen by the Minneapolis Lakers in the 1958 **National Basketball Association (NBA) draft** as the first overall selection.

Baylor played in the NBA from 1958–1972 for the Lakers, who moved from Minneapolis to Los Angeles in 1960. In 1959, he was

NBA Rookie of the Year. In his first three years in Los Angeles, he averaged better than 34 points per game in each of the three years. In **Wilt Chamberlain**'s first year in the NBA, 1959–1960, it was Baylor not Chamberlain who broke the single-game scoring record by scoring 64 points on 8 November 1959. The previous record of 63 was set by **Joe Fulks** in 1949 and had lasted for more than 10 years. The next year, it was again Baylor and not Chamberlain who was the first NBA player to score more than 70 points in one game. On 15 November 1960, Baylor scored 71 points in a game to break his own single-game scoring record. Baylor played in the NBA Finals with the Lakers eight times from 1959–1970 and was on the losing team each time. On 14 April 1962, Baylor scored 61 points in an NBA Finals game against Boston to set the all-time record for individual scoring in an NBA Finals game. He retired in November 1971, due to multiple injuries after playing just nine games that season and only two the previous season. Ironically, the Lakers won their game the following night and began a record-setting 33 game winning streak, the longest in league history. The Lakers went on to set a league record with 69 victories that season and won the NBA Championship, something that had eluded Baylor his entire career.

Baylor's NBA career totals for 14 years are 846 regular-season games and a 27.4 points and 13.5 rebounds per game average. He was selected for 11 NBA **All-Star Games** and was the Co-Most Valuable Player in 1959. He was named to the All-NBA First Team 10 times. After retiring from active play, he became assistant **coach** of the New Orleans Jazz. From 1976–1979, he was head coach of the Jazz. He was enshrined in the **Naismith Memorial Basketball Hall of Fame** in 1977. In 1980, he was one of 10 players selected to the NBA 35th Anniversary Team. In 1986, he became vice president of **basketball** operations for the **Los Angeles Clippers** and remained with them until his resignation in October 2008. In 1996, he was named one of the 50 Greatest Players in NBA History, and in 2006 he was named NBA Executive of the Year.

BAYLOR UNIVERSITY. Baylor University in Waco, Texas, began its men's **basketball** program in 1906 but has not had the same glory from its basketball teams as other major **National Collegiate Athletic Association (NCAA)** schools. From 1906–2010, the school has won less than half its games, with a record of 1,144–1,268. Home games since 1988 have been played at the 10,284-seat Ferrell Center. In 1948, the Bears reached the NCAA Championship final game, where they lost to the **University of Kentucky**. Among the best players in school history have been Carroll Dawson, Darrell Hardy, Vinnie Johnson, John Lucas III, Brian Skinner, Terry Teagle, David Wesley, and Micheal Williams.

The Baylor women's basketball program began in 1974. In 2005, the Lady Bears won the NCAA Championship and in 2010 they reached the semi-finals where they were defeated by eventual champion Connecticut. The best players in the school's history include Steffanie Blackmon; Mary Lowry; LaNita Luckey; Bernice Mosby; Debbie Polk; Suzie Snider-Eppers, who scored 3,861 points from 1973–1977, and Sophia Young. Kim Mulkey has been the most effective Baylor **coach**.

BEE, CLAIR FRANCIS. B. 2 March 1896, Grafton, West Virginia. D. 20 May 1983, Cleveland, Ohio. Clair Bee attended high school in West Virginia and then served in the military in Europe during World War I. In 1922, he enrolled at Waynesburg College in Pennsylvania. By the time he graduated in 1925, he was registrar of the college. He was hired by Rider College as chairman of its Accounting Department and in 1926 became Rider's **coach** of baseball, **basketball**, and football. In 1931, he became football and basketball coach at **Long Island University (LIU)**, where he had his greatest coaching success, leading the basketball team to 43 consecutive wins from 1934–1936 and the **National Invitation Tournament** championship in 1939 and 1941. In the early 1950s, the LIU team was affected by the point-shaving scandals, and their star player, Sherman White, was one of the players indicted. LIU dropped their basketball program, and Bee retired from coaching but remained at LIU as controller until June 1952. His coaching record at LIU was 370–80.

In November 1952, Bee was hired as coach of the **Baltimore Bullets** of the **National Basketball Association (NBA)** and coached them until November 1954. He became director of athletics at the New York Military Academy and owned and ran a summer sports camp. He worked at Kutsher's Country Club in the Catskills, was a cofounder in 1968 of Kutsher Sports Academy, and was a director of their summer sports camps. He was also a prolific author and wrote more than 50 books on sports, including a fictional sports series for boys featuring Chip Hilton, an All-American boy based on NBA player **Bob Davies**. Bee was enshrined in the **Naismith Memorial Basketball Hall of Fame** in 1968 as a contributor. Since 1996, the **National Collegiate Athletic Association** has presented the Clair Bee Coach of the Year Award to an active Division I men's coach.

BELLAMY, WALTER JONES "WALT." B. 24 July 1939, New Bern, North Carolina. Walt Bellamy attended J. T. Barber High School in New Bern and **Indiana University**. He won a **gold medal** with the 1960 U.S. **Olympic basketball** team and was chosen by the expansion Chicago Packers as the number one overall **draft** selection in the 1961 **National Basketball Association (NBA)** draft. He was named Rookie of the Year after recording one of the best rookie seasons in the history of the league—31.6 points and 19.0 **rebounds** per game. After his rookie season, his points-per-game average decreased annually for the next six seasons, although he was still one of the premier centers in the NBA. The six-foot, 11-inch **center** was named to the NBA **All-Star Game** in each of his first four NBA seasons. The Chicago team became the **Baltimore Bullets** in 1963, and he played with them until November 1965, when he was traded to the **New York Knickerbockers**.

Bellamy was with the Knicks until December 1968, when he was traded to the **Detroit Pistons**. That trade paved the way for the Knicks to move **Willis Reed** to center and helped lead the Knicks to the NBA Championship. In the 1968–1969 season, Bellamy played in an all-time league record 88 games, although the league schedule was just 82 games at the time due to the Pistons having played several fewer games than the Knicks at the time of the trade. In February 1970, he was traded by the Pistons to the **Atlanta Hawks**, and in May 1974 he was chosen by the expansion team New Orleans Jazz in an expansion draft. He concluded his professional career with one game for the Jazz on 17 October 1974, in which he made both **field goal** attempts and both **free throw** attempts and had five **rebounds** in just 14 **minutes** of play.

Bellamy is one of few basketball players whose last professional game had perfect shooting. In his 14-year NBA career, he played in 1,043 regular-season games and averaged 20.1 points and 13.7 rebounds per game. He is one of only seven NBA players to have scored more than 20,000 points and have 14,000 rebounds for his career. He was elected to the **Naismith Memorial Basketball Hall of Fame** in 1993. His 25-year-old younger half brother, Ron Bellamy, was a collegiate basketball player who became a professional boxer at the age of 35.

BELOV, ALEXANDER ALEXANDROVICH "SASHA." B. 11 November 1951, Leningrad, **Russia**, Union of Soviet Socialist Republics (USSR). D. 3 October 1978, USSR. Alexander Belov played **basketball** for Spartak Leningrad but is best known as the player who scored the winning basket for the USSR in the 1972 **Olympic Games** final against the **United States**. Also on their team at that time was **Sergei Belov**, but the two players were not related. The six-foot, eight-inch **forward** played in both the 1972 and 1976 Olympic Games for the USSR. In 1976, he won an Olympic **bronze medal** and is the only man to record a **triple-double** in Olympic basketball. On 27 July 1976, in a game against **Canada**, he scored 23 points with 14 **rebounds** and 10 **assists.** He also played in the 1970 and 1974 **World Championships,** helping the Soviet Union win a bronze medal in 1970 and the **gold medal** in 1974. In 1969, 1971, and 1975, he played on the Soviet Union team in the European Championships and led them to gold medals in 1969 and 1971 and a **silver medal** in 1975. Belov was awarded the Merited Master of Sport of the USSR in 1972 and was enshrined in the **Fédération Internationale de Basketball** Hall of Fame in 2007.

BELOV, SERGEI ALEXANDROVICH. B. 23 January 1944, Asheboro, **Russia, Union of Soviet Socialist Republics (USSR).** Sergei Belov attended Trud Voluntary Sports Society and the Armed Forces Sports Society. He played with Uralmash Sverdlovsk from 1964–1967 and with the Central Sports Army Club (CSKA) Moscow from 1968–1980, leading them to 11 USSR championships and Euroleague championships in 1969 and 1971. The six-foot, three-inch **guard** played with the Soviet national team in four **Olympic Games** from 1968–1980 and won four Olympic medals, gold in 1972 and bronze in 1968, 1976, and 1980. He was given the honor of lighting the Olympic torch in the Moscow Olympics, the only **basketball** player ever to do so. He also played in four **World Championships** and won **gold medals** in 1967 and 1974, silver in 1978, and bronze in 1970. He played in seven biennial European Championships from 1967–1979 and won four gold medals, two **silver medals** in 1975 and 1977, and bronze in 1973. In these three major **Fédération Internationale de Basketball (FIBA)** championships, he won more total medals than any other individual. Although **Alexander Belov** was his Soviet teammate for much of this time, the two men were not related.

In 1969, Belov was awarded the Merited Master of Sport of the USSR. In 1991, FIBA organized a vote by journalists for the century's best player, and Belov won. He was the first international player enshrined in the **Naismith Memorial Basketball Hall of Fame** when he was inducted in 1992. After retiring from active play, he became a **coach**. From 1993–1998, Belov was the president of the Russian Basketball Federation and coach of the Russian national team, leading them to silver medals in 1994 and 1998, the World Championships, and a **bronze medal** at the 1997 European Championship. Since 2005 he has been president of the Ural Great Perm club. Belov was inducted into the FIBA Hall of Fame in 2007.

BIASONE, DANIEL "DANNY." B. 22 February 1909, Miglianico, Chieti, **Italy**. D. 25 May 1992, Syracuse, New York. Dan Biasone came to the **United States** as a 10-year-old boy and grew up in Syracuse, New York. The owner of Eastwood Sports Center, a Syracuse bowling alley, in 1946, he and Syracuse businessman George Mangin purchased a franchise in the **National Basketball League (NBL)** and started the Syracuse Nationals **basketball** team. After playing three seasons in the NBL, the Nationals joined the **National Basketball Association (NBA)** in 1949 and remained in Syracuse until 1962, with Biasone acting as the team's general manager for most of that time.

Biasone's major contribution to basketball was convincing the other league owners to adopt the 24-second **shot clock** in 1954. In the summer of 1954, he set up an exhibition game in Syracuse to demonstrate its use and invited the other owners to watch. This convinced them, and the shot clock was incorporated in the NBA rules for the 1954–1955 season. Although he was not the inventor of the shot clock, he was a strong advocate of its use and is generally associated with its inception. In 1982, he was awarded the John Bunn award from the **Naismith Memorial Basketball Hall of Fame** for his service to basketball. He was enshrined in the hall in 2000 as a contributor.

BING, DAVID "DAVE." B. 24 November 1943, Washington, D.C. Dave Bing attended Spingarn High School in Washington and **Syracuse University**. He was selected by the **Detroit Pistons** in the 1966 **National Basketball Association (NBA) draft** and played from 1966–1975 for the Pistons. In 1975, he was traded to the Washington Bullets, played with them for two years and concluded his NBA career with one year with the **Boston Celtics**. His best year was 1967–1968, when he led the NBA in scoring with 2,142 points and a 27.1 points-per-game average. In 1967, he was named Rookie of the Year.

Bing's NBA career totals for 13 years are 901 regular-season games and a 20.3 points-per-game average. The six-foot, three-inch **guard** was selected for seven NBA **All-Star Games** and named its Most Valuable Player in 1976. He was also voted to the All-NBA First Team twice and the All-NBA Second Team once. In 1977, he was the recipient of the **J. Walter Kennedy** Citizenship Award. After retiring from active play, he founded the Bing Group in Detroit in 1980, a company that manufactures steel components for the automotive industry. It has grown to be one of the largest African American–owned firms in the **United States**. In 1990, he was enshrined in the **Naismith Memorial Basketball Hall of Fame** and in 1996 was named one of the 50 Greatest Players in NBA History. On 5 May 2009, he was elected mayor of the city of Detroit, Michigan.

BIRD, LARRY JOE. B. 7 December 1956, West Baden, Indiana. Larry Bird attended Springs Valley High School in French Lick, Indiana. He briefly attended **Indiana University**, then Northwood Institute, and finally **Indiana State University**. He led Indiana State to the **National Collegiate Athletic Association** Championship final game in 1979, where they were defeated by **Michigan State University**. He was the recipient of the Naismith College Player of the Year Award and the John R. Wooden Award as the best college **basketball**

player in 1979 and was drafted by the **Boston Celtics** in the first round of the 1978 **National Basketball Association (NBA) draft.**

The six-foot, nine-inch **forward** played in the NBA from 1979–1992 for the Celtics. Bird was voted Rookie of the Year in 1980; to the All-NBA First Team in each of his first nine years from 1980–1988; to the All-NBA Second Team in 1990; and NBA Most Valuable Player in 1984, 1985, and 1986. He was chosen for the NBA **All-Star Game** in every one of his 13 seasons except 1988–1989, when he was injured, and was named All-Star Game Most Valuable Player in 1982. From 1981–1987, he helped lead the Celtics to three NBA Championships and two NBA Finals and was twice named Finals Most Valuable Player. He led the NBA in **free throw** percentage four times. On 12 March 1985, he scored 60 points in one game, the most for any Celtics player. He was also a member of the **gold medal-**winning 1992 U.S. **Olympic** basketball **Dream Team.** Following the Olympics, on 18 August 1992, he announced his retirement from active play due to recurring back problems.

Bird's NBA career totals for 13 years and 897 regular-season games were 24.3 points per game, 10.0 **rebounds** per game, 6.3 **assists** per game, a free throw percentage of.886, and a **field goal** percentage of .496. After retiring from active play, he became a special consultant for the Celtics from 1992–1997. In 1996, he was named one of the 50 Greatest Players in NBA History. In 1997, he was hired as **coach** of the **Indiana Pacers.** He coached them for three seasons and compiled a record of 147–67 during that time. In 2000, they reached the NBA Championship Finals but lost to the **Los Angeles Lakers.** He resigned from coaching following that series but in 2003 was hired as the president of Basketball Operations of the Pacers and still held that position in 2010. Bird was enshrined in the **Naismith Memorial Basketball Hall of Fame** in 1998.

BLAZEJOWSKI, CAROL ANN "BLAZE." B. 29 September 1956, Elizabeth, New Jersey. Carol Blazejowski attended Cranford High School in Cranford, New Jersey, and Montclair State College. After graduating college in 1978, she was **drafted** in the first round by the New Jersey Gems of the **Women's Professional Basketball League (WBL)** but did not sign with them. She retained her amateur status and played **Amateur Athletic Union (AAU) basketball** for the Allentown Crestettes in 1978 and 1979, leading them to the semifinals of the national AAU tournament both years.

Known as "The Blaze," Blazejowski won a **silver medal** with the U.S. national team in the 1979 Pan American Games and a **gold medal** with them at the 1979 **World Championships**. She was selected for the ill-fated 1980 U.S. **Olympic** basketball team that boycotted the Moscow Olympics. When she signed a three-year, $150,000 contract with New Jersey in 1980, she became the WBL's highest-paid player. The five-foot, 10-inch **guard** averaged 30 points per game in the 1980–1981 season, but the WBL folded shortly thereafter.

Blazejowski worked as a promotional representative for Adidas, and, in 1997, when the **Women's National Basketball Association** began, was named vice president and general manager of the New York Liberty. In 2008, she was promoted to president and general manager. She was enshrined in the **Naismith Memorial Basketball Hall of Fame** in 1994 and in the **Women's Basketball Hall of Fame** in 1999.

BLOCKED SHOT. A blocked shot is one in which the defensive team alters the flight of the **basketball** by deflecting it after it has left the offensive player's hand. It must be done while the ball has not begun its downward flight to the basket, otherwise it is considered to be "goaltending." If the official determines that it was goaltending. a field goal is credited to the player shooting the ball. In 1973, the **National Basketball Association (NBA)** began officially recording blocked shots. Elmore Smith of the Buffalo Braves holds the NBA single-game record with 17 against the **Portland Trail Blazers** on 28 October 1973. In 1984–1985, Mark Eaton of the **Utah Jazz** blocked 456 shots in one season for an average of 5.56 blocks per game. Both **Bill Russell** and **Wilt Chamberlain** were extremely proficient shot-blockers. Had blocks been recorded while they were playing, most likely one or the other or both would be NBA record holders.

BOGUES, TYRONE CURTIS "MUGGSY." B. 9 January 1965, Baltimore, Maryland. Although he was only five-feet, three-inches tall, Muggsy Bogues was a professional basketball player for 14 years. His **National Basketball Association (NBA)** career was longer than

90 percent of the players who have reached that level. He attended Southern High School and Dunbar High School in Baltimore. At Dunbar, playing with three other players who also would reach the NBA—David Wingate, Reggie Williams, and Reggie Lewis—the team was undefeated in 1981 and 1982. Bogues then attended Wake Forest University. In 1986, he was a member of the U.S. national team that won a **gold medal** at the **World Championships**. In the first eight minutes of the semifinal game in that tournament, the diminutive Bogues held the six-foot, five-inch future Hall of Famer **Dražen Petrović** scoreless as the **United States** got off to a 19–2 lead. After his senior year in college, he won the Frances Pomeroy Naismith Award as the best male collegian under six feet tall.

Bogues was selected by the Washington Bullets in the 1987 NBA **draft**. The shortest player ever to play in the NBA, Bogues played for Washington, the Charlotte Hornets, the **Golden State Warriors**, and the **Toronto Raptors** from 1987–2001. With Washington, in 1986–1987, his teammate was **Manute Bol**, the tallest NBA player in history at seven-feet, seven-inches tall. Bogues's best year was 1993–1994, when he averaged a career-high 10.8 points and 4.1 **rebounds** along with 10.1 **assists** per game. His NBA career totals for 14 years are 889 regular-season games and a 7.7 points and 7.5 assists per game average. He was an excellent ball handler and committed few **turnovers** and is among the all-time NBA leaders in best assist-to-turnover ratio.

After retiring from active play, Bogues worked in real estate and then **coached** the Charlotte Sting **Women's National Basketball Association** team from August 2005 until they folded in January 2007. He then worked for the **Charlotte Bobcats** in their front office.

BOL, MANUTE. B. 16 October 1962, Gogrial, Sudan. D. 19 June 2010, Charlottesville, Virginia. Manute Bol was the son of a Dinka tribal chief and was discovered by American **coach** Don Feeley at a **basketball** clinic in Khartoum. At seven-feet, seven-inches tall, Bol weighed only 185 pounds when he was brought to the **United States**. He has extremely long arms and legs and could touch the rim of the **basket** without jumping. He was brought to play basketball at Cleveland State University, but after it was discovered that he could not read or write English sufficiently to meet the school's entrance requirement, he spent a year at Case Western Reserve English Language School in Cleveland, Ohio.

Although Bol had not played basketball in the United States, he was selected by the San Diego Clippers in the 1983 **National Basketball Association (NBA) draft**, but the selection was nullified by the league. He enrolled at the University of Bridgeport and averaged 22.5 points, 13.5 **rebounds**, and seven **blocked shots** per game and led Bridgeport to a 26–6 record and conference championship in 1984–1985. In 1985, he was selected by the Washington Bullets in the NBA draft. He played in the **United States Basketball League** in the summer of 1985 and in 25 games had 358 rebounds and 281 blocked shots, an average of more than 11 blocks per game.

With Washington in the 1985–1986 season, Bol became the tallest player ever to play in the NBA. In his first year, he blocked 397 shots (the second highest total of blocks in one season in NBA history) in 80 games for an average of 4.96 blocks per game. He only averaged 3.7 points per game and 6.0 rebounds per game, but on 12 December 1985, he scored 18 points in one game. On 25 January 1986, he blocked 15 shots in one game, the second highest single game total in NBA history. He remained with Washington for three seasons. In his last season with the Bullets, 1987–1988, one of his teammates was **Tyrone "Muggsy" Bogues**, at five-feet, three-inches tall the shortest player ever to play in the NBA.

In June 1988, Bol was traded to the **Golden State Warriors**. With the Warriors, Coach **Don Nelson** encouraged Bol to play away from the basket on offense since Bol was not a good shooter and was in the way of his teammates when he played near the basket. He taught Bol to stand back by the three-point line and encouraged him to shoot **three-point field goals**. In 80 games that season, Bol attempted 91 three-point field goals and made 20. He played one more season with the Warriors and was traded to the **Philadelphia 76ers** in August 1990.

Bol played three seasons for the 76ers before being released in July 1993. In the 1993–1994 season, he played briefly with the **Miami Heat**, Bullets, and 76ers. With the Bullets and 76ers, he was hired primarily to teach their giant players, seven-foot, seven-inch **Gheorghe Muresan** at Washington and seven-foot, six-inch Shawn Bradley at Philadelphia. On 18 October 1994, he was signed by the

Golden State Warriors but played only five games before retiring. In one of those five games, however, on 15 November 1994, he made three three-point field goals in three attempts within about five minutes during the game. His NBA career totals for 10 years are 624 regular-season games and a 2.6 points, 4.2 rebounds, and 3.3 blocks per game average. He was named to the NBA All-Defensive Second Team in 1986.

After retiring from active play, Bol returned to his native Sudan and worked with Sudanese refugees in attempts to rebuild the war-torn country. He established the Ring True Foundation to aid them and became involved with various promotions to raise money for his foundation. The promotions included a celebrity boxing match with 350-pound ex-pro football player William "The Refrigerator" Perry, an ice hockey appearance, and a stint as a jockey (although he did not get on horseback). Bol was seriously injured in an auto accident in 2004 and suffered a broken neck, although he recovered. In May 2010, he contracted Stevens-Johnson syndrome, a rare and painful skin condition after a reaction to a kidney medication. He died from kidney failure shortly afterward on 19 June 2010.

BOSTON CELTICS. The Boston Celtics are a team in the **National Basketball Association (NBA)**. They joined the **Basketball Association of America** in the initial year, 1946, and were originally owned by **Walter A. Brown**. The franchise was sold after his death in 1965 to the Ruppert Knickerbocker Breweries. Since then, the franchise has changed hands more than half a dozen times. Home games were played at the 14,890-seat **Boston Garden** from 1946–1995, although in 1946 some games were also played at the 6,000-seat Boston Arena. Since 1995, home games have been played at the 18,624-seat Fleet Center (recently renamed the TD Banknorth Garden). The Celtics have also played home games in Hartford, Connecticut, and in Providence, Rhode Island. Their **coaches** have included **John "Honey" Russell**, Alvin "Doggie" Julian, **Arnold "Red" Auerbach**, **Bill Russell**, **Tom Heinsohn**, Tom Sanders, **Dave Cowens**, Bill Fitch, **K. C. Jones**, Jimmy Rodgers, Chris Ford, M. L. Carr, Rick Pitino, Jim O'Brien, John Carroll, and Glenn "Doc" Rivers.

The Celtics were the first team to draft a black player, **Chuck Cooper**, in 1950, and also the first to play five black starters. In 1966,

Russell became the NBA's first black head coach. In 1985–1986, the Celtics proved that color didn't matter, when the league at that time was more than 75 percent black and the Celtics won the league championship by having a black coach play eight white players and four blacks.

Among their most notable players have been Hall of Famers **Nate "Tiny" Archibald, Dave Bing, Larry Bird, Bob Cousy,** Dave Cowens, **Wayne Embry** (enshrined as a contributor), **John Havlicek,** Tom Heinsohn, **Bailey Howell,** K. C. Jones, **Sam Jones, Clyde Lovellette, Ed Macauley, Pete Maravich, Kevin McHale, Robert Parish, Andy Phillip, Frank Ramsey, Arnie Risen,** John "Honey" Russell, **Bill Sharman, John Thompson** (enshrined as a coach), **Bill Walton,** and **Dominique Wilkins.** In addition, coaches Red Auerbach, Alvin Julian, and owner Walter A. Brown have also been enshrined in the **Naismith Memorial Basketball Hall of Fame.**

The Celtics have won 17 league championships—more than any other team in the league—and from 1956–1957 through 1968–1969 won 11 championships in 13 seasons, including a record eight consecutive from 1959–1966. They also won in 1974, 1976, 1981, 1984, 1986, and 2008. They lost in the NBA Championship Finals four times. Their record for their first 64 years in the league through the 2009–2010 season is 2,972–2,031.

BOSTON GARDEN. Boston Garden was an indoor arena in Boston, Massachusetts, built in 1928, and was the home of the **Boston Celtics** from 1955–1995. Its seating capacity for **basketball** was 14,890. Known for its parquet floor and lack of air conditioning, it was replaced by the Fleet Center (now renamed TD Banknorth Garden) in 1995 and demolished in 1997.

BRADLEY, WILLIAM WARREN "BILL." B. 28 July 1943, Crystal City, Missouri. Bill Bradley attended Crystal City High School and Princeton University. He won a Rhodes Scholarship and spent two years at Oxford University after his graduation from Princeton. While at Rhodes, he played for Milan Simmenthal of the Italian league in 1965–1966 and helped lead them to the **European Cup** Championship. In his three varsity years at Princeton, he averaged 30.2 points per game and led them to the **National Collegiate Athletic**

Association Final Four in 1965, where although they lost in the semifinal round he was named the tournament's Most Outstanding Player. He was also the recipient of the Sullivan Award in 1965 and was the first **basketball** player to win this award, presented by the **Amateur Athletic Union** since 1930 to the nation's best amateur athlete. In 1964, he won a **gold medal** with the **U.S. Olympic** basketball team.

Selected by the **New York Knickerbockers** in the 1965 **National Basketball Association (NBA) draft** as a **territorial** choice, the six-foot, five-inch **forward-guard** played in the NBA from 1967–1977 with the Knicks. Nicknamed "Dollar Bill" for his lucrative initial professional contract, Bradley was a member of the 1970 and 1973 NBA champions. In 10 NBA seasons, he played in 742 regular-season games and averaged 12.4 points per game. He also played in the 1973 NBA **All-Star Game.**

After retiring from basketball, Bradley became a U.S. Senator as a democratic representative from the state of New Jersey and served three terms from 1979–1996. He ran unsuccessfully for the democratic nomination for president of the United States in 2000. Since then he has worked as a corporate consultant and investment banker. He was enshrined in the **Naismith Memorial Basketball Hall of Fame** in 1982.

BRADLEY UNIVERSITY. Bradley University was founded in 1897 in Peoria, Illinois, as Bradley Polytechnic Institute and began a men's **basketball** program in 1902. From 1949–1982, home games were played at Robertson Memorial Field House. Since 1982, home games have been played at Peoria Civic Center's 11,164-seat Carver Arena. Bradley's most outstanding **coaches** have been Forrest A. "Forddy" Anderson, Chuck Orsborn, Alfred J. "A. J." Robertson, and Dick Versace. The Braves were runners-up to **City College of New York** in both the 1950 **National Collegiate Athletic Association (NCAA)** Championship and **National Invitation Tournament (NIT).** In 1954, they were second to **La Salle University** in the NCAA Championships. They won the NIT three times, in 1957, 1960, and 1964. Among the Braves' best players have been Hersey Hawkins, one of the NCAA's all-time leading scorers with 3,008 points in his four year career; Steve Kuberski; Bobby Joe Mason; Shellie McMillon; Roger Phegley; Paul Unruh; and Chet Walker.

BRAZIL. Brazil joined the **Fédération Internationale de Basketball (FIBA)** in 1935 and is a member in the FIBA Americas zone. The men's team competed in 13 **Olympic** tournaments and won the **bronze medal** three times. In the FIBA **World Championships**, they competed 16 times and won the tournament twice, finished second twice, and placed third twice. In the FIBA Americas Championships, they entered all 13 tournaments and won three times. In the South American Championships, they entered 41 of the 43 tournaments and medaled in 38 of them, with 17 **gold medals**, 12 **silver medals**, and nine bronze medals. In the Pan American Games, they entered all 15 times and have 13 medals, five gold, two silver, and six bronze. In the 1987 Pan American Games, they recorded a major upset by overcoming a 14-point **halftime** deficit to defeat the **United States** in Indianapolis, Indiana, 120–115.

There have been eight players from Brazil in the **National Basketball Association**: Rafael Araujo; Leandro Barbosa; Rolando Ferreira; Alex Garcia; Anderson Varejão; João José Vianna; Marcus Vinicius Vieira de Souza; and Maybyner Rodney Hilario, better known as Nenê. One of the greatest international players of all time was Brazilian **Oscar Schmidt**, one of only three men to compete in five Olympic Games and holder of numerous Olympic records.

The Brazilian women's team competed in five Olympic tournaments from 1992–2008 and won the silver medal in 1996, the bronze in 2000, and finished fourth in 2004. They competed in 14 of 15 FIBA World Championships, won in 1994, and finished third in 1971. In the FIBA Americas Championships, they entered eight of the nine tournaments and medaled each time they entered. In the South American Championships, they entered 30 of the 31 tournaments and medaled in 29 of them with, 22 gold, five silver, and two bronze. In the Pan American Games, the Brazilian women's team entered all 13 competitions and won three times, were second four times, and third three times. There have been 10 Brazilian players in the **Women's National Basketball Association**: **Janeth Arcain**, who played in four Olympic Games and holds numerous Olympic records; Iziane Castro Marques; Erika Desouza; Cintia Dos Santos; Helen Luz; Adriana Moisés Pinto; Cláudia Maria Neves; Kelly Santos; Alessandra Santos de Oliveira; and Leila Sobral. Possibly the two greatest Brazilian women basketball players were **Hortência Maria de Fátima Marcari**, known simply as Hortência, and Maria Paula Gonçalves da Silva, known as Magic Paula.

BRIGHAM YOUNG UNIVERSITY (BYU). Brigham Young University (BYU) in Provo, Utah, began its men's **basketball** program in 1903. Home games since 1971 have been played at the 22,700-seat Marriott Center, which when it first opened was the largest college basketball arena in the **United States**. Prior to 1971, home games were played at George Albert Smith Fieldhouse. One of the differences between BYU and most other schools is that the school, in keeping with its Mormon traditions, will not play games on Sunday. This can potentially become an issue in the **National Collegiate Athletic Association (NCAA)** Championship tournament, but so far it has not. The most accomplished **coaches** in the school's history have been LaDell Andersen, Frank Arnold, Roger Reid, G. Ott Romney, and Stan Watts. In 1951 and 1966, the Cougars won the **National Invitation Tournament**, but they have never reached the NCAA **Final Four**. The best players in school history include Danny Ainge, Shawn Bradley, **Krešimir Ćosić**, Bernie Fryer, Mel Hutchins, Timo Lampen, Craig Raymond, and Brady Walker.

BRONZE MEDAL. In **Fédération Internationale de Basketball** competition, for example, the **Olympic Games** and **World Championships**, the third place team is awarded bronze medals. In some tournaments, the semifinal losers play a match to determine the bronze medal winner. In other tournaments, a round-robin tournament is played, with the team with the third-best record receiving the bronze medal. *See also* GOLD MEDAL; SILVER MEDAL.

BROWN, HUBERT JUDE "HUBIE." B. 25 September 1933, Hazleton, Pennsylvania. Hubie Brown attended St. Mary's High School in Elizabeth, New Jersey, and Niagara University. The six-foot-tall **guard** played **basketball** at Niagara from 1951–1955 but averaged only 3.9 points per game in 82 games. After serving in the U.S.

Army, he played briefly in the Eastern Basketball Association. He **coached** high school basketball at several schools in New York and New Jersey and was assistant coach at William and Mary College and **Duke University** and for the **Milwaukee Bucks** of the **National Basketball Association (NBA)**. From 1974–1976, he was head coach of the **Kentucky Colonels** of the **American Basketball Association** and led them to the 1974 championship. He coached the **Atlanta Hawks** from 1976–1981 and **New York Knickerbockers** from 1982–1986.

Brown became a television analyst and has worked in television since coaching the Knicks, with the exception of the 2002–2003 and 2003–2004 seasons, when he returned to the NBA as coach of the **Memphis Grizzlies**. He was NBA Coach of the Year in both 1978 and 2004. In 2000, Brown was the recipient of the Curt Gowdy Media Award from the **Naismith Memorial Basketball Hall of Fame** and in 2005 was enshrined in the hall in the category of contributor.

BROWN, LAWRENCE HARVEY "LARRY." B. 14 September 1940, Brooklyn, New York. Larry Brown attended Long Beach High School in Long Beach, New York, and the **University of North Carolina**. After graduation from college, the five-foot, nine-inch Brown was drafted by the **Baltimore Bullets** in the 1963 **National Basketball Association (NBA) draft** but chose to play **Amateur Athletic Union basketball** for the Akron Goodyear team since the NBA rarely employed anyone under six feet tall during that era. He won a **gold medal** with the 1964 U.S. **Olympic** basketball team and in 1967 joined the New Orleans Buccaneers of the **American Basketball Association (ABA)** and played in the ABA from 1967–1972. In 1968, he helped lead the Bucs to the ABA Championship Finals. In 1968, he was traded to the Oakland Oaks and helped lead them to the 1969 ABA Championship. In his five-year playing career in the ABA, he played in 376 regular-season games, averaged 11.2 points per game, played in three ABA **All-Star Games**, and set the ABA record with 23 assists in one game on 20 February 1972.

In the ABA, Brown **coached** the Carolina Cougars from 1972–1974 and the **Denver Nuggets** from 1974–1976. Since 1976, he has coached in the NBA with **Denver, New Jersey, San Antonio,** the **Los Angeles Clippers, Indiana, Philadelphia, Detroit, New**

York, and the **Charlotte Bobcats,** and in college at the **University of California, Los Angeles (UCLA)** and the **University of Kansas.** He led UCLA to the 1980 **National Collegiate Athletic Association (NCAA)** Tournament Final game, where they lost to the **University of Louisville,** and led Kansas to the 1988 NCAA Championship. In the NBA, he led Detroit to the league championship in 2004. In 2001, with Philadelphia, and 2005, with Detroit, he was the losing coach in the NBA Finals. His NBA career coaching record through the 2009–2010 season is 1,089–885.

In 2000, Brown was assistant coach of the gold medal-winning U.S. Olympic team, and in 2004 he was the coach of the U.S. Olympic team that had a disastrous tournament, losing three games, but that still won the **bronze medal.** He was named Coach of the Year in three of his four ABA seasons and also in the NBA in 2001. He was enshrined in the **Naismith Memorial Basketball Hall of Fame** in 2002 as a coach. His brother, Herb, has also coached in the NBA.

BROWN, WALTER A. B. 10 February 1905, Hopkinton, Massachusetts. D. 7 September 1964, Hyannis, Massachusetts. Walter Brown attended Boston Latin School, Hopkinton High School, and Exeter Academy. His father, George Brown, was general manager of the Boston Arena and president of the **Boston Garden-**Arena Corporation. After graduating school, Walter began working for his father. In 1931, Walter worked as secretary of the Boston Tigers of the Canadian-American Hockey League. In 1933, he was the **coach** of the U.S. national team that won the world amateur hockey title.

In 1937, after his father's death, Brown was named president of the Boston Garden-Arena Corporation and retained that position until his own death. During World War II, he served in the U.S. Army and held the rank of lieutenant colonel. In 1946, he was one of the founders of the **Basketball Association of America.** He was coowner and president of the Boston Celtics and retained that position until his death. As owner of the Celtics, he drafted the league's first black player, **Chuck Cooper,** in 1950. He was president of the Boston Bruins National Hockey League team and treasurer of the Ice Capades. In 1947, he was named president of the International Hockey Federation. He promoted boxing and was involved in coordinating the Boston Marathon. From 1961–1964, he was chairman of the **Naismith**

Memorial Basketball Hall of Fame board of directors. In 1962, he was inducted into the Hockey Hall of Fame in Toronto and in 1965 was enshrined in the **basketball** Hall of Fame. After his death in 1964, the **National Basketball Association** named its championship trophy the Walter A. Brown Trophy.

BRYANT, KOBE BEAN. B. 23 August 1978, Philadelphia, Pennsylvania. Kobe Bryant (named for the **Japanese** delicacy Kobe beef) is the son of Joe "Jellybean" Bryant, a former **National Basketball Association (NBA)** player. At the age of six his family moved to **Italy**, where his father was playing. Kobe spent the next several years there and learned to speak fluent Italian. Upon returning to the **United States,** he attended Lower Merion High School in Ardmore, Pennsylvania, but did not go to college. He was chosen in the 1996 NBA **draft** by the Charlotte Hornets. Shortly afterward his **draft rights** were traded by the Hornets to the **Los Angeles Lakers.**

Bryant, a six-foot, six-inch **guard**, has played with the Lakers from the 1996–1997 season through the 2009–2010 season. As an 18-year old with the Lakers in 1996, his career started slowly, and he only averaged 7.6 points per game, playing about 15 **minutes** per game, but he was named to the NBA All-Rookie Second Team. Since then he has become one of the league's stars. He helped lead the Lakers to three consecutive NBA Championships from 2000–2002 and two more in 2009 and 2010.

Bryant has accumulated many individual honors including, **All-Star Game** Most Valuable Player in 2002, 2007, and 2009; league scoring leader in 2005–2006 and 2006–2007; Most Valuable Player in 2008; and NBA Finals Most Valuable Player in 2009 and 2010. From 1999–2010, he was named to the All-NBA First Team eight times, Second Team twice, and Third Team twice and the All-NBA Defensive First Team eight times and Second Team twice. On 22 January 2006, he scored 81 points in a game against the **Toronto Raptors,** the second highest single-game total in league history. In that game, he also scored 55 points in the second half, also the second best in that category. On four other occasions he scored between 60 and 65 points in a game. Through the 2009–2010 season, he had 24 games of 50 or more points (10 coming in the 2006–2007 season, when he averaged 35.4 points per game). Although not known as a

three-point field goal shooter, he set the record of 12 three-pointers in a game on 7 January 2003, since tied by Donyell Marshall in 2005.

Bryant's career has not been without controversy. In the summer of 2003, he was arrested for sexual assault in Colorado, but the complaint was later dropped before the case came to trial. His relationship with teammate **Shaquille O'Neal** deteriorated to the point that O'Neal was traded. His relationship with **coach Phil Jackson** also was not smooth, and Jackson left the team. In 2007, Bryant demanded to be traded, as he was unhappy with the quality of play of his teammates, but his request was not honored. In 2008, after previously refusing to play, he helped lead the U.S. **Olympic** team to the **gold medal**.

BUFFALO BISONS. *See* ATLANTA HAWKS.

BUFFALO BRAVES. *See* LOS ANGELES CLIPPERS.

BUFFALO GERMANS. Fred Burkhardt, who learned the game under Dr. **James Naismith**, organized a boys' **basketball** team in 1895 at the German YMCA in Buffalo, New York. By 1900, the group, with Allie Heerdt as captain, claimed a record of 87–6 and the Western New York championship. They never joined a non-YMCA league, but as they became more successful they began traveling. They won tournaments at the 1901 Pan American Exposition in Buffalo and the 1904 St. Louis Exposition and Fair. Some authors have mistakenly credited that with being an **Olympic Games** event, but most Olympic historians consider it to have been an exhibition or demonstration tournament and not part of the Olympic Games proper. They continued traveling and winning and claimed 111 consecutive victories from 1908–1911. In 1925, when the **American Basketball League** was organized, they entered, calling themselves the Buffalo Bisons, but they won only 10 of 30 games and disbanded shortly afterward. They claimed an overall record of 792 wins and only 86 losses during their 30-year existence.

At times, especially during and after World War I, the team was known as the Buffalo Orioles. Among the players on the team at one point or another were Allie Heerdt, Philip Dischinger, Henry J. Faust, Edward Linneborn, John I. Maier, Albert W. Manweiler, brothers

Edward C. and Harry J. Miller, Charles P. Monahan, George L. Redlein, Edmund Reimann, William C. Rohde, and George Schell. They were enshrined as a team in the **Naismith Memorial Basketball Hall of Fame** in 1961.

BULGARIA. Bulgaria joined the **Fédération Internationale de Basketball (FIBA)** in 1935 and is a member in the FIBA Europe zone. The men's team competed in four **Olympic** tournaments from 1952–1968. Their best result was in 1956, when they finished in fifth place. Georgi Marinov Panov was their only player to compete in three Olympic tournaments. In the FIBA **World Championships**, they competed only in 1959 and finished seventh. In the FIBA European Championships, they entered 22 times and won the **silver medal** in 1957 and the **bronze medal** in 1961. In the FIBA World Championships, they competed six times and finished second in 1959 and third in 1964. In the FIBA European Championships, they competed 22 times, won the **gold medal** in 1958, finished second five times, and placed third four times.

The women's team competed in three Olympic tournaments, 1976, 1980, and 1988. In 1976, they won the bronze medal and in 1980 the silver medal. Their overall Olympic Games record is 10–6, and their winning percentage is fourth behind the **United States**, the **Union of Soviet Socialist Republics**, and **Australia**. Their best female Olympic **basketball** player has been Evladia Slavcheva Stefanova, who played in the 1980 and 1988 Games and averaged 19.1 points per game.

Georgi Glouchkov, one of the first Europeans to play in the **National Basketball Association (NBA)**, played for the **Phoenix Suns** in the 1985–1986 season and is the only Bulgarian native thus far to compete in the NBA. Polina Tzekova played in the **Women's National Basketball Association** in 1999 for the Houston Comets.

– C –

CAGE. In the early days of **basketball**, between 1895–1925, the basketball court was surrounded by a wire or net cage. This was done to keep the ball in play and prevent spectator interference. The Trenton team originated its use and other teams followed suit. Since that time basketball players have been referred to as "cagers."

CALIFORNIA, LOS ANGELES, UNIVERSITY OF (UCLA). *See* UNIVERSITY OF CALIFORNIA, LOS ANGELES (UCLA).

CALIFORNIA, UNIVERSITY OF. The main campus of the University of California is located in Berkeley, California. The men's intercollegiate **basketball** program was begun in 1908. Home games since 1999 have played at the 11,877-seat Walter A. Haas Jr. Pavilion. Prior to its construction, home games beginning in 1933 were played at the much smaller Harmon Gymnasium. The Golden Bears were **National Collegiate Athletic Association (NCAA)** semifinalists in 1946, finishing in fourth place, and they won the NCAA Championship in 1959 by one point over West Virginia University and were runners-up in 1960. Their **coach**, Pete Newell, was inducted into the **Naismith Memorial Basketball Hall of Fame** in 1979. Among their more noted players have been Phil Chenier, Larry Friend, Darrall Imhoff, Charles Johnson, Kevin Johnson, **Jason Kidd**, Bill McClintock, Lamond Murray, and Leon Powe. In addition to Newell, other outstanding coaches have been Ben Braun and Clarence M. "Nibs" Price.

CANADA. Canada joined the **Fédération Internationale de Basketball (FIBA)** in 1936 and is a member in the FIBA Americas zone. The men's team competed in nine **Olympic** tournaments and won the **silver medal** in the very first Olympic Games in 1936, losing the final game to the **United States** outdoors in the rain. They also finished fourth in both 1976 and 1984. In the FIBA **World Championships**, they competed 13 times, with a best finish of sixth twice. In the FIBA Americas Championships, they entered all 13 times and finished second twice and third three times. In the Pan American Games, they entered 12 times, with fourth as their best effort.

The women's team competed in four Olympic tournaments, where their best finish was fourth in 1984. They competed eight times and finished third twice in the FIBA World Championships. In the FIBA Americas Championships, they competed nine times, won in 1995, and were third five times. In the Pan American Games, they competed in all 13 tournaments and were second in 1999 and third three times.

Among the native Canadians to play in the **National Basketball Association, Basketball Association of America**, or **American Basketball Association** have been Joel Anthony, Norm Baker, Ron Crevier, Bobby Croft, Rick Fox, Stewart Granger, Bob Houbregs, Todd MacCulloch, Jamaal Magloire, Leo Rautins, Mike Smrek, Gino Sovran, **Ernie Vandeweghe**, Bill Wennington, and Jim Zoet. In addition, several players born outside of Canada were raised in Canada, including Hank Biasatti, Samuel Dalembert, and Steve Nash, who have played professional **basketball** in the United States. Canadians Kelly Boucher, Stacy Dales, Amber Hall, Merlelynn Lange-Harris, Kim Smith, and Tammy Sutton-Brown have all played in the **Women's National Basketball Association (WNBA)**. Shona Thornburn, another WNBA player, was born in England but raised in Canada.

CAPITOL BULLETS. *See* WASHINGTON WIZARDS.

CARNESECCA, LUIGI P. "LOU." B. 5 January 1925, New York, New York. Lou Carnesecca graduated from St. Ann's High School in New York, in 1943, and served in the **U.S.** Coast Guard from 1943–1946. He enrolled at **St. John's University** and only played three games of **basketball** for the junior varsity team but starred in baseball and played in the College World Series in 1949. He **coached** basketball at St. Ann's from 1950–1957, while earning a master's degree in educational guidance at St. John's and also working as a scholastic baseball umpire and basketball **referee**. In 1957, he was hired by St. John's as an assistant to basketball coach **Joe Lapchick**. When Lapchick retired in 1965, Carnesecca became head coach and served in that capacity until 1992 (with the exception of 1970–1973, when he coached the New York Nets of the **American Basketball Association [ABA]**). He had a won–lost record of 526–200 for 24 seasons at St. John's. In 1985, he led St. John's to the **National Collegiate Athletic Association Final Four**, where they lost in the semifinal round. He was named National Coach of the Year in 1983 and 1985 by the United States Basketball Writers Association. With the Nets, in three seasons, his record was 114–138, but he led them to the ABA Championship Finals in 1972.

Known as "Looie" by fans and media, Carnesecca was known for wearing colorful sweaters while coaching. He was enshrined in the **Naismith Memorial Basketball Hall of Fame** in 1992. In November 2004, St. John's Alumni Hall was rededicated as the Lou Carnesecca Arena.

CAROLINA COUGARS. *See* SPIRITS OF ST. LOUIS.

CARR, AUSTIN GEORGE. B.10 March 1948, Washington, D.C. Austin Carr attended Mackin Catholic High School in Washington, D.C., and **Notre Dame University**. In college, he averaged 38.1 and 38.0 points per game in his final two seasons and 34.6 points per game for his three years of varsity play. In the 1970 **National Collegiate Athletic Association (NCAA)** Tournament, he scored 61 points in a first-round game against Ohio University on 7 March 1970, still the all-time tournament scoring record. In that tournament, he also scored 52 points in Notre Dame's second round loss to the University of Kentucky. His total of 158 points for the tournament and an average of 52.7 points per game is another NCAA record. In seven NCAA Tournament games from 1969–1971, he scored a record 289 points for an average of 41.3 points per game.

The six-foot, four-inch **guard** was selected by the **Cleveland Cavaliers** in the 1971 **National Basketball Association (NBA) draft** as the first overall selection and played for them from 1971–1980. Carr's professional career was never quite as spectacular as his college days, as he broke his foot early in his first year and injured a knee in the 1974–1975 season. In 1980–1981, he concluded his NBA career by playing for **Dallas** and **Washington**. His best year was 1973–1974, when he averaged 21.9 points per game and played in the 1974 NBA **All-Star Game**. In 1980, he was the recipient of the **J. Walter Kennedy** Citizenship Award from the NBA. His NBA career totals for 10 years are 682 regular-season games and a 15.4 points per game average. After retiring from active play, Carr worked as director of Community Relations for the Cavaliers and as a color commentator for their telecasts.

CARTER, VINCENT LAMAR "VINCE." B. 26 January 1977, Daytona Beach, Florida. Vince Carter attended Daytona Beach Mainland

High School and the **University of North Carolina**. He left school after his junior year and was chosen in the 1998 **National Basketball Association (NBA) draft** by the **Golden State Warriors**. His **draft rights** were immediately traded to the **Toronto Raptors**. The six-foot, six-inch **forward** played for the Raptors from 1998–2004.

Carter was Rookie of the Year in 1999 and was selected for the NBA **All-Star Game** each year from 2000–2007. In 2000, he won the **Slam Dunk** Contest with some spectacular moves that earned him the nickname "Half-man, half-amazing" from former player and television commentator Kenny Smith. Carter carried those abilities to the 2000 **Olympic Games** where, as a member of the **gold medal**-winning U.S. team, he leaped over the head of his seven-foot, two-inch French opponent, Frédéric Weis, and dunked the ball in a memorable play. From 2004–2009, he played for the **New Jersey Nets** and was traded to the **Orlando Magic** for the 2009–2010 season. In his first 12 NBA seasons, he has played in 852 regular-season games and has averaged 22.9 points per game. He is a cousin of **Tracy McGrady**.

CENTER. The center position is one of the five **basketball** positions and is sometimes referred to as the "**pivot**." It is usually played by the tallest player on the team. The center's role was originally to contest the jump ball that took place after each made basket. With the elimination of the **center jump**, the center's role was to play near the basket, **rebound**, and shoot within a few feet of the basket. **Bill Russell** recreated the center's role and made it a shot-blocking, defensive one as well. *See also* FORWARD; GUARD.

CENTER JUMP. The start of a **basketball** game is accomplished by an official putting the ball into play by throwing it in the air between two opponents in a circle at the middle court. Until the late 1930s, this was also done following every successful **field goal** as well. It was also done to begin each period of play, but in recent years this has been eliminated and teams have alternated beginning play by passing the ball in from out-of-bounds.

CENTRAL BASKETBALL LEAGUE (CBL). The Central Basketball League (CBL) was a men's professional **basketball** major league that was organized in the fall of 1906, in Pittsburgh, Pennsylvania, and lasted until 1912. There were six teams in the league the first season, including East Liverpool in Ohio and five teams in the Pittsburgh area—Pittsburgh, Greensburg, Homestead, Butler, and McKeesport. The league played a 30-game regular season and a 20-game postseason.

East Liverpool won the regular season and Pittsburgh the postseason. Over the next few years, the league played a 70-game schedule with minimal franchise changes. In the 1908–1909 season, the East Liverpool franchise was sold, and the new owners were unable to field a winning team. After beginning the season with a record of only four wins and 57 losses, they dropped out of the league and were replaced for the last 10 games of the season by an amateur team from Alliance, Ohio. On 16 March 1909, Johnstown defeated Alliance by the score of 110–9 on 55 **field goals**. Bill Keenan scored 38 field goals for 76 points. This amount of individual total field goals has never been surpassed in professional basketball, and the individual total points was the record until 1961.

The league attempted to play the 1912–1913 season but after playing just a few exhibition games disbanded on 12 November 1912. In its six-year history, the CBL attracted many of the top players of the day, including Ed Ferat, Joe Fogarty, **Harry Hough**, Jimmy Kane, Bill Keenan, Winnie Kincaide, Bill Kummer, Chief Muller, Andy Sears, Roy Steele, and **Dutch Wohlfarth**. *See also* APPENDIX B (for a list of league champions).

CERVI, ALFRED NICHOLAS "AL," "DIGGER." B. 12 December 1917, Buffalo, New York. D. 9 November 2009, Rochester, New York. Al Cervi attended East High School in Buffalo, left school after his junior year to help with the family business, and did not go to college. He began his professional **basketball** career with the Buffalo Bisons of the **National Basketball League (NBL)** in 1937. He then played for several independent teams, including the Newark Pros from 1939–1941, Syracuse Reds from 1939–1940, and Rochester Seagrams and Rochester Pros from 1943–1945. He also served five years in the U.S. Army Air Force. The five-foot, 11-inch **guard-forward** played in the NBL from 1945–1948 for the Rochester Royals and was a member of the league championship team in 1946. In

1948, he was named player-**coach** of the Syracuse Nationals. The Nationals joined the **National Basketball Association (NBA)** in 1949, and he remained with them as player-coach through 1953. After retiring as a player in 1953, he continued as coach of the Nationals until 12 games into the 1956–1957 season. He led the Nats to the 1950, 1954, and 1955 NBA Championship Finals and won the championship in 1955. In 1958–1959, he coached the Philadelphia Warriors.

Cervi's NBL/NBA career totals for nine years are 389 regular-season games and a 10.1 points per game average. He was named to the All-NBL First Team three times and the All-NBL Second Team and All-NBA Second Team once each. In 1949, he was NBL Coach of the Year. After retiring from active play he ran a basketball camp and worked as regional sales manager and public relations director of Eastern Freightways in Rochester, New York. Cervi was enshrined in the **Naismith Memorial Basketball Hall of Fame** in 1985.

CHAMBERLAIN, WILTON NORMAN "WILT." B. 21 August 1936, Philadelphia, Pennsylvania. D. 12 October 1999, Bel Air, California. Wilt Chamberlain attended Overbrook High School in Philadelphia and the **University of Kansas**. He was seven-feet, one-inch tall while still in high school and dominated the opposition to the extent that his high school teams had a record of 56–3, and he had games in which he scored 90, 74, and 71 points. He was recruited by more than 100 colleges but chose Kansas.

In college, Chamberlain averaged 29.9 points per game in two seasons of varsity play. In his junior year, 1957, he led Kansas to the **National Collegiate Athletic Association (NCAA)** Championship game, where they were defeated by the **University of North Carolina** in triple **overtime**. He was also an exceptional track and field athlete in high school and college and won the conference track and field high jump championship in college. He left school after his junior year and played one season with the **Harlem Globetrotters**.

His Globetrotter experience was so enjoyable that for the first part of his professional career, Chamberlain would play for the Trotters each summer after the **National Basketball Association (NBA)** season was concluded. He was one of the physically strongest players in NBA history and was selected by the Philadelphia Warriors in the 1959 NBA **draft** as a high school **territorial draft** overall selection, the only high school player ever designated a territorial choice. When he entered the NBA in 1959, the individual season scoring record had been set the previous season by **Bob Pettit** at 29.2 points per game and 2,105 total points.

In his first season, Chamberlain had 2,707 points and averaged 37.6 points per game, breaking the record by more than 600 points and eight points per game. He continued scoring at an astronomical pace and, in 1961–1962, he had his best year statistically when he averaged an unheard of 50.4 points per game, scoring 4,029 points for the season and playing every minute of every game except for one game in Los Angeles on 3 January 1962, when he was ejected with 8:38 remaining in the fourth quarter. During that season, he also set the individual game scoring record by scoring exactly 100 points in a game in Hershey, Pennsylvania, on 2 March 1962, against the **New York Knickerbockers**, breaking his own record of 78 set earlier that season. In the 100-point game, he also set league records for most **field goals** made and attempted in a game and a half. His NBA career totals for 14 years are 1,045 games and a 30.1 points, 22.9 **rebounds**, and 4.4 assists per game average. He scored more than 50 points in one game 118 times and more than 60 points 32 times.

During his career, Chamberlain also was an outstanding rebounder and holds the career record with 23,924 rebounds, more than 2,000 better than second-best **Bill Russell**. Wilt led the league for 11 seasons in rebounds, even though he played at the same time as Bill Russell, considered to be one of the league's best rebounders in its history. On 24 November 1960, in a game against Russell and the Boston Celtics, Chamberlain had a league record 55 rebounds. Chamberlain's Achilles' heel was free throws, and during his career he tried several methods but could never shoot better than 61 percent for a season, although ironically in his 100-point game he was successful with 28 of 32 **free throw** attempts and set the record for most free throws in one game (since tied). One other statistic in which Wilt was extremely proud was the fact that although he played nearly every minute of every game, he was never disqualified on personal **fouls**.

Chamberlain was selected for every NBA **All-Star Game**, except for 1970, when he was injured early in the season, and was named the All-Star Game Most Valuable Player in 1960. In 1962, he scored an All-Star Game record 42 points. He was voted as the NBA's Rookie of the Year in 1960 and its Most Valuable Player in 1960, 1966, 1967, and 1968. He was selected to the All-NBA First Team seven times and All-NBA Second Team three times. Although he had exceptional offensive years, he played at the time that the **Boston Celtics** dominated the league and was never able to win a championship with the Warriors either in Philadelphia or San Francisco, where they moved in 1962.

On 15 January 1965, Chamberlain was traded by the San Francisco Warriors back to Philadelphia to the former Syracuse Nationals team that had become the **Philadelphia 76ers**. In 1966–1967, with the Philadelphia 76ers, he modified his game from being an overwhelming offensive threat to a playmaking center, averaged 7.8 assists per game, and led the 76ers to a record 68 victories in the regular season and the NBA title. He remained with the 76ers for one more season and then was traded on 9 July 1968, to the **Los Angeles Lakers** to join future Hall of Famers **Jerry West**, and **Elgin Baylor**. Chamberlain played with the Lakers for five seasons and played in the NBA Finals in four of those five seasons, although the Lakers only won the championship in 1972, with Chamberlain being named the NBA Finals Most Valuable Player. In that season, the Lakers won 33 consecutive games and finished the season with a record 69 regular-season victories, breaking the 76ers record that Wilt had helped to set five years prior.

After the 1972–1973 NBA season, he was offered a job by the San Diego Conquistadors of the **American Basketball Association (ABA)** as a player-**coach**. To entice him, the ABA adopted a rule in which a player could not be disqualified from a game for excessive personal fouls. Wilt accepted the offer, but the Lakers and NBA prevented him from playing in the ABA, citing the reserve clause in his Laker contract. Chamberlain contented himself with just coaching for that season but then retired following it.

After retiring, Chamberlain formed a professional volleyball league in California. Although he was nicknamed "Wilt the Stilt" by sportswriters, he disliked that name and preferred the nickname of Dip or Dippy, short for the nickname "The Big Dipper." He was enshrined in the **Naismith Memorial Basketball Hall of Fame** in 1979. In 1980, he was selected to the NBA 35th Anniversary Team, and in 1996 he was named one of the 50 Greatest Players in NBA History. He died on 12 October 1999, due to heart failure, at his home in Bel Air, California, which he named Ursa Major (the constellation that contains the seven stars known as The Big Dipper).

CHANCELLOR, VAN. B. 27 September 1943, Louisville, Mississippi. Van Chancellor attended Nanih Waiya School in Louisville, East Central Junior College, and Mississippi State University, graduating in 1965 with bachelor's degrees in mathematics and physical education. In 1973, he earned a master's degree in physical education from the University of Mississippi. He began **coaching** boys' high school **basketball** at Noxapater High School while still a senior at Mississippi State. After graduation he coached both boys' and girls' basketball at Horn Lake High School and Harrison Central High School in Mississippi. He was the head coach of the women's basketball team at the University of Mississippi from 1978–1997 and compiled a record of 439–154.

From 1997–2006, Chancellor coached the Houston Comets of the **Women's National Basketball Association**; led them to four consecutive league championships from 1997–2000; and was named Coach of the Year in 1997, 1998, and 1999. As coach of the U.S. women's national team, he led them to **gold medals** in both the 2002 **World Championships** and 2004 **Olympic Games**. He was enshrined in the **Women's Basketball Hall of Fame** in 2001 and **Naismith Memorial Basketball Hall of Fame** in 2007 as a coach. In 2007, he was hired as head coach of the women's team at **Louisiana State University** and led them to the **National Collegiate Athletic Association Final Four** in 2008, where they lost in the semifinal round.

CHANEY, JOHN. B. 21 January 1932, Jacksonville, Florida. John Chaney attended Benjamin Franklin High School in Philadelphia and Bethune-Cookman College. He played **basketball** in school and also in the Eastern Professional Basketball League. He began **coaching** at Sayre Junior High School in 1963, then coached at Simon Gratz High School in Philadelphia. He coached Cheyney State University from 1972–1982 and led them to the **National Collegiate Athletic Association** Division II national championship in 1978. He finished his coaching career at **Temple University** from 1982–2006, retiring in 2006 with a record of 516–253. He was known as a disciplinarian who held 6 a.m. practices and demanded excellence from his players. In 2001, he was enshrined in the **Naismith Memorial Basketball Hall of Fame** as a coach.

CHARLOTTE BOBCATS. The Charlotte Bobcats are a team in the **National Basketball Association (NBA)**. They joined the league as an expansion franchise in 2004, and were owned by Robert L. Johnson, founder of Black Entertainment Television. In 2006, **Michael Jordan** purchased part of the team and was named head of basketball operations. On 17 March 2010, Jordan purchased the team from Johnson for $275 million. Home games were played at Charlotte Coliseum from 2004–2005 and the new Charlotte Bobcats Arena since 2005 (renamed Time Warner Cable Arena in 2008). Their **coaches** have been Bernie Bickerstaff, Larry Brown, and Sam Vincent. Among their most notable players have been Raja Bell; Primoz Brezec; Boris Diaw; Jared Dudley; Raymond Felton; Stephen Jackson; Sean May; Adam Morrison; **Emeka Okafor**, their first **draft** choice in 2004 and NBA Rookie of the Year in 2005; Bernard Robinson; and Gerald Wallace. Their best season was in 2009–2010, when they reached the playoffs for the first time and won 44 games for their first winning season. Their record for their first six NBA seasons is 188–304.

CHARLOTTE HORNETS. *See* NEW ORLEANS HORNETS.

CHICAGO AMERICAN GEARS. The Chicago American Gears were a team in the **National Basketball League (NBL)** from 1944–1947, owned by Maurice A. White, owner of the American Gear and Manufacturing Company. Home games were played at the Chicago Coliseum. Jack Tierney was **coach**, and players included Elmer Gainer, Ray Krzoska, Bill McDonald, Vince McGowan, Johnny Orr, Stan Patrick, Swede Roos, and Dick Triptow. Triptow later published an excellent account of the Gears in his 1996 book *The Dynasty That Never Was*.

The best collegiate **basketball** player in 1946 was the six-foot, 10-inch **George Mikan** of **DePaul University**. White signed him to a $60,000, five-year contract in March 1946, but shortly after the NBL season began, Mikan sued the team for breach of contract, and the season was spent in legal battles, with Mikan only playing in 25 games. The Gears added future Hall of Famer **Bobby McDermott** midway through the season as player-coach and won the 1946 NBL Championship. In 1947, White decided to capitalize on the success of his team and created his own league, the **Professional Basketball League of America**. He took the Gears, with Mikan and McDermott, and established a league with 15 other teams throughout the midwestern and southern part of the **United States**.

The league's first game was 24 October 1946, but after less than one month of play, the Gears were bankrupt. The league had lost $600,000 and on 13 November 1946 discontinued operations. On 14 November 1946, the NBL owners met and offered to place a franchise in Chicago, but neither White nor any of his players would be allowed to be involved with the team. The Gears did not reenter the NBL, but their players were distributed to the other NBL teams.

CHICAGO BULLS. The Chicago Bulls are a team in the **National Basketball Association (NBA)**. On 27 January 1966, a group headed by Dick Klein purchased an expansion franchise in the NBA and began league play in the 1966–1967 season. Home games were played at the 9,000-seat International Amphitheatre in their first season, at 18,000-seat Chicago Stadium from 1967–1994, and at the 21,500-seat United Center since 1994. In their first 44 years, the Bulls have employed 20 **coaches**, including three who were named NBA Coach of the Year. The most notable ones were **Doug Collins**, **Phil Jackson**, **Johnny "Red" Kerr**, Dick Motta, and **Jerry Sloan**. Among their best players were B. J. Armstrong, Tom Boerwinkle, **Artis Gilmore**, Ben Gordon, Horace Grant, **Michael Jordan**, Bob Love, John Paxson, **Scottie Pippen**, Jerry Sloan, Reggie Theus, Norm Van Lier, and Chet Walker.

Their best seasons were 1990–1991, 1991–1992, and 1992–1993, when they won three consecutive NBA Championships, and 1995–1996, 1996–1997, and 1997–1998, when they also won three consecutive titles. In 1995–1996, they had a regular-season record of 72–10, the best in NBA history, and a playoff record of 15–3. The following season was almost as good, with a regular-season record of 69–13 and a playoff record of 15–4. Their overall record for their first 44 years in the league through the 2009–2010 season was 1,818–1,757.

CHICAGO PACKERS. *See* WASHINGTON WIZARDS.

CHICAGO STAGS. The Chicago Stags were a team in the **Basketball Association of America (BAA)** from 1946–1950. They were owned by James D. Norris and Arthur Wirtz, owners of the 21,000-seat Chicago Stadium, where home games were played. Their **coaches** were Phil Brownstein and Harold "Ole" Olsen. Among their most notable players were Chuck Gilmur, Chick Halbert, Stan Miasek, Ed Mikan, **Andy Phillip**, Kenny Rollins, Jim Seminoff, Odie Spears, Gene Vance, and **Max Zaslofsky**. Their best season was their first, in 1946–1947, when they finished first in the Western Division but lost in the BAA Championship finals to the Philadelphia Warriors in five games. In 1950, they were purchased by **Abe Saperstein** and renamed the Chicago Bruins but were disbanded prior to the 1950–1951 season. In their four seasons in the league, their record was 145–92.

CHICAGO STUDEBAKER FLYERS. The Chicago Studebaker Flyers were a team in the **National Basketball League (NBL)** in the 1942–1943 season. Although they only played one season, they earned a place in **basketball** history as the first racially integrated team in professional basketball. (The Toledo Jim White Chevrolet NBL team was also integrated that season but disbanded after just four games.) The United Auto Workers union acquired the Chicago franchise in the NBL and sponsored a team consisting of basketball players who were working at the Studebaker factory converted for war production.

Included on that team were nine former members of the **Harlem Globetrotters** and four white players. Ex-Trotters Sonny Boswell, Hilary Brown, Duke Cumberland, Roosie Hudson, Al Johnson, Tony Peyton, Babe Pressley, Bernie Price, and Ted Strong were joined by white players Dick Evans, Mike Novak, Johnny Orr, and Paul Sokody. Their **coach** was Johnny Jordan. Surprisingly, with this much talent the team should have done better than an 8–15 won–lost record, but reportedly there was dissension among the players, which contributed to the team's poor showing. It has been said that the dissension was racial, but it was also reported that the problems were just conflicts over style of play.

CHICAGO ZEPHYRS. *See* WASHINGTON WIZARDS.

CHILE. Chile joined the **Fédération Internationale de Basketball (FIBA)** in 1935 and is in the FIBA Americas zone. The men's team competed in the first four **Olympic basketball** tournaments from 1936–1956. Their best showing was in 1948 and 1952, when they finished in fifth place each time. They entered the first three **World Championships** and finished third in both 1950 and 1959. Santiago, Chile, was the site for the 1959 tournament. They competed in only the first Pan American Games in 1951 and finished fifth. They have never competed in the FIBA Americas tournament. In the South American Championships, they were **gold medalists** in 1937, **silver medalists** twice, and **bronze medalists** four times.

In 1953, the inaugural women's World Championships was held in Santiago, and the home team finished in second place, the only time they have medaled in three tournaments. The women's team has competed in five FIBA Americas tournaments but have been unable to finish higher than fifth. In Pan American Games competition, the Chilean women's team was second in 1955 and third in 1959 and 1963, their only appearances in that tournament. In the South American Championships, the Chilean women have done quite well, with four gold medals, five silver medals, and five bronze medals.

There has yet to be a Chilean in either the **National Basketball Association** or **Women's National Basketball Association**. Among the better players for the Chilean Olympic teams of the 1950s were Rufino Bernedo Zorzano, Rolando Etchepare, Victor Mahaña Badrie, Juan Ostoic, Hernán Raffo Abarca, and Orlando Silva Infante.

CHINA. China joined the **Fédération Internationale de Basketball (FIBA)** in 1936 and was a member in the FIBA Asia zone until 1958. The government of the Republic of China was overthrown in 1949, and the People's Republic of China was established on the mainland, as the Republic of China (ROC) relocated to the island of

Taiwan. Although both entities were recognized by the International Olympic Committee (IOC) in 1954 and both were invited to the 1956 **Olympic Games**, the People's Republic withdrew after the Taiwan government accepted. The ROC competed in the men's **basketball** competition as "Formosa," the only time that they have participated in Olympic basketball. Although they won five of eight matches, they placed 11th of the 16 teams competing. In 1958, the People's Republic withdrew from the IOC and FIBA.

Taiwan has not competed in any other Olympic basketball tournaments but did enter the 1954 and 1959 men's **World Championships**, where they finished in fifth place in 1954 and fourth in 1959. They've competed in 16 men's Asia Championships and won the silver medal in 1960 and 1963 and bronze medal twice. The women's team, competing as "Chinese Taipei," entered four World Championship tournaments, with a best finish of 12th. They also entered the Asia Championships 17 times and won the silver medal in 1972 and the bronze medal eight times. American Joe Alexander, born in Taiwan and raised in Hong Kong and the People's Republic of China, played in the National Basketball Association (NBA) from 2008–2010.

In 1974, the People's Republic rejoined the FIBA and have competed since just as "China." The men's team from China competed in nine Olympic tournaments (1936 and 1948 as the ROC and 1984–2008 as the People's Republic of China) and are the only country other than the **United States** to appear in every Olympic basketball competition since 1984. Their best finish was in 2008, when as host nation they reached the quarterfinal round, lost to the United States, and were placed in a tie for fifth place even though they only won two of six games. In the 1948 Olympic Games tournament, the Republic of China won five of eight games, but the structure of the tournament was such that they only finished in 18th place despite that record.

In the FIBA World Championships, the People's Republic of China competed eight times, with a best finish of eighth in 1994. In the FIBA Asia Championships, they entered every event since 1975 and have won 14 **gold medals** and two **bronze medals** in their 17 appearances. The women's team competed in six Olympic Games and won the bronze medal in 1984 and the **silver medal** in 1992. In the FIBA World Championships, they competed seven times and finished second in 1994 and third in 1983. In the FIBA Asia Championships, they have entered every one of the 17 tournaments since 1976 and have won the gold medal nine times, silver medal six times, and bronze medal once. In 1999, they finished fourth.

There have been five players from China in the NBA: **Wang Zhi Zhi**, Batere Mengke, **Yao Ming**, Yi Jianlian, and Sun Yue. In addition, American Tom Meschery was born in Harbin, Manchuria, China, to missionary parents. The **Women's National Basketball Association** has had three Chinese players: **Zheng Haixia**, Miao Lijie, and Sui Feifei.

CINCINNATI, UNIVERSITY OF. The University of Cincinnati in Ohio began its men's **basketball** program in 1900. Home games since 1989 have been played at 13,176-seat Fifth Third Arena at Shoemaker Center. Prior to 1989, home games were played at several locations, including Riverfront Coliseum, Cincinnati Gardens, Armory Fieldhouse, and Schmidlapp Gym. In 1959 and 1960, they lost in the **National Collegiate Athletic Association (NCAA)** semifinal round, but in 1961 and 1962, the Bearcats defeated **Ohio State University** in the NCAA Championship final. In 1963, they lost in **overtime** to **Loyola University Chicago**, 60–58, in the NCAA final. They are one of only three schools to reach the **Final Four** in five consecutive years, one of only five schools to play in three consecutive NCAA finals, and one of only seven schools to win two consecutive championships.

The most accomplished **coaches** in the school's history have been Tay Baker, Gale Catlett, Bob Huggins, Ed Jucker, George Smith, and John Wiethe. The best players in Cincinnati's history were Hall of Famers **Oscar Robertson** and **Jack Twyman**. Other notable players include Jim Ard, Ron Bonham, Pat Cummings, Derrek Dickey, Connie Dierking, Danny Fortson, Paul Hogue, Rick Roberson, Nick Van Exel, and George Wilson.

CINCINNATI ROYALS. *See* SACRAMENTO KINGS.

CITY COLLEGE OF NEW YORK (CCNY). City College of New York (CCNY) is located in New York City. It was established in 1847, as the first free public institution of higher learning in the

United States and began its men's **basketball** program in 1905. Many of their home games during the 1940s were played at **Madison Square Garden**. The most accomplished **coach** in the school's history was **Nat Holman** (422–188). In 1950, the Beavers won the **National Invitation Tournament (NIT)** championship by defeating **Bradley University**. Two weeks later they again defeated Bradley for the **National Collegiate Athletic Association (NCAA)** Championship. They are the only school to win both major tournaments in the same year, a feat that will probably not be duplicated, as the tournaments are now run concurrently. They also finished third in the 1941 NIT. Among the best players in school history were Herb Cohen, Irwin Dambrot, Phil Farbman, Joe Galiber, Sidney "Sonny" Hertzberg, **William "Red" Holzman**, Hal Korovin, Floyd Lane, Norm Mager, Lionel Malamed, Ed Roman, Al Roth, and Ed Warner.

In 1951, a major scandal occurred in college sports, with more than 30 players from several colleges being accused of accepting bribes from gamblers for deliberately losing games or winning by fewer points than the gambling point spread. CCNY was one of the schools hit hardest by the scandal. Cohen, Dambrot, Lane, Mager, Roman, Roth, and Warner were all implicated and convicted, with penalties ranging from six months in prison to suspended sentences. Coach Nat Holman was suspended from his position pending an investigation but was eventually cleared and reinstated. Following the scandal, CCNY was banned from playing at Madison Square Garden and deemphasized its basketball program.

CLEVELAND CAVALIERS. The Cleveland Cavaliers are a team in the **National Basketball Association (NBA)**. On 6 February 1970, a group headed by Nick Mileti purchased an expansion franchise in the NBA and began league play in the 1970–1971 season. Home games were played at the 9,900-seat Cleveland Arena from 1970–1974, the 20,273-seat Coliseum at Richfield from 1974–1994, and the 20,562-seat Gund Arena (now known as Quicken Loans Arena) since then. Both the Cleveland Arena and the Gund Arena are in Cleveland, Ohio. The Coliseum was located in Richfield, Ohio, about 20 miles south of Cleveland.

They have employed 17 **coaches**, the most notable being Mike Brown, Bill Fitch, Mike Fratello, and **Lenny Wilkens**. Among their most notable players have been **Austin Carr**, Brad Daugherty, Craig Ehlo, Danny Ferry, Žydrūnas Ilgauskas, **LeBron James,** Larry Nance, Mark Price, Bobby "Bingo" Smith, and John "Hot Rod" Williams.

Their best seasons were 2006–2007, when they finished with a regular-season record of 50–32 but were defeated in the NBA Championship Finals by the **San Antonio Spurs**, and 2008–2009, when they won a team-record 66 games in the regular season but lost in the Eastern Conference Finals to the **Orlando Magic**. Their overall record for their first 40 years in the league through the 2009–2010 season is 1,521–1,727.

CLEVELAND REBELS. Al Sutphin, president of the Cleveland Arena, was awarded one of the **Basketball Association of America**'s charter franchises on 6 June 1946. Former **Original Celtic** player **Henry "Dutch" Dehnert** began as their **coach** but was replaced midway through the season by Roy Clifford. The team won half of their 60 games and finished third in the Western Division but lost to the **New York Knickerbockers** in the first round of the playoffs. Among the star players for Cleveland were Frank Baumholtz, Leo Mogus, and Mel Riebe. On 11 December 1946, the Rebels took part in an experimental game played with 15-**minute** quarters (instead of the customary 12-minute ones) but lost to the **Chicago Stags**, 88–70. On 10 June 1947, Sutphin withdrew his franchise.

CLIFTON, NATHANIEL "SWEETWATER" "NAT." B. Clifton Nathaniel 13 October 1922, England, Arkansas. D. 31 August 1990, Chicago, Illinois. Nat Clifton attended Dusable High School in Chicago, Illinois, and Xavier University in New Orleans, Louisiana. After college he served in the U.S. Army for three years. He played **basketball** for the **New York Rens**, **Harlem Globetrotters**, and Dayton Metropolitans. He played baseball in the Negro Leagues in 1949 and in organized baseball's minor leagues in 1949 and 1950. He was acquired by the **New York Knickerbockers** from the Globetrotters in September 1950.

The six-foot, seven-inch Clifton had huge hands and was one of the first **National Basketball Association (NBA)** players to hold the ball in one hand as he played the **center** or **forward** position. One of the first four black players in the NBA, he was actually the third to play in a game when he made his debut on 4 November 1950 and scored 16 points. He played in the NBA from 1950–1957 for the Knicks and played on the losing side in three NBA Finals. He also played in the 1957 NBA **All-Star Game**. In 1957, he was traded to the **Detroit Pistons** and played his last NBA season with them. His NBA career totals for eight years are 544 regular-season games and a 10.0 points per game average.

Clifton spent the summer of 1958 with former Trotter **Reece "Goose" Tatum**'s baseball team, the Detroit Clowns. In 1961, his former Globetrotter employer, **Abe Saperstein**, rehired Clifton for his Chicago Majors team in the new **American Basketball League**. Sweetwater played in 61 games that year and averaged 8.5 points per game. After retiring from active play, he owned and drove a taxicab in Chicago.

COACH. In **basketball**, the coach is the team's leader. He will decide which players start the game, which substitutes to employ, and what **offense** and **defense** should be used. In scholastic basketball, he is also a teacher. In the early days of basketball, one of the team's players would often also double as a coach and was designated a "player-coach," but in recent years player-coaches have been rare. Modern basketball also often employs several assistant coaches as well, with the primary coach designated as "head coach."

Some of the most accomplished high school coaches have been Ernest Blood, who from 1915–1924 led Passaic High School (New Jersey) to a record of 200 wins and only one loss, including 159 consecutive victories; Edna Tarbutton, whose Baskin High School (Louisiana) girls' teams won 315 and lost only two games from 1945–1955, including a record 218 consecutive wins; and **Morgan Wootten**, coach of DeMatha Catholic High School (Maryland) from 1956–2002 whose record was 1,274–192. Legendary college coaches include **John Wooden, Adolph Rupp, Forrest "Phog" Allen, Bobby Knight**, and **Mike Krzyzewski**. In 1996, the **National Basketball Association (NBA)** selected its Top 10 Coaches in NBA History. They include **Red Auerbach, Chuck Daly**, Bill Fitch, **Red Holzman, Phil Jackson**, John Kundla, **Don Nelson, Jack Ramsay, Pat Riley**, and **Lenny Wilkens**. *See also*

ATTLES, ALVIN A., JR. "AL"; BEE, CLAIR FRANCIS; BROWN, HUBERT JUDE "HUBIE"; BROWN, LAWRENCE HARVEY "LARRY"; CARNESECCA, LUIGI P. "LOU"; CHANCELLOR, VAN; CHANEY, JOHN; CRUM, DENZIL EDWIN "DENNY"; ECKMAN, CHARLES MARKWOOD, JR. "CHARLEY"; FERRÁNDIZ GONZÁLEZ, PEDRO; GAINES, CLARENCE EDWARD "BIG HOUSE"; HANNUM, ALEXANDER MURRAY "ALEX"; HEAD SUMMITT, PATRICIA SUE "PAT"; HOLMAN, NATHAN "NAT"; IBA, HENRY PAYNE "HANK"; LAPCHICK, JOSEPH BOHOMIEL "JOE"; MCGUIRE, ALFRED JAMES "AL"; MEYER, RAYMOND JOSEPH "RAY"; POPOVICH, GREGG CHARLES; RIPLEY, ELMER HORTON; SHARMAN, WILLIAM WALTON "BILL"; SLOAN, GERALD EUGENE "JERRY"; SMITH, DEAN EDWARDS; THOMPSON, JOHN R., JR.; VALVANO, JAMES THOMAS ANTHONY "JIM," "JIMMY V."

COLLEGE OF THE HOLY CROSS. *See* HOLY CROSS, COLLEGE OF THE.

COLLINS, PAUL DOUGLAS "DOUG." B. 28 July 1951, Christopher, Illinois. Doug Collins attended Benton High School in Benton, Illinois, and Illinois State University. He was a member of the 1972 **U.S. Olympic basketball** team that was defeated in the controversial final game with the Union of Soviet Socialist Republics. **U.S.** players felt they were cheated and refused to accept the second place **silver medals.** In that game, Collins was fouled with three seconds remaining and the United States losing by one point. He made two **free throws** to give the American team the lead. The final three seconds were played three times, until the Soviets won on a last second shot after a court-length pass.

Collins was drafted by the **Philadelphia 76ers** in the 1973 **National Basketball Association (NBA) draft** as the first overall selection and played eight years with them. In 1977, the 76ers reached the NBA Championship Finals. He concluded his NBA career with a points per game average of 17.9 in 415 regular-season games, with foot injuries limiting his play in several seasons. The six-foot, six-inch **guard-forward** was selected for four NBA **All-Star Games** from 1977–1980. After retiring from basketball, he was assistant coach at the University of Pennsylvania in 1981–1982 and Arizona State University from 1982–1984, and head coach in the NBA with the **Chicago Bulls** from 1986–1989, the **Detroit Pistons** from 1995–1998, and the **Washington Wizards** from 2001–2003. When not coaching he worked as a television analyst. On 21 May 2010, he was hired as the head coach of the Philadelphia 76ers.

COMMONWEALTH OF INDEPENDENT STATES (CIS). In December 1991, after the breakup of the former **Union of Soviet Socialist Republics**, 11 of the former Soviet republics, including **Russia**, Belarus, Ukraine, Armenia, Azerbaijan, Kazakhstan, Kyrgyzstan, Moldova, Tajikistan, Turkmenistan, and Uzbekistan, affiliated to form the Commonwealth of Independent States (CIS). The three Baltic republics, Estonia, **Lithuania**, and Latvia, did not. Since the newly established states did not have adequate time to prepare for the 1992 Barcelona **Olympic Games**, the International Olympic Committee permitted the CIS to enter as a team.

The CIS, sometimes referred to as the "Unified Team," did well. The 1992 Olympic **basketball** team consisted of seven Russians, an Azerbaijani, a Kazak, a Ukrainian, and two Latvians. The Latvians, Igors Miglinieks and Gundars Vētra, chose to play for the Unified Team because they realized that the Latvian team would not be strong enough to qualify for the Olympic Games, and they wanted the opportunity to compete in Barcelona. Both players faced strong criticism from the Baltic natives for what was considered an unpatriotic selfish action. The Unified Team advanced to the semifinal round but lost to **Croatia** by one point. In the match for third place, the CIS team faced the Lithuanian team, which had several of their former teammates on it. In a closely contested game, the Lithuanians prevailed, 82–78. The women's Olympic tournament did not have quite the same drama, as there were no former Soviet republics entered, and the women's Unified Team defeated **China** for the **gold medal**.

CONNECTICUT, UNIVERSITY OF (UCONN). The University of Connecticut (UConn) in Storrs began its men's **basketball** program in 1901. Home games since 1990 have been played at the 10,167-seat Harry A. Gampel Pavilion. Prior to 1990, home games were played at the Hugh S. Greer Field House. Hall of Famer Jim Calhoun (575–221 from 1986–2010) has been their most notable **coach**. He led them to their two **National Collegiate Athletic Association (NCAA)** titles in 1999 and 2004. The best players in the Huskies' history include **Ray Allen**, Wes Bialosuknia, Ben Gordon, Richard Hamilton, Toby Kimball, Donyell Marshall, **Emeka Okafor**, Art Quimby, Cliff Robinson, and Chris Smith.

The women's basketball program began in 1974. Geno Auriemma (735–122 from 1985–2010) has been their most accomplished coach. The UConn women's basketball program has been one of the most successful NCAA Division I programs, as they have been national champions seven times from 1995–2010. They reached the NCAA **Final Four** four other times between 1991–2008. They were undefeated in 39 games in each of 2008–2009 and 2009–2010 and hold the NCAA record of 78 consecutive victories. The best players in school history include Svetlana Abrosimova, Sue Bird, Swin Cash, Rebecca Lobo, Jennifer Rizzotti, Nykesha Sales, Kelly Schumacher, Ann Strother, and Kara Wolters.

CONNORS, KEVIN JOSEPH ALOYSIUS "CHUCK." B. 10 April 1921, Brooklyn, New York. D. 10 November 1992, Los Angeles, California. Chuck Connors attended Erasmus High School in Brooklyn; Adelphi Academy in Garden City, New York; and Seton Hall University. After two years in college he served in the U.S. Army. While in the service, he played **basketball** in the **American Basketball League** with Brooklyn in 1943–1944, with Wilmington in the 1944–1945 season, and with Paterson in 1945–1946. After being discharged, the six-foot, six-inch, **left-handed forward** played in the **National Basketball League (NBL)** with the Rochester Royals in the 1945–1946 season. In 1946, he signed with the **Boston Celtics** of the new **Basketball Association of America (BAA)** and, in their very first game on 5 November 1946 in Boston Arena, broke the **backboard** while warming up, causing the game to be delayed. After playing just four games for Boston the following year he was released. In three years in the NBL and BAA, he played in 67 games and averaged 4.0 points per game.

Connors played minor league baseball in 1949 and 1950, and in 1951 he played with the Chicago Cubs in the major leagues. While playing baseball and basketball, he was the team's clown and would take the slightest opportunities to entertain his teammates by reciting "Casey at the Bat," "The Face on the Barroom Floor," or soliloquies from Shakespeare. In 1952, he played minor league baseball for the Los Angeles Angels. There he was able to realize his dream of being a professional actor and began a successful Hollywood career with a speaking role in the sports film *Pat and Mike*, starring Spencer Tracy and Katherine Hepburn. He appeared in more than 20 motion pictures, with the highlight of his acting career coming from 1958–1963, when he starred in the television series *The Rifleman*. He continued to pursue his acting career until his death from lung cancer. An interesting sidelight to his career is that an individual was named for him who became a **National Basketball Association (NBA)** player. Chuck Connors Person played in the NBA from 1986–2000 and was appropriately nicknamed "The Rifleman."

CONTINENTAL BASKETBALL ASSOCIATION (CBA). The Continental Basketball Association (CBA) was a men's professional **basketball** minor league that began operation as the Eastern Pennsylvania Basketball League on 23 April 1946 (six weeks before the **Basketball Association of America** began). The league was renamed the Eastern Professional Basketball League in 1947, the Eastern Basketball Association in 1970, and the Continental Basketball Association in 1978. Prior to 1978, the league was usually referred to just as the Eastern Basketball League (EBL).

Teams in 1946 were the Wilkes-Barre Barons, Hazleton Mountaineers, Lancaster Red Roses, Reading Keys, Allentown Rockets, and the Binghamton Triplets. The league was integrated from the start, as Hazleton had former **New York Rens** players Bill Brown, Zack Clayton, and **John Isaacs** on their team. From 1947–1970, the league usually had from eight to 10 teams, mostly in Pennsylvania, and played approximately 30 games annually, usually on weekends. During the late 1940s and early 1950s, some teams served as farm clubs for **National Basketball Association (NBA)** teams, but in 1953 the EBL began accepting players that were involved in the college scandals, and the NBA distanced itself from the league. Among the players involved in the scandals who played in the EBL were Floyd Layne, **Jack Molinas**, Ed Roman, **Bill Spivey**, Ed Warner, and Sherman White. During that time, the NBA also had an unwritten quota system for black players, and many players who in future generations would have played in the NBA found work in the EBL. Such players as Wally Choice, Dick Gaines, **Sonny Hill**, Julius Mc-Coy, Jay Norman, and Roman Turman were talented enough to play in the NBA.

From 1970–1976, the league suffered due to the competition for players by the **American Basketball Association (ABA)** and NBA, and in 1974–1975 only four teams remained in the EBL. After the ABA was dissolved, the EBL experienced a resurgence and in 1977 expanded to include a team in Alaska. As the CBA during the 1980s and early 1990s, the league enjoyed its greatest success and progressed from an eight-team league in 1978, with teams primarily in the eastern part of the **United States**, to a 16-team league in 1989, with teams in Alaska, Hawaii, Puerto Rico, and Mexico at times. It was known for its innovations and in 1981 introduced the seven-point scoring system. Teams received one point for winning each quarter and three points for winning a game. This concept was proposed by league commissioner Jim Drucker to add interest in games where one team had a huge lead early on. During the mid-1980s, a sudden-death **overtime** rule was used, where the first team to score three points in overtime won the game.

On 3 August 1999, former NBA player **Isiah Thomas** purchased the entire league. In March 2000, the NBA attempted to purchase the league from Thomas, who refused to sell. In June 2000, he was offered a head **coaching** job in the NBA, but if he accepted the position he would have had to divest his interest in the CBA. He attempted to sell it to the NBA Players' Association but was unsuccessful. The NBA announced that it was forming its own developmental league and would no longer use the CBA to develop players. In October 2000, Thomas, unable to sell the league, placed it into a blind trust and became coach of the **Indiana Pacers**. On 8 February 2001, the league discontinued operations, unable to pay its players, and a few weeks later declared bankruptcy. Several of the original team owners repurchased their franchises and joined the International Basketball League (IBL) for the rest of that season. Later in 2001, the IBL discontinued operations, and the CBA resurfaced as an eight-team league. It continued to operate but abbreviated its 2008–2009 season due to economic problems and held a three-game championship playoff from 5–8 February as its final games. In November 2009, the league was sold. The new owners have announced plans to resume activity in the 2011–2012 season.

COOPER, CHARLES HENRY "CHUCK." B. 29 September 1926, Pittsburgh, Pennsylvania. D. 5 February 1984, Pittsburgh, Pennsylvania. Chuck Cooper attended Westinghouse High School in Pittsburgh, Pennsylvania, and **Duquesne University**. Selected by the **Boston Celtics** in the 1950 **National Basketball Association (NBA) draft**, he was the first black player to be drafted by the league. He was not the only one, however, as **Earl Lloyd** was also selected in a later round by the Washington Capitols. Cooper was actually the second black to appear in an NBA game, when he debuted for the Celtics on 1 November 1950, as Lloyd had played the day before. In Cooper's first game, he scored seven points as the Celtics lost to the Fort Wayne Pistons.

The six-foot, five-inch **forward** played in the NBA from 1950–1956 for the Celtics, Milwaukee (later St. Louis) Hawks, and Fort Wayne Pistons. His best year was his rookie year in 1950–1951, when he averaged 9.3 points and 8.5 **rebounds** per game. His NBA career totals for six years are 409 games and a 6.7 points and 5.9 rebounds per game average. After retiring from basketball, Connors was urban affairs officer at the Pittsburgh National Bank. *See also* CLIFTON, NATHANIEL "SWEETWATER" "NAT."

COOPER, CHARLES THEODORE "TARZAN." B. 30 August 1907, Newark, Delaware. D. 19 December 1980, Philadelphia, Pennsylvania. Tarzan Cooper should not be confused with **Charles Henry "Chuck" Cooper**, the first black player to be drafted by the **National Basketball Association (NBA)**. Tarzan Cooper attended Central High School in Philadelphia, Pennsylvania, and began playing professional **basketball** with the Philadelphia Panthers in 1925. He then played with the Philadelphia Giants and was hired by the **New York Renaissance** in 1929.

At six-foot, four-inches, weighing between 215–235 pounds, Cooper became one of the best **centers** of his era and was named by New York Celtics rival center **Joe Lapchick** as the greatest center.

He played with the Rens for the next 12 years and was a member of the team when they won 88 straight games in 1932–1933 and the World's Professional Championship in 1939. From 1940–1946, he played for the Washington Bears and helped lead them to the World's Professional Championship in 1943. He was enshrined in the **Naismith Memorial Basketball Hall of Fame** in 1977.

COOPER (-DYKE), CYNTHIA LYNNE. B.14 April 1963, Chicago, Illinois. Cynthia Cooper was raised in Southern California and attended Alan Leroy Locke High School in Los Angeles, California, and the **University of Southern California (USC)**. She led her high school team to the 1981 state 4A championship and led USC to the **National Collegiate Athletic Association (NCAA)** Championship in her freshman and sophomore years in 1983 and 1984. As a college senior in 1986, she played on the losing side in the NCAA Championship game. She was selected for the U.S. national team in 1986 and played in seven major international tournaments, winning six **gold medals** at the 1986 and 1990 Goodwill Games, the 1986 and 1990 **World Championships**, the 1987 Pan American Games, and 1988 and 1992 **Olympic Games**. In 1992, the U.S. team won the **bronze medal** and gold medals in the other six tournaments. The five-foot, 10-inch guard played professionally in **Italy** and **Brazil** from 1987–1998.

Cooper played in the **Women's National Basketball Association (WNBA)** from 1997–2000 for the Houston Comets, was a member of the WNBA Championship team in each of those years, and was the Finals Most Valuable Player all four years. She was the WNBA Most Valuable Player for both the 1997 and 1998 seasons. She also **coached** the Phoenix Mercury in the WNBA in 2001 and 2002. She attempted a brief playing comeback in 2003 with Houston but only played four games before retiring. In her WNBA career, she played in 124 regular-season games and averaged 21.0 points per game. After retiring from active play, she worked as a television analyst for **Houston Rockets** NBA games. From 2005–2010, she was head coach of Prairie View A&M University. On 10 May 2010, she accepted the head coaching position at the University of North Carolina-Wilmington. She was enshrined in the **Women's Basket-**

ball Hall of Fame in 2009 and in the Naismith Memorial Basketball Hall of Fame in 2010.

ĆOSIĆ KREŠIMIR. B. 26 November 1948, Zagreb, **Croatia, Yugoslavia. D.** 25 May 1995, Baltimore, Maryland. Krešimir Ćosić attended high school in Croatia, Yugoslavia, and **Brigham Young University (BYU)** in the United States. In his junior and senior years, he was one of the first international players to be selected for an **All-American** college team. The six-foot, 10-inch **center** was one of the first non-Americans to be drafted by the **National Basketball Association (NBA)**. In 1972, he was selected by the **Portland Trail Blazers**. He remained in school and was **drafted** in 1973 by the **Los Angeles Lakers** and by the **Carolina Cougars** in the **American Basketball Association (ABA)** draft.

Ćosić did not play professional **basketball** in the United States but returned to Croatia to play for KK Zadar and retain his eligibility for **Fédération Internationale de Basketball (FIBA)** play. During his career, he played for one of the most powerful international teams in history. He played in four **Olympic Games** for Yugoslavia from 1968–1980 and helped them win the **gold medal** in 1980, win the **silver medal** in 1968 and 1976, and finish fifth in 1972. In four Olympic tournaments, he played in 31 games and averaged 11.0 points per game. In four **World Championships** from 1967–1978, Yugoslavia won two gold medals, won two silver medals, and finished ahead of the U.S. team in all four of those tournaments. He played in a record nine biennial European Championships from 1967–1983, and Yugoslavia medaled in each of the seven tournaments from 1969–1981, winning three gold, three silver, and one **bronze medal**. In the Yugoslavian basketball league, he played for Zadar from 1964–1969 and 1973–1976, for Olimpija Ljubljana from 1977–1978, and for Cibona from 1981–1983. He also played two seasons for Bologna in the Italian League in 1979–1980.

While attending BYU, Ćosić converted to the Mormon faith and became influential in introducing the Church of Latter Day Saints to his native country upon his return home. After retiring from active play, he became a **coach** and led Yugoslavia to the bronze medal at the 1986 World Championships and 1987 European Championships.

He also coached teams in Bologna, **Italy**, and Athens, **Greece**. After Croatia became independent, Ćosić was named deputy ambassador to the United States and worked in the Croatian Embassy in Washington, D.C. He was the third international player to be included when he was enshrined in the **Naismith Memorial Basketball Hall of Fame** in 1996. In 2007, he was one of the inaugural class inducted in the FIBA Hall of Fame and in 2008 was named as one of the Euroleague's 50 Greatest Contributors.

COUSY, ROBERT JOSEPH "BOB." B. 9 August 1928, New York, New York. Bob Cousy attended Andrew Jackson High School in Cambria Heights, New York, and **Holy Cross College**. In 1947, as a college freshman, he was a member of the **National Collegiate Athletic Association (NCAA)** national champions, and in 1948 his team finished in third place in that tournament. The six-foot, one-inch **guard** was an excellent ball handler but was flashy and earned himself the nickname "Houdini of the Hardwood." He used behind-the-back **dribbling** and passing in an era when that type of showmanship was frowned upon.

Selected by the Tri-Cities Blackhawks in the first round of the 1950 **National Basketball Association (NBA) draft**, Cousy was traded to the **Chicago Stags**. The Stags franchise dissolved before the start of the 1950 season, and a dispersal draft of their players was held. The rights to Cousy went to the **Boston Celtics**, although he was not their first choice. He played for the Celtics from 1950–1963. In 1969, he was named head **coach** of the Cincinnati Royals and during that season attempted a brief comeback at the age of 41, playing in seven games.

For 10 seasons, from 1951–1952 through 1960–1961, Cousy averaged between 18.0–21.7 points and between 6.7–9.5 **assists** per game each year. His NBA career totals for 14 years are 924 regular-season games and an 18.4 points and 7.5 assists per game average. He also appeared in 109 playoff games and averaged 18.5 points and 8.6 assists per game. In a postseason playoff game on 21 March 1953 that lasted four **overtime** periods, he scored 50 points and had a record 30 free throws. One of the league's best passers, he led the NBA in assists eight times. He was selected for the NBA **All-Star Game** in every one of his first 13 seasons and was named the All-Star Game

Most Valuable Player in 1954 and 1957. He was named to the All-NBA First Team 10 times, was selected for the All-NBA Second Team twice, and was the league's Most Valuable Player in 1957. With the Celtics, he was a member of the NBA Championship team six times from 1957–1963. In 1954, he became the first president of the newly formed NBA Players Association.

After retiring from active play, Cousy coached Boston College from 1963–1967, coached the NBA Cincinnati Royals from 1969–1974 (the last two seasons the franchise was relocated to Kansas City/Omaha), was commissioner of the American Soccer League from 1975–1980, and was a television broadcaster with the Celtics. He was enshrined in the **Naismith Memorial Basketball Hall of Fame** in 1971. In 1996, he was named one of the 50 Greatest Players in NBA History and was one of only four players named to the 25th and 35th anniversary teams.

COWENS, DAVID WILLIAM "DAVE." B. 25 October 1948, Newport, Kentucky. Dave Cowens attended Newport Central Catholic High School and Florida State University and was selected by the **Boston Celtics** in the 1970 **National Basketball Association (NBA) draft**. Although considered by some to be too short, at six-feet, nine-inches, to play **center**, he played in the NBA from 1970–1980 for the Celtics, retired, and then made a comeback in 1982–1983 with the **Milwaukee Bucks**.

The **left-handed** red head's best year was 1972–1973, when he had career-high averages in points, with 20.5, and **rebounds**, with 16.2, and was named the league's Most Valuable Player as well as Most Valuable Player in the NBA **All-Star Game**. In 1971, he was Co-Rookie of the Year with Geoff Petrie. Cowens's NBA career totals for 11 years are 766 regular-season games and a 17.6 points and 13.6 rebounds per game average. He was selected for seven NBA All-Star Games and was named to the All-NBA Second Team three times, the NBA All-Defensive First Team in 1976, and NBA All-Defensive Second Team twice. He was a member of the 1974 and 1976 NBA champion team.

Cowens was named player-**coach** of the Celtics for the 1978–1979 season but after a record of 27–41 returned to just being a player the following year. He later coached the Bay State team in the

Continental Basketball Association in 1984–1985, the NBA's Charlotte Hornets from 1996–1998, the **Golden State Warriors** from 2000–2002, and the Chicago Sky of the **Women's National Basketball Association** in 2005–2006. He was an assistant coach with the **San Antonio Spurs** from 1994–1996 and Golden State from 31 January 2000–20 April 2000, when he was named head coach. In 2006, he was hired by the Detroit Pistons organization. He was enshrined in the **Naismith Memorial Basketball Hall of Fame** in 1991. In 1996, Cowens was named one of the 50 Greatest Players in NBA History.

CROATIA. Croatia is a former part of **Yugoslavia** that became independent in 1991. In 1992, they joined the **Fédération Internationale de Basketball (FIBA)** and are a member in the FIBA Europe zone. In 1994, the men's team finished third in the **World Championships**. They have competed in eight European Championships, with two third place finishes being their best efforts. In 1992, they competed in the **Olympic Games** for the first time. With a one-point victory over the **Commonwealth of Independent States** team in the semifinals, they reached the finals, where they were defeated by the U.S. **Dream Team** and won the **silver medal**. In 1996, they placed seventh and in 2008 finished in a tie for fifth place. The Croatian women's team has competed three times in the European Championships, with a best finish of eighth. They have not yet qualified for either the World Championships or the Olympic Games.

There have been eleven Croatians who have played in the **National Basketball Association (NBA)**, including Gordan Giriček, Mario Kasun, **Toni Kukoč**, Kosta Perović, **Dražen Petrović**, Dino Rađa, Predrag Savovic, Bruno Šundov, Žan Tabak, Roko-Leni Ukić, and Stojko Vranković. When the area was still a part of Yugoslavia, there were several Croatians who played for the Yugoslavian Olympic teams. Among them were Franjo Arapović; **Krešimir Ćosić**; Zdravko Radulović ; Petar Skansi, who later **coached** the 1992 and 1996 Olympic teams; Rato Tvrdić; and the aforementioned Kukoč, Rađa, and Vranković. Croatian members of the silver medal-winning 1988 Yugoslavian women's Olympic team were Žana Lelas and Danira Nakić.

CRUM, DENZIL EDWIN "DENNY." B. 2 March 1937, San Fernando, California. Denny Crum attended San Fernando High School, Pierce Junior College, and the **University of California, Los Angeles (UCLA)**. He achieved a modicum of success as a scholastic **basketball** player, winning the Southern California Junior College Player of the Year award in 1956–1957. After his graduation, he was assistant basketball **coach** at UCLA under Coach **John Wooden**, spent four years as head coach at Pierce Junior College, and returned to UCLA as assistant coach in 1968 during the team's remarkable reign as **National Collegiate Athletic Association (NCAA)** national champions. In 1971, he became head coach at the **University of Louisville**. His record at Louisville from 1971–2001 was 675–295. They were national champions in 1980 and 1986 and reached the **Final Four** in 1972, 1975, 1982, and 1983. Crum was enshrined in the **Naismith Memorial Basketball Hall of Fame** in 1994.

CRUZ DOWNS, TEÓFILO "TEO." B. 8 January 1942, Santurce, Puerto Rico. D. 30 August 2005, Trujillo Alto, Carolina, **Puerto Rico**. Teo Cruz played **basketball** in the Puerto Rican League from 1957–1982 for Cangrejeros de Santurce, Indios de Canóvanas, Mets de Guaynabo, Cardenales de Rio Piedras, and Tainos de Mayagüez. In his 25-year career in the Puerto Rican League, he was voted Most Valuable Player in four different seasons, was voted Best Defensive Player in six seasons, and twice led the league in scoring. In the 1967–1968 season, he played in Spain for the Picadero Damm team.

The six-foot, eight-inch **center** played with the Puerto Rican national team in five **Olympic Games** from 1960–1976 and is one of only three men to appear in five Olympic basketball tournaments. Had the team not boycotted the 1980 Moscow Games, Cruz would have played in six Olympics. In 39 games in the Olympics, he scored 437 points. In 1976, he was the Puerto Rico flag bearer for the Olympic Games in Montreal. He also played in the 1974 **World Championships**. After his death, the Santurce Sports Complex was renamed in his honor. In 2007, he was enshrined in the **Fédération Internationale de Basketball (FIBA)** Hall of Fame.

CUBA. Cuba has been a **Fédération Internationale de Basketball (FIBA)** member since 1937 and is in the FIBA Americas zone. The men's team competed in six **Olympic Games**, with a **bronze medal** in 1972 being their best effort. In the 1980 Olympic Games, Félix Martínez **blocked** 30 shots in the tournament—an all-time Olympic record. Ruperto Herrera, who played in four Olympic Games from 1968–1980, is among the all-time leaders in games played, with 32, and total points, with 440. Miguel Calderon, Pedro Chappé, Tomas Herrera, and Alejandro Urgelles all played in three Olympic tournaments. Cuba has competed in four **World Championships**, and their fourth place finish in 1974 is their best result. In eight Pan American Games competitions, their best result was the bronze medal in 1971. They have also competed in eight FIBA Americas tournaments, with fifth place twice being the best effort. The Cuban women's team has competed in four Olympic tournaments. In 1992, they finished fourth—their best Olympic performance.

The women's team has competed in 10 World Championship tournaments and won the bronze medal in 1990. The women's team has also competed in 10 Pan American Games and has won it three times, finished second twice, and placed third three times. In FIBA Americas' tournaments, they are tied with **Brazil** for the most medals, with eight, having won three times, placed second four times, and finished third once. Five of the members of the Cuban women's Olympic team each played in three Olympics from 1992–2000. They were Milayda Enríquez, Dalia Henry, Grisel Herrera, María Elena León, and Yamilé Martínez. Lazaro Borrell and Andres Guibert have played in the **National Basketball Association** and Alfonso Cueto in the **American Basketball Association**. Borrell's sister, Leonor, was just 16 years and 253 days old when she played in Moscow in 1980—the youngest to compete in women's Olympic **basketball**.

CUNNINGHAM, WILLIAM JOHN "BILLY," "THE KANGA-ROO KID." B. 3 June 1943, Brooklyn, New York. Billy Cunningham attended Erasmus Hall High School in Brooklyn and the **University of North Carolina**. Known as "The Kangaroo Kid" for his jumping ability, the six-foot, seven-inch **forward** was selected by the **Philadelphia 76ers** in the 1965 **National Basketball Association (NBA) draft**, played in the NBA from 1966–1972 for them, and was a member of their 1967 NBA Championship team. In 1969, he signed with the Carolina Cougars of the **American Basketball Association (ABA)** and after completing his NBA obligations was able to play for Carolina in the 1972–1973 season. He played two years in the ABA and then returned to the 76ers for the 1974–1975 and 1975–1976 seasons. On 5 December 1975, he suffered torn ligaments and cartilage in his left knee, and his playing career ended.

Cunningham's NBA career totals for nine years are 654 regular-season games and a 20.8 points and 10.1 **rebounds** per game average. He was selected for four NBA **All-Star Games** and was named to the All-NBA First Team three times and All-NBA Second Team in 1972. In his two years in the ABA, he was named the league's Most Valuable Player in 1973, was voted to the All-ABA First Team, and played in the ABA All-Star Game. He played in 116 regular-season ABA games and averaged 23.1 points and 11.6 rebounds per game. In 1977, he was hired as **coach** of the 76ers and coached them for the next eight seasons, with a cumulative record of 454–196. They won the NBA Championship in 1983 and were runners-up in 1980 and 1982. From 1987–1994, he was a minority owner of the **Miami Heat**. He was enshrined in the **Naismith Memorial Basketball Hall of Fame** in 1986. In 1996, Cunningham was named one of the 50 Greatest Players in NBA History.

CZECH REPUBLIC. The Czech Republic joined the **Fédération Internationale de Basketball (FIBA)** in 1993 and is a member in the FIBA Europe zone. The men's team has not yet competed in the **Olympic** tournament or FIBA **World Championships**. In the FIBA European Championships, they entered twice and had a best finish of ninth. The women's team competed in the 2004 and 2008 Olympic tournaments, where they finished in fifth place each time. In 2006, in the FIBA World Championships, they finished seventh in their only appearance. In the FIBA European Championships, they won the championship in 2005 and were second in 2003. There have only been two players born in what is now the Czech Republic in the **National Basketball Association**, Jiří Welsch and Jiří Zidek, and six players in the **Women's National Basketball Association**, Romana Hamzová, Zuzi Klimešová, Eva Němcová, Michaela Pavlíčková, Jana Vesela and Kamila Vodičková .

CZECHOSLOVAKIA. The country of Czechoslovakia joined the **Fédération Internationale de Basketball (FIBA)** in 1932 and was a member in the Europe zone. The men's team competed in seven **Olympic** tournaments, with a fifth place finish in 1960 being their best effort. In the FIBA **World Championships**, they competed four times, with a best finish of sixth in 1970. In the FIBA European Championships, they entered 24 times and won the tournament in 1946, finished second six times, and placed third five times.

The women's team competed in three Olympic tournaments, where their best showing was fourth in 1976. In the FIBA World Championships, they competed eight times. From 1957–1975, they finished either second or third in each tournament. In the European Championships, they entered 22 times and were second seven times and third eight times. From 1950–1966, they were either second or third in each tournament. There have been three players from Czechoslovakia in the **National Basketball Association**, including Jiří Welsch, Rich Petruška, and Jiří Zidek. The **Women's National Basketball Association** has featured Andrea Kuklová, Zuzana Zirková, Romana Hamzová, Zuzi Klimešová, Eva Němcová, Michaela Pavlíčková, Jana Vesela, and Kamila Vodičková. All eight women also played in the Olympic Games. In 1993, the country split into the Czech Republic and Slovakia.

– D –

D-LEAGUE. *See* NBA DEVELOPMENT LEAGUE (NBADL).

DALLAS CHAPARRALS. *See* SAN ANTONIO SPURS.

DALLAS MAVERICKS. The Dallas Mavericks are a team in the **National Basketball Association (NBA)**. On 20 April 1980, a group headed by Donald Carter purchased an expansion franchise and began play in the 1980–1981 season. Home games were played at the 17,293-seat Reunion Arena from 1980–2001 and at the 20,000-seat American Airlines Center since then.

Their **coaches** have included Rick Carlisle, Avery Johnson, Dick Motta, and **Don Nelson**. Among their most notable players have been Mark Aguirre, Rolando Blackman, Shawn Bradley, Brad Davis, James Donaldson, Michael Finley, Derek Harper, **Steve Nash, Dirk Nowitzki**, Sam Perkins, and Jay Vincent. From 1992–1994, they won only 24 and lost 140 games, the fewest wins of any team in league history in a two-year period. Their best season was 2005–2006, when they had a record of 60–22 in the regular season but lost in the NBA Finals to the **Miami Heat** in six games. In 2006–2007, they had their best regular-season won–lost record at 67–15 but were upset in the first round of the playoffs by the **Golden State Warriors**. Their overall record for their first 30 years in the league through the 2009–2010 season is 1,207–1,221.

DALY, CHARLES JEROME "CHUCK." B. 20 July 1930, St. Mary's, Pennsylvania. D. 8 May 2009, Jupiter, Florida. Chuck Daly attended Kane Area High School in Kane, Pennsylvania; St. Bonaventure University; and Bloomsburg State University. At Bloomsburg, he played **basketball** from 1950–1952 and averaged 13.1 points per game in 32 games. He **coached** Punxsutawney High School from 1955–1963; was assistant coach at **Duke University** from 1963–1969; was head coach at Boston College from 1969–1971 and Pennsylvania University from 1971–1977; was assistant coach with the **Philadelphia 76ers** of the **National Basketball Association (NBA)** from 1978–1981; and was head coach of the **Cleveland Cavaliers** in 1981–1982, **Detroit Pistons** from 1983–1992, **New Jersey Nets** from 1992–1994, and **Orlando Magic** from 1997–1999. He led the Pistons to the NBA Finals from 1988–1990 and won championships in 1989 and 1990. In 1992, he was named head coach of the U.S. **Olympic Dream Team** and led them to the **gold medal**.

Daly's record as college head coach was 151–62 and as professional head coach 638–437. In 1996, he was selected as one of the top 10 coaches in NBA history. When he was not employed as a coach, he worked in television broadcasting as an analyst. In May 2000, he was hired as special consultant to the president of the Vancouver (later **Memphis**) **Grizzlies** and retained that position until his death. He was enshrined in the **Naismith Memorial Basketball Hall of Fame** in 1994 as coach.

DAMPIER, LOUIS "LOUIE." B. 20 November 1944, Indianapolis, Indiana. Louie Dampier attended Southport High School in Indianapolis and the **University of Kentucky**. In 1967, the six-foot-tall **guard** was selected by the Cincinnati Royals in the **National Basketball Association (NBA) draft** and by the **Kentucky Colonels** in the **American Basketball Association (ABA) draft**. He signed with the Colonels and played for them from 1967–1976—one of only two players to play every ABA season for the same team. He scored 54 points in one game on 22 March 1968, and for a brief time he held the league single-game scoring record. One of the first **three-point field goal** specialists, in 1968–1969 he set the ABA season record for most three-point field goals made, 199, and attempted, 552. When the Colonels were dissolved in 1976, Dampier went to the **San Antonio Spurs** and played for them from 1976–1979.

Dampier was in seven ABA **All-Star Games**; was selected to the All-ABA Second Team four times; and is the ABA career record holder for games, **minutes** played, total **field goals**, total field goal attempts, three-point field goals, three-point field goal attempts, **assists**, and total points. He played in the ABA Championship Finals three times and was a member of the league champions in 1975. His 12-year professional totals are 960 games, 15.9 points, and 4.9 assists per game. After retiring from active play, he was assistant **coach** with the **Denver Nuggets**.

DANIELS, MELVIN JOE "MEL." B. 20 July 1944, Detroit, Michigan. Mel Daniels attended Pershing High School in Detroit, Burlington Junior College, and the University of New Mexico. In 1967, the six-foot, nine-inch **center** was selected by the Minnesota Muskies in the **American Basketball Association (ABA) draft** and the Cincinnati Royals in the **National Basketball Association (NBA)** draft. He signed with Minnesota—one of the first college stars to select the ABA over the NBA. He played in the ABA from 1967–1975, for the Muskies, **Indiana Pacers**, and **Memphis Sounds**, and led the Pacers to the ABA Championship three times. In the 1976–1977 season, he played in the NBA briefly for the New York Nets.

Daniels was ABA Rookie of the Year in 1968 and was twice the ABA's Most Valuable Player. His ABA career totals for eight years are 628 regular-season games and an 18.7 points and 15.1 **rebounds** per game average. He is the ABA career leader in **offensive** rebounds, **defensive** rebounds, total rebounds, and personal **fouls.** He played in seven ABA **All-Star Games** and was named the All-Star Game Most Valuable Player in 1971. He was selected for the All-ABA First Team four times and All-ABA Second Team once. After completing his playing career, he was assistant **coach** at Indiana State University. From 1986–2009, Daniels was director of player personnel for the Pacers.

DANTLEY, ADRIAN DELANO. B. 28 February 1956, Washington, D.C. Adrian Dantley attended DeMatha Catholic High School in Hyattsville, Maryland, and **Notre Dame University.** After his junior year in college, he was selected for the 1976 U.S. **Olympic basketball** team. The six-foot, five-inch **forward-guard** was the team's leading scorer, with an average of 19.3 points per game, and scored 30 points in the final game against **Yugoslavia,** the most points to that date by an American basketball player in an Olympic game. As an undergraduate, he was chosen by the Buffalo Braves in the 1976 **National Basketball Association (NBA) draft** and was named 1977 NBA Rookie of the Year. He played in the NBA from 1976–1991, for seven teams, and in **Italy** in the 1991–1992 season.

From 1980–1981 through 1983–1984, with the **Utah Jazz,** Dantley averaged 30 or more points per game each season and was the NBA scoring leader in 1981 and 1984. He was selected for the NBA **All-Star Game** in six of the seven seasons from 1980–1986, missing only the 1983 game, when he was injured. On 4 January 1984, he tied **Wilt Chamberlain**'s regular-season NBA record by making 28 **free throws** in one game. His NBA career average for 955 games was 24.3 points per game. After retiring from basketball he became assistant **coach** for the **Denver Nuggets** and was enshrined in the **Naismith Memorial Basketball Hall of Fame** in 2008.

DAVIES, ROBERT EDRIS "BOB." B. 15 January 1920, Harrisburg, Pennsylvania. D. 22 April 1990, Hilton Head, South Carolina. Bob Davies attended John Harris High School in Harrisburg, Franklin & Marshall College, and Seton Hall University. He served in the U.S. Navy and played part-time with the Brooklyn Indians and New York Gothams in the **American Basketball League** from 1943–1945, before joining the Rochester Royals of the **National Basketball League (NBL)** in 1945. He was head **coach** at Seton Hall University in the 1946–1947 season, while an active player with the Royals. He remained with the Royals through 1955, as they progressed from the NBL to the **Basketball Association of America (BAA)** to the **National Basketball Association (NBA)**, and helped lead Rochester to league championships in 1946 and 1951.

The six-foot, one-inch **guard** was one of the best ball handlers of his era, was one of the first to use a behind-the-back **dribble**, and was nicknamed "The Harrisburg Houdini." His career record in the NBL/BAA/NBA was 569 regular-season games and a 13.7 points per game average. He was selected for the first four NBA **All-Star Games** from 1951–1954 and was named to the All-League (NBL, BAA, or NBA) First Team five times and to the All-League Second Team twice. He was chosen as the NBL Most Valuable Player in 1947 and named to the NBA 25th Anniversary Team in 1971. After retiring from active play he coached at Gettysburg University from 1955–1957 and then worked for the Converse Rubber Company in sales and promotion. **Clair Bee** used Davies as the model for his Chip Hilton sports series. Davies was enshrined in the **Naismith Memorial Basketball Hall of Fame** in 1970.

DAWKINS, DARRYL "CHOCOLATE THUNDER." B. 11 January 1957, Orlando, Florida. Darryl Dawkins attended Maynard Evans High School in Orlando and led them to the state championship in 1975. He did not go to college and was selected by the **Philadelphia 76ers** in the 1975 **National Basketball Association (NBA) draft**. He began playing for the 76ers at the age of 18 and later played with the **New Jersey Nets, Utah Jazz**, and **Detroit Pistons** before retiring from the NBA in 1989.

The six-foot, 11-inch, 270-pound Dawkins was best known for his thunderous **slam dunks,** and he broke two glass **backboards** in one season. With his playful character, he gave names to his dunks, called himself "Chocolate Thunder," and invented a biography that had him coming from the planet "Lovetron." He led the NBA in personal **fouls** three times and set the league season record, with 386. With the 76ers he played on the losing side in three NBA Finals. His NBA career totals for 14 years are 726 games and a 12.0 points per game average.

After leaving the NBA, he played in **Italy** from 1989–1994. While there, he became obsessed with **field goal** percentage and seldom took a shot that wasn't from point-blank range. As a result, his field goal percentages in Italy ranged from .775 to .855. In 1995–1996, he played in the **Continental Basketball Association** and in subsequent years **coached** minor league teams in other leagues.

DAYTON UNIVERSITY. Dayton University in Ohio began its men's **basketball** program in 1903. Home games since 1969 have been played at the 13,409-seat University of Dayton Arena. The playing court is the Blackburn Court, named for former **coach** Tom Blackburn, who died of cancer on 6 March 1964, while still coaching at Dayton. The most accomplished coaches in the school's history have been Blackburn, Don Donaher, Brian Gregory, and Oliver Purnell. From 1951–1968, the Flyers reached the **National Invitation Tournament** championship final game seven times and won the tournament in 1962 and 1968. They won the NIT again in 2010. In 1967, the Flyers reached the **National Collegiate Athletic Association** Championship final game, where they lost to the **University of California, Los Angeles**. Among the best players in school history have been Arlen Bockhorn, Johnny Davis, Henry Finkel, John Horan, Don May, Don Meineke, John Paxson Sr., and John Paxson Jr., and Bill Uhl.

DEBUSSCHERE, DAVID ALBERT "DAVE." B. 16 October 1940, Detroit, Michigan. D. 14 May 2003, New York, New York. Dave DeBusschere attended Austin Catholic High School in Detroit and the University of Detroit. One of the few athletes to play two professional sports, he was a pitcher for the Chicago White Sox Major League Baseball team in 1962 and 1963 and the minor league Indianapolis Indians Pacific Coast League team in 1964 and 1965. He played in the **National Basketball Association (NBA)** from 1962–1974 for the **Detroit Pistons** and **New York Knickerbockers**. With the Pistons he was named player-**coach** in 1964 at the age of 24 and was the youngest coach in NBA history. He coached Detroit from 1964–1967. With the Knicks, he helped lead them to NBA Championships in 1970 and 1973. His NBA career totals for 12 years are 875 regular-season games and a 16.1 points and 11.0 **rebounds** per game average. He was selected for eight NBA **All-Star Games**

and was named to the All-NBA Second Team in 1969 and the NBA All-Defensive Team six times.

After retiring from the Knicks, DeBusschere was hired by the New York Nets of the **American Basketball Association (ABA)** as their general manager. In 1975, he was named commissioner of the ABA and helped bring about the merger with the NBA in 1976. In 1978, he and a few business partners purchased the boxing magazine, *Ring*. From 1982–1986, DeBusschere was general manager of the Knicks. He was enshrined in the **Naismith Memorial Basketball Hall of Fame** in 1983 and named one of the 50 Greatest Players in NBA History in 1996.

DEFENSE. In **basketball**, the team not in possession of the ball is considered to be on defense (pronounced with the accent on the first syllable) and their opponents on **offense**. While on defense, a team cannot score points. **Coaches** will generally design techniques for their teams on defense. Playing defense is generally considered more difficult (and less rewarding) than playing offense, and few players excel in defense. Certain statistics, such as **rebounds**, are recorded separately for the defense, and offense and defensive personal **fouls** are treated differently than those committed on offense.

DEHNERT, HENRY GEORGE "DUTCH." B. 5 April 1898, New York, New York. D. 20 April 1979, Far Rockaway, New York. Dutch Dehnert began playing professional **basketball** in 1917 and played in all the major basketball leagues for the next five years. In 1922, he signed an exclusive contract with the **Original Celtics**. He was the developer of the **pivot** play, in which he played with his back to the basket and would pass the ball out to his teammates or, if his opponent wasn't alert, would himself pivot and lay the ball in.

In 1928, the Celtics were broken up and players redistributed to the other teams in the **American Basketball League (ABL)** to provide a more balanced league. Dehnert was signed by the Cleveland Rosenblums and helped lead them to ABL titles in 1929 and 1930. The Rosenblums folded in 1930, and Dehnert was named player-**coach** of the Toledo Red Men Tobaccos team in 1930. After the ABL suspended operations in 1931, he joined the reorganized Celtics and played with them until 1939.

Dehnert then turned to coaching and was a professional basketball head coach in four different leagues in the 1940s. He led the Detroit Eagles to the **World Professional Basketball Tournament** Championship in 1941 and the **Sheboygan Redskins** to the **National Basketball League** Championship Finals in 1945 and 1946. After retiring from active play, Dehnert worked as a mutual clerk at New York area racetracks. He was enshrined in the **Naismith Memorial Basketball Hall of Fame** in 1969.

DENVER LARKS. *See* DENVER NUGGETS (ABA-NBA).

DENVER NUGGETS (ABA-NBA). The Denver Nuggets are a team in the **National Basketball Association (NBA)**. They originated in the **American Basketball Association (ABA)** as the Kansas City Larks in 1967, but before league play began the team was relocated to Denver and renamed the Denver Larks. Shortly afterward the team was sold and renamed the Denver Rockets. In 1974, they became the Denver Nuggets, and in 1977 they joined the NBA.

Kansas City Larks. On 2 February 1967, a franchise in the newly formed ABA was acquired for $35,000 by James J. Trindle of Kansas City, Missouri, who planned to call his team the Kansas City Larks. On 1 April 1967, the franchise was relocated to Denver and renamed the Denver Larks, as the team's owners were unable to obtain an adequate arena in Kansas City.

Denver Larks. On 14 June 1967, a majority share of the ownership was sold to J. William Ringsby, owner of Rocket Trucking, and the team was renamed the Denver Rockets.

Denver Rockets. Home games were played at the 6,900-seat Denver Auditorium Arena and the 10,200-seat Denver Coliseum. On 23 August 1969, the Rockets did something unprecedented—they signed 20-year-old **Spencer Haywood**, star of the 1968 U.S. Olympic team who had just completed his second year of college. Since the early days of the NBA, professional teams were required to wait until a player was four years removed from high school. The league's rationale was that its bylaws permitted the signing of an undergraduate in cases of "extreme hardship," and Haywood supported his mother and nine brothers and sisters. On 7 August 1974, the team was renamed the Denver Nuggets.

Denver Nuggets, ABA. In 1974–1975, the team won nearly all their home games, winning 40 and losing only two but losing in the second round of the playoffs to the Indiana Pacers. With the completion of the new 18,000-seat McNichols Arena, the Nuggets and New York Nets applied for admission to the NBA in 1975 but were not admitted. The Nuggets had just acquired **Dan Issel** and signed rookie **David Thompson**. Those two, along with **Bobby Jones**, provided a front line of three future Hall of Famers, one of the best in basketball history. The Nuggets finished the 1975–1976 season with the league's best record, 60–24, but lost in the ABA Finals. In 1976, with the ABA–NBA merger, the Nuggets joined the NBA. Among the Rockets/Nuggets best players, in addition to Haywood, Issel, Jones, and Thompson, were Byron Beck, Larry Jones, Julius Keye, Ralph Simpson, and Lonnie Wright.

Denver Nuggets, NBA. Their **coaches** have included **Larry Brown**, Dan Issel, George Karl, and Doug Moe. Among their most notable players have been **Mahmoud Abdul-Rauf**, Michael Adams, Carmelo Anthony, T. R. Dunn, Alex English, Bill Hanzlik, Dan Issel, Fat Lever, **Dikembe Mutombo**, Danny Schayes, David Thompson, and **Kiki Vandeweghe**. Their best season was 1984–1985, when they had a record of 52–30 and reached the Conference Finals. Their overall record for their first 34 years in the NBA through the 2009–2010 season is 1,319–1,437.

DENVER NUGGETS (NBL-NBA). The Denver Nuggets were a team in the **National Basketball League (NBL)** in the 1948–1949 season. They had previously competed successfully under the sponsorship of the Piggly Wiggly food stores as an **Amateur Athletic Union** team. They played home games at the University of Denver Field House and were **coached** by player-coach Ralph Bishop, a member of the 1936 U.S. **Olympic** team. Others on the team included Jimmy Darden; Ward Gibson; Robert "Ace" Gruenig; Al Guokas; and one-eyed Morris "Mo" Udall, who later became a U.S. congressman. The team was not successful and finished in last place in the Western Division. On 3 August 1949, they joined the **National Basketball Association (NBA)**, as the NBL and **Basketball Association of America** merged. Players on that team included Bob Brown, Jack Cotton, Dillard Crocker, Ken Sailors, Jack Toomay, and Floyd

Volker. They began their NBA season playing and losing their first 14 games on the road and started the season with a record of 0–15. They concluded the season with another 11-game losing streak and had a record of only 11–51 for the season. In April 1950, they left the NBA to join the new **National Professional Basketball League.**

DENVER ROCKETS. *See* DENVER NUGGETS (ABA-NBA).

DEPAUL UNIVERSITY. DePaul University in Chicago, Illinois, began its men's **basketball** program in 1923. Since 1980, home games have been played at the 17,500-seat Rosemont Horizon (now renamed the Allstate Arena). Prior to 1980, home games were played at Alumni Hall. The most accomplished **coaches** in the school's history have been **Ray Meyer** and his son, Joey. In 1944, the Blue Demons reached the **National Invitation Tournament (NIT)** championship final game where, led by **George Mikan**, they were defeated by **St. John's University.** The next year, again with Mikan, they won the NIT. In 1943 and 1979, they reached the **National Collegiate Athletic Association (NCAA) Final Four** but were defeated in the semifinal round. Among the best players in school history were George Mikan, his brother Ed, Mark Aguirre, Emmette Bryant, Howie Carl, Terry Cummings, Quentin Richardson, Ron Sobieszczyk, Rod Strickland, and Dick Triptow.

DETROIT FALCONS. The Detroit Falcons were a charter member of the **Basketball Association of America (BAA)** in 1946. Team owners James D. Norris and Arthur Wirtz had originally planned to play in Indianapolis but had problems switching the Indianapolis arena from ice hockey to **basketball** and moved the franchise to Detroit. The Falcons had a record of 20–40 and finished fourth in the five-team Western Division. Their main players were Hal Brown, Bob Dille, John Janisch, Tom King, Grady Lewis, Ariel Maughan, and Stan Miasek. Lewis later became president of the Converse Shoe Company. King, although not the best player in the league, was its highest paid player, since he received $8,500 as a player and another $8,000 for the jobs of publicity director, business manager, and traveling secretary. Playing their home games at the 14,000-seat Olympia Stadium, the Falcons' attendance of only 62,885 fans for

30 home games caused the franchise to withdraw from the BAA on 9 July 1947.

DETROIT GEMS. *See* LOS ANGELES LAKERS.

DETROIT PISTONS. The Detroit Pistons are a team in the **National Basketball Association (NBA)**. The team had its origin in the **National Basketball League (NBL)** in 1941, as the Fort Wayne Zollner Pistons. In 1948, they moved to the **Basketball Association of America (BAA)** and played as the Fort Wayne Pistons. They became members of the NBA with the merger of the BAA and NBL in 1949 and moved to Detroit in 1958.

Fort Wayne Zollner Pistons. The Fort Wayne Zollner Pistons played in the NBL from 1941–1948. They were owned by **Fred Zollner** and had previously played as an independent team. Home games were played at the 3,800-seat North Side High School gymnasium. Among their most notable players were Paul "Curly" Armstrong, Paul Birch, Jerry Bush, **Bobby McDermott**, Jake Pelkington, Herm Schaefer, and Carlisle "Blackie" Towery. In 1942, and again in 1943, they reached the NBL Championship series but were defeated. In 1944 and 1945, they won the NBL Championship. Their overall record for seven seasons in the NBL was 166–71. In 1948, they joined the BAA and became known as the Fort Wayne Pistons, since the BAA did not allow sponsors' names to be part of the team's name.

Fort Wayne Pistons. They continued to play at North Side High School gymnasium from 1948–1952 and then moved to the Fort Wayne Memorial Coliseum from 1952–1957. On 22 November 1950, before the 24-second **shot clock** was implemented, they were involved in the lowest-scoring game in league history. In an attempt to stop **George Mikan** and the Minneapolis Lakers, the Pistons froze the ball for most of the game and defeated the Lakers, 19–18. In a surprising move, former NBA **referee Charley Eckman** was hired as the Pistons' **coach** for the 1954–1955 season. The Pistons' best NBA seasons were 1954–1955 and 1955–1956, when they reached the NBA Championship Finals but lost both years. Among their most notable players in the NBA were Paul "Curly" Armstrong, Frankie Brian, Larry Foust, Mel Hutchins, Ralph Johnson, Don Meineke, **Andy Phillip**, Fred Schaus, and **George Yardley**.

Detroit Pistons. Home games were played at the 15,000-seat Olympia Stadium from 1957–1961, the 12,000-seat Cobo Arena from 1961–1978, the 80,000-seat Pontiac Silverdome from 1978–1988, and the 22,076-seat Palace of Auburn Hills since 1988. The most notable coaches have been **Larry Brown, Doug Collins, Chuck Daly,** and Phillip "Flip" Saunders. Among their best players in Detroit have been **Dave Bing, Joe Dumars,** Richard Hamilton, **Grant Hill,** Lindsey Hunter, Bill Laimbeer, **Bob Lanier,** John Long, **Dennis Rodman, Isiah Thomas,** and Vinnie Johnson. Their best seasons were 1988–1989, 1989–1990, and 2003–2004, when they won the NBA Championship. Their overall record since 1949 in the NBA through the 2009–2010 season is 2,427–2,465.

DISQUALIFICATION. *See* FOUL.

DIVAĆ, VLADE. B. 3 February 1968, Prijepolje, Serbia, **Yugoslavia.** Vlade Divać attended high school in Belgrade, Yugoslavia, and did not go to college. He began playing **basketball** with KK Elan in Prijepolje and in 1986 signed with KK Partizan Belgrade. He helped lead the Yugoslavian national team to **gold medals** in the 1990 and 2002 **World Championships** and 1989, 1991, and 1995 European Championships; **silver medals** at the 1988 and 1996 **Olympic Games;** and **bronze medals** in the 1986 World Championship and 1987 and 1999 European Championships. He was selected by the **Los Angeles Lakers** in the 1989 **National Basketball Association (NBA) draft** and played in the NBA from 1989–2005 for the Lakers, Charlotte Hornets, and **Sacramento Kings.** Although seven-feet, one-inch tall, he was an excellent ball handler for a **center.**

Divać s NBA career totals for 16 years are 1,134 regular-season games and an 11.8 points and 8.2 **rebounds** per game average. He was selected for the 2001 NBA **All-Star Game.** In 2000, he was presented with the **J. Walter Kennedy** Citizenship Award by the NBA. After retiring from active play, he has been involved in many business and humanitarian projects, including purchasing the KK Partizan sports club along with former teammate Sasha Danilović. In 2009, Divać was elected as president of the Serbian Olympic Committee. In 2010, he was inducted into the **Fédération Internationale de Basketball** Hall of Fame.

DONOVAN, ANNE THERESA. B. 1 November 1961, Ridgewood, New Jersey. Anne Donovan attended Paramus Catholic High School and **Old Dominion University**. She led Old Dominion to the **Association for Intercollegiate Athletics for Women (AIAW)** National Championship in 1979 and 1980 and the **National Collegiate Athletic Association (NCAA) Final Four** in 1983. She was the first recipient of the Naismith College Player of the Year in 1983. One of the tallest American women to play basketball at six-feet, eight-inches, she was selected as **center** for the 1980 **U.S. Olympic** team that boycotted the Moscow Olympics, but she played on the **gold medal**-winning 1984 and 1988 U.S. Olympic teams. She also played on the **U.S.** team in the 1983 and 1987 Pan American Games, 1983 and 1986 **World Championships**, and 1986 Goodwill Games. She played professional basketball in **Japan** from 1983–1988 and in **Italy** in 1989.

Donovan's **coaching** resume includes assistant coach for the 1998 and 2002 U.S. World Championship teams and 2004 Olympic team; head coach for the 2006 World Championship and 2008 Olympic teams; assistant coach at Old Dominion from 1989–1995; head coach at East Carolina University from 1995–1998; head coach of Philadelphia in the **American Basketball League** in 1998; **Women's National Basketball Association (WNBA)** head coach of Indiana in 2000, Charlotte in 2001–2002, and Seattle in 2003–2007; and assistant coach of the New York Liberty in 2009. On 31 July 2009, she was named head coach of the Liberty. On 29 March 2010, she was named head coach of Seton Hall University to take effect following the 2010 WNBA season. In 2004, she led Seattle to the WNBA title and was the first female coach to win a WNBA championship. She was enshrined in the **Naismith Memorial Basketball Hall of Fame** in 1995 and the **Women's Basketball Hall of Fame** in 1999.

DOUBLE DRIBBLE. A double **dribble** (also referred to as a discontinued dribble) occurs when the player dribbling the **basketball** stops dribbling and then resumes dribbling. This is a violation. Possession of the ball is transferred to the opposing team, who then puts it in play from out-of-bounds.

DOUGLAS, ROBERT L. "BOB." B. 4 November 1882, St. Kitts, British West Indies. D. 16 July 1979, New York, New York. Bob Douglas came to the **United States** at the age of four. His major contribution to the sport of **basketball** was as founder in 1922 and **coach** of the **New York Renaissance basketball** team. From 1922–1949, the all-black Rens were one of the best independent basketball teams in the country and had an 88-game consecutive winning streak in 1932–1933. Unlike the **Harlem Globetrotters**, they played straight basketball and in 1939 were the winners of the invitational **World Professional Basketball Tournament** in Chicago, Illinois. During the Rens' existence, their record was a reported 2,318–381. In 1948–1949, they were invited to join the **National Basketball League** mid-season and played league games as the Dayton Rens while continuing to barnstorm as the New York Renaissance.

Douglas has been called the "Father of Black Professional Basketball." In 1972, in the role of contributor, he was the first African American enshrined in the **Naismith Memorial Basketball Hall of Fame**. He was the first president of the New York Pioneer Athletic Club and manager of the Renaissance Ballroom until the age of 90.

DRAFT. The draft is a process whereby all teams in a league take turns selecting prospective players from a pool. The selection is usually done in inverse order to the team's recent performance. The drafted player may then only sign a contract with the team that selects him. The annual college draft was begun in July 1947, by the **Basketball Association of America** and continued by the **National Basketball Association (NBA)**. Until the mid-1960s, the NBA allowed teams to have "territorial draft selections." Players that attended college in a city with an NBA franchise could be reserved by that NBA team. During most of the years that the draft was held, it continued until the teams had selected all the players they desired. Since 1989, the draft has been limited to just two rounds. Originally the draft was a closed meeting of team representatives, but in recent years it has been held in large arenas with the public invited to attend. Drafts are also conducted to distribute players from disbanded teams and to stock expansion teams.

DRAFT RIGHTS. Once a team has selected a prospective player in a **draft**, that team owns what are called the "draft rights" to that player. Only that team may negotiate a contract with him. A team may trade those rights to other teams in exchange for other players or other players' draft rights.

DREAM TEAM. The 1992 **Olympic Games** were the first in which professional **basketball** players were allowed to participate. The U.S. Olympic Committee, in an attempt to avenge their 1988 Olympic loss and third-place finish, put together possibly the greatest basketball team ever assembled. The team, **coached** by **Chuck Daly**, was dubbed the "Dream Team" by sportswriters and consisted of **National Basketball Association** stars **Charles Barkley, Larry Bird, Clyde Drexler, Patrick Ewing, Earvin "Magic" Johnson, Michael Jordan, Karl Malone, Chris Mullin, Scottie Pippen, David Robinson,** and **John Stockton.** Collegian **Christian Laettner** was also added to the team. They won their eight Olympic games by an average score of 117–73 and easily won the **gold medal.** In 2010, the Dream Team was enshrined in the **Naismith Memorial Basketball Hall of Fame.**

DREXLER, CLYDE AUSTIN. B. 22 June 1962, New Orleans, Louisiana. Clyde Douglas attended Ross Sterling High School in Houston, Texas, and the **University of Houston.** He was drafted by the **Portland Trail Blazers** in the 1983 **National Basketball Association (NBA) draft** and played with the Blazers and **Houston Rockets** from 1983–1998. Nicknamed "Clyde the Glide" for his smooth style of play, he was a member of the NBA Championship team in 1995 with Houston. His all-around ability twice nearly resulted in **quadruple-doubles**, a feat only accomplished four times in NBA history. In 1992, he was a member of the U.S. **Olympic** basketball **Dream Team.**

   In 1996, Drexler was named one of the 50 Greatest Players in NBA History. In his 15-year NBA career, he played in 1,086 regular-season games and averaged 20.4 points per game. He was named to the All-NBA First Team in 1992, was selected to the All-NBA Second Team and All-NBA Third Team twice each, and was chosen for

10 NBA **All-Star Games**. After retiring from active play he became head **coach** at the University of Houston from 1998–2000. He then worked for the **Denver Nuggets** as assistant to the general manager and then as assistant coach. He was enshrined in the **Naismith Memorial Basketball Hall of Fame** in 2004. *See also* PHI SLAMA JAMA.

DRIBBLE. To retain possession of the **basketball**, a player must bounce the ball while moving. This is called a dribble. Once the player stops dribbling the ball he is allowed to take no more than two steps. In the early days of basketball, players were allowed to use two hands to dribble the ball, but since the mid-1920s only one hand can touch the ball while bouncing it, although the player may use either hand at any time to do so. *See also* TRAVELING.

DUKE UNIVERSITY. Duke University in Durham, North Carolina, began its men's **basketball** program in 1906. Since 1940, home games have been played at Duke's Indoor Stadium (renamed Cameron Indoor Stadium in 1972), as a tribute to former Duke athletic director and basketball **coach** Edmund M. "Eddie" Cameron. The Blue Devils have had many outstanding basketball players in the school's history, including nine who were named "National Player of the Year": Shane Battier, Elton Brand, Johnny Dawkins, Danny Ferry, Dick Groat, Art Heyman, **Christian Laettner**, J. J. Redick, and Jason Williams.

Their most accomplished coach, by far, has been Hall of Famer **Mike Krzyzewski**. From 1981–2010, he compiled a record of 795–220 and reached the **Final Four** 11 times, winning four **National Collegiate Athletic Association (NCAA)** Championships and finishing second four times. Other outstanding coaches have been Harold Bradley, Vic Bubas, and Bill Foster.

The women's basketball program began in 1975. The school's most successful women's coach has been Gail Goestenkoers. In 1999 and 2006, the Blue Devils reached the NCAA Championship final game but were defeated both times. The best players in school history include Alison Bales, Alana Beard, Monique Currie, Lindsey Harding, Katie Meier, Iciss Tillis, and Mistie Williams.

DUMARS III, JOE. B. 24 May 1963, Shreveport, Louisiana. Joe Dumars attended Natchitoches High School in Natchitoches, Louisiana, and McNeese State University. He was selected by the **Detroit Pistons** in the 1985 **National Basketball Association (NBA) draft** and played from 1985–1999 for the Pistons. He played on the NBA Championship team in 1989 and 1990 and was named the Finals Most Valuable Player in 1989.

Dumars was selected for six NBA **All-Star Games**, the NBA All-Defensive First Team four times, the NBA All-Defensive Second Team once, the All-NBA Second Team in 1993, and the All-NBA Third Team twice. His NBA career totals for 14 years are 1,018 games and a 16.1 points per game average. In 1996, he was the first winner of the NBA Sportsmanship Award, which has since been renamed the Joe Dumars Trophy. Playing for the U.S. national team in the 1994 **World Championships**, he won a **gold medal.**

Dumars is currently on the board of directors of the First Michigan Bank. He was named president of Basketball Operations of the Detroit Pistons in 2000 and has since guided the Pistons to the NBA Championship in 2004 and Eastern Conference Finals six times. He was enshrined in the **Naismith Memorial Basketball Hall of Fame** in 2006.

DUNCAN, TIMOTHY THEODORE "TIM." B. 25 April 1976, St. Croix, U.S. Virgin Islands. Tim Duncan attended St. Dunstan's Episcopal High School in St. Croix and Wake Forest University. In college, he won both the John R. Wooden Award and the Naismith College Player of the Year Award in 1997. He was the first overall selection in the 1997 **National Basketball Association (NBA) draft** and was chosen by the **San Antonio Spurs**. The six-foot, 10-inch **forward-center** is one of the few modern players who uses the **backboard** for most of his shots. He has led the Spurs to four NBA Championships.

Among Duncan's many honors have been 1998 NBA Rookie of the Year, NBA Most Valuable Player in both 2002 and 2003, NBA **All-Star Game** co-Most Valuable Player in 2000, All-NBA First Team nine times, All-NBA Second Team three times and All-NBA Third Team once, and NBA All-Defensive First Team eight times and NBA All-Defensive Second Team five times. He has been selected to play in the NBA All-Star Game each year he has been in the league. In his first 13 NBA seasons, he has averaged 21.1 points, 11.6 **rebounds**, and 2.3 **blocks** per game and been remarkably consistent with similar averages in all 13 seasons. He won a **bronze medal** with the 2004 **U.S. Olympic** team. His six-foot-tall sister, Tricia, competed in the 1988 Olympic Games for the Virgin Islands as a swimmer in both the 100- and 200-meter backstroke events.

DUNK. A dunk is achieved by holding the **basketball** above the rim and throwing the ball down through the **basket** with one or both hands. In the early days of basketball, this was not considered as a sporting move, and players who did so were subject to physical abuse by their opponents. Since the 1960s, however, it has been accepted and its use encouraged by professional leagues. From the 1967–1968 season through the 1975–1976 season, the **National Collegiate Athletic Association** banned dunking the ball. The **American Basketball Association** popularized the move and at their **All-Star Game** in 1976 held a "**slam-dunk**" contest. Since the mid-1980s, the **National Basketball Association** has also done so, and it has proved to be among the most popular events.

DUQUESNE UNIVERSITY OF THE HOLY SPIRIT. Duquesne University in Pittsburgh, Pennsylvania, began its men's **basketball** program in 1913. Home games since 1988 have been played at the 5,358-seat A. J. Palumbo Center. The most accomplished **coaches** in the school's history have been Charles "Chick" Davies, John "Red" Manning, Reverend Eugene N. McGuigan, and Donald "Dudey" Moore. Father McGuigan, who coached from 1915–1923, was listed in newspaper reports as "Coach Gene Martin" to avoid publicizing the fact that a Roman Catholic priest was associated with the then "rowdy" sport of basketball.

In 1940, the Dukes reached the **National Invitation Tournament (NIT)** championship final game, where they were defeated by the University of Colorado. They also reached the NIT final in 1954 and 1955. In 1954, they lost to **Holy Cross College**, but in 1955 they won the NIT by defeating **Dayton University**. The best players in school history include Moe Becker, Paul Birch, Herb Bonn, **Chuck Cooper**,

Sihugo Green, Walt Miller, brothers Dick and Dave Ricketts, Willie Somerset, Jim Tucker, and Paul Widowitz.

DYDEK, MAŁGORZATA TERESA "MARGO." B. 28 April 1974, Poznań, **Poland**. Margo Dydek is a graduate of Akademia Wychowania Fizycznego in Wrocław, Poland, and was selected for the 2000 Polish **Olympic basketball** team. The seven-foot, two-inch **center** is the tallest female athlete to ever appear in the Olympic Games. (**Uljana Semjonova** was probably about the same height but was always listed as six-feet, 10-inches tall.) Margo appeared in all seven games for the eighth-place Polish team and averaged 20.4 points, 12.1 **rebounds**, and 3.0 **blocks** per game. She tied the Olympic Games tournament record with 44 **free throws** and, in the game against the **United States** on 24 September 2000, made 10 free throws in 10 attempts. She ranks second all-time for one Olympic tournament in several categories, including blocks, total rebounds, defensive rebounds, and free throw attempts. She had five blocks in one game three times—the only player ever to do so more than once.

Dydek played for Poland in the 1994 **World Championships** and in four European Championships, leading her country to their greatest success in its basketball history, a **gold medal** in 1999. She played in the **Women's National Basketball Association (WNBA)** from 1998–2008, with Utah, San Antonio, Connecticut, and Los Angeles, is the all-time leader in blocked shots, with 877, and is one of only four players to record a **triple-double** in the WNBA. She has played in Europe in Poland, **France**, **Spain**, and **Russia**, and speaks five languages as a result. Her sister, Katarzyna, was also a member of the 2000 Polish Olympic team and played in the **American Basketball League**.

– E –

EARLY, PENNY ANN. B. 30 May 1943, Chicago, Illinois. Penny Ann Early was not a **basketball** player, yet she appeared in a regularly scheduled **American Basketball Association** game for the **Kentucky Colonels** on 27 November 1968. In the second quarter, after a time-out, she entered the game and inbounded the ball to teammate Bobby Rascoe. The Colonels then called time–out, and she was removed from the game. In doing so, she became the first female to play in a men's professional basketball game.

Early attended Chicago's Graeme Stewart Elementary School and Senn High School and quit high school her junior year to get married. The five-foot, three-inch, 114-pound Early was not an athlete and did not play high school sports, but she loved horses. She attempted to be a jockey, was rebuffed on several occasions, and finally received a chance to ride in a special match race in Tijuana, Mexico, on 2 February 1969, but she lost the six-furlong race by three lengths to male jockey Alvaro Pineda. She subsequently competed in several other races as a jockey.

EASTERN BASKETBALL ASSOCIATION (EBA). *See* CONTINENTAL BASKETBALL ASSOCIATION (CBA).

EASTERN BASKETBALL LEAGUE (EBL). The Eastern Basketball League (EBL) was a men's professional **basketball** major league organized by Philadelphia sportswriter William J. Scheffer. It began operation in 1909. Initially there were three teams from the Philadelphia area, including DeNeri, Jasper, and Germantown; two teams from New Jersey, Trenton and Elizabeth; and one team from Reading, Pennsylvania. After the league's first season, the Philadelphia-based team Greystock and the Camden, New Jersey, team replaced Germantown and Elizabeth. For the next eight years, there were no franchise changes. This league stability was unheard-of in professional basketball and was unmatched by any professional basketball league (including the **National Basketball Association**) in the 20th century.

In four of the first six seasons, the 40-game regular season ended in a tie. World War I caused league play to be suspended on 3 December 1917. The league resumed play in the 1919–1920 season and, for the first time since the 1910–1911 season, several franchises were moved but the league remained at six teams. The EBL continued until the 1922–1923 season. Play was suspended on 18 January 1923, with plans to reorganize the following season, but it was unable to do so. During its 14-year life span, the EBL featured most of the top professional players of the era. *See also* APPENDIX B (for a list of league champions).

EASTERN PENNSYLVANIA BASKETBALL LEAGUE. *See* CONTINENTAL BASKETBALL ASSOCIATION (CBA).

EASTERN PROFESSIONAL BASKETBALL LEAGUE. *See* CONTINENTAL BASKETBALL ASSOCIATION (CBA).

ECKMAN, CHARLES MARKWOOD, JR. "CHARLEY." B. 10 September 1921, Baltimore, Maryland. D. 3 July 1995, Glen Burnie, Maryland. Charley Eckman was the only **National Basketball Association (NBA) referee** to be hired as an NBA **coach**—and he was hired without any previous coaching experience. He attended Baltimore City College, a public high school, despite its name, and did not go to college. He was signed by the Class D Mooresville minor league baseball team as an infielder. Charley best described his baseball career by saying, "not only could I not hit the high, hard one, I couldn't hit the low, soft ones." He worked for Westinghouse in Baltimore and refereed **basketball** part-time.

After a strike at Westinghouse, Eckman became a full-time referee for the **Basketball Association of America**. On 18 April 1954, **Fred Zollner**, disillusioned with the way his Fort Wayne Pistons had been playing, decided to hire the 32-year-old Eckman as the Pistons' head coach. Eckman's pet phrase was "it's a very simple game," and he proved that to be true as he led the Pistons to the NBA Finals in 1955 and 1956, losing in the seventh and deciding game in 1955 by one point in the last 12 seconds. He was asked to resign as coach in December 1957, after the team had won just nine of their first 27 games. He returned to college refereeing and retired in 1967. During the 1960s, he began a successful career as a radio sports announcer. His personable style and sense of humor made him an extremely popular after-dinner speaker as well.

EDMONTON GRADS. The Edmonton Grads were a women's **basketball** team that had its origins with the 1915 senior girls' team at McDougall Commercial High School in Edmonton, Alberta, **Canada**. After winning the Provincial Championship, they remained together after graduating, were **coached** by their high school coach, J. Percy Page, and became world-famous. Their record for the 25-year period was 522–20. Although women's basketball was not an

Olympic sport, they defeated international teams in demonstration tournaments at Olympic Games from 1924–1936, winning all 27 games in those four years. Page later became the lieutenant governor of Alberta. The team was recognized by the **Women's Basketball Hall of Fame** in 2010 with a special display entitled "Trailblazers of the Game."

EDWARDS, LEROY "COWBOY," "LEFTY." B. 11 April 1914, Indianapolis, Indiana. D. 25 August 1971, Lawrence, Indiana. Leroy Edwards attended Arsenal Tech High School in Indianapolis and led his team to the city championship from 1931–1933. He enrolled at the **University of Kentucky,** played on the undefeated freshman team, and then played one season of varsity **basketball.** In each of his first five varsity games, he singlehandedly outscored the opposing team. He left Kentucky to play professional basketball and played in the **Midwest Basketball Conference** and its successor, the **National Basketball League (NBL),** from 1935–1949. From 1937–1949, with the **Oshkosh All-Stars,** he was the only player in NBL history to play for the same team in every season.

The six-foot, five-inch **left-handed center** led the NBL in scoring and was named its Most Valuable Player in each of his first three seasons in the league. In 1938, Edwards set the league individual game scoring record with 30 points, although the record was later broken. He helped lead Oshkosh to the NBL Championship in 1941 and 1942 and to the NBL Championship Finals four other times. Oshkosh entered the **World Professional Basketball Tournament** each year from 1939–1948, winning in 1942 and placing second four other years. In his 12-year NBL career, Edwards scored 3,221 points in 322 games. After retirement from basketball, he owned a tavern in Oshkosh, Wisconsin. He moved to Indianapolis in 1953 and worked for Chrysler Corporation until his death.

EDWARDS, TERESA. B. 19 July 1964, Thomasville, Georgia. Teresa Edwards attended Cairo High School in Cairo, Georgia, and the University of Georgia. She helped lead the University of Georgia to the **National Collegiate Athletic Association (NCAA) Final Four** twice. In 1984, as a college junior, she was selected for the U.S. **Olympic basketball** team—the first of five Olympic appearances.

The five-foot, 11-inch **guard** is the only female basketball player to play in five Olympic tournaments and one of only four people to play in five Olympic basketball tournaments. She is the only Olympian, male or female, to win four **gold medals** in basketball and the only one to win a total of five medals. At the Atlanta Olympic Games in 1996, she was chosen to take the Athlete's Oath—the only basketball player ever to do so. She also played for the U.S. national team at the 1986 and 1990 Goodwill Games; the 1986, 1990, and 1994 **World Championships**; and the 1987 and 1991 Pan American Games. She was named Female Athlete of the Year by USA Basketball four times.

During the 1980s and 1990s, Edwards played professionally for nine years in **Italy, Japan, Spain,** and **France**. From 1996–1998, she played in the **American Basketball League** and was player-**coach** with the Atlanta Glory in the 1997–1998 season. She was coaxed into playing for the Minnesota Lynx in the **Women's National Basketball Association** in 2003 at the age of 39 and played two seasons with them before retiring. In 2006, she became an assistant coach with Minnesota and has since worked as a television color analyst as well. She was enshrined in the **Women's Basketball Hall of Fame** in 2010.

EGYPT. The first African nation to join the **Fédération Internationale de Basketball (FIBA)** was Egypt in 1934. Due to the country's proximity to Europe and the lack of many African nations in FIBA, Egypt competed in the FIBA European Championships in 1937, 1947, 1949, and 1953. The 1949 European Championships were held in Cairo, Egypt, and were won by the host country. Since the advent of the FIBA African Men's Championships in 1962, Egypt has competed with its continental neighbors. Egypt won the African Championship four times, was runner-up six times, and placed third six other times. They also competed in five **World Championships**, with their fifth place finish in 1950 being their best. (For the 1959 and 1970 tournaments they were known as the United Arab Republic.)

As Egypt they competed in six **Olympic basketball** tournaments. Their best finish was in 1952, when they finished in a tie for ninth place. Some of the better players to play for the Egyptian national team have been Alain Attalah, Gaby Catafogo, Hesham Khalil, Mohamed Soliman, Albert Tadros, Abdel Moneim Wahby, and Medhat Warda. Wahby, after competing in 1936 as a player, also served as a **referee** in 1948 and 1952 and was FIBA president from 1968–1976. Soliman led all players in the 1984 tournament, with a 25.6 points per game average. The only Egyptian-born player in the **National Basketball Association** has been Alaa Abdelnaby, who moved to the **United States** at an early age but still retains his Egyptian heritage.

EMBRY, WAYNE RICHARD. B. 26 March 1937, Springfield, Ohio. Wayne Embry attended Tecumseh High School in New Carlisle, Ohio, and Miami of Ohio University. Chosen in the 1958 **National Basketball Association (NBA) draft** by the St. Louis Hawks, he was traded to the Cincinnati Royals shortly before the season began. The six-foot, eight-inch, 255-pound **center** played with the Royals from 1958–1966, was traded to the **Boston Celtics** in 1966, played two seasons there, and was a member of the 1968 NBA Championship team. He was selected by the **Milwaukee Bucks** in the 1968 expansion draft and played for them in his final professional season. In his 11-year NBA career, he played in 831 regular-season games, averaged 12.5 points and 9.1 **rebounds** per game, and was selected to the NBA **All-Star Game** each season from 1961–1965. His best individual season was 1961–1962, with the Royals, when he averaged career-highs with 19.8 points, 13.0 rebounds, and 2.4 **assists** per game.

Embry became the first black general manager of a North American major league sports franchise when he was hired by the Bucks in 1971. He remained with the Bucks through 1979; was general manager of the **Cleveland Cavaliers** from 1986–1992; and was promoted to vice president of Cleveland in 1992 and team president and chief operating officer in 1994, the first black in that role in the NBA. In 2004, he was hired as senior basketball advisor to the general manager of the **Toronto Raptors**. He is also a member of the board of directors of the Federal Reserve Bank of Cleveland. He was twice voted the NBA Executive of the Year. In 1999, he was enshrined in the **Naismith Memorial Basketball Hall of Fame** as a contributor.

ERVING II, JULIUS WINFIELD "DR. J." B. 22 February 1950, East Meadow, New York. Julius Erving attended Roosevelt High

School in Roosevelt, New York, and the University of Massachusetts. He was signed by the **Virginia Squires** of the **American Basketball Association (ABA)** during his junior year of college, played with them from 1971–1973, and was traded to the New York Nets in 1973. Known as "Dr. J.," the six-foot, six-inch **forward-guard** is best known for his leaping ability and spectacular **dunks**. In three seasons with the Nets, he was named Most Valuable Player each year. He led the league in scoring, took the Nets to the ABA Championship in 1974 and 1976, and was named the Most Valuable Player of the playoffs in both seasons. In his five-season ABA career, he played in 407 regular-season games, established the league record with a career average of 28.7 points per game, and played in the **All-Star Game** each year.

When the **National Basketball Association (NBA)** and ABA merged following the 1975–1976 season, the Nets franchise was required to pay eight million dollars to join the NBA. This caused them to sell Erving and several other players to raise the cash. He was sold to the **Philadelphia 76ers**, played with them from 1976–1987, and led them to four NBA Finals and the 1983 NBA Championship.

Erving was named to the NBA All-Star Game in each of his 11 seasons in the NBA and was twice voted its Most Valuable Player. In 1981, he was named the league's Most Valuable Player. He was named to the All-NBA First Team five times, selected for the All-NBA Second Team twice, and in 1983 received the **J. Walter Kennedy** Citizenship Award. His combined totals for 16 professional seasons and 1,243 regular-season games were 30,026 points and a 24.2 points per game average. In 1993, he was enshrined in the **Naismith Memorial Basketball Hall of Fame**. He was named one of the 50 Greatest Players in NBA History in 1996. After retiring from active play, he became owner of a Coca-Cola bottling plant in Philadelphia, was an analyst for televised **basketball** games, and from 1997–2008 was employed by the **Orlando Magic** in an executive capacity. His daughter, Alexandra Stevenson, is a tennis professional that reached the semifinal round at Wimbledon.

EUROLEAGUE. *See* EUROPEAN CUP.

EUROPEAN CUP. The **Fédération Internationale de Basketball (FIBA)** European Cup championship (also known as European Champions' Cup and Euroleague) is a club competition for **basketball** teams throughout FIBA Europe (which also includes Israel). It was established in 1958 and held until the 1999–2000 season. In the 2000–2001 season, a second European international club competition was created by an organization known as the Union of European Leagues of Basketball (ULEB), and it was also called Euroleague. The FIBA then changed the name of their competition to Suproleague. In that year, there were two leagues and two continental champions. By the following season, the FIBA acquiesced and allowed the ULEB to be the administrators for the professional club championship, while retaining authority over other such competitions as the European, World, and **Olympic** championships.

EWING, PATRICK ALOYSIUS. B. 5 August 1962, Kingston, Jamaica. Patrick Ewing's family came to the **United States** when he was 11 years old, and he was raised in Cambridge, Massachusetts. He attended Cambridge Rindge and Latin School and **Georgetown University**, where he helped lead his team to the 1984 **National Collegiate Athletic Association (NCAA)** Championship and the **Final Four** in 1982 and 1985. As a seven-foot-tall college junior, he was selected for the 1984 U.S. **Olympic basketball** team and won a **gold medal** with them. He was drafted by the **New York Knickerbockers** in the 1985 **National Basketball Association (NBA) draft** as the first overall selection, where he played from 1985–2000. In 1986, he was named NBA Rookie of the Year. He led the Knicks to the NBA Finals in 1994. In 1996, he was named one of the 50 Greatest Players in NBA History. He played the 2000–2001 season with the Seattle Supersonics and the 2001–2002 season with the **Orlando Magic**. He won his second Olympic gold medal as a member of the 1992 U.S. Olympic basketball **Dream Team**.

In his 17-year NBA career, Ewing played in 1,183 regular-season games and averaged 21.0 points, 9.8 **rebounds**. and 2.4 **blocks** per game. He was named to the All-NBA First Team in 1990, the All-NBA Second Team six times, the and NBA All-Defensive Second Team three times, and he was selected to play in 11 NBA **All-Star**

Games. After retiring from basketball, he became assistant **coach** with the **Washington Wizards** in 2002–2003, the **Houston Rockets** from 2003–2006, and the Orlando Magic from 2007–2010. In 2008, Ewing was enshrined in the **Naismith Memorial Basketball Hall of Fame**.

– F –

FÉDÉRATION INTERNATIONALE DE BASKETBALL (FIBA). The Fédération Internationale de Basketball (FIBA) is the international association that governs **basketball** worldwide. Created in Geneva, Switzerland, in 1932, with eight founding members: **Argentina, Czechoslovakia, Greece, Italy**, Latvia, Portugal, Romania, and Switzerland, it has grown to 213 members and is organized into five zones, Africa, Americas, Asia, Europe, and Oceania. The original name was the Fédération Internationale de Basket-Ball (FIBB), and it was later changed to the Fédération Internationale de Basketball Amateur, but in 1989 the word "amateur" was dropped from its name. It oversees competition for both men and women in the **Olympic Games**, **World Championships**, Zone Championships, and other championships of lesser importance. Since 2002, the FIBA's headquarters has been in Geneva. In 2007, a FIBA Hall of Fame was created. *See also* JONES, RENATO WILLIAM; APPENDIX K (for a list of Hall of Fame inductees).

FERRÁNDIZ GONZÁLEZ, PEDRO. B. 20 November 1928, Alicante, **Spain**. Pedro Ferrándiz began **coaching basketball** in 1955. As coach of the Real Madrid senior team from 1959–1962, 1964–1965, and 1966–1975, he had the remarkable record of 437–90, with three undefeated seasons in the Spanish League. He introduced a fast break style of play, and from 1961–1975, Real Madrid was nearly unbeatable. They won the championship of the Spanish League 12 times and had a consecutive game-winning streak of 71 games. They also won the **European Cup** tournament four times.

In 1964–1965, Ferrándiz coached the Spanish national team. In 1976, he was cofounder, along with **Italian** coach Cesare Rubini, of the World Association of Basketball Coaches. Ferrándiz, a recipient of the **Olympic** Order from the International Olympic Committee, is the only basketball coach ever to receive this honor. He created the Pedro Ferrándiz Foundation in the Madrid suburb of Alcobendas. The foundation's buildings contain a basketball library, a publishing house, and the **Fédération Internationale de Basketball (FIBA)** Hall of Fame. In 2000, he received the FIBA Order of Merit, in 2007 he was enshrined in the **Naismith Memorial Basketball Hall of Fame** in the category of coach and in 2009 he was enshrined in the FIBA Hall of Fame.

FIELD GOAL. A field goal is a successful shot from the field during the course of play in **basketball**. It is worth two points, although since the 1960s, three points have been awarded for successful shots taken beyond an arc of about 25 feet from the **backboard**. *See also* THREE-POINT FIELD GOAL.

FINAL FOUR. The Final Four is a phrase used to describe the four remaining teams in a tournament. It has usually been associated with the **National Collegiate Athletic Association (NCAA)** Championships but has also been used in others. The NCAA has trademarked the phrase and uses it extensively in promoting its tournament. *See also* MARCH MADNESS.

FLORIDA, UNIVERSITY OF. The University of Florida in Gainesville began its men's **basketball** program in 1915. Home games since 1980 have been played at the 12,000-seat Stephen C. O'Connell Center. From 1949–1980, home games were played at the 7,000-seat Florida Gym, better known as "Alligator Alley." Billy Donovan has been their most accomplished **coach**. His record from 1996–2010 was 331–139, and he led the team to the **National Collegiate Athletic Association (NCAA)** finals three times. Florida won the NCAA Championship in 2006 and 2007, one of only seven schools to win consecutive titles. Other coaches of note have been Lon Kruger, Sam McAllister, and Norm Sloan. The best players in the Gators' history include Corey Brewer, Udonis Haslem, Al Horford, David Lee, Mike Miller, Joakim Noah, Neal Walk, and Jason Williams.

FLORIDIANS, THE. *See* MIAMI FLORIDIANS.

FORT WAYNE PISTONS. *See* DETROIT PISTONS.

FORT WAYNE ZOLLNER PISTONS. *See* DETROIT PISTONS.

FORUM. The Forum is an indoor arena in Inglewood, California, a suburb of Los Angeles, completed in 1967. Until 1999, it was the home of the **Los Angeles Lakers**. Its seating capacity for **basketball** was 17,505. Called the "Fabulous Forum" when it first opened and renamed the "Great Western Forum" from 1988–2003, it was replaced as the Lakers' home in 1999 by the Staples Center. The Forum, sold to the Faithful Central Bible Church in 2000, is now primarily used for religious services.

FORWARD. The forward position is one of the five **basketball** positions. It is usually played by taller players who are the best **rebounders** and medium-range shooters. Initially forwards were described as left forward or right forward but no distinction was made in their roles. Since the mid-1970s, forwards have been classified as "**power forwards**" or "**small forwards**," with distinct differences in their functions. *See also* CENTER; GUARD.

FOUL. A personal foul can be called by the **referee** in a **basketball** game for one of several infractions, including illegal contact with an opponent. It can be assessed to either an **offensive** or **defensive** player and on rare occasions can be assessed to both players and is called a "double foul." Depending on the circumstances, a foul can result in the offended player receiving one or more **free throws**. An individual player is usually limited in the number of personal fouls he is allowed to commit in the game (six in most professional leagues and five in **Fédération Internationale de Basketball [FIBA]** and **National Collegiate Athletic Association [NCAA]** play), and exceeding the limit results in disqualification from the game.

Technical fouls can also be assessed by the referee for various acts, including unsportsmanlike conduct, and can range from abusive language toward a player or official to simply such technical infractions as too many players on the court. In FIBA play, technical fouls against a player are added to personal fouls in determining disqualification for excessive fouls. Two technical fouls on one individual will also generally result in ejection from the game. The penalty for a technical foul is one or two free throws for the opponent, with possession out-of-bounds after the free throws. In professional play, technical fouls are additionally penalized by a fine from the league. A technical foul is sometimes referred to as a "T."

FOUL SHOT. *See* FREE THROW.

FRANCE. France joined the **Fédération Internationale de Basketball (FIBA)** in 1933 and is a member in the FIBA Europe zone. The men's team competed in seven **Olympic** tournaments and won **silver medals** in 1948 and in 2000. In the FIBA **World Championships**, they competed six times, with a best finish of fourth in 1954. In the FIBA European Championships, they entered 33 of the 35 tournaments and finished second in 1949 and third five times.

The only Olympic tournament that the French women's team competed in was in 2000, where they finished in fifth place. In the FIBA World Championships, they competed seven times, with third place in 1953 being their best showing. In the European Championships, they competed 26 times and were champions in 2001 and were second in 1970, 1993, and 1999.

There have been 16 players born in France (including the French West Indies islands of Guadeloupe and Martinique) in the **National Basketball Association**, including Nicholas Batum, Rodrigue Beaubois, Boris Diaw, Mickaël Gelabale, Jérôme Moïso, Johan Petro, Mickaël Piétrus, Antoine Rigaudeau, and Ronny Turiaf. **Tony Parker**, who was born in Belgium, was raised in France. French **Women's National Basketball Association** players include Isabelle Fijalkowski, Sandrine Gruda, Edwige Lawson-Wade, Sabrina Palié, Audrey Sauret, and Laure Savasta.

FRANCIS, CLARENCE "BEVO." B. 4 September 1932, Hammondsville, Ohio. Bevo Francis attended Irondale High School in Hammondsville and Wellsville High School in Wellsville, Ohio. He was encouraged by his high school **coach**, Newt Oliver, to attend Rio (pronounced Rye-oh) Grande College, a small school in southeastern Ohio with only 37 male students. Their schedule during the 1952–1953 season included junior colleges and military teams as well as four-year colleges, and Oliver encouraged the six-foot, nine-inch Francis to score as many points as possible.

Rio Grande won all 39 games that season, and Francis averaged 50.1 points per game, including 116 points on 9 January 1953, against Ashland Junior College, bringing the school national acclaim. After the season, the **National Collegiate Athletic Association (NCAA)** ruled that only games between four-year-degree granting institutions would be recognized and that this policy was retroactive, in effect disallowing the achievements of Rio Grande, Oliver, and Francis. The following year, Rio Grande scheduled games against such larger schools as Wake Forest University and **North Carolina State University** and played in **Madison Square Garden**. Their record was 21–7, and Francis averaged 47.1 points. On 2 February 1954, he scored 113 points in a game against Hillsdale College.

After the season, Oliver, following a conflict with the Rio Grande school authorities, signed a contract with the **Harlem Globetrotters** for $50,000 for Francis to play on the Globetrotters opponents' team to be coached by Oliver. In 1956, after two years of constant travel with that team, Francis had enough and quit **basketball**. Since his college class had graduated, he was eligible for the **National Basketball Association (NBA) draft** and was selected by the Philadelphia Warriors in 1956. As he was offered only $10,000 by the Warriors, less than he had been earning, Francis decided he would not play in the NBA and instead worked in the shipping department of a pottery manufacturer and played on weekends in the Eastern Professional Basketball League. In 1961, he played briefly with the Cleveland Pipers in the new **American Basketball League** but was no longer in proper condition to play and retired. He then worked for Crucible Steel until the company folded in the mid 1980s and then at a division of the Akron Goodyear Corporation until his retirement in 1994.

FRAZIER, WALTER, JR. "WALT," "CLYDE." B. 29 March 1945, Atlanta, Georgia. Walt Frazier attended David Howard High School in Atlanta and Southern Illinois University. In 1967, he led Southern Illinois to the **National Invitation Tournament** championship. He was selected by the **New York Knickerbockers** in the first round of the 1967 **National Basketball Association (NBA) draft**, was with them from 1967–1977, and helped lead them to the NBA Championship in 1970 and 1973. In 1977, he was traded to the **Cleveland Cavaliers** and played his last three NBA seasons there.

Frazier's NBA career totals for 13 years are 825 regular-season games, 5.9 **rebounds**, 6.1 **assists**, and 18.9 points per game. His statistics were even better in 93 playoff games, when he had 7.2 rebounds, 6.4 assists, and 20.7 points per game. He was selected for seven NBA **All-Star Games** and was named the Most Valuable Player of the 1975 All-Star Game. He was named to the All-NBA First Team four times, the All-NBA Second Team twice, and the NBA All-Defensive Team seven times. He was an excellent defender and was one of the best at stealing the ball from an opponent, although **steals** were not officially recorded during the first six years of his NBA career, when he was at the height of his game.

After retiring from active play, Frazier became a broadcaster with the Knicks and was still with them in 2010. His style is distinctive. He enjoys using rhyming phrases to describe the action, for example, "dishing and swishing," "hustling and muscling," "slicing and dicing," and so forth. He was enshrined in the **Naismith Memorial Basketball Hall of Fame** in 1987 and in 1996 was named one of the 50 Greatest Players in NBA History.

FREE THROW. After a player has been **fouled**, he is generally awarded one, two, or three free throws from a line 15 feet away from the basket. Each successful free throw is worth one point. During a free throw, the game clock is stopped, and players from each team line up on either side of the free throw lane. If the final free throw is unsuccessful, players may then contest the **rebound**. A good professional player will generally succeed in 80 percent or more of his free throw attempts. The **National Basketball Association (NBA)** season record is 98.1 percent, set in 2009 by Jose Calderon of the **Toronto Raptors**, who made 151 of 154 free throw attempts. The NBA record for most consecutive successful free throw attempts is 97, set by Micheal Williams in 1993. Ted St. Martin claimed an unofficial record of 5,221 consecutive free throws on 28 April 1996, in a free throw shooting exhibition that lasted seven hours and 20 minutes.

FRIEDMAN, MAX H. "MARTY." B. 12 July 1889, New York, New York. D. 1 January 1986, New York, New York. The five-foot, seven-inch Max Friedman, a 1908 graduate of the Hebrew Technical Institute, was one of the best defensive players of his era. He began playing in 1908 with the University Settlement House amateur team called the "Busy Izzies." He went on to play professionally from 1909–1927 in most of the major leagues of the era and was on championship teams with Utica in 1914 and Albany in 1920 and 1921 in the **New York State League**. He and teammate **Barney Sedran** were often referred to as "The Heavenly **Twins**." In 1926, he was player-**coach** of the Cleveland Rosenblums and helped lead them to the **American Basketball League (ABL)** title. After retiring from active play, he continued coaching in the ABL during the 1930s and worked in the garage business with Sedran until 1958. Friedman was enshrined in the **Naismith Memorial Basketball Hall of Fame** in 1971.

FRONTCOURT. A **basketball** court is divided into two halves. The frontcourt is the half that contains the basket that the **offense** shoots at. The **backcourt** is the half that contains the opponent's **basket**. Teams change ends after the first half of the game. **Forwards** and **centers** are referred to as "frontcourt" players, since they spend most of their time in that end of the court. In the rules for girls' six-player basketball, certain players are prohibited from crossing from frontcourt to backcourt.

FULKS, JOSEPH FRANKLIN "JOE." B. 26 October 1921, Birmingham, Kentucky. D. 21 March 1976, New Eddyville, Kentucky. Joe Fulks attended Birmingham High School in Birmingham; Kuttawa High School in Kuttawa, Kentucky; and Murray State College. After playing basketball in college for two years, he enlisted in the U.S. Marines and served from 1943–1946. Signed by the Philadelphia Warriors of the **Basketball Association of America (BAA)** in 1946, he played with them until 1954. As one of the first **basketball** players to use a **jump shot**, he was known as "Jumpin' Joe." His first year in the BAA was his best year, as he led the league in scoring with a 23.2 points per game average and helped lead the Warriors to the 1947 BAA Championship. On 10 February 1949, the six-foot, five-inch **forward-center** scored 63 points in one game for a league record that was not surpassed for 10 years. His professional career totals for eight years are 489 games and a 16.4 points per game average.

After he retired, Fulks worked at the Kentucky State Penitentiary as the prison recreation director. He died after being shot during an argument. His murderer was convicted of "reckless homicide" and served less than two years of a four and one-half year sentence. Fulks was enshrined in the **Naismith Memorial Basketball Hall of Fame** in 1978. An excellent detailed account of his tragic life appears in John Christgau's 1999 book *The Origins of the Jump Shot*.

– G –

GAINES, CLARENCE EDWARD "BIG HOUSE." B. 21 May 1923, Paducah, Kentucky. D. 18 April 2005, Winston-Salem, North Carolina. Clarence Gaines attended Lincoln High School in Paducah. He played **basketball** and football in school and qualified for a football scholarship at Morgan State University. At six-foot, three-inches, and 265 pounds, he acquired the nickname "Big House" at Morgan State and was known by that name the rest of his adult life.

Gaines graduated in 1945 with a bachelor's degree in chemistry and planned to be a dentist but was hired as assistant **coach** for all sports at Winston-Salem State University. In 1946, he was given the head coach position for football and basketball along with responsibilities as teacher, team trainer, athletic director, and ticket manager. He coached both sports until 1949, when he became solely the basketball coach. In 1950, he earned a master of arts in education degree from Columbia University. He continued as basketball coach until 1993 and had a record of 828–447 when he retired at age 70. In 1967, Winston-Salem State won the **National Collegiate Athletic Association** Division II national basketball title and became the first historically black school to do so. An active member of the Boy Scouts of America for most of his life, Gaines was enshrined in the **Naismith Memorial Basketball Hall of Fame** in 1982 as a coach.

GALLATIN, HARRY J. "THE HORSE." B. 26 April 1927, Roxana, Illinois. Harry Gallatin attended Wood River High School and Roxana High School, both in Illinois, and Northeast Missouri State

Teachers College. He was selected by the **New York Knickerbockers** in the 1948 **Basketball Association of America draft**. After missing the first eight games of the season, he did not miss a game for the rest of his professional career, playing in 682 consecutive games and earning him the nickname "The Horse."

Gallatin's professional career totals for 10 years from 1948–1958 with the Knicks and **Detroit Pistons** are 682 games and a 13.0 points per game average. An excellent **rebounder**, he averaged 10 or more in each season in which the statistic was kept. He was selected for each **National Basketball Association (NBA) All-Star Game** from 1951–1957 and was voted to the All-NBA First Team in 1954 and the All-NBA Second Team in 1955.

From 1958–1962, Gallatin was **coach** of the Carbondale branch of Southern Illinois University. He coached the St. Louis Hawks of the NBA from 1962–1965 and was named Coach of the Year in 1963. From January to November 1965, he coached the Knicks. He then was basketball coach at the Edwardsville branch of Southern Illinois University until 1970. He remained there as a physical education teacher and golf coach until his retirement in 1991 and was enshrined in the **Naismith Memorial Basketball Hall of Fame** that same year. Gallatin is director of the First Clover Leaf Financial Corporation in Edwardsville, Illinois.

GARNETT, KEVIN MAURICE "THE BIG TICKET." B. 19 May 1976, Mauldin, South Carolina. Kevin Garnett attended Mauldin High School and Farragut Academy in Chicago, Illinois. He was named National High School Player of the Year in 1995 by *USA Today*. He did not go to college and was drafted in the 1995 **National Basketball Association (NBA) draft** by the **Minnesota Timberwolves**. The six-foot, 11-inch, 220-pound **forward** played for the Timberwolves from 1995–2007 and was the NBA Most Valuable Player in 2004. Traded to the **Boston Celtics** in 2007, he joined two other star players who also had never won an NBA Championship, **Paul Pierce** and **Ray Allen**. The three combined their talents to defeat the **Los Angeles Lakers** and win the league championship in 2008, and Garnett was named the NBA's Defensive Player of the Year.

In his first 15 NBA seasons, Garnett was voted to the All-NBA First Team four times, All-NBA Second Team three times, and

All-NBA Third Team twice. He has played in 1,124 regular-season games and averaged 19.8 points and 10.8 **rebounds** per game. He has been selected for 13 **All-Star Games** and was voted its Most Valuable Player in 2003. In 2000, he won a **gold medal** with the U.S. **Olympic** team.

GASOL SÁEZ, PAU. B. 6 July 1980, Barcelona, **Spain.** As with most European players, Pau Gasol's early **basketball** experience was gained with **sports clubs,** Alvirne, C. B. Cornellà, and FC Barcelona. He was drafted in the 2001 **National Basketball Association (NBA) draft** by the **Atlanta Hawks,** and his rights were traded to the **Memphis Grizzlies.** The seven-foot-tall, 240-pound **forward** played for Memphis from 2001–2008, when he was traded to the **Los Angeles Lakers.** In 2002, he was named the NBA Rookie of the Year. In 2008, 2009, and 2010, he helped the Lakers reach the NBA Championship Finals. They were defeated in 2008 but won the NBA title in 2009 and 2010.

In 2006, 2009, and 2010, Gasol was selected to play in the NBA **All-Star Game.** He has played in 649 regular-season games in his first nine NBA seasons and has averaged 18.8 points and 9.0 **rebounds** per game. With the Spanish national team, he won the **silver medal** at the 2008 **Olympic Games.** In 2006, he helped lead Spain to the **Fédération Internationale de Basketball World Championships** and was named Most Valuable Player of the tournament. He also played for Spain in the European Championships and won a **bronze medal** in 2001 and silver medals in 2003 and 2007. Gasol's brother Marc joined the NBA in 2008 and plays for the Memphis Grizzlies.

GATES, WILLIAM P. "POP." B. 30 August 1917, Decatur, Alabama. D. 1 December 1999, New York, New York. William Gates was raised in New York City and attended Benjamin Franklin High School. A member of the New York Public School Athletic League champions, he was named to the All-City First Team. He enrolled at Clark College but dropped out after one month in 1938 and began playing with the **New York Renaissance.** He was with them off and on until 1949. In his first year with the Rens, in 1939, they won the **World Professional Basketball Tournament.** During World

War II, he played for Grumman Aviation in 1941–1942 and the Washington Bears from 1942–1944, winning the World Professional Basketball Tournament with them in 1943. He returned to Grumman for the 1944–1945 season. In 1946–1947, the six-foot, two-inch **forward** was signed by the Buffalo Bisons of the **National Basketball League (NBL)** and remained with them when they relocated to Moline, Illinois, to become the Tri-Cities Blackhawks.

In 1948, when the Rens joined the NBL and played in Dayton, Gates was their player-**coach**. He won the league championship with Scranton in the **American Basketball League** in 1950. He was a player-coach with the **Harlem Globetrotters** from 1950–1955. After retiring from **basketball** in 1955, he worked for 23 years as a special officer for the Housing Authority in New York and was enshrined in the **Naismith Memorial Basketball Hall of Fame** in 1989.

GAZE, ANDREW BARRY CASSON. B. 24 July 1965, Melbourne, **Australia**. Andrew Gaze played for the Melbourne Tigers in the Australian National Basketball League (NBL) from 1984–2005. He was named the league's Rookie of the Year in 1984, was the league's top scorer in 14 of his 22 seasons, and led the Tigers to league titles twice. He was voted as the NBL's "Most Efficient Player" each season from 1990–1997. He is one of only four people to play **basketball** in five **Olympic Games**. In 2000, Gaze was the flag-bearer for Australia in the Games in his home country. The six-foot, seven-inch **guard** appeared in all eight games in each of the Olympic tournaments from 1984–2000 and is the only person to play in 40 Olympic basketball games. In Olympic career records, he is second in nine categories. Australia finished fourth in three of his five Olympic tournaments. He was also a member of the Australian national team in the 1986, 1990, 1994, and 1998 **World Championships** and 1990 and 1998 Goodwill Games.

Gaze played one season at Seton Hall University in the **United States** and helped lead them to the **National Collegiate Athletic Association (NCAA)** Championship finals, where they lost in **overtime**. He also played briefly in the **National Basketball Association (NBA)** in 1993–1994 with the **Washington Bullets** and in 1998–1999 with the **San Antonio Spurs** and was a member of the NBA champion team in 1999, although he did not play in any playoff games. In addition to playing in the NBA, he also played in **Italy**, **Spain**, and **Greece**.

Since retiring from active play, Gaze has been a television commentator and is **coach** of the Melbourne Tigers junior team. His father, Lindsay Gaze, was an Olympic basketball player, coach of the Australian Olympic team in four Olympic Games, and coach of the Melbourne Tigers for 35 years.

GEORGETOWN UNIVERSITY. Georgetown University is located in the Georgetown section of Washington, D.C. A Jesuit school, the oldest Catholic university in the nation, established in 1789, it began its men's **basketball** program in 1906. Home games since 1997 have been played at the 20,600-seat Verizon Center. Led by **coach John Thompson**, the most outstanding coach in the school's history (596–239 from 1972–1999), the Hoyas won the **National Collegiate Athletic Association (NCAA)** Championship in 1984 and finished second in 1982 and 1985. They were also NCAA runners-up in 1943. Thompson, a six-foot, 10-inch former **National Basketball Association (NBA)** player, was one of the first black coaches at a major college. His son, John Thompson III, became Georgetown coach in 2004. Georgetown alumni who played in the NBA include **Patrick Ewing**, Eric "Sleepy" Floyd, Othella Harrington, **Allen Iverson**, **Alonzo Mourning**, **Dikembe Mutombo**, Jahidi White, Jerome Williams, Reggie Williams, and David Wingate.

GERMANY. Germany joined the **Fédération Internationale de Basketball (FIBA)** in 1934 and is a member in the FIBA Europe zone. The men's team competed in five **Olympic** tournaments, in 1972 and 1984 as West Germany, and in 1936, 1992, and 2008 as a united country. Their best finish was seventh place in 1992. In the FIBA **World Championships**, they competed five times and won the **bronze medal** in 2002. In the FIBA European Championships, they entered 19 times, won the tournament in 1993, and were second in 2005. The women's team has not yet competed in the Olympic tournament. In the FIBA World Championships, they entered only in 1998 and finished in 11th place. In the FIBA European Championships, they entered 14 times, and third place in 1997 was their best effort.

There have been four **National Basketball Association (NBA)** players from Germany, including Uwe Blab, **Dirk Nowitzki**, Detlef Schrempf, and Chris Welp. There also have been several Americans born in Germany but raised in the **United States** who played in the NBA, for example, Shawn Bradley. German-born Marlies Askamp, Linda Frohlich, LaToya Pringle, and Martina Weber have played in the **Women's National Basketball Association.**

GERVIN, GEORGE "THE ICEMAN." B. 27 April 1952, Detroit, Michigan. George Gervin attended Martin Luther King High School in Detroit and Eastern Michigan University. He was signed by the **Virginia Squires** of the **American Basketball Association (ABA)** in 1972 as an undergraduate. The six-foot, seven-inch **guard-forward** played with them until 1974, when he went to the **San Antonio Spurs.** He remained with the Spurs in the ABA and continued with them in the **National Basketball Association (NBA)** until 1985. He played his final NBA season with the **Chicago Bulls** in 1985–1986. In 1986–1987, he played in **Italy,** and in 1989–1990, in **Spain.**

Nicknamed "The Iceman" for his cool demeanor, Gervin's favorite shot was the "finger roll," in which he extended his arm and let the ball roll off his fingertips into the **basket.** He was selected for three ABA **All-Star Games** and the All-ABA Second Team in 1975 and 1976. He played in every NBA All-Star Game from 1977–1985 and was its Most Valuable Player in 1980. He was named to the All-NBA First Team each year from 1978–1982, was selected for the All-NBA Second Team in 1977 and 1983, and won the NBA scoring championship four times. In 1996, he was enshrined in the **Naismith Memorial Basketball Hall of Fame** and was named one of the 50 Greatest Players in NBA History. He was assistant **coach** and community relations representative for the Spurs from 1992–2000. Gervin's brother, Derrick, also played in the NBA.

GILMORE, ARTIS. B. 21 September 1949, Chipley, Florida. Artis Gilmore attended Roulhac High School in Chipley; Carver High School in Dothan, Alabama; Gardner-Webb Junior College; and Jacksonville University. He led Jacksonville to the 1970 **National Collegiate Athletic Association (NCAA)** National Championship game, where they were defeated by the **University of California,**

Los Angeles. In 1971, he was selected by the **Kentucky Colonels** in the **American Basketball Association (ABA) draft** and the **Chicago Bulls** in the **National Basketball Association (NBA)** draft. Nicknamed "The A-Train," the seven-foot, two-inch **center** played in the ABA from 1971–1976 for the Colonels and in the NBA from 1976–1988 for the Bulls, **San Antonio Spurs**, and **Boston Celtics.** In 1988–1989, he played in **Italy.** He won the 1975 ABA Championship with Kentucky and was named the Playoffs Most Valuable Player.

Gilmore's combined professional totals for 17 seasons are 1,329 games, 12.3 **rebounds**, and 18.8 points per game. He was ABA Rookie of the Year and Most Valuable Player in 1972 and was voted to the All-ABA First Team in each of five seasons in the league and to the ABA All-Defensive Team from 1973–1976. He set the ABA single-game record with 40 rebounds and also holds the ABA season record for **blocks.** He played in the ABA **All-Star Game** in each one of his five seasons and was named its Most Valuable Player in 1974. In the NBA, he was voted to the All-Defensive Second Team in 1978, played in six All-Star Games, and holds the record for career **field goal** percentage, at .599. Gilmore is arguably the greatest modern-day American player not in the **Naismith Memorial Basketball Hall of Fame.**

GINÓBILI, EMANUEL DAVID "MANU." B. 28 July 1977, Bahía Blanca, **Argentina.** Emanuel Ginóbili played with Estudiantes in Argentina and Reggio Calabria in **Italy** before being drafted by the **San Antonio Spurs** in the 1999 **National Basketball Association (NBA) draft**. He remained in Italy for the next three years before joining the Spurs for the 2002–2003 season. With Kinder Bologna, he won the 2001 Italian league championship, the 2001 and 2002 Italian Cups, and the 2001 Euroleague championship. The six-foot, six-inch **left-handed guard-forward** has played for the Spurs from 2003–2010. With the Spurs, he raised his scoring average from 7.6 points per game in his first year to 19.5 in 2008 and helped lead them to NBA Championships in 2003, 2005, and 2007. He was selected to play in the 2005 NBA **All-Star Game.** In 2008, he was named NBA **Sixth Man** of the Year.

Ginóbili helped lead Argentina to the **silver medal** at the 2002 **World Championships** and the **gold medal** at the 2004 **Olympic**

Games and was named Most Valuable Player of the 2004 Olympic Games. In the 2008 Beijing Olympic Games, he was injured in the semifinal game with the **United States**, which Argentina lost, but his teammates rallied to win the **bronze medal** despite his absence.

GLICKMAN, MARTIN IRVING "MARTY." B. 14 August 1917, Bronx, New York. D. 3 January 2001, New York, New York. Marty Glickman attended James Madison High School in Brooklyn, New York, and **Syracuse University**, where he played football and ran track. Selected for the 1936 U.S. **Olympic** track team, he was one of only a few American Jewish athletes there. Scheduled to compete on the 400-meter relay team, he and Sam Stoller, both Jewish athletes, were removed from the relay team a few days prior to the event. Glickman has claimed that the move was anti-Semitic, since the chairman of the U.S. Olympic Committee, Avery Brundage, was a supporter of the Hitler regime. In 1998, the president of the **U.S.** Olympic Committee, citing "great evidence of anti-Semitism," presented Glickman and Stoller with a special plaque "in lieu of **gold medals** they didn't win."

Glickman began a sportscasting career in 1937 and for more than 50 years was one of the top sportscasters in the United States, covering **basketball**, football, ice hockey, track and field, and harness racing. He began working at a time when only one announcer covered the games. He was the voice of the **New York Knickerbockers** for most of their first 20 years and helped train his successor, Marv Albert, in that role. In 1991, he was given the Curt Gowdy Media Award from the **Naismith Memorial Basketball Hall of Fame.**

GOALTENDING. *See* BLOCKED SHOT.

GOLA, THOMAS JOSEPH "TOM." B. 13 January 1933, Philadelphia, Pennsylvania. Tom Gola attended La Salle High School in Philadelphia and **La Salle University**. As a college freshman, he led La Salle to the **National Invitation Tournament** title in 1952. They won the **National Collegiate Athletic Association (NCAA)** National Championship in 1954, and he was named Most Outstanding Player. In 1955, they were defeated in the National Championship game by the **University of San Francisco**. He averaged 20.9

points and 18.7 **rebounds** per game in four years of varsity play and was the first collegiate player with more than 2,000 points and 2,000 rebounds. Six-foot, six-inch Gola played all positions and was nicknamed "Mr. All-Around" by his college **coach.**

Chosen by the **Philadelphia Warriors** in the 1955 **National Basketball Association (NBA) draft** as a **territorial** selection, Gola played until 1966 for the Warriors and **New York Knickerbockers** and was a member of the NBA champions in 1956. His NBA career totals for 10 years are 698 games and an 11.3 points per game average. He was selected for five NBA **All-Star Games** and the 1958 All-NBA Second Team. From 1968–1970, he coached La Salle University.

In 1966, Gola was elected to the Pennsylvania State Legislature, was reelected in 1968, and in 1970 was elected as Philadelphia comptroller. In 1983, he ran for mayor of Philadelphia but was defeated in the primary election. He was enshrined in the **Naismith Memorial Basketball Hall of Fame** in 1976.

GOLD MEDAL. In **Fédération Internationale de Basketball** competition, for example, the **Olympic Games** and **World Championships**, the first place team is awarded gold medals. In some tournaments, the semifinal winners play a match to determine the gold medal winner. In other tournaments, a round-robin tournament is played, with the team with the best record receiving the gold medal. *See also* BRONZE MEDAL; SILVER MEDAL.

GOLDEN STATE WARRIORS. The Golden State Warriors are a team in the **National Basketball Association (NBA)**. They originally played as the Philadelphia Warriors and were a charter member of the **Basketball Association of America (BAA)** in 1946. In 1962, they moved to San Francisco and in 1971 were renamed the Golden State Warriors.

Philadelphia Warriors. Home games were played at the 7,777-seat Philadelphia Arena and the 9,200-seat Convention Hall. Among their most notable players were **Paul Arizin**, Ernie Beck, **Wilt Chamberlain**, Walt "Buddy" Davis, **Joe Fulks**, Jack George, **Tom Gola**, Joe Graboski, **Neil Johnston, Guy Rodgers**, Woody Sauldsberry, and George Senesky. The 1947 Warriors were BAA champions. In 1956, they were NBA champions. On 23 May 1962, the franchise was moved to San Francisco.

San Francisco Warriors. From 1962–1971, home games were played at four different venues in the San Francisco area. Among their most notable players then were **Al Attles**, **Rick Barry**, Wilt Chamberlain, Joe Ellis, Rudy LaRusso, Clyde Lee, Tom Meschery, Jeff Mullins, Guy Rodgers, **Nate Thurmond**, and Ron "Fritz" Williams. Their best seasons were 1963–1964 and 1966–1967, when they lost in the NBA Finals. In 1971, the team changed its name to the Golden State Warriors.

Golden State Warriors. Home games are played at the Oakland-Alameda County Coliseum (recently renamed the Oracle Arena) in Oakland, California. Among their most notable players were Rick Barry, Joe Barry Carroll, Eric "Sleepy" Floyd, Adonal Foyle, Tim Hardaway, Antawn Jamison, **Chris Mullin**, Sonny Parker, Clifford Ray, Jason Richardson, Mitch Richmond, Purvis Short, Larry Smith, Phil Smith, and Latrell Sprewell. Their best season was 1974–1975, when they won the NBA Championship. Their overall record for their 64 years in the league through the 2009–2010 season is 2,293–2,705.

GOTTLIEB, EDWARD "EDDIE," "THE MOGUL." B. 15 September 1898, Kiev, Ukraine. D. 7 December 1979, Philadelphia, Pennsylvania. Eddie Gottlieb emigrated with his family to the **United States** when he was only a few years old. He attended South Philadelphia High School and the Philadelphia School of Pedagogy. He organized the **Philadelphia SPHAs** in 1918, played with them until 1925, and was the team owner and **coach** from 1925–1946. The SPHAs won 11 league championships in the Eastern Basketball League and **American Basketball League**. He was the top booking agent and sports promoter in the Philadelphia area, promoting baseball, **basketball**, football, and professional wrestling, and was schedule maker and booking agent for the Negro National Baseball League.

One of the founders of the **Basketball Association of America (BAA)** in 1946, Gottlieb coached the Philadelphia Warriors from 1946–1955; led them to the league's first title in 1947; and was team owner and general manager, although not the coach, when they again won the **National Basketball Association (NBA)** Championship in 1956. From 1952–1962, he was the owner of the Warriors. He also helped promote the **Harlem Globetrotters'** international tours. He was chairman of the NBA Rules Committee for 25 years, and for most of the BAA/NBA's first 25 years he was the league's schedule maker. Gottlieb was enshrined in the **Naismith Memorial Basketball Hall of Fame** in 1972 as a contributor. The NBA Rookie of the Year award has been renamed the Eddie Gottlieb Trophy in his honor.

GREECE. Greece joined the **Fédération Internationale de Basketball (FIBA)** in 1932 and is a member in the FIBA Europe zone. The men's team competed in three **Olympic** tournaments—in 1996, 2004, and 2008—and finished in fifth place each time. In the FIBA **World Championships,** they competed six times and won the **silver medal** in 2006. In the FIBA European Championships, they entered 22 times and won the tournament in 1987 and 2005, were second in 1989, and placed third in 1949. As host nation, the women's team competed in the 2004 Olympic Games and finished in seventh place. They have yet to compete in the FIBA World Championships. In the FIBA European Championships, they entered four times, with ninth place in 2003 being their best showing.

There have been four players born in Greece who played in the **National Basketball Association (NBA),** including Antonis Fotsis, Andreas Glyniadakis, Efthimios Rentzias, and Vassilious Spanoulis. Iakovos "Jake" Tsakalidis, born in the Georgian Soviet Republic but raised in Greece, also played in the NBA. Anastasia Kostaki and Evanthia Maltsi both competed in the 2004 Olympic Games and played in the **Women's National Basketball Association.** Among the best players in Greece who were drafted but did not play in the NBA were Panagiotis Giannakis; Panagiotis Fasoulas; Sofoklis Schortsanitis, a 375-pound Greek born in the Cameroon; Fanis Christodoulou; and Nick Galis.

GREER, HAROLD EVERETT "HAL." B. 26 June 1936, Huntington, West Virginia. Hal Greer attended Frederick Douglass High School in Huntington and Marshall University. At Marshall, he was the first black to play **basketball** for a major college team in West Virginia. He was selected by the Syracuse Nationals in the 1958

National Basketball Association (NBA) draft and played from 1958–1973 for the Nationals franchise that moved to Philadelphia in 1963 and became the **Philadelphia 76ers**. The six-foot, two-inch **guard** is one of only five players to play 15 or more NBA seasons with just one franchise. He had the unorthodox method of shooting **jump shots** for **free throws**, one of very few professionals to use that method.

Greer's NBA career totals for 15 years are 1,122 regular-season games and a 19.2 points per game average. At the time of his retirement, Greer had played in more NBA games than anyone else, but the record has since been broken. He was selected for all 10 NBA **All-Star Games** from 1961–1970, was named the All-Star Game Most Valuable Player in 1968, and was nominated for the All-NBA Second Team each year from 1963–1969. In 1967, he was a member of the NBA Championship team. He was enshrined in the **Naismith Memorial Basketball Hall of Fame** in 1982 and in 1996 was named one of the 50 Greatest Players in NBA History.

GROZA, ALEX JOHN. B. 7 October 1926, Martins Ferry, Ohio. D. 21 January 1995, San Diego, California. Alex Groza attended Martins Ferry High School and the **University of Kentucky**, where he was a member of the 1948 **National Collegiate Athletic Association (NCAA)** champion team. He won a **gold medal** with the 1948 U.S. **Olympic basketball** team. The six-foot, seven-inch **center-forward** also helped Kentucky win the 1949 NCAA Championship. He, along with several other Kentucky teammates, joined the **National Basketball Association (NBA)** as player-owners of the **Indianapolis Olympians** in 1949. In 1951, he appeared in the NBA's first **All-Star Game**.

After playing in the NBA for two seasons, it was discovered that Groza was one of several players accused of shaving points while in college and was banned from the NBA for life by Commissioner **Maurice Podoloff**. In his two seasons in the NBA, he averaged 22.5 points per game and was second to **George Mikan** in scoring in each season. Groza later served as business manager for the **Kentucky Colonels** of the **American Basketball Association (ABA)** and general manager of the San Diego Conquistadors in the ABA. His brother, Lou, was a professional football star for 21 years and is a member of the Pro Football Hall of Fame. In a statistical oddity, both brothers led their leagues in **field goal** percentage in 1950, although basketball and football field goals are completely different.

GUARD. The guard position is one of the five **basketball** positions. It is usually played by the shorter, quicker players on the team and traditionally the ones with the best outside shots. Initially, guards were described as left guard or right guard, but no distinction was made in their roles. Since the 1970s, guards have been designated as "**point guards**" and "**shooting guards**," with distinct differences in their duties. *See also* CENTER; FORWARD.

– H –

HAGAN, CLIFFORD OLDHAM "CLIFF." B. 9 December 1931, Owensboro, Kentucky. Cliff Hagan attended Owensboro High School and the **University of Kentucky** and was a member of the 1951 **National Collegiate Athletic Association (NCAA)** National Championship team as a sophomore. Selected by the **Boston Celtics** in the 1953 **National Basketball Association (NBA) draft**, he remained in college until after the 1953–1954 season. He spent 1954–1956 in military service and played service basketball for Andrews Air Force Base. On 29 April 1956, his **draft rights** were traded to the St. Louis Hawks with **Ed Macauley** for the draft rights to **Bill Russell**.

Hagan played in the NBA from 1956–1966 for the Hawks. His NBA career totals for 10 years are 745 regular-season games and an 18.0 points and 6.9 **rebounds** per game average. The six-foot, four-inch **forward** was selected for five NBA **All-Star Games** and was named to the All-NBA Second Team in 1958 and 1959. With the Hawks, in 1958, he was a member of the NBA Championship team. In 1967, he became player-**coach** of the Dallas Chaparrals of the **American Basketball Association (ABA)**. In three years in the ABA, he played in 94 games, averaged 15.1 points and 4.7 rebounds per game, and played in the 1968 ABA All-Star Game. In 1972, Hagan became assistant athletic director at the University of Kentucky, was promoted to athletic director in 1975, and held that position until 1988. He was enshrined in the **Naismith Memorial Basketball Hall of Fame** in 1978.

HAIXIA, ZHENG. *See* ZHENG, HAIXIA.

HALFTIME. Halftime is the intermission between the first and second halves of a **basketball** game. The length of the intermission varies but is generally between 10 and 20 **minutes**. In **Fédération Internationale de Basketball, National Basketball Association**, and **National Collegiate Athletic Association** rules, the length is officially 15 minutes. Examples of halftime entertainment include dance teams, kids' abbreviated basketball games, vaudeville acts, fan participation events, and ceremonies honoring former players. At times there is no scheduled entertainment. Such touring teams as the **Harlem Globetrotters** often featured elaborate entertainment during halftime and would often extend the duration for the added entertainment.

HANNUM, ALEXANDER MURRAY "ALEX." B. 19 July 1923, Los Angeles, California. D. 18 January 2002, San Diego, California. Alex Hannum attended Hamilton High School in Los Angeles and the **University of Southern California**, with his college years interrupted by a stint in the U.S. Army from 1943–1945. In 1945–1946, he played **Amateur Athletic Union (AAU) basketball** for the Los Angeles Shamrocks. In 1948, although drafted by the **Indianapolis Jets** of the **Basketball Association of America (BAA)**, he played with the **Oshkosh All-Stars** of the **National Basketball League (NBL)**. From 1949–1957, he was in the **National Basketball Association (NBA)** with the Syracuse Nationals, **Baltimore Bullets**, Rochester Royals, Fort Wayne Pistons, and the Hawks, both in Milwaukee and St. Louis. In nine years of play in the NBL and NBA, the six-foot, seven-inch **forward-center** appeared in 578 regular-season games and averaged 6.0 points per game.

A prematurely bald, hard-nosed **rebounder** often called "Sarge," in reference to his military rank, Hannum was player-**coach** of the St. Louis Hawks and led them to the seventh game of the 1957 NBA Finals, where they lost in double **overtime** to the **Boston Celtics**. In 1958, he coached the Hawks from the bench and defeated the

Celtics to win the NBA Championship. Following the season, he resigned as coach to spend time with his construction business. Over the next decade, he coached in the **National Industrial Basketball League**, NBA, and **American Basketball Association (ABA)** and won championships in the AAU with the 1959 Wichita Vickers, in the NBA with the 1967 **Philadelphia 76ers**, and in the ABA with the 1969 Oakland Oaks. He also coached Syracuse in the NBA and the **Denver Nuggets** in the ABA.

Hannum was NBA Coach of the Year in 1964 and ABA Coach of the Year in 1969. After coaching at Denver, he returned to his construction business. He was enshrined in the **Naismith Memorial Basketball Hall of Fame** in 1998 as a coach.

HARLEM GLOBETROTTERS. The Harlem Globetrotters began playing in 1927 and are still going strong today. For years, their "official" history was that **Abe Saperstein** organized an all-black team known as the Savoy Big Five that played its first game in Hinckley, Illinois, on 7 January 1927. He began to bill the team as Saperstein's New York Globe Trotters, which eventually became simply the Harlem Globetrotters. In 2005, historian Ben Green, doing extensive research for his book entitled *Spinning the Globe*, showed that this "official history" was a myth. The team, however, by 1929, was established and playing for Saperstein as the Harlem Globe Trotters.

Among the team's earliest members were Albert "Runt" Pullins, Toots Wright, Fat Long, Kid Oliver, Inman Jackson, and Andy Washington. They traveled extensively throughout the Midwest, and when the local opposition proved to be ineffective the Globetrotters gradually added some comedy and fancy ball handling to maintain the crowd's interest. By 1939, they had been established as one of the better independent professional **basketball** teams and were one of 11 teams invited to play in the first **World Professional Basketball Tournament**. They advanced to the semifinal round, where they were defeated by another all-black team, the **New York Renaissance**. In 1940, they were again invited to the World Professional Basketball Tournament, and this time they defeated the Rens in the quarterfinals and went on to win the tournament.

In 1942, the Trotters signed Negro League baseball player **Reece "Goose" Tatum**. He had a flair for showmanship and soon enlarged the comedy aspect of Trotters' games. In 1947, **Marques Haynes**, a **dribbling** specialist, was added. By the late 1940s, the Trotters had established themselves as the top independent barnstorming basketball team. In February 1948, they challenged the leading team in the **National Basketball League**, the Minneapolis Lakers, and defeated them on a last-second shot by Ermer Robinson.

During the early 1950s, the Trotters often performed as part of a **National Basketball Association (NBA)** doubleheader, and their games usually attracted the largest attendance of the season for NBA teams. In 1950, as the NBA began to integrate, Saperstein sold the contract of one of his stars, **Nat "Sweetwater" Clifton**, to the **New York Knickerbockers**. Also in 1950, the Globetrotters made their first international tour, visiting 14 countries in Europe and North Africa. They were enthusiastically received and, in 1951, in Berlin, **Germany**, they set the all-time attendance record for a basketball game, when 75,000 people saw them play in a game at the **Olympic Stadium**.

They were the subject of two Hollywood films in the early 1950s and were at that time probably at their highest level of popularity. In 1953, Trotter costar Marques Haynes left the team following a salary dispute, and the team's star, Goose Tatum, left in 1955. Tatum was replaced by **Meadowlark Lemon** and Haynes by Fred "Curly" Neal. The NBA began employing more and more of the best black basketball players, and the Globetrotters, although still successful, began to rely mainly on comedy. By the 1960s, they were strictly a form of comedic entertainment, with opponents led by **Louis "Red" Klotz**, and billed as the **Washington Generals**, Boston Shamrocks, or Rhode Island Reds.

The Trotters continued to be extremely popular and are still a major attraction in the 21st century. One feature associated with the Trotters since the early 1950s has been the warm-up circle prior to the game in which the starting five players stand around the midcourt circle and pass the ball to one another, demonstrating their ball handling ability. This is done to a 1940s recording of *Sweet Georgia Brown* whistled by Freeman Davis (aka Brother Bones). Included among the Trotters "Legends" are Hubert "Geese" Ausbie, **Wilt Chamberlain**, "Sweet Lou" Dunbar, Bob "Showboat" Hall, Charles "Tex" Harrison, **Connie Hawkins**, Jackie Jackson, Bobby Joe Mason, and James "Twiggy" Sanders, in addition to the aforementioned players. As a team, they were enshrined in the **Naismith Memorial Basketball Hall of Fame** in 2002.

HARRIS-STEWART, LUSIA MAE "LUCY." B. 10 February 1955, Minter City, Mississippi. Lusia Harris-Stewart attended Amanda Elzy High School in Greenwood, Mississippi, and Delta State University. She led Delta State to the **Association for Intercollegiate Athletics for Women (AIAW)** National Championship from 1975–1977 and was named the tournament's most valuable player each year. She also played for the **United States** in the 1975 **World Championships** and Pan American Games and was the leading scorer on the 1976 U.S. **Olympic basketball** team. The six-foot, two-inch **forward** had the distinction of scoring the first points in women's Olympic basketball competition on 19 July 1976, in the match with **Japan**.

Harris-Stewart was drafted by the men's **National Basketball Association (NBA)** New Orleans Jazz team in the 1977 **draft**, although the selection was disallowed by the NBA's commissioner. She played one season in the **Women's Professional Basketball League** in 1979–1980 for Houston. She returned to Delta State and earned a master's degree in education in 1984, **coached** two years at Texas Southern University, and was admissions counselor and assistant coach at Delta State. She taught special education at Greenwood High School and was their assistant basketball coach. In 1992, she became the first female basketball player enshrined in the **Naismith Memorial Basketball Hall of Fame** and in 1999 was a member of the inaugural class of the **Women's Basketball Hall of Fame**.

HAVLICEK, JOHN J. "HONDO." B. 8 April 1940, Martins Ferry, Ohio. John Havlicek attended Bridgeport High School in Bridgeport, Ohio, and **Ohio State University**. In college, he was a member of the **National Collegiate Athletic Association (NCAA)** 1960 national champions and 1961 and 1962 NCAA national runners-up. The six-foot, five-inch **forward-guard** was selected by the **Boston Celtics** in the 1962 **National Basketball Association (NBA) draft** and by the Cleveland Browns of the National Football League (NFL) in the NFL draft. After going to training camp with the Browns, he decided to concentrate on basketball. Nicknamed "Hondo" after the

John Wayne character, Havlicek played in the NBA from 1962–1978 for the Celtics.

Havlicek's NBA career totals for 16 years are 1,270 games and a 20.8 points per game average. He was selected for 13 NBA **All-Star Games** and was named to the All-NBA First Team four times, the All-NBA Second Team seven times, the NBA All-Defensive First Team five times, and the NBA All-Defensive Second Team three times. He was a member of eight NBA Championship teams and was the Finals Most Valuable Player in 1974. Named to the NBA 35th Anniversary Team in 1980, he was enshrined in the **Naismith Memorial Basketball Hall of Fame** in 1984 and was named one of the 50 Greatest Players in NBA History in 1996. The owner of three Wendy's restaurants, Havlicek also does public relations work.

HAWKINS, CORNELIUS L. "CONNIE." B. 17 July 1942, Brooklyn, New York. Connie Hawkins attended Boys High School in Brooklyn and led them to the New York City Public School Athletic League title in 1959 and 1960. The six-foot, eight-inch **forward-center** has huge hands and would often palm the ball as he played the **pivot** position. He enrolled at the University of Iowa but was expelled from school for alleged association with gamblers before he played any college **basketball**. He was blacklisted by the **National Basketball Association (NBA)**, even though he was never officially charged with any wrongdoing.

Hawkins played with the Pittsburgh Rens of the **American Basketball League (ABL)** in 1961 until the league's demise on 31 December 1962. In one and one-half seasons in the ABL, he played 94 games, averaged 27.6 points and 13.2 **rebounds** per game, led the league in scoring, and was the league's Most Valuable Player. He then played with the **Harlem Globetrotters** until the **American Basketball Association (ABA)** was formed in 1967. While with the Globetrotters, he filed suit against the NBA for not allowing him to compete in their league. In the ABA, in 1967–1968, he played for the Pittsburgh Pipers, was the league's Most Valuable Player, led the league in scoring, led his team to the league title, and won the playoffs Most Valuable Player award. In 1969, the NBA settled the suit, and Hawkins was signed by the **Phoenix Suns**. He played with the Suns, **Los Angeles Lakers**, and **Atlanta Hawks** from 1969–1976.

Hawkins's NBA career totals for seven seasons were 499 games and 16.5 points and 8.0 rebounds per game. He played in four NBA **All-Star Games** and was selected to the 1970 All-NBA First Team. His ABA career totals were 117 games in two seasons and 28.2 points and 12.6 rebounds per game averages. He was named to the All-ABA Team in both of his ABA seasons and played in the 1968 ABA All-Star Game. He was enshrined in the **Naismith Memorial Basketball Hall of Fame** in 1992 and has worked as a community relations representative for the Suns.

HAYES, ELVIN ERNEST "THE BIG E." B. 17 November 1945, Rayville, Louisiana. Elvin Hayes attended Eula D. Britton High School in Rayville and led them to the state championship in 1964. He later enrolled at the **University of Houston**, where he and Don Chaney were the first two black players. The school reached the **National Collegiate Athletic Association (NCAA) Final Four** in 1967 and 1968 but lost in the semifinal round each year. In college, he averaged 31.0 points and 17.2 **rebounds** per game for three varsity seasons.

The six-foot, nine-inch **forward**, known as "The Big E," was selected by the San Diego Rockets in the 1968 **National Basketball Association (NBA) draft** as the first overall selection and played from 1968–1984 for the Rockets and Washington Bullets franchises. Hayes's NBA regular-season career totals for 16 years are 1,303 games, exactly 50,000 **minutes** played, and a 21.0 points and 12.5 rebounds per game average. Selected for the NBA **All-Star Game** each year from 1969–1980, he was named to the All-NBA First team and All-NBA Second Team three times each and was twice named to the NBA All-Defensive Second Team. With the Bullets, he was a member of the NBA Championship team in 1978.

After retiring from active play, Hayes returned to the University of Houston to complete his undergraduate degree requirements. He owned a car dealership in Texas and in 2007 graduated from the Law Enforcement Academy in Houston and became a Liberty County, Texas, sheriff's deputy, fulfilling a childhood dream. He was enshrined in the **Naismith Memorial Basketball Hall of Fame** in 1990. In 1996, he was named one of the 50 Greatest Players in NBA History.

HAYNES, MARQUES OREOLE. B. 3 October 1926, Sand Springs, Oklahoma. Marques Haynes attended Booker T. Washington High School in Sand Springs and led them to the state (colored) championship as a senior. He later attended Langston University and led their **basketball** team to a record of 112–3. After Langston had defeated the **Harlem Globetrotters** in an exhibition game, he was signed by the Trotters and became their **dribbling** specialist. When the other players needed a rest, he would start dribbling the ball in circles around the opposition.

During Haynes's time with the Globetrotters, they were at the height of their popularity, and he and **Reece "Goose" Tatum** were their two stars. In November 1953, his contract was sold to the Philadelphia Warriors of the **National Basketball Association (NBA)**, but Haynes turned down the chance to play in the NBA and formed his own barnstorming team, the Harlem Magicians. He rejected a second NBA offer in 1955 from the Minneapolis Lakers. In 1972, he sold the Magicians to the Globetrotter organization and went into the clothing business, establishing a black-owned company called Biella. From 1972 until his retirement in 1992, he played for the Globetrotters, **Meadowlark Lemon**'s Bucketeers, and the Magicians. His dribbling antics became one of the Trotters' best routines, and after Haynes left them, the Trotters always had a player fulfill that role. He was enshrined in the **Naismith Memorial Basketball Hall of Fame** in 1998.

HAYWOOD, SPENCER. B. 22 April 1949, Silver City, Mississippi. Spencer Haywood attended McNair High School in Belzoni, Mississippi; Pershing High School in Detroit, Michigan; Trinidad State Junior College; and the University of Detroit. After his first year of junior college he was selected for the 1968 U.S. **Olympic basketball** team. Although just 19 years old, the six-foot, eight-inch **forward-center** led them to the **gold medal** as the team's leading scorer. He returned to school after the Olympics but before he graduated was signed by the Denver Rockets of the **American Basketball Association (ABA)** in 1969.

Haywood played one season in the ABA; led the league in scoring; and was Most Valuable Player, Rookie of the Year, and Most Valuable Player in the ABA **All-Star Game**. He set league records for minutes played, field goals, and rebounds. Following the season, he was signed by the Seattle Supersonics of the National Basketball Association (NBA), although at the time the NBA had a rule forbidding the signing of players before their college class had graduated. He successfully sued the NBA, with the case reaching the U.S. Supreme Court.

Haywood played for Seattle from 1970–1975, was selected for the NBA All-Star Game in four of those years, and was twice named to the All-NBA First Team and twice to the All-NBA Second Team. He played for the New York Knickerbockers and New Orleans Jazz from 1975–1979. In 1979, the Jazz moved to Utah. Haywood did not want to play there and was traded to the Los Angeles Lakers. While in Los Angeles, he became addicted to cocaine and was released by the Lakers in 1980. Haywood played in Italy from 1980–1981 and returned to the NBA with the Washington Bullets from 1981–1983 before retiring. He has since become involved in real estate development.

HEAD SUMMITT, PATRICIA SUE "PAT." B. 14 June 1952, Henrietta, Tennessee. Pat Head attended Cheatham County High School in Ashland City, Tennessee, and the University of Tennessee at Martin. In 1974, she became the head coach of the women's basketball program at the University of Tennessee. A five-foot, 10-inch forward, she played for the U.S. national team in the 1975 World Championships, the gold medal-winning team in the 1975 Pan American Games, and the silver medal-winning 1976 U.S. Olympic team.

Head became the first National Collegiate Athletic Association (NCAA) Division I coach (man or woman, men's teams or women's teams) to record 1,000 victories, and through 2010 her record was 1,035–196. Since 1980, Tennessee has reached the NCAA Final Four a record 18 times, with eight National Championships and five second-place finishes. In 1980, she married R. B. Summitt and was then known as Patricia Head Summitt. (They filed for divorce in 2007.) She was assistant coach of the U.S. national team for the 1980 Olympic Games, which the United States boycotted, and was head coach of the gold medal-winning 1984 U.S. Olympic team. She was also head coach for the 1979 and 1983 World Championships and the

1979 Pan American Games. She was enshrined in the **Women's Basketball Hall of Fame** in 1999 and **Naismith Memorial Basketball Hall of Fame** in 2000.

HEARN, FRANCIS DAYLE "CHICK." B. 27 November 1916, Aurora, Illinois. D. 5 August 2002, Encino, California. Chick Hearn attended Marmion Academy in Aurora and **Bradley University.** His major contribution to **basketball** was as a radio and television broadcaster. He began working **Los Angeles Lakers'** games in 1961. After missing the Lakers' game on 20 November 1965, due to being stranded by inclement weather, he did not miss another game until he underwent cardiac bypass surgery in 2001. In that span, he worked 3,338 consecutive games.

Known for his colorful phrases, Hearn has been credited as the originator of many that are in popular use today. Among them are **air ball** (a shot that misses rim and **backboard**), charity stripe (**free throw** line), garbage time (time left in the game after one team has a decided advantage), leaping leaner (off-balance **jump shot**), no harm, no foul (contact that game officials deem incidental and don't penalize), **slam dunk** (powerful dunk shot), and ticky-tack foul (slight contact penalized by the official). When he felt that the game's outcome had been decided, he would usually say, "This game's in the refrigerator, the door's closed, the lights are out, the eggs are cooling, the butter's getting hard, and the Jell-O's jigglin'."

In 1992, Hearn was the recipient of the Curt Gowdy Media Award from the **Naismith Memorial Basketball Hall of Fame** for outstanding contributions to basketball via electronic media. He was enshrined in the hall in 2003 as a contributor.

HEINSOHN, THOMAS WILLIAM "TOM." B. 26 August 1934, Jersey City, New Jersey. Tom Heinsohn attended St. Michael's High School in Union City, New Jersey, and **Holy Cross College**, where he was a member of the **National Invitation Tournament** championship team in 1954. Selected by the **Boston Celtics** in the 1956 **National Basketball Association (NBA) draft** as a **territorial** selection, he played for them from 1956–1965, winning eight championships in his nine-year professional career, losing only in 1958. His NBA career totals for nine years are 654 games and an 18.6 points and 8.8 **rebounds** per game average. He was selected for six NBA **All-Star Games** and was named to the All-NBA Second Team four times. In 1957, he won the NBA Rookie of the Year award.

Heinsohn was the president of the NBA Players Association and played an important role in obtaining a pension plan. He **coached** the Celtics from 1969 until January 1978, leading them to NBA Championships in 1974 and 1976 and being named NBA Coach of the Year in 1973. He was enshrined in the **Naismith Memorial Basketball Hall of Fame** in 1986. He has been a member of the Celtics broadcast team since 1981, often working with former Celtics teammate **Bob Cousy**. Heinsohn is also an accomplished oil painter and has had his work displayed at galleries in New York City.

HILL, GRANT HENRY. B. 5 October 1972, Dallas, Texas. Grant Hill's father, Calvin, was a running back for the Dallas Cowboys of the National Football League. His mother, Janet, was a Wellesley graduate who was a roommate of Hillary Rodham (the future wife of President Bill Clinton). Grant attended South Lake High School in Reston, Virginia, and **Duke University**, where he helped them win the **National Collegiate Athletic Association (NCAA)** National Championship in 1991 and 1992 and reach the NCAA Championship game in 1994.

Hill was chosen in the 1994 **National Basketball Association (NBA) draft** by the **Detroit Pistons** and played for them from 1994–2000. The six-foot, eight-inch **forward** was named NBA Co-Rookie of the Year in 1995. In 1996, he was a member of the **gold medal–winning** U.S. **Olympic** team. He was traded to the **Orlando Magic** in 2000 but played sparingly over the next five seasons, as severe ankle injuries and other ailments limited his play. In July 2007, he was signed by the **Phoenix Suns** as a free agent and was with them from 2007-2010. He received the 2008 NBA Sportsmanship Award. In his first 16 years in the NBA, he played in 868 regular-season games; averaged 17.8 points, 6.5 **rebounds**, and 4.5 **assists** per game; and was selected to seven NBA **All-Star Games**.

HILL, WILLIAM RANDOLPH "SONNY." B. 1937, Philadelphia, Pennsylvania. Sonny Hill graduated from Northeast High School in Philadelphia in 1955 and then spent two years at Central State

University. He played at a time when the **National Basketball Association (NBA)** had unwritten quotas of two or three blacks per team and as a result played professionally in the Eastern Professional Basketball League (EBL), where he was one of the leading scorers. His full-time regular job was as a business agent for a union local. He also was a part-time **coach** in the EBL and coached an amateur team as well.

Hill's major contribution to **basketball** has been the creation and administration of two Philadelphia basketball leagues, the Charles Baker Memorial League, a summer league for professional players, and the Sonny Hill Community Involvement League, a year-round league for amateur players. The latter league was created in 1968 as a means of combating street gangs and has grown to its present size of more than 60 teams. He also has a radio show and during the 1970s did television color commentary for the weekly NBA games. He has worked with and/or coached just about every basketball player from Philadelphia in the past 50 years, including such legends as **Wilt Chamberlain**, **Earl Monroe**, and **Guy Rodgers**. In 2008, Hill was awarded the Mannie Jackson Humanitarian of the Year Award by the **Naismith Memorial Basketball Hall of Fame**.

HOLMAN, NATHAN "NAT." B. 19 October 1896, New York, New York. D. 12 February 1995, Bronx, New York. Nat Holman attended Commerce High School in New York, playing both football and **basketball**. He enrolled at the Savage School of Physical Education, graduated in 1917, and then earned a master's degree from New York University. In 1917, he was hired as professor of physical education at the **City College of New York (CCNY)** and **coached** the basketball team until 1960. His overall record was 422–188, and he led CCNY to both the **National Collegiate Athletic Association (NCAA)** and **National Invitation Tournament** championships in 1950—the only school ever to win both tournaments in the same year.

In 1951, it was discovered that several players on the CCNY team and other college teams had accepted bribes to adjust the point spread on games. A few of the players were later convicted. The school deemphasized its sports program, and Holman resigned as coach, although at no time was he ever accused of any wrongdoing. He returned as coach for the 1955–1956 and 1959–1960 seasons.

During the 1920s, the five-foot, 11-inch Holman was one of the top professional basketball players, playing for several teams, including the **Original Celtics** from 1916–1930. The author of four books on basketball, he founded a camp for boys and girls in 1921 in upstate New York and owned it until 1964. He was enshrined in the **Naismith Memorial Basketball Hall of Fame** in 1964.

HOLY CROSS, COLLEGE OF THE. The College of the Holy Cross is a Jesuit undergraduate college founded in 1843, in Worcester, Massachusetts. It began its men's **basketball** program in 1901. Since 1975, home games have been played at the 3,600-seat Hart Recreation Center. Among the school's most successful **coaches** are Jack Donohue; Alvin "Doggie" Julian; Roy Leenig; Frank Oftring; and former player George Blaney, the longest tenured coach, who compiled a record of 357–276 from 1972–1994. The best players in the Crusaders' history were Hall of Famers **Bob Cousy** and **Tom Heinsohn**. Other players of note were Rob Feaster, Jack Foley, George Kaftan, Togo Palazzi, Dwight Pernell, Ron Perry, Chris Potter, and Ed Siudut. Holy Cross won the **National Collegiate Athletic Association (NCAA)** Championship in 1947 and the **National Invitation Tournament** in 1954.

HOLZMAN, WILLIAM "RED." B. 10 August 1920, Brooklyn, New York. D. 13 November 1998, Manhasset, New York. Red Holzman attended Franklin K. Lane High School in Brooklyn, the University of Baltimore, and **City College of New York**. Although only five-feet, 10-inches tall, he was a reliable **guard** for nine seasons of professional major league **basketball**. He played for Albany in the minor league **New York State League** in 1941–1942 and then spent three years in the U.S. Navy, where he played on the Norfolk Naval Base team.

In 1945–1946, Holzman played briefly for the New York Gothams of the **American Basketball League** and then joined the Rochester Royals of the **National Basketball League (NBL)**. He played with them in the NBL from 1945–1948, in the **Basketball Association of America** in 1948–1949, and in the **National Basketball Association (NBA)** from 1949–1953. In the 1953–1954 season, he concluded his playing career as player-**coach** of the Milwaukee Hawks but continued as nonplaying coach of the Hawks until 1957. From 1959–1967, he was the chief scout for the **New York Knickerbockers**. He coached the Knicks from 1967–1977 and 1978–1982 and led them to championships in 1970 and 1973 and the NBA Finals in 1972. In 1970, he was NBA Coach of the Year.

Holzman played in 496 regular-season games in nine seasons in three leagues and averaged 7.4 points per game. He was a member of the NBL Championship team in 1946, the NBA Championship team in 1951, and was selected to the All-NBL First Team in 1946 and 1948 and the All-NBL Second Team in 1947. He was enshrined in the **Naismith Memorial Basketball Hall of Fame** in 1986 as a coach. In 1996, Holzman was selected as one of the Top 10 Coaches in NBA History.

HOOK SHOT. A hook shot is an attempt at a **field goal** taken by a player with one hand, sweeping the ball over his head at the **basket**. It was formerly a basic shot for most **centers** using either right or left hand, but in recent times is rarely used. **George Mikan** was one of the best proponents of the shot, and more recently **Kareem Abdul-Jabbar** was also proficient at it.

See also JOHNSTON, DONALD NEIL; TATUM, REECE "GOOSE.

HOOP. The round metal circle through which the **basketball** must pass is called a hoop or rim. The game of basketball is often referred to as "hoops." A successful **field goal** is also sometimes referred to as a made hoop. There is also a basketball magazine called *Hoop*.

H-O-R-S-E. H-O-R-S-E is a **basketball** game often played in practice. The first player will attempt a shot and, if successful, his opponent must duplicate the shot. If the opponent fails, he is given the letter "H." On the next failure, he receives the letter "O" and so on. When the first player misses, his opponent then takes the initiative. The game is over when a player has missed five times and has received the five letters in the word horse. Players will often take trick shots not normally used in an actual game and can specify whether the ball hits the rim or **backboard**. Variants of the game are played regionally using different words, once such variant being the New York City game SPOT.

HOUGH, HARRY DOUGLASS. B. 1 June 1883, Trenton, New Jersey. D. 20 April 1935. Harry Hough is possibly the greatest professional **basketball** player of the 20th century not yet inducted into the **Naismith Memorial Basketball Hall of Fame.** He had a career than spanned three decades. A five-foot, eight-inch **forward-guard,** he began in 1900 with Bristol in the **National Basketball League.** In 1908, he received $300 per month to play for Pittsburgh in the **Central Basketball League (CBL)** and was the highest paid player of his era.

In the 1909–1910 season, while playing for Pittsburgh in the CBL, Hough made 963 **free throws** in 64 games, the most free throws made by an individual in any professional league ever and 123 more than the **National Basketball Association**'s individual season record. In that era, each player had a designated **foul** shooter who shot all of his team's free throws. He also played in the **Eastern Basketball League** and the **Pennsylvania State League,** concluding his career in 1922. Acknowledged by his contemporaries as one of the greats, aspiring players were billed as "the next Harry Hough." After retirement, Hough was involved in politics in New Jersey.

HOUSTON, UNIVERSITY OF. The University of Houston, located in Houston, Texas, began its men's **basketball** program in 1946. Since 1969, home games have been played at the 8,500-seat Hofheinz Pavilion. Prior to 1969, they were played at Jeppesen Fieldhouse and Delmar Fieldhouse. Guy Lewis, **coach** from 1956–1986 with a record of 592–279, was the Cougars' most notable coach.

From 1982–1984, Houston had one of the best basketball teams in the country, led by **Hakeem Olajuwon** and **Clyde Drexler** and nicknamed **"Phi Slama Jama."** They reached the **National Collegiate Athletic Association (NCAA) Final Four** in all three years but came up short each year. The best players in school history include Greg "Cadillac" Anderson, Otis Birdsong, Don Chaney, Clyde Drexler, **Elvin Hayes,** Carl Herrera, Dwight Jones, Hakeem Abdul Olajuwon, Ken Spain, and Ollie Taylor.

HOUSTON MAVERICKS. *See* SPIRITS OF ST. LOUIS.

HOUSTON ROCKETS. The Houston Rockets are a team in the **National Basketball Association (NBA)**. They joined the NBA as the San Diego Rockets, an expansion team, in 1967, and moved to Houston in 1971.

San Diego Rockets. Home games were played at the 14,000-seat San Diego International Sports Arena. Among their most notable players were Jim Barnett, John Block, **Elvin Hayes**, Toby Kimball, Don Kojis, Stu Lantz, **Pat Riley**, John Trapp, Art Williams, and Bernie Williams. Their best year was the 1968–1969 season, when they finished fourth in the Western Division and lost in the first round of the playoffs to the **Atlanta Hawks** in six games. In June 1971, Rockets' owner Robert Breitbard sold a majority interest in the team to Texas Sport Investments, and the team was moved to Houston.

Houston Rockets. In their first season in Houston, 1971–1972, home games were played at several arenas, including Astrohall, the Astrodome, and Hofheinz Pavilion. From 1972–1975, they played at the 10,000-seat Hofheinz Pavilion. In 1975, they moved to the 16,000-seat Summit (later renamed the Compaq Center) and played there until 2003, when they moved to the 18,300-seat Toyota Center. Among their most notable players have been **Charles Barkley**, Allen Leavell, **Moses Malone**, **Tracy McGrady**, **Calvin Murphy**, Mike Newlin, **Hakeem Olajuwon**, Kenny Smith, Otis Thorpe, **Rudy Tomjanovich**, and **Yao Ming**. Their best seasons were 1993–1994 and 1994–1995, when they won the NBA Championship each season, defeating the New York Knickerbockers in 1994 and the Orlando Magic in 1995. Their overall record for their 43 years in the NBA through 2010 is 1,779–1,715.

HOWARD, DWIGHT DAVID. B. 8 December 1985, Atlanta, Georgia. Dwight Howard attended high school at Southwest Atlanta Christian Academy and did not go to college. In 2004, he received the Naismith Prep Player of the Year award and was the second player to be drafted directly from high school as the first overall **National Basketball Association (NBA) draft** selection when the **Orlando Magic** chose him. The six-foot, 11-inch, 240-pound **center** played 351 consecutive games for the Magic in his first five seasons before missing a game and has averaged 17.5 points, 12.7 **rebounds**, and 2.1 **blocks** per game through the 2009–2010 season.

Howard has been selected for four NBA **All-Star Games** and won the **Slam Dunk** Championship in 2007. He has been named to the All-NBA First Team three times twice to the All-Defensive First Team and once each to the All-NBA Third Team, and All-Defensive Second Team. In 2009 and 2010, he was the NBA Defensive Player of the Year. He played with the U.S. **bronze medal**-winning national team in the 2006 **World Championships** and won a **gold medal** as a member of the 2008 team at the Beijing **Olympics**. In 2009, the Magic reached the NBA Finals but lost to the **Los Angeles Lakers**.

HOWELL, BAILEY E. B. 20 January 1937, Middleton, Tennessee. Bailey Howell attended Middleton High School and Mississippi State University. The six-foot, seven-inch **forward** was selected by the **Detroit Pistons** in the 1959 **National Basketball Association (NBA) draft** and played from 1959–1971 for the Pistons, **Baltimore Bullets, Boston Celtics**, and **Philadelphia 76ers**.

Howell's NBA career totals for 12 years are 950 regular-season games and an 18.7 points and 9.9 **rebounds** per game average. He was selected for six NBA **All-Star Games** and was named to the All-NBA Second Team in 1963. With Boston in 1968 and 1969, he was a member of the NBA Championship team. After retiring from active play, he pursued a master's degree at Mississippi State, was assistant **coach** there, and worked for the Converse Rubber Company as a salesman. Howell was enshrined in the **Naismith Memorial Basketball Hall of Fame** in 1997.

HUDSON RIVER LEAGUE (HRL). On 18 September 1909, John H. Poggi of New York City helped organize the Hudson River League (HRL). In the league's first season there were eight teams, including the Troy Trojans, Paterson Crescents, Kingston Wild Cats, Catskill Mystics, Yonkers Fourth Separates, Hudson Mixers, Poughkeepsie Bridge Jumpers, and the Newburgh Rose Buds. All were New York state teams, except for the Paterson (New Jersey) Crescents.

Troy won the league championship the first two years but then left the league to join the **New York State League (NYSL)**. At an HRL league meeting prior to the start of the 1911–1912 season, four of the eight teams withdrew in a dispute over the league presidency. Creation of the rival NYSL added to the HRL's problems. After the withdrawal of Troy, Catskill, Hudson, and the Schenectady Indians (who replaced the Poughkeepsie Bridge Jumpers during the season and assumed their league record), teams from White Plains, New York, and Trenton, New Jersey, were added to fill out the now six-team league. The Paterson team attempted to play in both leagues and represented the city of Cohoes, New York, in the NYSL. By 20 January 1912, White Plains, Trenton, and Yonkers had all dropped out, and the league was abruptly terminated. *See also* APPENDIX B (for a list of league champions).

HUNDLEY, RODNEY CLARK "ROD," "HOT ROD." B. 26 October 1934, Charleston, West Virginia. Rod Hundley attended Charleston High School and West Virginia University. In college, he averaged 24.5 points per game in three years of varsity competition but was best remembered for his **Harlem Globetrotter–like** ball handling and showmanship. He was selected by the Cincinnati Royals in the 1957 **National Basketball Association (NBA) draft** as the first overall selection but was immediately traded to the Minneapolis Lakers.

Hundley played from 1957–1963 for the Lakers, in Minneapolis from 1957–1960, and in Los Angeles from 1960–1963. He played in the NBA Finals with the Lakers three times, but they lost to the **Boston Celtics** each time. He was chosen for the NBA **All-Star Games** in 1960 and 1961. His NBA career totals for six years are 431 games and an 8.4 points per game average. After retiring from active play, he became a television broadcaster for the Lakers, **Phoenix Suns**, and **Utah Jazz**, retiring from broadcasting after the 2008–2009 season. In 2003, Hundley received the Curt Gowdy Media Award from the **Naismith Memorial Basketball Hall of Fame**.

HUNGARY. Hungary joined the **Fédération Internationale de Basketball (FIBA)** in 1935 and is a member in the FIBA Europe zone. The men's team competed in four **Olympic** tournaments, with a ninth-place finish in 1960 being their best effort. They have never competed in the FIBA **World Championships**. In the FIBA European Championships, they entered 14 times and won the tournament in 1955, finished second in 1953, and placed third in 1946. The women's team's only appearance in the Olympic Games was in 1980, when they were fourth. They competed five times in the FIBA World Championships, with fifth place in 1957 being their best effort. In the FIBA European Championships, they entered 27 times and finished second in 1950 and 1956 and placed third five times. The only Hungarian to play in the **National Basketball Association** has been Kornél Dávid, who played from 1999–2001. Dalma Ivanyi played in the **Women's National Basketball Association** from 1999–2006.

– I –

IBA, HENRY PAYNE "HANK." B. 6 August 1904, Easton, Missouri. D. 15 January 1993, Stillwater, Oklahoma. Hank Iba attended Easton High School, Westminster College, and Maryville College. He played **basketball** in both high school and college and in the **Amateur Athletic Union**. From 1926–1970, he **coached** basketball at Classen High School in Oklahoma City, Oklahoma; Maryville College; the University of Colorado; and Oklahoma A&M College. At Oklahoma A&M (renamed **Oklahoma State University** in 1957), he compiled a record of 650–317 from 1934–1970. In 1945 and 1946, Oklahoma A&M won the **National Collegiate Athletic Association (NCAA)** National Championship and in 1949 lost the NCAA Championship final game to the **University of Kentucky.**

In 1959, the **United States** Basketball Writers Association established the Henry Iba Award for the best college basketball coach in the United States. He was coach of the U.S. **Olympic** team in 1964, 1968, and 1972, and led them to the **gold medal** in 1964 and 1968. In the 1972 Olympic Games, the United States suffered a controversial loss in the final game to the **Union of Soviet Socialist Republics.** Iba was enshrined in the **Naismith Memorial Basketball Hall of Fame** in 1969 as a coach.

IMMACULATA COLLEGE. Immaculata College (Immaculata University since 2003) is located in Malvern, Pennsylvania. It was founded in 1920 as Villa Maria College by the Catholic Sisters of the Immaculate Heart of Mary as a women's school. In 2005, it became coeducational. During the early years of women's intercollegiate **basketball**, Immaculata had some of the best women's basketball teams and won the **Association for Intercollegiate Athletics for Women** national championship each year from 1972–1974. They were runners-up in 1975 and 1976.

What made their triumph so remarkable was the size of their school, at only about 1,000 students, and the fact that they had no home court. Players practiced in the basement of a convent for novice nuns. The team's cheerleaders were nuns hitting metal buckets. When the team qualified for the national championships, players had to sell toothbrushes and pencils to earn enough to travel to the tournament in Normal, Illinois. They could only afford to take eight players and flew standby.

On 22 February 1975, they defeated Queens College at **Madison Square Garden** in a rematch of their 1973 championship game. It was the first women's collegiate basketball game ever played at the Garden. It drew 11,969 spectators and was part of a college doubleheader. More than half of the spectators left before the second game, a men's game between Fairfield and Massachusetts, was played.

Their **coach, Cathy Rush**, is now a member of the **Naismith Memorial Basketball Hall of Fame**, and players Marianne Crawford Stanley and Theresa Shank Grentz are enshrined in the **Women's Basketball Hall of Fame**. In the seven seasons, from 1970–1971 to 1976–1977, that Rush coached the team, known as the Mighty Macs, their record was 149–15. Others on the team included Judy Marra Martelli, Sue Martin, Rene Muth Portland, Mary Scharff, and Maureen Stuhlman. Their story was made into a film released in 2009 originally entitled *Our Lady of Victory* but later changed to *The Mighty Macs*.

INDIANA PACERS. The Indiana Pacers are a team in the **National Basketball Association (NBA)**. The team was founded by a group of Indiana businessmen on 2 February 1967, as a charter franchise in the **American Basketball Association (ABA)**. Home games were played at the 11,000-seat Fairgrounds Coliseum in Indianapolis, Indiana. In 1974, the 17,389-seat Market Square Arena was built in Indianapolis and was the Pacers' home until 1999. In 1999, they began playing home games at the 18,345-seat Conseco Fieldhouse.

The Pacers first major acquisition was Roger Brown, a New York City high school star who was blacklisted by the NBA. In one of the Pacers' first games, on 13 November 1967, Pacer Jerry Harkness threw the **basketball** the length of the court (later measured at 88 feet) at the final buzzer. The ball went in the **basket** and gave the team the victory, 119–118, over the Dallas Chaparrals in Dallas. Harkness never made another **three-point field goal** in his two years in the league. The Pacers were one of the most successful teams in the ABA. They qualified for the playoffs each of their nine seasons, won the league championship three times, and were losing finalists in two other years. Bob "Slick" Leonard was their **coach** for the most of their ABA games. In addition to Brown, other players who starred for the Pacers in the ABA included Don Buse, **Mel Daniels**, Donnie Freeman, Darnell Hillman, Bill Keller, Billy Knight, Freddie Lewis, **George McGinnis**, and Bob Netolicky.

Following the 1975–1976 season, the ABA merged with the NBA, and the Pacers joined the NBA. Among their most notable players in the NBA have been Travis Best, Antonio Davis, Dale Davis, Vern Fleming, Jeff Foster, **Reggie Miller**, Jermaine O'Neal, Chuck Person, Jalen Rose, Detlef Schrempf, Rik Smits, and Herb Williams. Their best NBA season was 1999–2000, when they lost in the NBA Championship Finals in six games to the **Los Angeles Lakers**. Their record for nine years in the ABA was 427–317 and for 34 years in the NBA through the 2009–10 season is 1,339–1,417.

INDIANA STATE UNIVERSITY. The Indiana State University men's **basketball** program is among the oldest in the **United States**, as it began play in 1896. Located in Terre Haute and formerly known as Indiana State Teachers College, it became Indiana State University in 1965. Since 1973, home games have been played at 10,200-seat Hulman Center. **Coaches** have included Birch E. Bayh, Glenn Curtis, Duane Klueh, John Longfellow, and **John Wooden**. The Sycamores' best player, by far, was **Larry Bird**, who led them to the **National Collegiate Athletic Association (NCAA)** Championship final in 1979, where they lost to **Michigan State University**. Other memorable players for Indiana State have included Dick Atha, Duane Klueh, Michael Menser, Carl Nicks, John Sherman Williams, and Rick Williams.

In 1947, coach Wooden's basketball team won their conference title and received an invitation to the National Association of Intercollegiate Basketball (NAIB) National Tournament in Kansas City. Wooden refused the invitation since African American team member Clarence Walker was not allowed to play due to the NAIB's policy. Wooden's actions caused them to change this policy, and in 1948 Walker became the first black to play in an intercollegiate postseason basketball tournament. In the inaugural Pan American Games in 1950, in Buenos Aires, Argentina, the U.S. team comprised Coach John Longfellow, seven Indiana State players, and seven members of the **Amateur Athletic Union** champion Oakland Blue 'n Gold team.

INDIANA UNIVERSITY. Indiana University has several campuses throughout the state of Indiana. The main one is at Bloomington. The men's **basketball** program was started in 1900. Among the most notable **coaches** have been Everett Dean, **Bobby Knight**, and Branch McCracken. McCracken led them to **National Collegiate Athletic Association (NCAA)** Championships in 1940 and 1953. Knight was the coach for their 1976, 1981, and 1987 titles. In 2002, Mike Davis was the coach when they finished second in the NCAA Championships. Home games since 1971 have been played at 17,000-seat Assembly Hall. The best players for the Hoosiers have included Steve Alford, **Walt Bellamy**, Kent Benson, Quinn Buckner, Archie Dees, Bob Leonard, **George McGinnis**, Don Schlundt, **Isiah Thomas**, **twins** Dick and Tom Van Arsdale, and Mike Woodson.

INDIANAPOLIS JETS. The Indianapolis Jets were a team in the **Basketball Association of America (BAA)** in the 1948–1949 season. They had played as the Indianapolis Kautskys in the **National Basketball League (NBL)** in previous years but, as the BAA did not allow sponsors' names to be used as team nicknames, they were renamed.

Indianapolis Kautskys. The Indianapolis Kautskys were initially an independent team owned by Indianapolis grocery store owner Frank H. Kautsky. They joined the NBL in 1937 and played from 1937–1940, 1941–1942, and 1945–1947 in that league. Home games were played at the 17,000-seat Butler Fieldhouse in Indianapolis, Indiana.

Among their most notable players were Ernie Andres, Frank Baird, Leo Crowe, **Arnie Risen**, Herm Schaefer, Johnny Sines, Homer Thompson, Johnny Townsend, **John Wooden**, and Jewell Young. Their best year was 1946–1947, when they finished in second place in the Western Division but lost in the first round of the playoffs. In 1948, they joined the BAA and were renamed the Indianapolis Jets.

Indianapolis Jets. The Jets finished in last place in 1948–1949 in the Western Division, with a record of 18–42. They employed 25 different players with the best being Charlie Black, Price Brookfield, Ralph Hamilton, Walt Kirk, Ray Lumpp, John Mandic, and Carlisle "Blackie" Towery. On 5 April 1949, the nearly bankrupt team was placed into receivership and was disbanded shortly afterward.

INDIANAPOLIS KAUTSKYS. *See* INDIANAPOLIS JETS.

INDIANAPOLIS OLYMPIANS. The Indianapolis Olympians were a team in the **National Basketball Association (NBA)** from 1949–1953. They were the only player-owned franchise in NBA history and were owned by former **University of Kentucky** players **Alex Groza**, Ralph Beard, Wallace Jones, Cliff Barker, and Joe Holland. Following the 1950–1951 season, Beard and Groza were banned by the league for point shaving in college and ordered to sell their interest in the team.

Home games were played at the 17,000-seat Butler Fieldhouse. In addition to their player-owners, other notable players were Leo Barnhorst, Joe Graboski, Bruce Hale, Bob Lavoy, **Bill Tosheff**, and Paul Walther. They won the longest game in NBA history on 6 January 1951, when they defeated the Rochester Royals, 75–73, in six **overtimes** in Rochester. Their best season was 1949–1950, when they reached the second round of the playoffs. Their overall record for four seasons was 132–137. On 23 April 1953, the team was disbanded.

INGLIS, JOHN "JACK." B.1888, Troy, New York D. October 1918, Troy, New York. Jack Inglis starred on the great Troy teams in the **Hudson River League (HRL)** and **New York State League (NYSL)**. He began playing in the HRL with Hudson in 1909 and moved to Troy the following season. Troy won the HRL championship in 1911, transferred leagues, and won the NYSL championship in 1912 and 1913. A graduate of Rensselaer Polytechnic Institute, he also **coached** them from 1911–1913 while playing professional **basketball**. He led the NYSL in scoring in 1912–1913 and also in a shortened 1914–1915 season. The following two seasons he played for Carbondale in the **Pennsylvania State League** and set that league record for most **field goals** in a season. Philadelphia writer–historian William J. Scheffer called Inglis the "greatest player outside of Philadelphia." Inglis was stricken with influenza during the epidemic and died in October 1918, while on furlough from the **U.S.** Navy.

IRISH, EDWARD SIMMONS "NED." B. 6 May 1905, Lake George, New York. D. 21 January 1982, Venice, Florida. Ned Irish attended Erasmus Hall High School in Brooklyn, New York, and the University of Pennsylvania. In 1928, he began working for the New York World-Telegram as a sportswriter. He especially enjoyed college **basketball** and convinced the president of **Madison Square Garden**, General John Reed Kilpatrick, to allow him to promote college basketball at the arena. The venture proved to be extremely successful, and Irish left his job to become basketball director at the Garden. In 1946, he helped found the **Basketball Association of America** and its New York entry, the **New York Knickerbockers**. He held various administrative positions in the Knicks organization from 1946–1974 and was enshrined as a contributor in the **Naismith Memorial Basketball Hall of Fame** in 1964.

ISAACS, JOHN "THE BOY WONDER." B. 15 September 1915, Panama. D. 26 January 2009, Bronx, New York. John Isaacs moved with his family to New York City at a young age and attended Textile High School, where he led them to the City High School championship in 1935 and was selected to the City High School All-Star Team. After high school, the six-foot, one-inch **guard** signed with the **New York Rens**, played for them from 1936–1940, and in 1942–1943 and was a member of the Rens team that won the 1939 **World Professional Basketball Tournament**.

During World War II, Isaacs worked at Grumman Aircraft and played on their company team. In 1943, he was with the Washington Bears and won a second World Professional championship with them. He played in the Eastern Pennsylvania Basketball League with Hazleton, in the **New York State League** with Utica, and in the **American Basketball League** with Brooklyn and Saratoga in the late 1940s and early 1950s.

Isaacs helped form a team called the Manhattan Nationals, whose sole purpose was to fight juvenile delinquency and promote the use of local youth teams in preliminaries to professional games. After retiring from active play, he continued working with youth for the next 50 years at the Madison Avenue Boys and Girls Club in the Bronx and **coached** at the Rucker Tournament in Harlem, New York.

ISSEL, DANIEL PAUL "DAN." B. 25 October 1948, Batavia, Illinois. Dan Issel attended Batavia High School and the **University of Kentucky**. In college, he averaged 33.9 points per game in his senior year and 25.8 for his three varsity years. In 1970, he was selected by the **Kentucky Colonels** in the **American Basketball Association (ABA) draft** and by the **Detroit Pistons** in the **National Basketball Association (NBA)** draft. He played in the ABA for Kentucky from 1970–1975 and was a member of the 1975 ABA Championship team.

In September 1975, Issel was traded to the Baltimore Claws and, as the Claws were going bankrupt, was traded again in October to the **Denver Nuggets**. He played the 1975–1976 season for the Nuggets and reached the ABA finals but lost to the New York Nets. Denver entered the NBA, and Issel remained with them through 1985.

In the ABA, he was named Co-Rookie of the Year in 1971, set the season record for most points in 1972, played in the ABA **All-Star Game** in each one of his six ABA seasons, and was the Most Valuable Player in the 1972 game. He played in the 1977 NBA All-Star Game and was awarded the **J. Walter Kennedy** Citizenship Award in 1985 by the NBA. His combined NBA-ABA totals were 27,482 points in 1,218 games for an average of 22.6 points per game. There have been only six players who have scored more career points in the NBA and ABA.

After retiring from active play, he devoted his time to raising thoroughbred horses in Kentucky. He **coached** the Nuggets from 1992–1995, was named president and general manager of the Nuggets in 1998, and hired himself as coach again in 1999. He coached the team until December 2001 and then resigned permanently. He was enshrined in the **Naismith Memorial Basketball Hall of Fame** in 1993.

ITALY. Italy joined the **Fédération Internationale de Basketball (FIBA)** in 1932 and is a member in the FIBA Europe zone. The men's team competed in 11 **Olympic** tournaments and won the **silver medal** in 1980 and 2004. **Dino Meneghin**, arguably the greatest Italian **basketball** player of all time, appeared in four Olympic Games from 1972–1984 and was drafted by the **Atlanta Hawks** in the 1970 **National Basketball Association (NBA) draft**, although he chose to remain in Italy. Pierluigi Marzorati also played in four Olympic Games from 1972–1984. Ottorino Flaborea, Gianfranco Lombardi, Massimo Massini, and Paolo Vittori all played in three Olympic Games. In the FIBA **World Championships**, Italy competed eight times, with a best finish of fourth in 1970 and 1978. In the FIBA European Championships, they entered 33 times, won in 1983 and 1999, finished second four times, and placed third four times.

The women's team competed in three Olympic tournaments, 1980, 1992, and 1996. They finished last in 1980 and 1992 and eighth in 1996. In the FIBA World Championships, they competed five times, with fourth place in 1975 being their best effort. In the FIBA European Championships, they entered 27 times and won the inaugural tournament in 1938. They were second in 1995 and third in 1974.

There have been six players from Italy who played in the NBA, including Andrea Bargnani, Marco Belinelli, Hank Biasatti, Vincenzo Esposito, Danilo Gallinari, and Stefano Rusconi, but there have been many Americans who played in the Italian professional leagues, for example, Mike Bantom, Jim Brewer, Mike D'Antoni, **Darryl Dawkins**, and Mike Sylvester, among others. Italian players in the **Women's National Basketball Association** include Susanna Bonfiglio, Laura Macchi, Raffaella Masciadri, Catarina Pollini, and Francesca Zara.

IVERSON, ALLEN EZAIL. B. 7 June 1975, Hampton, Virginia. Allen Iverson attended Bethel High School in Hampton and **Georgetown University**. He left school after his sophomore season and was chosen by the **Philadelphia 76ers** as the first overall selection in the 1996 **National Basketball Association (NBA) draft**. The six-foot-tall, 165-pound **guard**, one of the smallest players in the NBA, played for the 76ers from 1996–2006 and was NBA Rookie of the Year in 1997. In 2001, after averaging a league-leading 31.1 points per game and a league-leading 2.51 steals per game and leading the 76ers to the NBA Championship Finals, he was named NBA Most Valuable Player.

In December 2006, he was traded to the **Denver Nuggets** and, in November 2008, to the **Detroit Pistons**. He did not do well in Detroit and in September 2009 was signed by the **Memphis Grizzlies** as a free agent but was released after playing in just three games. On 25 November 2009, he announced his retirement, but one week later he signed a one-year contract with the 76ers. After playing just 25 games with Philadelphia, he retired permanently.

In his 14 years in the NBA, he played in 914 regular-season games and averaged 26.7 points per game. He was selected to 11 NBA **All-Star Games** and was its Most Valuable Player in 2001 and 2005; was the NBA scoring champion in 1999, 2001, 2002, and 2005; and was named to the All-NBA First Team three times, All-NBA Second Team three times, and All-NBA Third Team once. On 12 February 2005, he scored 60 points in an NBA game, one of only 19 players to score 60 or more in an NBA game and the shortest player ever to do so. With the **bronze medal**-winning **U.S.** team in the 2004 **Olympic Games**, he was their leading scorer.

– J –

JACKSON, CHRIS. *See* ABDUL-RAUF, MAHMOUD.

JACKSON, LAUREN ELIZABETH. B. 11 May 1981, Albury, New South Wales, **Australia**. Lauren Jackson attended Murray High School in Albury and the Australian Institute of Sport. She was selected for the 2000, 2004, and 2008 Australian **Olympic** basketball teams and is arguably Australia's greatest female basketball player. In three Olympic tournaments, the six-foot, five-inch **center** appeared in all 24 games for the Australian team, averaged 18.7 points per game, and led her country's team to three **silver medals**. She holds the Olympic Games career records for most **blocks** and is in the top 10 in nearly all individual career statistics.

She played in the **Women's National Basketball Association (WNBA)** from 2001–2010 for Seattle, was the league's Most Valuable Player in 2003, 2007, and 2010 and was Defensive Player of the Year in 2007. She led the WNBA in scoring in 2003 and 2004 and in **rebounds** in 2007. In her first ten seasons in the league, she played in 295 games and averaged 19.5 points, 7.9 **rebounds**, and 1.9 blocks per game and was selected to the All-WNBA First Team seven times, the All-WNBA Second Team once, the WNBA All-Defensive First Team twice, and the WNBA All-Defensive Second Team three times. During the WNBA off-season, she has played in **Russia**, **Korea**, and Canberra in Australia.

JACKSON, PHILIP DOUGLAS "PHIL." B. 17 September 1945, Deer Lodge, Montana. Phil Jackson attended Williston High School in Williston, North Dakota, and led them to two state championships. After graduating from the University of North Dakota, he was taken by the **New York Knickerbockers** in the 1967 **National Basketball Association (NBA) draft**. He played with the Knicks from 1967–1978 and was a player and assistant **coach** with the **New Jersey Nets** from 1978–1980. His long arms helped to make him an exceptional defensive player. He was a member of the 1970 Knicks NBA Championship team but did not play that season while recovering from a back operation. He did play for the 1973 Knicks NBA Championship team. In his 13-year NBA career, he played in 807 regular-season games and had a 6.7 points per game average.

From 1982–1987, Jackson was head coach of the Albany Patroons in the **Continental Basketball Association** and led them to the league championship in 1984. In 1987, he became an assistant for the **Chicago Bulls** and in 1989 was made head coach. With the Bulls, he won six NBA Championships from 1992–1998. In 1995–1996, the Bulls set the NBA record with a record of 72–10 in the regular season and 15–3 in the playoffs, winning 87 out of 100 games. Nicknamed the "Zen Master" for his cerebral approach to the game and ability to relate to various individual personalities, he retired from coaching after the 1997–1998 season, when tensions in his relationship with Bulls' general manager Jerry Krause reached a climax.

Jackson returned as head coach of the **Los Angeles Lakers** and coached them from 1999–2006, winning three more NBA Championships. After the Lakers lost in the 2004 NBA Finals, the first time that Coach Jackson had ever lost an NBA Final, he resigned. After taking a year off, he came back in 2005 and won a record 10th NBA Championship as coach in 2009. In 2010, he extended his record to 11 NBA Championships. He was enshrined in the **Naismith Memorial Basketball Hall of Fame** in 2007 in the category of coach.

JAMES, LEBRON RAYMONE. B. 30 December 1984, Akron, Ohio. LeBron James attended St. Vincent-St. Mary's High School in Akron. He was voted "Mr. Ohio" in high school each of his last three years and was the first overall selection in the **National Basketball Association (NBA) draft,** when he was chosen by the **Cleveland Cavaliers** in 2003. The six-foot, eight-inch **forward** has played for the Cavaliers since 2003.

In 2004, he was NBA Rookie of the Year. In his first seven seasons in the NBA, he has averaged 27.8 points, 7.0 **assists**, and 7.0 **rebounds** per game. Selected to the NBA **All-Star Game** in every season except his first, he has averaged 23.7 points per game in his first six All-Star appearances. In 2007–2008, he led the league in scoring, with a 30.0 points per game average, and was the Most Valuable Player in 2009 and 2010. Since he played his first NBA game at the age of 18, he holds numerous records as the youngest NBA player to achieve various milestones. He was the youngest player to record a **triple-double**; the youngest to score 30, 40, and 50 points in one game; the youngest to record 1,000 NBA career points; and the youngest for every 1,000-point interval up to 10,000 points.

Known as "King James," he was voted to the All-NBA First Team four times, All-NBA Second Team twice, and NBA All-Defensive First Team twice. He played for the **U.S.** national team in the 2004 **Olympic Games** and the 2006 **World Championships** and was cocaptain of the 2008 U.S. Olympic team. He became a free agent at the conclusion of his contract with Cleveland on 30 June 2010. On 8 July 2010, on a one-hour television special entitled "The Decision" he announced that he would be signing a contract with the Miami Heat for the coming season joining his Olympic teammates, **Dwyane Wade** and Chris Bosh.

JAPAN. Japan joined the **Fédération Internationale de Basketball (FIBA)** in 1936 and is a member in the Asia zone. Their men's team has competed in the FIBA Asia Championships in 23 of the 24 tournaments and have won the event twice, finished in second place five times, and placed third seven times. They have competed in the **World Championships** four times, with 11th place in 1967 being their best effort. They have also appeared in six **Olympic Games.** In 1964, as host country, they had their best result, finishing in 10th position. Since the reentry of **China** into international **basketball,** Japan has not qualified for the Olympic Games.

In the FIBA Asia Championships, the Japanese women's team has won eight **silver medals** and 10 **bronze medals.** They have been entered in nearly every World Championship since 1964 and have a second place in 1975 as their best effort. In the Olympic Games, the women's team competed three times, with a fifth place finish in 1976 being their best effort. Keiko Namai led all scorers in 1976 with 102 points and a 20.6 points per game average. She also holds the all-time women's Olympic basketball record for most **free throws** in one game, with 19, and is tied for most free throw attempts in one game, with 20. Misako Satake made all eight of her **field goal** attempts in one game and is tied for the all-time women's Olympic record for that feat. Mikiko Hagiwara played two years in the **Women's National Basketball Association,** from 1997–1998, and Yuko Oga played in 2008.

The only native Japanese male basketball player to play in the **National Basketball Association (NBA)** has been Yuta Tabuse, who played in the 2005–2006 season for the **Phoenix Suns.** American-born Japanese **Wataru "Wat" Misaka** played briefly for the **New York Knickerbockers** in 1947 in the **Basketball Association of America,** the NBA's predecessor.

JEANNETTE, HARRY EDWARD "BUDDY." B. 15 September 1917, New Kensington, Pennsylvania. D. 11 March 1998, Nashua, New Hampshire. Buddy Jeannette attended New Kensington High School and Washington and Jefferson College. He began playing professional **basketball** with the Warren Penns in the **National Basketball League (NBL)** in 1938. The five-foot, 11-inch **guard** played in the NBL from 1938–1946 for Warren, the Cleveland White

Horses, the Detroit Eagles, the **Sheboygan Redskins**, and the Fort Wayne Pistons.

In 1946, he was with the **Baltimore Bullets** of the **American Basketball League (ABL)**, and he remained with them when they moved to the **Basketball Association of America (BAA)** in 1947. In that year, as player-**coach**, he led them to the championship. He was with the Bullets through the 1949–1950 season as player-coach and retired from playing in 1950 but remained on as coach. He was replaced as coach in the 1950–1951 season.

From 1952–1956, he was head coach at **Georgetown University**. He coached Baltimore in the Eastern Professional Basketball League from 1959–1961 and returned to the **National Basketball Association (NBA)** as coach of a new Baltimore Bullets franchise in 1964–1965. He served as general manager of the Bullets from 1965–1968. In 1969, he coached the Pittsburgh Pipers of the **American Basketball Association (ABA)** for 45 games.

In 329 regular-season games as a player in the NBL, ABL, BAA, and NBA, he scored 2,661 points for an average of 8.1 points per game. He played on three NBL Championship teams, in 1943 with Sheboygan and in 1944 and 1945 with Fort Wayne. He was enshrined in the **Naismith Memorial Basketball Hall of Fame** in 1994.

JOHNSON, EARVIN, JR. "MAGIC." B. 14 August 1959, Lansing, Michigan. Earvin Johnson attended Everett High School in Lansing and **Michigan State University**. As a college sophomore, he led Michigan State to the **National Collegiate Athletic Association (NCAA)** Championship in 1979 and was named the tournament's Most Outstanding Player. In the final, Michigan State defeated **Larry Bird's Indiana State University** team. This began a friendly rivalry between Johnson and Bird that culminated with the two being teammates on the **gold medal**-winning **U.S. Olympic Dream Team** in 1992.

The six-foot, nine-inch **guard** (one of the tallest players in **basketball** history to play the guard position) was drafted by the **Los Angeles Lakers** as the first overall selection in the 1979 **National Basketball Association (NBA) draft**, and he played with them from 1979–1991. On 7 November 1991, Johnson announced that he had tested positive for the Human Immunodeficiency Virus and was retiring from basketball. Even though he did not play in the 1991–1992 season, he was still voted to the NBA **All-Star Game** by the fans. He scored 25 points and was named the game's Most Valuable Player. He became **coach** of the Lakers on 23 March 1994, coached the last 16 games of the 1993–1994 season, and discovered that coaching was not for him. In June 1994, he became a minority owner of the Lakers. On 30 January 1996, he returned as an active player, although about 50 pounds heavier than when he first began in the NBA, and played in 32 games in his last season.

In Johnson's 13-season NBA career, he played in 906 regular-season games and averaged 19.5 points, 7.2 **rebounds**, and 11.2 **assists** per game. He was a member of five NBA Championship teams and was named the NBA Finals Most Valuable Player three times. He was selected for 12 NBA All-Star Games and was named the All-Star Game Most Valuable Player twice. He was named to the All-NBA First Team nine consecutive years, from 1983–1991 and the All-NBA Second Team in 1982 and was the league's Most Valuable Player in 1987, 1989, and 1990. In 1996, he was named one of the 50 Greatest Players in NBA History. He remains a vice president of the Lakers and is a business entrepreneur with diverse interests, including a chain of movie theaters, a movie studio, and a promotional company. Johnson was enshrined in the **Naismith Memorial Basketball Hall of Fame** in 2002.

JOHNSTON, DONALD NEIL "NEIL." B. 4 February 1929, Chillicothe, Ohio. D. 27 September 1978, Irving, Texas. Neil Johnston attended Chillicothe High School and **Ohio State University**. He pitched minor league baseball in the Philadelphia Phillies organization from 1949–1951. He was not selected in the **National Basketball Association (NBA) draft** but signed with the Philadelphia Warriors in 1951 and played with them until a serious knee injury in the 1958–1959 season caused him to retire. On 16 February 1954, he scored 50 points in a game against the **New York Knickerbockers**, only the fourth **Basketball Association of America (BAA)**/NBA player to reach that amount.

Johnston was known for his **hook shot** and was quite accurate with it, leading the league in **field goal** percentage three times. He also led the league in **rebounds** in 1955 and in points and scoring average from 1953–1955. He was selected for the All-NBA First Team from 1953–1956 and the All-NBA Second team in 1957 and played in the NBA **All-Star Game** each year from 1953–1958. His NBA career totals for eight years are 516 games and a 19.4 points and 11.3 rebounds per game average. In 1956, he led the Warriors to the NBA Championship.

After retiring in 1959, he was named **coach** of the Warriors and coached them for two years. In 1961, he coached the Pittsburgh Rens of the new **American Basketball League (ABL)**. He attempted to play a few games and scored 49 points in five games that season. After the ABL folded in 1962, he coached Wilmington in the Eastern Professional Basketball League from 1964–1966 and was assistant coach at Wake Forest University from 1966–1972. In 1972, he was assistant coach with the **Portland Trail Blazers**. His final job was as athletic director at North Lake Community College in Irving, Texas. He was enshrined in the **Naismith Memorial Basketball Hall of Fame** in 1990.

JONES, K. C. B. 25 May 1932, Taylor, Texas. K. C. Jones attended Commerce High School in San Francisco and the **University of San Francisco**. He was a member of the 1955 and 1956 **National Collegiate Athletic Association (NCAA)** champion teams and won a **gold medal** in 1956 with the **U.S. Olympic basketball** team. The six-foot, one-inch **guard** was drafted by the Minneapolis Lakers in the 1955 **National Basketball Association (NBA) draft** but chose to remain in college. In 1956, he was drafted by the **Boston Celtics** and also by the Los Angeles Rams of the National Football League. He signed with the Celtics but first spent two years in the U.S. Army. In 1958, he began his professional basketball career and played nine seasons with the Celtics, helping them win eight consecutive NBA Championships. As a defensive specialist, he never averaged more than nine points per game in his career and never scored more than 20 points in a game. He later **coached** in the NBA with the Washington Bullets and Celtics and led the Celtics to the 1984 and 1986 NBA Championships. He was elected to the **Naismith Memorial Basketball Hall of Fame** in 1988.

JONES, RENATO WILLIAM. B. 5 October 1906, Rome, **Italy**. D. 22 April 1981, Munich, **Germany**. R. William Jones received a bachelor of science degree from the International YMCA College in Springfield, Massachusetts, in the **United States** in 1928. From 1929–1930, he attended the Deutsche Hochschule für Leibesubüngen in Berlin, Germany; the Niels Bukh School of Physical Education in Denmark; and the Royal Institute in Stockholm, Sweden. In 1930, he also received a certificate in pedagogy from the University of Geneva in Switzerland.

On 18 June 1932, Jones was one of the cofounders of the **Fédération Internationale de Basketball (FIBA)** and worked toward **basketball**'s inclusion in the 1936 **Olympic Games** in Berlin. He was the secretary general of FIBA from 1932–1976. In that role, he helped create the European Championships and **World Championships**. He was also the European secretary of the YMCA World Alliance in Geneva from 1940–1956. From 1956–1966, he was director of the United Nations Youth Institute in Gauting, Germany. From 1957–1968, he was also secretary general of the International Council of Sports and Physical Education.

Jones is best remembered in the United States for his interference in the 1972 Olympic Final game between the United States and the **Union of Soviet Socialist Republics**, in which he demanded that the last three seconds of the game be replayed after the United States thought they had won the game. Although he had no official authority to interfere, the game officials bowed to his position and forced the replay. In that replay, the Soviet Union scored the winning basket and became Olympic basketball champions. He was enshrined in the **Naismith Memorial Basketball Hall of Fame** in 1964 in the category of contributor. The R. William Jones Cup, a women's international tournament, has been played almost every year since 1977, in Taiwan. In 2007, he was inducted into the FIBA Hall of Fame in the Gold Contributor category, making him one of only three individuals to be awarded that status.

JONES, ROBERT CLYDE "BOBBY." B. 18 December 1951, Charlotte, North Carolina. Bobby Jones attended South Mecklenburg High School in Charlotte and was an excellent high jumper, twice state champion, and holder of the state record. In addition to suffering from asthma and an irregular heartbeat, he is also an epileptic, but he has never let these conditions disrupt his ability to play sports. He attended the **University of North Carolina** and helped lead them to the **National Invitation Tournament** championship in 1971 and to the **National Collegiate Athletic Association (NCAA)** Championship semifinals in 1972. He was a member of the 1972 **U.S. Olympic basketball** team that was defeated in a controversial game with the **Union of Soviet Socialist Republics.**

The six-foot, nine-inch **forward** returned to school after the Olympic Games and was drafted by the Carolina Cougars in the 1973 **American Basketball Association (ABA)** special circumstance **draft** and the **Houston Rockets** in the first round of the 1974 **National Basketball Association (NBA)** draft. Jones began his professional career in the ABA with the **Denver Nuggets** in 1974. He played with them for two seasons and helped lead them to the ABA Championship Finals in 1976. An excellent shooter, he led the ABA in **field goal** percentage in both years and set a league record with a .605 field goal percentage in his rookie season. He remained with Denver when they joined the NBA in 1976 and played with them until 1978, when he was traded to the **Philadelphia 76ers.** With Philadelphia, he helped lead them to three NBA Championship Finals and the 1983 NBA Championship. In that year, he also received the NBA **Sixth Man** of the Year award.

Jones retired from active play after the 1985–1986 season. In his 10 years in the NBA, he played in 774 regular-season games and averaged 11.5 points per game. As one of the best defensive players in the league, he was selected to the NBA All-Defensive First Team each year from 1977–1984 and the All-Defensive Second Team in 1985. He also played in four NBA **All-Star Games.** After retiring from basketball, he became a teacher and **coach** at the Carmel Christian School in Charlotte, North Carolina.

JONES, SAMUEL "SAM." B. 24 June 1933, Wilmington, North Carolina. Sam Jones attended Laurinburg Institute in Laurinburg, North Carolina, and North Carolina Central College. He attended college from 1951–1954 and then enlisted in the **U.S.** Army, where he served two years. He was selected by the Minneapolis Lakers in the 1956 **National Basketball Association (NBA) draft** but chose to return to school for his senior year.

After his graduation, Jones was selected by the **Boston Celtics** in the 1957 NBA draft and played for them from 1957–1969. He played in the postseason playoffs each year and won 10 NBA titles in his 12-year professional career. His favorite shot was a **jump shot** that used the **backboard**. On 29 October 1965, he scored 51 points and became the first Celtic player to exceed 50 points in a game. He matched that total two years later, on 28 March 1967, in a playoff game. He was selected for the NBA **All-Star Game** five times and was named to the All-NBA Second Team three times.

Jones's NBA career totals for 12 years are 871 regular-season games and 17.7 points per game average. In 154 playoff games, he had an 18.9 points per game average. After retiring from active play, he **coached** at Federal City College from 1969–1973 and at North Carolina Central from 1973–1974. In 1974–1975, he served as an assistant coach for the New Orleans Jazz in the NBA. He was enshrined in the **Naismith Memorial Basketball Hall of Fame** in 1984. He was also selected to the NBA 25th Anniversary Team in 1970 and in 1996 was named one of the 50 Greatest Players in NBA History.

JORDAN, MICHAEL JEFFREY. B. 17 February 1963, Brooklyn, New York. Michael Jordan is arguably the best **basketball** player of all time and has become one of the wealthiest due to his playing and self-marketing abilities. Raised in North Carolina, he attended Emsley A. Laney High School in Wilmington and the **University of North Carolina**. As a freshman, he hit the game-winning shot in the 1982 **National Collegiate Athletic Association (NCAA)** Championship game. He was named college player of the year in 1984 and won both the Naismith College Player of the Year Award and John R. Wooden award as the best college basketball player and a **gold medal** with the 1984 **U.S. Olympic** team.

After the Olympics, although only a college junior, he was drafted by the **Chicago Bulls** in the 1984 **National Basketball Association (NBA) draft** and played with them from 1984–1998. He returned to school and received his degree in 1986. The six-foot, six-inch **guard** was the league's scoring leader each season from 1987–1993, averaging better than 30 points per game in each of those seven years, but it was not until the 1990–1991 season that he played in the NBA Championship Finals. He helped lead his team to the NBA title in

1991, 1992, and 1993, and then surprised everyone by announcing his retirement so that he could pursue another challenge and play professional baseball.

In the summer of 1994, he played for the minor league Birmingham Barons, a Chicago White Sox farm team in the Double-A classification and batted just .202 with three home runs while playing the outfield. As Major League Baseball prepared to go on strike for the 1995 season, Jordan announced his return to basketball on 18 March 1995, with the two-word press release, "I'm Back."

Jordan played the final 17 games of the season for the Bulls and led them into the playoffs, but they were defeated by the **Orlando Magic** in the second round. The next season, 1995–1996, the Bulls had the best season in NBA history, as they won a record 72 of 82 games in the regular-season and 15 of 18 in the playoffs to again win the NBA title. The following year was almost as exceptional, as they compiled records of 69–13 in the regular season and 15–4 in the playoffs to repeat as NBA champions. In 1997–1998, they slipped slightly statistically, with records of 62–20 and 15–6, but were NBA champions for the third consecutive year. Following this season, however, **coach Phil Jackson** resigned after conflicts with the Bulls' general manager Jerry Krause and as the NBA was in the midst of a dispute between the NBA Players Association and the league owners that resulted in a lockout. Jordan, on 13 January 1999, decided to retire again, stating he was 99.9 percent sure he would not return.

The following year, Jordan became a part owner of the **Washington Wizards** NBA franchise and was named their president of Basketball Operations. After watching the Wizards finish in last place in the Atlantic Division of the NBA in 1999–2000 and 2000–2001 seasons, he decided to return as a player in an attempt to lead the team. He hired **Doug Collins** to coach the Wizards. Collins had previously coached Jordan in Chicago, and Jordan respected his abilities. In the 2001–2002 season, Jordan, at the age of 38, was still the best player on his team, even though his skills had eroded somewhat, and he led the team in scoring, **assists**, and **steals**, but after playing 60 games, he tore a cartilage in his knee that ended his season.

Prior to that injury, on 29 December 2001, he scored 51 points in a game to become the oldest player ever to top 50 points in one game. He played one more season with the Wizards and, after he celebrated his 40th birthday on 27 February 2003, he still managed to score 43 points in a game four days later. The Wizards still didn't reach the playoffs, and Jordan retired from active play after the season. He intended to return to his position as an executive with the Wizards but was fired by owner Abe Pollin shortly after the season ended. In 2006, Jordan became part owner of the **Charlotte Bobcats** and was named as a managing member of Basketball Operations. In 2010, he became the majority owner of the team, the first former NBA player to be an NBA team's majority owner.

In the 15 seasons in which he appeared in NBA games, Jordan played in 1,072 regular-season games and averaged 6.2 **rebounds**, 5.3 assists, 2.3 steals, and a career record 30.1 points per game. The Bulls made the playoffs each of the 13 years he was on the team, and in 179 playoff games he averaged 6.4 rebounds, 5.7 assists, 2.1 steals, and an NBA career record 33.4 points per game. He was the league's Most Valuable Player five times, the NBA Finals Most Valuable Player in each of the six finals in which he participated, and **All Star Game** Most Valuable Player three times. He was selected for the NBA All-Star Game in every season in which he played. He was named to the All-NBA First Team 10 times and the All-NBA Second Team once, was the NBA Rookie of the Year in 1985, and was NBA Defensive Player of the Year in 1988. He won a second Olympic gold medal with the 1992 U.S. Olympic basketball **Dream Team**. In 1996, he was named one of the 50 Greatest Players in NBA History. In 2009, Jordan was enshrined in the **Naismith Memorial Basketball Hall of Fame**.

JUMP SHOT. A jump shot is an attempt at the **basket** taken with both feet off the ground. Until the 1940s, players usually kept both feet on the floor when shooting. By jumping while shooting, there is less chance that a player's shot will be **blocked** by the defense. Some of the first players to popularize the jump shot were **Joe Fulks**, Davage "Dave" Minor, John "Bud" Palmer, Kenny Sailors, Myer "Whitey" Skoog, and Belus Smawley. Most outside **field goal** attempts since the 1960s have been jump shots. A few players, notably **Hal Greer**, even used a jump shot when attempting **free throws**.

– K –

KANSAS, UNIVERSITY OF. The University of Kansas in Lawrence began its men's **basketball** program in 1898 under **coach James Naismith**, inventor of the game. Home games since 1955 have been played at the 16,000-seat Allen Fieldhouse (named for former coach **Forrest "Phog" Allen**). Prior to 1955, the 3,500-seat Hoch Auditorium was the school's basketball venue. The eight coaches in the school's history have been James Naismith, Forrest "Phog" Allen, William Hamilton, Dick Harp, Ted Owens, **Larry Brown**, Roy Williams, and Bill Self.

Kansas has had one of the most illustrious collegiate programs in basketball history and have won more than 71 percent of their games with a record of 2,003–796 from 1898–2010. Sixteen of their former players or coaches have been enshrined in the **Naismith Memorial Basketball Hall of Fame**. The Jayhawks reached the **Final Four** in the **National Collegiate Athletic Association (NCAA)** Championships 13 times. They won the NCAA Championships three times—in 1952, 1988, and 2008—and were runners-up in the final round in 1940, 1953, 1957 (when **Wilt Chamberlain**'s team lost in triple **overtime**), 1991, and 2003.

In 1952, seven players from the Kansas team were selected to represent the **United States** in the **Olympic Games**. The best players in school history have included Charlie Black, B. H. Born, Bill Bridges, Wilt Chamberlain, Paul Endacott, Maurice King, Arthur "Dutch" Lonborg, **Clyde Lovellette**, Danny Manning, Greg Ostertag, **Paul Pierce**, Scot Pollard, Rex Walters, and **Joseph "Jo Jo" White**.

KANSAS CITY KINGS. *See* SACRAMENTO KINGS.

KANSAS CITY LARKS. *See* DENVER NUGGETS (ABA-NBA).

KANSAS CITY-OMAHA KINGS. *See* SACRAMENTO KINGS.

KENNEDY, JAMES WALTER "WALTER." B. 8 June 1912, Stamford, Connecticut. D. 26 June 1977, Stamford, Connecticut. As a youngster, Walter Kennedy had polio and was unable to participate in sports. He attended high school in Stamford and at the **University of Notre Dame**, graduating in 1934 with bachelor's degrees in journalism and business administration. He became sports information director for Notre Dame and was later a high school **basketball coach** at St. Basil's Preparatory School in Stamford and correspondent for *The Sporting News*.

When the **Basketball Association of America** began, Kennedy was public relations director from 1946–1949. He opened his own public relations firm and had the **Harlem Globetrotters** as a client. In 1959, he was elected mayor of Stamford and in 1962 was campaign manager for U.S. senator Abraham Ribicoff. He was chosen to succeed **Maurice Podoloff** as **National Basketball Association (NBA)** commissioner in 1963 and held that position until his retirement in 1975. While commissioner, the NBA faced the challenge of the new and competitive **American Basketball Association**. After retiring as commissioner, he spent much of his time as chairman of the board for the Special **Olympics**, chairman of the board of the First Stamford Bank and Trust Company, and president of the **Naismith Memorial Basketball Hall of Fame**. In 1974, the NBA instituted the J. Walter Kennedy Award, given to a player, coach, or trainer who shows "outstanding service and dedication to the community," as selected by the Professional Basketball Writers Association. He was enshrined in the hall in 1981 as a contributor.

KENNEDY, MATTHEW PATRICK "PAT." B. 28 January 1908, Hoboken, New Jersey. D. 16 June 1957, Mineola, New York. Pat Kennedy was one of the most capable and colorful **basketball referees** of all time. He attended Demarest High School in Hoboken and Montclair State College. As a physical education instructor, he supplemented his income by refereeing basketball games, officiating in the **American Basketball League** at only 20 years of age. He officiated for college basketball as well as in all the major professional leagues. In addition, he umpired minor league baseball in the Interstate and International leagues.

Kennedy was famous for calling a foul and then yelling at the perpetrator in a very animated style, "No, no, no, you can't do that!" Although he was criticized by some for his theatrics, no one ever accused him of not being an extremely competent official who was in total control of the game. He was one of the two officials for the very first **Basketball Association of America** game on 1 November 1946, between the **New York Knickerbockers** and **Toronto Huskies**. He was the league's first supervisor of officials and held that position from 1946–1950. He then worked for the **Harlem Globetrotters** and accompanied them on their round-the-world tour in 1952. He remained with them until 1956, when he took ill. In 1959, as a member of the inaugural class, he was the first referee inducted into the **Naismith Memorial Basketball Hall of Fame**.

KENTUCKY, UNIVERSITY OF. The University of Kentucky in Lexington began its men's **basketball** program in 1904. The school has won more basketball games than any other **National Collegiate Athletic Association (NCAA)** school and has the highest winning percentage (.760) with a record of 2,023–638–1 from 1904–2010. Home games since 1976 have been played at the 23,500-seat Rupp Arena. Prior to 1976, home games were played at Memorial Coliseum. The most accomplished **coaches** in the school's history have been Joe B. Hall, Rick Pitino, **Adolph Rupp**, Eddie Sutton, and Orlando "Tubby" Smith.

The Wildcats have reached the **Final Four** 13 times. They won the NCAA Championship seven times and were runners-up three times. In 1948, five members of the team played on the **U.S. Olympic** team. The best players in school history have included Cliff Barker, Ralph Beard, Sam Bowie, **Louie Dampier**, **Leroy "Cowboy" Edwards**, **Alex Groza**, **Cliff Hagan**, Joe Holland, **Dan Issel**, Wallace "Wah Wah" Jones, Jamal Mashburn, Tayshaun Prince, **Frank Ramsey**, **Pat Riley**, Rick Robey, Ken Rollins, Rajon Rondo, **Bill Spivey**, Mel Turpin, and Kenny Walker.

KENTUCKY COLONELS. The Kentucky Colonels were a team in the **American Basketball Association (ABA)** for the entire nine years of the league, from 1967–1976. Their record of 448–296 in that time was the best in the league. Home games for the first three years were played at the 5,900-seat Convention Center in Louisville, but from 1970 onward home games were played at the 16,000-seat Freedom Hall in Louisville. The Colonels won the league title in 1975, lost in the championship finals in two other years, and never failed to qualify for the playoffs.

The Colonels' **backcourt** of **Louie Dampier** and Darel Carrier were proficient **three-point field goal** shooters and were usually among the leaders in three-pointers made, three-pointers attempted, and three-point field goal percentage. The Colonels made history in their second season when, as a publicity stunt, they signed **Penny Ann Early**, a five-foot, three-inch female jockey, to a one-game contract and actually used her, very briefly, in a league game. In 1970, the Colonels signed **Dan Issel** and, the following year, **Artis Gilmore**, two of the nation's best collegians. Other players who starred for the Colonels were Les Hunter, Wendell Ladner, Jim "Goose" Ligon, Gene Moore, Cincy Powell, Bobby Rascoe, Walt Simon, and Sam Smith.

In the 1971–1972 season, the Colonels compiled a record of 68–16, the best ever in the ABA. In 1973, the franchise was sold to John Y. Brown, owner of Kentucky Fried Chicken. His wife, Ellie, was named chairman of the board, and a 10-woman board of directors was established. The Colonels were one of the seven ABA franchises in existence at the close of the 1975–1976 season. Brown decided to sell the team to the ABA for $3 million dollars and disbanded it on 17 June 1976, rather than accept the **National Basketball Association**'s terms to join their league.

KERR, JOHN GRAHAM "JOHNNY," "RED." B. 17 August 1932, Chicago, Illinois. D. 26 February 2009, Chicago, Illinois. Johnny Kerr attended Tilden High School in Chicago and led them to the 1950 Chicago Public School Championship. As a sophomore in 1952 at the University of Illinois, he helped his team reach the **National Collegiate Athletic Association (NCAA) Final Four**, where they finished in third place. Selected by the Syracuse Nationals in the 1954 **National Basketball Association (NBA) draft**, he played with the franchise from 1954–1966 in Syracuse and in **Philadelphia** as the **76ers**. In 1955, he won the NBA Championship with the Nationals. As a National and 76er, he did not miss a game and played in 844 consecutive games to set the NBA record (since broken). The six-foot, nine-inch, red-headed **center** finished his playing career with the **Baltimore Bullets** in the 1965–1966 season. He was selected from the Bullets by the **Chicago Bulls** in the expansion draft in 1966 but instead of playing for the Bulls **coached** them for two seasons.

The NBA Coach of the Year in 1967, he led the Bulls to the playoffs in their first season in the league. He then coached the expansion **Phoenix Suns** for their first two seasons. Kerr's NBA career totals for 12 years are 905 games and a 13.8 points per game average. He played in three NBA **All-Star Games**. After retiring from active play, he became a television announcer for the Suns, was business manager with the **Virginia Squires** of the **American Basketball Association** for two seasons, then returned to the Bulls to work in their front office. In 1975, he began as a Bulls television announcer and remained with them until his death. For a time, the Bulls had the world's tallest broadcasting team, with the six-foot, nine-inch Kerr; seven-foot, two-inch Tom Dore; and six-foot, 11-inch Stacey King as their announcers. Kerr received the John Bunn Lifetime Achievement Award from the **Naismith Memorial Basketball Hall of Fame** just two weeks before his death.

KEYHOLE. The keyhole is the area on a **basketball** court consisting of the **foul** circle, foul lane, and **free throw** line. It was originally shaped like a keyhole, with the width at the narrowest part being only six feet wide. To minimize congestion under the **basket** and the consequent rough play, the rules have changed through the years to widen the lane to its present width of 16 feet in **National Basketball Association** and **Women's National Basketball Association** play, 12 feet in **National Collegiate Athletic Association** play, and a trapezoid-shaped lane for **Fédération Internationale de Basketball** play, with the width ranging from 12 feet at the free throw line to six meters (19 feet, 8.25 inches) at the baseline. This area is also known as the "key" or "paint" due to the fact that it is painted a different color than the rest of the playing surface. *See also* POINTS IN THE PAINT.

KIDD, JASON FREDERICK. B. 23 March 1973, San Francisco, California. Jason Kidd attended St. Joseph of Notre Dame High School in Alameda, California, and the **University of California**. He left school after his sophomore year and was **drafted** in the 1994 **National Basketball Association (NBA)** draft by the **Dallas Mavericks**. The six-foot, four-inch **point guard** played for the Mavericks from 1994–1996, the **Phoenix Suns** from 1996–2001, the **New**

Jersey Nets from 2001–2008, and he returned to Dallas in 2008. He was still with them in 2009–2010.

With the Mavericks in 1995, Kidd was named co-Rookie of the Year with **Grant Hill**. He led the Nets to the NBA final round in 2002 and 2003. He was selected for 10 NBA **All-Star Games**. Although not an exceptional shooter, he averaged more than 10 points per game in each one of his first 14 NBA seasons and has averaged 13.6points per game for the first 16 seasons of his NBA career. He is second in NBA career assists. He led the league in **assists** three times and **steals** once. He was named to the All-NBA First Team five times, the All-NBA Second Team once, the All-Defensive First Team four times, and the All-Defensive Second Team five times. He played for the **U.S.** national team in the 2000 and in the 2008 **Olympic Games** and is one of the few men to have won two Olympic **gold medals** in **basketball**.

KING, WILLIAM "DOLLY." B. 15 November 1916. D. 29 January 1969, Binghamton, New York. Dolly King attended Alexander Hamilton High School in Brooklyn, New York, and **Long Island University**. In college, he was a football, baseball, and **basketball** star and after graduation played in the Negro Baseball League with the Homestead Grays. He played basketball with the New York Flashes semipro team, then formed his own team, "Dolly King's Blackbirds." In the fall of 1941, he played semipro football for the Long Island Indians. He also played basketball with Grumman Aviation and the **New York Rens** for several seasons during the 1940s and was with the league-leading Rochester Royals of the **National Basketball League** in the 1946–1947 season. He also played in the **American Basketball League** with Scranton from 1948–1951.

After retiring as an active player, King became a high school and college basketball **referee** in the New York City area. From 1948–1964, he was director of recreational programs for residents at the Riverton Housing Project in Harlem. In 1961, he received his master's degree from New York University, and in 1964 he became director of intercollegiate athletics and intramurals and professor of student life at Manhattan Community College. He was a consultant to President Lyndon B. Johnson's Council on Physical Fitness and was part of Vice President Hubert Humphrey's Summer Youth Sports and Recreation Program.

KLOTZ, LOUIS HERMAN "RED." B. 21 October 1921, Philadelphia, Pennsylvania. Red Klotz attended South Philadelphia High School and **Villanova University.** He led his high school team to the city championship in 1939 and 1940 and was named Philadelphia High School Player of the Year both years. After serving in World War II, he played in the **American Basketball League** for the **Philadelphia SPHAs** from 1946–1948. He was signed by the **Baltimore Bullets** in 1948 and was a member of their **Basketball Association of America** champion team that year, although he only played in 11 regular-season games and scored just 15 points. He did play in six of their 11 playoff games. He later bought the SPHAs franchise and renamed them the **Washington Generals,** and they became the regular opponent of the **Harlem Globetrotters.** Klotz played with the Generals until the age of 62. Although only five-feet, seven-inches tall, he had an outstanding set shot from long range. In retirement, he still continued to play schoolyard basketball into his 80s in southern New Jersey. On 10 March 2007, he was honored by the Globetrotters with their "Legend" award, making him the first non-Globetrotter to be so honored.

KNIGHT, ROBERT MONTGOMERY "BOBBY." B. 25 October 1940, Massillon, Ohio. Bobby Knight attended Orrville High School in Orrville, Ohio, where he played **basketball** and football. At **Ohio State University,** he played on the 1960 **National Collegiate Athletic Association (NCAA)** Championship team and the 1961 and 1962 NCAA runner-up teams as a reserve. He began his **coaching** career at Cuyahoga Falls High School in 1962. In 1963, he became an assistant coach at the **U.S.** Military Academy at West Point and from 1965–1971 was head coach. He had a record of 102–50 there and reached the **National Invitation Tournament** semifinal round three times.

From 1971–2000, Knight was head coach of **Indiana University.** At Indiana, he had a record of 661–240, won the NCAA national title three times, and reached the **Final Four** two other times. From

1974–1976, his teams lost only one of 64 games. Knight's volatile personality caused problems at times and, on 10 September 2000, he was fired by Indiana University. In 2001, he became coach of **Texas Tech University** and coached them until midway through the 2007–2008 season, with a record of 138–82. He also coached the **gold medal**-winning 1979 U.S. Pan American Games team and 1984 U.S. **Olympic** team. Although his personality caused controversy at times, he was never accused of improper recruiting activities. and most of his players earned their degrees. In 1991, he was enshrined in the **Naismith Memorial Basketball Hall of Fame** in the category of coach.

KOREA. Korea joined the **Fédération Internationale de Basketball (FIBA)** in 1947 and is a member in the FIBA Asia zone. The men's team has competed in six **Olympic** tournaments, with a best finish of eighth in 1948. In that tournament, they defeated the hapless team from Iraq, 120–20, and set the Olympic record for largest margin of victory, subsequently tied by **China** later in that year's tournament. In the FIBA **World Championships**, they competed six times, with a best finish of 11th in 1970. In the FIBA Asia Championships, they have entered in every one of the 24 events and have won 22 medals, two **gold medals**, 11 **silver medals**, and nine **bronze medals**.

The women's team competed in six Olympic tournaments and won the silver medal in 1984. In the FIBA World Championships, they competed 12 times and won silver medals twice, in 1967 and 1979. They competed in every one of the 22 events in the FIBA Asia Championships and won a medal each time, 12 gold, eight silver, and two bronze.

The only **National Basketball Association** player born in Korea has been the seven-foot, three-inch Ha Seung-Jin, who played for the **Portland Trail Blazers** from 2004–2006. His sister, six-foot, eight-inch Ha Eun-Joo, was on the Korean roster in the 2008 Olympic Games for Korea but did not play. She is a professional player who was offered a **Women's National Basketball Association (WNBA)** contract by the Los Angeles Sparks but has yet to play in the WNBA. Korean Olympian Sun-Min Jung played in the WNBA in 2003.

KORFBALL. Korfball is a sport that originated in the Netherlands and is similar to **netball**. It is contested between teams of eight players, four men and four women. The object is to throw a ball through a ring attached to a three-meter-high post. It is played worldwide and was included in the **Olympic Games** of 1920 and 1928 as a demonstration sport.

KRZYZEWSKI, MICHAEL WILLIAM "MIKE." B. 13 February 1947, Chicago, Illinois. Mike Krzyzewski (pronounced sha-shef-ski) attended Weber High School in Chicago and the **U.S.** Military Academy. He graduated in 1969 and served in the U.S. Army until 1974. While in the army, he **coached** service teams for three years and was head coach at the United States Military Academy Prep School for two years.

In the 1974–1975, season Krzyzewski was assistant coach at **Indiana University**, and from 1975–1980, he was head coach at the United States Military Academy. In 1980, he became head coach at **Duke University** and was still there in 2010. In his first 30 years at Duke, from 1980–2010, his record is 795–220. He led the Blue Devils to the **National Collegiate Athletic Association (NCAA) Final Four** 11 times, winning four championships and finishing second four times.

Krzyzewski has also coached the U.S. national team at the 1990 Goodwill Games, 1990, 2006, and 2010 **World Championships**, and 2008 **Olympic Games**. He was assistant coach for the 1979 Pan American Games and 1992 Olympic Games. His teams won **gold medals** in 1979, 1992, and 2008; won a **silver medal** at the 1990 Goodwill Games; and garnered **bronze medals** at the two World Championships. In 2001, "Coach K" was enshrined in the **Naismith Memorial Basketball Hall of Fame** in the category of coach.

KUKOČ, TONI. B. 18 September 1968, Split, **Croatia, Yugoslavia.** Toni Kukoč attended high school in Split and did not go to college. In 1987, he began his professional **basketball** career with Jugoplastika Split in the Yugoslavian league and helped them win the European Cup in 1989, 1990, and 1991. From 1991–1993, he was with Benetton Treviso in **Italy**. He was selected by the **Chicago Bulls** in the

1990 **National Basketball Association (NBA) draft** but remained in Europe until 1993, when he signed with them.

Kukoč played with Chicago from 1993–2000 and was a member of their NBA Championship teams in 1996, 1997, and 1998. He played for the **Philadelphia 76ers** from 2000–2001, the **Atlanta Hawks** from 2001–2002, and concluded his NBA career with the **Milwaukee Bucks** from 2002–2006. Although six-feet, 11-inches tall, the **left-handed** Kukoč was an excellent ball handler and passer and would sometimes play the role of **point guard**, even though his normal position was **forward**.

Kukoč's NBA career totals for 13 years are 846 regular-season games and an 11.6 points per game average. He won the NBA **Sixth Man** of the Year Award in 1996. He had an outstanding record internationally and competed for Yugoslavia in the 1988 **Olympic Games** and Croatia in the 1992 and 1996 Olympic Games. In 22 games in three Olympic tournaments, he averaged 11.3 points per game and was a member of the **silver medal**-winning team in 1988 and 1992. He also won medals at four European Championships (**bronze** in 1987, **gold** in 1989 and 1991 with Yugoslavia, and bronze in 1995 with Croatia) and two **World Championships** (gold in 1990 with Yugoslavia and bronze in 1994 with Croatia). In 2008, he was named one of the 50 Greatest Contributors in Euroleague History.

KURLAND, ROBERT ALBERT "BOB," "FOOTHILLS." B. 23 December 1924, St. Louis, Missouri. Bob Kurland attended Jennings High School in Jennings, Missouri, and **Oklahoma A&M College**. He led Oklahoma A&M to the **National Collegiate Athletic Association (NCAA)** Championship in 1945 and 1946 and to the **National Invitation Tournament** semifinals in 1944. While in college, the six-foot, 10-inch **center** had some memorable battles with **DePaul University** and their six-foot, 10-inch center, **George Mikan**. His shot-blocking abilities caused the NCAA to revise their **goaltending** rules.

Kurland was selected by the **St. Louis Bombers** in the 1947 **Basketball Association of America draft** but elected to remain an amateur and played with the Phillips 66ers **Amateur Athletic Union** team. Nicknamed "Foothills," he was selected for the 1948 and 1952

U.S. Olympic basketball teams. Prior to the use of professional basketball players in the Olympic Games, he was one of only three players to play for the U.S. Olympic team twice and also win two **gold medals**. He played in 14 of 16 games in the 1948 and 1952 Olympics and averaged 9.4 points per game.

After retiring from basketball, he continued to work for the Phillips Petroleum Company as a general sales manager. He was enshrined in the **Naismith Memorial Basketball Hall of Fame** in 1961, becoming the first Olympian to be enshrined in the hall.

– L –

LAETTNER, CHRISTIAN DONALD. B. 17 August 1969, Angola, New York. Christian Laettner attended the Nichols School in Buffalo, New York, and **Duke University**. He was one of only four players to play in the **National Collegiate Athletic Association (NCAA)** Championship **Final Four** all four years while in college. As a college sophomore, he won a **bronze medal** with the1990 **U.S. World Championships** team. In 1991, Duke won the NCAA Championship, and Laettner was named the tournament's Most Outstanding Player.

Laettner won a second bronze medal with the U.S. team in the 1991 Pan American Games. In the NCAA tournament regional final game in 1992 against the **University of Kentucky**, his last second **jump shot** at the buzzer enabled Duke to win the game, and the shot became one of the most dramatic in NCAA tournament history. Duke continued in the tournament and won it a second consecutive time. Laettner played 148 collegiate games and averaged 16.6 points per game. He won the John R. Wooden award as the best college **basketball** player, the Naismith College Player of the Year Award, and numerous other awards as the best college player in 1992. He was also the only collegian selected for the 1992 **gold medal**-winning U.S. **Olympic basketball Dream Team**.

The six-foot, 11-inch **forward-center** was drafted by the **Minnesota Timberwolves** in the 1992 **National Basketball Association (NBA) draft** and played from 1992–2005 for six NBA teams but never quite lived up to expectations. He was selected for the 1997

NBA **All-Star Game** but achieved no other professional milestones. In his 13-year professional career, he played in 868 games and averaged 12.8 points per game. Before retiring from basketball, he became coowner of a company that is developing a community in Durham, North Carolina.

LANIER, ROBERT JERRY, JR. "BOB." B. 28 September 1948, Buffalo, New York. Bob Lanier attended Bennett High School in Buffalo and St. Bonaventure University, where he averaged 27.6 points per game in three varsity seasons and led them to the **National Collegiate Athletic Association (NCAA) Final Four** in 1970. He was selected by the **Detroit Pistons** in the 1970 **National Basketball Association (NBA) draft** as the first overall selection. The six-foot, 11-inch, 265-pound **center** played from 1970–1980 for the Pistons and **Milwaukee Bucks**.

Lanier's NBA career totals for 14 years are 959 regular-season games and a 20.1 points and 10.1 **rebounds** per game average. Selected for eight NBA **All-Star Games**, he was named the Most Valuable Player in the 1974 game. The recipient of the NBA's **J. Walter Kennedy** Citizenship Award in 1978, he was president of the NBA Players Association from 1980–1985 and chairman of the NBA Stay in School Program from 1989–1994. In 1992, he was enshrined in the **Naismith Memorial Basketball Hall of Fame**, along with his size 22 shoe, the largest in the league to that date. He was assistant **coach** of the **Golden State Warriors** in the 1994–1995 season, was briefly interim head coach of the Warriors, and then worked as special assistant to the NBA commissioner.

LAPCHICK, JOSEPH BOHOMIEL "JOE." B. 12 April 1900, Yonkers, New York. D. 10 August 1970, Monticello, New York. Joe Lapchick did not go to high school, as he began working at age 15 as an apprentice machinist to contribute to the family's income. He began supplementing his income by playing **basketball** for five dollars a game, one-third of his weekly salary as an apprentice. By age 17, he had grown to his full six-feet, five-inch height—a giant in those days—and was getting seven to 10 dollars per game playing for whatever team needed him and could afford him. Never a high scorer, he was an excellent defensive player and was considered by his contemporaries as one of the best players in his era.

From 1920–1937, he played in most of the major professional leagues and was also a member of the **Original Celtics**. In 1937, he was hired as head basketball **coach** at **St. John's University**, even though he had not attended high school or college. He coached St. John's through the 1946–1947 season and led them to **National Invitation Tournament (NIT)** championships in 1943 and 1944.

In 1947, Lapchick was hired to coach the **New York Knickerbockers** of the **Basketball Association of America** and coached them through the 1956 season. He led them to the **National Basketball Association (NBA)** Championship Finals in 1951, 1952, and 1953, although they lost all three times. He resigned from the Knicks on 28 January 1956, due to "poor health and too many sleepless nights," but remained with the team for the rest of that season. Less than one month later, on 15 February 1956, he was given his former job back at St. John's and coached there from the 1956–1957 season until his compulsory retirement at age 65 in 1965.

St. John's won the NIT in 1959, were runners-up in 1962, and placed fourth in 1958. His final season as a coach was a memorable one, as St. John's again won the NIT, although they were not among the favorites. His overall record at St. John's was 334–130. He was enshrined in the **Naismith Memorial Basketball Hall of Fame** in 1966. After retiring from coaching at St. John's, he was sports coordinator at Kutsher's Country Club in Monticello, New York. His son, Richard Lapchick, is a social scientist who has been a spokesman for equality in sport.

LA SALLE UNIVERSITY. La Salle University is a Christian Brothers college located in Philadelphia, Pennsylvania. Although the school was founded in 1863, they did not play intercollegiate **basketball** until 1930. Since 1998, the Explorers have played their home games at Tom Gola Arena, a 4,000-seat facility at Hayman Center. The most accomplished **coaches** at the school have been Ken Loeffler, Donald "Dudey" Moore, William "Speedy" Morris, **Jim Pollard**, and Paul Westhead. By far, their most notable player has been **Tom Gola**, who led them to the 1952 **National Invitation Tournament**

championship, to the 1954 **National Collegiate Athletic Association (NCAA)** Championship, and to second place behind **Bill Russell'**s **University of San Francisco** team in 1955. Among their best players have been Lionel Simmons, whose 3,217 career points is the third highest in NCAA history; Steve Black; Michael Brooks; Rasual Butler; Larry Cannon; Donnie Carr; Ken Durrett; Norm Grekin; Tim Legler; Bill Raftery; Bob Walters; and Randy Woods.

LEFT-HANDED PLAYERS. Unlike such sports as baseball, tennis, and bowling, being left-handed has no particular advantage for **basketball** players. Many good players will develop the ability to shoot with either hand, especially near the **basket**, and most players can **dribble** and pass the ball with either hand. Some well-known left-handed players have been Dick Barnett, **Leroy Edwards**, **Artis Gilmore**, **Phil Jackson**, **Toni Kukoč**, **Chris Mullin**, **Willis Reed**, **Guy Rodgers**, **Bill Russell**, and **Lenny Wilkens**.

LEMON III, MEADOW GEORGE "MEADOWLARK." B. 25 April 1935, Wilmington, North Carolina, or B. 25 April 1933 or 1932, Lexington, South Carolina (biographies differ as to Meadowlark Lemon's birthdate and birthplace). He was raised in Wilmington and graduated from Williston High School in 1952, playing both football and **basketball** there. After seeing the film *The Harlem Globetrotter Story*, he decided that he wanted to be a Globetrotter. The six-foot, two-inch Lemon enrolled at Florida A8M University in 1952 but was drafted by the **U.S.** Army after spending just two weeks in school. Stationed in **Germany**, he contacted Trotters' owner **Abe Saperstein** and received a tryout there. He impressed Saperstein and after his discharge in 1954 joined the team, changing his first name to Meadowlark.

Lemon got his opportunity to shine when Globetrotters' chief clown **Reece "Goose" Tatum** left the team and Tatum's two backups were incapacitated. He soon became the Globetrotters main comedic star and was dubbed the "Clown Prince of Basketball." He remained with the Trotters until 1978, when he left to form his own team, the Bucketeers. He played with the Bucketeers from 1980–1983, renamed them the Shooting Stars in 1984, and in 1988 renamed them once more as the Meadowlark Lemon Harlem All-Stars. He retired in 1998.

He became an ordained minister in 1986. In 1998, he received a doctor of divinity degree and formed Meadowlark Lemon Ministries. In 2000, he was the recipient of the **Naismith Memorial Basketball Hall of Fame**'s prestigious John Bunn Award for outstanding lifetime contributions to basketball and was enshrined there in 2003 in the category of contributor.

LESLIE (LOCKWOOD), LISA DESHAUN. B. 7 July 1972, Gardena, California. Lisa Leslie attended Morningside High School in Inglewood, California. In a deliberate attempt to break **Cheryl Miller**'s single game scoring record of 105 points in a game, she scored 101 points in the first half of a high school game that was forfeited by the opposing team at **halftime**. She attended the **University of Southern California** and as a college senior won the Naismith College Player of the Year Award. In 1994–1995, she played for Sicilgesso in the Italian League. She has been selected for four **U.S. Olympic** basketball teams from 1996–2008 and is only the second American basketball player, man or woman, to compete in four Olympic Games. The six-foot, five-inch **center-forward** has averaged 15.3 points per game for 32 games and has won four **gold medals**. She holds the following Olympic basketball career records: most gold medals, most games (tied with **Teresa Edwards**), most two-point **field goals**, most defensive **rebounds**, most total rebounds, most personal **fouls**, most total field goals, and most **turnovers**. Although a natural **left-hander**, as a youth she developed the use of her right hand and is now ambidextrous.

Leslie played in the **Women's National Basketball Association (WNBA)** from 1997–2009 with the Los Angeles Sparks but sat out the 2007 season. In 363 regular-season games, she has averaged 17.4 points, 9.1 rebounds, and 2.2 **blocks** per game. A member of the WNBA champions in 2001 and 2002, she was the Finals Most Valuable Player both years and the league's Most Valuable Player in 2001, 2004, and 2006. She played in the WNBA **All-Star Game** seven times, was its Most Valuable Player three times, and was named to the All-WNBA First Team seven times and All-WNBA

Second Team three times. She works as a fashion model for the Wilhelmina Models modeling agency.

LEW, HARRY HASKELL "BUCKY." B. 4 January 1884, Lowell, Massachusetts. D. 22 October 1963, Springfield, Massachusetts. Harry "Bucky" Lew was the first black player to play in a professional **basketball** game, when he played for Lowell against Marlborough on 2 November 1902, in a New England League game. He was able to trace his roots back to the Revolutionary War to his ancestor, Barzillai Lew, a free black man, who was at the Battle of Bunker Hill. Bucky Lew was a graduate of Lowell High School and was a talented musician as well as a talented athlete. He was a competitive cyclist and basketball player. He began playing for his YMCA team in 1898 in Lowell and in 1902 joined the Pawtucketville Athletic Club in the New England League. The five-foot, eight-inch Lew was an excellent defensive player. He also played for Haverhill, until the New England League disbanded, and he then formed his own team and played and **coached** until 1926.

After his retirement from basketball, he had a dry cleaning business. Both his sister and brother were accomplished as well. His sister earned a law degree, and his brother, Gerard, played college football and was one of the founders of the DuSable Museum in Chicago, the country's first museum of African American history and art.

LIEBERMAN (-CLINE), NANCY ELIZABETH. B. 1 July 1958, Brooklyn, New York. Nancy Lieberman attended Far Rockaway High School in Far Rockaway, New York. The five-foot, nine-inch redhead, known as "Fire," "Flame," "Big Red," and "Lady Magic," developed her game by playing against males in playgrounds throughout New York City. She was selected for the 1976 **U.S. Olympic basketball** team, although only an 18-year-old recent high school graduate. After the Olympic Games, she played at **Old Dominion University**. She was named to the 1980 U.S. Olympic basketball team but left after the boycott was announced. She also was a member of the 1975 and 1979 U.S. **World Championships** teams and Pan American Games teams. She played in the **Women's Professional Basketball League** from 1980–1981 for Dallas; in the men's **United States Basketball League** in 1986; and with the

Harlem Globetrotters' opponents, the Washington Generals, in 1987–1988.

At the age of 39, Lieberman played for the Phoenix Mercury in the **Women's National Basketball Association (WNBA)** in 1997. She was head **coach** and general manager of the Detroit Shock in the WNBA in 1998 and 1999. In 2008, she was signed to a seven-day contract and played nine **minutes** of a WNBA game at the age of 50, registering two **assists**, two **turnovers**, and missing her only **field goal** attempt. In 1996, she was enshrined in the **Naismith Memorial Basketball Hall of Fame** and, in 1999, the **Women's Basketball Hall of Fame**. On 20 November 2009, it was announced that she will be the coach of the Texas Legends of the **NBA Development League** beginning in the 2010–11 season. She will become the first female head coach of a men's professional basketball team.

LITHUANIA. Lithuania joined the **Fédération Internationale de Basketball (FIBA)** in 1935 and was a member until 1947. They then became part of the **Union of Soviet Socialist Republics (USSR)**, and their athletes competed for the USSR. In 1992, they regained their independence and rejoined FIBA as a member in the FIBA Europe zone. When Lithuanians competed for the Soviet Union, some of the best players included Stepas Butautus, Valdemaras Chomičius, Sergėjus Jovaiša, Rimas Kurtinaitis, **Šarūnas Marčiulionis**, Modestas Paulauskas, Kazys Petkevičius, **Arvydas Sabonis**, and Stanislovas Stonkus. Soviet Lithuanian women's players include Vida Bėselienė and Vitalija Tuomaitė.

The men's team has competed in all five **Olympic** tournaments since 1992, with excellent results. They won the **bronze medal** in 1992, 1996, and 2000, and finished fourth in 2004 and 2008. In 2000, they nearly defeated the **United States** in the semifinal game, as Šarūnas Jasikevičius missed a **three-point field goal** attempt at the final buzzer that would have won them the game. They defeated the United States in a preliminary round game in 2004 but lost to them in the **bronze medal** match. In the FIBA **World Championships**, they competed three times, finished seventh in 1998 and 2006, and were third in 2010. In the FIBA European Championships, they won the event in 1937 and 1939 and, after regaining independence, competed in every tournament from 1995–2007, winning in 2003, finishing second in 1995, and placing third in 2007.

The women's team has not yet competed in the Olympic Games. In the FIBA World Championships, they competed three times and finished sixth in both 1998 and 2006 and 11th in 2002. In the FIBA European Championships, they were second in 1938 and, after regaining independence, have competed in six of seven events from 1995, winning the tournament in 1997.

There have been eight players from Lithuania in the **National Basketball Association**, including several who reached star status: Martinas Andriuškevičius, Žydrūnas Ilgauskas, Šarūnas Jasikevičius, Linas Kleiza, Arvydas Macijauskas, Šarūnas Marčiulionis, Arvydas Sabonis, and Darius Songaila. Jurgita Streimikyte played in the **Women's National Basketball Association** from 2000–2005 and Aneta Kausaite in 1998.

LLOYD, EARL FRANCIS. B. 3 April 1928, Alexandria, Virginia. Earl Lloyd attended Parker-Gray High School in Alexandria and West Virginia State College. He led West Virginia State to an undefeated record and conference and tournament championships in 1948 and 1949. In college, he acquired the nickname "Moon Fixer." Selected by the **Washington Capitols** in the 1950 **National Basketball Association (NBA) draft**, he was the first black player to play in the NBA. On 31 October 1950, in an otherwise uneventful game, Lloyd scored six points in his professional debut. There was little mention of the historic occasion, and it was in no way comparable to Jackie Robinson's first game in Major League Baseball.

The six-foot, six-inch **forward-center** played seven games for Washington before being drafted into the **U.S.** Army. After the Washington franchise disbanded, his contract was acquired by the Syracuse Nationals. After being discharged in 1952, he joined the Nationals and played with them through the 1957–1958 season. Known as "Big Cat," he was traded to the **Detroit Pistons** in 1958 and concluded his playing career with them in 1960. His best year was 1954–1955, when he averaged 10.2 points and 7.7 **rebounds** per game and was a member of the NBA champions. He and teammate Jim Tucker were the first black players to play on an NBA Championship team. When their Syracuse Nationals won the 1955 league championship.

His NBA career totals for nine years are 560 regular-season games and an 8.4 points and 6.4 rebounds per game average. After retiring from active play, he was hired as assistant **coach** with the Detroit Pistons in 1960 (the NBA's first black assistant coach) and from 1960–1972 worked as assistant coach or scout for them. On 3 November 1972, he was named head coach of the Detroit Pistons (only the NBA's fourth black head coach).

During the 1960s, he also worked for the Dodge division of the Chrysler Corporation in dealer relations. He later worked for the Detroit public school system as a job placement administrator and ran programs teaching job skills. In the 1990s, he worked as community relations director for the Bing Group, a company owned by former Piston **Dave Bing**. He was enshrined in the **Naismith Memorial Basketball Hall of Fame** in 2003 in the category of contributor.

LONG ISLAND UNIVERSITY (LIU). Long Island University (LIU) is located in Brooklyn, New York. Although the New York City borough of Brooklyn is not commonly thought of as being on Long Island, it is in fact located on the western end of the island. LIU began its men's **basketball** program in 1928. Home games since 2006 have been played at the 3,000-seat Wellness, Recreation, and Athletic Center. Prior to 2006, home games were played at Arnold and Marie Schwartz Athletic Center. The most notable **coaches** in the school's history have been **Clair Bee**, Paul Lizzo, and Roy Rubin.

In 1939, the Blackbirds won the second **National Invitation Tournament (NIT)** championship. They also won the NIT two years later, in 1941. The point-shaving scandals of 1951 affected LIU severely, and LIU's Sherman White was one of those found guilty. As a result, Coach Bee resigned. The school did not field a basketball team from 1951–1957. The best players in school history have included Cliff Culuko, Ray Felix, Albie Grant, Luther Green, Art Hillhouse, Jules Kasner, **William "Dolly" King**, Barry Liebowitz, Larry Newbold, **twins** Howie and Lennie Rader, Rubin Rodriguez, Irv Rothenberg, Ossie Schectman, and Irv Torgoff.

LOS ANGELES CLIPPERS. The Los Angeles Clippers are a team in the **National Basketball Association (NBA)**. They began as the Buffalo Braves in 1970. In 1978, the team was sold, moved to San

Diego, and renamed the Clippers. After six seasons there, they relocated to Los Angeles.

Buffalo Braves. Home games were played at the 18,000-seat Buffalo Memorial Auditorium in Buffalo, New York, with a few home games played in Toronto, Ontario, **Canada**, at the 16,000-seat Maple Leaf Gardens. Among their most notable players were Ernie DiGregorio, Garfield Heard, John Hummer, Bob Kauffman, **Bob McAdoo**, Jim McMillian, Elmore Smith, Randy Smith, and John Shumate. On 20 October 1972, the Braves scored a record 58 points in the fourth quarter of a game at Boston. The following night they only scored four points in the third quarter in a home game with Milwaukee, an NBA record for fewest points in a quarter. In that game, they also had a seven-point quarter and finished with only 63 points, the third lowest total at the time in the 24-second **shot clock** era. On 7 June 1978, in an unprecedented move, owners John Y. Brown and Harry T. Mangurian traded the Buffalo franchise to Irving H. Levin and Harold Lipton for the Boston franchise. The new owners moved the Buffalo team to San Diego for the 1978–1979 season and renamed them the San Diego Clippers.

San Diego Clippers. Home games were played at the 14,500-seat San Diego Sports Arena. Among their most notable players were Michael Brooks, World B. Free, Swen Nater, Randy Smith, **Bill Walton**, Sidney Wicks, and Freeman Williams. In May 1984, the team moved to Los Angeles.

Los Angeles Clippers. The Los Angeles Clippers are owned by Donald T. Sterling. Home games were played at the 16,161-seat Los Angeles Memorial Sports Arena from 1984–1999 and have been played at the 18,997-seat Staples Center since 1999. Some games from 1994–1999 were played at the 17,600-seat Arrowhead Pond of Anaheim in Anaheim, California. Among their most notable players have been Benoit Benjamin, Elton Brand, Ron Harper, Chris Kaman, Corey Maggette, Danny Manning, Ken Norman, Eric Piatkowski, Charles E. Smith, and Loy Vaught. In the 25 years that they have played in Los Angeles, the Clippers have won more games than they lost only twice, have reached the playoffs only four times, and only in 2005–2006 did they win a playoff series and advance to the second round. The franchise overall record from 1970–2010 is 1,175–2,073, the worst in the league during this time.

LOS ANGELES LAKERS. The Los Angeles Lakers are a team in the **National Basketball Association (NBA)**. The franchise began as the Detroit Gems in the **National Basketball League (NBL)** in 1946. Following a season in which they compiled one of the worst records in professional basketball history, the franchise was sold and the team restarted as the Minneapolis Lakers. The Lakers were NBL champions, moved to the **Basketball Association of America (BAA)** that became the NBA, and relocated to Los Angeles in 1960.

Detroit Gems. In direct competition with the **Detroit Falcons** of the BAA, the Detroit Gems played in the NBL in the 1946–1947 season and established a record for futility in that league. They managed to win only four of 44 games, one of the lowest winning percentages ever in a major sports league. Dearborn businessman C. King Boring and jeweler Maurice M. Winston were the team owners. Home games were played at Lincoln High School in Ferndale, Michigan. The main players were Paul Juntunen, Dave Latter, Del Loranger, Tom Meyer, Ed Parry, and Herb Scheffler. After the season, the franchise was sold to Minneapolis businessmen Ben Bergen and Morris Chalfen and moved to Minneapolis for the 1947–1948 season.

Minneapolis Lakers. Home games were played at the Minneapolis Auditorium. The Lakers' stroke of fortune occurred when the new **Professional Basketball League of America** folded and its players were made available to NBL teams in a special draft. Since the Lakers were operating the Detroit Gems franchise and the Gems had the worst record in the league the previous season, the Lakers received first choice. **George Mikan** was their choice. Over the next decade, Mikan became the most dominant player in professional basketball and was voted as the greatest player of the first half-century in a 1950 poll. With the six-foot, 10-inch Mikan at **center**; Jack Dwan and **Jim Pollard** at **forward**; Don "Swede" Carlson and Herm Schaefer at **guard**; and Bill Durkee, Tony Jaros, Johnny Jorgensen, Paul Napolitano, and Don Smith as reserves, the Lakers became 1948 NBL champions. Following the season, the Lakers, along with three other NBL teams, were enticed to switch leagues and joined the rival BAA. The Minneapolis Lakers were one of the most successful teams in the early BAA and NBA and won five league titles from 1949–1954. Among their most notable players were future Hall of Famers **Elgin Baylor**, **Clyde Lovellette**, **Slater Martin**, George

Mikan, **Vern Mikkelsen**, and Jim Pollard. Other notable players were Dick Garmaker, Bob Harrison, Bob Leonard, Dick Schnittker, and Myer "Whitey" Skoog. In 1960, new owners Bob Short and Francis Ryan moved the team to Los Angeles.

Los Angeles Lakers. Home games were played at the 16,161-seat Los Angeles Memorial Sports Arena from 1960–1967, the 17,505-seat **Forum** from 1967–1999, and the 18,997-seat Staples Center since 1999. Their most notable players include Hall of Famers **Kareem Abdul-Jabbar**, Elgin Baylor, **Wilt Chamberlain**, Gail Goodrich, **Connie Hawkins, Earvin "Magic" Johnson, Bob McAdoo, Jerry West**, and **James Worthy. Coaches Phil Jackson, Pat Riley**, and **Bill Sharman**, and broadcaster **Chick Hearn** are also in the hall. Potential future Hall of Famers include **Kobe Bryant** and **Shaquille O'Neal**. They have been one of the most successful franchises in NBA history and have won 10 league championships since moving to Los Angeles. In addition, they have been defeated in the NBA Championship Finals on 14 other occasions. In the 1971–1972 season, they set the NBA record with a 33 consecutive game winning streak from 5 November 1971 until 7 January 1972. Their overall record for their 62 years in the league through the 2009–2010 season is 3,027–1,866, the best in the league. In 2010, they became the first NBA franchise to win 3,000 games.

LOS ANGELES STARS. *See* UTAH STARS.

LOUISIANA BUCCANEERS. *See* MEMPHIS SOUNDS.

LOUISIANA STATE UNIVERSITY (LSU). Louisiana State University in Baton Rouge began its men's **basketball** program in 1921. Home games since 1972 have been played at the 13,472-seat LSU Assembly Center (renamed the **Pete Maravich** Assembly Center in 1988 shortly after Maravich's death). Prior to 1972, home games were played at the 6,756-seat James M. Parker Agricultural Coliseum. The most notable **coaches** in the school's history have been John Brady, Dale Brown, Press Maravich (Pete's father), and Harry Rabenhorst. The Tigers have reached the **National Collegiate Athletic Association (NCAA) Final Four** four times but have never advanced past the semifinal round. The best players in school history include

Frankie Brian, **Chris Jackson** (aka **Mahmoud Abdul-Rauf**), **Pete Maravich**, **Shaquille O'Neal**, **Bob Pettit**, Jerry Reynolds, Collis Temple, and John Williams.

The women's basketball program began in 1975. They were originally nicknamed the Ben-Gals. The most notable coach has been Sue Gunter, who compiled a record of 442–221 from 1982–2004. In 1977, the Lady Tigers reached the **Association for Intercollegiate Athletics for Women** Championship final game, where they were defeated by Delta State. For five consecutive years, from 2004–2008, they reached the NCAA Championship Final Four but were defeated each year in the semifinal round. The best players in school history include Seimone Augustus, Dana "Pokey" Chatman, Madeline Doucet, Sylvia Fowles, and Roneeka Hodges.

LOUISIANA TECH UNIVERSITY. Louisiana Tech University in Ruston began its women's **basketball** program in 1974, and it has become one of the best in the nation. Home games since 1982 have been played at the 8,098-seat Samuel M. Thomas Assembly Center. In 1979, the Lady Techsters were the national runners-up in the **Association for Intercollegiate Athletics for Women (AIAW)** National Championship tournament. In 1981, they were AIAW national champions.

Louisiana Tech competed in every **National Collegiate Athletic Association** women's National Championship tournament from 1982–2006, were national champions in 1982 and 1988, were runners-up four times, and reached the **Final Four** on four other occasions. Most of their success came as the result of two **coaches**, Sonja Hogg and Leon Barmore. Hogg coached from 1974–1985 and had a record of 307–55. Barmore began in 1977 as an assistant and in 1982 was named co-head coach. His record from 1982–2002 was 576–87. The best players in school history include Janice Lawrence Braxton, Tamicha Jackson, Vickie Johnson, Venus Lacy, Betty Lennox, Kim Mulkey, Angela Turner, Teresa Weatherspoon, and Jennifer White.

LOUISVILLE, UNIVERSITY OF. The University of Louisville in Kentucky began its men's **basketball** program in 1911. Home games since 1956 have been played at 18,865-seat Freedom Hall but will move to a new 22,000 seat facility for the 2010–2011 season. The most accomplished **coaches** in the school's history have been **Denny Crum**, Bernard "Peck" Hickman, and Rick Pitino. In 1980 and 1986, the Cardinals won the **National Collegiate Athletic Association (NCAA)** Championship. They also reached the NCAA **Final Four** six other times. In 1956, they were **National Invitation Tournament** champions. Among the best players in school history have been Alfred "Butch" Beard, Ulysses "Junior" Bridgeman, Pervis Ellison, Darrell Griffith, brothers Carlton "Scooter" and Rodney McCray, Jim Price, Phil Rollins, Derek Smith, Felton Spencer, Charlie Tyra, and **Wes Unseld**.

LOVELLETTE, CLYDE EDWARD. B. 7 September 1929, Petersburg, Indiana. Clyde Lovellette attended Garfield High School in Terre Haute, Indiana, and the **University of Kansas**. Selected for the 1952 **U.S. Olympic basketball** team as a member of the **National Collegiate Athletic Association (NCAA)** Championship Kansas team, he was the leading scorer for the **gold medal**-winning team. The Minneapolis Lakers chose him in the 1952 **National Basketball Association (NBA) draft**, and after playing one year with the Phillips 66ers and leading them to the **Amateur Athletic Union (AAU)** championship, he joined the Lakers in 1953. He played in the NBA from 1953–1964 with the Lakers, Cincinnati Royals, St. Louis Hawks, and **Boston Celtics**.

In 704 regular-season games, he averaged 17.0 points and 9.5 **rebounds** per game. He played in four NBA **All-Star Games** and was voted to the All-NBA Second Team in 1956. The six-foot, 10-inch **center** was a member of the Lakers NBA Championship team in his rookie year of 1954 and was a member of the Boston Celtics NBA Championship teams in his final two NBA seasons, 1963 and 1964. In 1952, 1953, and 1954, he was on championship teams in the NCAA, Olympic Games, AAU, and NBA, an unprecedented feat. At one time he was a sheriff in Terre Haute, and after retiring from basketball he became an auto dealer in Charleston, Illinois. In 1988, he was enshrined in the **Naismith Memorial Basketball Hall of Fame.**

LOYOLA UNIVERSITY CHICAGO. There are several Jesuit universities in the **United States** named for St. Ignatius of Loyola. The one located in Chicago, Illinois, has had the most illustrious **basket-**

ball program. It began in 1913 and culminated with the **National Collegiate Athletic Association (NCAA)** Championship in 1963, when the Ramblers defeated the **University of Cincinnati**, 60–58, in **overtime**, to win the title. This was Loyola's only appearance in the NCAA **Final Four**, but they were losing finalists in the 1939 and 1949 **National Invitation Tournaments**.

Among the most celebrated players in the Ramblers' history have been John Egan, Jerry Harkness, Alfrederick Hughes, Les Hunter, LaRue Martin, Ron Miller, Charlie "Feed" Murphy, Mike Novak, Vic Rouse, and Wayne Sappleton. Home games have been played at Joseph J. Gentile Center since 1996. From 1923–1996, they were played at Alumni Gym. Among the more illustrious **coaches** at Loyola have been Hall of Famer Leonard Sachs and George Ireland, who was the coach from 1951–1975 and who coached the NCAA champion team.

LUCAS, JERRY RAY. B. 30 March 1949, Middletown, Ohio. Jerry Lucas attended Middletown High School and led them to the state championship as a sophomore and as a junior. In his senior year, the team's only loss was in the semifinals of the state tournament. They recorded a remarkable 76-game winning streak while he was a member of the team. He went to **Ohio State University** on an academic scholarship, helped lead them to the national title as a sophomore in 1960, and was selected for the 1960 **U.S. Olympic basketball** team. After winning the **gold medal** at the Olympics, he returned to Ohio State and in 1961 and 1962 again helped them reach the **National Collegiate Athletic Association (NCAA)** National Championship game, where they were defeated both times by the **University of Cincinnati**.

Lucas graduated Phi Beta Kappa in 1962 and was selected by the Cincinnati Royals as a **territorial** selection in the **National Basketball Association (NBA) draft** but signed a contract with the Cleveland Pipers **American Basketball League (ABL)** team. The NBA attempted to get the Pipers to move to their league, but the deal did not work out and the Pipers, as well as the ABL, folded. As a result, Lucas did not play during the 1962–1963 season. The following year, Lucas signed with the Royals and played in the NBA from 1963–1974. The six-foot, eight-inch **forward-center** was the

NBA Rookie of the Year in 1964. He remained with the Royals until October 1969, when new Royals head **coach, Bob Cousy**, did not see eye to eye with him and traded him to the San Francisco Warriors. He was with the Warriors until May 1971, when he was traded to the **New York Knickerbockers**. He helped to lead the Knicks to the NBA Finals in 1972 and the NBA Championship in 1973. He became the first player to win championships at all four levels of play—high school, college, Olympic, and NBA.

In his 11-year NBA career, from 1963–1974, Lucas played in 829 regular-season games and averaged 17.0 points and 15.6 **rebounds** per game. On 29 February 1964, he recorded 40 rebounds in one game, the only forward ever to do so and one of only four players to reach 40. He was named to the All-NBA First Team three times, was nominated for the All-NBA Second Team twice, was selected for seven NBA **All-Star Games**, and was named the Most Valuable Player of the 1965 All-Star Game. In both the 1964–1965 and 1965–1966 seasons, he averaged more than 20 points and 20 rebounds per game. Only **Wilt Chamberlain** ever averaged 20 points and 20 rebounds in more than one NBA season.

Lucas is an accomplished magician and has a remarkable memory. After retiring from basketball, he wrote two books on memory improvement and is an educator and a public speaker. He was enshrined in the **Naismith Memorial Basketball Hall of Fame** in 1980 and in 1996 was named one of the 50 Greatest Players in NBA History.

LUISETTI, ANGELO GIUSEPPE "HANK." B. 16 June 1916, San Francisco, California. D. 17 December 2002, San Mateo, California. Hank Luisetti attended Galileo High School in San Francisco and **Stanford University**. At Stanford, the six-foot, two-inch Luisetti helped his team end **Long Island University**'s 43-game winning streak on 30 December 1936. He was one of the first collegiate players to score 50 points in one game, doing so on 1 January 1938, against **Duquesne University**. He popularized a running one-handed shot in an era when most players used a two-handed set shot and was one of the first players to **dribble** and pass behind his back. After graduating college, he played and **coached** in **Amateur Athletic Union (AAU)** competition. In 1938, he starred in the Hollywood film *Campus Confessions*, with Betty Grable. Because of this he was suspended by the AAU for one year. In 1939, he was reinstated and was named the outstanding player in the AAU national tournament.

During World War II, while in the U.S. Navy, he developed spinal meningitis that effectively terminated his athletic career. After his time in the service, he was hired by the Stewart Chevrolet Company in San Francisco to coach their AAU team. He later became their sales manager and then worked for the E. F. MacDonald Travel Company in San Francisco and eventually became president of their West Coast Region. In an Associated Press poll in 1950, he was voted the second greatest **basketball** player of the first half-century (behind **George Mikan**) and was enshrined in the **Naismith Memorial Basketball Hall of Fame** in 1959.

– M –

MACAULEY, CHARLES EDWARD, JR. "EASY ED." B. 22 March 1928, St. Louis, Missouri. Ed Macauley attended St. Louis University High School and St. Louis University, leading them to the **National Invitation Tournament** championship in 1948 and being named Player of the Year by the Associated Press in 1949. The six-foot, eight-inch **center-forward** was a **territorial** selection by the **St. Louis Bombers** in the 1949 **Basketball Association of America draft** and played from 1949–1959 with the Bombers, **Boston Celtics**, and St. Louis Hawks. He was traded by the Celtics to the Hawks on 29 April 1956, with the rights to **Cliff Hagan** in exchange for the rights to **Bill Russell**. The trade benefited both clubs, as Russell led the Celtics to 10 championships over the next 12 seasons and Macauley led the Hawks to the 1958 **National Basketball Association (NBA)** Championship.

In his 10-year NBA career, he played in 641 regular-season games, averaged 7.5 **rebounds** and 17.5 points per game, played in seven NBA **All-Star Games**, was the Most Valuable Player in the 1951 All-Star Game, was selected to the All-NBA First Team three times, and was chosen for the All-NBA Second Team once. In 1960, he was enshrined in the **Naismith Memorial Basketball Hall of Fame**. After retiring from **basketball**, he became sports director for a St. Louis television station.

MADISON SQUARE GARDEN. Madison Square Garden is an indoor arena in New York, New York. The first Madison Square Garden was a 10,000-seat arena built in 1879 and situated on Madison Avenue and 26th Street at Madison Square. It was primarily used as a velodrome. It was replaced by a new Madison Square Garden in 1890 at the same location. The second Garden was designed by famed architect Stanford White and had a seating capacity of 8,000. It was replaced in 1925 by the third Madison Square Garden, which was not located in Madison Square but moved uptown to 50th Street and 8th Avenue. This Garden was built by boxing promoter Tex Rickard and was the site of many important boxing events.

College **basketball** doubleheaders, popularized by promoter **Ned Irish**, began in the 1930s and were the Garden's second most popular attraction. In 1946, the Garden, with a seating capacity of 18,496 for basketball, became the home of the **New York Knickerbockers**, although due to scheduling conflicts they often played home games at the much smaller **69th Regiment Armory**, especially during the first few years of their existence.

In 1967, the fourth Madison Square Garden was built. The fourth Garden, still in use in 2010, is located on 33rd Street and 7th Avenue. The third Garden closed in 1968 and was later demolished and the site used as a parking lot. The current Garden, still the home of the Knickerbockers, has a seating capacity for basketball of 19,763 and is often referred to as "The World's Most Famous Arena."

MALONE, KARL ANTHONY "THE MAILMAN." B. 24 July 1963, Summerfield, Louisiana. Karl Malone attended Summerfield High School and **Louisiana Tech University**. After his junior year, he was drafted by the **Utah Jazz** in the 1985 **National Basketball Association (NBA) draft**. Nicknamed "The Mailman" because he always delivered, he played in the NBA from 1985–2003 for the Jazz. The six-foot, nine-inch **forward** signed with the **Los Angeles Lakers** for the 2003–2004 season to play alongside **Kobe Bryant**, **Shaquille O'Neal**, and **Gary Payton** in a quest for a championship ring that had eluded him in his previous 18 seasons, but the Lakers lost in the NBA Championship Final to the **Detroit Pistons**. Malone had played in the NBA finals in 1997 and 1998 with the Jazz, but they were defeated by the **Chicago Bulls** each time.

Malone won a **gold medal** with the 1992 **U.S. Olympic basket-ball Dream Team** and was one of five Dream Team players who also played in the 1996 Olympics and won a second gold medal. In 1996, he was named one of the 50 Greatest Players in NBA History. In his 19-year NBA career, he played in 1,476 games and averaged 25.0 points per game. One of the most durable players in league history, in his first 18 seasons he never missed more than two games in any one season, playing in 1,434 of a possible 1,444 games. His total of 36,928 points scored in regular-season games is second only to **Kareem Abdul-Jabbar**'s total of 38,387. Malone is first in NBA career **minutes** played, at 54,852; first in **free throws** made and attempted; and first in defensive **rebounds** (although defensive rebounds have only been recorded since the 1973–1974 season and both **Wilt Chamberlain** and **Bill Russell** probably had more).

Malone was named the NBA's Most Valuable Player in 1997 and 1999. He was named to the All-NBA First Team 11 consecutive years from 1989–1999, the All-NBA Second Team in 1988 and 2000, and the All-NBA Third Team in 2001. He was selected for 13 NBA **All-Star Games** and was the Most Valuable Player in the 1989 game and co-Most Valuable Player, along with John Stockton, in the 1993 game. After retiring from **basketball,** he was hired by Louisiana Tech to be in charge of promotion and as assistant strength and diet **coach.** In 2010, he was enshrined in the Naismith Memorial Basketball Hall of Fame. His daughter, Cheryl Ford, played in the **Women's National Basketball Association.**

MALONE, MOSES EUGENE. B. 23 March 1955, Petersburg, Virginia. Moses Malone attended Petersburg High School and did not go to college. He was selected by the **Utah Stars** in the 1974 **American Basketball Association (ABA) draft** and was the first player to be drafted directly out of high school. The six-foot, 10-inch **center-forward** played in the ABA in 1974–1975 for the Stars and was traded to the **Spirits of St. Louis** for the 1975–1976 season. He played in the 1975 ABA **All-Star Game** and in two ABA seasons played in 126 regular-season games and averaged 17.2 points and 12.9 **rebounds.** Following the 1975–1976 season, the ABA merged with the **National Basketball Association (NBA),** but St. Louis was not one of the merged teams.

On 5 August 1976, he was selected by the **Portland Trail Blazers** of the NBA in the ABA dispersal draft. Before he played in a regular-season game, he was traded to the Buffalo Braves. He played in the NBA from 1976–1995 for Buffalo, the **Houston Rockets**, the **Philadelphia 76ers**, the Washington Bullets, the **Atlanta Hawks**, the **Milwaukee Bucks**, and the **San Antonio Spurs**. His NBA career totals for 19 years are 1,329 regular-season games and a 20.6 points and 12.2 rebounds per game average. He was a member of the 1983 NBA Championship team with Philadelphia that won 12 of 13 games in the postseason playoffs, missing his prediction (Fo', Fo', Fo') of the length of the three best-of-seven series by one game.

Malone was voted the Most Valuable Player of the 1983 Finals and was also the league's Most Valuable Player three times. Selected for 12 NBA All-Star Games, he was named to the All-NBA First Team four times, All-NBA Second Team four times, NBA All-Defensive First Team in 1983, and NBA All-Defensive Second Team in 1979. He was an exceptional offensive rebounder and holds the single-game, single-season, and career records in that category (although offensive rebounds have only been recorded since the 1973–1974 season and **Bill Russell** or **Wilt Chamberlain** would have likely bettered Malone's marks). Malone also holds the unusual distinction of most consecutive games played without being disqualified on excessive personal **fouls**. He was disqualified five times in his first two NBA seasons but then played 1,212 games over the rest of his career without being disqualified. In 1996, he was named one of the 50 Greatest Players in NBA History. He was enshrined in the **Naismith Memorial Basketball Hall of Fame** in 2001.

MARAVICH, PETER PRESS "PETE," "PISTOL PETE." B. 22 June 1947, Aliquippa, Pennsylvania. D. 5 January 1988, Pasadena, California. Pete Maravich attended Daniel High School in Central, South Carolina; Needham Broughton High School in Raleigh, North Carolina; and Edwards Military Institute in Salemburg, North Carolina. He spent his youth constantly practicing shooting and ball handling under the tutelage of his father, Press Maravich, a former **Basketball Association of America** player. Pete played college **basketball** at **Louisiana State University**, where his father was head **coach**. In three years of varsity basketball, he scored a **National**

Collegiate Athletic Association record 3,667 points and averaged a record 44.2 points per game. He was known for his fancy ball handling, amazing passing ability, and wide variety of shots.

Selected by the **Atlanta Hawks** in the 1970 **National Basketball Association (NBA) draft**, the six-foot, five-inch **guard** played in the NBA until 1980 for the Hawks, New Orleans Jazz, and **Boston Celtics**. Maravich's best year was 1976–1977 with the Jazz, when he led the league in scoring with an average of 31.1 points per game. On 25 February 1977, he scored 68 points in a game against the **New York Knickerbockers**. Only six other players have ever scored more points in an NBA game. A leg injury helped to bring about his retirement from the game after just 10 seasons.

Maravich's NBA career totals are 658 regular-season games and a 24.2 points per game average. He was selected for five NBA **All-Star Games,** was twice named to the All-NBA First Team, and was twice nominated to the All-NBA Second Team. His career was disappointing in that he never played on a team in which his talents were best used, and he never won a college or professional championship. After retiring he became a recluse and searched for life and its meaning in various ways. He was enshrined in the **Naismith Memorial Basketball Hall of Fame** in 1987. He died at the age of 40 of a heart attack while playing a pickup game of basketball. An autopsy disclosed that he had a congenital defect and was missing the left coronary artery, which supplies blood to the heart. In 1996, he was named one of the 50 Greatest Players in NBA History.

MARCARI OLIVA, HORTÊNCIA MARIA DE FÁTIMA. B. 23 September 1959, Potirendaba, São Paulo, **Brazil**. Only five-feet, eight-inches tall, Hortência is one of the candidates for the title of greatest female **basketball** player of all time. Known only by her first name throughout the basketball world, she is a basketball legend in Brazil, rivaled only by **Oscar Schmidt**. She possessed the ability to shoot from anywhere on the court and, like Oscar, never hesitated to do so. In fact, she once scored 121 points in a game in Brazil.

Hortência joined the Brazilian national team in 1975 at the age of 15 and played with them for 21 years, culminating in an **Olympic silver medal** in Atlanta in 1996. Along the way, she participated in four Pan American Games and won a **bronze medal** in Caracas in

1983, a silver medal in Indianapolis in 1987, and a **gold medal** with the defeat of **Cuba** in Havana in 1991. She was on the 1994 **World Championships** team and competed in two Olympic Games. She retired in 1994 and had given birth to a son in February 1996, but was persuaded to come out of retirement for the Atlanta Games. At 36 years and 302 days of age, she became the oldest female Olympic basketball player when she stepped on the court in Atlanta. The Queen of Brazilian basketball was elected to the **Women's Basketball Hall of Fame** in 2002 and in 2005 became only the second female player from outside the United States to be elected to the **Naismith Memorial Basketball Hall of Fame**. In 2007, when the **Fédération Internationale de Basketball (FIBA)** Hall of Fame was opened she was a member of its inaugural class.

MARCH MADNESS. March Madness is a term that has been used by sportswriters to describe the season when high school and college **basketball** tournaments are held, usually during the month of March. Although it has been the title of more than one book, in recent years the **National Collegiate Athletic Association** has managed to acquire a trademark for the phrase. *See also* FINAL FOUR.

MARČIULIONIS, RAIMONDAS ŠARŪNAS, "ROONEY." B. 13 June 1964, Kaunas, **Lithuania, Union of Soviet Socialist Republics (USSR)**. Šarūnas Marčiulionis attended the State University of Vilnius in Lithuania. He began playing with Statyba Vilnius in Lithuania in 1981 and played for them until 1989. The six-foot, five-inch **left-handed guard** was selected by the **Golden State Warriors** in the 1987 **National Basketball Association (NBA) draft** and played from 1989–1997 for the Warriors, Seattle Supersonics, **Sacramento Kings**, and **Denver Nuggets**. His NBA career totals for seven years are 363 regular-season games and a 12.8 points per game average. He played for the Soviet Union national team and helped lead them to the **silver medal** at the 1987 European Championships, the **bronze medal** at the 1989 European Championships, and the **gold medal** at the 1988 **Olympic** Games. He was also awarded the Merited Master of Sport of the USSR in 1988.

In 1990, after Lithuania's independence, he helped organize a Lithuanian national team and was one of their key players in the

1992 and 1996 Olympic Games, winning bronze medals at both tournaments and a silver medal at the 1995 European Championships. He opened the Šarūnas Hotel in Vilnius in 1992. In 1993, he began the Lithuanian Basketball League and was its president. In 1999, he founded the North European Basketball League and became commissioner. He is also the president of the Šarūnas Marčiulionis Basketball Academy.

MARQUETTE UNIVERSITY. Marquette University in Milwaukee, Wisconsin, began its men's **basketball** program in 1910. Home games since 1988 have been played at the 19,000-seat Bradley Center. Prior to 1988, home games were played at the 11,000-seat Milwaukee Arena. The most noteworthy **coaches** in the school's history have been **Al McGuire** and Hank Raymonds. The team's nickname was the Warriors but was changed to Golden Eagles in 1994, when the **National Collegiate Athletic Association (NCAA)** decided that political correctness was in vogue. In 1974, the Warriors finished second in the NCAA National Championships, but in 1977 they won the tournament. In 2003, they again reached the **Final Four** but lost in the semifinal round. They won the **National Invitation Tournament** in 1967 and 1970. The best players in school history include Jim Chones, Maurice "Bo" Ellis, Alfred "Butch" Lee, Maurice Lucas, Dean Meminger, Larry McNeill, Glenn "Doc" Rivers, and **Dwyane Wade.**

MARTIN, SLATER NELSON, JR. "DUGIE." B. 22 October 1925, El Mina, Texas. Slater Martin attended Jefferson Davis High School in Houston, Texas, and led them to the state **basketball** championship in 1942 and 1943. He attended the **University of Texas** for one year, served two years in the **U.S.** Navy, and returned to school in 1946. In 1947, he led Texas to a third place finish in the **National Collegiate Athletic Association (NCAA)** National Championship tournament.

After graduation, Martin was signed by the Minneapolis Lakers and played with them from 1949–1956, winning four **National Basketball Association (NBA)** Championships. At just five-feet, 10-inches tall, he was the shortest NBA player of his era. In 1956, he was traded to the **New York Knickerbockers** and, after just 13 games with them, was traded to the St. Louis Hawks. He played with the Hawks through the 1959–1960 season and won another NBA Championship in 1958.

Martin's NBA career totals for 11 years are 745 regular-season games and a 9.8 points and 4.2 **assists** per game average. He was selected for seven NBA **All-Star Games** and was named to the All-NBA Second Team five times. He **coached** the Houston Mavericks in the **American Basketball Association**'s first season, 1967–1968, but was replaced after just 12 games in the 1968–1969 season. He has worked in public relations, building construction, and restaurant businesses. In 1982, he was enshrined in the **Naismith Memorial Basketball Hall of Fame**.

MARYLAND, UNIVERSITY OF. The University of Maryland in College Park began its men's **basketball** program in 1918. Home games since 2002 have been played at the 17,950-seat Comcast Center. Prior to 2002, home games were played at the 12,500-seat William J. Cole Fieldhouse. The most accomplished **coaches** in the school's history have been Charles "Lefty" Driesell, H. A. "Bud" Millikan, and Guy Williams. In 2002, the Terrapins won the **National Collegiate Athletic Association (NCAA)** Championship. Their only other **Final Four** appearance was in 2001, when they lost in the semifinals but they won the **National Invitation Tournament** in 1972. The best male players in school history include Len Bias, Steve Blake, Len Elmore, Steve Francis, **Lithuanian Olympian** Šarūnas Jasikevičius, Albert King, John Lucas, Tom McMillen, Gene Shue, and Charles "Buck" Williams.

The women's basketball program began in 1971. Chris Weller (499–286 from 1975–2002) has been the most notable coach. In 1978, the Lady Terrapins reached the **Association for Intercollegiate Athletics for Women** National Championship final game, where they lost to the **University of California, Los Angeles**. In 2006, they won the NCAA National Championship. In 1982 and 1989, they reached the NCAA Final Four but lost in the semifinal round. The best female players in school history have been Vicky Bullett, Shay Doron, Tara Heiss, Jessie Hicks, Kris Kirchner, Crystal Langhorne, **Yugoslavian** Olympian Jasmina Perazic, Kristi Toliver, Myra Waters, and Christy Winters.

McADOO, ROBERT ALLEN, JR. "BOB." B. 25 September 1951, Greensboro, North Carolina. Bob McAdoo attended Ben Smith High School in Greensboro, Vincennes Junior College, and the **University of North Carolina.** The six-foot, nine-inch **center-forward** was selected after his junior season by the Buffalo Braves in the 1972 **National Basketball Association (NBA) draft** and played from 1972–1986 for the Braves, **New York Knickerbockers, Boston Celtics, Detroit Pistons, New Jersey Nets, Los Angeles Lakers,** and **Philadelphia 76ers.**

McAdoo's best year was 1974–1975, when he led the league in scoring with an average of 34.5 points per game, while also recording 14.1 **rebounds** per game. That same year he was voted the league's Most Valuable Player and named to the All-NBA First Team. He was the NBA's scoring leader in 1974, 1975, and 1976. His NBA career totals for 14 years are 852 regular-season games and a 22.1 points per game average. Selected for five NBA **All-Star Games,** he was also named to the All-NBA Second Team in 1974 and was chosen as the Rookie of the Year in 1973. With the Lakers, in 1982 and 1985, he was a member of the NBA Championship team.

After retiring from the NBA, he played in **Italy** from 1986–1993 and averaged 26.6 points per game in seven seasons. In 1988, he won the Euroleague Finals Most Valuable Player award and in 2008 was named as one of the 50 Greatest Contributors in Euroleague History. He was enshrined in the **Naismith Memorial Basketball Hall of Fame** in 2000. He was assistant **coach** with the **Miami Heat** from 1995–2010.

McDERMOTT, ROBERT FREDERICK "BOBBY." B. 7 January 1914, Whitestone, New York. D. 3 October 1963, New York, New York. Bobby McDermott attended Flushing High School in Flushing, New York, but dropped out of school after just one year and did not play **basketball** there. He began playing semiprofessional basketball for the Whitestone Separates Juniors at the age of 15. From 1934–1941, he played with the Brooklyn Visitations, New York Celtics, and Baltimore Clippers of the **American Basketball League.** From 1941–1949, he played in the **National Basketball League (NBL)** with the Fort Wayne Pistons, **Chicago American Gears, Sheboygan Redskins,** Tri-Cities Blackhawks, and Hammond Ciesar All-Americans.

As player-**coach**, he led Fort Wayne to the 1944 and 1945 NBL league championships and played on the 1947 NBL champion Gears.

McDermott's hotheadedness was the major cause of his frequent movement, although he was arguably the league's best player. The six-foot-tall **guard** had an excellent two-handed set shot with deep range. Had the **three-point** line been in effect in that era, many of his **field goals** would have earned three instead of two points. His NBL career totals for eight seasons were 287 regular-season games and a 12.5 points per game average. McDermott played for Wilkes-Barre of the Eastern Professional Basketball League in 1949–1950 and concluded his professional basketball career by playing five games as player-coach with the Grand Rapids Hornets of the **National Professional Basketball League** in 1950–1951, before being suspended for the season in November by league commissioner Doxie Moore "for conduct unbecoming a coach." Mrs. Doxie Moore, wife and assistant to the commissioner, provided the details. After a game at Casper, Wyoming, on 14 November 1950, which Grand Rapids lost to the Denver Refiners, the league office was "deluged with telegrams from the Casper chamber of commerce, the game officials and spectators. They agreed that McDermott's profanity could be heard all over the gymnasium and that he ripped doors off lockers in the dressing room after shouting that his team had been robbed."

After retiring from basketball, he worked as a salesman for Security Cartridge Trucking in Fort Wayne and then returned to Flushing, where he worked as a life insurance salesman. He also worked part-time at night at Yonkers Raceway for the Pinkerton Agency, counting the day's receipts. He died of injuries from an auto accident in 1963. He was enshrined in the **Naismith Memorial Basketball Hall of Fame** in 1988. In an ironic note, the author of this book was raised in Whitestone and graduated from Flushing High School a generation after McDermott but in his 32 years of living there never once heard of McDermott.

McGINNIS, GEORGE F. B. 12 August 1950, Indianapolis, Indiana. George McGinnis attended Washington High School in Indianapolis and led his team to an undefeated season, took his team to the Indiana state high school championship, and was named Mr. Basketball in 1969. He enrolled at **Indiana University** but signed with the **Indiana Pacers** of the **American Basketball Association (ABA)** after his sophomore year. The six-foot, eight-inch **forward-center** played in the ABA from 1971–1975 for the Indiana Pacers and in the NBA from 1975–1982 for the **Philadelphia 76ers, Denver Nuggets**, and Pacers. McGinnis was known for holding and shooting the **basketball** with just one hand. His best year was 1974–1975, when he averaged 29.8 points, 14.3 **rebounds**, 6.3 **assists**, and 2.6 **steals** for the Pacers; led the league in scoring; and was named the ABA's co-Most Valuable Player. He was twice selected for the All-ABA First team, once nominated for the All-NBA First Team, and also chosen once each for the All-ABA Second Team and All-NBA Second Team. He was selected for six **All-Star Games**, three in each league.

His ABA career totals for four seasons are 314 regular-season games and 25.2 points and 12.9 rebounds per game. He was a member of the ABA Championship team in 1972 and 1973. His NBA career totals for seven years are 528 regular-season games and a 17.2 points and 9.8 rebounds per game average. In 1977, he reached the NBA Championship Finals with Philadelphia. His overall professional career totals for 11 years are 842 regular-season games with 11.0 rebounds and 20.2 points per game averages. After retiring from basketball, he founded a company in Indianapolis that deals in automotive parts and components.

McGRADY, TRACY LAMAR, JR. B. 24 May 1979, Bartow, Florida. Tracy McGrady attended Auburndale High School in Auburndale, Florida, and Mount Zion Christian Academy in Durham, North Carolina. He did not attend college and was taken in the 1997 **National Basketball Association (NBA) draft** by the **Toronto Raptors**. The six-foot, eight-inch **forward** played for the Raptors from 1997–2000. In 2000, he was traded to the **Orlando Magic**. His game improved dramatically, and he was voted the NBA's Most Improved Player in 2001, after he raised his scoring average from 15.4 to 26.8 points per game. On 10 March 2004, he scored 62 points in one game against the **Washington Wizards**, one of only 12 players to score 62 or more points in a single NBA game. In 2003 and 2004, he led the NBA in scoring, with scoring averages of 32.1 and 28.0. In 2004, he was traded to the **Houston Rockets** and was with them until 18 February 2010, when he was traded to the New York Knickerbockers. On 16 August 2010, he signed a one-year contract to play for the Detroit Pistons.

In his first 13 NBA seasons, he played in 814 regular-season games and averaged 21.5 points per game. He was named to the NBA **All-Star Game** seven times, each year from 2001–2007. He was twice chosen for the All-NBA First Team, three times to the All-NBA Second Team, and twice to the All-NBA Third Team. He is a cousin of **Vince Carter**.

McGUIRE, ALFRED JAMES "AL." B. 7 September 1928, New York, New York. D. 26 January 2001, Milwaukee, Wisconsin. Al McGuire attended St. John's Prep in Long Island City, New York, and **St. John's University**. Chosen by the **New York Knickerbockers** in the 1951 **National Basketball Association (NBA) draft**, he played from 1951–1954 for the Knicks and **Baltimore Bullets**. The six-foot, two-inch **guard** was a defensive specialist and complemented his brother, Dick, who was the playmaker and scorer in the Knicks **backcourt**.

Al's NBA career totals for four years are 191 regular-season games and a 4.0 points per game average. After retiring from active play, he became a **coach**. From 1954–1957, he was assistant coach at Dartmouth College. From 1957–1964, he was head coach at Belmont Abbey College. In 1964, he was named head coach of **Marquette University** and led them to the 1970 **National Invitation Tournament** title, 1974 **National Collegiate Athletic Association (NCAA)** Championship runner-up position, and 1977 NCAA Championship, retiring from coaching after the 1977 season with a record of 295–80. He became one of the most popular college **basketball** broadcasters and in 1992 was enshrined in the **Naismith Memorial Basketball Hall of Fame** as a coach.

McGUIRE, RICHARD JOSEPH "DICK." B. 25 January 1926, New York, New York. D. 3 February 2010, Huntington, New York. Dick McGuire attended La Salle Academy in New York and **St. John's University**. In his freshman year in college, he had the unique distinction of playing for two different schools, one the **National Invitation Tournament (NIT)** champion and the other the **National Collegiate Athletic Association (NCAA)** runner-up. At St. John's, he helped his team earn an entry into the NIT (which they eventually won) but was required to leave the team in February to attend Dartmouth College for training for the **U.S.** Navy. Although he did not play in the NIT, he was voted to the New York Basketball Writers all-star team. He played for Dartmouth in March 1944, and helped lead them to the NCAA Championship game, where they were defeated by the **University of Utah** in **overtime**. After completing his naval service, he resumed his college education in 1946, graduating in 1949.

McGuire was selected by the **New York Knickerbockers** in the 1949 **Basketball Association of America draft**. The six-foot-tall **guard**, known as "Tricky Dick" for his excellent ball handling abilities, played from 1949–1960 for the Knicks and **Detroit Pistons**. His **National Basketball Association (NBA)** career totals for 11 years are 738 regular-season games and an 8.0 points and 5.7 **assists** per game average. Selected for seven NBA **All-Star Games**, he was named to the All-NBA Second Team in 1951.

In 1959, McGuire was made player-**coach** of the Pistons. He completed the season in the dual roles but the following year retired as a player and just coached the team until 1963. From 1965–1967, he was Knicks coach. He was replaced in December 1967, and for the next 40 years was director of scouting for the Knicks. In 1993, McGuire was enshrined in the **Naismith Memorial Basketball Hall of Fame**. His brother, Al, was a Knick teammate, and Al's son, Allie, Dick's nephew, later briefly played for the Knicks.

McHALE, KEVIN EDWARD. B. 19 December 1957, Hibbing, Minnesota. Kevin McHale attended Hibbing High School and the University of Minnesota. In high school, he was named Mr. Basketball for the state of Minnesota, as he led Hibbing to the state championship game in 1976. The six-foot, 10-inch **forward** was selected by the **Boston Celtics** in the 1980 **National Basketball Association (NBA) draft** and played for them from 1980–1993. His best year was 1986–1987, when he averaged 26.1 points and 9.9 **rebounds** per game, led the league in **field goal** percentage, and was named to the All-NBA First Team.

McHale's NBA career totals for 13 years are 971 regular-season games and a 17.9 points and 7.3 rebounds per game average. He has extremely long arms that helped make him an excellent defensive player. He was selected for seven NBA **All-Star Games** and was named to the NBA All-Defensive First Team three times and NBA All-Defensive Second Team three times. He was twice the recipient of the NBA **Sixth Man** of the Year Award. A member of three NBA Championship teams and two NBA runners-up, he teamed with **Larry Bird** and **Robert Parish** to form one of the best **frontcourts** in NBA history.

After retiring from active play, he became assistant general manager of the **Minnesota Timberwolves** in 1994 and then vice president of Basketball Operations from 1995–2009. In 2008–2009, he was also their **coach**. In 1996, he was named one of the 50 Greatest Players in NBA History and was enshrined in the **Naismith Memorial Basketball Hall of Fame** in 1999.

McLENDON, JOHN B., JR. B. 5 April 1915, Hiawatha, Kansas. D. 8 October 1999, Cleveland Heights, Ohio. John McLendon's father was an African American who could trace his family back to pre–Civil War times, while McClendon's mother was a full-blooded Delaware Indian. He attended Kansas City Junior College and the **University of Kansas**, where he met **James Naismith**, who was a professor at the university. Although McLendon was the only black physical education student at the school, he was shielded from discrimination by his relationship with Naismith. McLendon did not play **basketball** for Kansas, since their basketball program had not yet been integrated. He graduated in 1936 and obtained a scholarship to the University of Iowa with Naismith's help.

In 1937, after graduating with a master's degree, McLendon accepted a position at the North Carolina College for Negroes (now known as North Carolina Central University) and worked as assistant **coach** in football, basketball, and track. In 1940, he was named head basketball coach. From 1940–1952, his basketball teams had a record of 264–60. From 1952–1954, he taught at Hampton Institute in Virginia and in 1954 was hired by Tennessee A&I College (later known as Tennessee State University). During his time there, he led them to consecutive **National Association of Intercollegiate Athletics** National Championships in 1957, 1958, and 1959.

In 1959, he was hired as coach of the Cleveland Pipers of the **National Industrial Basketball League (NIBL)**. He coached the Pipers in the NIBL for two seasons. When the Pipers joined the new professional **American Basketball League** in 1961, McLendon became the first black coach of an integrated U.S. major league professional sports team. In January 1962, a situation occurred where his players were not paid, and he resigned from the team in their support. He then worked for the U.S. Department of State teaching basketball in Malaya and Indonesia as part of a cultural exchange program. In 1966, he became the first black coach hired by a predominantly white university when he was chosen by Cleveland State University as their head coach.

After three years there, he accepted a job as coach of the Denver Rockets of the **American Basketball Association**. The team got off to a slow start, and after just 28 games he was fired. He was then hired by the Converse Rubber Company as the company's national and international promotional representative. Although he was primarily a coach, he was enshrined in the **Naismith Memorial Basketball Hall of Fame** in 1978 in the category of contributor. His main contribution was in successfully working toward the breaking of racial segregation barriers.

MEMPHIS GRIZZLIES. The Memphis Grizzlies are a team in the **National Basketball Association (NBA)**. They were formerly known as the Vancouver Grizzlies and moved to Memphis in 2001.

Vancouver Grizzlies. The Vancouver Grizzlies entered the NBA in 1995 as an expansion team along with the **Toronto Raptors**, another **Canadian** team. Home games were played at the newly constructed 20,000-seat General Motors Place. The Grizzlies won their first two games and are only the second of the league's 18 expansion teams to do so. After winning those two games, they lost their next 19. Later that same season, they set the NBA record for team futility, since tied by the 1997–1998 **Denver Nuggets**, by losing 23 consecutive games. Their most notable players include Shareef Abdur-Rahim, Greg Anthony, Mike Bibby, Othella Harrington, Lee Mayberry, Anthony Peeler, and Bryant Reeves. Chicago businessman Michael Heisley purchased the team in 2000 for $160 million and promised to keep the team in Vancouver, even though their attendance was declining. After the Grizzlies lost $40 million in his first year, Heisley reneged on his promise and moved the team to Memphis in 2001.

Memphis Grizzlies. Home games were played at the 20,142-seat Pyramid Arena from 2001–2004 and the 18,119-seat FedEx Forum since then. Among their most notable players have been Shane Battier, Mike Conley, **Pau Gasol**, his brother Marc, Rudy Gay, Mike Miller, Hakim Warrick, Jason Williams, and Lorenzen Wright. Their best regular-season record, 50–32, was in 2003–2004. They reached the postseason playoffs three straight years, from 2004–2006, but lost all four games in the first round each time. In Vancouver, they never reached the playoffs, and through 2010, the franchise has never won a playoff game. The franchise record from 1995–2010 is 404–794.

MEMPHIS PROS. *See* MEMPHIS SOUNDS.

MEMPHIS SOUNDS. The Memphis Sounds were a team in the **American Basketball Association (ABA)**. As the New Orleans Buccaneers, they were a charter member of the league. They relocated to Memphis in 1970 and played as the Memphis Pros, Tams, and Sounds. In 1975, they moved to Baltimore as the Claws but after three exhibition games were disbanded. In eight ABA seasons, the overall franchise record was 275–385.

New Orleans Buccaneers. The New Orleans Buccaneers began in the ABA in 1967, when a Louisiana group of owners, including Sean Morton Downey Jr., received a league franchise. Home games were played at the 6,500-seat Loyola Field House for the first two seasons and the 6,650-seat Municipal Auditorium and 4,650-seat Tulane University Field House their last season. One of the first players signed by the Buccaneers was Doug Moe, who had been implicated in the 1960 college scandals and blacklisted by the **National Basketball Association (NBA)** although never indicted. **Larry Brown**, a five-foot, nine-inch **guard** who had starred in the **Amateur Athletic Union** but was considered "too short" for the NBA, was also signed. Others on the team included Jess Branson, Gerald Govan, Jimmy Jones, Jackie Moreland, and Austin "Red" Robbins. Their best season was their first, when they lost to the **Pittsburgh Pipers** in the ABA Championship Finals. Following the 1969–1970, season the team was renamed the Louisiana Buccaneers in anticipation of playing future home games in several Louisiana cities, but in August the franchise was sold to P. L. Blake, who moved the team to Memphis, renaming them the Memphis Pros.

Memphis Pros/Tams/Sounds. Home games were played at the 10,753-seat Mid-South Coliseum. The team included Wendell Ladner, an extremely aggressive player and a fan favorite; Gerald Govan; Craig Raymond; and the unrelated Jones boys, Steve, Jimmy, and Wil. Also on the team were Al Cueto, Lee Davis, Bobby Warren, and Charlie Williams. On 14 January 1972, the Pros scored 52 points in the fourth quarter to set a league record. During the season, owner Blake gave up on the franchise and turned it over to the league, claiming losses of more than $200,000. Shares in the team were then sold to more than 4,000 Tennessee residents in an attempt to save the franchise. Charles Finley, owner of the Kansas City Athletics' Major League Baseball team, purchased the franchise and renamed it the TAMS, for Tennessee, Arkansas, and Mississippi. After two seasons in last place, Finley gave up on the team, and the league again took over the franchise. In July 1974, a group headed by ABA commissioner Mike Storen, who resigned his position, and including entertainer Isaac Hayes, purchased the franchise and renamed the team the Memphis Sounds. Storen, as general manager, made substantial player acquisitions and fielded a virtually new team. Following the season, the ABA required the team to meet certain financial requirements by 1 June 1975, and when they were unable to do so, the league once more took over the team. In August, a group headed by David Cohan of Baltimore, Maryland, acquired the team and moved it to Baltimore.

Baltimore Claws. As the Baltimore Claws they played three exhibition games (losing all three) but disbanded before the start of the regular season and never played a regular-season game. ABA commissioner **Dave DeBusschere**, on 16 October 1975, gave the Baltimore management four days to raise $500,000 as a performance bond to be held by the league. When they failed to do so, the league terminated the franchise four days later.

MEMPHIS TAMS. *See* MEMPHIS SOUNDS.

MENEGHIN, DINO. B. 18 January 1950, Alano di Piave, **Italy**. Although never a prolific scorer, Dino Meneghin was known for his aggressive play and champion's demeanor. He began playing **bas-ketball** for Varese at the age of 16 in 1966, and helped lead them to the **European Cup** Championship final game 10 consecutive years from 1970–1979. He moved to Milan in 1980 and led them twice to the European Cup championship. He played for Trieste from 1990–1993 and concluded his professional career playing for Milan in 1993–1994, retiring at the age of 44 after playing 836 games in Italian League competition. In the 21 years from 1969–1989, his team won the Italian League championship 12 times and was the runner-up team the other nine times. He was selected by the **Atlanta Hawks** in the 1970 **National Basketball Association (NBA) draft** as the 182nd overall selection but never played in the NBA.

The six-foot, eight-inch **center** played in four **Olympic Games** from 1972–1984 and won a **silver medal** in 1980. An aggressive defensive player, Meneghin is second all-time in Olympic Games total **rebounds** and first in personal **fouls**. He also played for Italy in the 1970 and 1978 **World Championships**. During his eight starts in the European Championships, he won a **bronze medal** in 1975 and a **gold medal** in 1983. He played 271 games for the Italian national team and scored 2,947 points during those games.

In 1983, Meneghin was also named the European Player of the Year by both *Superbasket* and *La Gazzetta dello Sport*. In 1991, he was selected as the "greatest player in European history" by the Italian basketball magazine *Giganti del Basket*. In Jim Patton's absorbing 1994 book on Italian League basketball, *Il Basket d'Italia*, Meneghin is described as "Il Monumento Nazionale" (the national monument). He was enshrined in the **Naismith Memorial Basketball Hall of Fame** in 2003. His son, Andrea, is a professional basketball player who also played for the Italian national team and played against his father in the Italian league. In 2008, Dino Meneghin was selected as one of the 50 Greatest Contributors in Euroleague History. In 2010, he was inducted into the **Fédération Internationale de Basketball** Hall of Fame.

MEXICO. Mexico joined the **Fédération Internationale de Basketball (FIBA)** in 1936 and is a member in the FIBA Americas zone. The men's team competed in seven **Olympic** tournaments and won the **bronze medal** in 1936. In the 1976 Olympic Games, Arturo Guerrero averaged 27.8 points per game and had individual games of 41 and 40 points, making him the first Olympian to record more than one game of 40 points or better. In the FIBA **World Championships**, Mexico competed four times, with a best finish of eighth in 1967. They entered the FIBA Americas Championships 10 times and had a best finish of fifth in both 1980 and 1984. In the Pan American Games, they have entered 13 times and won the **silver medal** in 1967 and 1991 and the bronze medal in 1983.

The women's team has yet to compete in the Olympic tournament. In the FIBA World Championships, they competed three times, with sixth place in 1975 being their best effort. In the FIBA Americas Championships, they have competed six times, with fourth place twice being their best showing. In the Pan American Games, the Mexican women have entered eight times, and their only medal was in 1975, when as host nation they finished second.

There have been two players from Mexico in the **National Basketball Association (NBA)**, Horacio Llamas and Eduardo Najera, and none thus far in the **Women's National Basketball Association**. Manuel Raga, in 1970, and Alberto Almanza, in 1961, were drafted by the NBA but did not play there.

MEYER, RAYMOND JOSEPH "RAY." B. 8 December 1913, Chicago, Illinois. D. 17 March 2006, Wheeling, Illinois. Ray Meyer began high school at Quigley Preparatory Seminary in Chicago studying for the priesthood but after two years transferred to St. Patrick's Academy, in Chicago, where he was a member of the national Catholic high school **basketball** champions in 1932. He enrolled at Northwestern University but transferred to **Notre Dame University**, graduating in 1938 with a bachelor's degree in social work.

Meyer played **Amateur Athletic Union** basketball for the La Salle Hotel Cavaliers after graduation. He began **coaching** as an assistant at Notre Dame but was given the head coach position at **DePaul University** in 1942. He coached DePaul from 1942–1984 and had a won–lost record of 724–354. In 1944, with **George Mikan** on the team, DePaul was the runner-up in the **National Invitation Tournament (NIT)**, and in 1945 they were NIT champions. In 1948, they finished in fourth place in the NIT, and in 1943 and 1979, they were semifinal losers in the **National Collegiate Athletic Association (NCAA)** National Championships.

During the 1950s, Meyer was coach of the College All-Stars, which played an annual series with the **Harlem Globetrotters**. He also ran a summer basketball camp in Wisconsin. Upon his retirement in 1984, his son, Joey, became head coach of DePaul. Another son, Tom, coached at the University of Illinois-Chicago Circle and in the 1981–1982 season coached his team against his father's DePaul team. After retiring from coaching, Ray Meyer worked as a broadcast analyst. He was enshrined in the **Naismith Memorial Basketball Hall of Fame** in 1979 as a coach.

MEYERS (DRYSDALE), ANN ELIZABETH. B. 26 March 1955, San Diego, California. Ann Meyers attended Sonora High School in La Habra, California, and the **University of California, Los Angeles (UCLA)**. She played for the U.S. national team in the 1975 and 1979 Pan American Games and the 1976 **Olympic Games** and was the flag bearer at the 1979 Pan Am Games. She led UCLA to the 1978 **Association for Intercollegiate Athletics for Women (AIAW)** National Championship. On 18 February 1978, at UCLA, she recorded a **quadruple-double**—20 points, 14 **rebounds**, 10 **assists**, and 10 **steals**—a rare feat only accomplished a few times in basketball history.

In 1979, Meyers was given a tryout with the **Indiana Pacers** of the men's **National Basketball Association (NBA)**. She played **Amateur Athletic Union (AAU)** basketball with a team called "Anna's Bananas" from 1977–1979 and won the national AAU Championship each year. The five-foot, eight-inch **guard** played professionally for New Jersey in the **Women's Professional Basketball League** in 1979–1980.

An all-around athlete, in 1980, 1981, and 1982, she won the made-for-television *Women's Superstars* competition each year by outscoring other female athletes in a combination of seven different athletic competitions. (In high school, besides **basketball**, she played softball, badminton, field hockey, and tennis and won 13 most valuable player awards). Her brother, Dave, played in the NBA from 1975–1980 with the **Milwaukee Bucks**. In 1986, she married former Major League Baseball player Don Drysdale and remained married to him until his death in 1993.

Meyers was enshrined in the **Naismith Memorial Basketball Hall of Fame** in 1993, the **Women's Basketball Hall of Fame** in 1999, and the **Fédération Internationale de Basketball** Hall of Fame in 2007. She has worked as a television analyst, is general manager of the Phoenix Mercury of the **Women's National Basketball Association**, and is a vice president of the NBA **Phoenix Suns**.

MIAMI FLORIDIANS. The Miami Floridians were a team in the **American Basketball Association (ABA)**. They began play in the league's first year as the Minnesota Muskies and moved to Florida in 1968. After two seasons in Miami, they were renamed simply "The Floridians," playing home games in several Florida cities. The franchise was disbanded in 1972, after compiling a record of 189–219 for five ABA seasons.

Minnesota Muskies. Home games were played at the 15,500-seat Metropolitan Sports Center in Bloomington, Minnesota. Their **coach** was former Minneapolis Laker **Jim Pollard**. In the 1967 ABA **draft**, they selected college star **Mel Daniels** as their first choice. He was one of the few college star players to sign with an ABA team in 1967. Other players on the Muskies that season included Donnie Freeman, Les Hunter, Erv Inniger, Ron Perry, and Sam Smith. Although the Muskies were successful on the court, they did not draw well and in May 1968 moved to Miami, Florida.

Miami Floridians/The Floridians. Home games were played at Miami Beach Convention Hall, a 9,500-seat arena. In a cost-saving move, the Floridians traded Daniels, their best player, for two lesser-known players and badly needed cash. Despite losing Daniels, they still finished in second place in the Eastern Division. Their second year, 1969–1970, home games were moved to the 6,000-seat Miami-Dade Junior College North Arena and the 6,900-seat Dinner Key Auditorium, a converted airplane hangar. Their one star player that season was Freeman, who averaged 27.4 points per game. At the conclusion of the season, the team was sold to Ned Doyle, who made some substantial changes and renamed the team simply The Floridians. As a regional franchise, home games were played at Tampa, St. Petersburg, West Palm Beach, and Jacksonville, in addition to Miami. Owner Doyle also made some additional promotional moves, including one of the ABA's most memorable ones—bikini-clad ball girls. None of the 22 players who appeared for the Miami Floridians in the 1969–1970 season played for the new team in 1970–1971.

Mack Calvin, Warren Davis, Carl Fuller, Ira Harge, Walter "Larry" Jones, Sam Robinson, and Tom "Trooper" Washington had the most playing time. On 13 June 1972, the franchise was purchased by the ABA and disbanded.

MIAMI HEAT. The Miami Heat is a team in the **National Basketball Association (NBA)**. On 22 April 1987, a group headed by Ted Arison purchased an expansion franchise to begin play in the 1988–1989 season. Home games were played at the 16,640-seat Miami Arena from 1988–1999 and the 20,000-seat American Airlines Arena since 1999. Among their most notable players have been Keith Askins, Bimbo Coles, Kevin Edwards, Tim Hardaway, Udonis Haslem, Eddie Jones, Grant Long, **Alonzo Mourning**, **Shaquille O'Neal**, Glen Rice, Rony Seikaly, and **Dwyane Wade**. Their best season was 2005–2006, when they defeated the **Dallas Mavericks** in the NBA Finals to win the NBA Championship. Their overall record for their first 22 years in the league through the 2009–2010 season is 861–911. On 8 July 2010, the Heat announced that they would sign **LeBron James** and Chris Bosh for the 2010–2011 season.

MICHIGAN, UNIVERSITY OF. The University of Michigan in Ann Arbor began its men's **basketball** program in 1908. Home games since 1967 have been played at the 13,751-seat Crisler Arena. The most accomplished **coaches** in the school's history have been Tommy Amaker, Steve Fisher, Bill Frieder, E. J. Mather, Johnny Orr, and Dave Strack. In 1989, the Wolverines reached the **National Collegiate Athletic Association (NCAA)** Championship final game, where they defeated Seton Hall University in **overtime**, 80–79. They also lost in the NCAA Final game in 1965, 1976, 1992, and 1993. In 1964, they reached the **Final Four** but lost in the semifinal round. The best players in school history include Bill Buntin, Bob Harrison, Juwan Howard, Phil Hubbard, Tim McCormick, Terry Mills, Glen Rice, Jalen Rose, Cazzie Russell, Campy Russell, **Rudy Tomjanovich**, Johnny Townsend, Robert "Tractor" Traylor, and Chris Webber.

MICHIGAN STATE UNIVERSITY. Michigan State University in East Lansing began its men's **basketball** program in 1898. Home games since 1989 have been played at the 16,280-seat Jack Breslin Student Events Center. Prior to 1989, home games were played at the 10,000-seat Jenison Fieldhouse. The most accomplished **coaches** in the school's history have been Jud Heathcote, Tom Izzo, and Benjamin F. VanAlstyne. In 1979, the Spartans reached the **National Collegiate Athletic Association (NCAA)** Championship final game, where, led by **Earvin "Magic" Johnson,** they defeated **Larry Bird**'s **Indiana State University** team. In 2000, they won their second NCAA Championship by defeating the **University of Florida**. In eight other years, they reached the NCAA semifinal round. The best players in school history include Chet Aubuchon, Charlie Bell, Bob Brannum, Mateen Cleaves, Johnny Green, Johnson, Greg Kelser, Ralph Simpson, Scott Skiles, Steve Smith, Eric Snow, Sam and Jay Vincent, and Kevin Willis.

The women's basketball program began in 1972. The most notable coaches have been Karen Langeland and Joanne Palombo McCallie. In 2005, the Spartans reached the NCAA Championship final game, where they lost to **Baylor University**. The best players in school history include Lindsay Bowen, Kristie Haynie, Carol Hutchins, Aisha Jefferson, Liz Moeggenberg, and Liz Shimek.

MIDWEST BASKETBALL CONFERENCE (MBC). The Midwest Basketball Conference (MBC) was a professional **basketball** league from 1935–1937. It can be considered the "grandfather" of the present-day **National Basketball Association (NBA),** since it evolved into the **National Basketball League**, which merged with the **Basketball Association of America** to form the NBA in 1949. The MBC was created by Akron Firestone Tire & Rubber Company athletic director Paul "Pepper" Sheeks and Indianapolis businessman Frank Kautsky in November 1935. Henry C. Carlson was the commissioner.

The nine-team league, consisting mostly of corporate-sponsored teams, did not have a fixed schedule, but teams were required to play a minimum of eight games against at least four league opponents. The league comprised the Akron Firestones, Pittsburgh YMHA, Buffalo Bisons, Dayton Metropolitans, Indianapolis Kautskys, Chicago Duffy Florists, Detroit Hed-Aids, Indianapolis U.S. Tire, and

Windsor Cooper Buses. Chicago was the 1936 league champion. The 1936–1937 season featured 12 teams, with the Akron Goodyears winning the championship. In October 1937, the league was renamed the National Basketball League. *See also* APPENDIX B (for a list of league champions).

MIKAN, GEORGE LAWRENCE, JR. "MR. BASKETBALL."

B.18 June 1924, Joliet, Illinois. D. 2 June 2005, Scottsdale, Arizona. George Mikan attended Joliet Catholic High School in Joliet, Illinois; Quigley Prep in Chicago, Illinois; and **DePaul University**. He led DePaul to the **National Collegiate Athletic Association (NCAA) Final Four** in 1943, the 1944 runner-up position in the **National Invitation Tournament (NIT)**, and the championship of the 1945 NIT.

The six-foot, 10-inch, 245-pound bespectacled **center** was signed by the **Chicago American Gears** of the **National Basketball League (NBL)** in March 1946 and played professionally from 1946–1956. After the Gears' championship season of 1946–1947, their owner, Maurice White, created a new professional league called the **Professional Basketball League of America (PBLA)**. The league lasted less than one month, and Mikan played in all eight games for the Gears in that league. When the PBLA folded, he was signed by the Minneapolis Lakers and led them to six championships over the next seven years. His best year statistically was 1950–1951, when he averaged 28.4 points and 14.1 **rebounds** per game, setting a new league record for points and scoring average.

Mikan's career totals for nine years are 520 regular-season games and a 22.6 points per game average. He was selected for four **National Basketball Association (NBA) All-Star Games**, was All-Star Game Most Valuable Player in 1953, and was named to the All-League First Team in each of his first eight seasons. He was the league scoring leader during each of his first five years and, on 20 January 1952, scored a career-high 61 points in one game. In 1950, he was voted by the Associated Press as the greatest **basketball** player in the first half of the 20th century. During the early years of the NBA, he was its biggest star and was known as "Mr. Basketball." **Madison Square Garden**, on its marquee, would advertise, "Tonite: Mikan vs. the Knicks." He retired in 1954, but attempted a comeback in the 1955–1956 season. Playing under the new 24-second **shot** clock rules that year proved to be too much for the lumbering giant, and he retired after playing just 37 games.

Mikan ran for U.S. Congress in 1956 and was narrowly defeated. In 1957, he began the season as **coach** of the Lakers but resigned after 39 games. He had a law practice and travel agency in Minneapolis and in 1967 was hired as the commissioner of the new **American Basketball Association.** In 1959, he was enshrined in the **Naismith Memorial Basketball Hall of Fame** and is one of only four players named to the NBA 25th Anniversary Team, nominated for the NBA 35th Anniversary Team, and selected as one of the 50 Greatest Players in NBA History in 1996. His brother, Ed, played professional basketball in the **Basketball Association of America** and NBA, and George's son, Larry, played one season in the NBA.

MIKKELSEN, ARILD VERNER AGERSKOV "VERN." B. 10 October 1928, Parlier, California. Vern Mikkelsen was raised in Askov, Minnesota, a small town with a population of 350, of which 99 percent were of Danish ancestry, and attended Askov High School and Hamline University. In 1949, he led Hamline to the **National Association of Intercollegiate Athletics** National Championship.

The six-foot, seven-inch **forward** was selected by the Minneapolis Lakers in the 1949 **Basketball Association of America draft** and played from 1949–1959 for the Lakers. Mikkelsen's best year was 1954–1955, when he averaged 18.7 points and 10.2 **rebounds** per game. He played in an era when **coaches** did not remove players from games to protect them from being disqualified on **fouls** and is the **National Basketball Association (NBA)** record holder, with 127 career disqualifications. He missed four games in his second season, the only games he missed in his entire NBA career.

Mikkelsen's NBA totals for 10 years are 699 games and a 14.4 points per game average. He was selected for six NBA **All-Star Games** and was named to the All-NBA Second Team four times. With the Lakers, he was a member of the NBA champion team four times and played on the losing side in the 1959 NBA Finals. After retiring from active play, he taught school. In the 1968–1969 season, he was an interim coach of the Minnesota Pipers of the **American Basketball Association.** He was enshrined in the **Naismith Memorial Basketball Hall of Fame** in 1995.

MILLER, CHERYL DEANNE. B. 3 January 1964, Riverside, California. Cheryl Miller is one of the most decorated players of all-time and arguably the best female **basketball** player of her generation. At Riverside Polytechnic High School, she was the first player, male or female, to be named to the *Parade* magazine High School All-America High School Girls Team four times. On 27 January 1983, she scored 105 points in a one-sided victory over Norte Vista High School. In that game, although standing only six-feet, two-inches tall, she became the first female to **dunk** a basketball in a high school game. In four years of high school, she averaged 32.8 points per game, with a high of 37.5 as a junior. Riverside compiled a record of 132–4 during that time, and she was twice named National High School Player of the Year. She also maintained a B average and played varsity softball.

Miller's college years brought more acclaim, as she led the **University of Southern California (USC)** to the **National Collegiate Athletic Association (NCAA) Final Four** three times, winning the NCAA Championship in 1983 and 1984 and finishing second in 1986. She was a four-time **All-American** and was named National Collegiate Player of the Year three times. While at USC, she set school records, with 45 points in one game, 24 **rebounds** in another, 10 **blocks** in a third contest, and 11 **steals** in a fourth game. The 19-year-old Miller, as a college freshman, won a **silver medal** with the **United States** in the 1983 **World Championships** at São Paulo, **Brazil** and a **gold medal** one week later in the Pan American Games at Caracas, Venezuela. In 1984, she led the **Olympic** team to the gold medal. She was drafted by the **United States Basketball League** (a men's league that had begun in 1985) but declined that opportunity to retain her amateur standing. In 1986, she played for the United States in the Goodwill Games and World Championships, both in Moscow, where the United States avenged their 1983 defeat to the **Union of Soviet Socialist Republics** by winning both tournaments. A knee injury and subsequent surgery caused her to end her playing career and deprived her of the opportunity to play in the 1988 Olympic Games.

Miller turned to sports broadcasting and has established herself as a premier female television analyst. From 1986–1991, she was an assistant **coach** at USC and from 1993–1995 was head coach. From 1997–2000, she was head coach and general manager of the Phoenix Mercury of the **Women's National Basketball Associa-**

tion. In 1995, she became one of the first women to be elected to the **Naismith Memorial Basketball Hall of Fame** and was in the inaugural class of the **Women's Basketball Hall of Fame** in 1999. In 1996, her younger brother, Reggie, won an Olympic Gold medal with the U.S. basketball team. Reggie, after his 18-year career in the **National Basketball Association**, is probably the only professional basketball player who can honestly say, "My sister is even better than me." In 2010, she was inducted into the **Fédération Internationale de Basketball** Hall of Fame.

MILLER, REGINALD WAYNE "REGGIE." B. 24 August 1965, Riverside, California. Reggie Miller attended Riverside Polytechnic High School and the **University of California, Los Angeles (UCLA)**. He was drafted by the **Indiana Pacers** in the 1987 **National Basketball Association (NBA) draft** and played for them from 1987–2005. He and **John Stockton** are the only two NBA players to play for 17 or more years with only one franchise. Stockton played 19 years with the **Utah Jazz**, and Miller played 18 years with the Indiana Pacers.

Miller, a six-foot, seven-inch **guard**, won **gold medals** with the **United States** in the 1994 **World Championships** and 1996 **Olympic Games**. In his NBA career, he played in 1,389 regular-season games and averaged 18.2 points per game. In the playoffs, he averaged 20.6 points per game in 144 games. In 2000, the Pacers reached the NBA Finals but were defeated by the **San Antonio Spurs**. He was selected for five NBA **All-Star Games** and to the All-NBA Third team Three times, and he holds the NBA career record for **three-point field goals**, with 2,560.

After retiring from **basketball**, he became a television broadcaster. His sister, **Cheryl Miller**, is a former Olympic basketball player and has been enshrined in the **Naismith Memorial Basketball Hall of Fame**. Their brother, Darrell, was a Major League Baseball player from 1984–1988.

MILWAUKEE BUCKS. The Milwaukee Bucks are a team in the **National Basketball Association (NBA)**. On 22 January 1968, a group headed by Marvin Fishman and Wesley Pavalon purchased an NBA expansion franchise and started play in the 1968–1969 season. In March 1985, future **U.S.** senator Herbert Kohl purchased the team. Home games were played at the 10,783-seat Milwaukee Arena (later known as the MECCA) from 1968–1988, and the 18,717-seat Bradley Center since 1988. In 1971, **Wayne Embry** was hired as general manager and became the league's first black general manager. Among their players have been Hall of Famers **Kareem Abdul-Jabbar**, **Dave Cowens**, Alex English, **Bob Lanier**, **Moses Malone**, and **Oscar Robertson**. Other notables include **Ray Allen**, Ulysses "Junior" Bridgeman, Bob Dandridge, Sidney Moncrief, Jon McGlocklin, Michael Redd, Glenn Robinson, and Brian Winters.

One of the highlights in their history occurred after their first year, when they won a coin flip with the **Phoenix Suns** for the right to have the first draft choice in the 1969 NBA **draft**. Lew Alcindor (later known as Kareem Abdul-Jabbar) became their choice and helped lead them to a championship shortly thereafter. Their best season was 1970–1971, when they defeated the **Baltimore Bullets** to win the NBA Championship. In 1973–1974, they also reached the NBA Finals but were defeated by the **Boston Celtics**. Their record for their first 42 years in the league through the 2009–2010 season is 1,790–1,622.

MILWAUKEE HAWKS. *See* ATLANTA HAWKS.

MING, YAO. *See* YAO, MING.

MINNEAPOLIS LAKERS. *See* LOS ANGELES LAKERS.

MINNESOTA MUSKIES. *See* MIAMI FLORIDIANS.

MINNESOTA PIPERS. *See* PITTSBURGH CONDORS.

MINNESOTA TIMBERWOLVES. The Minnesota Timberwolves are a team in the **National Basketball Association (NBA)**. Owners Harvey Ratner and Marv Wolfenson purchased the franchise on 22 April 1987, and the team began play in the 1989–1990 season. Home games were played at the 50,000-seat Metrodome in 1989–1990, and have been played at the 20,500-seat Target Center since then. Both venues are located in Minneapolis, Minnesota. Among their most notable players have been Tony Campbell, **Kevin Garnett**, Tom Gugliotta, Trenton Hassell, **Christian Laettner**, Sam Mitchell, Anthony Peeler, Isaiah "J. R." Rider, Wally Szczerbiak, and Doug West. Their best season was 2003–2004, when they had a regular-season record of 58–24, first in their division, and reached the Western Conference Finals. Their record for their first 21 years in the NBA through the 2009–2010 season is 688–1,002.

MINUTES. Professional **basketball** games since the inception of the **Basketball Association of America (BAA)** in 1946 have been scheduled for four quarters of 12 minutes each. **Fédération Internationale de Basketball, Women's National Basketball Association**, and college games have usually been scheduled for 40 minutes. In some years, games were played in two 20-minute halves, while at other times four 10-minute quarters were played. High school games are often scheduled for four eight-minute quarters. During the 1930s, some **American Basketball League** games were played in three 15-minute periods. During its first season, the BAA played a few experimental games of 60 minutes in four 15-minute quarters.

One of the statistics maintained by the **National Basketball Association (NBA)** since 1951 has been individual minutes played. On 9 November 1989, Dale Ellis of the Seattle Supersonics set the NBA record for a game by playing in 69 minutes of a 73-minute, five-**overtime** game against the **Milwaukee Bucks**. An NBA six-overtime game was played on 6 January 1951, but individual minutes played were not recorded then and it is not known whether Ellis's feat was surpassed. In college, Ed Fleming of Niagara University played all 70 minutes of a six-overtime game against Siena University on 21 February 1953. In the 1961–1962 season, **Wilt Chamberlain** of the Philadelphia Warriors played every minute of every game, except for one game when he was ejected by the **referee**. Chamberlain's total minutes for that season were 3,882, an average of 48.5 for the 80 games played.

MISAKA, WATARU "WAT." B. 21 December 1923, Ogden, Utah. Wat Misaka is a Japanese American who attended Ogden High School, Weber Junior College, and the **University of Utah.** In school, he also played football and baseball and ran track. After helping to lead Utah to the **National Collegiate Athletic Association**

(NCAA) National Championship in 1944, he served in the **U.S. Army** in 1945 and 1946. He returned to school and led Utah to the **National Invitation Tournament** championship in 1947.

In the 1947 **Basketball Association of America (BAA) draft**, the **New York Knickerbockers** made Misaka their first draft choice, even though he is only five-feet, seven-inches tall. The first player of Asian descent to play in the BAA when he played with the Knicks in 1947, he was released after playing in just three games and scoring seven points. His size seven shoe may possibly be the smallest ever worn by a professional **basketball** player. He used his degree in mechanical engineering to work for the Sperry Corporation as an engineer. In 2009, a documentary film, *Transcending: The Wat Misaka Story*, was released.

MOKRAY, WILLIAM GEORGE "BILL." B. 6 June 1907, Passaic, New Jersey. D. 21 March 1974, Revere, Massachusetts. From 1915–1924, Passaic High School's "Wonder Teams" lost only one game, while winning 200, and won 159 consecutive games from 17 December 1919 until 6 February 1925. Bill Mokray attended Passaic High during this time but had weak eyesight and did not play **basketball**, although he was very interested in the sport. He attended Rhode Island State College, was a member of their cross-country team, and graduated with a bachelor of science degree in 1929. He was hired by Rhode Island State as their sports publicity director and was also sports correspondent for the *Providence Journal-Bulletin*. His major contribution to basketball was as a statistician.

In 1944, he was hired as director of college basketball for **Boston Garden**. He worked for the **Boston Celtics** as public relations director from 1946 and was the editor of their annual yearbook, a more comprehensive one than any of the other teams had. He was editor of the annual **National Basketball Association** Guide and wrote the first encyclopedia of basketball, *Ronald Encyclopedia of Basketball*, published in 1963, the only basketball encyclopedia with detailed game-by-game scores for most major colleges. He was also editor of the annual Converse Basketball Yearbook, by far the most complete record of all basketball—scholastic, collegiate, professional, and international—for that era, from 1946 until his death. After Mokray's death, the quality of the Converse Yearbook declined substantially and was discontinued in 1984.

Mokray was chairman of the **Naismith Memorial Basketball Hall of Fame** Honors Committee and helped lead the effort to have a commemorative postage stamp issued in 1961 honoring basketball. He was enshrined in the Naismith Memorial Basketball Hall of Fame in 1965 in the category of contributor. He built one of the largest collections of basketball books that after his death was donated to the hall and forms the basis of its library, which is open to the public.

MOLINAS, JACOB LOUIS "JACK." B. 16 April 1932, New York, New York. D. 4 August 1975, Hollywood Hills, California. Jack Molinas led a fascinating but tragic life. He attended Stuyvesant High School in New York, New York, and Columbia University. At Stuyvesant, he set the New York City Public School Athletic League individual scoring record with 37 points in a game. He received an academic scholarship to attend Columbia University which, as an Ivy League school, did not award athletic scholarships. At Columbia, he led the team to 31 consecutive victories from 1949–1951.

The six-foot, six-inch **forward** was an outstanding shooter and all-around player and was selected by the Fort Wayne Pistons in the 1953 **National Basketball Association (NBA) draft**. Molinas began playing for the Pistons in the 1952–1953 season but, on 10 January 1953, was suspended by the league for life for betting on his own team. Since the college point-shaving scandal had occurred just two years previously, the NBA was extra sensitive to the situation, thus the heavy penalty. On 25 March 1953, a Bronx grand jury found no evidence of a crime committed by Molinas. In 29 NBA regular-season games, Molinas averaged 12.1 points and 7.2 **rebounds** when his NBA career was abruptly terminated. He had been selected to play in the NBA **All-Star Game** but was not allowed to once he was suspended. He played in the Eastern Professional Basketball League from 1954–1955 until 1961–1962 and was the league's first or second leading scorer in several seasons.

While attempting to have his suspension lifted, he enrolled in Brooklyn Law School and graduated in 1956 in the top 10 percent of his class. In 1958, he filed a $3 million dollar suit against the NBA for blacklisting him, but the case was dismissed. In May 1962, he was back in court, as he was indicted on charges of bribing college basketball players to fix games. The bribery investigation cited 49 players in 25 colleges in 18 states. On 11 February 1963, he was sentenced to 10–15 years in prison for the crimes. After appeals failed, he began his sentence on 10 July 1964.

Four years later, he was paroled and moved to California, where he became involved in producing pornographic films. He died on 4 August 1975, in what reportedly was a gangland-style execution. Charley Rosen has written an excellent account of Molinas' life, *The Wizard of Odds*, which disclosed that Molinas had been gambling and fixing games, including ones he played in since high school.

MONROE, VERNON EARL "EARL," "THE PEARL," "BLACK JESUS." B. 21 November 1944, Philadelphia, Pennsylvania. Earl Monroe attended John Bartram High School in Philadelphia and Winston-Salem State University. The six-foot, three-inch **guard** averaged 41.5 points per game and led Winston-Salem State to the 1967 **National Collegiate Athletic Association (NCAA)** College Division National Championship. In four years of varsity play, he averaged 26.7 points per game. He was selected by the **Baltimore Bullets** in the 1967 **National Basketball Association (NBA) draft** and played from 1967–1980 for the Bullets and **New York Knickerbockers**. His best year was 1968–1969, when he averaged 25.8 points per game.

Monroe's NBA career totals for 13 years are 926 regular-season games and an 18.8 points per game average. He was selected for four NBA **All-Star Games** and named to the All-NBA First Team in 1969. In 1968, he won the NBA Rookie of the Year award. With the Knicks in 1973, he helped them win the NBA Championship. He was known for his numerous one-on-one moves and flamboyant style of ball handling, shooting, and passing. After retiring from active play, he became involved in various activities, including being a record producer with his own label, doing television commentary work, and working as commissioner of the New Jersey Urban Development Corporation. He was enshrined in the **Naismith Memorial Basketball Hall of Fame** in 1990. In 1996, he was named one of the 50 Greatest Players in NBA History.

MOURNING, ALONZO HARDING, JR. "ZO." B. 8 February 1970, Chesapeake, Virginia. Alonzo Mourning attended Indian River High

School in Chesapeake and **Georgetown University**. In 1987, he led his high school team to the state championship. The six-foot, 10-inch **center** was drafted by the Charlotte Hornets in the 1992 **National Basketball Association (NBA) draft** and played from 1992–2008 for Charlotte, the **Miami Heat**, and the **New Jersey Nets**.

On 25 November 2003, Mourning retired, as he was suffering from a kidney disease known as focal segmental glomerular sclerosis. On 19 December 2003, he received a kidney transplant from a cousin who he had not seen for 25 years and was able to return to play in the 2004–2005 season. With Miami in 2005–2006, he was the backup center to **Shaquille O'Neal** and when O'Neal was injured became the starting center and helped lead Miami to the 2006 NBA Championship. On 19 December 2007, he tore a tendon in his knee that effectively terminated his career.

In his 16-year NBA career, Mourning played in 838 regular-season games and averaged 17.1 points, 8.5 **rebounds**, and 2.8 **blocked shots** per game. He was selected to play in seven NBA **All-Star Games** but due to injuries only played in four of them. He was the NBA Defensive Player of the Year in 1999 and 2000 and was named to the All-NBA First Team in 1999 and All-NBA Second Team in 2000. He was also the NBA leader in blocks those two seasons. He played on the **U.S.** team at the 1990 **World Championships** and won a **bronze medal**. Four years later, as a professional, he won a **gold medal** as a member of the U.S. team at the 1994 World Championships. He won another gold medal in 2000 with the U.S. **Olympic basketball** team. After retiring from basketball, Mourning became involved with charitable organizations, including a youth center in Miami and Athletes for Hope, an organization that helps professional athletes get involved in charitable work.

MULLIN, CHRISTOPHER PAUL "CHRIS." B. 30 July 1963, New York, New York. Chris Mullin attended Power Memorial High School in New York; Xaverian High School in Brooklyn, New York; and **St. John's University**. As a collegian, he won a **gold medal** with the 1984 **U.S. Olympic basketball** team. He helped St. John's reach the **National Collegiate Athletic Association (NCAA) Final Four** in 1985, where they were defeated by **Georgetown University** in the semifinal round. The recipient of the John R. Wooden Award as the nation's best college player in 1985, he was drafted by the **Golden State Warriors** in the 1985 **National Basketball Association (NBA) draft** and played from 1985–2001 for the Warriors and **Indiana Pacers**.

In 1992, Mullin was selected to the All-NBA First Team, in 1989 and 1991 to the All-NBA Second Team, and in 1990 to the All-NBA Third Team. The six-foot, seven-inch **left-handed forward** was selected to the NBA **All-Star Game** in each season from 1989–1993. An excellent shooter, he led the league in **free throw** percentage in 1997–1998, with a .939 mark. His NBA career totals for 16 seasons are 986 regular-season games, an 18.2 points per game average, and a .865 free throw percentage. He won a second Olympic gold medal as a member of the 1992 **U.S.** Olympic basketball **Dream Team**. After retiring from active play, Mullin was a special assistant with the Warriors from 2002–2004 and was executive vice president of Basketball Operations for the Warriors from 2004–2009.

MURESAN, GHEORGHE DUMITRU "GHITA." B. 14 February 1971, Triteni, Romania. Gheorghe Muresan attended the University of Cluj in Cluj-Napoca, Romania. At seven-feet, seven-inches tall he is tied with **Manute Bol** as the league's tallest player in history and outweighs Bol by nearly 100 pounds. In the 1992–1993 season, Muresan played in **France** with Pau Orthez. He was selected by the Washington Bullets in the 1993 **National Basketball Association (NBA) draft** and played from 1993–2000 for the Bullets and **New Jersey Nets**. After being injured in 1997, he only played a few NBA games until his retirement in 2000. He returned to Europe and briefly played for Pau Orthez and the Romanian national team. In 2003, he returned to the **United States** and now lives in New Jersey.

Muresan's best year was 1995–1996, when he averaged 14.5 points per game, led the league in **field goal** percentage, and was named the NBA's Most Improved Player. His NBA regular-season career totals for six years are 307 games and a 9.8 points, 6.4 **rebounds**, and 1.5 **blocks** per game average.

On 11 March 2007, in Rockville, Maryland, Muresan played one game for the Maryland Nighthawks minor league team, which featured the world's tallest lineup, and Muresan, for the first time in his life, was not the tallest player on the team. The Nighthawks center was the seven-foot, nine-inch Sun Ming-Ming. Also on the team were seven-foot, one-inch Ayo Adigun; seven-foot-tall Deng D'Awol; and six-foot, eight-inch Barry Mitchell. In 1998, Muresan starred with Billy Crystal in the Hollywood film *My Giant*.

MURPHY, CALVIN JEROME. B. 9 May 1948, Norwalk, Connecticut. Calvin Murphy attended Norwalk High School and Niagara University. In college, he averaged 48.9 points per game in 1966–1967, playing on the freshman team. On the varsity team for three seasons, he averaged 33.1 points per game, including an average of 38.2 in his sophomore year. On 7 December 1968, he scored 68 points in a game against **Syracuse University**. He was also an outstanding baton twirler and was national baton twirling champion as an eighth-grader in 1963. In 1977, after he had been an established professional **basketball** player, he won the Texas State Baton Twirling Championship.

Murphy was selected by the San Diego Rockets in the 1970 **National Basketball Association (NBA) draft**. Although only five-feet, nine-inches tall (he was the shortest NBA player since the early days of the league), he played **guard** with the Rockets from 1970–1983, in 1970–1971 in San Diego, and for the remainder of the time in Houston after the team moved there in 1971. His best year was 1977–1978, when he averaged 25.6 points per game. On 18 March 1978, he scored 57 points in one game, the most points ever scored in an NBA game by a player less than six feet tall. In 1981, he made 206 of 215 **free throws** for a NBA season record free throw percentage of .958, broken in 2009 by Jose Calderon. During that season, Murphy made 78 consecutive free throws, another NBA record that has since been broken. In 1981, the Rockets reached the NBA Finals but lost to the **Boston Celtics**. In the playoffs that year, Murphy made 58 of 60 free throws.

Murphy's NBA career totals for 13 years are 1,002 regular-season games, a 17.9 points per game average, and a .892 free throw percentage. He was selected for the 1979 NBA **All-Star Game**. After retiring from active play, he was employed by the Rockets as a community services adviser and television broadcaster and was enshrined in the **Naismith Memorial Basketball Hall of Fame** in 1993.

MUTOMBO, DIKEMBE. B. 25 June 1966, Kinshasa, Congo. Dikembe Mutombo attended the Institute Boboto in Kinshasa and then came to the **United States** to attend **Georgetown University** and play **basketball** for them, although at the time he had a very limited knowledge of English. His complete name is Dikembe Mutombo Mpolondo Mukamba Jean-Jacques Wamutombo. He graduated with bachelor's degrees in linguistics and diplomacy. As a linguist, he speaks English, Spanish, and Portuguese, in addition to his native French and five African languages.

The seven-foot, two-inch, 265-pound **center** was chosen in the 1991 **National Basketball Association (NBA) draft** by the **Denver Nuggets** and played in the NBA from 1991–2009 for Denver, the **Atlanta Hawks**, the **Philadelphia 76ers**, the **New Jersey Nets**, the **New York Knickerbockers**, and the **Houston Rockets**. In the 1994 playoffs, Mutombo helped Denver record one of the greatest upsets in NBA history. The eighth-seeded Nuggets came from two games down to defeat the league-leading Seattle Supersonics in **overtime** in the fifth and deciding game. One of the classic sports photos is Mutombo, lying on his back exhausted at the end of the game, clutching the ball in disbelief. He also helped lead the 76ers to the NBA Championship Finals in 2001, where they lost to the **Los Angeles Lakers**. He came out of retirement at the age of 42 to play for the Rockets in the 2008–2009 season, but after being injured in the first playoff game, he announced his retirement.

Mutombo was one of the league's most effective defensive players and as a shot blocker would wag his finger at his opponent after blocking one of their shots. The NBA originally considered the finger wagging as taunting but allowed Mutombo to just wag the finger at the crowd. He led the NBA in **blocked shots** three times and was NBA Defensive Player of the Year in 1995, 1997, 1998, and 2001. He was selected for the NBA **All-Star Game** eight times in his 18-year career. A true humanitarian, he helped finance the 1996 Zaire women's **Olympic** basketball team and has devoted much of his time, finances, and energy to building a hospital in his native Congo, which opened in Kinshasa in 2007.

– N –

NAISMITH, JAMES A. B. 6 November 1861, Almonte, Ontario, **Canada**. D. 28 November 1939, Lawrence, Kansas. James Naismith was the inventor of **basketball**. He graduated from Almonte High School in 1883 and graduated with honors from McGill University in Montreal, Quebec, Canada, with a bachelor's degree in philosophy in 1887. At McGill, the five-foot, 10-inch Naismith participated in football, soccer, and gymnastics. He originally intended to be a clergyman, studied theology at the Presbyterian Theological College in Montreal, and was licensed for the ministry in 1890. He was an advocate of "muscular Christianity" and decided to couple his religious calling with physical education and become an instructor for the YMCA.

In 1890, Naismith enrolled at the International YMCA Training School in Springfield, Massachusetts. During the summer, he was given the assignment of creating a physical activity to be played indoors during the winter months. He invented the game of basket ball (two words at first) and had a demonstration game played in December 1891. For that game, a peach **basket** was suspended from a balcony in the gymnasium, a soccer ball was used, and the simple task of throwing the ball into the basket was the object. The class of 18 students was divided in half, and Naismith's Original 13 Rules for the game were applied. The game quickly caught on and was spread by YMCAs throughout the country.

In 1895, Naismith moved to Denver, Colorado, to direct their YMCA. There he attended the Gross Medical School and became a licensed physician in 1898. He moved to Kansas and became director of chapel and director of physical education at the **University of Kansas**. He introduced his new game to his students and was **coach** of the varsity team from 1899–1909. One of his students was **Forrest "Phog" Allen**, who succeeded Naismith as varsity coach. During World War I, as an ordained minister, Naismith served as chaplain with the YMCA in France. In 1925, he became a naturalized **U.S.** citizen. He retired from his position at Kansas in 1937.

During his lifetime, Naismith received little public acclaim as the "Father of Basketball" and did not do much toward refining the game with rule changes or coaching techniques. He was invited to Berlin in 1936 for the introduction of basketball at the **Olympic Games**. In 1937, he helped create the National Association of Intercollegiate Basketball (later known as the **National Association of Intercollegiate Athletics**) and helped organize the first national collegiate tournament that year. In his obituary, it was stated that he played the game of basketball only twice in his life, in 1892 and in 1898. In 1941, his book *Basketball: Its Origins and Development* was published posthumously. The basketball hall of fame in Springfield, Massachusetts, bears his name, and he was enshrined in its inaugural class in 1959 in the category of contributor. *See also* APPENDIX A (for the Original 13 Rules).

NAISMITH MEMORIAL BASKETBALL HALL OF FAME. The Naismith Memorial Basketball Hall of Fame was established in 1959 and is located in Springfield, Massachusetts. Inductions have been performed annually since 1959, and through 2010 there have been 303 **coaches**, players, **referees**, contributors, and teams enshrined in the Hall. The current building housing the exhibits was completed in 2002. The Hall also maintains a library that is open to the public. *See also* APPENDIX J (for inductees).

NASH, STEPHEN JOHN "STEVE." B. 7 February 1974, Johannesburg, South Africa. Steve Nash was raised in **Canada** and attended St. Michael's High School in Victoria, British Columbia, and Santa Clara University in the United States. He was drafted in the 1996 **National Basketball Association (NBA) draft** by the **Phoenix Suns**. The six-foot, three-inch **point guard** played for the Suns from 1996–1998 and was used primarily as a backup player. He was traded to the **Dallas Mavericks** in 1998, and with the Mavericks his professional career blossomed. He was with Dallas from 1998–2004 and then was resigned by the Suns as a free agent.

Nash was named the NBA's Most Valuable Player in 2005 and 2006. In his first 14 years in the NBA, through 2009–2010, he played in 1,015 regular-season games and averaged 14.6 points and 8.3 **assists** per game and had a **free throw** percentage of .903—the second-highest for an NBA career. He was selected for seven NBA **All-Star Games**, the All-NBA First Team three times, the All-NBA Second Team twice, and the All-NBA Third Team twice. He has led the league in assists four times and in free throw percentage twice. Nash played for Canada in the 2000 **Olympic Games** and played on Canadian teams in other international tournaments for 12 years. His brother Martin is a professional soccer player with the Vancouver Whitecaps, and Steve is a part owner of that franchise. Their father was also a professional soccer player, and had Steve not chosen basketball, he probably would also have been one.

NASHVILLE BUSINESS COLLEGE (NBC). Nashville Business College is located in Nashville, Tennessee. Herman O. Balls, the owner of the college, began his sponsorship of women's **basketball** in 1923. Games were played under **Amateur Athletic Union (AAU)** jurisdiction, and the teams comprised both students and women who worked at the school. Leo Long was one of the team's first **coaches**. He coached the team until 1947, when John Head took over. Under Head's direction, the team won 11 AAU championships and were runners-up six times. They were AAU champions in 1950, 1958, 1960, and eight consecutive years from 1962–1969. Among the most notable players were Joan Crawford, Sue Gunter, Rita Horky, Doris Weems Light, Betty Murphy, Fern Nash, Margaret Sexton Petty, Doris Rogers, Alline Banks Sprouse, Jill Upton, Katherine Washington, and Nera White. *See also* WAYLAND BAPTIST UNIVERSITY.

NATIONAL AAU BASKETBALL LEAGUE (NABL). *See* NATIONAL INDUSTRIAL BASKETBALL LEAGUE (NIBL).

NATIONAL ASSOCIATION OF INTERCOLLEGIATE ATHLETICS (NAIA). The National Association of Intercollegiate Athletics was founded in 1937 as the National Association of Intercollegiate Basketball (NAIB). **James Naismith** and others organized a tournament for small colleges to be held in Kansas City, Missouri, to determine a national champion. Eight schools were invited to that first tournament, which was won by Central Missouri State University. The NAIB was renamed the National Association of Intercollegiate Athletics (NAIA) in 1952, and sponsorship of tournaments in other sports was begun. In 1953, the association became the first organization to invite historically black schools to its tournaments, and in 1957, Tennessee State University became the first school to win a national championship. In 1981, the NAIA began holding tournaments for women's **basketball**. In 1992, two divisions were established for both men's and women's basketball. The NAIA sponsors events in more than 20 sports and has more than 300 member schools.

NATIONAL ASSOCIATION OF INTERCOLLEGIATE BASKETBALL (NAIB). *See* NATIONAL ASSOCIATION OF INTERCOLLEGIATE ATHLETICS (NAIA).

NATIONAL BASKETBALL ASSOCIATION (NBA). The National Basketball Association (NBA) is a men's professional **basketball** major league that began operation as the result of the merger between its predecessor, the **Basketball Association of America** and the rival **National Basketball League** on 3 August 1949. In its first season, it contained an unwieldy 17 teams as the new league tried to incorporate most of the teams from the two leagues. After the 1949–1950 season, six teams were eliminated, and by 1955 the league was down to an eight-team league. Of these eight teams, only two have not relocated, the **Boston Celtics** and **New York Knickerbockers**. The other six teams were the **Milwaukee Hawks**, which began as the Tri-Cities Blackhawks and later moved to St. Louis and then Atlanta; the Fort Wayne Pistons, which moved to Detroit; the Philadelphia Warriors, which moved to San Francisco and then changed their name to the **Golden State Warriors**; the **Syracuse Nationals**, which moved to **Philadelphia** and play as the **76ers**; the Minneapolis Lakers, which moved to Los Angeles; and the **Rochester Royals**; which moved to Cincinnati, then Kansas City and Omaha, then just Kansas City, and are now in **Sacramento** as the **Kings**.

For the 1954–1955 season, the league made a significant rule change that likely saved the league's future. To combat stalling and unnecessary **fouling** that existed, the NBA adopted a **shot clock**. Teams had to shoot the ball and hit the **backboard** or rim within 24 seconds after gaining possession. This change revolutionized the way the game was played and renewed interest.

In 1961, the league decided to expand and added a team in Chicago. Since then, a continual expansion program has been in effect, with the league adding one or two teams every few years, and in the 2010–2011 season, there are 30 teams in the league. In 1976, the NBA absorbed four teams from the **American Basketball Association**, their prime competition from 1967–1976. During the 1950s, many of the teams played in arenas seating less than 10,000 people, and they were seldom able to sell out those venues. Now virtually every team plays in an arena with a capacity of more than 15,000, and the league's average attendance is in excess of 17,000.

During the league's 50 plus years, the Boston Celtics have won more titles, at 17, than any other team, with the Lakers, in Minneapolis and Los Angeles, at 15, a close second. During the 1990s, the **Chicago Bulls** won six titles in eight seasons. The **San Antonio Spurs**, with four titles from 1999–2007, have won the fourth most NBA Championships. In its first 61 years, the NBA has grown from a small operation in which many of the league's employees, players, officials, and team management required second jobs in the off-season, to one where the average player's annual salary exceeds $1 million. *See also* APPENDIX B (for a list of league champions).

NATIONAL BASKETBALL DEVELOPMENT LEAGUE. *See* NBA DEVELOPMENT LEAGUE (NBADL).

NATIONAL BASKET BALL LEAGUE (NBL) (1898–1904). The first professional **basketball** league, the National Basket Ball League (NBL), was organized on 30 July 1898, in Philadelphia, by William E. Morgenweck of Camden, New Jersey; James McMurray of Millville, New Jersey; H. W. Junghurth and Horace S. Fogel of Philadelphia; and Peter E. Wurfflein of Trenton, New Jersey. Fogel was elected league president. The league initially comprised three teams from New Jersey, Trenton, Millville, and Camden, and three from Philadelphia, Germantown, Clover, and Hancock.

The first game was played on Thursday, 1 December 1898, at Textile Hall in Philadelphia. Trenton defeated the Hancock A.A., 21–19. Two 20-minute halves were played, and E. C. Rutschman was the **referee**. The first NBL season ended on 8 April 1899. By season's end, both Germantown and Hancock had dropped out of the league. A total of 48 games were played, with three ending in ties.

Although several other professional leagues were attempted, the NBL continued as the main one until the **Philadelphia Basket Ball League** began play in 1902. Competition from that league caused the NBL to terminate on 3 January 1904. Among the league's stars during its five and one-half year existence were Al Cooper, John Deal, Ed Ferat, **Harry Hough**, Charlie Klein, Sandy Shields, and Steve White. *See also* APPENDIX B (for a list of league champions).

NATIONAL BASKETBALL LEAGUE (NBL) (1937–1949). The National Basketball League (NBL) was a men's professional **basketball** major league that began operation in 1935 as the **Midwest Basketball Conference** and changed its name to the National Basketball League in 1937. The 1937–1938 season had 13 teams divided into an Eastern Division and Western Division. There was no fixed league schedule, and teams played between nine and 20 league games. Even the rules varied from team to team, with the home team having the final say. Some games were played using the **center jump** after each successful **field goal**. The 13 teams that began play in the NBL's first year included the Akron Firestone Non-Skids, Akron Goodyear Wingfoots, Pittsburgh Pirates, Buffalo Bisons, Warren Penns, Columbus Athletic Supply, **Oshkosh All-Stars**, Whiting Ciesar All-Americans, Fort Wayne General Electrics, Indianapolis Kautskys, Richmond King Clothiers, Kankakee Gallagher Trojans, and Dayton Metros. The Firestone Non-Skids and All-Stars won their divisions, and the second place Wingfoots defeated both the Firestone Non-Skids and All-Stars to claim the league championship.

By the league's second year, there were only eight teams, but the schedule and rules were uniform. During the life of the league, its size varied from a minimum of four teams in the 1943–1944 season to a maximum of 13 teams in 1937–1938, and the schedule varied from 22 to 64 games. Teams were generally based in the Midwest, with Syracuse, New York, being the eastern-most team, and Denver, Colorado, the western-most. Teams in the league for the most seasons were Oshkosh, which played every season; the **Sheboygan Redskins**, from 1938–1949; Indianapolis, which played most years from 1938–1948, and the Fort Wayne Pistons, from 1942–1948.

In the 1942–1943 season the league integrated, as both the Chicago and Toledo teams employed black players. In November 1946, a rival professional major league, the **Basketball Association of America (BAA)**, began operations. Although the BAA played in larger cities, the NBL had the better players. Following the 1947–1948 season, four of the NBL's best teams, Fort Wayne, the Minneapolis Lakers, Indianapolis, and the Rochester Royals, left the NBL to join the BAA. The NBL managed to replace them for the 1948–1949 season. That season, after playing 19 mostly road games with a record of 2–17, the Detroit franchise dropped out of the league, as it could not find a useable arena, and the **New York Renaissance**, an all-black independent barnstorming team, was invited to join the league. The Rens played the remainder of the season's schedule and had a record of 14–26. Following that season, talks were held with the BAA, and a merger effected on 3 August 1949, forming the **National Basketball Association**. *See also* APPENDIX B (for a list of league champions).

NATIONAL COLLEGIATE ATHLETIC ASSOCIATION (NCAA). The National Collegiate Athletic Association (NCAA) is an organization of more than 1,200 **U.S.** colleges and universities that coordinates athletic activities in these schools. It administers programs in approximately 25 different sports and organizes national championships. The NCAA was founded on 3 February 1906, as the Intercollegiate Athletic Association of the United States (IAAUS) as a result of President Theodore Roosevelt requesting the presidents of three major Ivy League schools to take steps to improve the safety of collegiate athletics. In 1910, the IAAUS was renamed the National Collegiate Athletic Association. In 1973, the NCAA organized competition into three divisions, Division I, Division II, and Division III, with Division III schools not permitted to offer athletic scholarships.

The NCAA did not administer women's athletics until 1980. In 1939, the NCAA began annual national **basketball** tournaments. Originally only eight schools competed, with the number of entrants increased to 16 in 1951, 32 in 1975, 64 in 1985, 65 in 2001, and 68 in 2011 with the tournament being gradually expanded in the intervening years. In 1982, the association began holding annual women's basketball championships. The NCAA was headquartered in the Kansas City metropolitan area from 1951–1999 but is now located in Indianapolis, Indiana. *See also* APPENDIX C and APPENDIX D (for a list of tournament champions).

NATIONAL INDUSTRIAL BASKETBALL LEAGUE (NIBL). The National Industrial Basketball League (NIBL) was organized in 1947 as an amateur **basketball** league consisting of company-sponsored employees' teams. The league provided graduating collegians with an alternative to professional basketball, as players in the NIBL were considered by the **Fédération Internationale de Basketball (FIBA)** as amateurs and remained eligible for **Olympic**

Games and other international competition. In addition, prospective collegians were offered an opportunity for a business career that could last after they were finished with basketball. One of the greatest collegiate players of that era, **Bob Kurland**, joined the Phillips Petroleum Company and became the first U.S. Olympian to compete in two Olympic tournaments.

In the league's first season, 1947–1948, five teams competed and played an eight-game schedule, meeting each other twice with each team playing one of the two games at home. The Milwaukee Harnischfegers, a manufacturer of mining equipment, won all eight games and were league champions. The Peoria Cats (sponsored by the Caterpillar Tractor Company of Peoria, Illinois) were second, Milwaukee Allen-Bradleys (manufacturer of sensing devices) third, Akron Goodyear (Tire and Rubber Company) Wingfoots fourth, and Fort Wayne General Electrics fifth and last.

By the 1950–1951 season, the league had expanded to eight teams and played a variable schedule ranging from 13 to 28 games. The 1951–1952 season had the most teams, 11 total, and each played a 22-game schedule. By 1955–1956, the league was back down to only five teams. The Bartlesville Phillips 66ers, sponsored by the Phillips Petroleum Company, joined the league in its second season and won championships each year from 1949–1958 and also in 1960.

NIBL teams were invited to participate in the Olympic trials, and several Olympians in 1948, 1952, and 1956, as well as the head **coaches** in each of those years, were representatives of the NIBL. The **U.S.** national team that competed in the first **World Championships** in 1950 comprised the entire NIBL Denver Chevrolets team, and the 1954 U.S. entry in that tournament was the entire Peoria Caterpillar team.

In 1961, the league was renamed the National AAU Basketball League (NABL). When **Abe Saperstein**'s **American Basketball League (ABL)** began in the 1961–1962 season, the Cleveland Pipers and New York Tuck Tapers of the NIBL both joined the ABL. The NABL declined in popularity during the 1960s as the **National Basketball Association (NBA)** became more stabilized and salaries in the NBA escalated. During its 13-year existence, the NIBL had 25 different members at various times, with teams ranging from coast to coast.

NATIONAL INVITATION TOURNAMENT (NIT). The National Invitation Tournament, more commonly referred to as the NIT, is a men's collegiate **basketball** tournament that was originated in 1938 by the Metropolitan Basketball Writers Association in New York City. The tournament was played at **Madison Square Garden** following the regular college basketball season. The tournament predates the **National Collegiate Athletic Association (NCAA)** National Championship tournament by one year.

Six teams were invited for the first NIT, including **Temple University**, the University of Colorado, Oklahoma A&M College, New York University, **Long Island University**, and **Bradley University**, with Temple emerging the winner of the initial tournament. The tournament gradually increased the number of invited teams, and by 1968 there were 16. In 1953, the NCAA required its schools to play in its postseason tournament, if eligible. Prior to 1953, teams could play in either event and in some years were able to play in both. In 1950, **City College of New York** won both tournaments, the only time in history that this was the case.

As the NCAA expanded its field and more and more NCAA schools belonged to conferences in which the winner automatically received an NCAA Championship berth, the NIT declined in stature. In 1970, **Marquette University**, which at that time was not aligned with a conference, chose to play in the NIT rather than the NCAA. Since then, the NIT has been classified as a consolation tournament, with only teams that did not qualify for the NCAA Championship participating. Although the NIT has expanded to include 32 teams and preliminary round games are no longer played at Madison Square Garden, playing in the NIT no longer carries much prestige. In 2005, the NCAA purchased the rights to the NIT tournament for 10 years to settle an antitrust lawsuit alleging that the NCAA, by requiring its members to participate in its tournament, was overextending its powers. *See also* APPENDIX E (for a list of tournament champions).

NATIONAL PROFESSIONAL BASKETBALL LEAGUE (NPBL). The National Professional Basketball League (NPBL) was a men's professional **basketball** league that played its first game on 1 November 1950. It was formed by several former **National Basketball League (NBL)** teams that had played in the **National Basketball**

Association (NBA) in 1949–1950 but were discarded by the NBA for the 1950–1951 season as not having a large enough arena or market. The league's commissioner was former NBL commissioner Doxie Moore. The former NBL/NBA teams the **Anderson Packers, Sheboygan Redskins, Waterloo Hawks,** and **Denver Nuggets** (renamed the Denver Frontier Refiners) were joined by the Louisville Alumnites, Grand Rapids Hornets, St. Paul Lights, and Kansas City Hi-Spots. Before the season ended, Denver disbanded and was replaced by the Evansville Agogans, and Louisville, Grand Rapids, St. Paul, and Kansas City had all disbanded.

The league had a few notable occurrences. On 21 January 1951, Milt Schoon of Denver scored 64 points in one game, the most that any one player had scored in a game since the early years of professional basketball. Schoon played in 31 NPBL games that season and never scored more than 21 points in any other game. He also played 215 games professionally in four other seasons and never exceeded 24 points in a game. On 27 January 1951, Sheboygan defeated Denver, 157–72. This was the most points scored in a professional basketball game to that date, and the 85 point margin of victory has never been equaled in any U.S. professional major league basketball game to date.

The last NPBL game was played on 14 March 1951. Both division leaders, Sheboygan and Waterloo, claimed the league championship, but plans for a playoff were canceled and the league disbanded on 24 March 1951. The league employed many players who had played in the NBL, **Basketball Association of America,** and/or NBA, including Bob Brannum, Joe Graboski, **Bobby McDermott,** Mike Novak, Mac Otten, Milt Schoon, and Murray Wier. *See also* APPENDIX B (for a list of league champions).

NBA DEVELOPMENT LEAGUE (NBADL). The NBA Development League (NBADL) is a professional minor league that had its beginning in 2001, as the National Basketball Development League, and it is also referred to as the "D-League." Sponsored by the **National Basketball Association (NBA),** it played a 56–game season with eight teams in the South Central area of the **United States,** including the Asheville Altitude and Fayetteville Patriots in North Carolina, Greenville Groove and North Charleston Lowgators in

South Carolina, Huntsville Flight and Mobile Revelers in Alabama, Columbus Riverdragons in Georgia, and Roanoke Dazzle in Virginia.

In 2005, the NBA decided to expand the scope of the league; changed its name to the NBA Development League; and made it into more of a true farm system, with NBA teams having a direct working relationship with NBADL teams. Since then, the league has had teams in 15 other states, mostly throughout the western part of the country, and in 2010 had 16 teams. On 1 April 2007, Jordan Farmar of the Los Angeles D-Fenders played a NBADL game in the afternoon and was called up by the **Los Angeles Lakers** of the NBA and played for them that same evening. He was the first player ever to play for these two leagues in the same day.

NELSON, DONALD ARVID "DON." B. 15 May 1940, Muskegon, Michigan. Don Nelson attended Rock Island High School in Rock Island, Illinois, and the University of Iowa. He was selected by the Chicago Zephyrs in the 1962 **National Basketball Association (NBA) draft**. The six-foot, six-inch **guard-forward** played in the NBA from 1962–1976 for the Zephyrs, **Los Angeles Lakers**, and **Boston Celtics**.

Nelson's NBA career totals for 14 years are 1,053 regular-season games and a 10.3 points per game average. He was a member of the NBA champions five times with the Celtics and played with the Lakers in the NBA Finals on the losing side in 1965. An excellent shooter, he led the NBA in **field goal** percentage in 1975. After retiring from active play, he became an NBA head **coach**.

Nelson began the 1976–1977 season as assistant coach for the **Milwaukee Bucks**, was promoted to head coach in November, and coached the Bucks through the 1986–1987 season. From 1988–1995, he coached the **Golden State Warriors**. In 1995–1996, he coached the **New York Knickerbockers** and, from 1997–2005, the **Dallas Mavericks**. From 2006–2010, he again coached Golden State. His overall record as an NBA head coach through the 2009–2010 season is 1,335–1,063, the most wins in NBA coaching history, but he has never reached the NBA Finals as a coach.

Nelson was named NBA Coach of the Year in 1983, 1985, and 1992, and in 1996 was selected as one of the Top 10 Coaches in NBA History. In 1994, he was also the coach of the **gold medal**-winning

U.S. national team at the **World Championships**. His son, Donnie Nelson, has been an NBA assistant coach and has, at times, filled in for his father as head coach.

NET. A net is the cording attached to the rim of the **basket** to make it easier to determine whether a **field goal** is successful.

NETBALL. Netball is a game similar to **basketball**, usually played by girls and women. It is most popular in British Commonwealth countries. The sport has been included in the Commonwealth Games since 1998 and since 1995 has been a recognized sport by the International Olympic Committee, although its inclusion in future **Olympic Games** is unlikely. The object of the game is to throw a ball through a raised hoop, but unlike modern basketball, there is no **backboard**.

The game was developed in 1895 and is a derivative of basketball. American Clara Gregory Baer is considered to be the game's originator. It was developed specifically for women as a noncontact version of basketball, with an emphasis on passing and shooting. There are seven players to a team and, depending on position, these players are only allowed in certain areas of the court. Participants wear vests with their position indicated on the garment to aid the umpire. The seven positions include GS-goal shooter, GA-goal attack, WA-wing attack, C-center, WD-wing defense, GD-goal defense, and GK-goal keeper. Goals may only be scored by certain players and only from certain areas on the court. Games usually consist of four 15-**minute** quarters.

NEVADA, LAS VEGAS (UNLV), UNIVERSITY OF. *See* UNIVERSITY OF NEVADA, LAS VEGAS (UNLV).

NEW JERSEY AMERICANS. *See* NEW JERSEY NETS.

NEW JERSEY NETS. The New Jersey Nets are a team in the **National Basketball Association (NBA)**. They began as the New Jersey Americans in the **American Basketball Association (ABA)** in 1967. In 1968, they moved to New York and were renamed the New York Nets. In 1976, the Nets were included in the merger with the

NBA, playing as the New York Nets in 1976–1977 and returning to New Jersey in 1978, where they have played since.

New Jersey Americans. The team originated on 2 February 1967, when Arthur J. Brown, owner of ABC Freight Forwarding company, was awarded a franchise for $30,000 in the newly created ABA, along with partner Mark Binstein, who was the acting ABA president. The team was originally to be known as the New York Freighters, and they were to play home games at the **69th Regiment Armory** in New York City, but due to pressure by the **New York Knickerbockers** of the NBA, home games were played at the Teaneck Armory in New Jersey. Their first game was played on 23 October 1967, at the Teaneck Armory, before 3,089 fans. Players on the team included Tony Jackson, who had been blackballed by the NBA for being involved with the point-shaving scandal of 1961; Stew Johnson; Bobby Lloyd; Mel Nowell; Walt Simon; and Bruce Spraggins. The Americans finished tied with the **Kentucky Colonels** for fourth place in the Eastern Division; requiring a playoff between the two teams. The Teaneck Armory was unavailable, and the game was moved to the Commack Arena in Commack, Long Island, New York. When the teams arrived at the arena, it was discovcered that the **basketball** court, which had been placed over the arena's ice without adequate insulation, was extremely wet and slippery and could not be used for the game. The game was postponed, rescheduled for Minneapolis, and then canceled by league commissioner **George Mikan**. The Colonels were awarded a forfeit victory. The next season, the New Jersey Americans moved to Commack and changed the team's name to the New York Nets (to be in line with New York's other professional sports teams, the baseball New York Mets and the football New York Jets).

New York Nets (ABA). Home games were played at the 6,000-seat Commack Arena in the 1968–1969 season. The team drew poorly there and for the next two and one-half seasons played home games at the 8,500-seat Island Garden in West Hempstead, New York, until the new 17,800-seat Nassau Coliseum in nearby Uniondale was available in February 1972. During their eight years as the New York Nets, the team ran the gamut from the worst record in the league (17–61 in 1968–1969) to twice being ABA Champions after acquiring **Julius Erving**. The playing personnel also varied, from virtually no recognizable names among the 23 players who played in 1968–1969 to future Hall of Famers **Rick Barry** (1970–1972) and Erving (1973–1976). Other players who later also succeeded in the NBA included Larry Kenon, Billy Paultz, Brian Taylor, and John Williamson. On 17 June 1976, upon payment of $3.2 million, the Nets became members of the NBA. In addition, they were required to pay the New York Knickerbockers $4.8 million for operating within a 50-mile radius of **Madison Square Garden**. These cash payments caused them to sell some of the best players, including Erving, with the result that their initial teams in the NBA were not nearly as competitive as the ones in the last few years of the ABA. Their overall ABA record for nine years was 374–370.

New York Nets (NBA). In the NBA in 1976–1977, the Nets finished in last place in the Atlantic Division of the Eastern Conference. Players included Mike Bantom, Tim Bassett, Jim Fox, Robert "Bubbles" Hawkins, Kim Hughes, Al Skinner, Chuck Terry, Jan Van Breda Kolff, John Williamson, and Dave Wohl. In February, they became the first NBA team to start five **left-handed** players, Bassett, Hawkins, Hughes, Skinner, and Wohl. In July 1977, they moved to New Jersey.

New Jersey Nets. Home games were played at the 8,000-seat Rutgers Athletic Center in Piscataway, New Jersey, from 1977–1981, and at the 20,049-seat Brendan Byrne Arena (also known as Continental Arena and Izod Center) in East Rutherford, New Jersey, since then. They were involved in one of the league's most unusual games with the **Philadelphia 76ers** in the 1978–1979 season. On 8 November 1978, the Nets played the 76ers in Philadelphia. The game was protested with 5:50 remaining in the third quarter with the 76ers ahead 84–81, because the **referees** had erroneously called a third technical **foul** on New Jersey's **coach**, Kevin Loughery, and his player, Bernard King. The protest was upheld and the last portion of the game replayed on 23 March 1979. In the interval, the two teams had made a trade, and in the replayed portion the traded players, Eric Money, Harvey Catchings, and Ralph Simpson, played for their new teams, resulting in a box score with these players appearing for both New Jersey and Philadelphia, the only game in NBA history in which players played for both teams in the same game. Among their most notable players have been **Vince Carter**, Derrick

Coleman, Mike Gminski, Richard Jefferson, **Jason Kidd**, Kerry Kittles, Kenyon Martin, Chris Morris, **Drazen Petrovic**, Keith Van Horn, and Buck Williams. Their best seasons were 2001–2002 and 2002–2003, when they reached the NBA Finals. Their overall record for their 34 years in the NBA including their year in New York, through the 2009–2010 season is 1,162–1,594. Their worst season was 2009–2010 when they set a league record by losing their first 18 games and finished with a 12–70 won–lost record. On 23 September 2009, Russian businessman Mikhail Prokhorov agreed to a plan to purchase the Nets, have a new arena built in Brooklyn and move the team there for the 2011–2012 season.

NEW ORLEANS BUCCANEERS. *See* MEMPHIS SOUNDS.

NEW ORLEANS HORNETS. The New Orleans Hornets are a team in the **National Basketball Association (NBA)**. They were originally the Charlotte Hornets and moved to New Orleans in 2002. They moved most of their home games to Oklahoma City, Oklahoma, when Hurricane Katrina destroyed the city of New Orleans in 2005 and for two seasons were known as the New Orleans-Oklahoma City Hornets. In 2007, they returned to New Orleans.

Charlotte Hornets. The Charlotte Hornets, owned by a group headed by George Shinn, received an NBA expansion franchise on 22 April 1987, and began play in the 1988–1989 season. Home games were played at the 23,500-seat Charlotte Coliseum. Among their most notable players were **Tyrone "Muggsy" Bogues**, Elden Campbell, Rex Chapman, Dell Curry, Baron Davis, Kenny Gattison, Kendall Gill, Larry Johnson, **Alonzo Mourning**, J. R. Reid, Glen Rice, Kelly Tripucka, and David Wesley. Their best season was 1997–1998, when they reached the second round of the playoffs. In 2002, they moved to New Orleans.

New Orleans Hornets. Home games were played at the 18,500-seat New Orleans Arena. As the New Orleans-Oklahoma City Hornets from 2005–2007, most home games were played at the 19,599-seat Ford Center in Oklahoma City, with the Lloyd Noble Center on the campus of the University of Oklahoma, the **Pete Maravich** Assembly Center on the campus of **Louisiana State University**, and the New Orleans Arena also used. After the city of New Orleans was rebuilt in 2007, the Hornets moved back and have since been known simply as the New Orleans Hornets. Among their most notable players have been Hilton Armstrong, P. J. Brown, Rasual Butler, Tyson Chandler, Baron Davis, George Lynch, Jamaal Magloire, Jamal Mashburn, Jannero Pargo, Chris Paul, **Peja Stojakovic**, David Wesley, and David West. Their best season was 2007–2008, when they won 56 and lost 26 in the regular season but lost in the second round of the playoffs. The Hornets overall record for their 22 years in the league through 2009–2010 is 867–905.

NEW ORLEANS JAZZ. *See* UTAH JAZZ.

NEW ORLEANS-OKLAHOMA CITY HORNETS. *See* NEW ORLEANS HORNETS.

NEW YORK FREIGHTERS. *See* NEW JERSEY NETS.

NEW YORK KNICKERBOCKERS. The New York Knickerbockers are a team in the **National Basketball Association (NBA)**. They were a charter franchise in the **Basketball Association of America (BAA)** in 1946 and had the distinction of playing in the very first league game on 1 November 1946, in Toronto, Ontario, **Canada**, which they won, 60–58. They were initially owned by the Madison Square Garden Corporation, James D. Norris, and Arthur Wirtz. Home games were played at **Madison Square Garden** on Eighth Avenue and 50th Street from 1946–1968 and at the new Madison Square Garden on Seventh Avenue and 33rd Street since 1968. From 1946–1960, occasional home games were played at the **69th Regiment Armory**.

The Knicks were the first team to employ a player of Asian descent, Japanese American **Wataru "Wat" Misaka**, in the 1947–1948 season. They also had one of the first three black players in the league, when they signed former **Harlem Globetrotter Nat "Sweetwater" Clifton**. Among their most notable players have been Hall of Famers **Walt Bellamy, Bill Bradley, Dave DeBusschere, Patrick Ewing, Walt Frazier, Harry Gallatin, Tom Gola, Phil Jackson, Jerry Lucas, Al and Dick McGuire, Earl Monroe,** and **Willis Reed**.

Their best season was 1969–1970, when they had a regular-season record of 60–22 and won the NBA Championship in seven games by defeating the **Los Angeles Lakers**. The seventh game was one of the most memorable in league history, as Reed, who had been injured in the fifth game of the series, made a dramatic entrance and made his first two **field goals** to spark the Knicks. They also won the NBA Championship in 1973, by defeating the Lakers in five games. They reached the NBA Championship Finals for the first time in the 1950–1951 season. In that series, they lost the first three games to the Rochester Royals, then won the next three and lost game seven by only four points. In 1952 and 1953, they again reached the Finals but were defeated by the Minneapolis Lakers each time. In 1971–1972, they lost to the Lakers in the Finals and, in 1998–1999, lost to the **San Antonio Spurs** in the Finals. Their overall record for their first 64years in the league through the 2009–2010 season is 2,483–2,516.

NEW YORK NETS. *See* NEW JERSEY NETS.

NEW YORK RENAISSANCE "RENS." The New York Rens began play in November 1923. They were organized by **Bob Douglas**, who originally wanted to call the team the Spartan Braves, but in exchange for the use of the Renaissance Casino in Harlem, New York, he agreed to call the team the New York Harlem Renaissance. They were an all-black independent barnstorming team that, unlike the **Harlem Globetrotters**, played straight **basketball** without clowning. Their initial roster consisted of Zach Anderson; Frank "Strangler" Forbes; Clarence "Fat" Jenkins; Leon Monde; Hy Monte; and Hilton "Kid" Slocum, their captain. In the next few years, they added James "Pappy" Ricks; Eyre Saitch, a champion tennis player as well as a basketball player; **Charles "Tarzan" Cooper**; and Bill Yancey.

In their first season, 1923–1924, they played only 23 games, winning 15 of them. By 1925, they were playing nearly 100 games in a season and winning about 80 percent of them. From 1932–1936 were their peak years, when they had a record of 497–58, including an 88-consecutive-game winning streak. In 1939, they won the first invitational **World Professional Basketball Tournament** in Chicago, Illinois. In the 1948–1949 season, they were invited to join the

National Basketball League after the Detroit Vagabond Kings dropped out of the league on 17 December 1946. They played as the Dayton Rens and assumed Detroit's record of 2–17. **Coached by William "Pop" Gates**, they compiled a record of 14–26 over the remainder of the league season, while also playing exhibition games as the New York Rens. Following the season, they were disbanded.

Among the players for the Dayton Rens were George Crowe, who later became a major league baseball player; Hank DeZonie, who later played briefly in the **National Basketball Association**; Tom Sealy; Wee Willie Smith; Jim Usry, later to be mayor of Atlantic City; and Sonny Wood. For their contribution to basketball, they were enshrined in the **Naismith Memorial Basketball Hall of Fame** in 1963 in the category of team. They have been credited with a record of 2,588–539 during their history, although a definitive game-by-game record does not exist. The most comprehensive work on the New York Renaissance is the doctoral dissertation written by Susan Rayl in 1996.

NEW YORK STATE LEAGUE (NYSL). The New York State League (NYSL) was a men's professional **basketball** league organized in October 1911, in Catskill, New York. Perry W. Decker of Catskill was elected league president. Charter members of the league were Troy, Catskill, Cohoes, Hudson, Schenectady, and Gloversville. (All of these cities are within a 50-mile radius of Albany, New York.) Games were played in armories that had **cages** but no **backboards**. Most teams featured preliminary (nonleague) games at 8 p.m., a NYSL game at 9 p.m., and dancing from 10 p.m. until midnight, with ticket prices of 25 cents for general admission and 35 cents for reserved seats. Gloversville withdrew from the league prior to its start and was replaced by Utica.

In the first season, the six teams played approximately 50 games each, and Troy was the league champion. The league continued through the 1916–1917 season, usually with six teams. On 17 February 1917, the league suspended operations due to World War I and the military's need to use the armories that had been the leagues playing sites. In 1919, after a two and one-half year hiatus due to the war, the league resumed with a 10-team league, including two western Massachusetts teams. The league continued through the 1922–23 season, but dwindling attendance caused it to discontinue operations.

During the 1930s and 1940s, there were at times minor leagues also known as the New York State League. During its 10-year span, the NYSL attracted most of the best professional players of the era, future Hall of Famers John Beckman, **Marty Friedman**, **Joe Lapchick**, Frank Morgenweck, **Barney Sedran**, and **Ed Wachter** among them. *See also* APPENDIX B (for a list of league champions).

NEW ZEALAND. New Zealand joined the **Fédération Internationale de Basketball (FIBA)** in 1951 and is a member in the FIBA Oceania zone. The men's team competed in the **Olympic Games** of 2000 and 2004, where they finished 11th and 10th, respectively. Their top players were Pero Cameron, Phill Jones, and Sean Marks. They competed four times in the FIBA **World Championships** and finished a surprising fourth in 2002. In the FIBA Oceania Championships, they entered 19 times, won the title in 1999 and 2001, and finished in second place 17 times. The women's team competed in three Olympic tournaments, where their best finish was eighth place in 2004. In the FIBA World Championships, they only competed in 1994 and finished 15th. In the FIBA Oceania Championships, they competed 14 times and were champions in 1993 and 1999. There have been two New Zealand natives in the **National Basketball Association**, Sean Marks and Kirk Penney. Megan Compain, a New Zealand Olympian in 2000 and 2004, has played in the **Women's National Basketball Association**.

NORTH CAROLINA, UNIVERSITY OF. The University of North Carolina in Chapel Hill began its men's **basketball** program in 1910. Home games since 1986 have been played at the 21,750-seat **Dean Smith** Center. Prior to 1986, home games were played at the 8,000-seat Carmichael Auditorium. In their first 100 years, the school has a won–lost record of 2,004–720. They are only the second college to achieve 2,000 victories and their won-lost percentage of .736 is the second-best of all colleges. The most accomplished **coaches** in the school's history have been Frank McGuire (164–58 from 1953–1961), Dean Smith (879–254 from 1961–1997), and Roy Williams

(196–54 from 2003–2010). The Tarheels have reached the **National Collegiate Athletic Association (NCAA) Final Four** 17 times. In 1957, the Tarheels defeated a **Wilt Chamberlain**-led **University of Kansas** team in triple **overtime**, 54–53, to win their first NCAA Championship. They won their second NCAA Championship in 1982 by one point over **Georgetown University**. They also won NCAA Championships in 1993, 2005, and 2009. They were NCAA runners-up four times and losing semifinalists nine times. The best players in school history include **Larry Brown**, Bill Bunting, **Vince Carter**, **Billy Cunningham**, Brad Doherty, Walter Davis, Phil Ford, **Bobby Jones**, **Michael Jordan**, George Karl, Mitch Kupchak, Sean May, **Bob McAdoo**, Sam Perkins, Lenny Rosenbluth, Charlie Scott, Lee Shaffer, Kenny Smith, Joe Wolf, and **James Worthy**.

The women's basketball program began in 1971. The most notable coach has been Sylvia Hatchell (559–214 from 1986–2010). In 1994, the lady Tarheels won the NCAA National Championship and in 2006 and 2007 reached the Final Four. The best players in school history have included Sylvia Crawley, Marion Jones, Ivory Latta, Marsha Mann, and Tracy Reid.

NORTH CAROLINA STATE UNIVERSITY. North Carolina State University in Raleigh began its men's **basketball** program in 1914. Home games since 1999 have been played at the 19,722-seat Raleigh Entertainment and Sports Arena. Prior to 1999, home games were played at the 14,000-seat Reynolds Coliseum. The most accomplished **coaches** in the school's history have been Everett Case, Norm Sloan, and **Jim Valvano**. In 1974, the Wolfpack won the **National Collegiate Athletic Association (NCAA)** Championship. They won a second NCAA Championship in 1983 and were losing semifinalists in 1950. The best players in school history include Ed Biedenbach, Tom Burleson, Kenny Carr, Lorenzo Charles, Chris Corchiani, Vinny Del Negro, Dick Dickey, Tom Gugliotta, Sidney Lowe, Ronnie Shavlik, **David Thompson**, Monte Towe, Chris Washburn, Anthony "Spud" Webb, and Charles "Hawkeye" Whitney.

NOTRE DAME UNIVERSITY. Notre Dame University in South Bend, Indiana, began its men's basketball program in 1897. Home games since 1968 have been played at the 9,800-seat Edmund P.

Joyce Center. The most notable **coaches** in the school's history have been George Keogan, Edward "Moose" Krause, and Richard "Digger" Phelps. In 1927 and in 1936, they were named as national champions, but this was prior to a national championship tournament. Their best showing in the NCAA tournament was in 1978, when they reached the **Final Four** but lost in the semifinal round. One of their most notable wins in history was on 19 January 1974, when the Fighting Irish defeated the **University of California, Los Angeles (UCLA)** and ended UCLA's winning streak of 88 consecutive games. Among the best players in the school's history have been Leo Barnhorst, **Austin Carr**, Sid Catlett, Leo Crowe, **Adrian Dantley**, LaPhonso Ellis, Bill Hanzlik, Tom Hawkins, Collis Jones, Leo Klier, Bill Laimbeer, Jay Miller, John Paxson, Chris Quinn, Ron Reed, David Rivers, Donald Royal, John Shumate, Kelly Tripucka, Monty Williams, and Orlando Woolridge.

The women's **basketball** program commenced in 1977. The most notable coach has been Muffet McGraw (525–203 from 1987–2010). In 2001, the Fighting Irish won the **National Collegiate Athletic Association (NCAA)** Championship and in 1997 lost in the semifinal round. The best players in school history have included Charel Allen, Jacqueline Batteast, Sandy Botham, Letitia Bowen, Beth Cunningham, Megan Duffy, Niele Ivey, Sheila McMillen, Alicia Ratay, and Ruth Riley.

NOWITZKI, DIRK WERNER. B. 19 June 1978, Würzburg, **Germany**. Dirk Nowitzki did not attend college but starting playing professional basketball with the DJK Würzburg team in Germany in 1994. He was chosen in the 1998 **National Basketball Association (NBA) draft** by the **Milwaukee Bucks** and his **draft rights** were immediately traded to the **Dallas Mavericks**. The seven-foot-tall **forward** has played for the Mavericks since 1998.

Nowitzki is an outstanding shooter and has recorded professional career averages of 38 percent **three-point field goal** accuracy, 47 percent overall **field goal** accuracy, and 88 percent **free throw** accuracy. He won the NBA All-Star Weekend Three Point Shooting Competition in 2006. In his first 12 NBA seasons, he played in 920 regular-season games and has averaged 22.9 points per game. He has played in the NBA **All-Star Game** in each season from 2002–2010 and was the league's Most Valuable Player in 2007. He was named to the All-NBA First Team four times, All-NBA Second Team four times, and All-NBA Third Team twice. In 2006, he led Dallas to the NBA Championship Finals, where they were defeated in six games by the **Miami Heat.**

The flag bearer for Germany at the 2008 Beijing **Olympic Games,** Nowitzki led them in scoring with 17 points per game, although they only won one game and finished tied for ninth position. He has played in five European and two **World Championships.** In the 2002 World Championship and 2005 European Championships, he led them to the **bronze medal** and **silver medal,** respectively, and was both the leading scorer and most valuable player in these two tournaments.

NUCATOLA, JOHN P. "JOHNNY." B. 17 November 1907, New York, New York. D. 9 May 2000, New York, New York. Johnny Nucatola was one of the best **basketball** officials in history. He attended Newtown High School in Elmhurst, New York, and served in the **U.S.** Air Force during World War II. He later became dean of boys at Bayside High School in Bayside, New York. He **refereed** in the **Basketball Association of America** and **National Basketball Association (NBA)** from its first year in 1946 until 1954, resigning on 27 January 1954, when he felt the league owners did not give the officiating staff proper respect, but he continued **coaching** high school and college games.

In 1959, Nucatola authored *Officiating Basketball.* He later became supervisor of officials for the Eastern College Athletic Conference in 1958. He was the founder of the College Basketball Officials Association. In 1970, he was named supervisor of officials in the NBA and held that position until 1977. An advocate of the three-man officiating crew that was finally adopted by the NBA in the mid-1990s, he was called "basketball's greatest official" by basketball coach **Clair Bee** and in 1978 was elected to the **Naismith Memorial Basketball Hall of Fame.**

– O –

O'BRIEN, JOHN JOSEPH. B. 4 November 1888, Brooklyn, New York. D. 9 December 1967, Oceanside, New York. John O'Brien attended Commercial High School in Brooklyn, where he played baseball, football, and **basketball**, and **St. John's University**. He joined Coverdale & Colpitts consulting engineers in 1913 and was manager from 1920–1958. From 1910–1930, he was also a basketball **referee** for high school, college, and professional games. He helped organize several basketball leagues, including the Interstate League, Metropolitan League, and **American Basketball League (ABL)** of 1925. When the ABL folded in 1931, he reorganized the league in 1933 and was its leader until its dissolution in 1953. He also was vice president, secretary, and treasurer of Pierce Oil Corporation from 1930–1940; vice president, director, and secretary of the Minneapolis and St. Louis Railway; and a trustee of the West Caddo Oil Syndicate. His son, John Jr., was captain of the Columbia University basketball team and played in the ABL. He was enshrined in the **Naismith Memorial Basketball Hall of Fame** in 1961 in the category of contributor.

O'BRIEN, LAWRENCE FRANCIS, JR. "LARRY." B. 7 July 1917, Springfield, Massachusetts. D. 27 September 1990, New York, New York. Larry O'Brien graduated from Northeastern University in 1942 with a bachelor of law degree and spent much of his life in politics. He was an administrative assistant to Congressman Foster Furcolo from 1948–1950, campaign director and advisor to Senator John F. Kennedy from 1952–1958, special assistant for congressional relations to President Kennedy and President Lyndon B. Johnson from 1961–1965, postmaster general of the **United States** from 1965–1968, and national chairman of the Democratic Party from 1968–1972.

O'Brien was **National Basketball Association (NBA)** commissioner from 1 June 1975 until 1 February 1984. He oversaw the merger with the **American Basketball Association (ABA)**, a collective bargaining agreement with the NBA Players Association, and television contracts with several networks. He also implemented an antidrug policy. During his administration, the NBA attained substantial increases in attendance and television revenue. O'Brien was president of the **Naismith Memorial Basketball Hall of Fame** from 1985–1987 and in 1991 was enshrined in the hall as a contributor.

O'NEAL, SHAQUILLE RASHAUN. B. 6 March 1972, Newark, New Jersey. Shaquille O'Neal attended Cole High School in San Antonio, Texas, and **Louisiana State University (LSU)**. He left LSU after his junior year and was selected by the **Orlando Magic** as the first player chosen in the 1992 **National Basketball Association (NBA) draft**. The seven-foot, two-inch, 300 plus-pound **center** (his weight has varied between 265–350 pounds during his NBA career) played for the Magic from 1992–1996. He was Rookie of the Year in 1993 and took the Magic to the NBA Championship Finals in 1995. On 20 November 1993, he became only the third NBA player to record 15 **blocks** in one game.

O'Neal played for the **Los Angeles Lakers** from 1996–2004, won three NBA Championships with them, and was named the NBA Finals Most Valuable Player all three years. He was also the NBA's Most Valuable Player in 2000. On 6 March 2000, he scored 61 points in a game, one of only 15 NBA players to score 61 or more in a single game. After a dispute with teammate **Kobe Bryant**, he asked to be traded and, in July 2004, was traded to the **Miami Heat**.

In his second year in Miami, O'Neal helped lead them to the 2006 NBA Championship. He was traded to the **Phoenix Suns** in February 2008, and to the **Cleveland Cavaliers** in June 2009. On 4 August 2010, he signed a two-year contract with the Boston Celtics. Since he is a notoriously poor foul shooter (slightly over 50 percent for his career), opposing **coaches** have often employed a "Hack-a-Shaq" strategy of deliberately fouling him. As a result, he holds the NBA record for most **free throws** attempted in a game, with 39, on 9 June 2000. On 20 May 2000, a similar strategy was employed, and he set the record of 25 free throws attempted in one quarter and 27 for one half. The three free throw records were set in playoff games but surpass any regular-season records.

O'Neal was named to the All-NBA First Team eight times, All-NBA Second Team twice, All-NBA Third Team four times, and All-NBA Defensive Second Team three times in his first 18 NBA seasons. He was selected for 15 NBA **All-Star Games** and was named All-Star Most Valuable Player three times. He played for the **gold medal**-winning **U.S.** team in the 1994 **World Championships** and was named the most valuable player. He also won a gold medal in the 1996 **Olympic Games**.

Known for his likable personality and sense of humor, he has appeared in several Hollywood films and has recorded several rap records. He has been interested in law enforcement and became a reserve officer for the Los Angeles Port Police. After he was traded to Miami, he became a Miami Beach reserve officer in 2005. In 1996, O'Neal was named one of the 50 Greatest Players in NBA History, even though he had only played for a little more than three seasons at that time.

OAKLAND OAKS. *See* VIRGINIA SQUIRES.

OBAMA, BARACK HUSSEIN, JR. B. 4 August 1961, Honolulu, Hawaii. The 44th President of the **United States**, Barack Obama attended the Punahou School in Hawaii and played **basketball** on the team that won the state high school championship in 1979. Although the six-foot, two-inch **left-handed** future president, nicknamed "Barry O'Bomber," only scored two points in the championship game, he was considered to be an above average player. As a law student at Harvard University, he met the future Mrs. Obama, Michelle Robinson, whose brother, Craig Robinson, was a star player at Princeton University and is the present basketball **coach** at Oregon State University. Obama's basketball abilities were described by former **National Basketball Association** player Rickey Green, who has played basketball with him: "He's above average . . . and has a nice little left-hand shot and some knowledge of the game."

OFFENSE. In **basketball**, the team in possession of the ball is considered to be on offense (pronounced with the accent on the first syllable) and their opponents on **defense**. A team can only score points while on offense. **Coaches** will usually design plays to be carried out while the team is on offense. Certain statistics, such as **rebounds**, are recorded separately for the offense and for the defense. Personal **fouls** committed while the team is on offense are treated differently than those committed on defense.

OHIO STATE UNIVERSITY. Ohio State University is located in Columbus, Ohio. (Its official name includes the article "the.") The school was one of the first in the nation to play intercollegiate **basketball** and began its men's program in 1898. Home games were played at St. John Arena from 1956–1998. Since 1998, the 19,200-seat Value City Arena (renamed the Jerome Schottenstein Center) has been the site of their home games. The most accomplished **coaches** were Harold G. Olsen (260–196 from 1923–46) and Fred Taylor (297–158 from 1959–76). Among their best players have been Gary Bradds, Jim Cleamons, Robin Freeman, **John Havlicek**, Bill Hosket, Jim Jackson, Clark Kellogg, **Jerry Lucas**, Greg Oden, Michael Redd, Dick Schnittker, Dave Sorenson, and Herb Williams. The Buckeyes finished second to Oregon in the first **National Collegiate Athletic Association (NCAA)** Championship in 1939. They were champions in 1960 and runners-up in 1961, 1962, and 2007.

The women's basketball program began in 1965. The most notable coach was Nancy Darsch (234–125 from 1985–97). In 1993, the Buckeyes reached the NCAA Championship Final game but lost to **Texas Tech University**. The best players in school history have included Yvette Angel, Jessica Davenport, Jantel Lavender, Marscilla Packer, Katie Smith, and Kim Wilburn.

OKAFOR, CHUKWUEMEKA NOUBUISI "EMEKA." B. 28 September 1982, Houston, Texas. The phrase African American is quite appropriate for Emeka Okafor, who was born in the **United States** to Nigerian parents. He attended Bellaire High School in Houston and the **University of Connecticut (UCONN)**. In college, he was a true student-athlete, graduating with a degree in finance and a 3.8 grade point average in just three years. He was named the Academic All-American of the Year in 2004, led UCONN to the **National Collegiate Athletic Association (NCAA)** Championships, and was named the Most Outstanding Player of the 2004 NCAA tournament.

The six-foot, 10-inch, 250-pound **forward** was selected by the **Charlotte Bobcats** in the 2004 **National Basketball Association (NBA) draft**, played for them from 2004–2009, and was Rookie of the Year in 2005. In July 2009, Okafor was traded to the **New Orleans Hornets**. In his first six seasons in the NBA, he has averaged 13.3 points and 10.3 rebounds per game. He was the only player selected to the U.S. team in the 2004 **Olympic Games** without NBA experience and won a **bronze medal** with them.

OKLAHOMA A&M COLLEGE. *See* OKLAHOMA STATE UNIVERSITY.

OKLAHOMA CITY THUNDER. The Oklahoma City Thunder are a team in the **National Basketball Association (NBA)**. They were known as the Seattle Supersonics from 1967–2008 and moved to Oklahoma City in 2008.

Seattle Supersonics. Home games were played at the 17,000-seat Seattle Center Coliseum (renamed Key Arena in 1995) from 1967–1978, 1985–1994, and 1995–2008; at the 60,000-seat Kingdome from 1978–1985; and at the 21,000-seat Tacoma Dome in Tacoma, Washington, in 1994–1995, while the Coliseum was being refurbished. Among their most notable players have been Fred Brown, Michael Cage, Tom Chambers, Dale Ellis, **Spencer Haywood**, Shawn Kemp, Rashard Lewis, Xavier McDaniel, Derrick McKey, Nate McMillan, **Gary Payton**, Jack Sikma, and Gus Williams. They reached the 1978 NBA Championship Finals but lost to the Washington Bullets. They defeated the Bullets in a rematch to win the 1979 NBA Championship. In 1996, they lost to the **Chicago Bulls** in six games in the Finals.

Oklahoma City Thunder. In 2006, the Seattle franchise was sold for $350 million to investors from Oklahoma City, led by Clay Bennett. After a lawsuit between the new owners and the city of Seattle, an agreement was reached allowing the team's lease at Key Arena in Seattle to be broken, and the team moved to Oklahoma City for the 2008–2009 season. Rights to the Supersonics nickname, logo, and team colors were to remain in Seattle. Home games are played at the 19,599-seat Ford Center. Their leading players are Nick Collison, Kevin Durant, Desmond Mason, Joe Smith, Earl Watson, and Russell Westbrook. Through 2009–2010, the franchise has a won–lost record of 1,818–1,676.

OKLAHOMA STATE UNIVERSITY. Oklahoma State University in Stillwater was originally known as Oklahoma Agricultural and Mechanical College. On 15 May 1957, the name was changed to Oklahoma State University. Their men's **basketball** program began in 1907, the same year that the Oklahoma Territory achieved statehood. Home games since 1937 have been played at Gallagher Hall.

In 1987, its name became Gallagher-Iba Arena. From 1934–1970, **Henry P. "Hank" Iba** was their **coach**. In that time, he compiled a record of 652–317. Eddie Sutton (1990–2006) was the only other man to coach them for more than eight seasons. His record was 519–368. Under Iba, the Cowboys won consecutive **National Collegiate Athletic Association (NCAA)** Championships in 1945–1946, with **Bob Kurland** as their star player. In 1949, they finished second to the **University of Kentucky**. Among the team's best players have been Jameson Curry, Richard Dumas, Andy Hopson, Byron Houston, Kurland, Ed Odom, Adrian Peterson, Bryant Reeves, and Randy Rutherford.

OLAJUWON, HAKEEM ABDUL "THE DREAM." B. 21 January, Lagos, Nigeria. As a youth, Hakeem Olajuwon played soccer and team handball and did not play **basketball** until he was 15 years old. He attended Muslim Teachers College (high school) in Lagos and the **University of Houston** in Texas. At Houston, he was a member of the team with the nickname **Phi Slama Jama** and reached the **National Collegiate Athletic Association (NCAA)** Championship **Final Four** three times but failed to win the NCAA title.

Selected by the **Houston Rockets** in the 1984 **National Basketball Association (NBA) draft** as the first overall selection, Olajuwon played from 1984–2001 with the Rockets and in 2001–2002 with the **Toronto Raptors**. In 1994 and 1995, he led the Rockets to the NBA Championship and was named the NBA Finals Most Valuable Player both times. On 1 April 1993, he became a **U.S.** citizen and in 1996 won a **gold medal** with the U.S. **Olympic** basketball team.

The tall **center** (listed at seven-feet but probably closer to six-feet, 10-inches) was named one of the 50 Greatest Players in NBA History in 1996. In his 18 year NBA career, he played in 1,238 regular-season games and averaged 21.8 points per game. He played in the NBA playoffs in 15 of his 18 seasons and averaged 25.9 points per game in 145 playoff games. He was selected for the NBA **All-Star Game** 12 times, was named the NBA Most Valuable Player in 1994, and was selected as the NBA Defensive Player of the Year in 1993 and 1994. He was on the All-NBA First Team six times, All-NBA Second Team three times, All-NBA Third Team three times, All-NBA Defensive First Team five times, and All-NBA Defensive Second

Team four times. He led the league in **blocked shots** three times and holds the NBA career record for most blocked shots.

After retiring from the NBA, Olajuwon has invested in real estate in the Houston area and has a residence in the country of Jordan, where he pursues Islamic studies. In 2008, he was enshrined in the **Naismith Memorial Basketball Hall of Fame**.

OLD DOMINION UNIVERSITY. Old Dominion University, located in Norfolk, Virginia, began its women's **basketball** program in 1969. Their overall record for their first 41 years is a remarkable 904–314. Home games since 2002 have been played at the 8,600-seat Ted Constant Convocation Center. Prior to 2002, home games were played at the 5,200-seat Old Dominion University Fieldhouse. The most notable **coaches** have been Wendy Larry and Marianne Stanley. In 1979 and 1980, the Lady Monarchs won the **Association for Intercollegiate Athletics for Women** National Championship and in 1985 they won the **National Collegiate Athletic Association** National Championship. In 1997, they were national runners-up. The best players in school history include Mery Andrade, Lucienne Berthieu, Monique Coker, Medina Dixon, **Anne Donovan**, Adrienne Goodson, **Nancy Lieberman**, Inge Nissen, **Ticha Penicheiro**, and Nyree Roberts.

OLYMPIC GAMES. The modern Olympic Games, which began in 1896, had its first **basketball** tournament in 1904, in St. Louis. Six teams, all from the **United States**, participated, but most Olympic historians classify the event as a demonstration. The first international Olympic Games basketball tournament took place at the Berlin Games in 1936. Twenty-three men's teams were entered, although only 21 actually played (both **Hungary** and **Spain** withdrew prior to their first match). The matches were contested outdoors, and the final, won by the United States over **Canada**, 19–8, was played in a rainstorm on a muddy court.

The next Olympic Games, held in 1948, in London, England, saw 23 teams play. Several of the teams were new to the sport and lost games by huge margins. The United States nearly lost a preliminary round game to **Argentina** but won by two points and won the championship. In 1952, in Helsinki, Finland, a preliminary pre-Olympic tournament was held to narrow the field to 16 teams. The **Union of Soviet Socialist Republics (USSR)** fielded its first Olympic basketball team in 1952 and quickly became the United States' top rival. From 1952–1972, 16 teams participated, and the United States did not lose a match until the 1972 final in Munich, Germany. In a very controversial game, the USSR defeated the United States, 51–50, in a match where the final three seconds was played three times.

In 1976, a women's Olympic tournament was added, and six teams participated, with the USSR winning. The 1976 men's tournament was reduced to 12 teams and has remained at that limit since then, although the women's tournament was gradually expanded and since 1996 also has 12 teams participating.

Prior to 1992, competition was limited to amateur players (although the definition of "amateur" varied from country to country). In 1992, the event was opened to professionals, and the U.S. team comprised 11 of the best players from the **National Basketball Association (NBA)** and the best collegiate player. That team was dubbed the "**Dream Team**" by sportswriters and easily dominated the competition. Since 1992, other countries have vastly improved, and the United States has not always sent their best men's players; consequently, in 2004, Argentina won the Olympic championship. The U.S. women's team has been exceptional, however, and from 1996–2008 has been undefeated. *See also* APPENDIX F and APPENDIX G (for a list of tournament champions).

OREGON, UNIVERSITY OF. The University of Oregon in Eugene began its men's **basketball** program in 1903. Its most accomplished **coaches** have been Dick Harter, Howard Hobson, Ernie Kent, and William Reinhart. Home games are played at McArthur Court, which was built in 1927 and is still used today. For the 2010–2011 season, the team will move to the new 12,541-seat Matthew Knight Arena. Among their best players have been Greg Ballard, Jim Barnett, Terrell Brandon, John Dick, Laddie Gale, Luke Jackson, Ron Lee, Jim Loscutoff, Stan Love, Anthony Taylor, Charlie Warren, and Urgel "Slim" Wintermute. Wintermute, Dick, and Gale led the Ducks (also called the Webfoots), under coach Hobson, to the first **National Collegiate Athletic Association (NCAA)** Championship in 1939. The team was nicknamed the "Tall Firs" because Wintermute was six-feet, eight-inches tall, and Gale and Dick were each six-feet, four-inches tall.

ORIGINAL CELTICS. The Original Celtics began in 1914 as a group of local Irish American teenagers from the west side of New York City playing settlement house **basketball**. As the New York Celtics, they were managed by Frank McCormack. When McCormack entered the U.S. Army in 1917, James and Thomas Furey took over the team and made it a professional one. Since McCormack refused to sell the rights to the name to the Furey brothers, they simply renamed the team The Original Celtics. They kept a couple of the original players, including Pete Barry and John Whitty, and added others. They played as an independent team but from time to time entered various professional leagues.

In the 1921–1922 **Eastern Basketball League**, they compiled a league-leading 16–4 second-half record and won the league championship. The next season they entered the Metropolitan League, compiled a 12–0 record in the first half, and dropped out of the league seeking stronger competition. In 1927, the Celtics entered the **American Basketball League** and easily won another league championship. In 1928, they dropped out of the league as their manager, James Furey, served time for embezzlement. During the 1930s, the Celtics returned to barnstorming, but the quality of the team was not quite the same as earlier.

From 1920–1928, the Celtics played roughly 100 games a year and won approximately 90 percent of the time. From 1919–1928, their roster included many of the best players of the era, including Davey Banks, Pete Barry, John Beckman, **Henry "Dutch" Dehnert**, Joe Dreyfuss, Oscar Grimstead, George Haggerty, **Nat Holman**, **Joe Lapchick**, Chris Leonard, Ernie Reich, **Elmer Ripley**, Eddie White, and Johnny Whitty. They were enshrined in 1959 in the **Naismith Memorial Basketball Hall of Fame** in the category of team.

ORLANDO MAGIC. The Orlando Magic is a team in the **National Basketball Association (NBA)**. They began as an expansion franchise in 1989. Home games are played at the 17,519-seat Orlando Arena. The arena has undergone several name changes since 1989 and is presently known as the Amway Arena. Among their most notable players have been Nick Anderson, Darrell Armstrong, **Vince Carter,** Pat Garrity, Horace Grant, Anfernee "Penny" Hardaway, **Dwight Howard,** Rashard Lewis, **Tracy McGrady, Shaquille O'Neal,** Dennis Scott, Scott Skiles, and **Hidayet "Hedo" Türkoğlu.** Their best seasons were 1994–1995, when they finished 57–25 in the regular season but lost to the **Houston Rockets** in the NBA Championship Finals, and 2008–2009, when their record was 59–23 but were defeated by the **Los Angeles Lakers** in the Finals. Their overall record for their first 21 years in the league is 870–820.

OSHKOSH ALL-STARS. The Oshkosh All-Stars were a team in the **National Basketball League (NBL).** They were organized in 1929 as an independent team by Lonnie Darling, who later helped found the NBL in 1937. The All-Stars joined the NBL in its first year and were the only team to compete in every one of the NBL's 12 seasons. They were unique in that unlike most of the other NBL teams that were corporate-owned, the All-Stars were owned by the citizens of Oshkosh. Home games were at the 2,200-seat South Side Junior High School Auditorium.

The All-Stars were one of the more successful teams in the league, finishing first in their division seven times. They failed to qualify for the postseason playoffs only once but lost four times in the first round and twice in the second round. They won two NBL titles and lost three times in the championship finals. In their first five years in the league, they won 82 games and lost only 36 and finished first in their division each year. In 12 years in the NBL, they compiled a won–lost record of 225–170 but in the playoffs were only 28–28.

From 1937–1941, George Hotchkiss was the team's **coach,** but then Darling took over as coach for the next seven years. Their star player was **Leroy "Cowboy" Edwards.** He played all 12 seasons, was the league's leading scorer each year from 1937–1940, and was named most valuable player each of those three years. Other players include Lou Barle, Bob Carpenter, Gene Englund, Bob Feerick, **Alex Hannum,** Eddie Riska, Charley Shipp, Ralph Vaughn, Clint Wager, and Herm Witasek.

Prior to the 1948–1949 season, the All-Stars attempted to join the **Basketball Association of America (BAA)** but were excluded. When the BAA merged with the NBL in July 1949, Oshkosh was included, but on 9 September 1949, the newly created **National Basketball Association (NBA)** announced that the Oshkosh franchise was forfeited since they failed to file the $7,200 league entry fee on time. NBA President **Maurice Podoloff** kept the door open for the team to enter the NBA at a future date, but that never happened. Later that summer the team was disbanded and players were made available to other NBA teams.

OVERTIME. When a **basketball** game ends in a tied score after the regulation amount of time has been played, an overtime period (usually five **minutes**) is played. The team ahead at the end of the overtime period is then the winner. If teams are still tied, additional overtime periods are played until a winner is determined. In basketball's earliest days, tie games were permitted and overtime was not played. In earlier days, in some high school leagues, teams could not play more than two overtime periods, after which the game would be settled by alternating free throws. Some leagues (notably the **Continental Basketball Association**) have experimented with sudden-death overtime. The first team to gain a three-point advantage in overtime is the winner.

Before the **shot clock** rules were instituted, teams in overtime would often keep possession of the ball until the period was nearly over before attempting a shot. The **National Basketball Association (NBA)** record of six overtime periods on 6 January 1951, between the **Indianapolis Olympians** and Rochester Royals was one such game. The score at the end of regulation play was tied at 65. The teams each scored a total of eight points in five overtime periods, and Indianapolis won the game, 75–73, by scoring the only two points in the sixth overtime. Since the shot clock was instituted in the 1954–1955 season, there has been one five-overtime game in the NBA. On 9 November 1989, the **Milwaukee Bucks** defeated the Seattle Supersonics, 155–154, after five overtime periods. Overtime is also abbreviated and occasionally referred to as "OT."

– P –

PALESTRA. The Palestra is an indoor arena on the campus of the University of Pennsylvania in Philadelphia built in 1927. It has been used primarily for college **basketball**, and the Big Five of Philadelphia (**La Salle University**, the University of Pennsylvania, **Temple University**, St. Joseph's University, and **Villanova University**) have all played here. It was also occasionally used for **National Basketball Association** games. It's seating capacity for basketball is 8,722. It is known as the "Cathedral of College Hoops."

PALMING. In **basketball**, palming is a violation resulting in loss of possession when the offensive player, while **dribbling** the ball, places his hand underneath the ball and momentarily holds it or carries it. It is seldom strictly enforced in modern professional basketball. *See also* TURNOVER.

PALUBINSKAS, EDWARD SEBASTIAN "EDDIE." B. 17 September 1950, Canberra, ACT, **Australia**. Eddie Palubinskas attended Ricks Junior College and **Louisiana State University**, graduating in 1974. The six-foot, two-inch **guard** was selected by the **Atlanta Hawks** in the 1974 **National Basketball Association (NBA) draft** but did not play in the NBA. On the 1972 and 1976 Australian **Olympic basketball** teams, he averaged 25.6 points per game in the two tournaments, the second highest Olympic career average for players who have competed in more than one Olympic Games. In seven games in 1976, he averaged 31.3 points per game, never scored less than 26 points, and on 21 July 1976 set the Olympic record, with 48 points in one game (broken in 1988 by **Oscar Schmidt**).

Palubinskas was also an outstanding **free throw** shooter, and his free throw percentage of .917 in 1976, making 55 of 60, ranks among the best Olympic performances. He became a free throw **coach** and has made an instructional video on the subject. In 1978, he became head coach of the handball team of Bahrain. In 1981, he earned a master's degree from **Brigham Young University**. He has worked as an artist and is the president of Universal Sports Art and Graphics, a company that specializes in painting large wall and floor murals for sports facilities.

Palubinskas's basketball coaching includes assistant basketball coach at Brigham Young University from 1986–1989; assistant coach at Louisiana State University from 1991–1992; head coach at Central Private High School in Central, Louisiana, from 1992–1996;

and assistant coach with the **Los Angeles Lakers** in 2000–2001. In 1996, he opened the Palubinskas Basketball Academy to teach shooting fundamentals.

PARISH, ROBERT LEE "THE CHIEF." B. 30 August 1953, Shreveport, Louisiana. Robert Parish attended Woodlawn High School in Shreveport and Centenary College. The seven-foot-tall **center** was selected by the **Golden State Warriors** in the 1976 **National Basketball Association (NBA) draft** and played in the NBA from 1976–1997 for Golden State, the **Boston Celtics**, the Charlotte Hornets, and the **Chicago Bulls**. He was nicknamed "The Chief" by teammate Cedric Maxwell, who thought that Parish reminded him of a Native American character from the film *One Flew over the Cuckoo's Nest*.

Parish's NBA career totals for 21 years are 1,611 regular-season games and a 14.5 points, 9.1 **rebounds**, and 1.5 **blocks** per game average. He played more years and in more NBA games than anyone else in the league and concluded his playing career at the age of 43, making him the third oldest player in league history. Selected for nine NBA **All-Star Games**, he was named to the All-NBA Second Team in 1982 and All-NBA Third Team in 1989. With the Celtics, he played in the NBA Finals five times and was a member of the NBA champions in 1981, 1984, and 1986. In his last year, 1997, he was a member of the NBA champion Bulls. In 1996, he was named one of the 50 Greatest Players in NBA History. In 2001, he was named **coach** of the year, when he coached the Maryland Mustangs in the minor league **United States Basketball League**. He was enshrined in the **Naismith Memorial Basketball Hall of Fame** in 2003.

PARKER, WILLIAM ANTHONY "TONY." B. 17 May 1982, Bruges, Belgium. Tony Parker was raised in **France**, where his father, Tony Parker Sr., an American, played professional **basketball**. He began playing for Centre Fédéral in the French league in 1997 and played two seasons with them and two seasons for Paris Basket Racing. He played for the French junior national team and won the **Fédération Internationale de Basketball (FIBA)** Under 18 Championship in 2000.

In the 2001 **National Basketball Association (NBA) draft**, Parker was chosen by the **San Antonio Spurs** and played with them from 2001–2010. In his first nine NBA seasons, the six-foot, two-inch **point guard** played in 668 regular-season games, averaged 16.6 points per game, and helped lead the Spurs to three NBA Championships. In 2007, he was named the NBA Finals Most Valuable Player. He was selected to play in the NBA **All-Star Game** three times and played in the European Championships with the French senior national team from 2001–2009, winning a **bronze medal** in 2005. In 2007, he married actress Eva Longoria.

PAYTON, GARY DWAYNE "THE GLOVE." B. 23 July 1968, Oakland, California. Gary Payton attended Skyline High School in Oakland and Oregon State University. He was drafted by the Seattle Supersonics in the 1990 **National Basketball Association (NBA) draft** and played with them from 1990–2003. The six-foot, four-inch **guard** played for the **Milwaukee Bucks, Los Angeles Lakers, Boston Celtics**, and **Miami Heat** from 2003–2007. With Miami, he was a member of the 2006 NBA Championship team. He also played on the losing team in the NBA Championship Finals for Seattle in 1996 and Los Angeles in 2004. Known as "The Glove" for his exceptional defensive play, he won **gold medals** with the 1996 and 2000 **U.S. Olympic basketball** teams.

Payton's NBA career totals for 1,335 games are 16.3 points and 6.7 **assists** per game. He was selected for the NBA **All-Star Game** nine times and named NBA Defensive Player of the Year in 1996. He was named to the All-NBA First Team twice, All-NBA Second Team five times, All-NBA Third Team twice, and All-Defensive First Team nine times. After retiring from basketball, he has worked in television as an analyst.

PENICHEIRO, PATRICIA NUNES "TICHA." B. 18 September 1974, Figueira da Foz, Portugal. Ticha Penicheiro graduated from **Old Dominion University** in 1998. There she was a member of the 1997 team that lost to the **University of Tennessee** in the **National Collegiate Athletic Association (NCAA)** National Championship game. Selected by the Sacramento Monarchs in the 1998 **Women's National Basketball Association (WNBA) draft**, she has played for them from 1998–2009 and was a member of the league champions in 2005. After the Sacramento franchise folded in November 2009, she signed with the Los Angeles Sparks and played with them in 2010.

Through the 2010 season, the five-foot, 11-inch **guard** has played in 401 regular-season games and scored 2,509 points for a career average of 6.3 points, 6.0 **assists**, and 1.8 **steals** per game. Penicheiro is the all-time career leader in assists and steals and was named to the All-WNBA First Team in 1999 and 2000, All-WNBA Second Team in 2001, and WNBA All-Defensive First Team in 2008. She has also played in Portugal, **Poland, France, Russia,** and **Italy.**

PENNSYLVANIA STATE LEAGUE (PSL). The Pennsylvania State League (PSL) was a men's professional **basketball** major league that began operation in 1914. It was organized by newspapermen Byron J. Lewis of Pittston, Pennsylvania, and Michael U. Coll of Hazleton, Pennsylvania. Six teams within 25 miles in the Wyoming Valley coal-mining region of northeastern Pennsylvania comprised the league that began play in 1914 and lasted until 1921, with no play during the 1918–1919 season due to World War I. The league's schedule varied from 20 to 40 games and the league's size from five to eight teams. Prior to the start of the 1921–1922 season, the PSL disbanded, with two of their teams, Scranton and Wilkes-Barre, joining the **Eastern Basketball League.**

The PSL had its share of top players, as John Beckman, Frank Bruggy, John Deal, Joe Dreyfus, Oscar Grimstead, **Jack Inglis,** Dick Leary, Chris Leonard, Chief Muller, **Elmer Ripley,** Garry Schmeelk, Lou Sugarman, and Andy Suils all played. One of the other top players in the league was Stan "Bucky" Harris, who gained more fame as a Major League Baseball player and manager. *See also* APPENDIX B (for a list of league champions).

PERSONAL FOUL. *See* FOUL.

PERU. Peru joined the **Fédération Internationale de Basketball (FIBA)** in 1936 and is a member in the FIBA Americas zone. They have entered the men's **Olympic Games basketball** tournament three times, in 1936, 1948, and 1964. In 1936, they won their first two games and were matched against **Poland** in the quarterfinal round. Their football (soccer) team meanwhile lost a disputed match, and consequently the entire Peruvian Olympic team withdrew from the Olympic Games in protest. Their quarterfinal basketball match with Poland was then considered as a forfeit loss, and the team finished in eighth place, even though they had not actually lost a competitive game.

In 1964, they had the distinction of playing four brothers: Raúl, Ricardo, Enrique, and Luis Duarte Mungi. Ricardo led all players in scoring and set the Olympic Games record for individual points in a game, with 44 points on 22 of 36 **field goals**. The record stood until 1976. The 22 field goals and 36 field goal attempts are still all-time Olympic records.

Peru entered four of the first five men's **World Championships** with limited success, with seventh place being their best effort. In Pan American Games competition, the Peruvian men's team entered three times, with fifth place in 1963 being their best. They have never entered the FIBA Americas tournament. In the 1938 South America Championships, they won the **gold medal** and have finished second twice and third four times in that tournament.

The women's team has never competed in the Olympic Games. They finished seventh twice in four appearances in the World Championships and finished eighth in their only FIBA Americas tournament and sixth in their only Pan American Games tournament. In the South American Championship, the Peruvian women's team won the gold medal in 1977, won **silver** four times, and earned **bronze** six times. There has never been a Peruvian native in either the **National Basketball Association (NBA)** or **Women's National Basketball Association**, although Raúl Duarte was drafted in 1969 by the San Diego Rockets but did not play in the NBA.

PETROVIC, DRAZEN. B. 22 October 1964, Sibenik, **Croatia, Yugoslavia**. D. 7 June 1993, Denkendorf, **Germany**. Dražen Petrović attended the University of Zagreb in Croatia. He played for Šibenka Šibenik from 1982–1983, Cibona Zagreb from 1984–1988, and Real Madrid in **Spain** from 1988–1989. He led Real Madrid to the **European Cup** in 1989. On 5 October 1985, he scored 112 points in one game for Cibona against Smelt Olimpija in a Yugoslavian league game. He was selected by the **Portland Trail Blazers** in the

1986 **National Basketball Association (NBA) draft** but remained in Europe until 1989. The six-foot, five-inch **guard** played in the NBA from 1989–1993 for the Trail Blazers and **New Jersey Nets**. His career was cut short when he was killed in an auto accident.

Petrović's NBA career totals for four years are 290 regular-season games and a 15.4 points per game average. He was named to the All-NBA Third Team in 1993. He was also a member of the **bronze medal**-winning Yugoslavian **Olympic** team in 1984, the **silver medal**-winning Yugoslavian Olympic team in 1988, and the silver medal-winning Croatian team in 1992. In two **World Championships** and four European Championships, he won a **gold medal** and bronze medal in both events. He was enshrined in the **Naismith Memorial Basketball Hall of Fame** in 2002. His brother, Aleksandar "Aco" Petrović, also played and **coached** professional basketball.

PETTIT, ROBERT E. LEE, JR. "BOB." B. 12 December 1932, Baton Rouge, Louisiana. Bob Pettit attended Baton Rouge High School and in his senior year led them to the state championship. At **Louisiana State University**, he averaged 27.4 points and 14.6 **rebounds** for three years of varsity play. Selected by the Milwaukee Hawks in the 1954 **National Basketball Association (NBA) draft,** he was NBA Rookie of the Year in 1955. The following season, the Hawks moved to St. Louis, where the six-foot, nine-inch **forward** spent the rest of his NBA career. His best year was 1958–1959, when he led the NBA in scoring with a record 2,105 points and averages of 29.2 points, 16.4 rebounds, and 3.1 assists. His scoring records were demolished the next season when **Wilt Chamberlain** entered the league and scored 2,707 points, averaging 37.6 points per game.

Pettit's NBA career totals for 11 years are 792 regular-season games and a 26.4 points and 16.2 rebounds per game average. He had a remarkably consistent career in which he averaged at least 12 rebounds and 20 points in every season. He appeared in 88 playoff games and averaged 25.5 points and 14.8 rebounds. He was selected for the NBA **All-Star Game** in each of his 11 NBA seasons and was All-Star Game Most Valuable Player four times. He was named to the All-NBA First Team every year for his first 10 seasons and to the All-NBA Second Team in his final season. He helped lead the Hawks to the 1958 NBA Championship and the NBA Finals three other times. In 1956 and 1959, he was the league's Most Valuable Player.

After he retired from active play, he became president of Jefferson Bank in Metairie, Louisiana. Enshrined in the **Naismith Memorial Basketball Hall of Fame** in 1971, he was named to the NBA's 25th Anniversary Team and 35th Anniversary Team and in 1996 was named one of the 50 Greatest Players in NBA History.

PHI SLAMA JAMA. The **University of Houston basketball** team from the 1981–1982 season through the 1983–1984 season was given the nickname of Phi Slama Jama by a Houston sportswriter. The name is a takeoff on a college Greek letter fraternity, but it was made in reference to their aggressive **slam-dunking** style of play. Houston reached the **National Collegiate Athletic Association Final Four** in each of the three seasons but lost once in the semifinal round and twice in the final round. Among the best players on those teams were Benny Anders, Greg "Cadillac" Anderson, **Clyde Drexler**, Larry Micheaux, **Hakeem Olajuwon**, Ricky Winslow, and Michael Young.

PHILADELPHIA 76ERS. The Philadelphia 76ers are a team in the **National Basketball Association (NBA)**. They began as the Syracuse Nationals in the **National Basketball League (NBL)** in 1946, moved to the NBA in 1949, and relocated to Philadelphia as the 76ers in 1963.

Syracuse Nationals (NBL). On 1 July 1946, Syracuse businessmen George Mingin and **Danny Biasone** purchased an NBL franchise from the Cleveland Allmen Transfers, although the purchase price did not include any Cleveland players. Nationals' home games were played in Syracuse, New York, at the Syracuse Armory from 1946–1948, and at the Syracuse Coliseum from 1948–1949. Among their most notable players were **Al Cervi**, Jim Homer, John "Whitey" Macknowski, Charles "Chick" Meehan, Mike Novak, Bob Nugent, Ed Peterson, Jerry Rizzo, **Dolph Schayes**, and Paul Seymour. Their best NBL season was 1948–1949, when they reached the second round of the playoffs. They joined the NBA on 3 August 1949, when the NBL and **Basketball Association of America** merged.

Syracuse Nationals (NBA). Home games were played at the Syracuse Coliseum until 1951, and the Onondaga County War Memorial

Auditorium was the site from 1951–1963. Among their most notable players were Al Bianchi, Larry Costello, Billy Gabor, Dave Gambee, **Hal Greer**, **Johnny "Red" Kerr**, George King, **Earl Lloyd**, Ephraim "Red" Rocha, Dolph Schayes, and Paul Seymour. On 24 November 1949, the Nationals defeated the **Anderson Packers** in a five-**overtime** game in Syracuse in which there were 122 personal **fouls** called against the two teams. Syracuse was also involved in games of 114 personal fouls and 97 personal fouls against two teams. As a result of these games (and others like them), Syracuse owner Danny Biasone proposed a 24-second **shot clock** to prevent the strategic use of deliberate fouls at the end of the game in an attempt to obtain possession of the **basketball**. The shot clock revolutionized the game and possibly saved the league from extinction. In 1950 and 1954, the Nationals reached the championship finals but were defeated by the Minneapolis Lakers. In 1955, the Nationals defeated the Fort Wayne Pistons to become NBA champions. Biasone sold the team in 1963 to Irv Kossloff and Ike Richman of Philadelphia, and the new owners moved the team to Philadelphia, renaming them the Philadelphia 76ers. The Nationals qualified for the playoffs in each of their 14 NBA seasons.

Philadelphia 76ers. Home games were played at the 9,600-seat Convention Hall and the Philadelphia Arena from 1963–1967; the 18,136-seat Spectrum from 1967–1996; and the 21,600-seat Wachovia Center since 1996. Among their most notable players have been **Charles Barkley**, Fred Carter, **Wilt Chamberlain**, Maurice Cheeks, **Billy Cunningham**, **Julius Erving**, Greer, **Allen Iverson**, Lucious Jackson, **Bobby Jones**, **George McGinnis**, and Chet Walker. The 76ers also have had one of the best-known and most colorful public address announcers in **Dave Zinkoff** and one of the most comprehensive statistical record keepers in **Harvey Pollack**. The 76ers best season was 1966–1967, when they set a league record for most regular-season victories, with a record of 68–13 (since broken by the **Chicago Bulls** in 1995–1996, with 72), and won the NBA title. Only six seasons later, in 1972–1973, they set the league record for futility by winning only nine of 82 games. They also won the NBA Championship in 1982–1983, with a playoff record of 12–1. They reached the Finals but were defeated in four other years. Their overall NBA record through the 2009–2010 season is 2,569–2,259.

PHILADELPHIA BASKET BALL LEAGUE (PBL). The Philadelphia Basket Ball League (PBL) was a men's professional league established in Philadelphia in 1902 by sportswriter William J. Scheffer. It competed directly with the **National Basket Ball League (NBL)** and established as its motto "Clean Sport." League rules stated that, "any player found slugging would be disqualified and suspended for one game for the first infraction, two games for the second infraction, and expelled for the season for the third."

Play began on 5 January 1903, with eight teams. Although the NBL terminated operations in 1904, a new competitor, the **Central Basketball League**, began play in 1906 and gradually attracted most of the PBL's best players, causing the PBL to fold midway through the 1908–1909 season. Professional **basketball**'s first recorded death occurred on 2 January 1909, as Charles Ritter of the North Wales team died during a game against Stratton. Jack Reynolds was the league's scoring leader, with 1,401 points in 106 games over six seasons. *See also* APPENDIX B (for a list of league champions).

PHILADELPHIA SPHAS. The Philadelphia SPHAs (pronounced "spahs") were organized by **Eddie Gottlieb** and Harry Passon in 1917 as an amateur team known as the DeNeri Juniors. In 1919, they acquired the sponsorship of the South Philadelphia Hebrew Association and became known as the SPHAs. They emphasized their Jewish background by having the team's name written in Hebrew letters on their uniforms. They competed as an independent team and also in the **Eastern Basketball League** from 1925–1926; the **American Basketball League** from 1926–1928 as the Philadelphia Warriors; the Eastern League from 1929–1933; and the reorganized American Basketball League from 1933–1949, winning three Eastern League and seven American League championships.

In 1950, the team name was sold to **Louis "Red" Klotz**, who reorganized them as an opponent team for the **Harlem Globetrotters** and later renamed them the **Washington Generals**. Among the team's best players were Tom Barlow, Mike Bloom, Cy Boardman, Gaza Chizmadia, Gil Fitch (who doubled as the bandleader for dances after the SPHAs' games), Dutch Garfinkel, Moe Goldman, Shikey Gothoffer, Art Hillhouse, Teddy Kearns, Inky Lautman, Harry Litwack, Chickie Passon, Ash Resnick, Red Rosan, Petey Rosenberg, Lou Schneiderman, Butch Schwartz, and Irv Torgoff.

PHILADELPHIA WARRIORS. *See* GOLDEN STATE WARRIORS.

PHILIPPINES. The Philippines is possibly the only country in the world in which **basketball** is the most popular sport. They joined the **Fédération Internationale de Basketball (FIBA)** in 1936 and are a member in the FIBA Asia zone. The men's team competed in seven **Olympic** tournaments, taking part in every Olympic tournament from 1936–1972, except 1964 (which ironically was held in nearby **Japan**). In the Olympic Games, their best finish was fifth place in 1936, the best ever for an Asian team in the Games. In 1936, they won four of five Olympic contests and were defeated only by the **United States** in the quarterfinal round. In the FIBA **World Championships**, they competed four times and won the **bronze medal** in 1954. In the FIBA Asia Championships, they entered 22 times and won five times, were second twice, and placed third once. The women's team has never competed in the Olympic Games or the FIBA World Championships. They entered the FIBA Asia Championships 10 times, with a best finish of fourth twice.

Although the Philippines has an excellent professional league and many U.S. players have played there, there has yet to be any native players from the Philippines to play in the **National Basketball Association** or **Women's National Basketball Association**. **Miami Heat** head **coach** Erik Spoelstra is an American with partial Filipino ancestry.

PHILLIP, ANDREW MICHAEL "ANDY." B. 7 March 1922, Granite City, Illinois. D. 29 April 2001, Rancho Mirage, California. Andy Phillip attended Granite City High School and the University of Illinois. He left college after his junior year to serve in the **U.S.** Marine Corps and returned to school in 1946. Selected by the **Chicago Stags** in the 1947 **Basketball Association of America (BAA) draft**, he played in the BAA and **National Basketball Association (NBA)** from 1947–1958 for the Stags, Philadelphia Warriors, Fort Wayne

Pistons, and **Boston Celtics**. He also played minor league baseball in the St. Louis Cardinals' farm system for three years.

Phillip's professional career totals for 11 years are 701 regular-season games and a 9.1 points per game average. He was selected for the NBA's first five **All-Star Games** from 1951–1955 and was a member of the All-NBA Second Team in 1952 and 1953. He led the league in **assists** in 1951 and 1952 and twice set the league record (since broken) for most assists in one game, with 17 in 1951 and 19 in 1954. In 1957, with the Celtics, he won an NBA Championship. He began the 1958–1959 season as **coach** of the St. Louis Hawks but after 10 games with a record of 6–4 was fired by owner Ben Kerner, who said that the Hawks "looked bad even when they were winning." In 1961–1962, he coached the Chicago Majors of the **American Basketball League**. After retiring from **basketball**, he was a probation officer in Indio, California, and was enshrined in the **Naismith Memorial Basketball Hall of Fame** in 1961.

PHOENIX SUNS. The Phoenix Suns are a team in the **National Basketball Association (NBA)**. On 22 January 1968, a group of investors headed by Richard L. Bloch and including entertainers Andy Williams, Tony Curtis, Ed Ames, Bobbie Gentry, and Henry Mancini, purchased an NBA expansion franchise to start play in the 1968–1969 season. Home games were played at the 14,870-seat Arizona Veterans Memorial Coliseum from 1968–1992 and at the 18,422-seat America West Arena (renamed US Airways Arena in 2005) since then. Among their most notable players have been Alvan Adams, **Charles Barkley**, Walter Davis, Kevin Johnson, Dan Majerle, Shawn Marion, Larry Nance, **Steve Nash**, Amar'e Stoudemire, Dick Van Arsdale, and Paul Westphal.

One of their best seasons was 1975–1976, when they reached the NBA Championship Finals but lost to the **Boston Celtics** in six games. Game five of that series, on 4 June 1976, was one of the greatest games in NBA history. It went to three **overtimes** and included several last-second **field goals**. Another of their best seasons was in 1992–1993, when they had their best regular-season record of 62–20 and lost to the **Chicago Bulls** in six games in the NBA Championship Finals, a series that also included a memorable three-overtime game.

Their overall record for their first 42 years in the league through the 2009–2010 season is 1,914–1,498.

PIERCE, PAUL ANTHONY "THE TRUTH." B. 13 October 1977, Oakland, California. Paul Pierce attended Inglewood High School in Inglewood, California, and the **University of Kansas**. He left school after his junior year and was **drafted** in the 1998 **National Basketball Association (NBA)** draft by the **Boston Celtics**. The six-foot, six-inch **forward** has played for the Celtics since 1998. In 2008, after the Celtics acquired all-stars **Kevin Garnett** and **Ray Allen**, the team won the NBA Championship and Pierce was named the NBA Finals Most Valuable Player.

In 11 of his first 12 seasons, Pierce averaged more than 18 points per game. On 19 April 2003, he set an all-time NBA playoff record by making all 21 **free throws** in a game, the most ever without a miss. He led the NBA in points scored in 2002 and in free throws made in 2003. He was named to the All-NBA Second Team in 2009 and All-NBA Third Team three times and was selected for the NBA **All-Star Game** eight times in his career. On 15 February 2006, he scored 50 points in one game. Through the 2009–2010 season, he has played in 884 games and averaged 22.5 points and 6.1 rebounds per game. He played for the **U.S.** team in the 2002 **World Championships**, where they finished a disappointing sixth. He was also selected for the 2006 team but due to an elbow injury did not play.

PIPPEN, SCOTTIE MAURICE B. 25 September 1965, Hamburg, Arkansas. Scottie Pippen attended Hamburg High School and the University of Central Arkansas. He was chosen by the Seattle Supersonics in the 1987 **National Basketball Association (NBA) draft**, but his **draft rights** were immediately traded to the **Chicago Bulls**. He played in the NBA from 1987–2004 with the Bulls, **Portland Trail Blazers**, and **Houston Rockets**. He was with Chicago from 1987–1998 and, along with teammate **Michael Jordan**, led the Bulls to six NBA Championships in that time.

From 1992–1998, Pippen was named to the All-NBA First Team three times, All-NBA Second Team twice, and All-NBA Third Team twice. He was also voted to the NBA All-Defensive First Team eight times and NBA All-Defensive Second Team twice, and he played in seven NBA **All-Star Games** and was the Most Valuable Player in the 1994 game. In his 17-year NBA career, he played in 1,178 regular-season games and averaged 16.1 points, 6.4 **rebounds**, and 5.2 **assists** per game. He played in 208 playoff games and averaged 17.5 points, 7.6 rebounds, and 5.0 assists per playoff game. He holds the NBA career records for assists and **steals** by a **forward** and playoff steals.

The six-foot, seven-inch **forward** was one of five 1992 **U.S. Olympic Dream Team** players who also won a **gold medal** on the 1996 Olympic team. In 1996, he was named one of the 50 Greatest Players in NBA History. After retiring from **basketball**, he was assistant **coach** for the **Los Angeles Lakers**. In 2010, he was enshrined in the **Naismith Memorial Basketball Hall of Fame**.

PITTSBURGH CONDORS. The Pittsburgh Condors were a team in the **American Basketball Association (ABA)**. They began play in 1967–1968 as the Pittsburgh Pipers. The following season, they moved to Minneapolis and played as the Minnesota Pipers. In 1969, they returned to Pittsburgh as the Pittsburgh Pipers. In 1970, they were renamed the Pittsburgh Condors. In five ABA seasons, the overall franchise record was 180–228.

Pittsburgh/Minnesota Pipers. On 2 February 1967, at the ABA's formation meeting, a franchise was acquired by Gabe Rubin, a Pittsburgh theater owner. Home games were played at the 12,000-seat Pittsburgh Civic Arena. One of the first players the Pipers signed was **Harlem Globetrotter Connie Hawkins**, who had starred in the **American Basketball League** in 1961–1962 and had been banned by the **National Basketball Association (NBA)** for his alleged association with gamblers. In addition to Hawkins, other starters on the team were Craig Dill; Jim Jarvis; Tom "Trooper" Washington; Charlie Williams, who also had been blacklisted by the NBA; and ex-NBA players Art Heyman and Chico Vaughn. The Pipers used 21 different players that year but won the league championship. Hawkins led the league in scoring, with 26.8 points per game, and was named its most valuable player. The team was sold 28 June 1968, and moved to Minneapolis. Home games were played at the 15,500-seat Metropolitan Sports Center in Bloomington and 6,919-seat Duluth Auditorium in

Duluth. **Coach** Jim Harding had a dispute with owner Gabe Rubin, physically attacked him, and consequently lost his job. After a year in Minnesota, the Pipers returned to Pittsburgh for the 1969–1970 season. The following season, the team remained in Pittsburgh but changed their nickname to the Condors.

Pittsburgh Condors. The team started slowly and, in an effort to stimulate interest, all tickets for the 17 November 1970 home game were given away for free. The 12,000-seat Pittsburgh Civic Arena was still only slightly more than half full, as only 8,074 fans showed up. The star of the team was **forward** John Brisker, who had a quick temper and ready fists and averaged 29.3 points per game when he wasn't physically attacking opponents. Even his own teammates were afraid of practicing against him. On 6 March 1971, Condors' forward Stew Johnson, who only averaged 16 points per game, set a league record by scoring 62 points in one game. During the 1971–1972 season, there were rumors that the team would move and finish the season in another city, but that didn't happen, although they did play a few "home" games in Tucson, Arizona, and Birmingham, Alabama. On 13 June 1972, the league purchased the franchise and disbanded the team.

PITTSBURGH IRONMEN. The Pittsburgh Ironmen were a team in the **Basketball Association of America (BAA)** in the 1946–1947 season. Home games were played at the Pittsburgh Arena. The team finished in last place in the Western Division, winning only 15 of 60 games. **Coach** Paul Birch employed 17 players, with John "Brooms" Abramovic, Coulby Gunther, and Stan Noszka being the team's leading scorers.

A unique occurrence in league history took place on 7 November 1946, when five of Pittsburgh's nine players were disqualified on personal **fouls**. Opposing coach **Eddie Gottlieb** of the **Philadelphia Warriors** offered Pittsburgh a chance to reinstate one of their players so that the required five players would be available, but Coach Birch refused the offer. Gottlieb then withdrew one of his players, and the remainder of the game was played with but four players on each side. The league subsequently changed the rule regarding that situation to prevent teams from playing shorthanded. On 27 July 1947, the Ironmen were disbanded.

PITTSBURGH PIPERS. *See* PITTSBURGH CONDORS.

PIVOT. While holding the **basketball** and not **dribbling**, a player may not move both feet. He may move one foot, but the other must maintain contact with the floor. This foot is called the pivot foot. The **center** position is also referred to as the pivot position, and the center is called the pivot man. *See also* DEHNERT, HENRY GEORGE "DUTCH."

PODOLOFF, MAURICE. B.18 August 1890, Elizabethgrad, **Russia.** D. 24 November 1985, New Haven, Connecticut. Maurice Podoloff's family emigrated to Connecticut when he was a youth. He attended Hillhouse High School in New Haven and Yale University, where he earned a bachelor of arts degree in 1913 and a law degree in 1915. He owned the New Haven franchise in the Canadian-American Hockey League and the New Haven Arena and was elected president of the American Hockey League in 1935.

When the **Basketball Association of America** was formed in 1946, Podoloff was chosen as its first president due to his organizational and administrative skills, although he knew very little about the game of **basketball**. In 1949, he helped to bring about a merger with the rival **National Basketball League** and formed the **National Basketball Association (NBA)**. He resigned in 1963 after having established the NBA as a major sports entity in the **United States**. Although barely five-feet, two-inches tall, he ruled the league with a firm hand and permanently banned players and a **referee** who were implicated in gambling scandals. The NBA's Most Valuable Player award is now known as the Maurice Podoloff Trophy. He was enshrined in the **Naismith Memorial Basketball Hall of Fame** in 1974 in the category of contributor. During his long life, he was also a banker and real estate entrepreneur.

POINT GUARD. Point **guard** is one of the five basketball positions. It is occasionally referred to as the "1" position. This nomenclature arises from **coaches** numbering the five positions on a play chart. The player at this position is usually responsible for **dribbling** the ball up the court and setting up a play by passing to a teammate. The point guard is generally one of the shorter players on the team and often the quickest. The terminology *point guard* is a relatively new one and dates back only to around 1970. *See also* SHOOTING GUARD.

POINTS IN THE PAINT. In recent years, **basketball** statisticians have kept track of teams' points scored from close range within the **keyhole**, or painted area of the floor. This has been commonly called "points in the paint." This statistic can be used to determine whether teams rely more on driving toward the **basket** to score or shooting from longer range.

POLAND. Poland joined the **Fédération Internationale de Basketball (FIBA)** in 1934 and is a member in the FIBA Europe zone. The men's team competed in six **Olympic** tournaments. In 1936, they finished in fourth place, their best Olympic showing. Mieczysław Łopatka competed in four Olympic Games for Poland from 1960–1972. In the FIBA **World Championships**, they competed only once and finished in fifth place in 1967. In the FIBA European Championships, they entered 23 times and were second in 1963 and third three times.

The women's team competed in the 2000 Olympic tournament and finished in eighth place. In the FIBA World Championships, they competed three times and finished in fifth place in 1959 as their best effort. In the FIBA European Championships, they entered 26 times and were European champions in 1999. They finished second twice and third twice.

There have been three players from Poland in the **National Basketball Association (NBA)**, including Marcin Gortat, Maciej Lampe, and Cezary Trybański. Szymon Szewczyk was selected by the **Milwaukee Bucks** in the 2003 NBA **draft** but has not played in the NBA. Seven-foot, two-inch **Margo Dydek** has had a substantial career in the **Women's National Basketball Association**, and Agnieszka Bibrzycka and Krystyna Lara played in that league as well.

POLLACK, HERBERT HARVEY "HARVEY." B. 9 March 1922, Camden, New Jersey. Harvey Pollack's major contribution to **basketball** was as the premier **National Basketball Association (NBA)** statistician from the league's inception in 1946 as the **Basketball Association of America (BAA)** until the present day. He attended

Simon Gratz High School in Philadelphia, Pennsylvania, and **Temple University**. After being discharged from the service, he worked as a sportswriter for the *Philadelphia Bulletin*. He was hired by the Philadelphia Warriors of the BAA in 1946 as statistician and publicity director. He remained with the Warriors until 1962, when they moved to San Francisco. The following year he became the chief statistician for the **Philadelphia 76ers**.

Since the mid-1990s, Pollack has published an annual statistical year book that tracks virtually everything that happened in the previous NBA season, including statistics not found elsewhere, such as longest **field goals** of the year, number of times ejected, technical and flagrant **fouls**, four point plays in the NBA from 1979 to date, jump balls won, and so forth. In 2002, he was the recipient of the prestigious John Bunn Award from the **Naismith Memorial Basketball Hall of Fame** for lifetime service.

POLLARD, JAMES CLIFFORD "JIM," "THE KANGAROO KID." B. 9 July 1922, Oakland, California. D. 22 January 1993, Stockton, California. Jim Pollard attended Oakland Technical High School and **Stanford University**, where he was a member of the 1942 **National Collegiate Athletic Association (NCAA)** national champions. He was signed by the Minneapolis Lakers of the **National Basketball League (NBL)** in 1947, after having played **Amateur Athletic Union (AAU)** basketball for the San Diego Dons in 1945–1946 and the Oakland Bittners in 1946–1947. He was Most Valuable Player in the national AAU tournaments in 1946 and 1947. The six-foot, five-inch **forward** played with the Lakers from 1947–1955 in the NBL, **Basketball Association of America (BAA)**, and **National Basketball Association (NBA)** and was a member of six league championship teams with them.

Pollard played in 497 regular-season games and averaged 13.1 points per game. Known for his extraordinary jumping ability, he was nicknamed "The Kangaroo Kid." Selected for four NBA **All-Star Games**, he was named to the All-BAA First Team in 1949, All-NBA first Team in 1950, and All-NBA Second Team in 1952 and 1954. After retiring from active play, he **coached La Salle University** from 1955–1958. He then coached the Lakers for the last part of the 1959–1960 season, the **Chicago Packers** in 1960–1961, and the

Minnesota Muskies and **Miami Floridians** in the **American Basketball Association** in 1967–1969. He later became athletic director and basketball coach at Florida Atlantic University. He was enshrined in the **Naismith Memorial Basketball Hall of Fame** in 1978.

POPOVICH, GREGG CHARLES. B. 28 January 1949, East Chicago, Indiana. Gregg Popovich attended Merrillville High School in Merrillville, Indiana, and the Air Force Academy. Following his graduation in 1970, with a Soviet studies major, he served in the **U.S.** Air Force for five years, played basketball on the Armed Forces **Amateur Athletic Union** team, and helped them win the 1972 AAU National Championship. From 1972–1978, he was also an assistant basketball **coach** at the Air Force Academy. While there, he attended the University of Denver and received a master's degree in physical education. From 1979–1986, he coached the Pomona-Pitzer **National Collegiate Athletic Association** Division III basketball team.

Popovich spent the 1986–1987 season as volunteer assistant coach with **Larry Brown** at the **University of Kansas**. In 1988, Brown became coach of the **San Antonio Spurs** of the **National Basketball Association (NBA)** and took Popovich with him as an assistant. Popovich remained with the Spurs through 1992, then went to the **Golden State Warriors** from 1992–1994 as an assistant. In 1994, he was hired by the Spurs as general manager. He retained that position until 10 December 1996, when he replaced the Spurs coach, Bob Hill, with himself. As coach of the Spurs from 1996–2010, his overall won–lost record is 736–362, with four NBA Championships. He was assistant coach of the **U.S.** men's team at the 2002 **World Championships** and 2004 **Olympic Games**.

PORTLAND TRAIL BLAZERS. The Portland Trail Blazers are a team in the **National Basketball Association (NBA)**. On 6 February 1970, an expansion franchise was purchased by a group headed by Herman Sarkowsky, Robert J. Schmertz, and Lawrence Weinberg, with the team to begin play in the 1970–1971 season. The Trail Blazers are the only major league sports franchise located in the state of Oregon. Home games were played at 12,888-seat Memorial Coliseum from 1970–1995 and the 20,630-seat Rose Garden since then.

Among their most notable players have been **Clyde Drexler,** Kevin Duckworth, Jerome Kersey, Maurice Lucas, Jim Paxson, Geoff Petrie, Terry Porter, **Arvydas Sabonis,** Larry Steele, Rasheed Wallace, **Bill Walton,** Sidney Wicks, and Buck Williams. Their best seasons were 1976–1977, when they won the NBA Championship, and 1989–1990 and 1991–1992, when they reached the Finals but were defeated. Their overall record for their first 40 years in the league through the 2009–2010 season is 1,733–1,515.

POWER FORWARD. The power **forward** is one of the five **basketball** positions. It is sometimes referred to as the "4" position. This designation comes from **coaches** numbering the five positions on a play chart. Players at this position are usually responsible for **rebounding** and shooting from near the **basket** and are normally among the taller, stronger players on the team. The phrase "power forward" is relatively new and dates back to the mid-1970s. *See also* SMALL FORWARD.

PROFESSIONAL BASKETBALL LEAGUE OF AMERICA (PBLA). The Professional Basketball League of America (PBLA) was a men's professional **basketball** major league that began operation on 25 October 1947, with 16 teams throughout the midwestern and southeastern parts of the **United States.** Organized by Maurice White, owner of the **National Basketball League's (NBL) Chicago American Gears**, it featured **George Mikan** of the Gears as the league's star attraction. Other top professionals such as Price Brookfield, Coulby Gunther, Bruce Hale, Noble Jorgensen, Fred Lewis, **Bobby McDermott,** Paul Seymour, Dick Triptow, and Stan Waxman also played. In less than one month, the league's losses surpassed $600,000, and the Gears filed for bankruptcy. On 13 November 1947, the league was disbanded, and many of the players returned to the NBL or **Basketball Association of America.** *See also* APPENDIX B (for a list of league champions).

PROVIDENCE COLLEGE. Providence College in Rhode Island began its men's **basketball** program in 1920. Home games since 1972 have been played at the 12,993-seat Providence Civic Center (renamed the Dunkin' Donuts Center in 2001). Prior to 1972, home games were played at the 2,620-seat Alumni Hall. The most accomplished **coaches** in the school's history have been Dave Gavitt, Albert McClellan, and Joe Mullaney. In the five years from 1959–1963, the Friars reached the **National Invitation Tournament** semifinal round four times and won it in 1961 and 1963. The best players in school history have included Marvin Barnes, Marty Conlon, Ernie DiGregorio, Billy Donovan, Johnny Egan, Vinnie Ernst, Jim Hadnot, Mike Riordan, Kevin Stacom, **John Thompson**, Jimmy Walker, and **Lenny Wilkens**.

PROVIDENCE STEAMROLLERS. The Providence Steamrollers were a team in the **Basketball Association of America (BAA)**. They were owned by Lou Pieri, who also owned the Providence Reds American Hockey League team, as well as the arena they played in, Providence Arena. In the three seasons of their existence, the Steamrollers had records of 28–32, 6–42, and 12–48. Players on the team included Hank Beenders; Ernie Calverley; Armand Cure; Johnny Ezersky; George Nostrand; Lee Robbins; Kenny Sailors; Earl Shannon; Bob Shea; and Jack Toomay, later to become a **U.S.** Air Force major general.

Their **coaches** included Bob Morris, a successful coach and physics teacher at Pawtucket High School; former National Football League player Albert "Hank" Soar, later to be a major league umpire; former **Original Celtic** Matthew "Nat" Hickey; and for their final year, Ken Loeffler, a former college coach who had coached the **St. Louis Bombers** of the BAA. During the 1947–1948 season, at one point the team was shorthanded and the 45-year-old Hickey added himself to the roster for one game. He entered the game with five **minutes** to play in the first half and Providence down by seven points. He committed four personal **fouls**, and the deficit grew to 19 points in that brief time. When the BAA and **National Basketball League** merged in 1949, the Providence team was disbanded.

PUERTO RICO. The Commonwealth of Puerto Rico joined the **Fédération Internationale de Basketball (FIBA)** in 1957 and is a member in the FIBA Americas zone. Although politically a part of the **United States**, they have their own National **Olympic** Committee and compete as an independent entity. The men's team competed in nine Olympic tournaments and finished fourth in 1964. They almost caused one of the biggest upsets in Olympic history in 1976, when they were defeated by only one point by the champion U.S. team, 95–94. In the 2004 Olympic Games, they did defeat the United States in the opening game of the tournament, 92–73, the largest margin of victory over the United States in Olympic **basketball** competition. Olympian **Teófilo Cruz Downs** is one of only three men to compete in five Olympic basketball tournaments. He played in every one from 1960–1976. José "Piculin" Ortiz competed in four Olympic basketball tournaments from 1988–2004. In the FIBA **World Championships**, they competed 12 times, with a best finish of fourth in 1990. In the FIBA Americas Championships, they have entered all 13 tournaments and won the event three times, were second three times, and placed third twice. In the Pan American Games, they have entered every tournament since 1959 and have 10 medals to show for their 13 attempts. They won the **gold medal** in 1991, the **silver medal** five times, and the **bronze medal** four times.

The women's team has yet to compete in either the Olympic Games or the FIBA World Championships. In the FIBA Americas Championships, they entered five times and won the bronze medal in 1995. In the Pan American Games, they entered twice and finished sixth both times.

There have been seven players from Puerto Rico in the **National Basketball Association (NBA)**, including Carlos Arroyo, José Juan Barea, Guillermo Diaz, Alfred "Butch" Lee, José Ortiz, Peter John Ramos, and Ramón Rivas. Héctor Blondet, Michael Vicéns, and Jerome Mincy were **drafted** by the NBA but did not play in the league.

PURDUE UNIVERSITY. Purdue University in Lafayette, Indiana, began its men's **basketball** program in 1896. Home games since 1967 have been played at the 14,123-seat Mackey Arena. Prior to 1967, home games were played at the 7,500-seat Lambert Fieldhouse. The most accomplished **coaches** in the school's history have been Gene Keady, George King, and Ward "Piggy" Lambert. In 1969, the Boilermakers lost the **National Collegiate Athletic Association (NCAA)** Championship final game to the **University of California, Los Angeles**. Among the best players in school history have been Joe Barry Carroll, Terry Dischinger, Herm Gilliam, Paul Hoffman, Billy

Keller, Brad Miller, Todd Mitchell, Rick Mount, Charles "Stretch" Murphy, Glenn Robinson, Dave Schellhase, Jerry Sichting, **John Wooden**, and Jewell Young.

The women's basketball program began in 1975. The school's most notable coaches have been Kristy Curry and Lin Dunn. In 1999, the Boilermakers won the NCAA National Championship. In 2001, they again reached the championship final game but lost to **Notre Dame University**. The best players in school history include Camille Cooper, Katie Douglas, Katie Gearlds, Joy Holmes, Stacey Lovelace, Brittany Rayburn, and Stephanie White.

– Q –

QUADRUPLE-DOUBLE. A quadruple-double is a relatively new term in basketball and refers to a player who has compiled double digits (10 or more) in four positive statistical categories in one game. It has been recorded only four times in **National Basketball Association (NBA)** competition. On 18 October 1974, **Nate Thurmond** of the **Chicago Bulls** recorded 22 points, 14 **rebounds**, 13 **assists**, and 12 **blocks**. On 18 February 1986, Alvin Robertson of the **San Antonio Spurs** had 20 points, 11 rebounds, 10 assists, and 10 **steals**. On 29 March 1990, **Hakeem Olajuwon** of the **Houston Rockets** scored 18 points and had 16 rebounds, 10 assists, and 11 blocks. And on 17 February 1994, **David Robinson** of the San Antonio Spurs, with 34 points and 10 each of rebounds, assists, and blocks, was the fourth player to accomplish this. On 3 March 1990, Olajuwon also recorded 29 points, 18 rebounds, 11 blocks, and 10 assists, but there was some controversy over one of the assists, and the NBA did not recognize this as a quadruple-double.

In the women's **American Basketball League**, on 8 December 1996, five-foot, three-inch **guard** Debbie Black of the Colorado Xplosion recorded a quadruple-double, with 10 points, 14 rebounds, 12 assists, and 10 steals, and **Ann Meyers** accomplished this in college play at the **University of California, Los Angeles** on 18 February 1978, with 20 points, 14 rebounds, 10 assists, and 10 steals.

Lester Hudson of the University of Tennessee at Martin recorded the first quadruple-double in **National Collegiate Athletic Association**

Division I men's competition on 13 November 2007, with 25 points, 12 rebounds, 10 assists, and 10 steals. *See also* TRIPLE-DOUBLE.

– R –

RAMSAY, JOHN T. "JACK." B. 21 February 1925, Philadelphia, Pennsylvania. Jack Ramsay attended Upper Darby High School in Upper Darby, Pennsylvania, and St. Joseph's College, graduating in 1949 with a bachelor's degree. He attended the University of Pennsylvania and received master's and doctorate degrees in 1952 and 1963. Although from 1949–1955, he played in the Eastern Professional Basketball League, his major contribution to **basketball** was as a **coach**. He coached St. Joseph's from 1955–1966. In 1956 and 1961, they finished in third place in the **National Invitation Tournament**.

Often referred to as "Dr. Jack," he became general manager of the **Philadelphia 76ers** in 1966 and from 1968–1972 was their head coach. He coached the Buffalo Braves from 1972–1976, the **Portland Trail Blazers** from 1976–1986, and the **Indiana Pacers** in 1986–1987. In 1977, his Trail Blazers won the **National Basketball Association (NBA)** Championship. His overall NBA coaching record was 864–783.

After retiring from coaching, he became a television analyst and worked for the **Miami Heat** and Philadelphia 76ers. He was enshrined in the **Naismith Memorial Basketball Hall of Fame** in 1992 as a coach. In 1996, he was named one of the Top 10 Coaches in NBA History.

RAMSEY, FRANK VERNON, JR. B. 13 July 1931, Corydon, Kentucky. Frank Ramsey attended Madisonville High School in Madisonville, Kentucky, and the **University of Kentucky**. In college, he was a member of the 1951 **National Collegiate Athletic Association** National Championship team. He was selected by the **Boston Celtics** in the 1953 **National Basketball Association (NBA) draft** and played for them from 1955–1964. The six-foot, three-inch **forward-guard** was used primarily as the **sixth man**.

Ramsey's NBA career totals for nine years are 623 regular-season games and a 13.4 points per game average. Despite being a member of the NBA Championship team, in seven of his nine years he was never selected for the NBA **All-Star Game** and was never named to the All-NBA First Team or All-NBA Second Team. In 1970–1971, he **coached** the **Kentucky Colonels** of the **American Basketball Association** and led them to the league championship finals, where they lost to the **Utah Stars** in seven games. After retiring from **basketball**, he owned a construction business in Madisonville. Since 1972, he has been president of the Dixon Bank in Madisonville and was appointed to the Financial Institutions Board of Kentucky in 2009. Ramsey was enshrined in the **Naismith Memorial Basketball Hall of Fame** in 1982.

REBOUND. A rebound occurs when the ball bounces off the **backboard** and/or the rim after a missed shot. Since the early 1950s, statisticians have tracked rebounds and, since the mid-1970s, they have also tracked whether the rebound was an offensive or defensive one.

REED, WILLIS, JR. B. 25 June 1942, Hico, Louisiana. Willis Reed attended West Side High School in Lillie, Louisiana, and Grambling State University. As a freshman at Grambling in 1961, he was a member of the **National Association of Intercollegiate Athletics** National Championship team. In four years at Grambling, he averaged 18.7 points and 15.2 rebounds per game.

The six-foot, 10-inch **left-handed center-forward** was selected by the **New York Knickerbockers** in the 1964 **National Basketball Association (NBA) draft** and played for them from 1964–1974. Reed's NBA career totals for 10 years are 650 regular-season games and an 18.7 points and 12.9 **rebounds** per game average. In 1965, he was named Rookie of the Year. He was injured in the fifth game of the 1970 NBA Championship Finals and did not play in the sixth game but made a dramatic appearance at the start of the seventh game, making his first two **field goals** and leading the Knicks to the NBA title. That season, he was the **All-Star Game** Most Valuable Player, NBA Finals Most Valuable Player, and the league's Most Valuable Player, and was named to the All-NBA First Team and

All-Defensive First Team. He was selected for seven NBA All-Star Games and named to the All-NBA Second Team four times. In 1973, he again led the Knicks to the NBA title and was again named the Finals Most Valuable Player.

After retiring as a player, Reed **coached** the Knicks from 1977–1979 and Creighton University from 1981–1985. He was an assistant with the **Atlanta Hawks** from 1985–1987 and **Sacramento Kings** in 1987–1988 and head coach of the **New Jersey Nets** from 1987–1989. From 1988–2004, he was a vice president of the Nets as well. In 2004, he became vice president of **Basketball** Operations for the **New Orleans Hornets**. He was enshrined in the **Naismith Memorial Basketball Hall of Fame** in 1982. In 1996, Reed was named one of the 50 Greatest Players in NBA History.

REFEREE. The referee is the individual who is the chief arbitrator of the **basketball** game. Since the 1920s, two referees have been used. At one time the second referee was designated as an "umpire" and had a slightly different role, but in recent years this distinction is no longer used. Since the 1990s, games often employ three referees, also referred to as "officials." Among the most notable referees have been **Pat Kennedy**, **Johnny Nucatola**, Sid Borgia, **Mendy Rudolph**, **Earl Strom**, Darrell Garretson, and Dick Bavetta. *See also* ECKMAN, CHARLES MARKWOOD, JR. "CHARLEY."

RILEY, PATRICK JAMES "PAT." B. 20 March 1945, Rome, New York. Pat Riley is the son of Lee Riley, a minor league baseball player who played briefly in the major leagues. Pat attended Linton High School in Schenectady, New York, and the **University of Kentucky**, where he was a member of the 1966 team that lost in the **National Collegiate Athletic Association (NCAA)** National Championship final game to **Texas Western University**. The six-foot, four-inch **guard** was selected by the San Diego Rockets in the 1967 **National Basketball Association (NBA) draft**. He was also selected by the Dallas Cowboys in the National Football League draft but did not sign with them. He played in the NBA from 1967–1976 for the Rockets, **Los Angeles Lakers**, and **Phoenix Suns** and was a member of the Lakers' NBA Championship team in 1972. In nine NBA seasons, his career totals are 528 regular-season games and a 7.4 points per game average.

Riley is best known for his **coaching** abilities. He was an assistant coach with the Lakers from 1979–1981 and their head coach from 1981–1990. In that time, the Lakers won at least 50 games and finished in first place in the Pacific Division each year. They were four-time NBA champions and three-time runners-up. In 1991, he was hired as coach of the **New York Knickerbockers** and led them to the 1994 NBA Championship Finals, where they lost to the **Houston Rockets**. He coached the **Miami Heat** from 1995–2003. In 2005–2006, as the Heat's president and general manager, he replaced Stan Van Gundy as coach and led them to the 2006 NBA title but resigned as coach after the 2007–2008 season, although he kept his role as team president. When not coaching, he worked as a television analyst. He was named NBA Coach of the Year in 1997 and was enshrined in the **Naismith Memorial Basketball Hall of Fame** in 2008 as a coach.

RIPLEY, ELMER HORTON. B. 21 July 1891, Staten Island, New York. D. 29 April 1982, Staten Island, New York. Elmer Ripley attended Curtis High School in Staten Island and did not go to college. As a five-foot, eight-inch **guard**, he played professionally from 1914–1929 in all the major leagues of his era for more than 20 different teams. He began **coaching** in 1922 at Wagner College while still an active player and coached there from 1922–1925, at **Georgetown University** from 1927–1929, at Yale University from 1929–1935, at Georgetown again from 1938–1943 (losing the 1943 **National Collegiate Athletic Association** National Championship game), at Columbia University from 1943–1945, at **Notre Dame University** in 1945–1946, at Georgetown for a third time from 1946–1949, at John Carroll University from 1949–1951, and at the **United States** Military Academy from 1951–1953. From 1953–1956, he even coached the **Harlem Globetrotters**.

In 1956, Ripley was the coach of the Israel **Olympic** team that withdrew just prior to the Games due to the Suez Conflict. In 1960, he coached the **Canadian** Olympic team that was eliminated in the Olympic qualifying tournament. In 1961, he coached the Washington

Tapers in the **American Basketball League** and in 1962 coached the Scranton Miners in the Eastern Professional Basketball League. From 1962–1973, he was the coach at the Englewood School for Boys. In 1973, he was enshrined in the **Naismith Memorial Basketball Hall of Fame** as a contributor.

RISEN, ARNOLD D. "ARNIE." B. 9 October 1924, Williamstown, Kentucky. Arnie Risen attended Williamstown High School, Eastern Kentucky State University, and **Ohio State University**. He began his professional **basketball** career with the Indianapolis Kautskys of the **National Basketball League** in 1945. He was with them for two seasons and then played for the Rochester Royals from 1948–1955. The six-foot, nine-inch **center**, nicknamed "Stilts," played on the **National Basketball Association (NBA)** Championship team in 1951 with the Royals. He was traded to the **Boston Celtics**, where he spent three years, retiring after the 1957–1958 season. In 1957, he was again a member of an NBA Championship team, when Boston won its first NBA title.

In 13 professional seasons, Risen played in 760 regular-season games and averaged 12.2 points per game. He was selected for four NBA **All-Star Games** and was named to the All-**Basketball Association of America** Second Team in 1949. After retiring from active play, he worked as a construction engineer in Rochester, New York. He was enshrined in the **Naismith Memorial Basketball Hall of Fame** in 1998.

ROBERTSON, OSCAR PALMER "THE BIG O." B. 24 November 1938, Charlotte, Tennessee. Oscar Robertson was raised in Indiana and attended Crispus Attucks High School in Indianapolis. He helped lead them to the Indiana State High School Championship in 1955 and 1956, the first Indiana State High School Championship won by an all-black school. The team lost only one game of 63 in those two seasons, with 45 straight victories. He attended the **University of Cincinnati** and led them to the **National Collegiate Athletic Association (NCAA) Final Four** in 1959 and 1960, where they finished in third place both years. He was selected for the 1959 Pan American Games and 1960 **U.S. Olympic** teams and won **gold medals** in both tournaments.

The six-foot, five-inch **guard** was chosen by the Cincinnati Royals as a **territorial** selection in the 1960 **National Basketball Association (NBA) draft** and played for them from 1960–1970 and with the **Milwaukee Bucks** from 1970–1974. In 1971, Robertson was a member of the NBA Championship team. In his 14-year NBA career, he played in 1,040 regular-season games and averaged 7.5 **rebounds**, 9.5 **assists**, and 25.7 points per game. In 1962, he set the NBA record (since broken) for most assists in a season, with 899. He was named NBA Rookie of the Year in 1961 and NBA Most Valuable Player in 1964. He was selected to the All-NBA First Team each year from 1961–1969, chosen for the All-NBA Second Team in 1970 and 1971, and was voted to the NBA **All-Star Game** in each of his first 12 seasons in the league and named All-Star game Most Valuable Player three times.

Robertson was a versatile player and, in the 1961–1962 season, averaged a **triple-double** with 12.5 rebounds, 11.4 assists, and 30.8 points per game, the only time in league history that a player has averaged double figures for a season in all three categories. In fact, after his first five years in the league, his NBA career averages were 10.4 rebounds, 10.6 assists, and 30.3 points per game. The expression triple-double and use of that statistic was not popularized, however, until Robertson had retired from play.

Robertson was president of the NBA Players Association and in 1971 led them in an antitrust suit against the NBA, which was settled in 1976 when the NBA and **American Basketball Association** merged. He was elected to the **Naismith Memorial Basketball Hall of Fame** in 1980 and the NBA 35th Anniversary Team in 1980. He was one of the 50 Greatest Players in NBA History in 1996. In 1998, the United States Basketball Writers Association renamed their annual trophy awarded to the best NCAA Division I player the Oscar Robertson Trophy. In 2009, he was elected to the **Fédération Internationale de Basketball** Hall of Fame. His brother, Bailey, played with the **Harlem Globetrotters**.

ROBINSON, DAVID MAURICE "THE ADMIRAL." B. 6 August 1965, Key West, Florida. David Robinson attended Osbourn Park High School in Manassas, Virginia, and the **United States** Naval Academy. He was an exceptional student and majored in mathematics.

In his senior year, in 1987, he was awarded the Naismith College Player of the Year Award and the **John R. Wooden** Award as outstanding collegiate player of the year. He was drafted by the **San Antonio Spurs** as the first overall selection in the 1987 **National Basketball Association (NBA) draft**, although he had not yet completed his military requirement. He served two years of active duty and then became a member of the Spurs in 1989.

Robinson played for the Spurs for the next 14 seasons, making him one of only nine players to play their entire NBA career with one franchise for 14 or more seasons. In that time, he received several individual honors, including Rookie of the Year in 1990, Defensive Player of the Year in 1992, Most Valuable Player in 1995, the Sportsmanship Award in 2001, and the **J. Walter Kennedy** Citizenship Award in 2003. He was also five times the winner of the International Business Machines award for all-around contributions to his team's success. In 1994, his best individual year statistically, his 29.8 points per game scoring average led the league, and he was also the league leader in total points, **free throws** made, and free throws attempted. On 17 February 1994, he recorded a **quadruple-double** with 34 points and 10 each of **rebounds**, **assists**, and **blocks**, making him one of only four NBA players to achieve this feat. In his final game that season, on 24 April 1994, he scored 71 points and became only the fourth NBA player to score 70 or more in a game. (**Kobe Bryant** has since joined this group.)

In his NBA career, Robinson played in 987 regular-season games and averaged 21.1 points, 10.6 rebounds, and 3.0 blocks per game. The seven-foot, one-inch **left-handed center** played in 10 NBA **All-Star Games** and was selected to the All-NBA First Team four times, All-NBA Second Team twice, All-NBA Third Team four times, NBA All-Defensive First Team four times, and NBA All-Defensive Second Team four times. He helped lead the Spurs to the NBA Championship in 1999 and 2003. While still an amateur, he was selected for the 1988 U.S. **Olympic basketball** team and won a **bronze medal**. He won **gold medals** as a member of the 1992 and 1996 U.S. Olympic basketball **Dream Teams** and is the only American male to play in three Olympic basketball tournaments. In 1996, he was named one of the 50 Greatest Players in NBA History. In 2001, he and his wife founded the Carver Academy, a nonprofit private elementary school in San Antonio. He was elected to the **Naismith Memorial Basketball Hall of Fame** in 2009.

ROCHESTER ROYALS. *See* SACRAMENTO KINGS.

RODGERS, GUY WILLIAM, JR. B. 1 September 1935, Philadelphia, Pennsylvania. D. 19 February 2001, Los Angeles, California. Guy Rodgers attended Northeast High School in Philadelphia and **Temple University**. In college, he was half of an all-**left-handed backcourt** with Hal Lear, averaged 19.6 points and 6.5 **rebounds** per game in his three varsity seasons, and was a member of the third place team in the 1956 and 1958 **National Collegiate Athletic Association (NCAA)** tournaments and 1957 **National Invitation Tournament**.

Rodgers was selected by the Philadelphia Warriors in the 1958 **National Basketball Association (NBA) draft** as a **territorial** selection. The six-foot-tall **guard** played in the NBA from 1959–1970 for the Warriors, **Chicago Bulls**, Cincinnati Royals, and **Milwaukee Bucks**. On 14 March 1963, he had 28 **assists** in one game, tying **Bob Cousy**'s NBA record, which remained until 1978. Rodgers's best year was 1965–1966, when he averaged 18.6 points and 10.7 assists per game and had his career high game of 47 points on 19 November 1965. His NBA career totals for 12 years are 892 regular-season games and an 11.7 points and 7.8 assists per game average. He played in four NBA **All-Star Games** and twice led the league in assists.

RODMAN, DENNIS KEITH "WORM." B. 13 May 1961, Trenton, New Jersey. Dennis Rodman attended South Oak Cliff High School in Dallas, Texas; Cooke County Junior College; and Southeastern Oklahoma State University. The six-foot, eight-inch **forward** was selected by the **Detroit Pistons** in the 1986 **National Basketball Association (NBA) draft** and played in the NBA from 1986–2000 for the Pistons, **San Antonio Spurs**, **Chicago Bulls**, **Los Angeles Lakers**, and **Dallas Mavericks**. His NBA career totals for 14 years are 911 regular-season games and a 7.3 points and 13.1 **rebounds** per game average. He played in two NBA **All-Star Games**, was named the NBA Defensive Player of the Year in 1990 and 1991, was chosen for the NBA All-Defensive First Team seven times, and was

312 • RUDOLPH, MARVIN "MENDY"

selected to the NBA All-Defensive Second Team in 1994. He was also selected for the All-NBA Third Team in 1992 and 1995. He led the NBA in offensive rebounds six times, defensive rebounds three times, total rebounds four times, and rebounds per game in every season from 1992–1998.

Rodman was a shy, introverted person as a youth and for the first seven years of his professional **basketball** career was an ordinary, talented defensive player who was a member of the 1988 NBA finalists and 1989 and 1990 NBA champions. In 1993, after going through a difficult divorce, Rodman developed a new persona and started dying his hair unusual colors, getting tattoos, and having his body pierced. He demanded a trade from the Pistons and, on 1 October 1993, was traded to the San Antonio Spurs. He still was an extremely hard competitor, but his outrageous behavior at times did not sit well with the Spurs management and he was traded to the Bulls on 2 October 1995. The Bulls also acquired journeyman Jack Haley, Rodman's best friend on the Spurs. Under **coach Phil Jackson**, a master at handling difficult individuals, Rodman blended in and became a valuable member of the Bulls. With **Michael Jordan** and **Scottie Pippen**, he helped lead them to NBA Championships in 1996, 1997, and 1998. Following the 1998 season, Jackson resigned, Jordan retired, and so did Rodman.

Rodman attempted comebacks with the Lakers in 1999 and the Mavericks in 2000, but after 12 games with Dallas his NBA career was over. Since then he has been involved in numerous activities, including professional wrestling; playing exhibition basketball games in Finland, England, and the **Philippines**; having a reality talk show; making an action film; and appearing on celebrity television shows.

RUDOLPH, MARVIN "MENDY." B. 8 March 1926, Philadelphia, Pennsylvania. D. 4 July 1979, New York, NewYork. Mendy Rudolph attended James M. Coughlin High School in Wilkes-Barre, Pennsylvania. His father, Harry, was an established **referee** in the Eastern Professional Basketball League and later became president of that league. After graduating from high school, Rudolph joined his father as a referee in the Eastern League. In 1953, he was added to the officiating staff of the **National Basketball Association (NBA)**. By 1955, he was refereeing the NBA Championship Final series. In 1961, he and **Earl Strom** worked all seven games of the NBA Championship Final series. In 1966, he was named referee in chief of NBA officials. He wrote the *National Basketball Association Case Book* in 1970. On 25 April 1975, he suffered a blood clot in his lung while officiating an NBA playoff game and had to be helped from the court.

Rudolph officially retired in November 1975. During his NBA career, he officiated in 2,113 games, eight NBA **All-Star Games**, and at least one playoff finals game in 22 straight seasons and was considered by most as one of the NBA's best officials. From 1975–1977, he was a color analyst for **basketball** games on television. Although he was a compulsive gambler at the race track and casinos, he never was involved in any situation where the game of basketball was compromised. In 2007, he was enshrined in the **Naismith Memorial Basketball Hall of Fame**.

RUPP, ADOLPH FREDERICK "THE BARON." B. 2 September 1901, Halstead, Kansas. D. 10 December 1977, Lexington, Kentucky. Adolph Rupp attended Halstead High School and the **University of Kansas**. He played **basketball** at Kansas from 1919–1923 under **coach Forrest "Phog" Allen** but was a reserve player. His major contribution to basketball was as a coach.

Rupp coached the **University of Kentucky** from 1930 until his mandatory retirement in 1972. Known as "The Baron of the Bluegrass" or "The Man in the Brown Suit," he amassed a record of 876–190 and led his team to the **National Collegiate Athletic Association (NCAA)** National Championship four times and was the runner-up in 1966. They were **National Invitation Tournament (NIT)** champions in 1946 and NIT runners-up in 1947. In 1952–1953, Kentucky did not field a team as a result of the point-shaving scandal of 1951. In 1953–1954, Kentucky compiled an undefeated 25–0 record but did not compete in a postseason tournament since three of their star players had exhausted their college eligibility. He was assistant coach of the 1948 **U.S. Olympic** team, with five players from his Kentucky team on the Olympic squad.

Rupp was enshrined in the **Naismith Memorial Basketball Hall of Fame** in 1969 in the category of coach. After his mandatory retirement, he was president of the Memphis Tams of the **American**

Basketball Association and vice chairman of the board of directors of the **Kentucky Colonels.**

RUSH, CATHERINE ANN COWAN "CATHY." B. 7 April 1947, Atlantic City, New Jersey. Cathy Cowan attended Oakcrest High School in Mays Landing, New Jersey, and West Chester University, graduating in 1968 with a bachelor's degree and in 1972 with a master's degree in education. She was also a member of the West Chester **basketball** team for two years. In 1968, she married **National Basketball Association referee** Ed T. Rush. She taught physical education in the Philadelphia area and in 1970 was hired as basketball **coach** at **Immaculata College**, a women's school in Philadelphia.

Rush coached them from 1971–1977 and had a won–lost record of 149–15. Immaculata won the national championship in 1972, 1973, and 1974, and was national runner-up in 1975 and 1976. In 1975, she was head coach of the **U.S.** national team at the Pan American Games, where they won the **gold medal**, and **World Championships**, where they finished in eighth place. In 1979, she was director of player personnel for the California Dreams in the **Women's Professional Basketball League**. She runs a basketball camp for both boys and girls in the Pocono Mountains, works as a motivational speaker, and does television commentary. In 2000, she was enshrined in the **Women's Basketball Hall of Fame** and in 2008 the **Naismith Memorial Basketball Hall of Fame.**

RUSSELL, JOHN DAVID "HONEY." B. 31 May 1902, Brooklyn, New York. D. 15 November 1973, Livingston, New Jersey. Honey Russell attended Alexander Hamilton High School in Brooklyn and Seton Hall University. He played professional **basketball** from 1920–1945 for more than two dozen teams and concluded his career by playing in the **American Basketball League (ABL)** from 1933–1945. He was a player-**coach** of the Chicago Bruins of the ABL from 1927–1930 and later coached Newark, Wilkes-Barre, Camden, Brooklyn, New York, and Trenton in the reorganized ABL. In the first two years of the **Basketball Association of America**, he was the **Boston Celtics'** coach. From 1936–1943 and 1949–1960, he was the coach of Seton Hall University and in the 1945–1946 season coached Manhattan College. In 1953, he led Seton Hall to the **National Invitation Tournament** championship.

Russell was also a baseball scout for 26 years; a football scout; and a sports promoter of boxing, wrestling, and other events. In 1964, he was enshrined in the **Naismith Memorial Basketball Hall of Fame**. An excellent 1986 biography written by his son, John Jr., is entitled *Honey Russell: Between Games, Between Halves*.

RUSSELL, WILLIAM FELTON "BILL." B. 12 February 1934, Monroe, Louisiana. Bill Russell's family moved to California when he was eight years old. He attended McClymonds High School in San Francisco and the **University of San Francisco**. He led the University of San Francisco to a then record 55-game winning streak and the **National Collegiate Athletic Association (NCAA)** Championships in both 1955 and 1956. Selected for the 1956 **U.S. Olympic basketball** team, he won a **gold medal** with them.

After the Olympics, the six-foot, nine-inch **center** signed with the **Boston Celtics** and played for them for 13 years, leading them to 11 **National Basketball Association (NBA)** Championships. Russell is arguably the greatest defensive player in NBA history. He revolutionized the game by blocking opponents' shots and keeping the ball in play and was an extremely effective rebounder, averaging more than 20 **rebounds** per game in 10 of his 13 NBA seasons. He and **Wilt Chamberlain** had some of the most memorable meetings in the history of the game.

In 1966, Russell was named by **Red Auerbach** as **coach** of the Boston Celtics and became the first African American NBA coach. As player-coach, he led the Celtics to two titles in three seasons. He was selected as the NBA's Most Valuable Player five times and was selected to play in the NBA **All-Star Game** every season from 1958–1969. He later coached the Seattle Supersonics for four seasons and the **Sacramento Kings** for one but did not have the same level of success that he had with the Celtics. He was elected to the **Naismith Memorial Basketball Hall of Fame** in 1974, named one of the 50 Greatest Players in NBA History in 1996, and in 2007 was elected to the **Fédération Internationale de Basketball** Hall of Fame. In 2009, the NBA Finals Most Valuable Player award was renamed the Bill Russell NBA Finals Most Valuable Player award.

RUSSIA. Russia joined the **Fédération Internationale de Basketball (FIBA)** in 1992 and is a member in the FIBA Europe zone. From 1947–1992, as a republic within the **Union of Soviet Socialist Republics**, their athletes competed for the Soviet Union. As independent Russia, the men's team competed in the **Olympic Games** of 2000 and 2008. In 2000, they finished in eighth place, and in 2008, they were tied for ninth place. In the FIBA **World Championships**, they competed four times and finished second in both 1994 and 1998. In the FIBA European Championships, they entered eight times and were champions in 2007, second in 1993, and third in 1997.

The women's team competed in four Olympic tournaments and won **bronze medals** in 2004 and 2008. In the FIBA World Championships, they entered three times from 1998–2006 and finished second each time. In the FIBA European Championships, they entered eight times and finished first, second, and third two times each. There have been seven Russian players in the **Women's National Basketball Association**, including Svetlana Abrosimova, Elen Bunatyants Chakirova, Ilona Korstine, Irina Osipova, Maria Stepanova, Natalia Vodopyanova, and Oksana Zakaluzhnaya. In the **National Basketball Association**, Sergei Bazarevich, Andrei Kirilenko, Yaroslav Korolev, Sergei Monia, Pavel Podkolzin, and Aleksandar Volkov were all born in Russia.

– S –

69TH REGIMENT ARMORY. The 69th Regiment Armory is located on Lexington Avenue in New York City between 25th and 26th streets. Due to previous bookings at **Madison Square Garden**, it was the home of 26 of the 30 **New York Knickerbocker** home games during their first season in 1946–1947. It also was used by the Knicks until 1960 on dates when the Garden was not available, even though its seating capacity for **basketball** was only about 5,000 and the Garden's was 18,000. In 1967, it was planned to be used by the New York entry in the **American Basketball Association**, but the franchise was moved to New Jersey to avoid direct confrontation with the Knicks. Until 1982, the armory continued to be used for college basketball. Construction of the armory was completed in 1906, and it was cited as a National Historic Landmark on 6 May 1996. It is still used by the New York National Guard's 69th Infantry Regiment for training purposes.

SABONIS, ARVYDAS ROMAS. B.19 December 1964, Kaunas, **Lithuania, Union of Soviet Socialist Republics (USSR).** Arvydas Sabonis played for Kaunas Žalgiris from 1981–1989, Forum Valladolid from 1989–1992, and Real Madrid from 1992–1995. The seven-foot, three-inch, 280-pound **center** was selected by the **Portland Trail Blazers** in the 1986 **National Basketball Association (NBA) draft**, did not join them until 1995, and played for them until 2003. By the time he played in the NBA, his best years were behind him and, although he could no longer run and jump as well as he once could, he still had an excellent shooting touch and was an accomplished passer. His NBA career totals for seven years are 470 regular-season games and a 12.0 points and 7.3 **rebounds** per game average.

In 2003, Sabonis returned to Žalgiris and played two more seasons with them before retiring. He played for the USSR team in the 1982 and 1986 **World Championships** and won a **gold medal** in 1982 and a **silver medal** in 1986. In 1983, 1985, and 1989, at the European Championships, he won **bronze**, gold, and bronze with the Soviet Union team. His most impressive international appearance was at the 1988 **Olympic Games**, where he teamed with fellow Lithuanians Valdemaras Chomičius, Rimas Kurtinaitis, **Šarūnas Marčiulionis**, and teammates from five other Soviet republics to defeat the **United States** and win the Olympic gold medal. In 1985, he was awarded the Merited Master of Sport of the USSR. After Lithuania received its independence, he won bronze medals with them in the 1992 and 1996 Olympic Games. In 1995, he won a silver medal as a member of the Lithuanian team in the European Championships. In three Olympic Games tournaments, he played in 23 games and averaged 18.2 points per game. He holds the Olympic career records for most defensive rebounds and total rebounds and is second in **blocked shots**. In 2008, he was named one of the 35 greatest players in the 50 years of the Euroleague. In 2010, he was inducted into the **Fédération Internationale de Basketball** Hall of Fame.

SACRAMENTO KINGS. The Sacramento Kings are a team in the **National Basketball Association (NBA)**. They began as the Rochester Seagrams independent team in the 1940s and joined the **National Basketball League (NBL)** as the Rochester Royals in 1945. They transferred to the **Basketball Association of America (BAA)** in 1948, which became the NBA in 1949. In 1957, they moved to Cincinnati, where they played until 1972, when they moved to Kansas City and Omaha and were known as the Kansas City–Omaha Kings. In 1975, their name was changed to the Kansas City Kings, and in 1985, they moved to Sacramento.

Rochester Royals (NBL). The Rochester Royals were owned by brothers Jack and Lester Harrison. Home games were played at the 4,200-seat Edgerton Park Sports Arena in Rochester, New York. Their 1945–1946 NBL Championship team featured several interesting players: In addition to future **basketball** Hall of Famers **Al Cervi, Bob Davies,** and **William "Red" Holzman,** they also had future football Hall of Famer Otto Graham and future Major League Baseball players **Kevin "Chuck" Connors** and Del Rice. Connors later became better known as a television actor in the *Rifleman* Western series. The 1946–1947 team included **William "Dolly" King,** one of the first black players in the NBL. Others who played with the Royals in the NBL included Andy Duncan, George Glamack, Arnie Johnson, Andrew "Fuzzy" Levane, John Mahnken, Al Negratti, **Arnie Risen,** and **Bobby Wanzer.** Their overall record for three seasons in the NBL was 99–39, and their overall playoff record was 18–11. On 10 May 1948, the Royals, along with the **Fort Wayne Pistons, Minneapolis Lakers,** and **Indianapolis Kautskys,** were enticed to switch leagues and joined the rival BAA.

Rochester Royals (NBA). Home games continued to be played at the Edgerton Park Sport Arena until 1954, and from 1954–1957, contests were held at the 10,000-seat Rochester War Memorial and Exhibit Hall. Among their most notable players were future Hall of Famers Bob Davies, Arnie Risen, **Maurice Stokes, Jack Twyman,** and Bobby Wanzer. Other Royals included Cal Christensen, Jack Coleman, William "Red" Holzman, Jack McMahon, and Art Spoelstra. In 1951 and 1952, they were involved in three home games that lasted four or more **overtimes,** including a six-overtime game on 6 January 1951. They won the NBA Championship in 1951. On 3 April 1957, they moved to Cincinnati.

Cincinnati Royals. Home games were played at the 11,650-seat Cincinnati Gardens. **Bob Cousy** was called out of retirement to be a player-**coach** in 1969, after retiring in 1963, but after playing in just seven games at the age of 41, he realized that he was best off as a nonplaying coach. Among their other notable players were Hall of Famers **Nate "Tiny" Archibald, Wayne Embry, Clyde Lovellette, Jerry Lucas, Oscar Robertson**, Maurice Stokes, and Jack Twyman. Others on the team included Arlen Bockhorn, Harold "Happy" Hairston, Adrian Smith, and Tom Van Arsdale. Their best season was 1963–1964, when they reached the Eastern Division Finals. On 14 March 1972, the team was sold and moved to Kansas City and Omaha for the 1972–1973 season.

Kansas City–Omaha Kings. For three seasons, the team split their home games between Kansas City, Missouri, and Omaha, Nebraska. Home games were played at the 10,000-seat Kansas City Municipal Auditorium from 1971–1974, the 16,000-seat Kemper Arena in Kansas City in 1974–1975, and the 9,000-seat Omaha Civic Auditorium. Their best players were Nate "Tiny" Archibald, Ron Behagen, Don Kojis, Sam Lacey, Jimmy Walker, and Nate Williams. In those three years, their best showing was 1974–1975, when they were second in the Midwest Division but lost in the first round of the postseason playoffs. In 1975–1976, they discontinued playing in Omaha on a regular basis.

Kansas City Kings. Home games were played at the Kemper Arena in Kansas City, Missouri. They also played a few home games at the 15,000-seat Checkerdome in St. Louis, Missouri, and at the Omaha Civic Auditorium. Among their most notable players were Otis Birdsong, Ron Boone, Phil Ford, Larry Drew, Sam Lacey, Scott Wedman, and Mike Woodson. On 16 April 1985, they moved to Sacramento.

Sacramento Kings. Home games were played at the 10,133-seat original ARCO Arena from 1985–1988 and have been played at the new 17,317-seat ARCO Arena since then. Among their most notable players have been Mike Bibby, **Vlade Divać**, Bobby Jackson, Kevin Martin, Brad Miller, Mitch Richmond, **Peja Stojaković**, Wayman Tisdale, and Chris Webber. Their best season was 2001–2002, when they reached the Western Conference Finals. The franchise record for their 62 years in the BAA/NBA through the 2009–2010 season is 2,300–2,593.

SAMPSON, RALPH LEE, JR. B. 7 July 1960, Harrisonburg, Virginia. Ralph Sampson attended Harrisonburg High School and led them to the state championship in 1978 and 1979. Highly recruited, he went to the University of Virginia, where he led them to the 1981 **National Collegiate Athletic Association Final Four**. He won the Naismith Award and United States Basketball Writers Association award as College Basketball Player of the Year three times and also twice won the John R. Wooden Award.

The seven-foot, four-inch **center-forward** was selected by the **Houston Rockets** as the first overall selection in the 1983 **National Basketball Association (NBA) draft** and played in the NBA until 1992 for the Rockets, **Golden State Warriors, Sacramento Kings**, and Washington Bullets. In his second season, the Rockets also acquired the seven-foot-tall **Hakeem Olajuwon**, and the combination of Sampson at forward and Olajuwon at center, called "The Twin Towers," worked well. Sampson's best years were his first three years with Houston, when he averaged between 10.4 and 11.1 **rebounds**, 18.9 and 22.1 points, and 1.6 and 2.4 **blocks** per game each season. In 1984, he was NBA Rookie of the Year and in 1985 was named to the All-NBA Second Team. In 1986, the Rockets reached the NBA Championship Finals. Injuries during the 1986–1987 season effectively ended Sampson's career. He continued playing until 1992 but was no longer effective.

Sampson's NBA career totals for nine years are 456 regular-season games and a 15.4 points, 8.8 rebounds, and 1.6 blocks per game average. He played in four NBA **All-Star Games** and was the 1985 All-Star Game Most Valuable Player. In 1992–1993, he was assistant **coach** at James Madison University.

SAN ANTONIO SPURS. The San Antonio Spurs are a team in the **National Basketball Association (NBA)**. They began in 1967 in the **American Basketball Association (ABA)** as the Dallas Chaparrals, became the Texas Chaparrals in 1970 as they attempted to operate regionally, and reverted back to the Dallas Chaparrals in 1971. In 1973, they moved to San Antonio as the San Antonio Spurs and joined the NBA in 1976 after the ABA–NBA merger.

Dallas/Texas Chaparrals. On 2 February 1967, a franchise in the new ABA was awarded to a group headed by Gary Davidson. Former NBA player **Cliff Hagan** was coaxed out of retirement to be the player-**coach** of the new team. Home games were played at the 9,305-seat Moody Coliseum in Dallas. Players included Charlie and John Beasley (no relation), Riney Lochmann, Cincy Powell, Bob Verga, and Bobby Wilson. In 1970, as the Texas Chaparrals, they scheduled home games in Dallas, Lubbock, and Fort Worth. The attempt failed, with less than 200 fans at one game in Fort Worth, and they returned to Dallas for the 1971–1972 season. Players included Donnie Freeman, Joe Hamilton, Simmie Hill, Collis Jones, Larry Jones, Rich Jones, Steve Jones, and Eugene "Goo" Kennedy. On 9 April 1973, the owners leased the team to a group of 36 San Antonio citizens led by Angelo Drossos. The group received the right to operate the team in San Antonio for three years, after which time they had the option to buy. The team was moved to San Antonio for the 1973–1974 season and renamed the San Antonio Spurs.

San Antonio Spurs (Aba). Home games were played at the 10,146-seat Hemisfair Arena. In November 1973, the Spurs made two major acquisitions by purchasing **George Gervin** and Swen Nater from the **Virginia Squires**. Since San Antonio did not have any other major league sports teams, the fans supported the Spurs, and their average attendance far exceeded that of the NBA's Texas team, the **Houston Rockets**. The San Antonio leasees were pleased with the response and, on 22 March 1974, exercised their option and purchased the team. On 17 June 1976, the Spurs entered the NBA. In nine years in the ABA, their record was 378–366.

San Antonio Spurs (NBA). Home games were played at the Hemisfair Arena until 1993, the 20,000 plus seat Alamodome from 1993–2002 and at the 18,797-seat AT&T Center (formerly the SBC Center) since then. Among their most notable players have been: Bruce Bowen, **Tim Duncan**, Sean Elliott, George Gervin, **Emanuel "Manu" Ginóbili**, Avery Johnson, Larry Kenon, Mike Mitchell, Johnny Moore, **Tony Parker**, **David Robinson**, and Malik Rose. Their best seasons have been 1999, 2003, 2005, and 2007, when they won the NBA Championship. Their overall record for their first 34 years in the NBA through the 2009–2010 season is 1,653–1,103.

SAN DIEGO CLIPPERS. *See* LOS ANGELES CLIPPERS.

SAN DIEGO CONQUISTADORS. *See* SAN DIEGO SAILS.

SAN DIEGO ROCKETS. *See* HOUSTON ROCKETS.

SAN DIEGO SAILS. The San Diego Sails were a team in the **American Basketball Association (ABA)** that only played 11 games in the 1975–1976 season before disbanding on 12 November 1975. They had played the previous three seasons as the San Diego Conquistadors. In their brief time in the ABA, the franchise record was 101–162.

San Diego Conquistadors "Qs." The San Diego Conquistadors were the only expansion team in the ABA. The franchise was purchased for $1 million by San Diego dentist Leonard Bloom in July 1972. Although San Diego had a new 14,400-seat arena, a conflict between Bloom and the arena's owner caused the team to play home games at the 4,500-seat Peterson Gymnasium at San Diego State University. They played from 1972–1975 and reached the playoffs in two of their three seasons. Among the team's best players were Simmie Hill, Stew Johnson, Larry Miller, Gene Moore, Austin "Red" Robbins, Ollie Taylor, and Chuck Williams. In September 1973, Bloom signed **National Basketball Association (NBA)** superstar **Wilt Chamberlain** to a three-year contract for $1,800,000 to be player-**coach**, but the **Los Angeles Lakers** exercised a clause in their previous year's contract with Chamberlain to prohibit him from playing for the Qs. As coach, Chamberlain was barely interested, and after coaching for one season resigned. In February 1975, the league assumed operation of the failing franchise and in June found a new owner, Frank Goldberg of San Diego. He renamed the team the San Diego Sails.

San Diego Sails. Attendance was poor, and Goldberg discovered that in the proposed merger with the NBA, San Diego would not be included, since the NBA had a team in Los Angeles and did not want additional competition. Upon learning this, coupled with the minimal attendance, Goldberg decided to cut his losses and disbanded the team on 12 November 1975, after just 11 games. Players on the team that season included Lee Davis, Tom Ingelsby, Stew Johnson, Caldwell Jones, Kevin Joyce, Bo Lamar, Mark Olberding, Dave Robisch, Bobby Warren, and Joby Wright.

SAN FRANCISCO, UNIVERSITY OF. The University of San Francisco in California began its men's **basketball** program in 1923.

Home games since 1958 have been played at the 5,300-seat War Memorial Gymnasium. Prior to 1958, their basketball teams had no permanent home, and practices and games were conducted at Kezar Pavilion or St. Ignatius High School. The most accomplished **coaches** in the school's history have been Pete Newell and Phil Woolpert.

San Francisco won the 1949 **National Invitation Tournament** by one point over **Loyola University Chicago**. In 1955 and 1956, the **Bill Russell**-led Dons won the **National Collegiate Athletic Association (NCAA)** Championship. In 1957, they reached the NCAA **Final Four** for the third straight year but lost in the semifinals. During the mid-1950s, San Francisco won 60 consecutive games, the most for a college team at that time. The record was topped by the **University of California, Los Angeles** in the 1960s, when they won 88 straight.

In 1980, after some infractions were disclosed, school president Reverend John LoSciavo discontinued the basketball program. It was resumed in 1985. The best players in school history include Bill Cartwright, Joe Ellis, Mike Farmer, **K. C. Jones**, Fred LaCour, Erwin Mueller, Paul Napolitano, Hal Perry, Kevin Restani, Abel Rodrigues, Bill Russell, Fred Scolari, and Phil Smith.

SAN FRANCISCO WARRIORS. *See* GOLDEN STATE WARRIORS.

SAPERSTEIN, ABRAHAM MICHAEL "ABE." B. 4 July 1902, London, England. D. 15 March 1966, Chicago, Illinois. Abe Saperstein graduated from Lake View High School in Chicago and spent one year at the University of Illinois from 1922–1923. His major contribution to the sport of **basketball** was the formation of the **Harlem Globetrotters** in the late 1920s in Illinois. The "official" Globetrotter history claims that Saperstein formed the team as the Savoy Big Five and, on 7 January 1927, they played their first game in Hinckley, Illinois. Modern historians have disputed these claims, and historian Ben Green published an excellent account of the Globetrotters in 2005 entitled *Spinning the Globe*, in which he writes that this story, "to put it mildly, . . . is utter nonsense." Nonetheless, by 1929, Saperstein did manage an independent black barnstorming team named the "New York Harlem Globe Trotters." During the team's early years, the five-foot, five-inch Saperstein not only managed and promoted the team, but he occasionally appeared as a substitute player.

In 1940, the Globetrotters won the **World Professional Basketball Tournament**. They continued barnstorming throughout the 1940s and gradually worked more comedy into their games after they acquired **Reese "Goose" Tatum** in 1941. In 1950, as the team's popularity continued to rise, Saperstein attempted to become an owner in the **National Basketball Association**. He purchased the **Chicago Stags** on 20 June 1950 but was not able to keep the franchise alive for the 1950–1951 season, and the team was disbanded on 25 September 1950.

In 1961, Saperstein organized a new basketball major league, the **American Basketball League,** and was league commissioner as well as owner of the Chicago franchise. The league was the first professional league to award three points for a field goal from behind an arc 25 feet from the basket. It lasted for one and one-half seasons and ended in 1962 midway through its second season. In 1971, Saperstein was enshrined in the **Naismith Memorial Basketball Hall of Fame** in the category of contributor.

SCHAYES, ADOLPH "DOLPH." B. 19 May 1928, New York, New York. Dolph Schayes attended DeWitt Clinton High School in the Bronx, New York, and New York University. He was selected by the **New York Knickerbockers** in the 1948 **Basketball Association of America (BAA) draft** and by the Tri-Cities Blackhawks in the **National Basketball League (NBL)** draft, but the Blackhawks sold his **draft rights** to the Syracuse Nationals. He played with the Nationals in the NBL in 1948–1949 and in the **National Basketball Association (NBA)** from 1949–1963. The Nationals moved to Philadelphia in 1963, and his final year was as a **Philadelphia 76er**.

In 1949, Schayes was the NBL Rookie of the Year. His professional career totals for 16 years are 1,059 games, an 18.2 points per game average, and a **free throw** percentage of .843. The six-foot, eight-inch **forward** was selected for every NBA **All-Star Game** from 1951–1962 and was named to the All-NBA First Team and All-NBA Second Team six times each. He played every league game from 17 February 1952 until 26 December 1961, for a total of 706 consecutive games, even though for some of that time he played wearing a heavy cast protecting a broken arm.

Known for his high-arcing, two-handed set shot from the perimeter, had Schayes played when the **three-point field goal** rule was in effect, he would have been among the league leaders in three pointers. He was an excellent free throw shooter and led the league three times and was second five times in that category.

In 1955, he was a member of the NBA Championship team. He was named player-**coach** of the 76ers in 1963 but after playing in just 24 games retired as a player but continued as coach until 1966. In 1966, he was NBA Coach of the Year. He also coached the Buffalo Braves in 1970–1971. In 1967, he was named NBA Supervisor of Officials and retained that position until March 1970. In 1970, he was named to the NBA 25th Anniversary Team. He was enshrined in the **Naismith Memorial Basketball Hall of Fame** in 1973 and in 1996 was named one of the 50 Greatest Players in NBA History. His son, Danny, played in the NBA from 1981–1999.

SCHMIDT BEZERRA, OSCAR DANIEL. B. 16 February 1958, Rio Grande do Norte, Natal, **Brazil**. At six-feet, eight-inches tall, playing both **guard** and **forward**, Oscar Schmidt was **basketball**'s most prolific scorer and was known simply as "Oscar" throughout the world, although he had the nickname "Mão Santa" (holy hand) in his native Brazil. He began playing basketball for Palmeiras in the Brazilian league in 1975 and played in Brazil for Sírio from 1975–1982 and in **Italy** for Caserta from 1982–1990 and Pavia from 1990–1993. From 1993–1995, he played for Fórum Valladolid in **Spain** and then returned to Brazil with Corinthians, Bandeirantes, Barueri, Mackenzie São Paulo, and Flamengo until 2003, when he retired at the age of 45.

In his nearly 30 years of playing, Schmidt has been credited with scoring an unofficial total of 49,703 points. He played for the Brazilian national team in the 1990 Goodwill Games, four **World Championships**, two Pan American Games, and a record five **Olympic Games** from 1980–1996. In 1978, he won a **bronze medal** at the World Championships with Brazil and at the 1979 Pan American Games as well. In the 1987 Pan American Games, he led a second-half comeback against the **United States** to win the **gold medal** for Brazil.

In his five Olympic Games tournaments, he played in 38 games and scored 1,093 points for a 28.8 points per game average, and he holds most of the career Olympic records. In the 1988 Olympic tournament, in eight games, he averaged an Olympic record 42.3 points per game, including a record 55 points in a losing effort against Spain on 24 September 1988. He was selected by the **New Jersey Nets** in the 1984 **National Basketball Association draft** but preferred to remain an amateur and did not sign with them. In retirement, he was the chief executive officer of the Brazilian league team Telemar Rio de Janeiro. In 2010, he was inducted into the **Fédération Internationale de Basketball** Hall of Fame.

SEATTLE SUPERSONICS. *See* OKLAHOMA CITY THUNDER.

SEDRAN (SEDRANSKY), BERNARD "BARNEY." B. 28 January 1891, New York, New York. D. 14 January 1969, New York, New York. Barney Sedransky attended DeWitt Clinton High School in the Bronx, New York, but was deemed too small to play for his high school team. He enrolled at **City College of New York** and played **basketball** there from 1909–1911. Although only five-feet, four-inches tall and 115 pounds, he played professional basketball from 1911–1924, was among the leading scorers in several of the leagues he played in, and was considered one of the best players of his era. He shortened his name to Sedran when he began playing with Newburgh in the **Hudson River League** in 1911.

For much of his career, Sedran was a teammate of **Max "Marty" Friedman**, and they were referred to as "The Heavenly Twins." Sedran was a player-**coach** for Passaic in the 1919–1920 Interstate League and in the 1930s and 1940s was a bench coach for several teams in the **American Basketball League (ABL)**. He led Wilmington to ABL Championships in 1942 and 1944. After retiring from active play, he was in the garage business in Manhattan before World War II, and after the war he and a partner were real estate owners in lower Manhattan. He was enshrined in the **Naismith Memorial Basketball Hall of Fame** in 1962.

SELVY, FRANKLIN DELANO "FRANK." B. 9 November 1932, Corbin, Kentucky. Frank Selvy attended Corbin High School and Furman University. On 13 February 1954, he scored 100 points for Furman in a game against Newberry College, and he is the only player in **National Collegiate Athletic Association (NCAA)** Division I history to reach that total. He averaged an NCAA record 41.7 points per game (later broken by **Pete Maravich** in 1968) in his senior year at Furman and 32.5 points per game for his three varsity seasons.

The six-foot, two-inch **guard** was chosen by the **Baltimore Bullets** in the 1954 **National Basketball Association (NBA) draft** as the first overall selection, and he played from 1954–1964 for the Bullets, Milwaukee Hawks, St. Louis Hawks, Minneapolis Lakers, **New York Knickerbockers**, and **Los Angeles Lakers**. Selvy's best year was his rookie year, in 1954–1955, when he averaged 19.0 points per game for the Bullets and Milwaukee Hawks, who acquired his contract after Baltimore disbanded.

Selvy's NBA career totals for nine years are 565 regular-season games and a 10.8 points per game average. With the Lakers, he played on the losing team in the NBA Championship Finals in 1962 and 1963, and he is remembered for making two baskets in the final **minute** of the seventh game of the 1962 NBA Finals to tie the score, but he missed the buzzer shot that would have given the Lakers the victory. After retiring from active play, he **coached** Furman from 1966–1970 and also worked in sales for the St. Joe Paper Company in Laurens, South Carolina.

SEMJONOVA, ULJANA LARIONOVNA. B. 9 March 1952, Medumi, Daugavpils, Latvia, **Union of Soviet Socialist Republics (USSR).** Uljana Semjonova towered over her competition. Officially listed as 2.10 meters (6 feet, 10 inches) she was probably closer to 2.18 meters (7 feet, 2 inches). Regardless of the official measurement, she was head and shoulders above her teammates and opponents. During her competitive era, only **Anne Donovan** of the **United States** and **Zheng Haixia** of China—both 6 feet, 8 inches tall—approached her size.

Semjonova was not just tall but was an effective player, shooting 65 percent from the **free throw** line and a record 72 percent from the field during her two **Olympic gold medal** performances. She competed for 18 seasons in international competition, winning two Olympic gold medals, three **World Championships** gold medals, and 10 European Cup Championships, never losing a game in these major competitions. She scored more than 15,000 points in her career.

Named the most popular athlete in Latvia 12 times from 1970–1985, in 1995, Semjonova received the highest honor of the

Republic of Latvia, "The Commander of the Order of the Three Stars." A member of the Latvian club TTT Riga in the former USSR, she won the championship of the USSR basketball league 15 times and the European Cup for women 11 times. She later played professionally in **Spain** and **France**. She was awarded the Merited Master of Sport of the USSR in 1971. In 1993, she became the first international woman enshrined in the **Naismith Memorial Basketball Hall of Fame** and was included in the first class of both the **Women's Basketball Hall of Fame** in 1999 and **Fédération Internationale de Basketball** Hall of Fame in 2007.

SENEGAL. Senegal joined the **Fédération Internationale de Basketball (FIBA)** in 1962 in the Africa zone and has competed in 23 of the 24 FIBA Men's Africa Championships since then. They have been champions five times, finished second six times, and placed third three times. They competed in the **World Championships** three times, with 14th in 1978 being their best showing.

They also competed in three **Olympic Games**. In 1968 and 1972, they finished 15th of 16. In 1980, they finished 11th of 12 teams. Their best players in the Olympic Games have been Oumar Dia, Bireyma Diagne, Babacar Seck, Assane Thiam, and Babacar Traore. **National Basketball Association** players born in Senegal include Desagana Diop, Mamadou N'Diaye, Boniface N'Dong, Makhtar Ndiaye, Pape Sow, Cheikh Samb, and Mouhamed Sene. Diop has been a useful backup center, but the others have only played sparingly.

SHARMAN, WILLIAM WALTON "BILL." B. 25 May 1926, Abilene, Texas. Bill Sharman attended Narbonne High School in Lomita, California, and Porterville High School in Porterville, California. He served in the **U.S.** Navy from 1944–1946 and then went to the **University of Southern California** from 1947–1950. He was an excellent baseball player and was with the Brooklyn Dodgers organization for five years from 1950–1955.

Selected by the **Washington Capitols** in the 1950 **National Basketball Association (NBA) draft**, Sharman played from 1950–1961 for Washington and the **Boston Celtics**. The six-foot, one-inch **guard** was a member of the NBA Championship team four times with the

Celtics. His best year was 1957–1958, when he averaged 22.3 points per game and set the NBA **free throw** percentage record, with .932. His NBA career totals for 11 years are 711 regular-season games, a 17.8 points per game average, and a free throw percentage of .883. He was selected for eight NBA **All-Star Games** and was named the Most Valuable Player in the 1955 game. He was also selected to the All-NBA First Team four times and the All-NBA Second Team three times. An excellent free throw shooter, he led the league in that category seven times. In 1955, he set the NBA record by making 50 consecutive free throws. He broke his own record by making 55 straight in 1956. He also made 56 consecutive playoff free throws.

After retiring from active play with the Celtics, Sharman became player-**coach** with the Los Angeles Jets of the newly formed **American Basketball League (ABL)** in 1961. The Jets folded after 39 games, and he was named head coach of the Cleveland Pipers for the remainder of the season and led them to the ABL Championship. After the season the Pipers folded, and Sharman became head coach of the California State University, Los Angeles college team for two seasons.

Sharman then coached the San Francisco Warriors in the NBA from 1966–1968, the Los Angeles Stars (the team moved to Utah in 1970) of the **American Basketball Association (ABA)** from 1968–1971, and the **Los Angeles Lakers** from 1971–1976. He led the Warriors to the 1967 NBA Finals, the Stars to the 1970 ABA Finals and 1971 ABA Championship, and the Lakers to the 1972 NBA Championship and 1973 NBA Finals. In the 1971–1972, season the Lakers set an NBA record (since broken by the **Chicago Bulls**) with 69 victories, including an NBA record 33 consecutive wins.

While coaching the record-breaking season, Sharman severely damaged his vocal cords and, after his coaching contract expired in 1976, resigned as coach and became general manager of the Lakers. In 1982, he was promoted to Lakers' president. He was enshrined in the **Naismith Memorial Basketball Hall of Fame** in 1975 as a player and in 2004 was enshrined a second time as a coach. In 1996, he was named one of the 50 Greatest Players in NBA History.

SHEBOYGAN REDSKINS. The Sheboygan Redskins were a team in the **National Basketball League (NBL)** from 1938–1949. They played in the **National Basketball Association (NBA)** in 1949–1950 and in the **National Professional Basketball League (NPBL)** in 1950–1951.

Sheboygan Redskins (NBL). The city of Sheboygan, Wisconsin, had an independent team owned by 120 local stockholders during the 1930s under various sponsorships known as the Ballhorns, Art Imigs, and Enzo Jels. In 1938, they joined the NBL as the Redskins. Home games were played at the 1,500-seat Eagle Auditorium from 1938–1942 and the 3,500-seat Sheboygan Municipal Auditorium and Armory from 1942–1949. Among their most notable players were Ed Dancker, Bobby Holm, Rube Lautenschlager, Bill McDonald, Mike Novak, Dick Schulz, Paul Sokody, and Kenny Suesens. Their best season was 1942–1943, when they won the league championship. For the next three years, they lost each year in the NBL Championship finals. Their overall record for 11 seasons in the NBL was 199–182. Following the season, they were included in the NBA when the NBL and **Basketball Association of America** merged.

Sheboygan Redskins (NBA). Although the Sheboygan Redskins played in the NBA for only one season and had a record of 22–40, they were involved in one of the more memorable games. On 10 March 1950, the Redskins defeated the **Denver Nuggets**, 141–104, and set several league records, including most points scored by one team, with 141; most points scored by two teams, with 245; most **field goals**, with 61; most field goals by two teams, with 107; most **assists**, with 51; and most assists by two teams, with 83. Most records were subsequently bettered, but the 51 assists remained the league record for 21 years and still is among the top five performances in NBA history. Among the Redskins' players with the most playing time were Bob Brannum, Jack Burmaster, Bobby Cook, Noble Jorgensen, Max Morris, Stan Patrick, Milt Schroon, and George Sobek. Following the season, the team dropped out of the NBA and played in the new NPBL in the 1950–1951 season.

SHOOTING GUARD. Shooting guard is one of the five basketball positions. It is sometimes referred to as "off guard" or "2" guard. The latter designation comes from **coaches** numbering the five positions on a play chart. The player at this position is usually one of the best outside shooters on the team and will often lead the team in **three-**

point field goals. Occasionally, the shooting guard will bring the ball up the floor, but that function is usually carried out by the point guard. The designation "shooting guard" is a relatively new one and dates back to the mid-1970s. *See also* GUARD; POINT GUARD.

SHOT CLOCK. In 1954, to speed up play and prevent stalling during the latter stages of the game, a 24-second shot clock was added to the **National Basketball Association** rules. The offensive team had to attempt a shot at the **basket** that was successful or hit the rim of the basket within 24 seconds after gaining possession, otherwise the defensive team would be given possession. Other leagues have used shot clocks with different times required to shoot. The **National Collegiate Athletic Association** adopted its use during the 1980s and, now virtually all organized **basketball** games are played with a shot clock. *See also* BIASONE, DANIEL "DANNY."

SILVER MEDAL. In **Fédération Internationale de Basketball (FIBA)** competition, such as the **Olympic Games** and **World Championships**, the second-place team is awarded silver medals. In some tournaments, the semifinal winners play a match to determine the **gold medal** winner. The losing team in that match receives the silver medal. In other tournaments, a round-robin tournament is played, with the team with the second-best record receiving the silver medal. *See also* BRONZE MEDAL.

SIXTH MAN. The sixth man is the team's first substitute and usually is one of the team's best players with the ability to quickly produce once he enters the game. A sixth man will often receive more playing time than one of the starting players. **Boston Celtics' coach Red Auerbach** was one of the first coaches to use this technique, and such players as **John Havlicek, Don Nelson,** and **Frank Ramsey** played this vital role on his teams. In 1983, the **National Basketball Association (NBA)** began presenting an annual award for the best sixth man in the league, as voted on by sportswriters and broadcasters. **Kevin McHale** of the Boston Celtics, Ricky Pierce of the **Milwaukee Bucks,** and Detlef Schrempf of the **Indiana Pacers** are the only players to win the award twice. The phrase "sixth man" is also occasionally used in reference to the home team's fans, who through vociferous cheering provide an edge to the team. Both the **Sacramento Kings** and **Orlando Magic** of the NBA have actually "retired" uniform number six in recognition of their fans.

SLAM DUNK. A "slam dunk" is a **dunk** thrown down with extra force. Slam dunk competitions have been held since the mid-1970s to reward individuals for creativity while dunking the basketball. *See also* DAWKINS, DARRYL "CHOCOLATE THUNDER"; ERVING II, JULIUS WINFIELD "DR. J."

SLOAN, GERALD EUGENE "JERRY." B. 28 March 1942, McLeansboro, Illinois. Jerry Sloan attended McLeansboro High School. He enrolled at the University of Illinois but left before the start of the **basketball** season; transferred to Evansville College; and played there from 1962–1965, leading his school to the **National Collegiate Athletic Association (NCAA)** Division II National Championship in 1964 and 1965. He was selected by the **Baltimore Bullets** in the 1964 **National Basketball Association (NBA) draft** but returned to school and was again chosen by the Bullets in the 1965 NBA draft.

The six-foot, five-inch **guard** played with the Bullets in the 1965–1966 season and was selected by the **Chicago Bulls** in the expansion **draft** and played for them from 1966–1976. His NBA career totals for 11 years are 755 regular-season games and a 14.0 points and 7.4 **rebounds** per game average. He was selected for two NBA **All-Star Games**, named to the NBA All-Defensive First Team four times, and nominated for the NBA All-Defensive Second Team twice. He **coached** the Bulls from 1979–1982 and has been coach of the **Utah Jazz** from 1988–2010. He has coached the same team for more consecutive years than anyone in NBA history. In 2009, he was enshrined in the **Naismith Memorial Basketball Hall of Fame** in the category of coach.

SMALL FORWARD. The "small" **forward** is one of the five **basketball** positions. It is sometimes referred to as the "3" position. This designation comes from **coaches** numbering the five positions on a play chart. The name "small" forward is a misnomer, since players at this position tend to be among the taller players on the team but are usually not as heavy as **power forwards** or **centers**. Small forwards are usually primarily responsible for shooting from medium range. Some have developed excellent **three-point** shots and will shoot from outside as well. The designation "small forward" is a relatively new one and dates back to the mid-1970s.

SMITH, DEAN EDWARDS. B. 28 February 1931, Emporia, Kansas. Dean Smith attended Topeka High School in Topeka, Kansas, and the **University of Kansas**. In high school, although only five-feet, 10-inches tall, he was a football quarterback, baseball catcher, and **guard** in **basketball**. He received an academic scholarship to Kansas and played basketball there under **coach Forrest "Phog" Allen**. Although only a substitute player, he was a member of the 1952 **National Collegiate Athletic Association (NCAA)** National Championship team and 1953 NCAA national runner-up team. He graduated in 1953 with bachelor's degrees in mathematics and physical education.

Smith's major contribution to basketball was as a coach. From 1954–1958, he was in the **U.S.** Air Force and, in 1957, was assigned as assistant basketball coach at the then new Air Force Academy. In 1959, he became assistant coach at the **University of North Carolina**, and in 1962, he was named its head coach, a position he held for the next 36 years. His record when he retired was 879–254, which at that time was the most wins for an NCAA Division I college basketball coach. His teams reached the NCAA Championship **Final Four** 11 times, winning the tournament twice and finishing second three times. His 1971 team was the **National Invitation Tournament** champion. From 1970 through his final season in 1997, Smith's North Carolina teams won at least 20 games in each season, an unprecedented feat. In 13 consecutive years, from 1981–1993, his teams reached at least round 16 in the NCAA National Championship tournament.

In addition to being an extremely successful coach, Smith is most proud of the fact that more than 95 percent of his players graduated. He developed the "four corners offense," a strategy originally designed by coach **John McClendon** to protect a lead in close games. Smith's successful use of this tactic eventually led to the NCAA adopting a **shot clock**. In 1976, he coached the **gold medal**-winning **U.S. Olympic** team. He was enshrined in the **Naismith Memorial**

Basketball Hall of Fame in 1982 as coach. The basketball arena at North Carolina, built in 1986, has been named the Dean Smith Center.

SOUTHERN CALIFORNIA, UNIVERSITY OF (USC). *See* UNIVERSITY OF SOUTHERN CALIFORNIA (USC).

SOVIET UNION. *See* UNION OF SOVIET SOCIALIST REPUBLICS (USSR).

SPAIN. Spain joined the **Fédération Internationale de Basketball (FIBA)** in 1934 and is a member in the FIBA Europe zone. The men's team competed in 10 **Olympic** tournaments and won the **silver medal** in 1984 and 2008. The great "Epi," Juan Antonio San Epifanio, appeared in four Olympic tournaments from 1980–1992. Spanish Olympians who played in three Olympic Games are Francisco Buscató, Juan Antonio Corbalán, Jorge Garbajosa, Andrés Jiménez, Carlos Jiménez, José Luis Llorente, Josep María Margall, Juan Carlos Navarro, and Ignacio "Nacho" Solozábal. In the FIBA **World Championships**, Spain competed 10 times and won the tournament in 2006. In the FIBA European Championships, they entered 26 times and finished second six times and third twice.

The women's team competed in three Olympic tournaments and finished fifth in 1992, sixth in 2004, and tied for fifth in 2008. In the World Championships, they competed four times and finished fifth in 1998 and 2002 as their best effort. In the FIBA European Championships, they entered 14 times and won the tournament in 1993, finished second in 2007, and placed third three times.

There have been nine players from Spain in the **National Basketball Association (NBA)**, including seven members of the 2008 Olympic team: José Calderón, Rudy Fernández, Jorge Garbajosa, brothers Marc and **Pau Gasol**, Raúl López, Fernando Martín, Juan Carlos Navarro, and Sergio Rodríguez. In addition, two Americans who played in the NBA, Wally Szczerbiak and Wallace Bryant, were born in Spain but raised in the **United States**. Roberto Dueñas was drafted by the **Chicago Bulls** in 1997 NBA **draft**, José Antonio Montero was drafted in 1987 by the **Atlanta Hawks**, and Ricky Rubio was drafted by the **Minnesota Timberwolves** and Sergio Llull by Denver in the 2009 draft but all four players preferred to remain in Spain. Americans Wayne Brabender and Clifford Luyk were also NBA draftees but chose to play in Spain, becoming Spanish citizens and Spanish Olympians. The **Women's National Basketball Association** has seen eight Spanish players, including Elisa Aguilar, Elisabeth Cebrián, Marta Fernández, Marina Ferragut, Begoña Garcia, Núria Martinez, Isabel Sánchez, and Amaya Valdemoro.

SPIRITS OF ST. LOUIS. The Spirits of St. Louis were a team in the **American Basketball Association (ABA)**. They began play in 1967 as the Houston Mavericks and after two years in Houston, Texas, became the Carolina Cougars, a regional franchise playing in four cities in North Carolina. They moved to St. Louis, Missouri, in 1974 and played there until 1976. In nine ABA seasons, the franchise overall record was 334–410.

Houston Mavericks. On 2 February 1967, William Whitmore, Charles Frazier, and former National Football League player Cloyce Box purchased a franchise in the newly created ABA and became charter members. Home games were played at the 8,925-seat Sam Houston Coliseum. Virtually none of the 14 players who played for Houston that season had previous **National Basketball Association (NBA)** experience. Only one of them played in the ABA past the 1968–1969 season and, for eight of them, the 1967–1968 season with the Mavericks was their only season of major league professional basketball in the **United States**. The team had Hal Hale, Darrell Hardy, Art Becker, Wil Frazier, Joe Hamood, Leary Lentz, DeWitt Menyard, Jerry Pettway, and Willie Somerset. The owners gave up on the team during its second season, and the league assumed ownership, finally selling the team to a group from North Carolina headed by James C. Gardner. Attendance during their two years in the league was abysmal, and after the team was sold, published attendance figures were no longer padded. On 2 April 1969, in a rescheduled game with the New York Nets, they drew exactly 89 spectators. The team moved to North Carolina and was renamed the Carolina Cougars.

Carolina Cougars. The Carolina Cougars was organized as a regional franchise with home games scheduled for four cities in North Carolina, including Charlotte, Greensboro, Raleigh, and Winston-Salem. The team drastically changed their roster of players, with only Bob Verga and Hank Whitney remaining from the previous year's Houston team. Bill Bunting, Calvin Fowler, Steve Kramer, Gene Littles, Randy Mahaffey, Larry Miller, Doug Moe, and Rich Niemann were added, most of whom had played college **basketball** in North Carolina. On 18 March 1972, Miller scored a league-record 67 points in one game. In the 1972–1973 season, ex-ABA player and future Hall-of-Fame **coach Larry Brown** began his coaching career with them. **Billy Cunningham** and Joe Caldwell moved from the NBA to join the team. In July 1974, Todd Munchak, owner of the Cougars, sold the team to four New York businessmen, who moved the team to St. Louis, Missouri.

Spirits of St. Louis. Home games were played at the 18,000-seat St. Louis Arena, also known as the Checkerdome. Collegian Marvin Barnes was signed to a $2 million contract, and the team acquired Gus Gerard, Steve Jones, Freddie Lewis, and Maurice Lucas. In November 1975, a possible merger with the failing **Utah Stars** was discussed, but it was not pursued. When the Stars were disbanded, the Spirits acquired Ron Boone, Randy Denton, Steve Green, and **Moses Malone**. St. Louis was one of seven franchises that survived the 1975–1976 season. On 17 June 1976, four ABA teams joined the NBA. St. Louis was not one of them, but the team's owners did negotiate one of the most lucrative deals ever in professional sports. They received $2.2 million and a one-seventh share of all television revenue of those four teams in perpetuity. At the time, the financial profits that the NBA would reach during the coming decades were unimaginable. Since then, there have been several unsuccessful attempts to break this contract.

SPIVEY, WILLIAM EDWIN "BILL." B. 19 March 1929, Lakeland, Florida. D. 8 May 1995, Quepos, Costa Rica. Bill Spivey attended Macon Jordan High School in Warner-Robins, Georgia, and the **University of Kentucky**, where he led them to the 1951 **National Collegiate Athletic Association (NCAA)** National Championship. The seven-foot-tall **center** missed the first half of the 1951–1952 season due to an injury and then went under investigation in a point-shaving scandal and sat out the remainder of the season. He refused to testify against his teammates and was indicted for perjury but acquitted by a jury. Although one of the best **basketball** players in the country, he was banned for life by the **National Basketball Association** and never played in that league, although he maintained his innocence until his death.

In October 1952, Spivey was signed by the Elmira Colonels of the **American Basketball League (ABL)** and played two games for them, but the other teams in the league objected to him playing and he was not allowed to play any further in the ABL. In 1952–1953, he played for the barnstorming Detroit Vagabond Kings. From 1953–1955, he played for the **Harlem Globetrotters'** opponents. In the 1955–1956 season, Spivey was signed by the Globetrotters' competition, the Harlem Magicians, to play opposite them. In 1957, he began playing in the Eastern Professional Basketball League and played in that league through the 1967–1968 season, averaging 35.9 and 36.3 points per game in the 1958–1959 and 1959–1960 seasons, respectively. When the ABL began in 1961, he played for the Los Angeles Stars and, when that team folded midseason, he moved to the Hawaii Chiefs.

Spivey averaged 22.7 points per game in his first ABL season and 29.2 points in the abbreviated second season. After his basketball career was over, he had various jobs. He ran a bar in Lexington, Kentucky, and sold insurance and real estate, but for most of his life he was extremely bitter over his missed opportunity.

SPORTS CLUBS. Throughout most countries outside of North America, **basketball** players learn the game by participating in sports clubs rather than through high school and college teams. Clubs have various junior and senior levels and play interclub matches in league formats. Most clubs usually sponsor professional teams as well. Competition is contested within nations in national leagues and also between clubs from various nations in such leagues as the Euroleague, a European equivalent of the **National Basketball Association**. Some of the best known sports clubs include Galatasaray, Fenerbahçe, and Efes Pilsen in Turkey; Maccabi Tel Aviv in Israel; Real Madrid and FC Barcelona in **Spain**; Bourges in **France**; Žalgiris Kaunas in **Lithuania**; Panathinaikos and Olimpiakos in **Greece**; CSKA Moscow and Spartak Moscow in **Russia**; KK (formerly Jugoplastika) Split in **Croatia**; Bayer Leverkusen and Alba Berlin in **Germany**; Cimberio (formerly Ignis), Varese, and Benetton Treviso in **Italy**; TTT Riga in Latvia; and Boca Juniors in **Argentina**.

ST. JOHN'S UNIVERSITY. St. John's University in Jamaica, Queens, New York, began its men's **basketball** program in 1907. Home games since 1961 have been played at the 6,008-seat Alumni Hall (renamed Carnesecca Arena in 2004) and also at **Madison Square Garden**. Prior to 1961, home games were played at DeGray Gymnasium and Madison Square Garden. On 19 January 1931, St. John's played in the first college game in the Garden.

The most accomplished **coaches** in the school's history have been **Lou Carnesecca**, James "Buck" Freeman, **Joe Lapchick**, and Frank McGuire. The school's greatest success in postseason play occurred in the **National Invitation Tournament (NIT)**, when the NIT was still a major tournament. St. John's won the tournament four times and was second three times, third three times, and fourth twice. After 1970, when the tournament was a much lesser event, they won the NIT twice and finished fourth twice.

In 1952, the Redmen reached the **National Collegiate Athletic Association (NCAA)** final game but lost to the **University of Kansas**. In 1985, they also reached the **Final Four** but lost in the semifinals. In August 1994, the school changed their nickname from Redmen to Red Storm in line with the NCAA's requirement for political correctness. The best players in school history include Harry Boykoff, Lloyd "Sonny" Dove, Dick Duckett, Leroy Ellis, Jack "Dutch" Garfinkel, Mark Jackson, Tony Jackson, Andrew "Fuzzy" Levane, Kevin Loughery, **Al** and **Dick McGuire**, Jack McMahon, **Chris Mullin**, Billy Paultz, and **Max Zaslofsky**.

ST. LOUIS BOMBERS. The St. Louis Bombers were a charter member of the **Basketball Association of America** in 1946. Home games were played at the 12,000-seat St. Louis Arena. Among their most notable players were Bob Doll, Johnny Logan, **Ed Macauley**, Don Martin, Ariel Maughan, George Munroe, Estes "Easy" Parham, Don Putnam, Ephraim "Red" Rocha, Gifford Roux, and Belus Smawley. Their best season was 1947–1948, when they finished first in the Western Division with a record of 29–19 but were defeated in their first playoff series. In four seasons in the league, they compiled a record of 122–115. On 22 April 1950, they disbanded.

ST. LOUIS HAWKS. *See* ATLANTA HAWKS.

STALEY, DAWN MICHELLE. B. 4 May 1970, Philadelphia, Pennsylvania. Dawn Staley attended Dobbins Tech High School in Philadelphia and the **University of Virginia**, where she led her team to the **National Collegiate Athletic Association (NCAA)** finals in 1990, 1991, and 1992. In 1991, they lost the championship game to the **University of Tennessee** in **overtime**. In 1990 and 1992, they were defeated in the semifinal round.

Staley was selected for the 1996, 2000, and 2004 **U.S. Olympic basketball** teams. The five-foot. six-inch **guard** appeared in all 24 games and scored nearly the same amount of points in each Olympic tournament, 33 in 1996, 32 in 2000, and 33 in 2004, for a 4.1 points per game average and three **gold medals**. In the 2004 Olympic Games, she was the flag bearer for the U.S. team at the Opening Ceremonies. In 2008, she was assistant **coach** for the U.S. Olympic team. She also played for the U.S. national team at the 1994 Goodwill Games, won a gold medal, and was named Most Outstanding Player of the tournament. She won a **bronze medal** and two gold medals at the 1994, 1998, and 2002 **World Championships** and was selected for the 1995 Pan American Games team that did not compete due to insufficient entries.

Staley played professionally in **France, Italy, Brazil**, and **Spain** and was part of the **American Basketball League** from 1996–1998 with Richmond and Philadelphia. In 263 regular-season **Women's National Basketball Association** games from 1999–2006 with Charlotte and Houston, she averaged 8.5 points per game. After retiring from active play, she was head coach at **Temple University** from 2000–2008. In 2008, she became head coach at the University of South Carolina.

STANFORD UNIVERSITY. Stanford University in Palo Alto, California, began its men's **basketball** program in 1913. Home games since 1969 have been played at the 7,329-seat Roscoe Maples Pavilion. The most accomplished **coaches** in the school's history have been John W. Bunn, Everett Dean, and Mike Montgomery. Former Stanford player Howie Dallmar coached the longest, from 1955–1975, but had a losing record. In 1942, the school won the **National Collegiate Athletic Association (NCAA)** Championship, when they defeated Dartmouth College. This was their only appearance in the

NCAA **Final Four**, although they had strong basketball teams during the 1930s prior to the inception of the NCAA tournament. In 1937–1938, led by **Angelo "Hank" Luisetti**, they won 25 of 27 games and were unofficially recognized as the top intercollegiate team in the country. In one game, Luisetti scored 50 points, a remarkable feat for that era and still the school record.

The team's nickname was originally the Indians, but when the NCAA made the move toward political correctness they became known as "the Cardinal," singular in reference to the team colors. The best players in school history include the Collins **twins**, Jarron and Jason; Howie Dallmar; Adam Keefe; the Lopez twins, Brook and Robin; Brevin Knight; Angelo "Hank" Luisetti; Mark Madsen; Paul Neumann; **Jim Pollard**; and **George Yardley**.

The women's basketball program began in 1974. The most notable coach has been Tara VanDerveer (605–142 from 1985–2010). VanDerveer coached the **U.S.** national team from 1995–1996. During her absence, assistant coaches Amy Tucker and Marianne Stanley ran the team and compiled a 29–3 record. They reached the NCAA Final Four nine times, winning the national title in 1990 and 1992 and being runners-up in 2008 and 2010. The best players in school history include Jennifer Azzi, Kristin Folkl, Sonja Henning, Carolyn Moos, Vanessa Nygaard, Kate Paye, Nicole Powell, Olympia Scott, Kate Starbird, Katy Steding, Val Whiting, Jamila Wideman, and Candice Wiggins.

STANKOVIĆ, BORISLAV "BORIS." B. 9 July 1925, Bihać, Bosnia and Herzegovina, **Yugoslavia**. Boris Stanković graduated from the University of Belgrade with a degree in veterinary medicine and worked as a veterinary inspector for meat control in Belgrade. He played **basketball** for Red Star Belgrade and was a member of the Yugoslavian league championship team in 1946 and 1947. He was also a member of the Yugoslavian national team and played in the first **World Championships** tournament in 1950 and the 1953 European Championship.

Stanković **coached** OKK Beograd from 1953–1963 and again in 1965 and led them to four Yugoslavian league championships. From 1966–1969, he coached Cantù in **Italy** and won the 1968 Italian league championship. From 1956–1966, he was secretary general of the Yugoslav Basketball Federation. He has been a member of the Yugoslavian **Olympic** Committee since 1988 and the International Olympic Committee from 1988–2006 and was secretary general of the **Fédération Internationale de Basketball (FIBA)** from 1976–2002, after having had lesser positions with the FIBA since 1960. He has worked with **National Basketball Association (NBA)** commissioner **David Stern** to help bring NBA teams to Europe for preseason games.

Stanković was enshrined in the **Naismith Memorial Basketball Hall of Fame** in 1991 in the category of contributor and in 2007 was a member of the inaugural class of the FIBA Hall of Fame. In 2005, the FIBA introduced the Stanković Continental Champions' Cup, an international tournament for men's national teams.

STEAL. A steal in basketball terminology is a statistical category used to record the interception of opponents' passes or simply legally taking the ball from an opponent's hands while he is holding or **dribbling** it. The **National Basketball Association (NBA)** has only been recording steals since the 1973–1974 season, although the **American Basketball Association** began the previous season. Ironically, the player who had the most steals that first NBA season was Larry Steele of the **Portland Trail Blazers**. The single game record is 11, held by Larry Kenon of San Antonio in 1976, and Kendall Gill of New Jersey in 1999. **John Stockton** holds the NBA career record, with 3,265, from 1984–2003. The most steals in an NBA season is 301 by Alvin Robertson of San Antonio in 1985–1986.

STERN, DAVID JOEL. B. 22 September 1942, New York, New York. David Stern was raised in Teaneck, New Jersey, and attended Teaneck High School, Rutgers University, and Columbia Law School. Upon graduation in 1966, he was admitted to the bar in New York. He joined the law firm of Proskauer, Rose, Goetz, and Mendelsohn, which at that time represented the **National Basketball Association (NBA)** as outside counsel. From 1974–1978, Stern worked on cases involving the NBA, including the **Oscar Robertson** case, settling a conflict between the league and its players. He also worked on the merger agreement between the **American Basketball Association** and NBA. In 1978, he was hired by the league as its general counsel.

In 1980, Stern was named executive vice president of the NBA, and on 1 February 1984, he became the NBA's fourth commissioner. During his administration, he has made the league into a worldwide marketer, seen it expand from 23 to 30 franchises, promoted international preseason play, and also has had regular-season games played in **Japan** and **China**. NBA offices have been established throughout the world to help promote the league. The **Women's National Basketball Association** and **NBA Development League** have been created, and the NBA has become a multibillion-dollar operation. He has accomplished this with a league in which more than 85 percent of the players are African American in a society that is more than 85 percent non-African American.

Stern solved several critical problems during this time, one during the 1980s when a large number of players were involved with drugs. A second was in 2007, when an NBA official was accused of gambling. A third occurred in 1999, when the NBA Players Union and NBA owners could not reach agreement and the first half of the season was canceled. In each of these situations, there was a minimum of backlash, and the league remains as popular as ever, with most games being sold out even though the price of tickets and players' salaries have risen astronomically.

STOCKTON, JOHN HOUSTON. B. 26 March 1962, Spokane, Washington. John Stockton attended Gonzaga Preparatory School in Spokane and Gonzaga University. Drafted by the **Utah Jazz** in the 1984 **National Basketball Association (NBA) draft**, he played for them from 1984–2003 and is the only player to play 19 seasons with only one team in the NBA. A member of the 1992 **U.S. Olympic basketball Dream Team**, he was injured for much of the tournament and only appeared in four games for the **gold medal**-winning U.S. team. He was one of five Dream Team players who also won a second gold medal in 1996. That year, he was named one of the 50 Greatest Players in NBA History.

In his 19-year NBA career, Stockton played in 1,504 of a scheduled 1,526 regular-season games, playing every game in 17 of his 19 seasons, and averaged 13.1 points and 10.5 **assists** per game. The six-foot, one-inch **guard** was selected for 10 NBA **All-Star Games** and was the co-Most valuable Player in the 1993 game, along with Utah teammate **Karl Malone**. He also played in the playoffs in every one of his 19 seasons, appearing in 182 playoff games and averaging 13.4 points and 10.1 assists per game. The Jazz reached the NBA Finals twice but lost to the **Chicago Bulls** both times.

Stockton led the league in assists nine times and holds the career record for assists with 15,806, almost 5,000 more than second-place **Jason Kidd**. Stockton also has the career record for steals, with 3,265, more than 700 more than second-place **Michael Jordan**. He is third on the career list of regular-season games played and fourth in **minutes** played. Despite these numbers, he was only named to the All-NBA First Team twice, in 1994 and 1995, both seasons during Michael Jordan's first retirement. He was selected for the All-NBA Second Team six times and All-NBA Third Team three times and was named to the NBA All-Defensive Second Team five times. In 2009, he was enshrined in the **Naismith Memorial Basketball Hall of Fame**.

STOJAKOVIĆ, PREDRAG "PEJA." B. 9 June 1977, Belgrade, Serbia, **Yugoslavia**. Peja Stojaković began his professional career in **Greece** with the PAOK team in 1995. In three seasons in the Greek league, he averaged 20.0 points per game. He was selected in the 1996 **National Basketball Association (NBA) draft** by the **Sacramento Kings** but remained in Greece for two more seasons.

The six-foot, nine-inch **forward** played for the Kings from 1998–2006. He was with the **Indiana Pacers** in 2006 and the **New Orleans Hornets** from 2006–2010. Stojaković was selected for three NBA **All-Star Games** and was named to the All-NBA Second Team in 2004. In 2002 and 2003, he won the **three-point** shootout competition at the All-Star weekend. He is one of the all-time NBA career leaders in **free throw** percentage, with an average of .895 after his first 12 seasons in the league. He played for the Yugoslavian national team in the 2000 **Olympic Games** and won **gold medals** with them in the 2001 European Championships and the 2002 **World Championships** and a **bronze medal** at the 1999 European Championship.

STOKES, MAURICE "MO." B. 17 June 1933, Rankin, Pennsylvania. D. 6 April 1970, Cincinnati, Ohio. Maurice Stokes attended Westinghouse High School in Pittsburgh, Pennsylvania, and St.

Francis College in Loretto, Pennsylvania. In college, he averaged 22.4 points and 17.8 **rebounds** per game. The six-foot, seven-inch, 235-pound **forward-center** was selected by the Rochester Royals in the 1955 **National Basketball Association (NBA) draft** and played with them from 1955–1958, in Rochester for his first two years and Cincinnati for the third.

All three years were fairly consistent, with averages ranging from 15.6 to 16.9 points and 16.3 to 18.1 rebounds per game. In his second year, Stokes recorded a league record 1,256 rebounds. His NBA career totals for three years are 202 regular-season games and a 16.4 points and 17.3 rebounds per game average. He was named NBA Rookie of the Year in 1956, selected for the NBA **All-Star Game** in each of his three seasons, and named to the All-NBA Second Team all three years.

In the last game of the regular-season, on 12 March 1958, while driving to the **basket**, Stokes was knocked to the floor, hit his head, and became unconscious. He was revived and returned to the game. Three days later, after the team's first playoff game, he took ill on the team's flight home and fell into a coma. He was hospitalized with a brain injury and spent the remainder of his life attempting to regain his abilities. Through hard work he eventually was able to speak some and had limited use of his hands and arms. Royals' teammate **Jack Twyman** became his legal guardian and spent much of the next 12 years involved in fund-raising activities to help pay for Stokes' care. Stokes was enshrined in the **Naismith Memorial Basketball Hall of Fame** in 2004. Their story was made into the 1973 movie *Maurie*.

STROM, EARL. B. 15 December 1927, Pottstown, Pennsylvania. D. 10 July 1994, Pottstown, Pennsylvania. Earl Storm attended Pottstown High School and played football, baseball, and **basketball**. After graduation, he joined the **U.S.** Coast Guard. He enrolled at Pierce Junior College after his discharge and graduated in 1951. He became a high school and college **referee** and worked for General Electric. In 1957, he was hired by the **National Basketball Association (NBA)**, and he worked his final NBA game in 1990. In 1961, he and **Mendy Rudolph** worked the entire Boston-St. Louis NBA Championship series. He was named NBA crew chief for 1967 and

1968. In 1969, Strom and three other NBA officials left to join the **American Basketball Association (ABA)** but returned to the NBA for the 1973–1974 season. As a result of his defection, the NBA significantly increased referee salaries and benefits.

During his career, Strom officiated more than 2,600 professional basketball games, including seven NBA **All-Star Games** and 29 NBA and ABA Finals. He was known for his neutrality in a sport where officials often favored the home team. A study showed that the visiting team won 43 percent of the games Strom worked, compared with 30 percent for games worked by other NBA officials. **Boston Celtics coach Red Auerbach** said that Strom "was probably the best official in the NBA." In retirement, Strom worked as a color commentator for basketball games, wrote a column for a local newspaper, and coauthored his biography. He was enshrined in the **Naismith Memorial Basketball Hall of Fame** in 1995.

SYRACUSE NATIONALS. *See* PHILADELPHIA 76ERS.

SYRACUSE UNIVERSITY. Syracuse University in New York began its men's **basketball** program in 1898. Home games since 1980 have been played at the Carrier Dome, one of the first multipurpose domed stadiums and the largest on-campus basketball arena in the country, with a capacity for basketball of 33,000. Home games were played at the Onondaga War Memorial Auditorium and at the Manley Field House prior to 1980. The most accomplished **coach** in the school's history has been Hall of Famer Jim Boeheim, who played at Syracuse from 1962–1966, began coaching at Syracuse in 1976, and was still active in 2010. His teams won 829 games and lost only 293 from 1976–2010. Other noteworthy coaches were Lew Andreas and Roy Danforth.

In 2003, the Orangemen won the **National Collegiate Athletic Association (NCAA)** Championship, when they defeated the **University of Kansas** in the final. In 1987, they lost the NCAA Final by one point to **Indiana University**, and in 1996, they reached the final game but lost to the **University of Kentucky**. Among the best players for the 'Cuse have been Carmelo Anthony, although he only played one season but led them to their only championship; **Dave Bing**; Roosevelt Bouie; Sherman Douglas; Billy Gabor; Vic Hanson;

Ed Miller; Louis Orr; Billy Owens; Leo Rautins; Danny Schayes; Rony Seikaly; Wilmeth Sidat-Singh; John Wallace; and Dwayne Washington.

– T –

TATUM, REECE "GOOSE." B. 3 May 1921, Calion, Arkansas. D. 18 January 1967, El Paso, Texas. The six-foot, six-inch Goose Tatum is best known for his years with the **Harlem Globetrotters** from 1942–1955 as their **center** and chief showman. He was also a good baseball player and played first base and outfield in the Negro Leagues from 1941–1949. His huge hands enabled him to easily palm the **basketball** and aided him in many of the tricks he performed. His favorite shot was a **hook shot.** As star of the Trotters, he was called the "Clown Prince of Basketball" and played for them at a time when the team was transitioning from a talented team that played legitimate basketball to a team that played purely to entertain the audience. He would occasionally not show up for a game and, in March 1955, was suspended by Trotters owner **Abe Saperstein.** One month later, Tatum was released.

Goose and ex-Trotter **dribbling** star **Marques Haynes** then formed the Harlem Magicians, a traveling basketball team that played the same entertaining style as the Globetrotters. In the 1960s, Tatum left the Magicians and formed the Harlem Road Kings featuring his son, Goose Tatum Jr. Tatum Sr. played with them into the mid-1960s until he suffered a liver ailment and retired.

TAURASI, DIANA LURENA. B. 11 June 1982, Glendale, California. Diana Taurasi attended Don Lugo High School in Chino, California, and won the Naismith Award as High School Player of the Year in 2000. She led the **University of Connecticut** to the **National Collegiate Athletic Association Final Four** in each of her four college years, losing in the semifinals in 2001 and winning national championships in each of the next three years. She again won the Naismith Award in 2003 and 2004 as the National College Player of the Year.

The six-foot-tall **guard** was chosen by the Phoenix Mercury as the first overall selection in the 2004 **Women's National Basketball**

Association (WNBA) draft and has played with them through 2010. In 2004, Taurasi was WNBA Rookie of the Year and in 2007 helped Phoenix win the WNBA Championship. She has been selected for the WNBA **All-Star Game** four times. On 10 August 2006, she scored a league-record 47 points in one game. In 2009, she led the WNBA in scoring, led Phoenix to the championship, and was the Most Valuable Player and Finals Most Valuable Player. She also holds the WNBA season record with 860 points in 2006 and was a member of the 2004 and 2008 **gold medal**-winning **U.S. Olympic** teams.

TECHNICAL FOUL. *See* FOUL.

TEMPLE UNIVERSITY. Temple University in Philadelphia, Pennsylvania, began its men's **basketball** program in 1894. Home games since 1997 have been played at the 10,224-seat Apollo of Temple (now known as the Peter J. Liacouras Center). Prior to 1997, home games were played at McGonigle Hall and at the **Palestra**. The most accomplished **coaches** in the school's history have been **John Chaney**, Harry Litwack, and James Usilton. In 1938, the Owls became the first **National Invitation Tournament (NIT)** champions. They also won the NIT championship in 1969. They have twice reached the **National Collegiate Athletic Association Final Four**. The best players in school history include John Baum, Meyer Bloom, Nelson Bobb, Eddie Jones, Hal Lear, Aaron McKie, Bill Mlkvy, Mark Macon, and **Guy Rodgers**.

TENNESSEE, UNIVERSITY OF. The University of Tennessee is located in Knoxville. The women's **basketball** program is the most successful in **National Collegiate Athletic Association (NCAA)** history. Tennessee began fielding a women's basketball team in 1903, although only a few games were played each year. In 1926, they dropped the sport and didn't resume until 1960, but it wasn't until 1969 that the sport became popular and national tournaments were held. Since then they have reached the NCAA **Final Four** a record 18 times. They won the tournament eight times and were second five times. They were also runners-up twice in the **Association for Intercollegiate Athletics for Women** tournament, the NCAA tournament's predecessor.

The main reason for the Lady Volunteers' success has been their **coach, Pat Head Summitt**. She played on the **U.S.** Olympic team in 1976 and has been the only head coach at Tennessee since 1974. In 2009, she became the first college basketball coach (male or female) of a four-year college to record 1,000 victories, and her record from 1974–2010 is 1,035 wins and only 196 losses. Home games since 1987 have been played at the 21,000-seat Thompson-Boling Arena. The best players for the Lady Vols include Tamika Catchings, Daedra Charles, Bridgette Gordon, Dena Head, Chamique Holdsclaw, Kara Lawson, Candace Parker, and Holly Warlick.

TERRITORIAL DRAFT. *See* DRAFT.

TEXAS, UNIVERSITY OF. The University of Texas in Austin began its men's **basketball** program in 1905. Home games since 1977 have been played at the 16,755-seat Frank Erwin Center. Prior to 1977, home games were played at Gregory Gymnasium. The most accomplished **coaches** in the school's history have been Rick Barnes, Jack Gray, and Tom Penders. The Longhorns reached the **National Collegiate Athletic Association (NCAA) Final Four** three times. The best players in school history include Jay Arnette, Kevin Durant, T. J. Ford, Royal Ivey, **Slater Martin**, Chris Mihm, Johnny Moore, Anthony Tucker, and B. J. Tyler.

The women's basketball program began in 1974. Jody Conradt compiled a record of 783–245 in 31 years at Texas from 1976–2007 and has been inducted into the **Naismith Memorial Basketball Hall of Fame**. In 1982, Texas lost to Rutgers University in the championship final game of the **Association for Intercollegiate Athletics for Women** national tournament. In 1986, Texas won the NCAA National Championship. Texas also reached the NCAA Final Four in 1987 and 2003. Among the best players at Texas have been Edna Campbell, Taj Dillard, Kamie Ethridge, Nell Fortner, Vicki Hall, Fran Harris, Angela Jackson, and Andrea Lloyd.

TEXAS AT EL PASO, UNIVERSITY OF (UTEP). *See* UNIVERSITY OF TEXAS AT EL PASO (UTEP).

TEXAS CHAPARRALS. *See* SAN ANTONIO SPURS.

TEXAS TECH UNIVERSITY. Texas Tech was founded in Lubbock in 1923 as Texas Technological College. In 1969, its name was changed to Texas Tech University. Home games since 1999 have been played at the 15,020-seat United Spirit Arena. The women's team, known as the Lady Raiders, began in 1975 and won the **National Collegiate Athletic Association (NCAA)** Championship in 1993, their only appearance in the NCAA **Final Four**. Among their most notable players are Erin Grant, Krista Kirkland-Gerlich, Reena Lynch, Sheryl Swoopes, Alicia Thompson, and Carolyn Thompson. Marsha Sharp was the **coach** from 1982–2006 and compiled a record of 572–189.

TEXAS WESTERN UNIVERSITY. Texas Western University is located in El Paso. It was renamed the University of Texas at El Paso in 1967, but it was as Texas Western University that made **basketball** history. The men's basketball program began in 1937. Home games since 1976 have been played at the 12,222-seat Don Haskins Center (formerly the Special Events Center but renamed in 1998). Prior to 1976, home games were played at Memorial Gym. The most notable **coach** in the school's history was Don Haskins (719–353 from 1961–1999). In 1966, the Miners won the **National Collegiate Athletic Association (NCAA)** Championship when they defeated the **University of Kentucky**. The game was historic in that Texas Western had a racially integrated team and started five black players, and Kentucky, which had never had a black basketball player to that date, had an all-white team. The historic game has been detailed in the 1999 book by Frank Fitzpatrick entitled *And the Walls Came Tumbling Down* and in the 2006 Hollywood film *Glory Road*.

Members of the 1966 team that played in the historic game were Jerry Armstrong, Orsten Artis, Louis Baudoin, Willie Cager, Harry Flournoy, Bobby Joe Hill, Dave Lattin, Nevil Shed, and Willie Worsley. Other notable players in school history have been **Nate Archibald**, Gus Bailey, Jim Barnes, Antonio Davis, Scott English, Greg Foster, Dick Gibbs, and Tim Hardaway. The 1966 team was enshrined in the **Naismith Memorial Basketball Hall of Fame** in 2007.

THOMAS III, ISIAH LORD "ZEKE." B. 30 April 1961, Chicago, Illinois. Isiah Thomas attended St. Joseph's High School in

Westchester, Illinois, and **Indiana University**. He was selected for the 1980 **U.S. Olympic basketball** team that did not compete due to the U.S. boycott of the Olympic Games. In 1981, he helped Indiana win the **National Collegiate Athletic Association** Championship and was named the tournament's Most Outstanding Player. The six-foot, one-inch **guard** was drafted by the **Detroit Pistons** in the 1981 **National Basketball Association (NBA) draft** and played with them from 1981–1994. In 1988, they reached the NBA Championship Finals but lost to the **Los Angeles Lakers**. The Pistons won NBA titles in 1989 and 1990.

In his 13-year NBA career, Thomas played in 979 regular-season games and averaged 19.2 points per game. Known to his teammates as Zeke, he was selected to the NBA **All-Star Game** each year in all but his final season and was twice named its Most Valuable Player. He was named to the All-NBA First Team three times and All-NBA Second Team twice. He was disappointed in not being chosen for the 1992 U.S. Olympic **Dream Team**. He was named to the 1994 **World Championships** team but was unable to play due to an injury. In 1996, he was named one of the 50 Greatest Players in NBA History.

After retiring from active play, Thomas was vice president and part owner of the **Toronto Raptors** from 1996–1998. He purchased the entire **Continental Basketball Association** in 1998, but the investment proved disastrous and the league failed. In 2000, he was enshrined in the **Naismith Memorial Basketball Hall of Fame**. That year he became **coach** of the **Indiana Pacers** and coached them for three seasons. In 2003, he became president and general manager of the **New York Knickerbockers** and from 2006–2008 was their coach. In 2009, he was hired as head coach at Florida International University.

THOMPSON, DAVID O'NEIL "SKYWALKER." B.13 July 1954, Shelby, North Carolina. David Thompson attended Crest High School in Shelby and **North Carolina State University**. He led North Carolina State to an undefeated 27–0 record in 1973 as a sophomore but, as the school was then on probation, it was not eligible for the **National Collegiate Athletic Association (NCAA)** Championship tournament. In 1974, they won the NCAA National Championship, and Thompson was the tournament's Most Outstanding Player.

Known as "Skywalker" for his outstanding leaping ability, Thompson was selected by the **Atlanta Hawks** in the 1975 **National Basketball Association (NBA) draft** as the first overall selection and was also chosen by the **Virginia Squires** in the **American Basketball Association** draft. Virginia traded his **draft rights** to the **Denver Nuggets**, and he signed with the Nuggets. The six-foot, four-inch **guard-forward** averaged 26.0 points per game that season, was named Rookie of the Year and **All-Star Game** Most Valuable Player, and helped lead the Nuggets to the ABA Championship finals, where they lost to the New York Nets. Following that season, the Nuggets joined the NBA. Thompson played in the NBA from 1976–1982 with the Nuggets, was selected for the NBA All-Star Game three times, and was voted its Most Valuable Player in 1979.

On 9 April 1978, Thompson scored 73 points in the final game of the season in an attempt to win the league's season scoring title, but later that day **George Gervin** scored 63 points to edge him out. Only **Wilt Chamberlain** and **Kobe Bryant** have ever scored more points in one NBA game. In that game, Thompson set an NBA record with 32 points in one quarter, but the record was broken by Gervin later that day, with 33. Thompson's record of 13 **field goals** in the quarter still stands, however.

In the 1981–1982 season, Thompson's performance declined due to substance abuse. He was traded to the Seattle Supersonics, was selected to the NBA All-Star Game in 1983, and concluded his NBA career in 1983–1984. In his eight years in the NBA, he played in 509 regular-season games and averaged 22.1 points per game. He was enshrined in the **Naismith Memorial Basketball Hall of Fame** in 1996. He eventually returned to college and in 2003 completed his degree in sociology.

THOMPSON, JOHN R., JR. B. 2 September 1941, Washington, D.C. John Thompson attended Archbishop Carroll High School in Washington and **Providence College**, where he led them to the 1963 **National Invitation Tournament** championship. He was selected in the 1964 **National Basketball Association (NBA) draft** by the

Boston Celtics and for two seasons was the backup **center** to **Bill Russell**. The six-foot, 10-inch Thompson only played in 74 regular-season games and averaged 3.5 points per game but was a member of two NBA Championship teams. He was selected by the **Chicago Bulls** in the expansion draft of 1966 but decided to become a **coach**.

In 1966, Thompson began his coaching career at St. Anthony's High School in Washington. From 1966–1972, his teams compiled a record of 122–28. He was hired by **Georgetown University** in 1972 and coached the Hoyas from 1972–1999, with a won–lost record of 596–239. In 1982, they reached the **National Collegiate Athletic Association (NCAA)** Championship Final game but lost. Two years later, Thompson became the first black coach to lead his team to the NCAA basketball championship, when Georgetown defeated the **University of Houston** in the final game. In 1985, Georgetown again reached the NCAA Championship final game but lost by only two points, 66–64. While at Georgetown, Thompson coached many future NBA players, including **Patrick Ewing, Allen Iverson, Alonzo Mourning**, and **Dikembe Mutombo**.

In 1988, Thompson was coach of the **U.S. Olympic** team, the last American team still composed of amateur players. They were defeated by the **Union of Soviet Socialist Republics** in the semifinal round and had to settle for the **bronze medal**. On 8 January 1999, he resigned from Georgetown and has since worked as a television analyst. In 2004, his oldest son, John Thompson III, was hired as basketball coach for Georgetown University. In 1999, John Thompson Jr. was enshrined in the **Naismith Memorial Basketball Hall of Fame** as coach.

THOMPSON, TINA MARIE. B. 10 February 1975, Los Angeles, California. Tina Thompson attended Morningside High School in Inglewood, California, and the **University of Southern California**. She was selected by the Houston Comets as the first overall choice in the inaugural **Women's National Basketball Association (WNBA) draft** in 1997. She played in the WNBA with Houston from 1997–2008 and is the only player to play in the league in each of its first 14 seasons. She was a member of the league champions in 1997, 1998, 1999, and 2000. After the Houston franchise was disbanded following the 2008 season, she played with the Los Angeles Sparks in 2009 and 2010. The six-foot, two-inch **forward** was selected for the All-WNBA First Team three times and the All-WNBA Second Team five times.

Thompson has also played overseas during the WNBA off-season in **Italy, Korea,** and **Russia**. She won **gold medals** with the 2004 and 2008 **U.S. Olympic basketball** teams, was an alternate for the 2000 U.S. Olympic team, and was selected for the team in the 1998 and 2002 **World Championships** but was unable to play due to injuries.

THREE-POINT FIELD GOAL. The three-point field goal is a relatively recent innovation in **basketball**. It was experimented with in a college game in 1945 between Columbia and Fordham on 7 February 1945. The first major league that employed it was the **American Basketball League** of 1961–1962. Any **field goal** from beyond 25 feet was rewarded with three points instead of the traditional two points. Tony Jackson of the Chicago Majors led the league with 141 in 383 attempts in 72 games and, on 14 March 1962, made a record 12 three-point field goals in one game. In the 1963–1964 season, the minor league Eastern Basketball Association adopted the rule. When the **American Basketball Association (ABA)** was established in 1967, they, too, used the three-point field goal rule. Les Selvage of Anaheim set the ABA record with 10 three-point field goals in 26 attempts on 15 February 1968. For the season, he made 147 in 461 attempts.

The **National Basketball Association (NBA)** did not adopt the rule until the 1979–1980 season, and it was seldom used for the first few years. By the mid-1990s, the three-point field goal had become an acceptable part of basketball strategy. In 1994, the NBA attempted to increase three-point field goal shooting and decreased the distance to a uniform 22 feet. This rule was used for three seasons and then changed back to the previous distance. The NBA record for three-point field goals in one game is 12, set by **Kobe Bryant** in 2003 and tied by Donyell Marshall in 2005.

College basketball first used the three-point field goal rule in 1980 in the Southern Conference. Other conferences adopted it over the next few years, and by 1986–1987, all college conferences used the rule. The **Fédération Internationale de Basketball (FIBA)** first used it in Olympic competition in 1988. FIBA uses a 20.5-foot distance, as does the **Women's National Basketball Association**. Most high schools use a 19.75-foot distance, as do the **National Collegiate Athletic Association (NCAA)** women's rules. NCAA men's rules previously used the 19.75-foot distance, but beginning with the 2008–2009 season, the distance was changed to 20.75 feet. When a player is attempting a three-point field goal, the **referee** raises one hand. If the shot is successful, the referee raises both hands.

THURMOND, NATHANIEL "NATE." B. 25 July 1941, Akron, Ohio. Nate Thurmond attended Central Hower High School in Akron and Bowling Green University. He was selected by the San Francisco Warriors in the 1963 **National Basketball Association (NBA) draft** and played from 1963–1977 for the Warriors, **Chicago Bulls**, and **Cleveland Cavaliers**. Thurmond was one of the few players who could guard **Wilt Chamberlain** and play him on an even basis. Thurmond was named to the NBA All-Defensive First Team twice and NBA All-Defensive Second Team three times. He was one of the best rebounders in league history and, on 9 November 1965, had 42 **rebounds** in a game. Only **Bill Russell** and Chamberlain have ever recorded more rebounds in one game. Thurmond still holds the NBA record for rebounds in one quarter, with 18, in 1965. He was selected for the NBA **All-Star Game** seven times. On 18 October 1974, while playing for the Bulls, he recorded the first **quadruple-double** in NBA history, with 22 points, 14 rebounds, 13 **assists**, and 12 **blocks**. There have still only been four quadruple-doubles in NBA history.

Thurmond's NBA career totals for 14 years are 964 regular-season games and a 15.0 points and 15.0 rebounds per game average. His best season was 1967–1968, when he averaged 20.5 points per game and 22.0 rebounds per game. Only Chamberlain ever averaged more than 20 rebounds and 20 points per game in an NBA season. After retiring from **basketball**, Thurmond opened a San Francisco restaurant called Big Nate's BBQ. In 1985, he was enshrined in the **Naismith Memorial Basketball Hall of Fame** and in 1996 was named as one of the 50 Greatest Players in NBA History.

TOMJANOVICH, RUDOLPH "RUDY." B. 24 November 1948, Hamtramck, Michigan. Rudy Tomjanovich attended Hamtramck High School and the **University of Michigan**. He was selected by the San Diego Rockets in the 1970 **National Basketball Association (NBA) draft** and played his entire professional career with the Rockets, who moved to Houston following the 1970–1971 season. The six-foot, eight-inch **forward**'s best year was 1973–1974, when he averaged 24.5 points and 9.0 **rebounds** per game. He was selected for the NBA **All-Star Game** five times.

On 9 December 1977, his career nearly ended. In a game between the Rockets and **Los Angeles Lakers**, a fight broke out, and Tomjanovich, in attempting to act as a peacemaker, ran across the court toward a Laker player. Kermit Washington thought that Tomjanovich was attempting to fight with him and turned and hit Tomjanovich in the face with a punch as Tomjanovich ran directly into his fist. Because of the momentum, Tomjanovich suffered multiple severe facial injuries, had shattered facial bones, was placed in intensive care, and required multiple operations. He was able to return to play the following year and played three more seasons. Washington, a generally mild-mannered person, played several more years in the NBA but was never the same. A full account of the incident and its aftermath is the subject of John Feinstein's 2002 book *The Punch*.

Tomjanovich's NBA career totals for 11 years from 1970–1981 are 768 regular-season games and a 17.4 points and 8.1 rebounds per game average. After retiring from active play in 1981, he was hired by the Rockets as a scout, promoted to assistant **coach** in 1983, and advanced to head coach in 1992. As head coach, he led the Rockets to NBA Championships in 1994 and 1995. He was the coach of the 1998 **U.S. World Championships** team and led them to the **bronze medal**. He then coached the 2000 U.S. **Olympic** team to a **gold medal**. He resigned from the Rockets after the 2002–2003 season after being diagnosed with bladder cancer. Hired by the Los Angeles Lakers as head coach in 2004, he resigned in February 2005 but remained as a consultant.

TORONTO HUSKIES. The Toronto Huskies were a **basketball** team in the **Basketball Association of America** in the 1946–1947 season. They had the honor of playing the very first game in league history on 1 November 1946, against the **New York Knickerbockers** at Maple Leaf Gardens in Toronto, Ontario, **Canada**, before a crowd of 7,090. The Knicks won that game 68–66.

The Huskies started the season with Ed Sadowski as player-**coach**, but after only 12 games he was dissatisfied with the team's management as well as his dual roles and was traded to the Cleveland Rebels. The team had two Canadians, Hank Biasatti and Italian-born Canadian Gino Sovran, but neither distinguished himself and both were released after each playing in only six games. The team's personnel changed frequently throughout the season, and of the 11 men who played in the initial game, only Dick Fitzgerald, Mike McCarron, and Harry Miller were with the team at the end of the season. The Huskies employed 20 players and four coaches in compiling a record of 22–38, good for a last-place tie in the league's Eastern Division. On 27 July 1947, the team disbanded.

TORONTO RAPTORS. The Toronto Raptors are a team in the **National Basketball Association**. They were awarded an expansion franchise on 30 September 1993, and joined the league in 1995. Home games were played at the 28,808-seat Sky Dome from 1995–1999 and the 19,800-seat Air **Canada** Centre from 1999 to date. They have also played some home games at Maple Leaf Gardens in Toronto and Copps Coliseum in Hamilton, Ontario. Among their most notable players have been Andrea Bargnani, Chris Bosh, José Calderón, **Vince Carter**, Doug Christie, Antonio Davis, **Tracy McGrady**, Anthony Parker, Morris Peterson, Jalen Rose, Damon Stoudamire, and Alvin Williams. Their best season was 2000–2001, when they finished in second place in their division, with a record of 47–35. In their first 15 years, the team has won 502 games and lost 696 in the regular season.

TOSHEFF, WILLIAM MARK "BILL," "TOSH." B. 2 June 1926, Gary, Indiana. Bill Tosheff attended Froebel High School in Gary and enlisted in the **U.S.** Army Air Corps and was a member of a B-17 bomber crew. After his discharge from the service, he enrolled at **Indiana University** and played **basketball** there from 1947–1951. He also played baseball and football at Indiana and six years of minor league baseball with Indianapolis in Class AAA, among other teams. The six-foot, one-inch **guard** was selected by the **Indianapolis Olympians** in the 1951 **National Basketball Association (NBA) draft** and played from 1951–1953 with them. He was Co-Rookie of the Year in 1952, with Mel Hutchins. The Indianapolis franchise disbanded following the 1952–1953 season, and Tosheff went to the Milwaukee Hawks in the dispersal draft.

Tosheff retired after one season with the Hawks, with NBA career totals for three years of 203 regular-season games and a 9.2 points per game average. After retiring from active play, he worked as a general contractor. He started the Pre–1965 NBA Players Association and spent about 20 years fighting with the NBA in an attempt to obtain pensions for former players, especially those whose careers were interrupted by military service. In 1998, he even went before Congress in his quest. In 2007, his efforts were finally acknowledged and rewarded, but by that time nearly half of the players he had been fighting for were deceased.

TRAVELING. Traveling is the word used in **basketball** to describe a type of rules infraction. It occurs when the player in possession of the ball illegally moves his feet. This could be because he takes more than the allowable number of steps without **dribbling** the ball. It is also called when a stationary player moves his **pivot** foot or when a player jumps into the air with the ball and lands on the ground still in possession without shooting or passing the ball. The penalty for traveling is loss of possession, with the ball given to the opposing team out-of-bounds. Traveling is recorded as a **turnover**.

TRI-CITIES BLACKHAWKS. *See* ATLANTA HAWKS.

TRIPLE-DOUBLE. A triple-double is a relatively new term in **basketball** and refers to the feat of a player who has compiled double digits (10 or more) in three positive statistical categories in one game, usually points, **rebounds**, and **assists**, but occasionally points, rebounds, and **blocks**, or points, assists, and **steals**. **Oscar Robertson**, with 181 in the regular season and eight more in playoffs, and **Earvin "Magic" Johnson**, with 30 in playoffs and 138 in regular-season play, have compiled the most in **National Basketball Association (NBA)** play, although the term was not in popular use when Robertson played.

A triple-double in the 48-minute-long NBA games is not uncommon. In 40-minute **Fédération Internationale de Basketball, Women's National Basketball Association**, and college games, it is much less common, and there have only been two in **Olympic Games** competition. **Aleksandr Belov** of the **Union of Soviet Socialist Republics** scored 23 points and had 14 rebounds and 10 assists on 27 July 1976, in a game with **Canada**. In women's Olympic play, **Korean** Joo-Weon Chun recorded 10 rebounds, 11 assists, and 10 points against **Cuba** on 24 September 2000. *See also* QUADRUPLE-DOUBLE.

TÜRKOĞLU, HIDAYET "HEDO." B. 19 March 1979, Istanbul, Turkey. Hedo Türkoğlu is one of only four **National Basketball Association (NBA)** players to have been born in Turkey. He began playing **basketball** for the Efes Pilsen club in Istanbul. He was with them from 1996–2000 and was chosen in the 2000 **NBA draft** by the **Sacramento Kings**. The six-foot, eight-inch **guard-forward** played for the Kings, **San Antonio Spurs**, and **Orlando Magic** from 2000–2009. Following the 2008–2009 season, in which the Magic reached the NBA Finals, he was traded to the **Toronto Raptors**. On 14 July 2010, he was traded to the Phoenix Suns.

In 2008, Türkoğlu was named the NBA's Most Improved Player, after raising his scoring average from 13.3 points per game in 2006–2007 to 19.7 points per game in 2007–2008. In his first 10 NBA seasons, he appeared in 752 games and averaged 12.2 points per game. He played for Turkey in six European Championships and the 2002 and 2010 **World Championships** and won a **silver medals** with them in the 2001 European Championship and 2010 World Championship.

TURNOVER. A turnover in **basketball** is a statistical category used when the team in possession of the ball loses it without attempting a shot at the basket. It can result from an errant pass that goes out of bounds, a pass intercepted by the opposition (usually referred to as a **steal**), a violation such as **traveling, palming**, or a **double dribble**, or an offensive **foul**. Official recording of turnovers only began in the 1970s. The **American Basketball Association** kept track of turnovers beginning with their first season in 1967–1968, although they called them "errors." The **National Basketball Association (NBA)** did not record individual turnovers until the 1977–1978 season, although they started recording team turnovers in 1970–1971.

The NBA record for most turnovers in a game is 14, held by John Drew and **Jason Kidd**. The individual season high for turnovers is 366, by **Artis Gilmore** in 1977–1978. The team record for most turnovers in a game is 45, by the San Francisco Warriors, on 9 March 1971, while the fewest team turnovers in a game is two by the **Milwaukee Bucks** on 1 April 2006.

TWINS. There have been several notable sets of twins who played **basketball**. The **National Basketball Association (NBA)** has had the Collins twins, Jason and Jarron; the Graham twins, Joey and Stephen; the Grant twins, Harvey and Horace; the Lopez twins, Brook and Robin; the Thomas twins, Carl and Charles; and the Van Arsdale twins, Tom and Dick. In addition, NBA player Bob Brannum's twin brother, Clarence, played professional basketball in the **National Professional Basketball League**. Howie Rader played in both the **Basketball Association of America** and **National Basketball League (NBL)**, while his twin brother, Lenny, only played in the NBL.

In the **Women's National Basketball Association (WNBA)**, Heather and Heidi Burge, Coco and Kelly Miller, and Doneeka and Roneeka Hodges are the three sets of twins who have played in that league. Pam McGee's twin, Paula, played with her at the **University of Southern California** but not in the **Olympic Games** or WNBA.

Early pro basketball had the Beaver twins, Jake and Dave; the Bradshaw twins, Howard and Raymond; and the Murnane twins, Jim and Eddie. **Barney Sedran** and **Max Friedman** were often teammates during basketball's early years and were referred to by sportswriters as "The Heavenly Twins," but they were unrelated. Possibly the best known set of twins in college basketball were the O'Brien twins, Johnny and Eddie, who played for the University of Seattle in the early 1950s. Neither played professional basketball, but both played Major League Baseball.

TWYMAN, JOHN KENNEDY "JACK." B. 11 May 1934, Pittsburgh, Pennsylvania. Jack Twyman attended Central Catholic High School in Pittsburgh and the **University of Cincinnati**. He led Cincinnati to third place in the 1955 **National Invitation Tournament.** Selected by the Rochester Royals in the 1955 **National Basketball Association (NBA) draft**, the six-foot, six-inch **guard-forward**

played with them from 1955–1957 in Rochester and in Cincinnati from 1957–1966. His best year was 1959–1960, when he averaged 31.2 points per game and was second to **Wilt Chamberlain** for league scoring honors. In his 11-year NBA career, he played in 823 regular-season games and averaged 19.2 points per game. He was twice selected to the All-NBA Second Team and played in six NBA **All-Star Games**.

Although he had an excellent NBA career, Twyman is best known for befriending teammate **Maurice Stokes**, who was stricken with a brain injury in 1958 and required hospitalization and constant care for the next 12 years. As Stokes' legal guardian, Twyman helped raised funds to pay Stokes' expenses. He organized an annual all-star game at Kutsher's Country Club in Monticello, New York, in which many of the best NBA players donated their services to raise money for Stokes' care. Twyman and Stokes' story was made into a 1973 film called *Maurie*. After retiring from active play, Twyman worked as a television analyst for ABC sports. He was enshrined in the **Naismith Memorial Basketball Hall of Fame** in 1983.

– U –

UNIFIED TEAM. *See* COMMONWEALTH OF INDEPENDENT STATES (CIS).

UNION OF SOVIET SOCIALIST REPUBLICS (USSR). The Union of Soviet Socialist Republics (USSR), more commonly known as the Soviet Union, joined the **Fédération Internationale de Basketball (FIBA)** in 1947 and was a member in the FIBA Europe zone. In 1991, the Union was dissolved, and its former republics became independent states. The men's team competed in nine of 10 **Olympic basketball** tournaments from 1952–1988, except 1984, which they boycotted, and they won a medal in every tournament. They won the event in 1972 in a controversial finish in the final game with the **United States**. They also won in 1988 without controversy. They were second four times and third three times. In the FIBA **World Championships**, they competed nine times and won eight medals. They won the tournament three times, were second three times, and placed third twice. In the FIBA European Championships, they entered 21 times and medaled every time, with 14 championships.

The women's team competed in every Olympic tournament from 1976–1988, except 1984. They were undefeated in 1976 and 1980, winning **gold medals** each time, led by their seven-foot, two-inch Hall of Fame **center Uljana Semjonova**, and third in 1988 after she had retired. In their nine appearances at the FIBA World Championships, they won the competition six times, including five consecutive from 1959–1975. In the 22 FIBA European Championships from 1950–1991, they won *every* tournament, except 1958, where they were second to **Bulgaria**. According to Tomasz Małolepszy, author of a book on the European Championships, between 1958–1986 in the FIBA major competitions (Olympic Games, European Championships, and World Championships), the women's Soviet national team won 168 consecutive games before they were defeated by the United States, 108–88, in the 1986 World Championship final.

There have been more than two-dozen players from the former Soviet Union in the **National Basketball Association**, including Russians and players from the former Soviet Republics of Latvia, Lithuania, Estonia, the Ukraine, and Georgia. The **Women's National Basketball Association** has had 12 players from the former Soviet Union. Among the best Soviet players of all time were four-time Olympians **Sergei Belov** and Gennady Volnov, and three-time Olympians Jānis Krūmiņš, Valdis Muižnieks, Alzhan Zharmukhamedov, and Maigonis Valdmanis. Lithuanians **Arvydas Sabonis** and **Šarūnas Marčiulionis** helped lead the Soviet team to the 1988 Olympic championship and are among the best to play for the USSR. *See also* RUSSIA.

UNITED STATES BASKETBALL LEAGUE (USBL). The United States Basketball League (USBL) was a summer men's professional **basketball** minor league that began operations in 1985. Billed as "The League of Opportunity," the league operated continuously since 1985, with the exception of the 1989 season, but suspended operations in 2007. Teams were mostly on the East Coast of the **United States** and ranged from Maine to Florida, although at times there were teams in Kansas, Oklahoma, and Indiana. Between 20–30 games were usually scheduled.

Many USBL players later played in the **National Basketball Association**, including Michael Adams, Darrell Armstrong, Raja Bell, **Tyrone "Muggsy" Bogues**, **Manute Bol**, Mario Elie, World B. Free, Adrian Griffin, Avery Johnson, John Lucas, and Anthony "Spud" Webb. The league has also employed such female players as **Nancy Lieberman** and Lynette Richardson, and professional boxing champion Roy Jones Jr. has also played. On 15 June 1996, Jones played a USBL game in the afternoon in Alabama and the same evening took part in a boxing match in Jacksonville, Florida. Football stars Randy Moss and Terrell Owens have also played in the league.

UNITED STATES OF AMERICA (USA). The United States of America joined the **Fédération Internationale de Basketball (FIBA)** in 1934 and is a member in the FIBA Americas zone. The men's team has competed in every **Olympic basketball** tournament, except 1980, when they boycotted the Moscow Olympic Games. They were undefeated from 1936–1972, winning the first seven Olympic championships. In 1972, they were defeated by the **Union of Soviet Socialist Republics** in a controversial finish and placed second but refused to accept their second-place medals. They won again in 1976 and 1984 but finished in third place in 1988. For the 1992 tournament, professional players were allowed to compete in the Olympic Games, and the 1992 U.S. Olympic team (called the **Dream Team** by the media) may have been the greatest team ever assembled. They won all eight games in that tournament by an average score of 117–73. The U.S. team won again in 1996 and 2000. They had their worst showing in Olympic competition in 2004 and lost three games but won the **bronze medal**. In 2008, the so-called "Redeem Team" showed that they still could play excellent basketball. and the United States once again won the Olympic championship, although **Spain** played well against them in the final game.

The United States has never given the proper importance to the other FIBA competitions and often has not sent their best players to compete. As a result, their record in non-Olympic international events does not reflect the same level of dominance. In the FIBA **World Championships**, they competed 16 times and have only won the tournament four times. In the FIBA Americas Championships, they only entered nine of the 13 tournaments and won six times. In the Pan American Games, they entered all 15 competitions and won only eight. The women's team competed in every Olympic tournament, except 1980, and have won in 1984, 1988, and 1996–2008. They finished second in 1976 and third in 1992. They have won 50 Olympic matches (33 consecutive) and lost only three. In the FIBA World Championships, the American women have done much better than the men and have seven **gold medals**, one **silver medal**, and two bronze medals to their credit in 14 appearances. In the FIBA Americas Championships, they entered four of the nine tournaments, winning twice, and in the Pan American Games, they have entered all 13 tournaments and medaled each time, with seven gold medals, four silver medals, and two bronze medals to their credit.

UNIVERSITY OF ARIZONA. *See* ARIZONA, UNIVERSITY OF.

UNIVERSITY OF ARKANSAS. *See* ARKANSAS, UNIVERSITY OF.

UNIVERSITY OF CALIFORNIA. *See* CALIFORNIA, UNIVERSITY OF.

UNIVERSITY OF CALIFORNIA, LOS ANGELES (UCLA). The University of California, Los Angeles, more popularly known as UCLA, is located in the Westwood section of Los Angeles and began its men's **basketball** program in 1919. Home games since 1965 have been played at the 12,829-seat Pauley Pavilion. The most accomplished **coach** in the school's history by far has been **John Wooden** (620–147 from 1948–1975) and, largely as a result of his tenure, the school holds many **National Collegiate Athletic Association (NCAA)** records for its basketball accomplishments. It reached the NCAA **Final Four** a record 18 times, including 10 consecutive years from 1967–1976. In 1964, the Bruins defeated **Duke University** and won their first championship. From 1965–1975, they won an unprecedented nine more NCAA Championships, including seven consecutive from 1967–1973. In 1995, they won once more. In 1980 and 2006, they were defeated in the NCAA Championship game.

The best players in school history have included Lew Alcindor (aka **Kareem Abdul-Jabbar**); Lucius Allen; Gail Goodrich; Walt Hazzard (aka Mahdi Abdul-Rahman); Marques Johnson; Dave Meyers; **Reggie Miller**; Willie Naulls; **Kiki Vandeweghe**; **Bill Walton**; and Mike Warren, who did not play pro basketball but went on to an acting career. More than 70 former UCLA Bruin basketball players have played in the **National Basketball Association**.

The women's basketball program began in 1974. In 1978, they won the **Association for Intercollegiate Athletics for Women (AIAW)** National Championship. Since the NCAA Women' National Championships began in 1982, they have not reached the Final Four. The most notable coach was Hall of Famer Billie Moore (296–181 from 1977–93). Their best players include Hall of Famers Denise Curry and **Ann Meyers**.

UNIVERSITY OF CINCINNATI. *See* CINCINNATI, UNIVERSITY OF.

UNIVERSITY OF CONNECTICUT. *See* CONNECTICUT, UNIVERSITY OF (UCONN).

UNIVERSITY OF FLORIDA. *See* FLORIDA, UNIVERSITY OF.

UNIVERSITY OF HOUSTON. *See* HOUSTON, UNIVERSITY OF.

UNIVERSITY OF KANSAS. *See* KANSAS, UNIVERSITY OF.

UNIVERSITY OF KENTUCKY. *See* KENTUCKY, UNIVERSITY OF.

UNIVERSITY OF LOUISVILLE. *See* LOUISVILLE, UNIVERSITY OF.

UNIVERSITY OF MARYLAND. *See* MARYLAND, UNIVERSITY OF.

UNIVERSITY OF MICHIGAN. *See* MICHIGAN, UNIVERSITY OF.

UNIVERSITY OF NEVADA, LAS VEGAS (UNLV). The University of Nevada, Las Vegas, more commonly known as UNLV, began in 1957 as the southern regional division of the University of Nevada. In 1965, the name was changed to Nevada Southern University and, in 1969, to its current title. The men's **basketball** program began in 1958. In their first 52 years, the Runnin' Rebels have won more than 70 percent of their games. Since 1983, the 18,500-seat Thomas and Mack Center has been their home court.

Among the best players in the school's history have been Greg Anthony, Stacey Augmon, Armon Gilliam, Glen Gondrezick, Sidney Green, Larry Johnson, Shawn Marion, Ricky Sobers, and Reggie Theus. They won the **National Collegiate Athletic Association** Championship in 1990 and were semifinalists in 1977, 1987, and 1991. Their most successful **coach** was Jerry Tarkanian, who won more than 80 percent of the games he coached (509–105 from 1973–1992) and changed the team's nickname from the Rebels to the Runnin' Rebels.

UNIVERSITY OF NORTH CAROLINA. *See* NORTH CAROLINA, UNIVERSITY OF.

UNIVERSITY OF OREGON. *See* OREGON, UNIVERSITY OF.

UNIVERSITY OF SAN FRANCISCO. *See* SAN FRANCISCO, UNIVERSITY OF.

UNIVERSITY OF SOUTHERN CALIFORNIA (USC). The University of Southern California in Los Angeles began its men's **basketball** program in 1906. Home games since 2006 have been played at the 10,258-seat Galen Center. From 1959–2006, home games were played at the 16,161-seat Los Angeles Sports Arena. In 1940 and 1954, the Trojans reached the **National Collegiate Athletic Association (NCAA) Final Four** but lost in the semifinal round. They have not advanced as far in the NCAA tournament since. The most notable **coaches** have been Justin "Sam" Barry, Bob Boyd, and Forrest Twogood. Among their best players have been Mack Calvin, **Alex Hannum**, Bill Hewitt, John Lambert, O. J. Mayo, Robert Pack, **Bill Sharman**, Paul Westphal, and Gus Williams.

The women's program began in 1977. The Women of Troy were NCAA national champions in 1983 and 1984 and lost in the championship final game in 1986. Their most notable coach was Linda Sharp (271–99 from 1977–89). Among their best players have been **Cynthia Cooper, twins** Pam and Paula McGee, **Cheryl Miller, Lisa Leslie**, and **Tina Thompson**.

UNIVERSITY OF TENNESSEE. *See* TENNESSEE, UNIVERSITY OF.

UNIVERSITY OF TEXAS. *See* TEXAS, UNIVERSITY OF.

UNIVERSITY OF TEXAS AT EL PASO (UTEP). *See* TEXAS WESTERN UNIVERSITY.

UNIVERSITY OF UTAH. *See* UTAH, UNIVERSITY OF.

UNIVERSITY OF WISCONSIN. *See* WISCONSIN, UNIVERSITY OF.

UNIVERSITY OF WYOMING. *See* WYOMING, UNIVERSITY OF.

UNSELD, WESTLEY SISSEL "WES." B.14 March 1946, Louisville, Kentucky. Although only six-feet, seven-inches tall, Wes Unseld proved he could more than hold his own as a **National Basketball Association (NBA) center** during his 13-year career. At 245 pounds, Unseld made up for his lack of height with his strength and bulk. After graduating from Seneca High School in Louisville and the **University of Louisville**, he was chosen by the **Baltimore Bullets** in the 1968 NBA **draft**. That season, he became only the second player to be named both Rookie of the Year and Most Valuable Player in the same year. During his 13 years with the Bullets, he led them to the NBA Finals four times and the 1978 NBA Championship. He was also named Finals Most Valuable Player in that year. In his NBA career, he played in 984 regular-season games, averaged 10.8 points and 14.0 **rebounds** per game, and played in five NBA **All-Star Games**. After his retirement in 1981, he was with the Bullets organization in various roles and served as head **coach** from 1988–1994. In 1988, he was elected to the **Naismith Memorial Basketball Hall of Fame** and in 1996 was named one of the 50 Greatest Players in NBA History.

URUGUAY. Although a relatively small country, with a population of approximately three and one-half million in 2009, Uruguay has a strong **basketball** tradition. They joined the **Fédération Internationale de Basketball (FIBA)** in 1936 and have competed in the **Olympic** men's basketball competition seven times and won the **bronze medal** in both 1952 and 1956. They have not fared as well in the **World Championships**, with a sixth place in 1954 being their best result in seven tournaments. They have entered all but one of the FIBA Americas tournaments, with second place in 1984 being their best result.

Among their best players have been Horacio López, who averaged 24.9 points per game in the 1984 Olympics; Oscar Moglia, who led all scorers in the 1954 World Championships and also in the 1956 Olympics; and Adesio Lombardo, their top player in 1952. Other top layers include Héctor Costa, Nelson DeMarco, Héctor Garcia, and Sergio Matto, each of whom competed in three Olympic Games. Esteban Batista, a Uruguayan native, appeared in 70 games in the **National Basketball Association** for the **Atlanta Hawks** from 2005–2007, with reasonable success.

USA BASKETBALL. The Amateur Basketball Association of the **United States of America** (ABAUSA) was formed in 1974. When the United States first joined **Fédération Internationale de Basketball (FIBA)** in 1934, the **Amateur Athletic Union (AAU)** was the organization recognized by FIBA as being responsible for U.S. international **basketball** competition. During the 1960s, the Basketball Federation of the USA (BFUSA) was organized in an attempt to gain control and replace the AAU as the recognized international organization. The BFUSA comprised representatives of various collegiate, high school, and **coaching** organizations. In 1972, the FIBA withdrew recognition of the AAU and instructed the United States to create a new organization. The resulting organization was known as ABAUSA and had representatives from the AAU, **Association**

for Intercollegiate Athletics for Women (AIAW), National Association of Intecollegiate Athletics (NAIA), National Collegiate Athletic Association (NCAA), and several other basketball organizations. It officially began operation on 1 January 1975. In 1979, it relocated to the U.S. Olympic Training Center in Colorado Springs, Colorado, and on 12 October 1989, it changed its name to USA Basketball and added the National Basketball Association as a member after the FIBA allowed professionals to compete in its events.

UTAH, UNIVERSITY OF. The University of Utah in Salt Lake City began its men's basketball program in 1908. In 1916, the team won the Amateur Athletic Union National Championship by defeating the Illinois Athletic Club, 28–27. The most outstanding coaches have been Jack Gardner, Rick Majerus, and Vadal Peterson. Among the best players have been Andrew Bogut, Art Bunte, Luther "Ticky" Burden, Jerry Chambers, Mike Doleac, Jeff Judkins, Billy McGill, Andre Miller, Mike Newlin, Keith Van Horn, and Danny Vranes. Since 1969, home games have been played at the 15,000-seat Jon M. Huntsman Center. The Utes, led by Arnie Ferrin and five-foot, seven-inch Japanese American Wat Misaka, won the National Collegiate Athletic Association Championship in 1944 with a 42–40 victory over Dartmouth College in overtime. They were runners-up to the University of Kentucky in 1998 and finished fourth in 1961 and 1966.

UTAH JAZZ. The Utah Jazz is a team in the National Basketball Association (NBA) formerly known as the New Orleans Jazz.
    New Orleans Jazz. The New Orleans Jazz joined the NBA as an expansion franchise in 1974. Home games were played at the 6,500-seat Loyola Field House and the 7,853-seat Municipal Auditorium in the 1974–1975 season and at the 55,675-seat Louisiana Superdome from 1975–1979. Among their most notable players were Gail Goodrich, Paul Griffin, Aaron James, Rich Kelley, Pete Maravich, Jim McElroy, Otto Moore, Louie Nelson, Leonard "Truck" Robinson, and Nate Williams. One of the team's few highlights occurred on 25 February 1977, when Maravich scored 68 points in a game against the New York Knickerbockers. In five seasons in New Orleans, they never had a winning record or reached the playoffs. On

8 June 1979, they moved to Salt Lake City, Utah. In an inexplicable move, they retained the team's nickname "Jazz," which was quite appropriate for the city of New Orleans but absurd for Utah.

Utah Jazz. Home games were played at the 12,212-seat Salt Palace in Salt Lake City from 1979–1991 and the 19,911-seat Delta Center (renamed the Energy Solutions Arena in 2006) from 1991 to date. The Utah Jazz have only had three **coaches** in their 30 years in the NBA: Tom Nissalke from 1979–1981, Frank Layden from 1981–1988, and **Jerry Sloan** from 1988–2010. Sloan holds the NBA record for most consecutive years coaching the same team. Among their most notable players have been Thurl Bailey, **Adrian Dantley**, Mark Eaton, Darrell Griffith, Jeff Hornacek, Andrei Kirilenko, **Karl Malone**, Mehmet Okur, Bryon Russell, and **John Stockton**. Their best seasons were 1996–1997 and 1997–1998. They reached the NBA Championship Finals each year and were defeated both times by the **Chicago Bulls**. The franchise overall record for 36 years from 1974–2010 is 1,594–1,326.

UTAH STARS. The Utah Stars were a team in the **American Basketball Association (ABA)**. They began play as the Anaheim Amigos in 1967, became the Los Angeles Stars in 1968, and moved to Salt Lake City in 1970.

Anaheim Amigos. On 2 February 1967, the Anaheim Amigos became a charter franchise team in the ABA. They played most home games at the 7,800-seat Anaheim Convention Center, although they also scheduled three games in Hawaii and five others throughout California. The team had the distinction of playing in the league's first game on 13 October 1967, losing, 134–129, to the Oakland Oaks in Oakland, California. The most impressive player on the Amigos was guard Les Selvage, who took advantage of the league's new **three-point field goal** rule and made a league-leading 147 three-pointers in a league-leading 461 attempts for the season. On 15 February 1968, he made 10 three-pointers in 26 attempts. His 10 successful three-pointers was not equaled in the **National Basketball Association (NBA)** until 1993. No one in the NBA has ever come close to Selvage's 26 three-point field goal attempts in one game. One of the season's oddities for the Amigos was the use of their public relations director, Dick Lee, as a substitute in two games when their team was shorthanded due to injuries. Other players on the team included Bob Bedell, Larry Bunce, Steve Chubin, Warren Davis, John Fairchild, and Ben Warley. On 27 March 1968, the Amigos were sold to James J. Kirst and moved to Los Angeles to play as the Los Angeles Stars.

Los Angeles Stars. Home games were played at the 15,325-seat Los Angeles Sports Arena. For the Stars' first season, they retained only three players from the Amigos, Steve Chubin, Warren Davis and Ben Warley, and added Dennis Grey, Merv Jackson, Ed Johnson, George Lehmann, Larry Miller, George Stone, and Bobby Warren. In 1970, they finished in fourth place in the Western Division but did surprisingly well in the playoffs and reached the league championship series. On 11 June 1970, the team was moved to Salt Lake City, Utah, and played as the Utah Stars.

Utah Stars. Home games were played at the 12,166-seat Salt Palace. The Stars acquired NBA star Zelmo Beaty, who had been required to sit out the 1969–1970 season. Donnie Freeman and Austin "Red" Robbins were also added prior to the season, and the team won the 1971 ABA Championship. As a result of Utah's success, **coach Bill Sharman** received an offer to coach the **Los Angeles Lakers** and left the team. On 21 February 1972, Beaty set the league single-game scoring record of 63 points, but the record lasted for less than one month, as Larry Miller with the Carolina Cougars scored 67 on 18 March 1972. The Stars finished in first place in the Western Division for the third consecutive season in 1973–1974 but lost to the New York Nets in the ABA Championship finals. On 29 August 1974, the team signed 19-year-old **Moses Malone** directly from high school to a seven-year, $3 million contract. On 2 December 1975, the team was disbanded with a record of 4–12. In their eight-plus ABA seasons, the franchise record was 366–310.

– V –

VALVANO, JAMES THOMAS ANTHONY "JIM," "JIMMY V."
B. 10 March 1946, New York, New York. D. 28 April 1993, Durham, North Carolina. Jim Valvano attended Seaford High School in Seaford, New York, and Rutgers University. Although he played **basketball** at Rutgers and helped lead the team to third place in the

1967 **National Invitation Tournament**, his major contribution to basketball was as a **coach**. He coached from 1969–1990 and had a won–lost record of 346–210. He was at Johns Hopkins University in 1969–1970, Bucknell University from 1972–1975, Iona College from 1975–1980, and **North Carolina State University** from 1981–1990. His greatest success was at North Carolina State, where he compiled a 209–114 record. In the 1982–1983 season, they won the **National Collegiate Athletic Association** Championship in an upset victory over the University of Houston on a last-second shot.

From 1990–1993, Valvano worked as a television basketball analyst. Shortly before his death from cancer, he created the The V Foundation for Cancer Research to help find a cure for cancer. Each year a Jimmy V celebrity golf tournament and a Jimmy V basketball classic are held to aid this cause.

VANCOUVER GRIZZLIES. *See* MEMPHIS GRIZZLIES.

VANDEWEGHE, ERNEST MAURICE, JR. "ERNIE." B. 12 September 1928, Montreal, Quebec, **Canada**. Ernie Vandeweghe was raised on Long Island, New York, and attended Oceanside High School in Oceanside, New York, and Colgate University. The six-foot, three-inch **forward-guard** was selected by the **New York Knickerbockers** in the 1949 **National Basketball Association (NBA) draft** and played for them from 1949–1956, while attending Columbia Medical School. His NBA career totals for six years are 224 regular-season games and a 9.5 points per game average. On 24 May 1953, he married Colleen Kay Hutchins, sister of NBA player Mel Hutchins and Miss America 1952. Vandeweghe left professional **basketball** in 1956 to become a pediatrician.

Vandeweghe began his practice for the **U.S.** Air Force Hospital in Wiesbaden, Germany, and he later settled in Los Angeles, California, where he was chief of pediatrics. He also was associate clinical professor of pediatrics, adolescent, and sports medicine at the **University of California, (UCLA)** Medical Center. In addition, he was the team physician for the **Los Angeles Lakers**.

Vandeweghe's son, **Ernest Vandeweghe III**, better known as "Kiki," played in the NBA from 1980–1993. His other son, Bruk, was a professional volleyball player. His daughter, Heather, is a pediatrician at the UCLA Medical Center. His other daughter, Tauna, won a **gold medal** in the 1976 **Olympics** in swimming and in 1984 won an Olympic **silver medal** with the U.S. volleyball team. Tauna's daughter, Coco, became a professional tennis player at the age of 16.

VANDEWEGHE III, ERNEST MAURICE "KIKI." B. 1 August 1958, Weisbaden, **Germany**. The son of former **National Basketball Association (NBA)** player **Ernie Vandeweghe**, Kiki Vandeweghe was born in Germany, where his father was working for the **U.S. Air Force** as a pediatrician. Kiki was raised in Southern California and attended Pacific Palisades High School in Pacific Palisades and the**University of California, Los Angeles**. Although selected by the expansion **Dallas Mavericks** in the 1980 NBA **draft**, he refused to play for them and was traded to the **Denver Nuggets**. From 1980–1993, he played for Denver, the **Portland Trail Blazers**, the **New York Knickerbockers**, and the **Los Angeles Clippers**. The six-foot, eight-inch **forward** was an excellent outside shot and led the NBA in **three-point field goal** percentage in 1986–1987. His NBA career totals for 13 years are 810 regular-season games and a 19.7 points per game average.

After retiring from active play, Vandeweghe became president of a Los Angeles-based sport drink company, was the shooting **coach** of the **United States Basketball League** Long Island Surf, was the player development assistant coach with the Dallas Mavericks in 1999–2001, was general manager of the Nuggets in 2001–2006, and later worked in television as an analyst. In 2008, he became a special assistant to the president of the **New Jersey Nets** and in 2009 was named their coach. His contract was terminated after the Nets ownership changed hands in 2010.

VILLANOVA UNIVERSITY. Villanova University, located in Villanova, Pennsylvania, a suburb of Philadelphia, began its men's **basketball** program in 1920. Home games since 1985 have been played at the 6,500-seat arena The Pavilion. Prior to 1985, home games were played at the 3,000-seat University Fieldhouse. The most accomplished **coaches** in the school's history have been Jack Kraft, Steve Lappas, Rollie Massimino, Alex Severance, and Jay Wright. In the very first **National Collegiate Athletic Association (NCAA)**

tournament in 1939, with only eight teams competing, they lost in the semifinal round; in 1971 they were defeated by **University of California, Los Angeles** in the championship final, but in 1985 the Wildcats won the NCAA Championship. In 2009, they again reached the Final Four but were defeated by the eventual champion North Carolina. The best players in school history include **Paul Arizin**, Chris Ford, Larry Hennessy, Chris Herren, Tom Ingelsby, Wally Jones, Kerry Kittles, Bill Melchionni, Ed Pinckney, John Pinone, Howard Porter, and Hubie White.

VIRGINIA SQUIRES. The Virginia Squires were a team in the **American Basketball Association (ABA)**. They began in 1967 as the Oakland Oaks, moved to Washington as the Washington Capitols in 1969, and vacated to Virginia in 1970 to play as a regional franchise. In nine years, their record was 326–417.

Oakland Oaks. On 2 February 1967, a California group headed by singer Pat Boone purchased a franchise in the ABA for $30,000. They signed future Hall of Famer **Rick Barry**, who had been with the San Francisco Warriors of the **National Basketball Association (NBA)**. In August 1967, a California court ruled that Barry's contract with San Francisco included a one-year option clause, and Barry was prohibited from playing for Oakland for the 1967–1968 season. Without Barry, the team finished last in the Western Division. They had several capable players, including Andy Anderson, Ron Franz, Jim Hadnot, Steve "Snapper" Jones, and Lavern Tart. Barry was able to play the following year, but an injury limited him to just 35 games, although he led the league in scoring. The Oaks acquired Doug Moe and **Larry Brown** from New Orleans and, with rookie Warren Armstrong, improved their record by 38 games and won the league championship. In August 1969, the Oaks were sold to an East Coast group who moved the team to Washington, D.C.

Washington Capitols. The team had some excellent players, including Warren Armstrong, Rick Barry, Larry Brown, and Roland "Fatty" Taylor, but they finished in third place, as injuries to key players hampered their success. Following the season, the team relocated and became known as the Virginia Squires.

Virginia Squires. As a regional franchise, the Virginia Squires played home games in four cities in Virginia, including Richmond,

Norfolk, Hampton Roads, and Roanoke, in arenas ranging in seating capacity from 5,200–10,745. In each of the team's six years in the league, they got progressively worse, even though at various times they had both future Hall of Fame players **Julius Erving** and **George Gervin**. On 11 May 1976, the franchise folded.

VITALE, RICHARD J. "DICK." B. 9 June 1939, Passaic, New Jersey. Dick Vitale attended East Rutherford High School in East Rutherford, New Jersey; Seton Hall University; and William Paterson College, where he received a master's degree. As a youth, he lost the sight in one eye, which prevented him from excelling at sports, so he decided to **coach** instead. He coached at Garfield High School in 1963, coached at East Rutherford High School from 1964–1970, was assistant coach at Rutgers University from 1971–1973, and was head coach at the University of Detroit from 1973–1977. He coached the **Detroit Pistons** in the **National Basketball Association** in the 1978–1979 season and for part of the 1979–1980 season.

Vitale began work as a broadcaster in December 1979, and it was as a broadcaster that he made his most significant contribution to **basketball**. He provided the color commentary for college basketball for the next 30 years and was known for his enthusiasm and colorful phrases. In Vitale's words, an outstanding freshman is a "diaper dandy," a star player is a "PTPer" (for prime-time player), a **three-point field goal** is "a trifecta." "It's awesome, baby" is another of his catch phrases. In 1998, he was the recipient of the Curt Gowdy Media Award given by the **Naismith Memorial Basketball Hall of Fame** for outstanding contributions in electronic media. In 2008, he was enshrined in the hall as a contributor.

– W –

WACHTER, EDWARD A. "ED." B. 30 June 1883, Troy, New York. D. 12 March 1966, Troy, New York. Ed Wachter did not attend high school or college but began playing **basketball** for the Troy YMCA team in 1896 and continued with the Columbia Athletic Club the following year. In 1900, the six-foot, six-inch **center** began his professional basketball career. He played for more than a dozen different teams in most of the leagues of his day and retired as a player after the 1923 season. With Troy, he was a member of the **Hudson River League** champions in 1910 and 1911 and the **New York State League (NYSL)** champions in 1912, 1913, and 1914. He had four brothers who also played professional basketball, Lew, Joe, Vic, and Charlie. On 11 December 1915, the game between Troy and Utica was one of several that season in which four of the brothers took part, two on each side. In nine years, from 1911–1923, Ed scored more than 1,100 points in the NYSL while playing for Troy, Utica, Hudson, Albany, and Cohoes.

Wachter **coached** the professional Utica Utes team in the NYSL in 1915–1916 and was a college coach at Rensselaer Polytechnic Institute in 1915, New York State Teachers College at Albany from 1915–1916, Williams College from 1916–1919, Harvard University from 1920–1933, and Lafayette College from 1936–1938. He was enshrined in the **Naismith Memorial Basketball Hall of Fame** in 1961.

WADE, DWYANE TYRONE. B. 17 January 1982, Chicago, Illinois. Dwyane Wade attended Harold L. Richards High School in Oak Lawn, Illinois; the University of Illinois; and **Marquette University**. In college, he led Marquette to the **National Collegiate Athletic Association (NCAA) Final Four** in 2003 and in that tournament recorded a **triple-double**, with 29 points, 11 **rebounds**, and 11 **assists**. This was just the third triple-double in NCAA tournament history. He left school after his junior year and was chosen in the 2003 **National Basketball Association (NBA) draft** by the **Miami Heat**. The six-foot, four-inch **guard** has played for them since then. He helped lead the Heat to the NBA championship in 2006 and was the NBA Finals Most Valuable Player that year.

In his first seven NBA seasons, Wade played in 471 regular-season games and averaged 25.4 points per game. He was named to the All-NBA First Team in 2009 and 2010, All-NBA Second Team twice, All-NBA Third Team once, and All-NBA Defensive Second Team three times. He was also selected for the NBA **All-Star Game** in each season from 2005–2010. He won **bronze medals** with the **United States** in the 2004 **Olympic Games** and 2006 **World Championships** and won a **gold medal** in the 2008 Olympic Games, when he led the team in scoring with an average of 16.0 points per game. On 8 July 2010, Olympic teammate **LeBron James** announced that he would be joining Wade and Chris Bosh on Miami for the coming NBA season.

WALTON III, WILLIAM THEODORE "BILL." B. 5 November 1952, San Diego, California. Bill Walton attended Helix High School in La Mesa, California, and the **University of California, Los Angeles (UCLA)**. In high school, he led his team to two state titles and a 49-game winning streak. At UCLA, he led the freshman team to a 20-game undefeated season. As a sophomore and junior, he led the UCLA varsity to two undefeated seasons and the **National Collegiate Athletic Association (NCAA)** National Championship in 1972 and 1973. In the 1973 NCAA Championship final game against Memphis State, Walton made 21 of 22 **field goal** attempts and scored 44 points in one of the most impressive individual performances in an NCAA Championship final.

Walton won the James E. Sullivan Award as the nation's top amateur athlete in any sport in 1973. He also won the Naismith College Player of the Year Award and United States Basketball Writers Association College Player of the Year awards in each of his three college varsity seasons. During his senior year, UCLA's record 88-game winning streak was ended by **Notre Dame University** on 19 January 1974. This also ended Walton's personal 157-game winning streak that began in the middle of his junior year in high school. UCLA's streak of seven national championships also ended that year, when they were defeated by **North Carolina State University** in double **overtime** in the NCAA semifinal round.

The six-foot, 11-inch **center**, known as "The Big Redhead," was chosen by the **Portland Trail Blazers** in the 1974 **National Basketball Association (NBA) draft** as the first overall selection. Walton played from 1974–1988 for the Trail Blazers, San Diego Clippers, **Los Angeles Clippers**, and **Boston Celtics**. His best year was 1976–1977, when he averaged 14.4 **rebounds** and 18.6 points per game, led the Trail Blazers to the NBA Championship, and was named the NBA Finals Most Valuable Player. His NBA career totals for 10 years are 468 regular-season games and a 13.3 points and 10.5 rebounds per game average. He was selected for two NBA **All-Star**

Games and was named to the All-NBA First Team in 1978, All-NBA Second Team in 1977, and NBA All-Defensive First Team in 1977 and 1978. In 1978, he was named the league's Most Valuable Player.

Walton was injury-prone as a professional and played only 209 games of 328 regular-season games in his first four years. From 1978–1982, he did not play in three of the four seasons and only played 14 games in the fourth season. He returned for the 1982–1983 season and played in 33 games. The following two years, he played in 55 and 67 games. On 6 September 1985, he was traded to the Boston Celtics and had one of his best professional seasons with them. He played in 80 games as a reserve center, was a member of the NBA Championship team, and won the NBA **Sixth Man** of the Year Award. The following year, he was only able to play in 10 games and, in 1987–1988, was on the Boston roster but did not play. In 13 NBA seasons, he played in only 468 of the scheduled 1,066 games.

After retiring from active play, Walton became a television broadcaster, a remarkable achievement for a person who had a severe stuttering problem until the age of 28. After meeting sportscaster **Marty Glickman** at a social function, Glickman counseled Walton and gave him six tips to overcoming his stuttering problem. Without the help of a doctor or speech therapist, Walton applied these tips and with much hard work became an accomplished speaker. He is now a spokesman for the National Stuttering Foundation and is one of the most popular television basketball analysts.

Walton was enshrined in the **Naismith Memorial Basketball Hall of Fame** in 1993. In 1996, he was named one of the 50 Greatest Players in NBA History. His brother, Bruce, played professional football in the NFL from 1973–1975. Bill's son, Luke, plays for the **Los Angeles Lakers**.

WANG, ZHI ZHI. B. 8 July 1977, Beijing, **China.** The **left-handed** Wang Zhi Zhi became the first native Chinese to play in the **National Basketball Association (NBA)** when he appeared for the **Dallas Mavericks** on 5 April 2001. He was selected by Dallas in the second round of the 1999 NBA **draft**. Although seven-feet tall, he is primarily an outside shooter with a good touch. Wang played for the Chinese Army Bayi Rockets team from 1994–2001 and was a member of the Chinese **Olympic** team in 1996 and 2000. Never a star in the

NBA, his best season was 2001–2002, when he averaged 5.6 points per game in 55 games for Dallas. He later played for the **Los Angeles Clippers** and **Miami Heat** in a five-year NBA career and had career totals of 604 points in 137 regular-season games. He fell out of favor with the Chinese National team for failure to attend practices in China and was not selected to the 2002 **World Championships** team or 2004 Olympic team but was later forgiven and played in the 2006 and 2010 World Championships and the 2008 Beijing Olympics. In 20 games in three Olympics, he scored 216 points.

WANZER, ROBERT FRANCIS "BOBBY," "HOOKS." B. 4 June 1921, New York, New York. Bobby Wanzer attended Benjamin Franklin High School in New York and Seton Hall University. After two years at Seton Hall, he enlisted in the **U.S.** Marine Corps, served from 1943–1946, and returned to Seton Hall for his final two years of college. He was selected by the Rochester Royals in the 1948 **Basketball Association of America (BAA) draft**. The six-foot-tall **guard** played from 1948–1957 for the Royals. His best year was 1951–1952, when he averaged 15.7 points, 5.0 **rebounds**, and 4.0 **assists** per game and became the first player in league history to shoot better than 90 percent for the season from the **free throw** line. His professional career totals for 10 years are 608 regular-season games and a 11.7 points per game average. He was selected for five **National Basketball Association (NBA) All-Star Games** and was named to the All-NBA Second Team three times. In 1951, he was a member of the NBA Championship team.

Wanzer was player-**coach** of the Royals from 1955–1957 and bench coach from 1957–1959. In 1962, he became head coach at St. John Fisher College, a **National Collegiate Athletic Association** Division III school in Pittsford, New York, a Rochester suburb. He coached there until 1986 and was also the athletic director and coach of the golf team. He was enshrined in the **Naismith Memorial Basketball Hall of Fame** in 1987.

WASHINGTON BULLETS. *See* WASHINGTON WIZARDS.

WASHINGTON CAPITOLS (ABA). *See* VIRGINIA SQUIRES.

WASHINGTON CAPITOLS (BAA). The Washington Capitols were a charter member of the **Basketball Association of America** in 1946 and were owned by Miguel J. "Mike" Uline. Home games were played at the 7,000-seat Uline Arena. They had the distinction of having the first black player play in a **National Basketball Association (NBA)** game on 31 October 1950, when **Earl Lloyd** played in an otherwise uneventful game. Among their most notable players were Bob Feerick, Kleggie Hermsen, Sonny Hertzberg, Horace "Bones" McKinney, John Mahnken, Jack Nichols, Fred Scolari, and Irv Torgoff. Their best seasons were 1946–1947, when they finished first in the Eastern Division but lost the playoff semifinal round, and 1948–1949, when they lost in the NBA Finals. After compiling a record of 10–25, they were disbanded on 9 January 1951. Their record for four and one-half seasons was 157–114.

WASHINGTON GENERALS. The Washington Generals are a barnstorming basketball team that have usually served as the opponents for the **Harlem Globetrotters**. They were organized in 1952 by **Louis "Red" Klotz**, a former player in the **Basketball Association of America** who was a member of the 1948 BAA champion **Baltimore Bullets**. They have also been billed as the Boston Shamrocks, New Jersey Reds, Baltimore Rockets, Atlantic City Seagulls, and New York Nationals.

WASHINGTON WIZARDS. The Washington Wizards are a team in the **National Basketball Association (NBA)**. They began play in 1961 as the Chicago Packers, changed their name to the Chicago Zephyrs in 1962, and moved to Baltimore as the Baltimore Bullets in 1963. In 1973, they were renamed the Capital Bullets and, in 1974, the Washington Bullets. In 1997, they became known as the Washington Wizards.

Chicago Packers/Zephyrs. On 16 September 1959, a group of Chicago businessmen headed by David C. Trager was awarded an expansion franchise to begin play in the 1961–1962 season. Home games were played at the International Amphitheatre. The team was stocked via an expansion **draft** in which the Packers selected nine second-line players. After the season began, Joe Graboski, Si Green,

Woody Sauldsberry, and Charlie Tyra were acquired by trade. In the college draft, their first selection was **Walt Bellamy**, who became Rookie of the Year, as he averaged 31.1 points per game. Despite Bellamy's excellent season, the team only won 18 of 80 games and finished last in their division. The Packers moved to the Chicago Coliseum the next season and were renamed the Zephyrs. In 1963, they moved to Baltimore and were known as the Baltimore Bullets.

Baltimore/Capital/Washington Bullets. Home games were played at the Baltimore Civic Center from 1963–1973. In 1973, their home court was the 17,500-seat Capitol Centre in Landover, Maryland, and they were renamed the Capitol Bullets. In 1974, they became the Washington Bullets, although they continued to play home games in Landover. Since 1997, home games are played at the 20,173-seat Verizon Center, located in Washington, D.C. Among their best players have been **Tyrone "Muggsy" Bogues**, **Manute Bol**, Phil Chenier, Archie Clark, **Elvin Hayes**, **Bailey Howell**, Juwan Howard, Gus Johnson, Bernard King, Kevin Loughery, Jack Marin, **Earl Monroe**, **Gheorghe Muresan**, Mike Riordan, and **Wes Unseld**. Their best season was 1977–1978, when they won the NBA Championship in seven games over the Seattle Supersonics. They were also losers in the Finals in 1971, 1975, and 1979. In 1997, they were renamed the Washington Wizards.

Washington Wizards. In 1999, **Michael Jordan** became a minority owner, but when he decided to return to play in 2001, he had to divest himself of team ownership. Among their most notable players have been Gilbert Arenas, Caron Butler, Richard Hamilton, Brendan Haywood, Larry Hughes, Antawn Jamison, Jared Jeffries, Jordan, Mitch Richmond, and Chris Whitney. The franchise's overall record from 1961–2010 is 1,801–2,174.

WATERLOO HAWKS. The Waterloo Hawks were a professional basketball team that played in the **National Basketball League (NBL)** in 1948–1949, the **National Basketball Association (NBA)** in 1949–1950, and the **National Professional Basketball League (NPBL)** in 1950–1951.

Waterloo Hawks (NBL). The Waterloo Hawks were originally an independent team and joined the NBL in 1948. Home games were played at the 7,500-seat Hippodrome in Waterloo, Iowa. Their playing-**coach** was Charley "JoJo" Shipp, and their most notable players were Harry Boykoff, Bill Brown, Les Deaton, Elmer Gainer, Leo Kubiak, Dick Mehen, Ben Schadler, and Rollie Seltz. Following the season, they were among the teams included in the merger that created the NBA.

Waterloo Hawks (NBA). In the 1949–1950 NBA season, the Hawks won 19 and lost 43 and finished in fifth place in the Western Division. Players with the most playing time that season were Don Boven, Harry Boykoff, Leo Kubiak, Dick Mehen, Johnny Payak, Wayne See, Charley "JoJo" Shipp, and Jack Smiley. After the season, the Hawks were dropped from the NBA and played the 1950–1951 season in the new NPBL.

WAYLAND BAPTIST UNIVERSITY. Wayland Baptist University in Plainview, Texas, began its women's **basketball** program in 1946. In the 1949–1950 season, Claude Hutcherson, owner of an air service, helped sponsor the teams and also provided transportation. They then became known as the Wayland Flying Queens. They won the national **Amateur Athletic Union** Championship 10 times and were national runners-up 10 times from 1951–1976, under **coach** Harley Redin. Unlike their rival **Nashville Business College** teams, all of Wayland's teams were composed of students of the school. Among their best players were Ruth Cannon, Lois Finley, Patsy Neal, Jill Rankin, and Laura Switzer.

WEST, JERRY ALAN "MR. CLUTCH." B. 28 May 1938, Cheylan, West Virginia. Jerry West attended East Bank High School in East Bank, West Virginia, and West Virginia University. He led his high school to the state championship in his senior year in 1956. He led his college to the **National Collegiate Athletic Association (NCAA)** Championship final game in 1959 and was voted the Most Outstanding Player of the NCAA **Final Four**. Selected to the 1959 **U.S.** Pan American Games team and 1960 U.S. **Olympic basketball** team, he won **gold medals** with both teams.

The six-foot, two-inch **guard** was drafted by the Minneapolis Lakers in the 1960 **National Basketball Association (NBA) draft** and, after the Lakers relocated to Los Angeles, played with them from 1960–1973. Nicknamed "Mr. Clutch" by sportswriters for his ability to score in close games, when West first came into the league, he was nicknamed "Zeke from Cabin Creek" by his teammates for his shy, retiring manner and Appalachian accent. On 17 January 1962, he scored 63 points in one game. At that time, only **Wilt Chamberlain** and **Elgin Baylor** had ever scored more in an NBA game.

In his 14 years as a player in the NBA, West was selected for the NBA **All-Star Game** each of his 14 years and was its Most Valuable Player in 1972. His NBA career statistics are 932 regular-season games and 25,192 points for an average of 27.0 points per game. He played in 153 playoff games and had 4,457 points, for an average of 29.1 points per game. He was named to the All-NBA First Team 10 times and All-NBA Second Team twice. The Lakers played in the NBA playoffs in each of his 14 years and reached the NBA Finals nine times but lost in eight of the nine series, winning only in 1972 against the Knicks. In 1965, he averaged 40.6 points per game for 11 playoff games, including an NBA record 46.3 in the six-game Western Division Finals with the **Baltimore Bullets**. He was voted the NBA Finals Most Valuable Player in 1969. In 1969, the NBA used his silhouette to create their logo.

In 1976, West was named head **coach** of the Lakers and coached them for three seasons. He remained with the Laker organization as a consultant and scout and, in 1982, became their general manager. In that role, he helped create teams that reached the NBA Finals seven times and won three NBA Championships. In 1994, he was promoted to vice president of Basketball Operations and remained with the Lakers until 2000.

From 2002 until his retirement in 2007, West was general manager of the **Memphis Grizzlies**. He was voted NBA Executive of the Year twice, in 1995 with the Lakers and in 2004 with the Grizzlies. He was enshrined in the **Naismith Memorial Basketball Hall of Fame** in 1980, and that year he was also named to the NBA 35th Anniversary Team. In 1996, he was named one of the 50 Greatest Players in NBA History.

WHEELCHAIR BASKETBALL. Wheelchair **basketball** was developed following World War II to aid disabled veterans in rehabilitation. Players are rated based on ability level, and teams are required to play a combination of players with different ability levels. The rules are similar to regular basketball, except that players must remain in wheelchairs throughout the game. The sport has grown, is now played internationally, and is one of the featured sports at the Quadrennial Paralympic Games. The International Wheelchair Basketball Federation administers the sport internationally, and the National Wheelchair Basketball Association administers it within the **United States**.

WHITE, JOSEPH HENRY "JO JO." B.16 November 1946, St. Louis, Missouri. Jo Jo White attended Vashon High School and McKinley High School in St. Louis and the **University of Kansas**. In 1968, he led Kansas to the **National Invitation Tournament** championship game, where they were defeated by **Dayton University**. He won a **gold medal** with the 1968 **U.S. Olympic basketball** team.

The six-foot, three-inch **guard** was selected by the **Boston Celtics** in the 1969 **National Basketball Association (NBA) draft** and played from 1969–1981 with the Celtics, **Golden State Warriors**, and Kansas City Kings. With the Celtics, White was a member of NBA Championship teams in 1974 and 1976 and was named the NBA Finals Most Valuable Player in 1976. He played in the NBA **All-Star Game** seven consecutive years from 1971–1977, and was twice voted to the All-NBA Second team. In his 12 seasons in the NBA, he played in 837 regular-season games and averaged 17.2 points per game. After retiring from basketball, he became director of special projects for the Celtics in 2000.

WILKENS, LEONARD RANDOLPH "LENNY." B. 28 October 1937, Brooklyn, New York. Lenny Wilkens attended Boys High School in Brooklyn and **Providence College**. At Providence, his team reached the semifinals of the 1959 **National Invitation Tournament** and was the losing finalist in the 1960 tournament. Selected by the St. Louis Hawks in the 1960 **National Basketball Association (NBA) draft**, he played from 1960–1975 for the Hawks, Seattle Supersonics, **Cleveland Cavaliers**, and **Portland Trail Blazers**. His NBA career totals for 15 years are 1,077 regular-season games and a 16.5 points and 6.7 **assists** per game average. In 1970 and 1972, he led the NBA in assists. The six-foot, one-inch **guard** was selected for nine NBA **All-Star Games** and was voted the Most Valuable Player in the 1971 game. In 1960 and 1961, with the Hawks, he was on the losing side in the NBA Championship Finals.

From 1969–2005, Wilkens **coached** in the NBA for Seattle, Portland, Seattle again, Cleveland, Atlanta, Toronto, and New York. He was player-coach with Seattle from 1969–1972 and Portland from 1974–1976 and bench coach for the other teams. He held the NBA record for most wins as a coach (surpassed in 2010 by Don Nelson), and Wilkens' won–lost record in 32 years of NBA coaching is 1,332–1,155. He was assistant coach of the 1992 **U.S. Olympic Dream Team** and head coach of the **gold medal**-winning 1996 U.S. Olympic team. He was enshrined in the **Naismith Memorial Basketball Hall of Fame** in 1989 as a player and in 1998 as a coach. In 1996, he was named one of the 50 Greatest Players in NBA History and one of the Top 10 Coaches in NBA History.

WILKINS, JACQUES DOMINIQUE "DOMINIQUE," "NIQUE."
B. 12 January 1960, Paris, **France**. Dominique Wilkins was born in France, as his father was stationed there while in the **U.S.** Air Force. Dominique attended Washington High School in Washington, North Carolina, and led them to the state high school championship in 1978 and 1979. He then attended the University of Georgia. He left college after his junior year and was selected by the **Utah Jazz** in the 1982 **National Basketball Association (NBA) draft** but was traded to the **Atlanta Hawks** prior to the start of the season. He played from 1982–1999 for the Hawks, **Los Angeles Clippers**, **Boston Celtics**, **San Antonio Spurs**, and **Orlando Magic**. He also played in Europe with Panathinaikos in **Greece** in 1995–1996 (winning a Euroleague championship with them) and Bologna in **Italy** in 1997–1998. His best year was 1985–1986, when he averaged a league-leading 30.3 points per game.

As one of the more spectacular dunkers in the league, Wilkins won the **Slam Dunk** Championship in 1985 and 1990 and was given the nickname "The Human Highlight Film." On 8 December 1992, he shot 23 **free throws** in one game without missing a single one, an NBA record for perfection in one game. His NBA career totals for 15 years are 1,074 regular-season games and a 24.8 points per game average. He is among the top 10 in NBA career points scored. He was selected for nine NBA **All-Star Games** and was named to the

All-NBA First Team in 1986, All-NBA Second Team four times, and All-NBA Third Team twice.

After retiring from active play, Wilkins was employed by the Hawks as a special assistant to the executive vice president. He was enshrined in the **Naismith Memorial Basketball Hall of Fame** in 2006. His brother, Gerald, also played in the NBA, and Gerald's son, Damien (Dominique's nephew), is also an NBA player.

WISCONSIN, UNIVERSITY OF. The University of Wisconsin in Madison began its men's **basketball** program in 1899. In the 1904–1905 season, Christian Steinmetz scored 50 points in a game, the most by a college player in that era. Home games since 1998 have been played at the 17,190-seat Kohl Center. Prior to 1998, home games were played at the Wisconsin Field House. The most prominent **coaches** in the school's history have been Harold E. "Bud" Foster, Walter Meanwell, and William "Bo" Ryan. Prior to the creation of a national championship tournament, Wisconsin was selected as national champion by the Helms Foundation in 1912, 1914, and 1916. They were undefeated with 15–0 records the first two seasons and had a 20–1 record in the third. The Badgers were **National Collegiate Athletic Association (NCAA)** tournament champions in 1941. Their only other appearance in the NCAA **Final Four** was in 2000, when they lost in the semifinals to eventual champion **Michigan State University**. The best players in school history include Bob Cook, Gene Englund, Michael Finley, Claude Gregory, Devin Harris, John Kotz, Wes Matthews, Brad Sellers, Christian Steinmetz, and Alando Tucker.

WOHLFARTH, WALTER F. "DUTCH." B. 8 September 1888. D. 25 January 1973, Shadyside, Pittsburgh, Pennsylvania. Dutch Wohlfarth was known as "The Blind Dribbler." In an era when two-handed **dribbling** was permitted, he was one of the first players to dribble the ball without looking at it. He played **guard**, primarily a defensive position, but was a top scorer and in 1911–1912 with Johnstown in the **Central Basketball League (CBL)**, where he was tied for the lead in **field goals**, with 233 in 58 games. His average of 4.02 field goals per game was considered a remarkable feat during a time when a guard who scored two field goals per game was thought to be exceptional. A dental student at the University of Pittsburgh, he played for Homestead in 1907–1911 and Johnstown in 1911–1912. After the CBL folded in 1912, Wohlfarth played with Jasper in the Eastern League from 1912–1914. He later owned a bakery.

WOMEN'S BASKETBALL HALL OF FAME. The Women's Basketball Hall of Fame is located in Knoxville, Tennessee, and was opened in June 1999. Its mission is to "honor the past, celebrate the present, promote the future." Induction ceremonies take place annually. *See also* APPENDIX L (for inductees).

WOMEN'S NATIONAL BASKETBALL ASSOCIATION (WNBA). The Women's National Basketball Association (WNBA) is a women's professional basketball major league that began operation in 1997. It was created on 24 April 1996, by the men's **National Basketball Association (NBA)**, to take advantage of the heightened interest in women's basketball as a result of the **United States'** success in the 1996 **Olympic Games**. Its first game was played on 21 June 1997, in Los Angeles, between New York and Los Angeles. The league began with eight teams placed in NBA cities, including the Charlotte Sting, Cleveland Rockers, Houston Comets, Los Angeles Sparks, New York Liberty, Phoenix Mercury, Sacramento Monarchs, and Utah Starzz, and during its existence it has had as many as 13 teams. The WNBA has survived longer than any other women's basketball league in the United States, as the 2010 season was the league's 14th.

Games are played during the summer months so as not to conflict with the NBA. League rules are generally the same as the NBA, although 40-**minute** games are played instead of the NBA's 48-minute games, the **three-point field goal** line is closer than in the NBA, and the ball is slightly smaller. Most of the teams in the league play in the same arenas as the NBA teams, but attendance is usually less than half of that for NBA games, with an average of about 8,000–9,000 per game. Since the NBA is sponsoring the league, there is little danger of the league dissolving, as was the case with its predecessors. From 1997–2000, the Houston Comets were league champions. Since then, the Detroit Shock have won three times, the Los Angeles Sparks, Phoenix Mercury, and Seattle Storm have won twice, and the

Sacramento Monarchs has won once. *See also* APPENDIX B (for a list of league champions).

WOMEN'S PROFESSIONAL BASKETBALL LEAGUE (WBL). The Women's Professional Basketball League (WBL) was organized by Bill Byrne and began operation in 1978 in an attempt to capitalize on the interest in women's **basketball** created by the 1976 **Olympic Games**. Teams in the league were the Chicago Hustle, Dayton Rockettes, Houston Angels, Iowa Cornets, Milwaukee Does, Minnesota Fillies, New Jersey Gems, and New York Stars. The league played a 34-game schedule. Its first game was played in Milwaukee on 9 December 1978. The second season saw the league expand to 14 teams, but by the league's third year only nine teams remained.

The league attracted most of the top women's players of the era and included eight of the 12 members of the 1976 **U.S.** Olympic Team, including Cindy Brogdon, Nancy Dunkle, **Lusia Harris**, Charlotte Lewis, **Nancy Lieberman**, Gail Marquis, **Ann Meyers**, and Trish Roberts. For the 1980–1981 season, four of the players on the 1980 U.S. Olympic team also joined the league, namely **Carol Blazejowski**, Tara Heiss, Rosie Walker, and Holly Warlick. The WBL player that received the most press, however, was "Machine Gun" Molly Bolin, an attractive blond who had only played the six-a-side girls' version in Iowa and was a prolific scorer.

During the WBL's third season, financial problems for most of the teams caused players to go without pay, go on strike, and refuse to play. League travel was difficult, as owners attempted to cut costs and players would be required to fly standby or drive eight hours by car to reach their destinations. Hotel rooms were also at a premium, and some teams placed six players in one room. Although attempts were made to keep the league going for a fourth season, it did not come to pass. *Mad Seasons*, an excellent account of the WBL and its personalities, written by Karra Porter, was published in 2006. *See also* APPENDIX B (for a list of league champions).

WOODARD, LYNETTE. B. 12 August 1959, Wichita, Kansas. Lynette Woodard attended Wichita North High School and the **University of Kansas**. A five-foot, 11-inch **guard**, she scored 3,649 points at Kansas and is the all-time leading scorer in women's major college **basketball**. She was selected for the 1980 **U.S. Olympic** basketball team that boycotted the Moscow Olympics. She retained her amateur status and was later selected for the 1983 Pan American Games **(gold medal)**, 1983 **World Championships (silver medal)**, 1984 Olympic Games (gold medal), 1990 Goodwill Games (gold medal), 1990 World Championships (gold medal), and 1991 Pan American Games **(bronze medal)**. In 1985, she became the first female to be signed by the **Harlem Globetrotters**. Her cousin, Hubert "Geese" Ausbie, was one of the Trotters' stars for 25 years and played his last Globetrotter season as her teammate. From 1987–1989, she played in the Italian league and, from 1990–1993, played in **Japan**.

At the age of 38, Woodard played in the **Women's National Basketball Association**'s initial season in 1997 with the Cleveland Rockers. Her final professional season was with the Detroit Shock in the 1998 WNBA. In 55 regular-season WNBA games, she averaged 5.7 points per game. She also worked as a stockbroker in New York and in 1999 became assistant **coach** at the University of Kansas. In 2004, she was enshrined in the **Naismith Memorial Basketball Hall of Fame** and in 2005 in the **Women's Basketball Hall of Fame**.

WOODEN, JOHN ROBERT. B. 14 October 1910, Hall, Indiana. D. 4 June 2010, Los Angeles, California. John Wooden attended Martinsville High School in Martinsville, Indiana, and **Purdue University**. He led Martinsville to the state championship in 1927 and the finals in 1926 and 1928. In 1932, he graduated from Purdue with a degree in English and was a member of the unofficial 1932 national championship team. The five-foot, 10-inch **guard** received the nickname "The India Rubber Man" for his ability to bounce off the floor diving for loose balls. He played professionally for the Indianapolis Kautskys in the **Midwest Basketball Conference** in 1936. In the 1937–1938 season, the league was renamed the **National Basketball League (NBL)**. Wooden played for Whiting, averaged 11.0 points per game, and was selected to the All-NBL First Team. In the 1938–1939 season of the NBL, he played for Hammond and Indianapolis, averaging 7.1 points per game.

Wooden began his **coaching** career at Dayton High School in Dayton, Kentucky. After spending two years there, he moved to South Bend Central High School in South Bend, Indiana. In 1942, he enlisted in the **U.S.** Navy. After the war, he was hired as athletic director, baseball coach, and **basketball** coach at **Indiana State University** in 1946. Although he coached at Indiana State for only two years, he made a major impact on basketball history while there. The school won their conference championship in 1947 and was invited to the National Association of Intercollegiate Basketball (NAIB) national tournament. One of Indiana State's players, Clarence Walker, was not allowed to play in the tournament, as the NAIB at that time had a rule banning black players, thus Wooden refused the invitation. The following year, the NAIB changed its rules and, Indiana State, along with Walker, competed in the tournament but lost the championship final game to the **University of Louisville**. Walker was the first African American to play in an intercollegiate postseason tournament.

In 1948, Wooden was hired by the **University of California, Los Angeles (UCLA)**. For the next 27 years, he was their head basketball coach, and his teams had winning records in all 27 years. In 1964, they won the **National Collegiate Athletic Association (NCAA)** National Championship and began an unprecedented string of championships. They repeated as champions in 1965, did not reach the tournament in 1966, and in 1967 won the first of seven consecutive championships. Their overall record for these seven years was 205–5. They had an 88-game winning streak that ended in 1974, when they were defeated by **Notre Dame University** on 19 January. In 1974, they were defeated in the semifinal round of the NCAA tournament in double **overtime** by **North Carolina State University** but won the consolation game and finished third. In 1976, Wooden's final year as head coach, UCLA again won the NCAA tournament. His career record at UCLA was 620–147, and his overall college coaching record was 664–162.

Wooden has been one of the most widely respected coaches and is known for teaching his "Pyramid of Success" philosophy. He was enshrined in the **Naismith Memorial Basketball Hall of Fame** in 1961 in the category of player and was enshrined a second time as a coach in 1973. In retirement, he held the title head coach emeritus at UCLA. He died of natural causes on 4 June 2010, four months shy of his 100th birthday.

WOOTTEN, MORGAN BAYARD. B. 21 April 1931, Durham, North Carolina. Morgan Wootten's major contribution to **basketball** was as a **coach**. He coached DeMatha Catholic High School in Hyattsville, Maryland, from 1956–2002, and had the remarkable won–lost record of 1,274–192, with two undefeated seasons and seven seasons with just one defeat. In 1965, DeMatha ended Power Memorial's 71-game winning-streak. In 1980, Wootten was reportedly offered the job as coach of **Duke University** (which **Mike Krzyzewski** eventually accepted) and **North Carolina State University** (which **Jim Valvano** took) but refused the positions, preferring to remain at DeMatha. In 1991, he was the recipient of the John W. Bunn Award for lifetime achievement from the **Naismith Memorial Basketball Hall of Fame**. The author of five books on basketball, he was enshrined in the hall in 2000 as a coach. In 2007, the Hall of Fame instituted the Morgan Wootten Award to honor both a boys' and a girls' high school basketball coach who "have had tremendous influence on the game."

WORLD BASKETBALL LEAGUE (WBL). The World Basketball League (WBL) was a men's professional **basketball** minor league that began operation in 1988. It was a summer league and featured several innovations. One was a maximum height for players. From 1988–1991, the maximum was six-feet, five-inches and, in 1992, it was raised to six-feet, seven-inches. Another innovation was the scheduling of regular-league games with international teams. The WBL began its first year with six teams, namely the Calgary 88s, Chicago Express, Fresno Flames, Las Vegas Silver Streaks, Vancouver Nighthawks, and Youngstown Pride, and teams played a 54-game schedule.

In 1989, international teams from Finland, **Greece**, **Italy**, the Netherlands, Norway, and the **Union of Soviet Socialist Republics (USSR)** were invited to play regular-league games with the five other league teams, but the internationals were only able to win one game of the 50 that they played. The league's final season, 1992, saw 10 North American teams, plus the Estonian Nationals; Abruzzo, Italy All-Stars; Kiev, USSR All-Stars; and Bahamas All-Stars compete. On 1 August 1992, after several teams had dropped out, the league disbanded. Many WBL players eventually played in the **National**

Basketball Association, including Vincent Askew, Mario Elie, Jim Les, Sidney Lowe, Kenny Natt, Keith Smart, and Mark Wade.

WORLD CHAMPIONSHIPS OF BASKETBALL. The World Championships of Basketball are organized by the **Fédération Internationale de Basketball (FIBA)**. Separate tournaments are held quadrennially for men and women. The first men's tournament was held in Buenos Aires, **Argentina**, and was won by the host nation. Ten nations competed. The tournament's size has varied, and as many as 24 teams entered in 1986, 2006, and 2010. The women's tournament began in 1953 in Santiago, **Chile**, with 10 nations participating. That tournament has since been expanded to 16 teams. *See also* APPENDIX H and APPENDIX I (for additional details).

WORLD PROFESSIONAL BASKETBALL TOURNAMENT. The World Professional Basketball Tournament was organized by Arch Ward of the *Chicago Herald-American* in 1939. Eight of the best professional teams were invited for the initial event, which took place in Chicago from 26–28 March 1939. The invitational tournament was contested annually in Chicago from 1939–1948, with as many as 16 teams entered. Such independent teams as the **New York Renaissance** and **Harlem Globetrotters** competed, as well as **National Basketball League** and **American Basketball League** teams. *See also* APPENDIX B (for a list of tournament champions).

WORTHY, JAMES AGER. B. 27 February 1961, Gastonia, North Carolina. James Worthy attended Ashbrook High School in Gastonia and the **University of North Carolina**. He led North Carolina to the 1981 **National Collegiate Athletic Association (NCAA)** Championship game, where they were defeated by **Indiana University**. The following year, North Carolina won the NCAA Championship, and Worthy was selected as the tournament's Most Outstanding Player. He dropped out of college following his junior year (but later completed his degree requirements in summer school) and was selected by the **Los Angeles Lakers** in the 1982 **National Basketball Association (NBA) draft** as the first overall selection. The six-foot, nine-inch **forward** played from 1982–1994 for the Lakers.

Worthy's NBA career totals for 12 years are 926 regular-season games and a 17.6 points per game average. In 143 playoff games in nine years, he averaged 21.1 points per game, earning himself the nickname "Big Game James." He played in seven NBA Finals and was a member of the NBA champions in 1985, 1987, and 1988. In 1988, he was also chosen as the Finals Most Valuable Player. He was selected for seven NBA **All-Star Games** and was named to the All-NBA Third Team in 1990 and 1991.

After retiring from active play, Worthy became the chief excutive officer of Worthy Enterprises and does television work for Laker games. In 1996, he was named one of the 50 Greatest Players in NBA History. He was enshrined in the **Naismith Memorial Basketball Hall of Fame** in 2003.

WYOMING, UNIVERSITY OF. The University of Wyoming in Laramie began its **basketball** program in 1904. The best players in the Cowboys' history include Fennis Dembo; Curt Gowdy, who became much more famous as a television sportscaster; Milo Komenich; Eric Leckner; John Pilch; Flynn Robinson; Kenny Sailors; Reggie Slater; Theo Ratliff; Floyd Volker; and Tony Windis. Wyoming became **National Collegiate Athletic Association** champions in 1943, the only trip to the **Final Four** in the school's history. Since 1982, the 15,028-seat Arena-Auditorium has been the site of Wyoming's home games. From 1951–1982, home games were played at the War Memorial Field House, and before that the Half-Acre Gym was used. The most noted **coaches** in the school's history have been Jim Brandenburg, Everett Shelton, and Willard "Dutch" Witte.

– Y –

YAO, MING. B. 12 September 1980, Shanghai, **China**. Yao Ming is the son of two former Chinese national team **basketball** players. From 1997–2002, he played for the Shanghai Sharks in the Chinese Basketball Association and was the first international player to be the first overall selection when he was selected in the 2002 **National Basketball Association (NBA) draft**. The seven-foot, six-inch,

300-pound **center** is one of the four tallest men to ever play in the NBA. He has a remarkable shooting touch for someone his size and, from 2005–2006 through 2007–2009, shot **free throws** with 86 percent accuracy. He has played for the **Houston Rockets** from 2002–2009. He suffered a fracture in his left foot at the end of the 2008–2009 season and was unable to play in 2009–2010 but plans to return to Houston for the 2010–2011 season.

In his first seven years in the NBA, Ming averaged 19.1 points per game, with a high of 25.0 points per game during the 2006–2007 season, and he was selected for the NBA **All-Star Game** each year. He was named to the All-NBA Second Team twice and All-NBA Third Team three times. With the Chinese national team in three **Olympic Games** from 2000–2008, he averaged 16.9 points per game in 19 games and was the country's flag-bearer in 2004 and 2008. On 6 August 2007, Yao married Chinese Olympic basketball player Ye Li.

YARDLEY III, GEORGE HARRY "BIRD." B. 3 November 1928, Hollywood, California. D. 12 August 2004, Newport Beach, California. George Yardley is best known as the man who first scored more than 2,000 points in a single **National Basketball Association (NBA)** season, gaining a total of 2,001 in 1957–1958. The six-foot, five-inch, prematurely bald **forward** saw his record stand for only a single year, as **Bob Pettit** broke it 1959 and **Wilt Chamberlain** shattered it the year after that. Yardley attended Balboa Newport Harbor High School in Balboa, California, and **Stanford University**. He was drafted by the Fort Wayne Pistons of the NBA in 1950 but decided to play amateur basketball for the Stewart Chevrolet team in the **National Industrial Basketball League** for a season while working toward his master's degree in engineering at Stanford. He followed that with two years in the Naval Air Corps.

Yardley's first NBA season was in 1953–1954. After five and one-half years with the Pistons, he was traded to the Syracuse Nationals. In 1960, he retired to devote more time to his engineering firm, the George Yardley Co. of Santa Ana, California, but returned to play the 1961–1962 season for Los Angeles of the new **American Basketball League (ABL)**. He was elected to the **Naismith Memorial Basketball Hall of Fame** in 1996.

YUGOSLAVIA. Yugoslavia joined the **Fédération Internationale de Basketball (FIBA)** in 1936 and was a member in the FIBA Europe zone until 2003, when the remaining republics of the country changed their name to Serbia and Montenegro. The men's team competed in all eight **Olympic** tournaments from 1960–1988, the only nation to do so. They won the tournament in 1980 in Moscow in an upset over the **Union of Soviet Socialist Republics.** They were second in 1968, 1976, and 1988 and third in 1984. After the breakup of the country in 1991, the republics of Serbia and Montenegro retained the name of Yugoslavia and competed in the 1996 and 2000 Olympic Games, where they finished second in 1996 and sixth in 2000. In the FIBA **World Championships,** they have the most outstanding record of all competitors, with five victories, three second-place finishes, and two third-place finishes in 12 competitions. In the FIBA European Championships, they entered 25 times and won eight times, were second five times, and placed third four times.

The women's team competed in three Olympic tournaments and won the **bronze medal** in 1980 and **silver medal** in 1988. In the FIBA World Championships, they have competed six times and finished second in 1990 as their best effort. In the FIBA European Championships, they entered 24 times and were second four times and placed third twice.

Among the most outstanding Olympians have been the four-time Olympian and Hall of Famer **Krešimir Ćosić** and three-time Olympians Dražen Dalipagić, Ivo Daneu, Andro Knego, Radivoje Korać, Damir Šolman, and Rajko Žižić. There have been more than two-dozen players from the former Yugoslavia in the **National Basketball Association,** including some of the league's best, such as **Vlade Divać,** Marko Jarić, Nenad Krstić, **Dražen Petrović,** Vladimir Radmanović, and **Peja Stojaković.** The **Women's National Basketball Association** has featured more than a dozen Yugoslavian players.

– Z –

ZASLOFSKY, MAX "SLATS," "THE TOUCH." B. 7 December 1925, Brooklyn, New York. D. 15 October 1985, New Hyde Park,

New York. Max Zaslofsky graduated from Thomas Jefferson High School in Brooklyn, was in the military for two years, and attended **St. John's University** for one year. One of the stars of the **Basketball Association of America**'s **(BAA)** first season in 1946–1947, he played for the **Chicago Stags** for four seasons before returning to his New York City home for three years with the **New York Knickerbockers**. He continued his pro career with a year split between Baltimore and Milwaukee and finished with three years in Fort Wayne. With the Stags, he led the BAA in scoring in the 1947–1948 season and finished in the top five the other three years.

The six-foot, two-inch **guard-forward** had an outstanding outside shot. In 1950, Zaslofsky led the **National Basketball Association** **(NBA)** in **free throw** percentage, becoming one of only three players to lead the league in both scoring and free throw percentage. He was selected for the All-League First Team four times and to the 1952 **All-Star Game**. When he retired after the 1955–1956 season, his regular-season total of 7,990 points in 540 games was the third highest career-scoring total in the NBA. After retiring from active play, he was manager of a bowling alley. When the **American Basketball Association** began in 1967, he was chosen as head **coach** and general manager of the New Jersey Americans/**New York Nets**, coaching them for two seasons.

ZHENG, HAIXIA. B. 7 March 1967, Tuocheng, Henan Province, **China**. There are very few female athletes who admit to weighing more than 250 pounds, but China's Zheng Haixia is one of them. With the nicknames "Baby Huey," "Big Girl," and "The Wall," she was the second heaviest **Olympic** women's **basketball** player, at 254 pounds (115 kilograms); however, on her six-foot, eight-inch frame with size 18 sneakers on her feet, that weight did not prohibit her from being one of the most effective players of all time.

Zheng was selected to the Chinese national team at the age of 15 and was on the **bronze medal**-winning team at the 1983 **World Championships**. In 1994, she was the Most Valuable Player of the World Championships, where China won the **silver medal**. She appeared in four Olympic tournaments from 1984–1996 and won a bronze medal in her first at the age of 17 years and 145 days, making her the youngest women's basketball Olympic medalist ever.

Ironically, on that 1984 team, she was not even the tallest player on her own team, as the six-foot, nine-inch Chen Yuefang held that distinction. In the Barcelona Olympics in 1992, Zheng helped lead China to the silver medal. In 1997, she became the first Chinese person (man or woman) to play professional basketball in the United States when she signed with the Los Angeles Sparks of the **Women's National Basketball Association (WNBA)**. She played one additional year in the WNBA and retired after the 1998 season. She later became head **coach** of the Bayi team in the Chinese professional women's basketball league.

ZHI ZHI, WANG. *See* WANG, ZHI ZHI.

ZINKOFF, DAVID "DAVE," "ZINK." B. 15 May 1910, Russia. D. 25 December 1985, Philadelphia, Pennsylvania. For four decades, Dave Zinkoff made watching Philadelphia **basketball** much more exciting than watching games in other cities. He was the public address announcer for most of Philadelphia's sports events from the mid-1940s until 1985. A 1932 graduate of the **Temple University** School of Commerce, he was the announcer at Temple University events and also announced for the baseball Philadelphia Phillies, the basketball Philadelphia Warriors and **Philadelphia 76ers**, and Convention Hall boxing and wrestling. He accompanied the **Harlem Globetrotters** on their first round-the-world tour in 1952 and wrote a book about his experiences.

Zinkoff's unique style added to the game's entertainment in an era when most announcers simply reported the facts. He would call a "Gola goal" when **Tom Gola** scored or a "Dipper dunk" when **Wilt Chamberlain** scored for the Warriors. In the **National Basketball Association**, when a player in certain situations received three attempts to make two **free throws**, if the 76ers Lloyd Free was the recipient, Zink would say, "Lloyd at the line, Free to make two." Crediting an **assist** from Fred Carter to **Billy Cunningham** was, "Caaaaahter from Cunning-haaaaaam." **Julius Erving** was always reported as "Errrrrrrving." On 25 March 1986, the 76ers held a ceremony in which his microphone was retired in the same manner that celebrated players' uniforms were retired—with a banner hung from the rafters of the 76ers arena.

ZOLLNER, FRED. B. 22 January 1901, Little Falls, Minnesota. D. 21 June 1982, North Miami, Florida. Fred Zollner earned an engineering degree from the University of Minnesota in 1927 and became coowner of the Zollner Machine Works with his father, Theodore. Engine pistons became the major product of the company, which relocated to Fort Wayne in 1931. Both father and son were avid sports fans, and the company sponsored softball and **basketball** teams in local industrial leagues.

In 1941, the Fort Wayne Zollner Pistons joined the **National Basketball League (NBL)**. With the company's success due to the heavy production requirements of World War II, and Fred Zollner's "quest for the best" attitude, he was able to hire some of the best basketball players to bolster his team. As a result, the Zollner Pistons finished second in the NBL in their first season and were league champions the following three years.

As the rival **Basketball Association of America (BAA)** began to succeed, the Pistons, along with three other strong NBL teams, the **Minneapolis Lakers**, **Rochester Royals**, and **Indianapolis Kautskys**, were enticed to join the BAA for the 1948–1949 season. Zollner helped orchestrate the BAA-NBL merger in 1949 that created the **National Basketball Association (NBA)**.

In 1952, Zollner, attempting to gain an edge on the competition, decided to charter a DC-3 airplane to ease the team's travel. The move proved to be successful, and Zollner then purchased a 21-passenger plane to transport the team, the first such acquisition in sports history. Zollner achieved another first in 1954, when he gave a three-year contract to **Charley Eckman** to be his head **coach**. Eckman had been an NBA **referee** with no prior coaching experience. He led the Pistons to the 1955 NBA Finals, where they lost the league championship in the seventh and final game to the **Syracuse Nationals**. Following the 1956–1957 season, the Pistons moved to Detroit, and in 1974, Zollner sold his interest in the team to William Davidson. On 1 October 1999, Fred Zollner was inducted into the **Naismith Memorial Basketball Hall of Fame** as a contributor.

Appendix A
Dr. James Naismith's Original
Thirteen Rules of Basketball

The ball is to be an ordinary association football (soccer ball).

1. The ball may be thrown in any direction with one or both hands.
2. The ball may be batted in any direction with one or both hands (never with the fist).
3. A player cannot run with the ball. The player must throw it from the spot on which he catches it; allowance to be made for a man who catches the ball when running at a good speed.
4. The ball must be held in or between the hands; the arms or body must not be used for holding it.
5. No shouldering, holding, pushing, tripping, or striking, in any way, the person of an opponent shall be allowed; the first infringement of this rule shall disqualify the player until the next goal is made, or if there was evident intent to injure the person for the whole of the game, no substitute allowed.
6. A foul is striking at the ball with the fist, violations of Rules 3 and 4 and such as described in Rule 5.
7. If either side makes three consecutive fouls, it shall count a goal for the opponents (consecutive means without the opponents in the meantime making a foul).
8. A goal shall be made when the ball is thrown or batted from the grounds into the basket and stays there, providing those defending the goal do not touch or disturb the goal. If the ball rests on the edge and the opponent moves the basket, it shall count as a goal.
9. When the ball goes out of bounds, it shall be thrown into the field and played by the person first touching it. In case of a dispute, the umpire shall throw it into the field. The thrower-in is allowed five seconds. If he holds it longer, it shall go to the opponent. If any side persists in delaying the game, the umpire shall call a foul on them.

10. The umpire shall be judge of the men and shall note the fouls and notify the referee when three consecutive fouls have been made. He shall have power to disqualify men according to Rule 5.
11. The referee shall be judge of the ball and shall decide when the ball is in play, in bounds, to which side it belongs, and shall keep the time. He shall decide when a goal has been made and keep account of the goals, with any other duties that are usually performed by a referee.
12. The time shall be two fifteen-minute halves, with five minutes rest between.
13. The side making the most goals in that time shall be declared the winners. In case of a draw, the game may, by agreement of the captains, be continued until another goal is made.

Appendix B
Major Professional
Basketball League Champions

National Basketball League

1898–1899	Trenton Nationals
1899–1900	Trenton Nationals
1900–1901	New York Wanderers
1901–1902	Bristol Pile Drivers
1902–1903	Camden Electrics
1903–1904	Camden Electrics

Disbanded on 18 January 1904

Philadelphia Basketball League

1902–1903	Columbia F.C.
1903–1904	Jasper A.C.
1904–1905	Conshohocken
1905–1906	De Neri
1906–1907	Conshohocken
1907–1908	Germantown
1908–1909	Germantown

Disbanded on 9 January 1909

Central Basketball League

1906–1907	East Liverpool
1907–1908	East Liverpool
1908–1909	Homestead
1909–1910	McKeesport
1910–1911	McKeesport

1911–1912   Johnstown
Disbanded on 12 November 1912

Hudson River League

1909–1910   Troy Trojans
1910–1911   Troy Trojans
1911–1912   Kingston Co. M
Disbanded on 12 January 1912

Eastern Basketball League

1909–1910   Trenton Potters
1910–1911   DeNeri
1911–1912   Trenton Potters
1912–1913   Reading Bears
1913–1914   Jasper Jewels
1914–1915   Camden Alphas
                 Reading Bears
1915–1916   Greystock Greys
1916–1917   Greystock Greys
1917–1918   Jasper Jewels
Suspended on 3 December 1917
1918–1919   No league
1919–1920   Camden Crusaders
1920–1921   Germantown
1921–1922   New York Celtics
1922–1923   Trenton Tigers
Disbanded on 18 January 1923

New York State League

1911–1912   Troy Trojans
1912–1913   Troy Trojans
1913–1914   Utica Indians
1914–1915   Troy Trojans
Season ended early on 2 January 1915
1915–1916   Schenectady

1916–1917	Schenectady

Suspended on 17 February 1917

1917–1918	No league
1918–1919	No league
1919–1920	Albany Senators
	Troy Trojans
1920–1921	Albany Senators
1921–1922	Cohoes
1922–1923	Kingston Colonials
1923–1924	Discontinued

Pennsylvania State League

1914–1915	Pittston
1915–1916	Wilkes-Barre
1916–1917	Carbondale
1917–1918	Pittston
1918–1919	No league
1919–1920	Nanticoke
1920–1921	Scranton
1921–1922	Disbanded

Interstate Basketball League

1915–1916	Paterson
1916–1917	Bridgeport
1917–1918	No league
1918–1919	No league
1919–1920	New York

Disbanded on 10 January 1920

Metropolitan Basketball League

1921–1922	Brooklyn Dodgers
1922–1923	Paterson Legionnaires
1923–1924	Brooklyn Visitations
1924–1925	Brooklyn Visitations

1925–1926	Greenpoint Knights
1926–1927	Brooklyn Visitations
1927–1928	Kingston Colonials

Disbanded in January 1928

American Basketball League

1925–1926	Cleveland Rosenblums
1926–1927	Brooklyn Celtics
1927–1928	New York Celtics
1928–1929	Cleveland Rosenblums
1929–1930	Cleveland Rosenblums
1930–1931	Brooklyn Visitations
1931–1933	Suspended operations

American Basketball League

1933–1934	Philadelphia SPHAs
1934–1935	Brooklyn Visitations
1935–1936	Philadelphia SPHAs
1936–1937	Philadelphia SPHAs
1937–1938	Jersey Reds
1938–1939	New York Jewels
1939–1940	Philadelphia SPHAs
1940–1941	Philadelphia SPHAs
1941–1942	Wilmington Bombers
1942–1943	Philadelphia SPHAs
1943–1944	Wilmington Bombers
1944–1945	Philadelphia SPHAs
1945–1946	Baltimore Bullets
1946–1947	Trenton Tigers
1947–1948	Wilkes-Barre Barons
1948–1949	Wilkes-Barre Barons
1949–1950	Scranton Miners
1950–1951	Scranton Miners
1951–1952	Wilkes-Barre Barons
1952–1953	Manchester British Americans
1953–1954	Disbanded

Midwest Basketball Conference

1935–1936   Chicago Duffy Florists
1936–1937   Akron Goodyears
Renamed the National Basketball League

National Basketball League

1937–1938   Akron Goodyears
1938–1939   Akron Firestones
1939–1940   Akron Firestones
1940–1941   Oshkosh All-Stars
1941–1942   Oshkosh All-Stars
1942–1943   Sheboygan Redskins
1943–1944   Fort Wayne Pistons
1944–1945   Fort Wayne Pistons
1945–1946   Rochester Royals
1946–1947   Chicago American Gears
1947–1948   Minneapolis Lakers
1948–1949   Anderson Packers
Merged with the Basketball Association of America on 3 August 1949

MAJOR PROFESSIONAL BASKETBALL LEAGUE CHAMPIONS

World Professional Basketball Tournament

1939   New York Renaissance
1940   Harlem Globetrotters
1941   Detroit Eagles
1942   Oshkosh All-Stars
1943   Washington Bears
1944   Fort Wayne Pistons
1945   Fort Wayne Pistons
1946   Fort Wayne Pistons
1947   Indianapolis Kautskys
1948   Minneapolis Lakers

Basketball Association of America

1946–1947   Philadelphia Warriors
1947–1948   Baltimore Bullets
1948–1949   Minneapolis Lakers
Merged with the National Basketball League on 3 August 1949

Professional Basketball League of America

1947–1948   Chicago Gears
                Houston Mavericks
Disbanded on 13 November 1947

National Professional Basketball League

1950–1951   Sheboygan Redskins
                Waterloo Hawks
Disbanded on 24 March 1951

American Basketball League

1961–1962   Cleveland Pipers
1962–1963   Kansas City Steers
Disbanded on 31 December 1962

American Basketball Association

1967–1968   Pittsburgh Pipers
1968–1969   Oakland Oaks
1969–1970   Indiana Pacers
1970–1971   Utah Stars
1971–1972   Indiana Pacers
1972–1973   Indiana Pacers
1973–1974   New York Nets
1974–1975   Kentucky Colonels
1975–1976   New York Nets
Merged with the National Basketball Association on 17 June 1976

National Basketball Association

1949–1950	Minneapolis Lakers
1950–1951	Rochester Royals
1951–1952	Minneapolis Lakers
1952–1953	Minneapolis Lakers
1953–1954	Minneapolis Lakers
1954–1955	Syracuse Nationals
1955–1956	Philadelphia Warriors
1956–1957	Boston Celtics
1957–1958	St. Louis Hawks
1958–1959	Boston Celtics
1959–1960	Boston Celtics
1960–1961	Boston Celtics
1961–1962	Boston Celtics
1962–1963	Boston Celtics
1963–1964	Boston Celtics
1964–1965	Boston Celtics
1965–1966	Boston Celtics
1966–1967	Philadelphia 76ers
1967–1968	Boston Celtics
1968–1969	Boston Celtics
1969–1970	New York Knickerbockers
1970–1971	Milwaukee Bucks
1971–1972	Los Angeles Lakers
1972–1973	New York Knickerbockers
1973–1974	Boston Celtics
1974–1975	Golden State Warriors
1975–1976	Boston Celtics
1976–1977	Portland Trail Blazers
1977–1978	Washington Bullets
1978–1979	Seattle Supersonics
1979–1980	Los Angeles Lakers
1980–1981	Boston Celtics
1981–1982	Los Angeles Lakers
1982–1983	Philadelphia 76ers
1983–1984	Boston Celtics
1984–1985	Los Angeles Lakers

1985–1986	Boston Celtics
1986–1987	Los Angeles Lakers
1987–1988	Los Angeles Lakers
1988–1989	Detroit Pistons
1989–1990	Detroit Pistons
1990–1991	Chicago Bulls
1991–1992	Chicago Bulls
1992–1993	Chicago Bulls
1993–1994	Houston Rockets
1994–1995	Houston Rockets
1995–1996	Chicago Bulls
1996–1997	Chicago Bulls
1997–1998	Chicago Bulls
1998–1999	San Antonio Spurs
1999–2000	Los Angeles Lakers
2000–2001	Los Angeles Lakers
2001–2002	Los Angeles Lakers
2002–2003	San Antonio Spurs
2003–2004	Detroit Pistons
2004–2005	San Antonio Spurs
2005–2006	Miami Heat
2006–2007	San Antonio Spurs
2007–2008	Boston Celtics
2008–2009	Los Angeles Lakers
2009–2010	Los Angeles Lakers

WOMEN'S LEAGUES

Women's Professional Basketball League

1978–1979	Houston Angels
1979–1980	New York Stars
1980–1981	Nebraska Wranglers

Disbanded in 1982

American Basketball League

| 1996–1997 | Columbus Quest |
| 1997–1998 | Columbus Quest |

1998–1999   Columbus Quest
                   Portland Power
Disbanded on 22 December 1998

Women's National Basketball Association

1997	Houston Comets
1998	Houston Comets
1999	Houston Comets
2000	Houston Comets
2001	Los Angeles Sparks
2002	Los Angeles Sparks
2003	Detroit Shock
2004	Seattle Storm
2005	Sacramento Monarchs
2006	Detroit Shock
2007	Phoenix Mercury
2008	Detroit Shock
2009	Phoenix Mercury
2010	Seattle Storm

Appendix C
National Collegiate Athletic
Association Champions: Men

DIVISION I

Year	Championship Final Game	Third-Place Game
1939	Oregon 46, Ohio State 33	*Oklahoma, Villanova
1940	Indiana 60, Kansas 42	*Duquesne, Southern California
1941	Wisconsin 39, Washington State 34	*Pittsburgh, Arkansas
1942	Stanford 53, Dartmouth 38	*Colorado, Kentucky
1943	Wyoming 46, Georgetown 34	*Texas, DePaul
1944	Utah 42, Dartmouth 40 (OT)	*Iowa State, Ohio State
1945	Oklahoma A&M 49, NYU 45	*Arkansas, Ohio State
1946	Oklahoma A&M 43, North Carolina 40	Ohio State 63, California 45
1947	Holy Cross 58, Oklahoma 47	Texas 54, CCNY 50
1948	Kentucky 58, Baylor 42	Holy Cross 60, Kansas State 54
1949	Kentucky 46, Oklahoma A&M 36	Illinois 57, Oregon State 53
1950	CCNY 71, Bradley 68	North Carolina State 53, Baylor 41
1951	Kentucky 68, Kansas State 58	Illinois 61, Oklahoma A&M 45
1952	Kansas 80, St. John's 63	Illinois 67, Santa Clara 64
1953	Indiana 69, Kansas 68	Washington 88, Louisiana St. 69

Year	Championship Final Game	Third-Place Game
1954	La Salle 92, Bradley 76	Penn State 70, Southern California 61
1955	San Francisco 77, La Salle 63	Colorado 75, Iowa 54
1956	San Francisco 83, Iowa 71	Temple 90, Southern Methodist 81
1957	North Carolina 54, Kansas 53 (3 OT)	San Francisco 67, Michigan State 60
1958	Kentucky 84, Seattle 72	Temple 67, Kansas State 57
1959	California 71, West Virginia 70	Cincinnati 98, Louisville 85
1960	Ohio State 75, California 55	Cincinnati 95, NYU 71
1961	Cincinnati 70, Ohio State 65 (OT)	St. Joseph's 127, Utah 120 (4 OT)
1962	Cincinnati 71, Ohio State 59	Wake Forest 82, UCLA 80
1963	Loyola Chicago 60, Cincinnati 58 (OT)	Duke 85, Oregon State 63
1964	UCLA 98, Duke 83	Michigan 100, Kansas State 90
1965	UCLA 91, Michigan 80	Princeton 118, Wichita State 82
1966	Texas Western 72, Kentucky 65	Duke 79, Utah 77
1967	UCLA 79, Dayton 64	Houston 84, North Carolina 62
1968	UCLA 78, North Carolina 55	Ohio State 89, Houston 85
1969	UCLA 92, Purdue 72	Drake 104, North Carolina 84
1970	UCLA 80, Jacksonville 69	New Mexico 79, St. Bonaventure 73
1971	UCLA 68, Villanova 62	W. Kentucky 77, Kansas 75
1972	UCLA 81, Florida State 76	North Carolina 105, Louisville 91
1973	UCLA 87, Memphis State 66	Indiana 97, Providence 79
1974	North Carolina State 76, Marquette 64	UCLA 78, Kansas 61
1975	UCLA 92, Kentucky 85	Louisville 96, Syracuse 88
1976	Indiana 86, Michigan 68	UCLA 106, Rutgers 92
1977	Marquette 67, North Carolina 59	UNLV 106, UNC Charlotte 94

Year	Championship Final Game	Third-Place Game
1978	Kentucky 94, Duke 88	Arkansas 71, Notre Dame 69
1979	Michigan State 75, Indiana State 64	DePaul 96, Pennsylvania 93
1980	Louisville 59, UCLA 54	Purdue 75, Iowa 58
1981	Indiana 63, North Carolina 50	Virginia 78, Louisiana State 74
1982	North Carolina 63, Georgetown 62	*Houston, Louisville
1983	North Carolina State 54, Houston 52	*Georgia, Louisville
1984	Georgetown 84, Houston 75	*Kentucky, Virginia
1985	Villanova 66, Georgetown 64	*Memphis State, St. John's
1986	Louisville 72, Duke 69	*Louisiana State, Kansas
1987	Indiana 74, Syracuse 73	*UNLV, Providence
1988	Kansas 83, Oklahoma 79	*Duke, Arizona
1989	Michigan 80, Seton Hall 79 (OT)	*Illinois, Duke
1990	UNLV 103, Duke 73	*Georgia Tech, Arkansas
1991	Duke 72, Kansas 65	*UNLV, North Carolina
1992	Duke 71, Michigan 51	*Indiana, Cincinnati
1993	North Carolina 77, Michigan 71	*Kansas, Kentucky
1994	Arkansas 76, Duke 72	*Arizona, Florida
1995	UCLA 89, Arkansas 78	*Oklahoma State, North Carolina
1996	Kentucky 76, Syracuse 67	*Massachusetts, Mississippi State
1997	Arizona 84, Kentucky 79	*North Carolina, Minnesota
1998	Kentucky 78, Utah 69	*Stanford, North Carolina
1999	Connecticut 77, Duke 74	*Ohio State, Michigan State
2000	Michigan State 89, Florida 76	*Wisconsin, North Carolina
2001	Duke 82, Arizona 72	*Maryland, Michigan State
2002	Maryland 64, Indiana 52	*Kansas, Oklahoma
2003	Syracuse 81, Kansas 78	*Texas, Marquette
2004	Connecticut 82, Georgia Tech 73	*Duke, Oklahoma State
2005	North Carolina 75, Illinois 70	*Michigan State, Louisville

Year	Championship Final Game	Third-Place Game
2006	Florida 73, UCLA 57	*George Mason, Louisiana State
2007	Florida 84, Ohio State 75	*UCLA, Georgetown
2008	Kansas 75, Memphis 68 (OT)	*North Carolina, UCLA
2009	North Carolina 89, Michigan State 72	*Villanova, Connecticut
2010	Duke 61, Butler 59	*West Virginia, Michigan State

* Third-place consolation game not played in 1939–1945 and 1982–2010.

Participation vacated for using ineligible players: St. Joseph's, 1961; Villanova, 1971; Western Kentucky, 1971; UCLA, 1980; Memphis State, 1985; Michigan, 1992, 1993; Massachusetts, 1996; Minnesota, 1997; Ohio State, 1999, Memphis 2008.

Appendix D
National Collegiate Athletic
Association Champions: Women

DIVISION I

Year	Championship Final Game	Semifinalists
1982	Louisiana Tech 76, Cheyney State 62	Tennessee, Maryland
1983	Southern California 69, Louisiana Tech 67	Georgia, Old Dominion
1984	Southern California 72, Tennessee 61	Louisiana Tech, Cheyney State
1985	Old Dominion 70, Georgia 65	Northeast Louisiana, W. Kentucky
1986	Texas 97, Southern California 81	Western Kentucky, Tennessee
1987	Tennessee 67, Louisiana Tech 44	Long Beach State, Texas
1988	Louisiana Tech 56, Auburn 54	Tennessee, Long Beach State
1989	Tennessee 76, Auburn 60	Maryland, Louisiana Tech
1990	Stanford 88, Auburn 81	Virginia, Louisiana Tech
1991	Tennessee 70, Virginia 67 (OT)	Stanford, Connecticut
1992	Stanford 78, Western Kentucky 62	Virginia, Southwest Missouri State
1993	Texas Tech 84, Ohio State 82	Vanderbilt, Iowa
1994	North Carolina 60, Louisiana Tech 59	Purdue, Alabama
1995	Connecticut 70, Tennessee 64	Stanford, Georgia
1996	Tennessee 83, Georgia 65	Connecticut, Stanford

Year	Championship Final Game	Semifinalists
1997	Tennessee 68, Old Dominion 59	Notre Dame, Stanford
1998	Tennessee 93, Louisiana Tech 75	Arkansas, North Carolina State
1999	Purdue 62, Duke 45	Louisiana Tech, Georgia
2000	Connecticut 71, Tennessee 52	Penn State, Rutgers
2001	Notre Dame 68, Purdue 66	Connecticut, Southwest Missouri State
2002	Connecticut 82, Oklahoma 70	Tennessee Duke
2003	Connecticut 73, Tennessee 68	Texas, Duke
2004	Connecticut 70, Tennessee 61	Minnesota, Louisiana State
2005	Baylor 84, Michigan State 62	Louisiana State, Tennessee
2006	Maryland 78, Duke 75 (OT)	North Carolina, Louisiana State
2007	Tennessee 59, Rutgers 46	North Carolina, Louisiana State
2008	Tennessee 64, Stanford 48	Louisiana State, Connecticut
2009	Connecticut 76, Louisville 54	Stanford, Oklahoma
2010	Connecticut 53, Stanford 47	Baylor, Oklahoma

Note: Loser to eventual champion listed first.

Appendix E
National Invitation Tournament Champions

Year	Championship Final Game	Third-Place Game
1938	Temple 60, Colorado 36	Oklahoma A&M 37, NYU 24
1939	Long Island 44, Loyola (IL) 32	Bradley 40, St. John's 35
1940	Colorado 51, Duquesne 40	Oklahoma A&M 23, DePaul 22
1941	Long Island 56, Ohio University 42	CCNY 42, Seton Hall 27
1942	West Virginia 47, Western Kentucky 45	Creighton 48, Toledo 46
1943	St. John's 48, Toledo 27	Washington & Jefferson 39, Fordham 34
1944	St. John's 47, DePaul 39	Kentucky 45, Oklahoma A&M 29
1945	DePaul 71, Bowling Green 54	St. John's 64, Rhode Island 57
1946	Kentucky 46, Rhode Island 45	West Virginia 65, Muhlenberg 40
1947	Utah 49, Kentucky 45	North Carolina State 64, West Virginia 52
1948	St. Louis 65, NYU 52	Western Kentucky 61, DePaul 59
1949	San Francisco 48, Loyola (IL) 47	Bowling Green 82, Bradley 77
1950	CCNY 69, Bradley 61	St. John's 69, Duquesne 67
1951	Brigham Young 62, Dayton 43	St. John's 70, Seton Hall 68
1952	LaSalle 75, Dayton 64	St. Bonaventure 48, Duquesne 34
1953	Seton Hall 58, St. John's 46	Duquesne 81, Manhattan 67

Year	Championship Final Game	Third-Place Game
1954	Holy Cross 71, Duquesne 62	Niagara 71, Western Kentucky 65
1955	Duquesne 70, Dayton 58	Cincinnati 96, St. Francis (PA) 91
1956	Louisville 93, Dayton 80	St. Joseph's 93, St. Francis (NY) 82
1957	Bradley 84, Memphis State 83	Temple 67, St. Bonaventure 50
1958	Xavier (OH) 78, Dayton 74	St. Bona. 84, St. John's 69
1959	St. John's 76, Bradley 71	NYU 71, Providence 57
1960	Bradley 88, Providence 72	Utah State 99, St. Bonaventure 83
1961	Providence 62, St. Louis 59	Holy Cross 85, Dayton 67
1962	Dayton 73, St. John's 67	Loyola (IL) 95, Duquesne 84
1963	Providence 81, Canisius 66	Marquette 66, Villanova 58
1964	Bradley 86, New Mexico 54	Army 60, NYU 59
1965	St. John's 55, Villanova 51	Army 75, NYU 74
1966	Brigham Young 97, NYU 84	Villanova 76, Army 65
1967	Southern Illinois 71, Marquette 56	Rutgers 93, Marshall 76
1968	Dayton 61, Kansas 48	Notre Dame 81, St. Peter's 78
1969	Temple 89, Boston College 76	Tennessee 64, Army 52
1970	Marquette 65, St. John's 53	Army 75, Louisiana State 68
1971	North Carolina 84, Georgia Tech 66	St. Bonaventure 92, Duke 88
1972	Maryland 100, Niagara 69	Jacksonville 83, St. John's 80
1973	Virginia Tech 92, Notre Dame 91	North Carolina 88, Alabama 69
1974	Purdue 87, Utah 81	Boston College 87, Jacksonville 77
1975	Princeton 80, Providence 69	Oregon 80, St. John's 76
1976	Kentucky 71, UNC Charlotte 67	North Carolina State 74, Providence 69
1977	St. Bonaventure 94, Houston 91	Villanova 102, Alabama 89

Year	Championship Final Game	Third-Place Game
1978	Texas 101, North Carolina State 93	Rutgers 85, Georgetown 72
1979	Indiana 53, Purdue 52	Alabama 96, Ohio State 86
1980	Virginia 58, Minnesota 55	Illinois 84, UNLV 74
1981	Tulsa 86, Syracuse 84	Purdue 75, West Virginia 72
1982	Bradley 67, Purdue 58	**Oklahoma, Georgia
1983	Fresno State 69, DePaul 60	**Wake Forest, Nebraska
1984	Michigan 83, Notre Dame 63	Virginia Tech 71, Louisiana, Lafayette 70
1985	UCLA 65, Indiana 62	Tennessee 100, Louisville 84
1986	Ohio State 73, Wyoming 63	Louisiana Tech 67, Florida 62
1987	Southern Mississippi 84, La Salle 80	Nebraska 76, Arkansas at Little Rock 67
1988	Connecticut 72, Ohio State 67	Colorado State 58, Boston College 57
1989	St. John's 73, Saint Louis 65	UAB 78, Michigan State 76
1990	Vanderbilt 74, Saint Louis 72	Penn State 83, New Mexico 81
1991	Stanford 78, Oklahoma 72	Colorado 98, Massachusetts 91
1992	Virginia 81, Notre Dame 76	Utah 81, Florida 78
1993	Minnesota 62, Georgetown 61	UAB 55, Providence 52
1994	Villanova 80, Vanderbilt 73	Siena 92, Kansas State 79
1995	Virginia Tech 65, Marquette 64	Penn State 66, Canisius 62
1996	Nebraska 60, St. Joseph's 56	Tulane 87, Alabama 76
1997	Michigan State 82, Florida State 73	Connecticut 74, Arkansas 64
1998	Minnesota* 79, Penn State 72	Georgia 95, Fresno State 79
1999	California 61, Clemson 60	Xavier 106, Oregon 75
2000	Wake Forest 71, Notre Dame 61	Penn State 74, North Carolina State 72
2001	Tulsa 79, Alabama 66	Memphis 86, Detroit 71
2002	Memphis 72, South Carolina 62	Temple 65, Syracuse 64
2003	St. John's* 70, Georgetown 67	Texas Tech 71, Minnesota 61

Year	Championship Final Game	Third-Place Game
2004	Michigan 62, Rutgers 55	**Oregon, Iowa State
2005	South Carolina 60, Saint Joseph's 57	**Maryland, Memphis
2006	South Carolina 76, Michigan 64	**Louisville, Old Dominion
2007	West Virginia 78, Clemson 73	**Mississippi State, Air Force
2008	Ohio State 92, Massachusetts 85	**Mississippi, Florida
2009	Penn State 69, Baylor 63	**Notre Dame, San Diego State
2010	Dayton 79, North Carolina 68	**Mississippi, Rhode Island

* Participation vacated for using ineligible players.

** Third-place game not played in 1982–1983 and 2004–2010.

Note: From 1971–2010, the National Invitation Tournament was a tournament of lesser prestige, as all NCAA schools from 1971 onward were required to play in the NCAA national championship tournament, if selected.

Appendix F
Olympic Games Basketball: Men

OLYMPIC GAMES COMPETITORS

Entries	Appearances	Best Year
ANG–Angola	5, 9th (tied)	2008
ARG–Argentina	5, 1st	2004
AUS–Australia	12, 4th	1988, 1996, 2000
BEL–Belgium	2, 11th	1948
BRA–Brazil	13, 3rd	1948, 1960, 1964
BUL–Bulgaria	4, 5th	1956
CAF–Central African Republic	1, 10th	1988
CAN–Canada	9, 2nd	1936
CHI–Chile	4, 5th	1952
CHN–China	8, 5th (tie)	2008
CRO–Croatia	3, 2nd	1992
CUB–Cuba	6, 3rd	1972
EGY–Egypt	7, 9th (tie)	1952
ESP–Spain	11, 2nd	1984, 2008
EST–Estonia	1, 9th (tie)	1936
EUN–Unified Team*	1, 4th	1992
FIN–Finland	2, 9th (tie)	1952
FOR–Formosa	1, 11th	1956
FRA–France	7, 2nd	1948, 2000
FRG–West Germany	2, 8th	1984
GBR–Great Britain	1, 20th	1948
GER–Germany	3, 7th	1992
GRE–Greece	3, 5th	1996, 2004, 2008
HUN–Hungary	5, 9th	1960
IND–India	1, 12th	1980
IRI–Islamic Republic of Iran	1, 9th (tie)	2008
IRN–Iran	1, 14th	1948
IRQ–Iraq	1, 22nd	1948
IRL–Ireland	1, 23rd	1948

Entries	Appearances	Best Year
ITA–Italy	11, 2nd	1980, 2004
JPN–Japan	6, 10th	1956, 1964
KOR–Korea	6, 8th	1948
LAT–Latvia	1, 15th (tie)	1936
LTU–Lithuania	5, 3rd	1992, 1996, 2000
MAR–Morocco	1, 16th	1968
MEX–Mexico	7, 3rd	1936
NZL–New Zealand	2, 10th	2004
PAN–Panama	1, 12th	1968
PER–Peru	3, 8th	1936
PHI–Philippines	7, 5th	1936
POL–Poland	6, 4th	1936
PUR–Puerto Rico	9, 4th	1964
RUS–Russia	2, 8th	2000
SCG–Serbia and Montenegro	1, 11th	2004
SEN–Senegal	3, 11th	1980
SIN–Singapore	1, 13th	1956
SUI–Switzerland	2, 9th (tie)	1936
SWE–Sweden	1, 10th	1980
TCH–Czechoslovakia	7, 5th	1960
THA–Thailand	1, 15th	1956
TUR–Turkey	1, 19th (tie)	1936
URS–Soviet Union	9, 1st	1972, 1988
URU–Uruguay	7, 3rd	1952, 1956
USA–United States	16, 1st	13 times
VEN–Venezuela	1, 11th	1992
YUG–Yugoslavia	10, 1st	1980

* Also known as the Commonwealth of Independent States.

TOURNAMENT LOCATIONS

1904	St. Louis, Missouri, United States*
1936	Berlin, Germany
1948	London, England
1952	Helsinki, Finland
1956	Melbourne, Australia
1960	Rome, Italy
1964	Tokyo, Japan
1968	Mexico City, Mexico

1972	Berlin, Germany
1976	Montreal, Canada
1980	Moscow, Soviet Union
1984	Los Angeles, California, United States
1988	Seoul, Korea
1992	Barcelona, Spain
1996	Atlanta, Georgia, United States
2000	Sydney, Australia
2004	Athens, Greece
2008	Beijing, China

* During the 1904 games in St. Louis, a tournament called the Olympic World's Basketball Championship was held. Most Olympic historians consider this tournament as a demonstration event rather than a true Olympic one.

MEN'S OLYMPIC BASKETBALL MEDALISTS, 1936–2008

Country	Gold	Silver	Bronze	Total
United States	13	1	2	16
Soviet Union	2	4	3	9
Yugoslavia	1	4	1	6
Brazil	0	0	3	3
Lithuania	0	0	3	3
Argentina	1	0	1	2
France	0	2	0	2
Italy	0	2	0	2
Spain	0	2	0	2
Uruguay	0	0	2	2
Canada	0	1	0	1
Croatia	0	1	0	1
Cuba	0	0	1	1
Mexico	0	0	1	1

MEN'S OLYMPIC BASKETBALL FINAL STANDINGS, 1936–2008

Finish	1936	1948	1952	1956	1960	1964	1968	1972	1976	1980	1984
1	USA	USA	USA	USA	USA	USA	USA	URS	USA	YUG	USA
2	CAN	FRA	URS	URS	USA	USA	YUG	USA	YUG	ITA	ESP
3	MEX	BRA	URU	URU	URS	URS	URS	CUB	URS	URS	YUG
4	POL	MEX	ARG	FRA	BRA	BRA	BRA	ITA	CAN	ESP	CAN
5	PHI	URU	CHI	BUL	ITA	PUR	MEX	YUG	ITA	BRA	ITA
6	URU	CHI	BRA	BRA	TCH	ITA	POL	PUR	TCH	CUB	URU
7	ITA	TCH	BUL	PHI	YUG	POL	ESP	BRA	CUB	POL	AUS
8	PER	KOR	FRA	CHI	POL	YUG	ITA	TCH	AUS	AUS	FRG
9	*BRA	CAN	*CAN	CAN	URU	URU	PUR	AUS	PUR	TCH	BRA
10	*CHI	PER	*CUB	JPN	HUN	AUS	BUL	POL	MEX	SWE	CHN
11	*TCH	BEL	*TCH	FOR	FRA	JPN	CUB	ESP	JPN	SEN	FRA
12	*EST	PHI	*EGY	AUS	PHI	FIN	PAN	FRG	EGY	IND	EGY
13	*JPN	CUB	*FIN	SIN	MEX	MEX	PHI	PHI			
14	*SUI	IRN	*HUN	KOR	PUR	HUN	KOR	JPN			
15	**CHN	ARG	*MEX	THA	ESP	CAN	SEN	SEN			
16	**EGY	HUN	*PHI	–	JPN	PER	MAR	EGY			
17	**GER	ITA			BUL	KOR					
18	**LAT	CHN									
19	***BEL	EGY									
20	***FRA	GBR									
21	***HUN	SUI									
22	***ESP	IRQ									
23	***TUR	IRL									

Finish	1988	1992	1996	2000	2004	2008
1	URS	USA	USA	USA	ARG	USA
2	YUG	CRO	YUG	FRA	ITA	ESP
3	USA	LTU	LTU	LTU	USA	ARG
4	AUS	EUN	AUS	AUS	LTU	LTU
5	BRA	BRA	GRE	ITA	GRE	GREx
6	CAN	AUS	BRA	YUG	PUR	CROx
7	PUR	GER	CRO	CAN	ESP	AUSx
8	ESP	PUR	CHN	RUS	CHN	CHNx
9	KOR	ESP	ARG	ESP	AUS	RUS*
10	CAF	ANG	PUR	CHN	NZL	GER*
11	CHN	VEN	ANG	NZL	SCG	IRI*
12	EGY	CHN	KOR	ANG	ANG	ANG*

x Tied for 5th.
* Tied for 9th.
** Tied for 15th.
*** Tied for 19th.

Appendix G
Olympic Games Basketball: Women

OLYMPIC GAMES COMPETITORS

Entries	Appearances	Best Year
AUS–Australia	6, 2nd	2000, 2004, 2008
BLR–Belarus	1, 5th (tie)	2008
BRA–Brazil	5, 2nd	1996
BUL–Bulgaria	3, 2nd	1980
CAN–Canada	4, 4th	1984
CHN–China	6, 2nd	1992
CUB–Cuba	4, 4th	1992
CZE–Czech Republic	2, 5th	2004, 2008
ESP–Spain	3, 5th	1992, 2008
EUN–Unified Team	1, 1st	1992
FRA–France	1, 5th	2000
GRE–Greece	1, 7th	2004
HUN–Hungary	1, 4th	1980
ITA–Italy	3, 6th	1980
JPN–Japan	3, 5th	1976
KOR–South Korea	6, 2nd	1984
LAT–Latvia	1, 9th (tie)	2008
MLI–Mali	1, 9th (tie)	2008
NGR–Nigeria	1, 11th	2004
NZL–New Zealand	3, 8th	2004
POL–Poland	1, 8th	2000
RUS–Russia	4, 3rd	2004, 2008
SEN–Senegal	1, 12th	2000
SVK–Slovakia	1, 7th	2000
TCH–Czechoslovakia	3, 4th	1976
UKR–Ukraine	1, 4th	1996
URS–Soviet Union	3, 1st	1976, 1980
USA–United States	8, 1st	6 times
YUG–Yugoslavia	3, 2nd	1988
ZAI–Zaire	1, 12th	1996

TOURNAMENT LOCATIONS

1976   Montreal, Canada
1980   Moscow, Soviet Union
1984   Los Angeles, California, United States
1988   Seoul, Korea
1992   Barcelona, Spain
1996   Atlanta, Georgia, United States
2000   Sydney, Australia
2004   Athens, Greece
2008   Beijing, China

WOMEN'S OLYMPIC BASKETBALL MEDALISTS, 1976–2008

Country	Gold	Silver	Bronze	Total
United States	6	1	1	8
Australia	0	3	1	4
Soviet Union	2	0	1	3
Brazil	0	1	1	2
Bulgaria	0	1	1	2
Yugoslavia	0	1	1	2
Russia	0	0	2	2
Unified Team	1	0	0	1
China	0	1	0	1
South Korea	0	1	0	1
Canada	0	0	1	1

WOMEN'S OLYMPIC BASKETBALL
FINAL STANDINGS, 1976–2008

Finish	1976	1980	1984	1988	1992	1996	2000	2004	2008
1	URS	URS	USA	USA	EUN	USA	USA	USA	USA
2	USA	BUL	KOR	YUG	CHN	BRA	AUS	AUS	AUS
3	BUL	YUG	CAN	URS	USA	AUS	BRA	RUS	RUS
4	TCH	HUN	CHN	AUS	CUB	UKR	KOR	BRA	CHN
5	JPN	CUB	AUS	BUL	ESP	RUS	FRA	CZE	ESP*
6	CAN	ITA	YUG	CHN	TCH	CUB	RUS	ESP	BLR*
7				KOR	BRA	JPN	SVK	GRE	KOR*
8				TCH	ITA	ITA	POL	NZL	CZE*
9						CHN	CUB	CHN	BRA**
10						KOR	CAN	JPN	LAT**
11						CAN	NZL	NGR	NZL**
12						ZAI	SEN	KOR	MLI**

* Tied for 5th.
** Tied for 9th.

Appendix H
FIBA World Championships: Men

FIBA WORLD CHAMPIONSHIP COMPETITORS

Entries	Best	Year
ALG–Algeria	1, 15th	2002
ANG–Angola	5, 10th	2006
ARG–Argentina	11, 1st	1950
AUS–Australia	9, 5th	1982, 1994
BRA–Brazil	15, 1st	1959, 1963
BUL–Bulgaria	1, 7th	1959
CAN–Canada	12, 6th	1978, 1982
CAF–Central African Republic	1, 14th	1974
CHI–Chile	3, 3rd	1950, 1959
CHN–China	7, 8th	1994
COL–Colombia	1, 7th	1982
CIV–Cote d'Ivoire	2, 13th	1982, 1986
CRO–Croatia	1, 3rd	1994
CUB–Cuba	4, 4th	1974
TCH–Czechoslovakia	4, 6th	1970
DOM–Dominican Republic	1, 12th	1978
ECU–Ecuador	1, 8th	1950
EGY–Egypt	3, 5th	1950
FOR–Formosa*	2, 4th	1959
FRA–France	5, 4th	1954
GER–Germany	4, 3rd	2002
GRE–Greece	5, 2nd	2006
ISR–Israel	2, 7th	1986
ITA–Italy	8, 4th	1970, 1978
JPN–Japan	4, 11th	1967
KOR–Korea	6, 11th	1970
LIB–Lebanon	2, 16th	2002
LTU–Lithuania	2, 7th	1998, 2006
MAS–Malaysia	1, 13th	1986

Entries	Best	Year
MEX–Mexico	4, 8th	1967
NED–Netherlands	1, 13th	1986
NZL–New Zealand	3, 4th	2002
NGR–Nigeria	2, 13th	1998, 2006
PAN–Panama	4, 9th	1970, 1982
PAR–Paraguay	2, 9th	1954
PER–Peru	4, 7th	1950
PHI–Philippines	4, 3rd	1954
POL–Poland	1, 5th	1967
PUR–Puerto Rico	11, 4th	1990
QAT–Qatar	1, 21st	2006
RUS–Russia	3, 2nd	1994, 1998
SEN–Senegal	3, 14th	1978
SCG–Serbia and Montenegro	1, 11th	2006
SLV–Slovenia	1, 12th	2006
URS–Soviet Union	9, 1st	1967, 1974, 1982
ESP–Spain	9, 1st	2006
TUR–Turkey	2, 6th	2006
UAR–United Arab Republic**	2, 11th	1959
USA–United States	15, 1st	1954, 1986, 1994
URU–Uruguay	7, 6th	1954
VEN–Venezuela	3, 11th	1990
YUG–Yugoslavia	12, 1st	5 times

* Former name of Taiwan
** United Arab Republic was a union between Egypt and Syria. The union began in 1958 and existed until 1961, when Syria seceded from the union. Egypt continued to be known officially as the United Arab Republic until 1971.

TOURNAMENT LOCATIONS

1950	Buenos Aires, Argentina
1954	Rio de Janeiro, Brazil
1959	Antofagasta, Concepcion, Santiago de Chile, Temuco, and Valparaiso, Chile
1963	Belo Horizonte, Curitiba, Petropolis, Rio de Janeiro, and Sao Paulo, Brazil

1967   Mercedes, Montevideo, and Salto, Uruguay; Cordoba,
          Argentina

1970   Karlovac, Ljubljana, Sarajevo, Skopje, and Split,
          Yugoslavia

1974   San Juan, Caguas, and Ponce, Puerto Rico

1978   Manila, Philippines

1982   Bogota, Bucaramanga, Cali, Cucuta, and Medellin,
          Colombia

1986   Barcelona, Ferrol, Madrid, Malaga, Oviedo, Zaragoza, and
          Teneryfa, Spain

1990   Buenos Aires, Cordoba, Rosario, Salta, Santa Fe, and Villa
          Ballester, Argentina

1994   Toronto and Hamilton, Canada

1998   Athens and Piraeus, Greece

2002   Indianapolis, Indiana, United States

2006   Hamamatsu, Hiroshima, Saitama, Sapporo, and Sendai,
          Japan

2010   Ankara, Istanbul, Izmir, and Kayseri, Turkey

MEDALISTS, 1950–2006

Country	Gold	Silver	Bronze	Total
Yugoslavia	5	3	2	10
United States	3	3	4	10
Soviet Union	3	3	2	8
Brazil	2	2	2	6
Argentina	1	1	0	2
Russia	0	2	0	2
Chile	0	0	2	2
Spain	1	0	0	1
Greece	0	1	0	1
Croatia	0	0	1	1
Germany	0	0	1	1
Philippines	0	0	1	1

FINAL STANDINGS, 1950–2006

Finish	1950	1954	1959	1963	1967	1970	1974	1978	1982	1986	1990	1994	1998	2002	2006
1	ARG	USA	BRA	BRA	URS	YUG	URS	YUG	URS	USA	YUG	USA	YUG	YUG	ESP
2	USA	BRA	USA	YUG	YUG	BRA	YUG	URS	USA	URS	URS	RUS	RUS	ARG	GRE
3	CHI	PHI	CHI	URS	BRA	URS	USA	BRA	YUG	YUG	USA	CRO	USA	GER	USA
4	BRA	FRA	FOR	USA	USA	ITA	CUB	ITA	ESP	BRA	PUR	GRE	GRE	NZL	ARG
5	EGY	FOR	PUR	FRA	POL	USA	ESP	USA	AUS	ESP	BRA	AUS	ESP	ESP	FRA
6	FRA	URU	URS	PUR	ARG	TCH	BRA	CAN	CAN	ITA	GRE	PUR	ITA	USA	TUR
7	PER	CAN	BUL	ITA	URU	URU	PUR	AUS	COL	ISR	AUS	CAN	LTU	PUR	LTU
8	ECU	ISR	PHI	ARG	MEX	CUB	CAN	PHI	BRA	CAN	ARG	CHN	ARG	BRA	GER
9	ESP	PAR	URU	MEX	ITA	PAN	MEX	TCH	PAN	CHN	ITA	ARG	AUS	TUR	ITA
10	YUG	CHI	ARG	URU	PER	CAN	TCH	PUR	TCH	GRE	ESP	ESP	BRA	RUS	ANG
11	–	YUG	UAR	CAN	JPN	KOR	ARG	CHN	URU	CUB	VEN	BRA	PUR	ANG	SCG
12	–	PER	CAN	PER	PUR	AUS	AUS	DOM	CHN	ARG	CAN	GER	CAN	CHN	SLV
13	–	–	MEX	JPN	PAR	UAR	PHI	KOR	CIV	FRA	ANG	KOR	NGR	CAN	AUS
14	–	–	–	–	–	–	CAF	SEN	–	NED	CHN	EGY	JPN	VEN	NGR
15	–	–	–	–	–	–	–	–	–	PUR	KOR	CUB	SEN	ALG	CHN
16	–	–	–	–	–	–	–	–	–	GER	EGY	ANG	KOR	LIB	NZL
17	–	–	–	–	–	–	–	–	–	AUS	–	–	–	–	PUR
18	–	–	–	–	–	–	–	–	–	URU	–	–	–	–	LIB
19	–	–	–	–	–	–	–	–	–	PAN	–	–	–	–	BRA
20	–	–	–	–	–	–	–	–	–	ANG	–	–	–	–	JPN
21	–	–	–	–	–	–	–	–	–	NZL	–	–	–	–	VEN
22	–	–	–	–	–	–	–	–	–	KOR	–	–	–	–	SEN
23	–	–	–	–	–	–	–	–	–	CIV	–	–	–	–	PAN
24	–	–	–	–	–	–	–	–	–	MAS	–	–	–	–	QAT

Note: No playoffs for 13–24 in 1986. No playoffs for 9–16, 17–20, and 21–24 in 2006.

Appendix I
FIBA World Championships: Women

FIBA WORLD CHAMPIONSHIP COMPETITORS

Entries	Appearances	Best Year
ARG–Argentina	7, 6th	1953
AUS–Australia	12, 1st	2006
BOL–Bolivia	1, 10th	1979
BRA–Brazil	14, 1st	1994
BUL–Bulgaria	6, 2nd	1959
CAN–Canada	8, 3rd	1979, 1986
CHI–Chile	3, 2nd	1953
CHN–China	7, 2nd	1994
TPE–Chinese Taipei	4, 12th	1986
COL–Colombia	1, 7th	1975
COD–Democratic	3, 14th	1983
Republic of Congo (Zaire)		
CUB–Cuba	10, 3rd	1990
CZE–Czech Republic	1, 7th	2006
TCH–Czechoslovakia	8, 2nd	1964, 1971
GDR–East Germany	1, 4th	1967
ECU–Ecuador	1, 12th	1971
FRA–France	7, 3rd	1953
GER–Germany	1, 11th	1998
HUN–Hungary	5, 5th	1957
ITA–Italy	5, 4th	1975
JPN–Japan	10, 2nd	1975
KEN–Kenya	1, 16th	1994
KOR–Korea	12, 2nd	1967, 1979
LTU–Lithuania	3, 6th	1998, 2006
MAD–Madagascar	1, 13th	1971
MAS–Malaysia	2, 11th	1979
MEX–Mexico	3, 6th	1975

Entries	Best	Year
NED–Netherlands	1, 8th	1979
NZL–New Zealand	1, 15th	1994
NGR–Nigeria	1, 16th	2006
PRK–North Korea	1, 8th	1959
PAR–Paraguay	3, 5th	1953
PER–Peru	4, 7th	1953, 1964
POL–Poland	3, 5th	1959
ROM–Romania	1, 6th	1959
RUS–Russia	3, 2nd	1998, 2002, 2006
SEN–Senegal	6, 12th	1979
SVK–Slovakia	2, 5th	1994
URS–Soviet Union	9, 1st	6 times
ESP–Spain	4, 5th	1998, 2002
SUI–Switzerland	1, 9th	1953
TUN–Tunisia	1, 16th	2002
USA–United States	14, 1st	7 times
YUG–Yugoslavia	6, 2nd	1990

TOURNAMENT LOCATIONS

1953	Santiago, Chile
1957	Rio de Janeiro, Brazil
1959	Moscow, Soviet Union
1964	Arequipa, Chiclayo, Iquitos, Lima, and Tacna, Peru
1967	Bratislava, Brno, Gottwaldow, and Prague, Czechoslovakia
1971	Araraquara, Brasilia, Niteroi, Recife, and Sao Paulo, Brazil
1975	Bogota, Bucaramanga, and Cali, Colombia
1979	Seoul, South Korea
1983	Brasilia, Porto Alegre, Rio de Janeiro, Sao Bernardo do Campo, and Sao Paulo, Brazil
1986	Vilnius, Minsk, and Moscow, Soviet Union
1990	Kota Kinabalu, Kuala Lumpur, and Kuching, Malaysia
1994	Adelaide, Hobart, Launceston, and Sydney, Australia
1998	Münster, Wuppertal, Rotenburg/Fulda, Karlsruhe, Dessau, Bremen, and Berlin, Germany
2002	Changshu, Changzhou, Huaian, Nanjing, Suzhou, Taicang, Wuzhong, Zhangjiagang, and Zhenjiang, China
2006	Barueri and Sao Paulo, Brazil
2010	Ostrava and Brno, Czech Republic

MEDALISTS, 1953–2006

Country	Gold	Silver	Bronze	Total
United States	7	1	2	10
Soviet Union	6	2	0	8
Czechoslovakia	0	2	4	6
Australia	1	0	2	3
Russia	0	3	0	3
Brazil	1	0	1	2
Korea	0	2	0	2
Bulgaria	0	1	1	2
China	0	1	1	2
Canada	0	0	2	2
Chile	0	1	0	1
Japan	0	1	0	1
Yugoslavia	0	1	0	1
Cuba	0	0	1	1
France	0	0	1	1

FINAL STANDINGS, 1953–2006

Finish	1953	1957	1959	1964	1967	1971	1975	1979	1983	1986	1990	1994	1998	2002	2006
1	USA	USA	URS	URS	URS	URS	URS	USA	URS	USA	USA	BRA	USA	USA	AUS
2	CHI	URS	BUL	TCH	KOR	TCH	JPN	KOR	USA	URS	YUG	CHN	RUS	RUS	RUS
3	FRA	TCH	TCH	BUL	TCH	BRA	TCH	CAN	CHN	CAN	CUB	USA	AUS	AUS	USA
4	BRA	BRA	YUG	USA	GDR	KOR	ITA	AUS	KOR	TCH	TCH	AUS	BRA	KOR	BRA
5	PAR	HUN	POL	BRA	JPN	JPN	KOR	ITA	BRA	CHN	URS	SVK	ESP	ESP	FRA
6	ARG	PAR	ROM	YUG	YUG	FRA	MEX	JPN	BUL	CUB	AUS	CUB	LTU	CHN	LTU
7	PER	CHI	HUN	PER	BUL	CUB	COL	FRA	POL	BUL	CAN	CAN	CUB	BRA	CZE
8	MEX	MEX	PRK	KOR	BRA	USA	USA	NED	YUG	HUN	BUL	ESP	SVK	FRA	ESP
9	SUI	ARG	–	JPN	ITA	AUS	HUN	BRA	CAN	AUS	CHN	FRA	JPN	CUB	ARG
10	CUB	AUS	–	FRA	AUS	CAN	AUS	BOL	CUB	KOR	BRA	KOR	HUN	ARG	CAN
11	–	PER	–	CHI	USA	ARG	CAN	MAS	AUS	BRA	KOR	ITA	GER	LTU	CUB
12	–	CUB	–	PAR	–	ECU	BRA	SEN	JPN	TPE	JPN	JPN	CHN	YUG	CHN
13	–	–	–	ARG	–	MAD	SEN	–	PER	–	ITA	POL	KOR	JPN	KOR
14	–	–	–	–	–	–	–	–	COD	–	SEN	TPE	SEN	TPE	TPE
15	–	–	–	–	–	–	–	–	–	–	COD	NZL	ARG	SEN	SEN
16	–	–	–	–	–	–	–	–	–	–	MAS	KEN	COD	TUN	NGR

Appendix J
Naismith Memorial Basketball
Hall of Fame Inductees

The Naismith Memorial Basketball Hall of Fame was established in 1959, and is located in Springfield, Massachusetts. Inductions have been performed annually since 1959. The current building housing the exhibits was completed in 2002.

PLAYER INDUCTEES

Player	Year Inducted
Kareem Abdul-Jabbar	1995
Nate Archibald	1991
Paul Arizin	1978
Charles Barkley	2006
Tom Barlow	1981
Rick Barry	1987
Elgin Baylor	1977
John Beckman	1973
Walter Bellamy	1993
Sergei Belov	1992
Dave Bing	1990
Larry Bird	1998
Carol Blazejowski	1961
Bernard "Benny" Borgmann	1961
Bill Bradley	1983
Joe Brennan	1975
Al Cervi	1985
Wilt Chamberlain	1979
Charles "Tarzan" Cooper	1977
Cynthia Cooper	2010

Player	Year Inducted
Krešimir Ćosić	1996
Bob Cousy	1971
Dave Cowens	1991
Joan Crawford	1997
Billy Cunningham	1986
Denise Curry	1997
Dražen Dalipagić,	2004
Adrian Dantley	2008
Bob Davies	1970
Forrest DeBernardi	1961
Dave DeBusschere	1983
Henry "Dutch" Dehnert	1969
Anne Donovan	1995
Clyde Drexler	2004
Joe Dumars	2006
Paul Endacott	1972
Alex English	1997
Julius Erving	1993
Patrick Ewing	2008
Harold "Bud" Foster	1964
Walt Frazier	1987
Max Friedman	1972
Joe Fulks	1978
Lauren "Laddie" Gale	1977
Harry Gallatin	1991
William "Pop" Gates	1989
George Gervin	1996
Tom Gola	1976
Gail Goodrich	1996
Hal Greer	1982
Robert "Ace" Gruenig	1963
Cliff Hagan	1978
Vic Hanson	1960
Lusia Harris-Stewart	1992
John Havlicek	1984
Connie Hawkins	1992
Elvin Hayes	1990
Marques Haynes	1998
Tom Heinsohn	1986
Nat Holman	1964
Bob Houbregs	1987
Bailey Howell	1997

Player	Year Inducted
Charles Hyatt	1959
Dan Issel	1993
Harry "Buddy" Jeannette	1994
Dennis Johnson	2010
Earvin "Magic" Johnson	2002
Gus Johnson	2010
William Johnson	1977
Neil Johnston	1990
K. C. Jones	1989
Sam Jones	1984
Michael Jordan	2009
Edward "Moose" Krause	1976
Bob Kurland	1961
Bob Lanier	1992
Joe Lapchick	1966
Nancy Lieberman	1996
Clyde Lovellette	1988
Jerry Lucas	1980
Angelo "Hank" Luisetti	1959
Ed Macauley	1960
Karl Malone	2010
Moses Malone	2001
Pete Maravich	1987
Hortência Marcari	2005
Slater Martin	1982
Bob McAdoo	2000
Branch McCracken	1960
Jack McCracken	1962
Bobby McDermott	1988
Dick McGuire	1993
Kevin McHale	1999
Dino Meneghin	2003
Ann Meyers	1993
George Mikan	1959
Vern Mikkelsen	1995
Cheryl Miller	1995
Earl Monroe	1990
Calvin Murphy	1993
Charles Murphy	1960
Hakeem Olajuwon	2008
Harlan Page	1962
Robert Parish	2003

Player	Year Inducted
Ubiritan Maciel Pereira	2010
Dražen Petrović	2002
Bob Pettit	1971
Andy Phillip	1961
Scottie Pippen	2010
Jim Pollard	1978
Frank Ramsey	1982
Willis Reed	1982
Arnie Risen	1998
Oscar Robertson	1980
David Robinson	2009
John Roosma	1961
John "Honey" Russell	1964
Bill Russell	1975
Dolph Schayes	1973
Ernest Schmidt	1974
John Schommer	1959
Barney Sedran	1962
Uljana Semjonova	1993
Bill Sharman*	1976
Christian Steinmetz	1961
John Stockton	2009
Maurice Stokes	2004
Isiah Thomas	2000
David Thompson	1996
John A. Thompson	1962
Nate Thurmond	1985
Jack Twyman	1983
Wes Unseld	1988
Robert "Fuzzy" Vandivier	1975
Ed Wachter	1961
Bill Walton	1993
Bobby Wanzer	1987
Jerry West	1980
Nera White	1992
Lenny Wilkens*	1989
Dominique Wilkins	2006
Lynette Woodard	2004
John Wooden*	1960
James Worthy	2003
George Yardley	1996

COACH INDUCTEES

Coach	Year Inducted
Forrest "Phog" Allen	1959
W. Harold Anderson	1985
Arnold "Red" Auerbach	1969
Geno Auriemma	2006
Leon Barmore	2003
Justin "Sam" Barry	1979
Ernest Blood	1960
Jim Boeheim	2005
Larry Brown	2002
Jim Calhoun	2005
Howard G. Cann	1968
Henry "Doc" Carlson	1959
Lou Carnesecca	1992
Pete Carril	1997
Bernard "Ben" Carnevale	1970
Everett Case	1982
Van Chancellor	2007
John Chaney	2001
Jody Conradt	1998
Denny Crum	1994
Chuck Daly	1994
Everett Dean	1966
Antonio Díaz-Miguel	1997
Edgar Diddle	1972
Bruce Drake	1973
Pedro Ferrándiz	2007
Clarence Gaines	1982
Sandro Gamba	2006
Jack Gardner	1984
Amory "Slats" Gill	1968
Alexandr Gomelsky	1995
Sue Gunter	2005
Alex Hannum	1998
Marv Harshman	1985
Don Haskins	1997
Pat Head Summitt	2000
Edgar Hickey	1979
Howard Hobson	1965
William "Red" Holzman	1986
Robert "Bob" Hurley, Sr.	2010

Coach	Year Inducted
Hank Iba	1969
Phil Jackson	2007
Alvin "Doggie" Julian	1968
Frank Keaney	1960
George Keogan	1961
Bobby Knight	1991
Mike Krzyzewski	2001
John Kundla	1995
Ward "Piggy" Lambert	1960
Harry Litwack	1976
Ken Loeffler	1964
Art Lonborg	1973
Arad McCutchan	1981
Al McGuire	1992
Frank McGuire	1977
Walter Meanwell	1959
Ray Meyer	1979
Ralph Miller	1988
Billie Moore	1999
Aleksandar Nikolić	1998
Mirko Novosel	2007
Lute Olson	2002
Jack Ramsay	1992
Pat Riley	2008
Cesare Rubini	1994
Adolph Rupp	1969
Cathy Rush	2008
Leonard Sachs	1961
Bill Sharman*	2004
Everett Shelton	1980
Jerry Sloan	2009
Dean Smith	1983
C. Vivian Stringer	2009
Fred Taylor	1986
John Thompson	1999
Margaret Wade	1985
Stan Watts	1986
Lenny Wilkens*	1998
Roy Williams	2007
John Wooden*	1973
Phil Woolpert	1992
Morgan Wooten	2000
Kay Yow	2002

CONTRIBUTOR INDUCTEES

Contributor	Year Inducted
Clair Bee	1968
Senda Berenson Abbott	1985
Danny Biasone	2000
Hubie Brown	2005
Walter A. Brown	1965
John Bunn	1964
Jerry Buss	2010
Jerry Colangelo	2004
William Davidson	2008
Robert L. Douglas	1972
Alva O. Duer	1982
Wayne Embry	1999
Clifford Fagan	1984
Harry Fisher	1974
Lawrence Fleischer	1991
Dave Gavitt	2006
Eddie Gottlieb	1972
Dr. Luther Gulick	1959
Lester Harrison	1980
Chick Hearn	2003
Ferenc Hepp	1981
Edward Hickox	1959
Paul Hinkle	1965
Edward "Ned" Irish	1964
R. William Jones	1964
J. Walter Kennedy	1981
Meadowlark Lemon	2003
Emil Liston	1975
Earl Lloyd	2003
John McLendon	1979
Bill Mokray	1965
Ralph Morgan	1959
Frank Morgenweck	1962
Dr. James Naismith	1959
Pete Newell	1979
Charles Newton	2000
John J. O'Brien	1961
Lawrence O'Brien	1991
Harold Olsen	1959

Contributor	Year Inducted
Maurice Podoloff	1974
Henry Porter	1960
William A. Reid	1963
Elmer Ripley	1973
Abe Saperstein	1971
Arthur Schabinger	1961
Lynn St. John	1962
Amos Alonzo Stagg	1959
Boris Stanković	1991
Edward Steitz	1984
Charles Taylor	1969
Bertha Teague	1985
Oswald Tower	1959
Arthur Trester	1961
Dick Vitale	2008
Clifford Wells	1972
Louis Wilke	1983
Fred Zollner	1999

REFEREE INDUCTEES

Referee	Year Inducted
James Enright	1979
George Hepbron	1960
George Hoyt	1961
Matthew "Pat" Kennedy	1959
Lloyd Leith	1983
Zigmund "Red" Mihalik	1986
John Nucatola	1978
Ernest Quigley	1961
Mendy Rudolph	2007
J. Dallas Shirley	1980
Earl Strom	1995
Dave Tobey	1961
David Walsh	1961

TEAM INDUCTEES

Team	Year Inducted
1960 U.S.A. Olympic Team	2010
1992 U.S.A. Olympic Team	2010
Buffalo Germans	1961
First Team	1959
Harlem Globetrotters	2002
New York Rens	1963
Original Celtics	1959
Texas Western	2007

* Inducted both as a player and a coach.

Appendix K
FIBA Hall of Fame Inductees

The FIBA Hall of Fame is located in Alcobendas, Spain, near Madrid. The building was completed in 2007 and is adjacent to the Pedro Ferrándiz Foundation. The first four contributors were awarded a special "gold" status.

PLAYER INDUCTEES

Player	Year Inducted
Alexander Belov	2007
Sergei Belov	2007
Jacky Chazalon	2009
Krešimir Ćosić	2007
Teófilo Cruz	2007
Dražen Dalipagić	2007
Ivo Daneu	2007
Mirza Delibašić	2007
Vlade Divac	2010
Oscar Furlong	2007
Nikos Galis	2007
Ricardo González	2009
Dragon Kicanovic	2010
Radivoj Korać	2007
Hortência Marcari	2007
Fernando Martín	2007
Pierluigi Marzorati	2007
Dino Meneghin	2010
Ann Meyers	2007
Cheryl Miller	2010
Amaury Pasos	2007
Ubiratan Maciel Pereira	2009
Dražen Petrović	2007

Oscar Robertson	2009
Emiliano Rodríguez	2007
Liliana Ronchetti	2007
Bill Russell	2007
Arvydas Sabonis	2010
Oscar Schmidt	2010
Uljana Semjonova	2007
Vanya Voynova	2007
Natalia Zassoulskaya	2010

CONTRIBUTOR INDUCTEES

Contributor	Year Inducted
8 Founding Federations	2007
Léon Bouffard	2007
R. William Jones	2007
George Killian	2010
James Naismith	2007
Eduardo Airaldi Rivarola	2007
Abdel Azim Ashry	2007
Turgut Atakol	2007
Robert Busnel	2007
Dionisio Calvo	2007
Antonio dos Reis Carneiro	2007
José Claudio Dos Reis	2007
Duk Joo Yoon	2007
Willard N. Greim	2007
Ferenc Hepp	2007
Marian Kozlowski	2007
Anselmo López	2007
Luis Martín	2009
Hans-Joachim Otto	2010
August Pitzl	2007
Nebojša Popović	2007
Al Ramsay	2009
Raimundo Saporta	2007
Decio Scuri	2007
Ernesto Segura De Luna	2010
Nikolai Semashko	2007
Abdoulaye Seye Moreau	2010
Radomir Shaper	2007

Contributor	Year Inducted
Boris Stanković	2007
Edward S. Steitz	2007
Yoshimi Ueda	2007
Abdel Moneim Wahby	2007

COACH INDUCTEES

Coach	Year Inducted
Lidia Alexeeva	2007
Antonio Díaz-Miguel	2007
Pedro Ferrándiz	2009
Lindsay Gaze	2010
Alexander Gomelsky	2007
Evgeny Gomelsky	2010
Henry Iba	2007
Vladimir Kondrashin	2007
Pete Newell	2009
Aleksandar Nikolić	2007
Mirko Novosel	2010
Giancarlo Primo	2007
Kay Yow	2009

TECHNICAL OFFICIALS INDUCTEES

Technical Official	Year Inducted
Artenik Arabadjian	2009
Jim Bain	2010
Obrad Belošević	2007
Konstantinos Dimou	2010
Mario Hopenhaym	2007
Ervin Kassai	2007
Vladimir Kostin	2007
Marcel Pfeuti	2009
Allen Rae	2007
Pietro Reverberi	2007
Renato Righetto	2007

Appendix L
Women's Basketball Hall of Fame Inductees

The Women's Basketball Hall of Fame is located in Knoxville, Tennessee. It was opened in June 1999. Its mission is to "honor the past, celebrate the present, promote the future." Induction ceremonies take place annually.

PLAYER INDUCTEES

Player	Year Inducted
Jennifer Azzi	2009
Alline Banks Sprouse	2000
Carol Blazejowski	1999
Ruthie Bolton	2011
Julienne Brazinski Simpson	2002
Cindy Brogdon	2002
Vicky Bullett	2011
Daedra Charles-Furlow	2007
Cynthia Cooper-Duke	2009
Joan Crawford	1999
Denise Curry	1999
Clarissa Davis-Wrightsil	2006
Anne Donovan	1999
Nancy Dunkle	2000
Teresa Edwards	2010
Kamie Ethridge	2002
Jennifer Gillom	2009
Paula Gonçalves da Silva	2006
Bridgette Gordon	2007
Lurlyne Greer Rogers	2004
Lusia Harris-Stewart	1999
Tara Heiss	2003

Player	Year Inducted
Rita Horky	2000
Pamela Kelly-Flowers	2007
Janice Lawrence Braxton	2006
Nancy Lieberman	1999
Kelli Litsch	2005
Andrea Lloyd Curry	2007
Rebecca Lobo	2010
Hortência Marcari	2002
Katrina McClain Johnson	2006
Suzie McConnell-Serio	2008
Ann Meyers-Drysdale	1999
Cheryl Miller	1999
Pearl Moore	2011
Kim Mulkey-Robertson	2000
Patsy Neal	2003
Lometa Odom	2011
LaTaunya Pollard	2001
Jill Rankin Schneider	2008
Patricia Roberts	2000
Doris Rogers	2003
Sue Rojcewicz	2000
Uljana Semjonova	1999
Margaret Sexton Greaves	2002
Bev Smith	2004
Olga Soukharnova	2000
Michele Timms	2008
Vanya Voynova	2001
Hazel Walker	2001
Rosie Walker	2001
Holly Warlick	2001
Katherine Washington	2000
Ora Washington	2009
Teresa Weatherspoon	2010
Nera White	1999
Lynette Woodard	2005

REFEREE INDUCTEES

Referee	Year Inducted
Patty Broderick	2008
Darlene May	1999
Marcy Weston	2000

COACH INDUCTEES

Coach	Year Inducted
Lidia Alexeeva	1999
Leta Andrews	2010
Geno Auriemma	2006
Leon Barmore	2003
Barbara "Breezy" Bishop	2000
Joanne Bracker	1999
Van Chancellor	2001
Joe Ciampi	2005
Jody Conradt	1999
Marianne Crawford Stanley	2002
Fran Garmon	2000
Dorothy Gaters	2000
Theresa Grentz	2001
Sue Gunter	2000
Sylvia Hatchell	2004
John Head	1999
Pat Head Summitt	1999
Sonja Hogg	2009
Jill Hutchison	2009
Andy Landers	2007
Lin Laursen	2008
Muffet McGraw	2011
Sandra Meadows	2002
Billie Moore	1999
Lorene Ramsey	2000
Harley Redin	1999
Amy Ruley	2004
Cathy Rush	2000
Debbie Ryan	2008
Linda Sharp	2001
Marsha Sharp	2003

Coach	Year Inducted
Jim Smiddy	1999
Barbara Stevens	2006
C. Vivian Stringer	2001
Edna Tarbutton	2005
Bertha Teague	1999
Tara VanDerveer	2002
Margaret Wade	1999
Marian Washington	2004
Dean Weese	2000
Chris Weller	2010
Dixie Woodall	2005
Kay Yow	2000

CONTRIBUTOR INDUCTEES

Contributor	Year Inducted
Val Ackerman	2011
Mildred Barnes	2000
Senda Berenson Abbott	1999
E. Wayne Cooley	2000
Carol Eckman	1999
Betty Jo Graber	1999
Mel Greenberg	2007
Phyllis Holmes	2001
Claude Hutcherson	2003
Betty Jaynes	2000
George Killian	2000
Hunter Low	2002
Shin-Ja Park	1999
Lee Plarski	2002
Gloria Ray	2010
Boris Stankovic	2000
William Wall	2004

Bibliography

I. INTRODUCTION

Basketball publications are quite extensive and have been published since shortly after the game was invented. In the early 1900s, the A. J. Reach Sporting Goods Company of Philadelphia and the A. G. Spalding Sporting Goods Company of New York published annual compilations of the previous year's basketball activity, basketball rules, and instructions on how to play the game. The Reach guides are an excellent source for early professional results, and the Spalding guides have a greater emphasis on amateur results. Various other instructional books were also published by Spalding. Although basketball books aren't nearly as numerous as books on other sports, such as baseball, in recent years there has been a growing number published each year. Nearly every major language contains basketball publications. A brief selection of books in other languages is included in section IIID3, and several non-English periodicals are listed in section IX.

The following list contains most of the more useful ones. Nearly all of the sources listed in this section are in the author's own library, and many have been consulted in the preparation of this book

Among basketball reference books, William G. Mokray's *Ronald Encyclopedia of Basketball* is the earliest comprehensive book that also includes an exceptional section on college basketball. Zander Hollander continued with several editions of his *Modern Encyclopedia of Basketball*, and in 1989 the National Basketball Association (NBA) began publishing their "Official" basketball encyclopedia. They continued under various editors until 2000. *The Sports Encyclopedia: Pro Basketball*, 5th edition, by David S. Neft and Richard M. Cohen was the first to contain individual statistics on the National Basketball League. *Total Basketball: The Ultimate Basketball Encyclopedia*, published in 2003 by Ken Shouler, contains more comprehensive statistical data. Robert Bradley's *Compendium of Professional Basketball* is an exceptional book containing a massive amount of historical information. Unfortunately, in recent years, publishers have shied away from this type of comprehensive basketball statistical books as the Internet gains in popularity as a reference source.

The Sporting News published an excellent *Official NBA Guide* and *Official NBA Register* but terminated publication in 2007 (although a limited amount are prepared for media use but are not sold to the public). Most teams now produce annual media guides, and print versions can usually be purchased.

There is no one book that stands out for general basketball history. The best way to acquire detailed knowledge of the sport's history is to delve into the various specialized books dedicated to individual leagues or teams. Surprisingly, there have been quite a few basketball books devoted to high school basketball, although, to my knowledge, there has not been one comprehensive book dedicated to general high school basketball history. High school books tend to concentrate on a specific school or state.

As for NBA history, Leonard Koppett is one of the most comprehensive as well as entertaining authors, and any of his works on basketball (or other sports for that matter) are worth reading. Among his basketball books are: *Championship NBA: Official 25th Anniversary*, *24 Seconds to Shoot: An Informal History of the National Basketball Association*, and *The Essence of the Game Is Deception: Thinking about Basketball*.

Since basketball has played a major role in race relations, there have been quite a few books about African Americans' rise to prominence in the sport. Ron Thomas's book *They Cleared the Lane: The NBA's Black Pioneers* is worth reading. Ben Green's book on the Harlem Globetrotters, *Spinning the*

Globe: The Rise, Fall, and Return to Greatness of the Harlem Globetrotters, is exceptionally well-researched and destroys some of the myths associated with the team. And Susan Rayl's doctoral dissertation *The New York Renaissance Professional Black Basketball Team, 1923–1950* is by far the most comprehensive work on that team.

Stanley Cohen's book *The Game They Played* and Charley Rosen's two books, *Scandals of '51: How the Gamblers Almost Killed College Basketball* and *The Wizard of Odds: How Jack Molinas Almost Destroyed the Game of Basketball* on the 1951 basketball scandal and Jack Molinas provide excellent accounts of a major event in basketball history.

Basketball biographies are one of the largest subgroups of basketball literature. Most tend to be relatively superficial. Both Neil D. Isaacs's *Vintage NBA: The Pioneer Era, 1946–1956* and Charles Salzberg's *From Set Shot to Slam Dunk: The Glory Days of Basketball in the Words of Those Who Played It* are excellent collections of interviews, but one wishes that they either lengthened the interviews or published sequels.

As women's basketball has gained in popularity, more and more books about that aspect of the sport have appeared. Two useful ones are Pamela Grundy and Susan Shackelford's *Shattering the Glass: The Remarkable History of Women's Basketball* and Karra Porter's *Mad Seasons: The Story of the First Women's Professional Basketball League, 1978–1981*.

Instructional books make up another large subgroup and have been published since the early days of the sport. For those interested in learning more about techniques and strategy, the suggestion is to read books by several different coaches to best discover various methods.

Compared to other sports, such as baseball and boxing, basketball fiction is virtually nonexistent, and the quality of authors certainly cannot be compared to Hemingway on boxing or Thurber and Lardner on baseball. Charley Rosen has written several entertaining fictional works and also one based on his experiences as a coach in the Continental Basketball Association entitled *The Cockroach Basketball League*. Neil D. Isaacs, an outstanding basketball historian, wrote an account of the controversial Jack Molinas entitled *The Great Molinas* but classified it as fiction (presumably to avoid lawsuits).

Sports historian Roger Meyer of Boxboro, Massachusetts, has done extensive research on 1940s and 1950s sports and has privately published monographs ranging from six to 100 pages on various teams and individuals of that era. For the serious researcher, his work is essential.

Basketball periodicals seem to come and go. Dell published a basketball annual for about 20 years from 1950–1970, and Street and Smith had basketball annuals for a slightly longer period. The nearly monthly *Basketball News* survived for 30 years from 1974–2004. Far and away the most useful annual basketball publication was the one issued by the Converse Rubber Company of Malden, Massachusetts, primarily as promotional material. Converse began the publication in 1924 and terminated it in 1983. When William G. Mokray became its editor in the mid-1940s until his death in 1974, the annual *Converse Yearbook* contained more useful information and photos than any other annual publication.

Today, much useful basketball information is contained on the Internet. Two competing websites, www.basketballreference.com and one with a similar name with a hyphen between the words basketball and reference, have basically supplanted the basketball encyclopedias. Denver attorney Arthur Hundhausen's website www.remembertheaba.com contains virtually everything on the now defunct American Basketball Association of 1967–1976, including many photographs. The website of the Association for Professional Basketball Research, founded by Robert Bradley, is at http://tss12.serverconfig.com/~orgapbr/ and contains a wealth of information not found elsewhere. The NBA's site, www.nba.com, is also an essential one for the basketball fan and researcher and contains up-to-date results and statistics, although the preponderance of advertising and promotional material occasionally make it difficult to navigate.

The library of the Naismith Memorial Basketball Hall of Fame in Springfield, Massachusetts, is the largest one in the United States devoted to basketball publications and may be consulted by the researcher by appointment.

The Pedro Ferrándiz Foundation in the Madrid, Spain, suburb of Alcobendas contains the largest basketball library in Europe.

The following listing provides a comprehensive selection of basketball resources.

II. REFERENCE

A. Encyclopedias

Bjarkman, Peter C. *The Biographical History of Basketball*. Lincolnwood, Ill.: Masters, 2000.

———. *The Encyclopedia of Pro Basketball Team Histories*. New York: Carroll & Graf, 1994.

Bradley, Robert. *Compendium of Professional Basketball*, Second Edition. Tempe, Ariz.: Xaler, 2010.

Brenner, Morgan G. *College Basketball's National Championships: The Complete Record of Every Tournament Ever Played*. Lanham, Md.: Scarecrow, 1999.

Douchant, Mike. *Encyclopedia of College Basketball*. Detroit: Visible Ink, 1995.

Hollander, Zander, ed. *The Modern Encyclopedia of Basketball*. New York: Four Winds, 1969.

———. *The Pro Basketball Encyclopedia*. Los Angeles: Corwin, 1977.

Hollander, Zander, and Alex Sachare, eds. *The Official NBA Basketball Encyclopedia*. New York: Villard, 1989.

Hubbard, Jan, ed. *The Official NBA Encyclopedia*, 3rd ed. New York: Doubleday, 2000.

Mokray, William G., ed. *Ronald Encyclopedia of Basketball*. New York: Ronald, 1963.

Neft, David S., and Richard M. Cohen. *The Sports Encyclopedia: Pro Basketball*, 5th ed. New York: St. Martins, 1992.

Neft, David S., Roland T. Johnson, Richard M. Cohen, and Jordan A. Deutsch. *The Sports Encyclopedia: Pro Basketball*. New York: Grosset & Dunlap, 1975.

Porter, David L., ed. *Biographical Dictionary of American Sports: Volume 4, Basketball and Other Indoor Sports*. New York: Greenwood, 1989.

Sachare, Alex, ed. *The Official NBA Basketball Encyclopedia*, 2nd ed. New York: Villard, 1994.

Savage, Jim. *The Encyclopedia of the NCAA Basketball Tournament: The Complete Independent Guide to College Basketball's Championship Event*. New York: Dell, 1990.

Shouler, Ken, ed. *Total Basketball: The Ultimate Basketball Encyclopedia*. Toronto: Sport Media, 2003.

Smith, Ron. *The Ultimate Encyclopedia of Basketball: The Definitive Illustrated Guide to the NBA*. Norfolk, England: Carlton, 1996.

B. Annuals and Yearbooks

Balzer, Howard M., ed. *Eastern Basketball Association, 1977–1978: Official Guide*. Philadelphia: Eastern Basketball Association, 1977.

Clary, Jack. *Pro Basketball Guide, 1978–1979*. Summit, N.J.: Snibbe, 1978.

Coates, Shawn. *The Official 1999–2000 IBA Player Registry*. Winnipeg, Manitoba, Canada: International Basketball Association, 1999.

Hepbron, George T. *Official Basket Ball Guide for 19xx*. New York: American Sports, annually from 1902–1948. (Spalding's Athletic Library), aka *Spalding Guide*. Later edited by Oswald Tower.

Hollander, Zander. *The Complete Handbook of College Basketball: 1980 Edition*. New York: New American Library, 1979.

———. *The Complete Handbook of Pro Basketball*. New York: New American Library, annually from 1975–1998.

———. *The NBA Book of Fantastic Facts, Feats, and Superstats, 1995 and 1996 Editions.* Mahwah, N.J.: Troll, 1995, 1996.

Jacobs, Barry, and Ron Morris. *ACC Basketball: A Fan's Guide 1985 Edition.* Durham, N.C.: Court, 1984.

Keith, Dwight, ed. *Prep All-America Basketball Yearbook 1973–1974 Edition.* Montgomery, Ala.: Coach & Athlete, 1974.

Lader, Martin, and Joe Carnicelli. *Pro Basketball '73–'74.* New York: Pocket, 1973.

Lattimore, Reuben, ed. *Street and Smith's Guide to Pro Basketball, 1994–1995, 1995–1996.* New York: CondeNast, 1994.

Marsom, Matt et al., eds. *1992–1993 Basketball Almanac.* Lincolnwood, Ill.: Publications International, 1992.

Miller, Chuck, ed. *2006–2007 CBA Media Guide and Register.* Albany, N.Y.: Continental Basketball Association, 2006.

Miller, Craig et al., eds. *The 1997 USA Basketball Fact Book.* Colorado Springs, Colo.: USA Basketball, 1996.

O'Brien, Jim. *The Complete Handbook of Pro Basketball 1971–1972 Edition.* New York: Lancer, 1971.

Olderman, Murray. *Pro Basketball, 1959–1960.* New York: Maco Magazine, 1959.

Orr, Jack. *Pro Basketball Factbook, 1971–1972, 1972–1973.* Ridgewood, N.J.: Sports Communications, 1971, 1972.

Pollack, Harvey. *Harvey Pollack's NBA Statistical Yearbook.* Philadelphia: Philadelphia 76ers, annually from 1996–2010.

Scheffer, William J. *Reach Official Basket Ball Guide.* Philadelphia: A. J. Reach, annually from 1903–1926.

Tower, Oswald. *The Official National Basketball Committee Basketball Guide, 1949–1950.* New York: A. S. Barnes, 1949.

Various editors. *American Basketball Association Guide.* St. Louis, Mo.: Sporting News, annually from 1968–1975.

Various editors. *Basketball Stars of 19XX.* New York: Pyramid, annually from 1961–1973.

Various editors. *Continental Basketball Association Official Guide.* Various cities, annually from 1978–2000.

Various editors. *The Official National Collegiate Athletic Association Basketball Guide.* New York: National Collegiate Athletic Bureau, annually from 1951–1979.

Various editors. *The Official NBA Guide.* St. Louis, Mo.: Sporting News, annually from 1958–2006.

Various editors. *The Official NBA Register.* St. Louis, Mo.: Sporting News, annually from 1980–2006.

Wallace, Chris, ed. *1984–1985 Blue Ribbon College Basketball Yearbook.* Buckhannon, W.V.: Christopher, 1984.

——. *European Register, 1997–1998.* San Marino: European Scouting Service, 1997.

Weber, Bruce. *All-Pro Basketball Stars, 1976, 1979, 1981.* New York: Scholastic, 1976, 1979, 1981.

C. Record Books

Benson, Marty, ed. *NCAA Official 2001 Men's Basketball Records.* Indianapolis, Ind.: National Collegiate Athletic Association, 2000.

Hagwell, Steven R, ed. *Official 1994 NCAA Final Four.* Overland Park, Kans.: National Collegiate Athletic Association, 1994.

Johnson, Gary K. et al. *NCAA Basketball: The Official 1995 College Basketball Records Book.* Overland Park, Kans.: National Collegiate Athletic Association, 1994.

D. Media Guides

Most professional basketball teams and many colleges produce an annual media guide, and many can now be found online.

III. HISTORY

A. General

Benagh, Jim. *Basketball: Startling Stories behind the Records.* New York: Sterling, 1992.

Camelli, Allen. *Basketball: Great Teams, Great Men, Great Moments.* New York: Bantam, 1972.

Clary, Jack. *Basketball's Great Moments.* New York: McGraw-Hill, 1988.

Devaney, John. *The Story of Basketball.* New York: Random House, 1976.

Dickey, Glenn. *The History of Professional Basketball since 1896.* New York: Stein and Day, 1982.

Fox, Larry. *Illustrated History of Basketball.* New York: Grosset & Dunlap, 1974.

Goldaper, Sam. *Great Moments in Pro Basketball.* New York: Grosset & Dunlap, 1977.

Healey, Jim. *St. Louis Hoops, 1904–2006: Compendium of St. Louis Basketball.* St. Louis, Mo.: Privately published, 2007.

Hugunin, Marc, and Stew Thornley. *Minnesota Hoops: Basketball in the North Star State.* St. Paul: Minnesota Historical Society, 2006.

Jares, Joe. *Basketball: The American Game.* Chicago: Follett, 1971.

Miers, Earl Schenck. *Basketball.* New York: Grosset & Dunlap, 1969.

Naismith, James. *Basketball: Its Origin and Development.* Lincoln: University of Nebraska Press, 1996. Reprinted from the original 1941 edition by Association Press, New York.

Snyder, John S. *Basketball! Great Moments and Dubious Achievements in Basketball History.* San Francisco: Chronicle, 1993.

Weyand, Alexander M. *The Cavalcade of Basketball.* New York: Macmillan, 1960.

B. Amateur

1. College

a. General

Bjarkman, Peter. *Big Ten Basketball.* Indianapolis, Ind.: Masters, 1995.

——. *Hoopla: A Century of College Basketball.* Indianapolis, Ind.: Masters, 1996.

Feinstein, John. *Forever's Team.* New York: Villard, 1989.

——. *The Last Amateurs: Playing for Glory and Honor in Division 1 Basketball's Least-Known League.* Boston: Little, Brown and Company, 2000.

——. *A March to Madness: The View from the Floor in the Atlantic Coast Conference.* Boston: Little, Brown and Company, 1998.

——. *A Season Inside: One Year in College Basketball.* New York: Simon & Schuster, 1988.

——. *A Season on the Brink: A Year with Bob Knight and the Indiana Hoosiers.* New York: Simon & Schuster, 1986.

Gutman, Bill. *The History of NCAA Basketball.* Greenwich, Conn.: Brompton, 1993.

——. *The Pictorial History of College Basketball.* New York: W. H. Smith, 1989.

Isaacs, Neil D. *All the Moves: A History of College Basketball.* New York: Harper & Row, 1984.

Jacobs, Barry. *Three Paths to Glory: A Season on the Hardwood with Duke, N.C. State, and North Carolina.* New York: Macmillan, 1993.

Kuska, Bob. *Cinderella Ball: A Look inside Small-College Basketball in West Virginia.* Lincoln: University of Nebraska Press, 2008.

McCallum, John D. *College Basketball U.S.A. since 1892.* New York: Stein and Day, 1978.

Monteith, Mike. *Passion Play: A Season with the Purdue Boilermakers and Coach Gene Keady*. Chicago: Bonus, 1988.

Packer, Billy, with Roland Lazenby. *50 Years of the Final Four*. Dallas, Tex.: Taylor, 1987.

———. *Hoops! Confessions of a College Basketball Analyst*. Chicago: Contemporary, 1986.

Phelps, Richard "Digger," and Larry Keith. *A Coach's World*. New York: Thomas Y. Crowell, 1974.

Pitino, Rick, with Dick Weiss. *Full-Court Pressure: A Year in Kentucky Basketball*. New York: Hyperion, 1992.

Reynolds, Bill. *Big Hoops: A Season in the Big East Conference*. New York: Penguin, 1989.

Shapiro, Leonard. *Big Man on Campus: John Thompson and the Georgetown Hoyas*. New York: Henry Holt, 1991.

Sloan, Norm, with Larry Guest. *Confessions of a Coach: A Revealing Tour of College Basketball's Backstage*. Nashville, Tenn.: Rutledge Hill, 1991.

Vitale, Dick, with Dick Weiss. *Holding Court: Reflections on the Game I Love*. Indianapolis, Ind.: Masters, 1995.

———. *Time Out, Baby!* New York: G. P. Putnam's Sons, 1991.

Wertheim, L. Jon. *Transition Game: How Hoosiers Went Hip-Hop*. New York: G. P. Putnam's Sons, 2005.

Yaeger, Don. *Shark Attack: Jerry Tarkanian and His Battle with the NCAA and UNLV*. New York: HarperCollins, 1992.

b. Specific Schools

i. Bard

Rosen, Charley. *Players and Pretenders: The Basketball Team That Couldn't Shoot Straight*. New York: Holt, Rinehart and Winston, 1981.

ii. Cincinnati

Grace, Kevin et al. *Bearcats!: The Story of Basketball at the University of Cincinnati*. Louisville, Ky.: Harmony House, 1998.

iii. Duke

Brill, Bill, and Mike Krzyzewski. *A Season Is a Lifetime: The Inside Story of the Duke Blue Devils and Their Championship Seasons*. New York: Simon & Schuster, 1993.

iv. Indiana

Marquette, Ray. *Indiana University Basketball*. New York: Alpine, 1975.

v. Kentucky

Rice, Russell. *Kentucky Basketball's Big Blue Machine.* Huntsville, Ala.: Strode, 1976.

vi. LaSalle, Pennsylvania, St. Joseph's, Temple, and Villanova

Hunt, Donald. *The Philadelphia Big 5: Great Moments in Philadelphia's Storied College Basketball History.* Champaign, Ill.: Sagamore, 1996.

vii. Syracuse

Snyder, Bob, ed. *Syracuse Basketball: A Century of Memories.* Champaign, Ill.: Sports, 1999.

Waters, Mike. *The Orangemen: Syracuse University Men's Basketball.* Portsmouth, N.H.: Arcadia, 2003.

viii. University of California, Los Angeles (UCLA)

Brondfield, Jerry. *The UCLA Story.* New York: Scholastic, 1973.

Heisler, Mark. *They Shoot Coaches, Don't They: UCLA and the NCAA since John Wooden.* New York: Macmillan, 1996.

Libby, Bill. *The Walton Gang.* New York: Coward, McCann & Geoghegan, 1974.

c. National Collegiate Athletic Association (NCAA) Tournament

Gergen, Joe. *The Final Four.* St. Louis, Mo.: Sporting News, 1987.

Minsky, Alan. *March to the Finals: The History of College Basketball's Illustrious Finale.* New York: Michael Friedman, 1999.

Vitale, Dick, with Mike Douchant. *Tourney Time.* Indianapolis, Ind.: Masters, 1993.

2. High School

Berkow, Ira. *The DuSable Panthers: The Greatest, Blackest, Saddest Team from the Meanest Street in Chicago.* New York: Atheneum, 1978.

Campbell, Nelson, ed. *Grass Roots and Schoolyards: A High School Basketball Anthology.* New York: Penguin, 1988.

———. *Illinky: High School Basketball in Illinois, Indiana, and Kentucky.* New York: Penguin, 1990.

Embry, Mike. *March Madness: The Kentucky High School Basketball Tournament.* South Bend, Ind.: Icarus, 1985.

Enright, Jim. *March Madness: The Story of High School Basketball in Illinois.* Bloomington: Illinois High School Association, 1977.

Frey, Darcy. *The Last Shot: City Streets, Basketball Dreams.* New York: Houghton Mifflin, 1994.

Gildea, William. *Where the Game Matters Most: A Last Championship Season in Indiana High School Basketball.* Boston: Little, Brown and Company, 1997.

Guffey, Greg. *The Greatest Basketball Story Ever Told: The Milan Miracle, Then and Now.* Bloomington: Indiana University Press, 1993.

Joravsky, Ben. *Hoop Dreams: A True Story of Hardship and Triumph.* Atlanta, Ga.: Turner, 1995.

Keown, Tim. *Skyline: One Season, One Team, One City.* New York: Macmillan, 1994.

Moran, Keith L. *The Roll of Champions: A Record of Montana High School State Basketball Tournaments from 1911 to 1969.* Missoula, Mont.: Privately published, 1970.

Plaiss, Mark, and Mike Plaiss. *The Road to Indianapolis: Inside a Season of Indiana High School Basketball.* Chicago: Bonus, 1991.

Propst, Nell Brown. *The Boys from Joes: A Colorado Basketball Legend.* Boulder, Colo.: Pruett, 1988.

Roberts, Randy. *"But They Can't Beat Us": Oscar Robertson and the Crispus Attucks Tigers.* Champaign, Ill.: Sports Publishing, 1999.

Rowland, E. Trasel. *The Pennsylvania Basketball Record Book, 1955.* Bryn Mawr, Pa.: Privately published, 1954.

Russell, Jim. *Indiana High School Basketball Tourney Record Book.* Indianapolis, Ind.: Indianapolis Newspapers, 1992.

Sheets, Harley. *Where in the World Is Westview, Wes-Del, and Wapahani.* Privately published, 1983.

Smith, Mike. *When Spirit Soared: The Legendary 1956–1957 Kentucky High School Basketball Season.* Louisville, Ky.: Concord, 1994.

Trogdon, Wendell. *Basket Cases: Stories and Glories of Indiana High School Basketball Coaches.* Evanston, Ill.: Highlander, 1989.

——. *No Harm, No Foul: Referees are People, Too.* Evanston, Ill.: Highlander, 1987.

Williams, Bob. *Hoosier Hysteria: Indiana High School Basketball.* South Bend, Ind.: Icarus, 1982.

Wojnarowski, Adrian. *The Miracle of St. Anthony: A Season with Coach Bob Hurley and Basketball's Most Improbable Dynasty.* New York: Gotham, 2005.

3. Industrial League

Buchan, Robin, and Bruce Kitts. *Longshot: The Story of the Buchan Bakers.* Seattle, Wash.: Classic Day, 2004.

Grundman, Adolph H. *The Golden Age of the AAU Tournament, 1921–1968.* Lincoln: University of Nebraska Press, 2004.

Kirkpatrick, Mac C., and Thomas K. Perry. *The Southern Textile Basketball Tournament: A History, 1921–1997.* Jefferson, N.C.: McFarland, 1997.

4. Armed Forces

Triptow, Dick, Seymour Smith, and Jack Rimer. *A Tribute to Armed Forces Basketball: 1941–1969.* Chicago: Privately published, 2003.

5. Playground

Telander, Rick. *Heaven Is a Playground.* Lincoln: University of Nebraska Press, 1995.

Valenti, John. *Swee'pea and Other Playground Legends: Tales of Drugs, Violence, and Basketball.* New York: Michael Kesend, 1990.

C. Professional

1. Early Professional

Bole, Robert D., and Alfred C. Lawrence. *From Peachbaskets to Slamdunks.* Lebanon, N.H.: Whitman, 1987.

Gould, Todd. *Pioneers of the Hardwood: Indiana and the Birth of Professional Basketball.* Bloomington: Indiana University Press, 1998.

Nelson, Murry. *The Originals: The New York Celtics Invent Modern Basketball.* Bowling Green, Ohio: Bowling Green State University Popular Press, 1999.

Nelson, Rodger. *The Zollner Piston Story.* Fort Wayne, Ind.: Allen County Public Library Foundation, 1995.

Peterson, Robert W. *Cages to Jumpshots: Pro Basketball's Early Years.* New York: Oxford University Press, 1990.

2. National Basketball Association

a. General

Feinstein, John. *The Punch: One Night, Two Lives, and the Fight That Changed Basketball Forever.* Boston: Little, Brown and Company, 2002.

Glass, Keith. *Taking Shots: Tall Tales, Bizarre Battles, and the Incredible Truth about the NBA.* New York: HarperCollins, 2007.

Jemas, William, Jr., and William M. Gray, eds. *NBA Jam Session: A Photo Salute to the NBA Dunk.* New York: National Basketball Association, 1993.

Koppett, Leonard. *24 Seconds to Shoot: An Informal History of the National Basketball Association.* New York: Macmillan, 1968.

———. *Championship NBA: Official 25th Anniversary.* New York: Dial, 1970.

Lazenby, Roland. *The NBA Finals: The Official Illustrated History.* Dallas, Tex.: Taylor, 1990.

Liss, Howard. *The Winners: National Basketball Association Championship Playoffs.* New York: Delacorte, 1968.

Pluto, Terry. *Falling from Grace: Can Pro Basketball Be Saved?* New York: Simon & Schuster, 1995.

Pomerantz, Gary M. *Wilt, 1962: The Night of 100 Points and the Dawn of a New Era.* New York: Three Rivers, 2005.

Rosen, Charley. *The First Tip-Off: The Incredible Story of the Birth of the NBA.* New York: McGraw Hill, 2009.

Ryan, Bob, and Terry Pluto. *Forty Eight Minutes: A Night in the Life of the NBA.* New York: Macmillan, 1987.

Simmons, Bill. *The Book of Basketball: The NBA According to the Sports Guy.* New York: Ballantine, 2009.

Taylor, John. *The Rivalry: Bill Russell, Wilt Chamberlain, and the Golden Age of Basketball.* New York: Random House, 2005.

Vancil, Mark. *The NBA at Fifty.* Avenel, N.J.: Random House, 1996.

Vancil, Mark, and Don Jozwiak. *NBA Basketball: An Official Fan's Guide.* London: Carlton, 1996.

Woten, Bill. *Game 7: Inside the NBA's Ultimate Showdown*, Second Edition. Self-published, 2010.

b. Specific Teams

i. Boston Celtics

Araton, Harvey, and Filip Bondy. *The Selling of the Green: The Financial Rise and Moral Decline of the Boston Celtics.* New York: HarperCollins, 1992.

Cousy, Bob, and Bob Ryan. *Cousy on the Celtic Mystique.* New York: McGraw-Hill, 1988.

Lazenby, Roland. *The Official Boston Celtics 1988–1989 Greenbook.* Dallas, Tex.: Taylor, 1988.

Shaughnessy, Dan. *Evergreen: The Boston Celtics: A History in the Words of Their Players, Coaches, Fans, and Foes from 1946 to the Present.* New York: St. Martins, 1990.

ii. Charlotte Hornets

Drape, Joe. *In the Hornets' Nest: Charlotte and Its First Year in the NBA.* New York: St. Martin's, 1989.

iii. Chicago Bulls

Logan, Bob. *The Bulls and Chicago: A Stormy Affair.* Chicago: Follett, 1975.

Sachare, Alex. *The Chicago Bulls Encyclopedia.* Lincolnwood, Ill.: Contemporary, 1999.

iv. Dallas Mavericks

Pate, Steve. *The Dallas Mavericks '88–'89.* Dallas, Tex.: Taylor, 1988.

v. Denver Nuggets

Monroe, Mike. *Hardwood Gold: The Rise and Fall . . . and Rise of the Denver Nuggets.* Dallas, Tex.: Taylor, 1994.

vi. Detroit Pistons

Lazenby, Roland. *The Detroit Pistons 1988–'89.* Dallas, Tex.: Taylor, 1988.

Stauth, Cameron. *The Franchise: Building a Winner with the World Champion Detroit Pistons, Basketball's Bad Boys.* New York: William Morrow and Company, 1990.

Thomas, Isiah, with Matt Dobek. *Bad Boys!* Grand Rapids, Mich.: Masters, 1989.

vii. Los Angeles Lakers

Clary, Jack. *Basketball's Great Dynasties: The Lakers.* New York: Smithmark, 1992.

Harris, Merv. *The Fabulous Lakers.* New York: Lancer, 1972.

Jackson, Phil, with Michael Arkush. *The Last Season: A Team in Search of its Soul.* New York: Penguin, 2004.

Libby, Bill. *We Love You Lakers.* New York: Sport, 1972.

Ostler, Scott, and Steve Springer. *Winnin' Times: The Magical Journey of the Los Angeles Lakers.* New York: MacMillan, 1986.

Riley, Pat. *Showtime: Inside the Lakers' Breakthrough Season.* New York: Warner, 1988.

viii. Milwaukee Bucks

Devaney, John. *The Champion Bucks.* New York: Lancer, 1971.

Doucette, Eddie. *The Milwaukee Bucks and the Remarkable Abdul-Jabbar.* Englewood Cliffs, N.J.: Prentice Hall, 1974.

ix. New York Knickerbockers

Albert, Marv, with Jim Benagh. *Krazy about the Knicks.* New York: Hawthorn, 1971.

Axthelm, Pete. *The City Game.* New York: Pocket, 1971.

Berger, Phil. *Miracle on 33rd Street: The N.Y. Knickerbockers' Championship Season*. New York: Simon and Schuster, 1970.

Cole, Lewis. *Dream Team*. New York: William Morrow and Company, 1981.

DeBusschere, Dave, Paul Zimmerman, and Dick Schaap, eds. *The Open Man: The Diary of the New York Knicks Championship Year*. New York: Grove, 1970.

Kalinsky, George. *The New York Knicks: The Official 50th Anniversary Celebration*. New York: Macmillan, 1996.

Pepe, Phil. *The Incredible Knicks*. New York: Popular, 1970.

Shatzkin, Mike. *The View from Section 111*. Englewood Cliffs, N.J.: Prentice Hall, 1970.

Spitz, Bob. *Shoot Out the Lights: The Amazing, Improbable, Exhilarating Saga of the 1969–70 New York Knicks*. New York: Harcourt Brace & Company, 1995.

x. Phoenix Suns

McCallum, Jack. *:07 Seconds or Less: My Season on the Bench with the Runnin' and Gunnin' Phoenix Suns*. New York: Simon & Schuster, 2006.

xi. Portland Trail Blazers

Cameron, Steve. *Rip City!: A Quarter Century with the Portland Trail Blazers*. Dallas, Tex.: Taylor, 1995.

Halberstam, David. *The Breaks of the Game*. New York: Alfred A. Knopf, 1981.

xii. Syracuse Nationals

Ramsey, David. *Nats: A Team. A City. An Era*. Utica, N.Y.: North Country Books, 1995.

3. Other Leagues

a. American Basketball Association

Pluto, Terry. *Loose Balls: The Short, Wild Life of the American Basketball Association as Told by the Players, Coaches, and Movers and Shakers Who Made It Happen*. New York: Simon & Schuster, 1990.

b. Continental Basketball Association

Levine, David. *Life on the Rim: A Year in the Continental Basketball Association*. New York: Macmillan, 1989.

c. National Basketball League

Nelson, Murry R. *The National Basketball League: A History, 1935–1949*. Jefferson, N.C.: McFarland, 2009.

Triptow, Richard F. *The Dynasty That Never Was.* Chicago: Privately published, 1996.

D. International

1. Olympic Games

Cunningham, Carson. *American Hoops: U.S. Men's Olympic Basketball from Berlin to Beijing.* Lincoln: University of Nebraska Press, 2009.

Daly, Chuck, with Alex Sachare. *America's Dream Team: The Quest for Olympic Gold.* Atlanta, Ga.: Turner, 1992.

Escamilla, Pedro. *The Olympic Basketball History.* Madrid, Spain: Fundacion Pedro Ferrándiz, 1994.

Layden, Joe. *USA Basketball.* New York: Scholastic, 1996.

Lyberg, Wolf. *The Athletes of the Summer Olympic Games, 1896–1996.* Stockholm, Sweden: Privately published, 1999.

Maritchev, Gennadi. *Who Is Who at the Summer Olympics, 1896–1992.* Latvia: Latvian Olympic Committee, 1994.

2. Other: English Language

Bocobo, Christian, and Beth Celis. *Legends and Heroes of Philippine Basketball.* Philippines: Privately published, 2004.

Colbeck, A. Leslie et al., eds. *The Basketball World.* Munich, Germany: International Amateur Basketball Federation, 1972.

Hernando, Mario, and José Luis Ortega. *The World Championships History.* Madrid, Spain: Fundacion Pedro Ferrándiz, 1995.

Jiménez, Carlos, and Barbara Jiménez. *The European Championships: 1935–1995.* Madrid, Spain: Fundacion Pedro Ferrándiz, 1997.

Jiménez, Carlos, and Suzy Calvon. *History of the European Cup.* Madrid, Spain: Fundacion Pedro Ferrándiz, 2001.

McGregor, Jim, and Ron Rapoport. *Called for Traveling.* New York: Macmillan, 1978.

Patton, Jim. *Il Basket d'Italia.* New York: Simon & Schuster, 1994.

Wanninger, Florian et al., eds. *FIBA Media Guide 2001.* Munich, Germany: Fédération Internationale de Basketball, 2001.

Wolff, Alexander. *Big Game, Small World: A Basketball Adventure.* New York: Warner, 2002.

3. Other: Non-English Language

a. Castilian

Rodríguez, Antonio. *La Leyenda Verde: Historia de Los Boston Celtics.* Madrid, Spain: Clementine, 2009.

b. French

Bosc, Gérard. *Une Historie du Basket Français*. Paris: AFEB, 1999.

Jordane, Francis, and Joseph Martin. *Basket: 150 Situations d'Entraînement*. Paris: Amphora, 1998.

LeFrère, Noël. *Les Fondamentaux du Basket*. Paris: Amphora, 2001.

Pain, Georges. *Basketball: Pour Une Autre Formation*. Montigny-Le-Bretonneux, France: Chiron, 2006.

Vincent, Pierre. *Basket: La Formation des Joueurs*. Montigny-Le-Bretonneux, France: Chiron, 2004.

c. German

Sauer, Holger R. *Dirk Nowitzki: German Wunderkind*. Munich, Germany: Stiebner Verlag, 2004.

d. Italian

Arceri, Mario, and Valerio Bainchini. *La Leggenda del Basket*. Milan, Italy: Baldini Castoldi Dalai, 2004.

Cacciuni-Angelone, Mimmo. *Recalcati: Head Coach and C.T.* Milan, Italy: Libreria Dello Sport, 2005.

Girelli, Andrea. *Il Libro Della Pallacanestro*. Milan, Italy: Garzanti, 1976.

Micalich, Davide. *Io Amo La Pallacanestro*. Milan, Italy: Libreria Dello Sport, 2006.

Peterson, Dan. *Basket Essenziale: N.E.* Milan, Italy: Libreria Dello Sport, 2003.

e. Latvian

Bērzzarņiš, Gunrs et al. *Latvijas Basketbola Vsture*. Riga, Latvia: Jumava, 1998.

f. Lithuanian

Bertašius, Arnoldas. *Krepšinio Zinyas: 1922–1998*. Kaunas, Lithuania: Gabija, 1999.

Stonkus, Stanislovas, and Arnoldas Bertašius. *Lietuvos Krepšinis*. Kaunas, Lithuania: Sviesa, 2007.

g. Polish

Małolepszy, Tomasz. *Historia Koszykówki i: Mistrzostwa Europy od Szwajcarii 1935 r. do Polski 2009 r.* Warsaw, Poland: Banigier Media, 2009.

h. Portuguese
Cunha, Odir. *Oscar Schmidt*. São Paulo, Brazil: Best Seller, 1996.
Ferreira Coutinho, Nilton. *Basquetebol na Escola da Iniciacao ao Treinamento*. Rio de Janeiro, Brazil: Sprint, 2003.

i. Russian
Genkin, Z. A., and E. R. Jachontov. *Basketbol-Spravocnik*. Moscow, Russia: Fizkultura i Sport, 1983.
Kvaskov, V. *100 let Rossijskogo Basketbola-Spravocnik*. Moscow, Russia: Sovietskij Sport, 2006.

j. Serbian
Bajrović, Vinko. *Almanah Košarkaškog Saveza Jugoslavije: 1945–1988*. Belgrade, Serbia: Košarkaški savez Jugoslavije, 1989.

k. Spanish
Escudero, Juan Francisco. *Drazen Petrovic: La Leyenda del Indomable*. Madrid, Spain: Clementine, 2006
———. *Generacion NBA: La Historia de la Mejor Liga de Baloncesto Del Mundo Desde 1980*. Madrid, Spain: Clementine, 2007.
———. *Históricos del Baloncesto Español*. Madrid, Spain: Clementine, 2008.
Sáenz-López Buñuel, Pedro. *La Formación del Jugador de Baloncesto de Alta Competicóon*. Seville, Spain: Wanceulen, 2006.

E. African-American Influence

Ashe, Arthur R., Jr. *A Hard Road to Glory: Basketball: The African-American Athlete in Basketball*. New York: Amistad, 1993.
Bayne, Bijan C. *Sky Kings: Black Pioneers of Professional Basketball*. New York: Franklin Watts, 1997.
Christgau, John. *Tricksters in the Madhouse: Lakers vs. Globetrotters, 1948*. Lincoln: University of Nebraska Press, 2004.
Fitzpatrick, Frank. *And the Walls Came Tumbling Down: Kentucky, Texas Western, and the Game That Changed American Sports*. New York: Simon & Schuster, 1999.
George, Nelson. *Elevating the Game: The History and Aesthetics of Black Men in Basketball*. New York: Simon & Schuster, 1993.
Green, Ben. *Spinning the Globe: The Rise, Fall, and Return to Greatness of the Harlem Globetrotters*. New York: Amistad, 2005.
Jacobs, Barry. *Across the Line: Profiles in Basketball Courage: Tales of the First Black Players in the ACC and SEC*. Guilford, Conn.: Lyons, 2008.

Katz, Milton S. *Breaking Through: John B. McLendon, Basketball Legend, and Civil Rights Pioneer*. Fayetteville: University of Arkansas Press, 2007.

Kuska, Bob. *Hot Potato: How Washington and New York Gave Birth to Black Basketball and Changed America's Game Forever*. Charlottesville: University of Virginia Press, 2004.

Menville, Chuck. *The Harlem Globetrotters*. New York: David McKay, 1978.

Rayl, Susan Jane. *The New York Renaissance Professional Black Basketball Team, 1923–1950*. Ann Arbor, Mich.: UMI, 1996. Doctoral diss., Pennsylvania State University.

Thomas, Ron. *They Cleared the Lane: The NBA's Black Pioneers*. Lincoln: University of Nebraska Press, 2004.

Vecsey, George. *Harlem Globetrotters*. New York: Scholastic, 1970.

Zinkoff, Dave, with Edgar Williams. *Around the World with the Harlem Globetrotters*. Philadelphia: Macrae Smith, 1953.

F. Corruption

Benedict, Jeff. *Out of Bounds: Inside the NBA's Culture of Rape, Violence, and Crime*. New York: HarperCollins, 2004.

Cohen, Stanley. *The Game They Played*. New York: Farrar, Straus and Giroux, 1977.

Golenbock, Peter. *Personal Fouls: The Broken Promises and Shattered Dreams of Big Money Basketball at Jim Valvano's North Carolina State*. New York: Carroll & Graf, 1989.

McMillen, Tom, with Paul Coggins. *Out of Bounds: How the American Sports Establishment Is Being Driven by Greed and Hypocrisy—and What Needs to Be Done about It*. New York: Simon & Schuster, 1992.

Rosen, Charley. *Scandals of '51: How the Gamblers Almost Killed College Basketball*. New York: Seven Stories, 1999.

——. *The Wizard of Odds: How Jack Molinas Almost Destroyed the Game of Basketball*. New York: Seven Stories, 2001.

Wetzel, Dan, and Don Yaeger. *Sole Influence: Basketball, Corporate Greed, and the Corruption of America's Youth*. New York: Warner, 2000.

Wolff, Alexander, and Armen Keteyian. *Raw Recruits: The High Stakes Game Colleges Play to Get Their Basketball Stars—and What It Costs to Win*. New York: Simon & Schuster, 1990.

IV. BIOGRAPHY

A. Collections

1. Interviews

Isaacs, Neil D. *Vintage NBA: The Pioneer Era, 1946–1956*. Indianapolis, Ind.: Masters, 1996.

Pluto, Terry. *Tall Tales: The Glory Years of the NBA, In the Words of the Men Who Played, Coached, and Built Pro Basketball*. New York: Simon & Schuster, 1992.

Salzberg, Charles. *From Set Shot to Slam Dunk: The Glory Days of Basketball in the Words of Those Who Played It*. New York: E. P. Dutton, 1987.

2. Individual Biographies

Christgau, John. *The Origins of the Jump Shot: Eight Men Who Shook the World of Basketball*. Lincoln: University of Nebraska Press, 1999.

Clary, Jack. *The NBA: Today's Stars, Tomorrow's Legends*. Greenwich, Conn.: Brompton, 1993.

Deutsch, Robin Jonathan. *Basketball Hall of Fame Class of 1994 Yearbook*. Springfield, Mass.: Naismith Memorial Basketball Hall of Fame, 1994.

Garber, Angus G. III. *Basketball Legends*. New York: W. H. Smith, 1989.

Harris, Merv. *On Court with the Superstars of the NBA*. New York: Pocket, 1974.

Heller, Bill. *Playing Tall: The 10 Shortest Players in NBA History*. Chicago: Bonus, 1995.

Hoffman, Anne Byrne. *Echoes from the Schoolyard*. New York: Hawthorn, 1977.

Hollander, Zander. *Pro Basketball: Its Superstars and History*. New York: Scholastic, 1971.

Holzman, Red, with Leonard Lewin. *A View from the Bench*. New York: W. W. Norton, 1980.

Mallozzi, Vincent M. *Basketball: The Legends and the Game*. London: Quintet, 1998.

Mendell, Ronald L. *Who's Who in Basketball*. New Rochelle, N.Y.: Arlington House, 1973.

Minsky, Alan. *Kings of the Court: Legends of the NBA*. New York: Michael Friedman, 1995.

Padwe, Sandy. *Basketball's Hall of Fame*. Englewood Cliffs, N.J.: Prentice Hall, 1970.

Patterson, Wayne, with Lisa Fisher. *100 Greatest Basketball Players.* New York: Crown, 1989.
Sachare, Alex. *100 Greatest Basketball Players of All Time.* New York: Pocket, 1997.

B. Single Individual

1. Players

a. Kareem Abdul-Jabbar (Lew Alcindor)

Abdul-Jabbar, Kareem, and Peter Knobler. *Giant Steps: The Autobiography of Kareem Abdul-Jabbar.* New York: Bantam, 1983.
Abdul-Jabbar, Kareem, with Mignon McCarthy. *Kareem.* New York: Random House, 1990.
Hano, Arnold. *Kareem!: Basketball Great.* New York: G. P. Putnam's Sons, 1975.
Haskins, James. *From Lew Alcindor to Kareem Abdul-Jabbar.* New York: Lothrop, Lee & Shepard, 1978.
Pepe, Phil. *Stand Tall: The Lew Alcindor Story.* New York: Grosset & Dunlap, 1970.

b. Charles Barkley

Barkley, Charles, and Roy S. Johnson. *Outrageous: The Fine Life and Flagrant Good Times of Basketball's Irresistible Force.* New York: Simon & Schuster, 1992.

c. Rick Barry

Barry, Rick, with Bill Libby. *Confessions of a Basketball Gypsy: The Rick Barry Story.* Englewood Cliffs, N.J.: Prentice Hall, 1972.

d. Len Bias

Cole, Lewis. *Never Too Young to Die: The Death of Len Bias.* New York: Pantheon, 1989.

e. Larry Bird

Bird, Larry, with Bob Ryan. *Drive: The Story of My Life.* New York: Bantam, 1990.
Bird, Larry, with Jackie MacMullan. *Bird Watching: On Playing and Coaching the Game I Love.* New York: Warner, 1999.

f. Manute Bol
Montville, Leigh. *Manute: The Center of Two Worlds.* New York: Simon & Schuster, 1993.

g. Bill Bradley
Bradley, Bill. *Life on the Run.* New York: Quadrangle, 1976.
McPhee, John. *A Sense of Where You Are: A Profile of William Warren Bradley.* New York: Bantam, 1970.

h. Kobe Bryant
Layden, Joe. *Kobe.* New York: Harper, 1998.
Lazenby, Roland. *Mad Game: The NBA Education of Kobe Bryant.* New York: Contemporary, 2000.

i. Wilt Chamberlain
Chamberlain, Wilt. *A View from Above.* New York: Villard, 1991.
Chamberlain, Wilt, and David Shaw. *Wilt: Just Like Any Other 7-Foot Black Millionaire Who Lives Next Door.* New York: MacMillan, 1973.
Cherry, Robert. *Wilt: Larger Than Life.* Chicago: Triumph, 2004.
Libby, Bill. *Goliath: The Wilt Chamberlain Story.* New York: Dodd, Mead & Company, 1977.
Sullivan, George. *Wilt Chamberlain.* New York: Grosset & Dunlap, 1966.

j. Bob Cousy
Cousy, Bob, as told to Al Hirshberg. *Basketball Is My Life.* New York: J. Lowell Pratt, 1963.
Cousy, Bob, with Edward Linn. *The Last Loud Roar.* Englewood Cliffs, N.J.: Prentice Hall 1964.
Cousy, Bob, with John Devaney. *The Killer Instinct.* New York: Random House, 1975.
Reynolds, Bill. *Cousy: His Life, Career, and the Birth of Big-Time Basketball.* New York: Simon & Schuster, 2005.

k. Darryl Dawkins
Dawkins, Darryl, and Charley Rosen. *Chocolate Thunder: The Uncensored Life and Times of the NBA's Original Showman.* Toronto: Sport Media, 2003.
Dawkins, Darryl, with George Wirt. *Chocolate Thunder: The In-Your-Face, All-Over-the-Place, Death-Defyin' Mesmerizin', Slam-Jam Adventures of Double-D.* Chicago: Contemporary, 1986.

l. Dike Eddleman
Lenzi, Diana Eddleman. *Dike Eddleman: Illinois' Greatest Athlete.* Champaign, Ill.: Sports, 1997.

m. Wayne Embry
Embry, Wayne, with Mary Schmitt Boyer. *The Inside Game: Race, Power, and Politics in the NBA.* Akron, Ohio: University of Akron Press, 2004

n. Julius Erving
Bell, Marty. *The Legend of Dr. J.* New York: Coward, McCann & Geoghegan, 1975.

o. Bevo Francis
Keiderling, Kyle. *Shooting Star: The Bevo Francis Story.* Toronto: Sport Media, 2005.
Oliver, Newt. *One Basketball and Glory.* Springfield, Ohio: Privately published, 1969.

p. Walt Frazier
Frazier, Walt, and Ira Berkow. *Rockin' Steady: A Guide to Basketball and Cool.* Englewood Cliffs, N.J.: Prentice Hall, 1974.
Frazier, Walt, and Joe Jares. *Clyde.* New York: Holt, Rinehart and Winston, 1970.
Frazier, Walt, with Neil Offen. *Walt Frazier: One Magic Season and a Basketball Life.* New York: Times, 1988.

q. Hank Gathers
Kimble, Bo. *For You, Hank: The Story of Hank Gathers and Bo Kimble.* New York: Delacorte, 1992.

r. Andrew Gaze
Gaze, Andrew, and Patrick Smith. *On the Road with Andrew Gaze.* Sydney, Australia: Pan McMillan, 1995.

s. Connie Hawkins
Wolf, David. *Foul! The Connie Hawkins Story.* New York: Holt, Rinehart, Winston, 1972.

t. Spencer Haywood
Haywood, Spencer, with Scott Ostler. *Spencer Haywood: The Rise, the Fall, the Recovery.* New York: Amistad, 1992.

u. Tom Heinsohn

Heinsohn, Tommy, and Joe Fitzgerald. *Give 'Em the Hook*. New York: Prentice Hall, 1988.

Heinsohn, Tommy, with Leonard Lewin. *Heinsohn, Don't You Ever Smile?: The Life and Times of Tommy Heinsohn and the Boston Celtics*. Garden City, N.Y.: Doubleday & Company, 1976.

v. Grant Hill

Hill, Grant. *Change the Game: One Athlete's Thoughts on Sports, Dreams, and Growing Up*. New York: Warner, 1996.

w. Rod Hundley

Libby, Bill. *Clown: Number 33 in Your Program, Number 1 in Your Heart— Hot Rod Hundley*. New York: Cowles, 1970.

x. Bobby Hurley

Hurley, Bob, Sr., with Phil Pepe. *Divided Loyalties: The Diary of a Basketball Father*. New York: Windsor, 1993.

y. Earvin "Magic" Johnson

Johnson, Earvin "Magic," and Roy S. Johnson. *Magic's Touch*. Reading, Mass.: Addison Wesley, 1989.

Johnson, Earvin "Magic," with William Novak. *My Life*. New York: Random House, 1992.

z. Michael Jordan

Clary, Jack. *Michael Jordan*. New York: Smithmark, 1992.

Greene, Bob. *Hang Time: Days and Dreams with Michael Jordan*. New York: St. Martin's, 1992.

Jordan, Michael, and Mark Vancil, ed. *For the Love of the Game: My Story, by Michael Jordan*. New York: Crown, 1998.

——. *Rare Air: Michael on Michael*. San Francisco: Collins, 1993.

Krugel, Mitchell. *Jordan: The Man, His Words, His Life*. New York: St. Martin's, 1994.

——. *Michael Jordan*. New York: St. Martin's, 1989.

Parker, Bobby. *Michael Jordan before the Legend*. Wilmington, N.C.: Wilmington Star-News, 1999.

Smith, Sam. *The Jordan Rules*. New York: Simon & Schuster, 1992.

——. *Second Coming: The Strange Odyssey of Michael Jordan—from Courtside to Home Plate and Back Again*. New York: HarperCollins, 1995.

aa. Joe Lapchick

Alfieri, Gus. *Lapchick: The Life of a Legendary Player and Coach in the Glory Days of Basketball.* Guilford, Conn.: Lyons, 2006.

ab. Meadowlark Lemon

Lemon, Meadowlark, with Jerry B. Jenkins. *Meadowlark.* Nashville, Tenn.: Thomas Nelson, 1987.

ac. Stan Love

Love, Stan, and Ron Rapoport. *Love in the NBA: A Player's Uninhibited Diary.* New York: E. P. Dutton & Co., 1975.

ad. Earl Manigault

Beckham, Barry. *Double Dunk.* Los Angeles: Holloway House, 1980.

ae. Pete Maravich

Federman, Wayne, and Marshall Terrill, in collaboration with Jackie Maravich. *Maravich.* Toronto: Sport Media, 2006.

Gutman, Bill. *Pistol Pete Maravich: The Making of a Basketball Superstar.* New York: Grosset & Dunlap, 1972.

Kriegel, Mark. *Pistol: The Life of Pete Maravich.* New York: Simon & Schuster, 2007.

af. George Mikan

Carlson, Bill (as told to). *Mr. Basketball: George Mikan's Own Story.* New York: Greenberg, 1951.

Schumacher, Michael. *Mr. Basketball: George Mikan, the Minneapolis Lakers, and the Birth of the NBA.* New York: Bloomsbury, 2007.

ag. Vern Mikkelsen

Egan, John. *The Vern Mikkelsen Story.* Minneapolis, Minn.: Nodin, 2006.

ah. Shaquille O'Neal

O'Neal, Shaquille, with Jack McCallum. *Shaq Attaq!* New York: Hyperion, 1993.

———. *Shaq Talks Back.* New York: St. Martin's, 2001.

ai. Hakeem Olajuwon

Olajuwon, Hakeem, with Peter Knobler. *Living the Dream: My Life and Basketball.* Boston: Little, Brown, 1996.

aj. Bob Pettit
Pettit, Bob, with Bob Wolff. *Bob Pettit: The Drive within Me*. Englewood Cliffs, N.J.: Prentice Hall, 1966.

ak. Willis Reed
Fox, Larry. *Willis Reed: The Knicks' Take-Charge Man*. New York: Grosset & Dunlap, 1970.

al. David Robinson
Savage, Jim. *The Force*. New York: Dell, 1992.

am. Dennis Rodman
Rodman, Dennis, with Tim Keown. *Bad as I Wanna Be*. New York: Delacorte, 1996.
Rodman, Dennis, Pat Rich, and Alan Steinberg. *Rebound: The Dennis Rodman Story*. New York: Crown, 1994.

an. Bill Russell
Russell, Bill, and Taylor Branch. *Second Wind: The Memoirs of an Opinionated Man*. New York: Random House, 1979.
Russell, Bill, as told to William McSweeny. *Go Up for Glory*. New York: Berkley, 1966.

ao. Paul Shirley
Shirley, Paul. *Can I Keep My Jersey?: 11 Teams, 5 Countries, and 4 Years in My Life as a Basketball Vagabond*. New York: Villard, 2007.

ap. Phil Smyth
Scholes, Gary. *The General, Phil Smyth*. Canberra, Australia: Canberra, 1987.

aq. Maurice Stokes
Morrow, Douglas. *Maurie*. New York: Grosset & Dunlap, 1973. Screenplay.

ar. David Thompson
Thompson, David, with Sean Stormes and Marshall Terrill. *David Thompson Skywalker*. Champaign, Ill.: Sports, 2003.

as. Rudy Tomjanovich
Tomjanovich, Rudy, with Robert Falkoff. *A Rocket at Heart: My Life and My Team*. New York: Simon & Schuster, 1997.

at. Tom and Dick Van Arsdale

Marshall, Kerry D. *Two of a Kind: The Tom and Dick Van Arsdale Story.* Indianapolis, Ind.: Scott, 1992.

au. Chet Walker

Walker, Chet, with Chris Messenger. *Long Time Coming: A Black Athlete's Coming-of-Age in America.* New York: Grove, 1995.

av. Bill Walton

Walton, Bill, with Gene Wojciechowski. *Nothing but Net: Just Give Me the Ball and Get Out of the Way.* New York: Hyperion, 1994.

aw. Spud Webb

Webb, Spud, with Reid Slaughter. *Flying High.* New York: Harper & Row, 1988.

ax. Jerry West

West, Jerry, with Bill Libby. *Mr. Clutch: The Jerry West Story.* Englewood Cliffs, N.J.: Prentice Hall, 1969.

ay. Lenny Wilkens

Wilkens, Lenny. *The Lenny Wilkens Story.* New York: Paul S. Eriksson, 1974.

az. Jayson Williams

Williams, Jayson, with Steve Friedman. *Loose Balls.* New York: Broadway, 2000.

ba. Johnny Wilson

Burdette, Dick, with Johnny Wilson and Gene Wilson. *Jump, Johnny, Jump.* Bloomington, Ind.: Author House, 2007.

2. Coaches

a. Forrest "Phog" Allen

Kerkhoff, Blair. *Phog Allen: The Father of Basketball Coaching.* Indianapolis, Ind.: Masters, 1996.

b. Arnold "Red" Auerbach

Auerbach, Arnold "Red," and Joe Fitzgerald. *Red Auerbach On and Off the Court.* New York: Bantam, 1986.

Auerbach, Arnold "Red," and John Feinstein. *Let Me Tell You a Story: A Lifetime in the Game.* New York: Little, Brown and Company, 2004.

Auerbach, Arnold "Red," and Paul Sann. *Red Auerbach: Winning the Hard Way.* Boston: Little, Brown and Company, 1966.

c. Ernest A. Blood

Hess, Charles "Chic." *Prof Blood and the Wonder Teams: The True Story of Basketball's First Great Coach.* Newark, N.J.: Newark Abbey, 2003.

d. Bill Frieder

Frieder, Bill, with Jeff Mortimer. *Basket Case: The Frenetic Life of Michigan Coach Bill Frieder.* Chicago: Bonus, 1988.

e. Clarence "Big House" Gaines

Gaines, Clarence E., with Clint Johnson. *They Call Me Big House.* Winston-Salem, N.C.: John F. Blair, 2004.

f. William "Red" Holzman

Holzman, Red, and Harvey Frummer. *Red on Red.* New York: Bantam, 1987.

g. Bob Huggins

Huggins, Bob, with Mike Bass. *Bob Huggins Pressed for Success.* Champaign, Ill.: Sagamore, 1995.

h. George Karl

Karl, George, with Don Yaeger. *This Game's the Best: So Why Don't They Quit Screwing with It?* New York: St. Martin's, 1997.

i. Bob Knight

Alford, Steve, with John Garrity. *Playing for Knight: My Six Seasons with Coach Knight.* New York: Simon & Schuster, 1989.

Knight, Bob, with Bob Hammel. *Knight: My Story.* New York: St. Martin's, 2002.

Mellen, Joan. *Bob Knight: His Own Man.* New York: Donald I. Fine, 1988.

Wolfe, Rich. *Oh, What a Knight!* (double book with *Knightmares*). Privately printed, 2001.

j. Tom Meschery

Meschery, Tom. *Caught in the Pivot: The Diary of a Rookie Coach.* New York: Dell, 1973.

k. Ray Meyer

Enright, James. *Ray Meyer: America's #1 Basketball Coach*. Chicago: Follett, 1980.

Meyer, Ray, with Ray Sons. *Coach*. Chicago: Contemporary, 1987.

l. Dick Motta

Motta, Dick, with Jerry Jenkins. *Stuff It: The Story of Dick Motta, Toughest Little Coach in the NBA*. Radnor, Pa.: Chilton, 1975.

m. Bill Musselman

Heller, Bill. *Timberwolves Stalk the NBA Obsession: Bill Musselman's Relentless Quest to Beat the Best*. Chicago: Bonus, 1989.

n. John "Honey" Russell

Russell, John. *Honey Russell: Between Games, Between Halves*. Washington: Dryad, 1986.

o. Dean Smith

Smith, Dean, with John Kilgo and Sally Jenkins. *A Coach's Life*. New York: Random House, 1999.

p. Jim Valvano

Valvano, Jim, and Curry Kirkpatrick. *Valvano: They Gave Me a Lifetime Contract and Then They Declared Me Dead*. New York: Simon & Schuster, 1991.

q. John Wooden

Chapin, Dwight, and Jeff Prugh. *The Wizard of Westwood: Coach John Wooden and His UCLA Bruins*. Boston: Houghton Mifflin, 1973.

Wooden, John, with Jack Tobin. *They Call Me Coach*. Lincolnwood, Ill.: Contemporary, 1988.

3. Others

a. Frank J. Basloe

Basloe, Frank J., with D. Gordon Rohman. *I Grew Up with Basketball: Twenty Years of Barnstorming with Cage Greats of Yesterday*. New York: Greenberg, 1952.

b. Charlie Eckman

Eckman, Charley, and Fred Neil. *"It's a Very Simple Game": The Life and Times of Charley Eckman*. Baltimore: Borderlands, 1995.

c. Eddie Gottlieb

Westcott, Rich. *The Mogul: Eddie Gottlieb, Philadelphia Sports Legend and Pro Basketball Pioneer*. Philadelphia, Pa.: Temple University Press, 2008.

d. Chick Hearn

Hearn, Chick, and Steve Springer. *Chick: His Unpublished Memoirs and the Memories of Those Who Knew Him*. Chicago: Triumph, 2004.

e. Spike Lee

Lee, Spike, with Ralph Wiley. *Best Seat in the House: A Basketball Memoir*. New York: Crown, 1994.

f. James Naismith

Webb, Bernice Larson. *The Basketball Man: James Naismith*, rev ed. Lawrence, Kans.: Kappelman's Historic Collections, 1994.

g. Richie Powers

Powers, Richie, with Mark Mulvoy. *Overtime!: An Uninhibited Account of a Referee's Life in the NBA*. New York: David McKay, 1975.

h. Dick Vitale

Vitale, Dick, with Curry Kirkpatrick. *Vitale: Just Your Average Bald, One-Eyed Basketball Wacko Who Beat the Ziggy and Became a PTP'er*. New York: Pocket Books, 1988.

i. Pat Williams

Williams, Pat, with James D. Denney. *Ahead of the Game: The Pat Williams Story*. Grand Rapids, Mich.: Fleming H. Revell, 1999.

V. WOMEN'S BASKETBALL

A. Reference

Jutilla, Dean. *The 1997–98 ABL Media Guide*. Palo Alto, Calif.: American Basketball League, 1997.

Various editors. *The Official WNBA Register*. St. Louis, Mo.: Sporting News, annually from 1999–2006.

B. History

Corbett, Sara. *Venus to the Hoop: A Gold Medal Year in Women's Basketball*. New York: Doubleday, 1997.

Grundy, Pamela, and Susan Shackelford. *Shattering the Glass: The Remarkable History of Women's Basketball*. Chapel Hill: University of North Carolina Press, 2005.

Ikard, Robert W. *Just for Fun: The Story of AAU Women's Basketball*. Fayetteville: University of Arkansas Press, 2005.

Kent, Richard. *Inside Women's College Basketball: Anatomy of a Season*. Dallas, Tex.: Taylor, 2007.

Kessler, Lauren. *Full Court Press: A Season in the Life of a Winning Basketball Team and the Women Who Made It Happen*. New York: Penguin, 1998.

McElwain, Max. *The Only Dance in Iowa: A History of Six-Player Girls' Basketball*. Lincoln: University of Nebraska Press, 2004.

Neal, Patsy. *At The Rim: A Celebration of Women's Collegiate Basketball*. Charlottesville, Va.: Thomasson-Grant, 1991.

Porter, Karra. *Mad Seasons: The Story of the First Women's Professional Basketball League, 1978–1981*. Lincoln: University of Nebraska Press, 2006.

Redin, Harley J. *The Queens Fly High*. Plainview, Tex.: Harley J. Redin, 1958.

VanDerveer, Tara, with Joan Ryan. *Shooting from the Outside: How a Coach and Her Olympic Team Transformed Women's Basketball*. New York: Avon, 1997.

Whiteside, Kelly. *WNBA: A Celebration: Commemorating the Birth of a League*. New York: HarperCollins, 1998.

C. Biography

Lieberman-Cline, Nancy, with Debby Jennings. *Lady Magic: The Autobiography of Nancy Lieberman-Cline*. Champaign, Ill.: Sagamore, 1992.

Summitt, Pat, with Sally Jenkins. *Reach for the Summit*. New York: Broadway, 1998.

D. Instructional

Bell, Mary M. *Women's Basketball*. Dubuque, Iowa: William C. Brown, 1964.

Brace, David K. *Basketball for Girls: Skills Test Manual*. Washington, D.C.: American Alliance for Health, Physical Education, and Recreation, 1966

Ebert, Frances H., and Billye Ann Cheatum. *Basketball—Five Player*. Philadelphia, Pa.: W. B. Saunders, 1972.

Galsworthy, Betty. *Netball*. London: Blanford, 1993.

Lieberman-Cline, Nancy, and Robin Roberts. *Basketball for Women*. Champaign, Ill.: Human Kinetics, 1996.

Loftin, Aimee. *Basketball Guide: August 1969–August 1970*. Washington, D.C.: American Association for Health, Physical Education, and Recreation, 1969.

Lowry, Carla. *Women's Basketball*. North Palm Beach, Fla.: Athletic Institute, 1974.

O'Brien, Maureen. *Who's Got the Ball (and Other Nagging Questions about Team Life)*. San Francisco: Jossey-Bass, 1995.

Rush, Cathy, with Lawrie Mifflin. *Women's Basketball*. New York: Hawthorn, 1976.

Schaafsma, Frances. *Basketball for Women*. Dubuque, Iowa: William C. Brown, 1966.

VI. INSTRUCTIONAL

A. Rules and Officiating

National Basketball Association Operations Department. *Official Rules of the National Basketball Association, 1993–94*. St. Louis, Mo.: Sporting News, 1993.

National Collegiate Athletic Association. *1993 Read-Easy Basketball Rules*. Overland Park, Kans.: National Collegiate Athletic Association, 1993.

———. *1994 NCAA Basketball Men's and Women's Rules and Interpretations*. Overland Park, Kans.: National Collegiate Athletic Association, 1993.

———. *1995 Basketball Statisticians' Manual*. Overland Park, Kans.: National Collegiate Athletic Association, 1994.

National Federation of State High School Athletic Associations. *1949–50 Basketball Casebook*. Chicago: National Federation of State High School Athletic Associations, 1949.

———. *Basketball Player Handbook, 1960–61*. Chicago: National Federation of State High School Athletic Associations, 1960.

———. *Basketball Rule Book, 1977–78*. Chicago: National Federation of State High School Associations, 1977.

Rudolph, Mendy. *National Basketball Association Casebook*. St. Louis, Mo.: Sporting News, 1970.

Steitz, Edward S. *Illustrated Basketball Rules*. Garden City, N.Y.: Doubleday & Company, 1976.

Stroher, Manfred. *Basketball: The Rules, 1931–2000*. Munich, Germany: Fédération Internationale de Basketball, 2001.

Tobey, Dave. *Basketball Officiating*. New York: A. S. Barnes and Company, 1943.

B. Coaching

Aaseng, Nate. *Basketball: You Are the Coach*. New York: Dell, 1983.

Allen, Forrest C. "Phog," with Harold E. "Bud" Foster, and Edward S. "Eddie" Hickey, consultants. *How to Improve Your Basketball*. Chicago: Athletic Institute, 1955.

Angell, E. D. *Basketball for Coach, Player, and Spectator*. New York: Thos. E. Wilson, 1921.

Auerbach, Arnold "Red." *Basketball for the Player, the Fan, and the Coach*. New York: Pocket, 1952.

Bee, Clair, and Ken Norton. *The Science of Coaching*. New York: Ronald, 1959.

Bird, Larry, with John Bischoff. *Bird on Basketball: How to Strategies from the Great Celtics Champion*. Reading, Mass.: Addison-Wesley, 1985.

Brown, Lyle. *Offensive and Defensive Drills for Winning Basketball*. Englewood Cliffs, N.J.: Prentice Hall, 1965.

Bunn, John W. *Basketball Methods*. New York: MacMillan, 1939.

Cooper, John M., and Daryl Siedentop. *The Theory and Science of Basketball*. Philadelphia: Lea & Febiger, 1969.

Cousy, Bob, and Frank Power Jr. *Basketball Concepts and Techniques*. Boston: Allyn & Bacon, 1970.

Cummins, Gloria, and Jim Cummins. *Basketball by the Pros*. New York: Mason/Charter, 1977.

Daher, Joseph G. *Fundamentals of Basketball*. Chelyan, W.Va.: Crowder, 1940.

Dean, Everett S. *Progressive Basketball: Methods and Philosophy*. Englewood Cliffs, N.J.: Prentice Hall, 1946.

Edmonston, Don, and Jack Lehane. *Progressive Basketball Drills: A Coach's Guide*. Boston: Allyn & Bacon, 1984.

Hobson, Howard A. *Scientific Basketball*. New York: Prentice Hall, 1949.

Holman, Nat. *Holman on Basketball*. New York: Crown, 1950.

Holzman, Red, and Leonard Lewin. *Holzman's Basketball: Winning Strategy and Tactics*. New York: MacMillan, 1973.

Hutton Joe, and Vern B. Hoffman. *Basketball*. Mankato, Minn.: Creative Education, 1962.

Isaacs, Neil D., and Dick Motta. *Sports Illustrated Basketball*. New York: Harper & Row, 1981.

Jagger, B., ed. *Basketball Coaching and Playing*. London: Faber and Faber, 1962.

Jourdet, Lon W., and Kenneth A. Hashagen. *Modern Basketball*. Philadelphia: W. B. Saunders, 1940.

Krause, Jerry. *Better Basketball Basics before the Xs and Os*. New York: Leisure, 1985.

Lai, William T. "Buck." *Winning Basketball*. New York: Stadia Sports, 1973.

Lapchick, Joe. *50 Years of Basketball*. Englewood Cliffs, N.J.: Prentice Hall, 1968.

Liss, Howard. *Basketball Talk*. New York: Pocket, 1973.

Marcus, Howard. *Basketball Basics: Drills, Techniques, and Strategies for Coaches*. Lincolnwood, Ill.: Contemporary, 1991.

Mather, Edwin J., and Elmer D. Mitchell. *Basketball: How to Coach the Game*. New York: A. S. Barnes, 1925.

McCracken, Branch. *Indiana Basketball*. New York: Prentice Hall, 1955.

Meanwell, Walter E. *The Science of Basket Ball for Men*. Madison, Wis.: Democrat, 1924.

Messer, Guerdon N. *How to Play Basketball*. New York: American Sports, 1919.

Morris, Donald. *Kentucky High School Basketball*. West Nyack, N.Y.: Parker, 1969.

Newell, Pete, and John Benington. *Basketball Methods*. New York: Ronald, 1962.

Nisenson, Sam. *A Handy Illustrated Guide to Basketball*. New York: Permabooks, 1949.

Pim, Ralph L. *Winning Basketball*. Lincolnwood, Ill.: Contemporary, 1994.

Ruby, J. Craig. *How to Coach and Play Basketball*. Champaign, Ill.: Bailey & Himes, 1926.

Training Division Aviation Office of the Chief of Naval Operations, U.S. Navy. *Basketball*. Annapolis, Md.: United States Naval Institute, 1943.

Wardlaw, Charles Digby, and Whitelaw Reid Morrison. *Basketball*. New York: Charles Scribner's Sons, 1923.

Wilkes, Glenn. *Basketball*. Dubuque, Iowa: Wm. C. Brown, 1990.

Williams, Joe, and Stan Wilson. *Youth League Basketball: Coaching and Playing*. Indianapolis, Ind.: Masters, 1998.

C. Analysis

Bellotti, Bob. *The Points Created Pro Basketball Book, 1993–94*. New Brunswick, N.J.: Night Work, 1994.

Heeren, Dave. *The Basketball Abstract*. Englewood Cliffs, N.J.: Prentice Hall, 1989.

Klein, Dave. *A Thinking Person's Guide to Pro Basketball.* New York: Grosset & Dunlap, 1978.

Koppett, Leonard. *The Essence of the Game Is Deception: Thinking about Basketball.* Boston: Little, Brown and Company, 1973.

Manley, Martin. *Martin Manley's Basketball Heaven, 1990 Edition.* New York: Doubleday, 1989.

Oliver, Dean. *Basketball on Paper: Rules and Tools for Performance Analysis.* Washington, D.C.: Brassey's, 2004.

Rosen, Charley. *God, Man, and Basketball Jones: The Thinking Fan's Guide to Professional Basketball.* New York: Holt, Rinehart and Winston, 1979.

D. Philosophy

Barkley, Charles, with Rick Reilly. *Sir Charles: The Wit and Wisdom of Charles Barkley.* New York: Warner, 1994.

Bradley, Bill. *Values of the Game.* New York: Broadway, 1998.

Green, A. C., with J. C. Webster. *Victory.* Lake Mary, Fla.: Creation House, 1994.

Jackson, Phil. *Sacred Hoops: Spiritual Lessons of a Hardwood Warrior.* New York: Hyperion, 1995.

Jordan, Michael. *I Can't Accept Not Trying: Michael Jordan on the Pursuit of Excellence.* San Francisco: Harper, 1994.

Riley, Pat. *The Winner Within: A Life Plan for Team Players.* New York: G. P. Putnam's Sons, 1993.

Wooden, John, with Steve Jamison. *Wooden: A Lifetime of Observations and Reflections On and Off the Court.* Lincolnwood, Ill.: Contemporary, 1997.

VII. OTHER BOOKS

A. Essays

Batchelor, Bob, ed. *Basketball in America: From the Playgrounds to Jordan's Game and Beyond.* New York: Haworth, 2005.

Ross, John, and Q. R. Hand Jr., eds. *We Came to Play: Writings on Basketball.* Berkeley, Calif.: North Atlantic, 1996.

B. Fiction

Carroll, Jim. *The Basketball Diaries.* New York: Penguin, 1978.

Isaacs, Neil D. *The Great Molinas.* Bethesda, Md.: WID Publishing, 1992.

Lupica, Mike. *Jump*. New York: Villard, 1995.
———. *Travel Team*. New York: Penguin, 2004.
Manus, Willard. *The Fixers*. New York: Ace, 1957.
Rosen, Charley. *The Cockroach Basketball League*. New York: Donald I. Fine, 1992.

C. Miscellaneous

Barzman, Sol. *505 Basketball Questions Your Friends Can't Answer*. New York: Walker and Company, 1981.
Beckett III, James. *Beckett's Official Price Guide Basketball Cards, Fifth Edition 1996*. New York: Random House, 1995.
Blythe, Will, and David Hirshey. *Rotisserie League Basketball, 1991 Edition*. New York: Bantam, 1990.
Boeldt, Troy et al. *1992 Fantasy Basketball Digest*. Minneapolis, Minn.: Lerner, 1992.
Martin, Clare. *Official NBA Trivia*. New York: HarperCollins, 1999.
Nash, Bruce, and Allan Zullo. *The Basketball Hall of Shame*. New York: Pocket, 1991.
Phelps, Richard "Digger." *Basketball for Dummies*. Foster City, Calif.: IDG, 1997.
Pollak, Mark. *Sports Leagues and Teams: An Encyclopedia, 1871 through 1996*. Jefferson, N.C.: McFarland, 1999.
Silberstang, Edwin. *Playboy's Guide to Basketball Betting*. New York: Wideview, 1982.
Sperling, Dan. *A Spectator's Guide to Basketball*. New York: Avon, 1983.
Wielgus, Chuck, Jr., and Alexander Wolff. *The In-Your-Face Basketball Book*. New York: Everest House, 1980.

VIII. MONOGRAPHS AND PAMPHLETS

Sports historian Roger Meyer of Boxboro, Massachusetts, has issued many useful privately published monographs ranging in length from 5–50 pages.

Grasso, John. *The Absurd "Official" Statistics of the 1954–55 NBA Season*. Guilford, N.Y.: Privately published, 2005.
———. *Olympic Games Basketball Records*. Guilford, N.Y.: Privately published, 2004.
Jones, Todd H. *1985–86 Pennsylvania High School Sports Record Booklet*. Nazareth, Pa.: Privately published, 1986.

Lamp, William R. *A History of Basketball at Rockwood*. Privately published, 1981.

Rumlow, Wayne. *Oshkosh All-Stars and the National Basketball League*. Privately published.

IX. PERIODICALS

A. English Language

ABA Pictorial, 1968–69. Revere, Mass.: William G. Mokray.

Athlon Sports Pro Basketball. 1995–1998. Nashville, Tenn.: Athlon, annually.

Basketball Digest. 1974–2004. Chicago: Century Sports, eight issues annually.

Basketball Illustrated. 1945–1949. Mt. Morris, Ill.: Elbak, annually.

Basketball News, 1971–1972. Pleasantville, N.Y.: Basketball News, twenty-eight issues annually.

Basketball News, 1999. Bannockburn, Ill.: Primedia, thirty-two issues annually.

Converse Basketball Yearbook. 1924–1983. Malden, Mass.: Converse Rubber, annually.

Dell Basketball. 1950–1964. New York: Dell, annually.

Indiana Basketball History Magazine, Fall 2000–Fall 2002. New Castle, Ind.: Indiana Basketball Hall of Fame, quarterly.

Official National Pro Basketball League, 1949. West Liberty, Iowa: Liberty, annually.

Pro Basketball Illustrated, 1969–70. Brooklyn, N.Y.: Complete Sports, annually.

Sporting News, College Basketball, 1997–98. St. Louis: Sporting News, annually.

Sporting News, Pro Basketball 19xx. St. Louis: Sporting News, annually.

Street & Smith's Basketball, 1957–1988. New York: Street & Smith, annually.

Street & Smith's College/Prep Basketball, 1988–1999. New York: Conde Nast, annually.

Street & Smith's Pro Basketball, 1988–1998. New York: Conde Nast, annually.

B. Foreign Language

French	*Mondial Basket*, 1999.
German	*Basket*, 2003.
	Basketball das Sonderheft, 2003.
	Five, 2003.
Greek	*Tripoito*, 2003.

Italian	*Giganti del Basket*, 1999.
	Superbasket, 1999.
Polish	*Basket News*, 2003–2005. Weekly.
Spanish	*Lea Deportes, Panama* 1981

X. WEBSITES

American Basketball Association, www.remembertheaba.com
Association for Professional Basketball Research,
    http://tss12.serverconfig.com/~orgapbr/
Basketball statistics, www.basketball-reference.com and
    www.basketballreference.com/
FIBA, www.fiba.com/
National Basketball Association, www.nba.com
NBA data, www.eskimo.com/~pbender/index.html

About the Author

John Grasso, an Olympic historian and treasurer of the International Society of Olympic Historians since 2004, was born in New York City, raised in Whitestone, New York, and educated as an accountant but spent most of his working life in data processing. He moved to Guilford in central New York state in 1980; has written on boxing and basketball; and has traveled extensively, visiting more than 35 countries and attending seven Olympic Games with his wife, Dorothy, and his two children, Steven and Laurel.

His published boxing work includes *505 Boxing Questions Your Friends Can't Answer*, with Bert R. Sugar; *The 100 Greatest Boxers of All Time*, with Bert R. Sugar; *The Olympic Games Boxing Record Book*; and *1984 Ring Record Book and Boxing Encyclopedia* (Olympic Editor). He also contributed boxing essays to the *Biographical Dictionary of American Sports* and *American National Biography*, as well as several columns to *Ring* magazine and *Boxing and Wrestling* magazine. He founded the International Boxing Research Organization in 1982.

He is a member of the Association for Professional Basketball Research, and his basketball work includes many statistical compilations on their website, as well as the section on early professional basketball with Robert Bradley in *Total Basketball* and two monographs, *The Absurd "Official" Statistics of the 1954–55 NBA Season* and *Olympic Games Basketball Records*. He has also contributed to several editions of *Harvey Pollack's NBA Statistical Yearbook* and Robert Bradley's *Compendium of Professional Basketball, 2nd Edition*.

Breinigsville, PA USA
01 November 2010
248303BV00001B/2/P